ADMINISTERING THE CALIFORNIA
SPECIAL NEEDS TRUST

ADMINISTERING THE CALIFORNIA
SPECIAL NEEDS TRUST

THIRD EDITION

A Guide for Trustees and Those Who Advise Them

KEVIN URBATSCH AND MICHELE FULLER

ISBN: 978-0-578-62071-8

Library of Congress Control Number: 2019920385

Author Introduction

For years, the authors have planned for persons with disabilities that included establishing special needs trusts, powers of attorney, advance health-care directives, and limited conservatorships and guardianships. All too often, once the documents were drafted and the clients left our office, there was little day-to-day guidance we could offer. In order to help our clients, we drafted a relatively short twenty-page (or so) document that discussed some details of managing a special needs trust. While it answered some questions, it also seemed to generate many follow-up questions due to the relative complex nature of special needs trust administration.

Over the years, we have heard a similar type of question from people confused about how special needs trust disbursements would affect the beneficiary's public benefits or whether a trustee was authorized to perform a certain action. It was not only trustees but also other attorneys (unfamiliar with public benefit rules) who sought advice on some of the unique issues that arose during special needs trust administration.

It is understandable that clients and attorneys who do not spend every day working on special needs issues are confused, but what is more troubling is that many public benefit agency caseworkers often misunderstand the rules governing their own public benefit programs and provide improper advice on how a special needs trust interacts with public benefit programs.

It was imperative that a resource be provided that would allow a trustee to feel more confident in his or her administration. We reviewed the existing publications, and none of them addressed the specific California issues that a special needs trust trustee would see on a day-to-day basis. Sometime in late 2009, Kevin tried expanding his client handout, but as he started working on it, he realized it was going to take a much more thorough treatment to provide the kind of guidance he felt was necessary. Thus, this book was born and since then has been updated, this being the second update.

In writing any book, the author needs to decide who the book's audience will be. In this case, we decided my audience is anyone who has taken on the responsibility of administering a California special needs trust. This could be a family member or friend who has never managed any kind of trust, a professional fiduciary who may manage a few or a lot of special needs trusts, up to national bank trust departments, which manage hundreds. Thus, the book provides some of the basics in special needs trust administration, but it also provides a relatively sophisticated level of coverage of all aspects of special needs trust administration.

A challenge with special needs trust administration is that the law is ever-changing. Public benefit rules change. Tax laws change. Trust laws change. Therefore, if you run into a question that may have a serious impact on the person with a disability's rights or with your role as trustee, it is important that you sign up for my monthly e-newsletter titled the *Special Needs News* at my website at www.Urblaw.com, which provides monthly updates and articles on helping trustees and people with disabilities. No book can ever replace the advice from an attorney with experience in special needs trust administration on specific trust administration issues.

For this book, we decided to use a question-and-answer format to address queries as we have received over the years. We have also provided a summary at the end of each Chapter that summarizes the Chapter's main points. We included footnotes of citations to legal authority, but this was really for the author's benefit, so we could keep track of any changes in the law and update those things as they arose. We also decided to add a variety of checklists, form documents, and law summaries some of my clients have found helpful over the years. We hope that you find them helpful.

If you have any other documents or forms that you have found helpful, please e-mail Kevin at Kevin@Urbatsch.com or Michele at Michele@Michiganlawcenter.com and I will include them on my website at www.UrbLaw.com or Michele's website at www.Michiganlawcenter.com for the benefit of all. Also, if you have any specific comments, concerns, or questions about this book, please contact me.

Finally, we want to thank you for taking on the responsibility of serving as a special needs trustee. It is a challenging but rewarding service you are providing to persons with disabilities, and we hope you find this book to be a valuable resource.

Kevin Urbatsch

Michele Fuller

Legal Disclaimer

This book was written with the intention of providing a resource for trustees of special needs trusts. It is not, and cannot, be a substitute for actual legal advice between an attorney and client. While the content of this book has been prepared by attorneys Kevin Urbatsch and Michele Fuller and contributing authors, it was done so for informational purposes only and should not be construed as legal advice but rather as the author's opinion concerning the law and practice at the time of this book's publication. The material posted in this book is not intended to create a lawyer-client relationship, and readers should not act upon it without seeking professional counsel.

I consider this book the beginning of a dialogue with the readers. If you are aware of an omission, error, or confusing section in this book, please share your knowledge with us. Send your comments to Kevin@Urbatsch.com or Michele@Michiganlawcenter.com.

Table of Contents

CHAPTER 1

Special Needs Trust Administration Overview

Administering a special needs trust (SNT) is an important job, which has a profound impact on the life of a person with disabilities. The person or entity who administers an SNT is called a "trustee." The trustee has the legal responsibility for managing a trust by following the rules set forth in the trust document, under federal law, and under California law for the benefit of the trust's beneficiary. The person with a disability is called the "beneficiary." This book describes the duties and responsibilities an SNT trustee must follow to comply with the law, but also describes best practices to better enhance the quality of life of the beneficiary.

In most cases, the SNT trustee is providing the beneficiary basic goods and services that improve and enhance the person with a disability's quality of life. In some cases, the SNT trustee may be the only person looking to the beneficiary's welfare. Thus, the role of SNT trustee is often a more substantial role than in many other types of trusteeships.

In order to do an excellent job, the SNT trustee must draw upon an impressive arsenal of skills to properly manage an SNT. The trustee must be comfortable navigating the multiple layers of rules and policies of various governmental agencies. The trustee must appreciate the beneficiary's disabilities that may limit the beneficiary's ability to communicate, manage their daily lives, locate housing, find employment, and become active citizens in the community. The SNT trustee is not only entrusted to assist with the financial management of a person with a disability's assets but may also be called upon to assist with the beneficiary's personal protection and development.

The ideal SNT trustee is one that:

1. Understands all laws (and changes to laws) necessary to manage a trust;
2. Understands all laws (and changes to laws) to qualify and maintain public benefits;
3. Always acts in the best interest of the beneficiary (no self-dealing or favoring others);
4. Has expertise in prudently investing funds for persons with disabilities and following investment limitations under trust law;
5. Comprehends tax ramifications for income, property, employment, and all possible trust transactions;
6. Maintains impeccable records and books;
7. Carries insurance or has deep pockets to refund trust in case of personal negligence;
8. Has ability to identify and rectify financial or physical abuse, discrimination or second-rate service for a person with a disability;
9. Understands all aspects of running and maintaining a primary residence for persons with disabilities;
10. Employs excellent care manager and caregivers for persons with disabilities;
11. Knowledgably follows all employment laws concerning employees and independent contractors;
12. Communicates well with everyone, is kind, but can be firm and say no when necessary; and
13. Is psychic, immortal, and omniscient.

It is not a job for the timid, nor is it typically a job for one person. It is one that requires a team. It is important that the trustee feel comfortable asking for help if he or she does not feel capable of properly handling any one of these roles.

In order to assist the SNT trustee in both directly handling these issues and knowing when (and where) to find help, this book is set up in a question-and-answer format to highlight the different issues that will arise for the SNT trustee.

> **Critical Pointer:** Please keep in mind that the guidelines laid out in this book are far from exhaustive. These guidelines are intended to alert trustees to their duties and to impress upon them the

significance of their responsibilities. Please do not hesitate to ask for legal, financial, tax, or other advice, especially if the trustee is not convinced he or she knows the right answer. That advice may cost something in the short run, but the cost can be far less than it takes to fix a mistake later on. Remember that the trust will pay reasonable costs associated with trustees obtaining advice, but trustees could end up paying out of their own pockets for their failure to secure advice when needed. Use Chapter 20 to find help in administering an SNT.

WHAT IS AN SNT?

An SNT is a type of trust designed to provide a person with a disability with assets to enhance his or her quality of life while at the same time allowing that person to remain eligible for needs-based public benefits. The two primary types of public benefit programs that are protected by use of an SNT are Supplemental Security Income ("SSI") and Medicaid (in California this program is called "Medi-Cal").

There are many other reasons why an SNT is valuable:

1. Providing supplemental lifetime support by purchasing additional items and services that make life more rewarding for the person with a disability;

2. Providing a system of advocacy to preserve the civil rights of the person with a disability;

3. Providing the funding for a safe and appropriate living arrangement so the person with a disability can live in the least restrictive environment;

4. Protecting the beneficiary from financial predators who take advantage of minors or vulnerable adults who may not have the capacity to protect themselves;

5. Investing the beneficiary's assets in a way that will best protect the beneficiary throughout his or her lifetime to the maximum extent possible especially when the beneficiary is unsophisticated in managing his or her own resources;

6. Providing a system to provide ongoing and safe caregiving services that may also supplement In-Home Supportive Services (IHSS);

[handwritten margin note: Reasons why SNT is valuable]

7. Offering opportunities so the person with a disability can enjoy all social and recreational activities that enhance his or her quality of life;

 8. Protecting the beneficiary's assets by having someone responsible for insuring and otherwise protecting trust assets;

 9. Paying all applicable taxes so the beneficiary is not later subject to penalties or fines for under reporting tax obligations; and

 10. Reporting to the proper government, legal, and family when required by law or policy when using the SNT for the benefit of the beneficiary.

Critical Pointer: An improperly drafted SNT will cause the beneficiary to lose his or her benefits. There are many ways to draft an improper SNT; it may require payments to the beneficiary or require that payments be used for the beneficiary's support. Thus, before someone agrees to take on the job of trustee, the trustee should have the trust reviewed by an experienced special needs trust attorney to make sure it was drafted and established correctly.

WHAT IS A SETTLOR, TRUSTEE, TRUST ADVISORY COMMITTEE, OR TRUST PROTECTOR?

In order to understand administration, it is important to know the terms for the different people who may be involved in the administration of the SNT:

- **Settlor, Trustmaker, Grantor, Trustor:** These are different names for the person or entity that created or established the trust. For example, if a parent created a trust for a child with a disability, then the parent would be named the settlor, grantor, trustmaker, or trustor of the trust, depending on the drafting attorney's own convention of use. In California law, the term *settlor* is used; however, there is no difference in treatment if a trust document uses a different name.

- **Trustee:** This is the person responsible for administering the trust once it is established. A trust may also name successor trustees, who would be the persons responsible for managing the trust if the originally named trustee could no longer serve. A trust can have more than one trustee at a time. Be aware that a cotrustee can be held responsible for another cotrustee's breach of a fiduciary duty. Thus, it is important that all cotrustees pay close attention to everything that is done in the administration of the trust. If there is any question or problem, it should be communicated to the other cotrustee or cotrustees immediately. As a general rule, where there are two or more cotrustees, all have to agree on all matters of trust administration. However, the trust document may create a different standard for agreement such as majority rule. In order to minimize the chances of being held responsible for someone else's poor judgment or breach of duty, a cotrustee should be sure to make a written record of any points of disagreement about trust business. In extreme cases, a cotrustee may be required to blow the whistle on other cotrustees' activities.

- **Beneficiary:** This is the person or entity that is to receive the benefit of the trust. The primary beneficiary of a SNT is the person with a disability. There may also be named remainder beneficiaries or sometime contingent beneficiaries; these are the persons who would receive the trust assets once the primary beneficiary either dies or there is a provision in the trust that would cause the assets to go to someone else. For example, an SNT could provide, "I leave my assets to be administered for the benefit of my child with a disability for as long as he is alive, but on his death or upon his no longer being disabled, the assets of the trusts shall be distributed to my grandchildren." In this example, the remainder beneficiaries would be the grandchildren.

- **Trust Advisory Committee:** In some SNTs, there will be a group of persons called a trust advisory committee. Typically, the committee will have the authority to speak on behalf of the beneficiary and make requests for disbursements. They may also have the authority to remove and replace a trustee. Attorneys include committees for a variety of reasons, but primarily to make sure there is a way for someone to oversee the trustee's actions. As with nearly all questions surrounding trust administration, it is

5

very important to read the document to understand what role the committee will serve.

- **Trust Protector**: As with the trust advisory committee, a trust protector is used in some SNTs. The protector will be given a series of responsibilities as spelled out in the trust document. Typically, these include the right to remove and replace trustees and the right to amend the trust if there are changes in the law that will require an amendment to the trust to keep it current.

For further explanations of legal terms used in the trust document please look at the Glossary of Legal Terms at the end of the book.

ARE THERE DIFFERENT TYPES OF SNTS?

Yes, there are two kinds of SNTs, commonly referred to as "first-party" and "third-party" SNTs. The distinguishing feature between the two is who is putting the money into the trust. The difference is set forth as follows:

- A **first-party SNT** is funded with the assets of the person with a disability.

- A **third-party SNT** is typically part of a parent or grandparent's estate plan for a child with a disability. However, it is not limited to them; any person other than the person with a disability can fund this type of trust. Such a trust is funded with the assets of a "third party," that is, parents, grandparents, or anyone else other than the person with a disability whom the trust benefits.

ARE THE DIFFERENT TYPES OF SNTS TREATED DIFFERENTLY BY AN SNT TRUSTEE?

Yes, the trustee must understand whether he or she is administering a first- or third-party SNT. While many of the duties and responsibilities of the trustee are the same for the two types of SNTs, there are duties and responsibilities that drastically change depending on whether the trust is a first- or third-party trust. Throughout the book, the discussion will indicate if there is a difference in the answer because of the different type of trust being administered.

> **Helpful Hint:** To determine which type of trust is being administered, the trustee needs to find out who provided the original money or assets to the trust. Generally, this is explained in the first few pages of the trust. For example, a trust may state that all funding of the trust is being done by a parent or grandparent, in which case it would be a third-party SNT. Another trust may state that all trust assets have come from the person with a disability, in which case it would be a first-party SNT.

> **Warning:** It may not be obvious from the trust document whose assets were used to fund the trust. It may require some investigation from the trustee to determine whose money was used. Some people would rather the trust be treated as a third-party SNT because the rules are generally more favorable and make various attempts to characterize money being used to fund the trust as coming from someone other than the beneficiary when it is really the beneficiary's money. For example, if an inheritance is to be received by a person with a disability, some people believe that if instead of writing a check to the person with a disability (as required by the trust) they write it directly to a third-party SNT that it will then not be treated as the person with a disability's assets because the person never placed the funds into their own name. This is not true because legally the money belonged to the person with a disability whether it was paid directly to them or not. To remain eligible for needs-based public benefits, the inheritance should have been paid to a properly established first-party SNT. If it is discovered that the inheritance is held in the wrong kind of trust and the SNT beneficiary is receiving needs-based public benefits, then there will be sanctions and possible damages awarded if the trustee was aware of this situation and did not do anything about it.

WHY SHOULD I AGREE TO BE AN SNT TRUSTEE?

Administering an SNT on behalf of a person with a disability can be very satisfying. The trustee can make a real difference in that person's quality of life and, sadly, may be the only person fighting for that person's proper care. The level of commitment can vary widely depending on who is the SNT beneficiary. On the most difficult end, there are SNT beneficiaries who are fully dependent on their trustee to make all their decisions and must be protected at all times. On the other end, the person with a disability may have full capacity to manage his or her affairs and only needs a modest amount of attention. In this case, the SNT is typically established only to keep the person eligible for public benefits. Regardless of the level of commitment, the trustee is doing a great service to this all-too-often neglected part of society.

[Correctly administering an SNT is a very important task. If the administration is done incorrectly, the trustee may cause the person with a disability to lose his or her eligibility for public benefits.] This results in substantial loss of assets and loss of access to health care. While the loss of financial benefits is important and can be devastating to ongoing care and comfort, the loss of health care can be life threatening. Thus, depending on the circumstance of the SNT, the trustee literally holds the key to the person with a disability's life, care, and comfort.

HOW DIFFICULT IS IT TO BE AN SNT TRUSTEE?

While it is important and satisfying to administer an SNT, it can also be very difficult. The trust rules and public benefits regulations are highly technical, often unclear, and frequently contradictory. Even small differences in a beneficiary's factual situation can significantly affect the trustee's duties. The most skilled and experienced trustees constantly review the trust document and have a system to keep current with changes in the trust and public benefits laws. The trustee should also understand the beneficiary's disability and know what types of agencies serve this population. Oftentimes, the trustee is asked to pay for services that can be obtained for free from not-for-profit agencies or the government.

Unless the SNT has a very small amount of assets, most SNT trustees retain professionals to assist in the administration, including SNT attorneys, private professional fiduciaries, corporate trust departments, financial advisers, tax professionals, professional caregivers, and public benefits advocates, just to name a few.

Helpful Hint: There are numerous resources in this book that will help you stay current with any significant changes in the law, see Chapter 20 for a list of websites and other resources for helping the SNT trustee.

WHAT ARE AN SNT TRUSTEE'S DUTIES?

The trustee has a "fiduciary duty" to the SNT beneficiary. A fiduciary duty is the highest duty one person can owe another under the law; it is much like the duty a parent owes to a child.

In general, the trust document itself provides a roadmap for the SNT trustee's responsibilities. However, other trustee duties are set forth in California law, which may not be discussed in the trust document at all.

A short summary of the SNT trustee's duties:

- Diversify SNT assets
- Administer SNT by its terms
- Make SNT property productive
- Defend actions against the SNT
- Enforce claims on behalf of the SNT
- Deal impartially with SNT beneficiary
- Take control and preserve SNT property
- Loyalty/confidentiality to the SNT beneficiary
- Avoid conflict of interest(s) with the SNT beneficiary
- Use any special skills the person serving has as SNT trustee
- Not require SNT beneficiary to relieve the trustee of liability
- Keep SNT beneficiaries reasonably informed of trust activities
- Keep SNT property separate from both the SNT trustee's assets and the SNT beneficiary's other assets
- Comply with prudent investor rule or other investment standard set forth in document
- Not delegate SNT trustee duties (with some exceptions that are explained in this book)
- Reasonably use SNT trustee's discretionary powers, such as deciding what type of disbursements the trust should make

Not to undertake role as trustee of an adverse trust interest like investing trust assets in a business that the trustee owns separately

These duties are listed with appropriate code sections in Appendix C and are further explained briefly below, and in much more detail in Chapter 2.

WHERE ARE THE RULES AND LAWS FOR AN SNT TRUSTEE LOCATED?

The SNT trustee's rules are set forth in a variety of places. Primarily, the trustee should review the trust document, which will have most of the information that the trustee will ever need to look up.

Other sources of law concerning trusts include

- California Probate Code
- California case law

Sources of law concerning public benefits laws include

- United State Code (USC)
- Code of Federal Regulations (CFR)
- Federal case law
- Social Security Administration's Program Operation Manual System (POMS)
- California Welfare and Institutions Code
- Medi-Cal's California regulations (CCR)
- All County Welfare Director's Letters (ACWDL)
- All County Letters (ACL)

These laws are discussed in more detail throughout this book and in Chapter 20 the website addresses are identified. This is how the trustee can look up these laws directly.

WHAT PUBLIC BENEFITS PROGRAM RULES WILL AN SNT TRUSTEE NEED TO UNDERSTAND?

A SNT trustee will primarily be concerned with the following types of public benefits:

- **Needs-Based Benefits.** The two "needs-based" programs that are the primary public benefit programs for persons with a disability who are also beneficiary's of an SNT are Supplemental Security Income (SSI) and Medi-Cal, which also pays for the In-Home Supportive Services (IHSS), program which is important to many SNT beneficiaries.

    > **Note:** As a result of the Affordable Care Act (Obamacare), California has expanded its Medi-Cal program so that someone can qualify for it even if they have resources. There are several limitations to the program that are discussed in detail in Chapter 3.

However, the trustee should understand how the SNT may (or may not) interact with other public benefits programs, including the following:

- **Entitlement Benefits.** Old Age, Survivors, and Disability Insurance (OASDI), which includes SSDI, Childhood Disability Beneficiary Benefits (CDB) or sometimes known as Disabled Adult Child (DAC), Social Security retirement benefits (often referred to as Social Security for short), and Medicare

- **Housing Benefits.** Housing Choice Voucher Program, more commonly known as Section 8 housing

- **Other Benefits.** Regional Center assistance for persons with developmental disabilities, veteran benefits, Healthy Families, catastrophic health-care coverage, CalWorks, and CalFresh (food stamps).

Public benefits will be discussed in greater detail in Chapter 3.

WILL THE SNT TRUSTEE'S DUTIES CHANGE IF THE PERSON WITH A DISABILITY IS ELIGIBLE FOR ONLY SOME OF THE AVAILABLE PUBLIC BENEFITS?

Yes. Generally, if the SNT beneficiary is an SSI recipient, then the trustee is only responsible for following the SSI rules. The reason that only SSI rules are important is that if the beneficiary is qualified for SSI, he or she automatically receives Medi-Cal. The Medi-Cal rules are then unimportant for continued eligibility. However, if the beneficiary does not qualify for SSI but is still otherwise eligible for Medi-Cal, then the SNT trustee must know the Medi-Cal rules, which can be different from SSI rules. When this happens, we will point this out in the book.

If the only government benefits involved are entitlement programs, such as Social Security Disability Insurance (SSDI), Social Security or Medicare, which have no resource limits, an SNT trustee will operate the trust pursuant to its terms and normal trust laws and will not need to be concerned with violating public benefits laws. There is nothing an SNT trustee can do to ruin eligibility for these entitlement public benefits.

> **Critical Pointer:** It is imperative that the SNT trustee determines which benefits the SNT beneficiary is receiving. The trustee's job can be fundamentally different depending on which benefits the SNT beneficiary is receiving. Many times, an SNT beneficiary will not know which public benefits programs he or she is receiving. It is easy to understand why there is confusion. The Social Security Administration (SSA) manages SSI, SSDI, CDB, and Social Security, and the checks come from the same place, so it is easy to be confused. Further, Medi-Cal and Medicare can cover identical types of medical care, and it can be difficult to know which program is covering the beneficiary.

If the SNT beneficiary is eligible for Section 8 housing, veteran benefits, or any other of the available government benefits, then the SNT trustee must know how these benefits may be affected by the existence of an SNT and whether distributions from the SNT will affect public benefits.

A further discussion of public benefits can be found in Chapter 3. For how to make an appropriate SNT distribution and how it will or will not affect public benefits, see Chapters 4, 11 - 16.

WHAT TYPE OF DISBURSEMENTS CAN AN SNT TRUSTEE MAKE FOR THE SNT BENEFICIARY?

It is a common misunderstanding that the SNT is very limited in what it can pay for when enhancing the quality of life of a person with a disability. Depending on the SNT terms, the SNT trustee can actually pay for anything that is not illegal or against public policy. This can include a huge variety of items that have no impact on public benefits at all, such as furniture, clothing, vacations, pet expenses, internet, computers, television, and all the things that many people without disabilities take for granted. For a much more complete list, see Appendix O.

Some SNT disbursements, most notably disbursements for food, shelter, or medical care already paid for by Medi-Cal, may affect eligibility for certain types of public benefits. However, the SNT trustee (when the SNT document allows such a disbursement) may still pay for these items if it is in the best interests of the beneficiary. See Chapter 12 for a discussion on making disbursements for food and shelter. This may reduce or eliminate public benefits; however, depending on the circumstances, this may be a good trade-off.

> **Example:** A beneficiary of an SNT wishes to have the SNT trustee pay for a new apartment where the rent is $2,000 per month. The beneficiary is an SSI recipient receiving the maximum amount of SSI ($958.63 per month in 2020 for California). The payment of rent by the SNT trustee will cause a reduction of the monthly SSI check to $685.63 per month in the year 2020. However, this is generally a good trade-off. The SNT beneficiary is able to live in a much nicer and safer apartment and only loses $281 per month of SSI. This formula is described in more detail in Chapters 3 and 12.

> **Critical Pointer:** It is important to know if the SNT document will allow a trustee to make disbursements that reduce or eliminate

eligibility for public benefits. Some SNTs do and some do not. To see whether the SNT allows it, please review Chapter 4, which discusses "distribution standards" and provides an explanation for the different types of distribution standards that allow such distributions.

For further discussion on making appropriate distributions, see Chapters 4, 11 - 16.

CAN AN SNT TRUSTEE BE RESPONSIBLE IF HE OR SHE MAKES A MISTAKE IN ADMINISTERING AN SNT?

Yes. But the type of actions that will cause the SNT trustee to be held responsible will depend on the terms of the SNT document. If the SNT is silent, then the trustee is liable if the SNT trustee commits a breach of trust. This typically means if the trustee acts (1) in bad faith, (2) knowingly but in good faith, or (3) negligently.

Negligence generally means the failure of the trustee to meet the applicable standard of care of a trustee. A trustee's standard of care will depend on the actions being taken by the trustee. An SNT trustee must do what a prudent person would do in the SNT trustee's situation and act in good faith and with reasonable prudence, discretion, and intelligence. The trustee must use reasonable skill, care, and caution when serving. If the trustee does not use this level of care, he or she will be held responsible for breach of trust. This, however, does not mean the SNT trustee is the insurer for all trust losses. Whether the trustee's conduct meets the requisite standard of care will be determined by the circumstances as they appear at the time the decision was made, not later, in hindsight. An SNT trustee is also not required to exercise extraordinary care in serving. He or she must exercise ordinary care.

> **Critical Pointer:** Some trustees believe that if they are not being paid that they cannot be held responsible for breaches of trust. This is incorrect. It makes no difference if the trustee is paid or not; he or she will still be fully responsible for any breaches of trust.

Courts have found trustees in breach of trust in the following situations:

- Failure to vigorously monitor and manage rental real property owned by the trust.[1]
- Delay in complying with trustee's duty to invest trust assets (5-year delay unreasonable as a matter of law).[2]
- Failure to obtain necessary assistance in subject area in which the trustee lacked expertise.[3]
- Failure to take action in general to protect the interest of the beneficiaries.[4]
- Accepting the suggestion of a beneficiary without exercising independent judgment.[5]

Some SNTs have provisions that may limit the trustee's liability. If the SNT document includes a provision that says the trustee's liability is absolutely limited, it may reduce the liability of the trustee to acts that are

1. Intentional breaches of trust, with gross negligence, in bad faith, or with reckless indifference to the interest of the beneficiary, or
2. For any profit that the trustee derives from a breach of trust.

In California, a trust document cannot limit a trustee's liability any further than this. In general, to be held responsible under these provisions, the SNT trustee must be doing something intentional to harm the beneficiary or with such indifference that the trustee should have known that something was being done that would either benefit the trustee at the expense of the SNT or harm the SNT beneficiary.

Some trustees try to limit their liability by forcing beneficiaries to sign agreements that the beneficiary will not sue the trustee for any actions taken by the trustee. These agreements are void, as they contradict public policy under California law.

Critical Pointer: Professional trustees are held to more stringent standards than nonprofessional trustees and are required to apply

---

1 *Estate of Gump* (1991) 1 Cal. App. 4th 582, 595
2 *Lynch v. John M. Redfield* (1970) 9 Cal. App. 3d 293, 302
3 *Estate of Gump* (1991) 1 Cal. App. 4th 582, 595
4 *Younglove v Hacker* (1936) 15 Cal. App. 2d 211, 217
5 *Estate of Talbot* (1956) 141 CA2d 309, 315

the knowledge and competence ordinarily possessed by professionals under similar circumstances. Thus, if the SNT trustee is holding him or herself out as an expert in financial matters, he or she will be held to a higher standard of care for the financial performance of the trust than someone who does not hold him or herself out as such an expert.

WHAT ARE THE PENALTIES IF AN SNT TRUSTEE MAKES A MISTAKE?

There are a host of penalties that an SNT trustee can receive for a breach of trust. A breach of trust is a violation by the trustee of any duty that the trustee owes a beneficiary. Depending on what happened, an SNT trustee may be held responsible for one or more of the following actions:

- an injunction entered stopping the trustee from breaching the trust;
- may be removed and another trustee may be appointed in his or her place;
- may have compensation set aside or denied;
- may have to pay back from their own assets to the SNT any amount of money that was lost as a result of the wrongful act or give back to the SNT any assets that were wrongfully taken;
- may have to pay a penalty out of their own pocket for their wrongful act, even if no money was lost by the SNT;
- a court may set aside the wrongful act of the SNT trustee as long as someone who is innocent is not harmed;
- may lose or have reduced any money that is owed to them for their services as trustee;
- the court may go after property that was improperly distributed out to someone else;
- in extreme cases, the SNT trustee can be held in contempt of court if the trustee refuses to provide an accounting of his or her actions or if the SNT trustee ignores a court order to perform a certain act; or
- in even more extreme cases, if the trustee ignores a court order, the SNT trustee can be imprisoned until he or she performs the tasks for which he or she had been held in contempt of court.

WHAT RECORDS DOES THE SNT TRUSTEE GENERALLY HAVE TO KEEP?

Trustees have a duty to keep accurate records of trust transactions. Not only is it a legal duty, but it is very prudent to do so. A trustee may be questioned years later by the SNT beneficiary or his or her legal representatives about trust actions. Further, it is not unusual for public benefits agencies, such as the Social Security Administration (SSA) or the Department of Health Care Services (DHCS), to request a review of the trustee's records. Finally, other government agencies, like the IRS, may audit trust tax returns. Without good records, it may be impossible to respond to these requests or remember why disbursements were made.

Without good records, if someone questions the SNT trustee's actions, all presumptions will be made against the SNT trustee as if he or she did something wrong. Records should be thorough, legible, and easily accessible and should provide a cumulative description of the trustee's administration. This can be done by a simple spreadsheet while requiring copies of all receipts.

> **Example:** One common mistake that SNT trustees make is paying a reimbursement to others for purchases made on the beneficiary's behalf but failing to keep an accurate record of what the underlying purchase was for. For example, trustee reimburses parent of beneficiary $800 for television purchased for beneficiary—a perfectly acceptable transaction. However, trustee only notes that $800 was paid as reimbursement to parents, failing to make sure that it was for a television. Years later, the SSA seeks an explanation of why cash was distributed. If the trustee is not able to adequately explain it, the SSA could take the position that a gift was made and penalize the beneficiary's SSI eligibility. The better practice is to make a short notation that it was for the purchase of a television and provide a copy of the receipt.

For a further discussion of the recordkeeping requirements of the SNT trustee, see Chapter 8.

DOES THE SNT TRUSTEE HAVE TO KEEP THE BENEFICIARY INFORMED OF TRUSTEE'S ACTIONS?

Yes. The SNT trustee has a legal duty to keep a beneficiary reasonably informed about the trustee's administrative decisions and acts and generally to account to beneficiaries on an annual basis. The type of account the SNT trustee must provide will depend on which type of SNT is being administered, for example, court-supervised trust or non–court supervised trust.

In general, if the SNT is not court supervised which includes all SNTs that are third-party SNTs (SNTs funded with money other than the beneficiary's) and some first-party SNTs (SNTs funded with money of the beneficiary), the accounting requirement is somewhat relaxed and can be done by sending an annual summary of the trustee's actions by letter to the beneficiaries and their legal representatives.

If the SNT is court supervised, which is generally a first-party SNT established by a court, then there are very formal legal requirements that must be followed, and the court account must be filed in a probate court on a periodic basis, generally one year after the trust is established and every two years thereafter. It is imperative that the trustee review the trust document and the court's order establishing the first-party SNT for direction on whether the trust must file accounts and reports for court approval.

For a further discussion of the accounting requirements of the SNT trustee, see Chapter 8.

DOES THE SNT TRUSTEE HAVE TO INVEST THE SNT ASSETS?

Yes. An SNT trustee must always invest SNT assets. However, the type of investments that are authorized depends on whether the trust is a first-party SNT that has been established by a court or a non–court supervised SNT.

Most SNTs are not court supervised, and the trustee's investment powers are derived from the SNT document, which will set forth the investment standard. If the SNT document is silent, the SNT trustee must comply with the Uniform Prudent Investor Act (UPIA), California case law, and the circumstances of the trust and its beneficiaries. All these sources of investment powers are considered in determining whether an investment is proper. In general, the UPIA investment standard of care states,

1. A trustee shall invest and manage trust assets as a prudent investor would, by considering the purposes, terms, distribution requirements, and other circumstances of the trust. In satisfying this standard, the trustee shall exercise reasonable care, skill, and caution.

2. A trustee's investment and management decisions respecting individual assets and courses of action must be evaluated not in isolation but in the context of the trust portfolio as a whole and as a part of an overall investment strategy, having risk and return objectives reasonably suited to the trust.

If the SNT is court supervised, the SNT trustee may only invest in a very limited way. The investment standard is identical to that of a court proceeding, called a conservatorship. The conservatorship investment standard authorizes only a short list of approvable investments. However, this limited list can be expanded by court order, so the SNT trustee should look at any court order that set up the trust to see if the investment standard was expanded.

The only trustee delegable duty is the right to delegate investment and management duty to another. Depending on the size of the SNT and the complexity of the assets, it may be crucial for an SNT trustee to delegate these functions to an experienced and trusted investment advisor. If a trustee decides to delegate investment or management responsibilities, the trustee must still exercise prudence in (1) selecting the agent, (2) establishing the scope and terms of the delegation of authority, and (3) periodically reviewing the agent's overall performance and complying with the terms of the delegation.

If SNT trustees decide to maintain these duties, they can still consult with other professionals, such as financial advisers, real estate brokers, accountants, tax attorneys, and other specialists to aid them in their investment responsibility and protect themselves from potential liability.

For further discussion of the SNT trustee's investment responsibility, see Chapter 9.

WHAT IS THE SNT TRUSTEE'S RESPONSIBILITY FOR FILING RETURNS AND PAYING TAXES?

The SNT trustee is responsible for the tax liabilities and reporting for the SNT to both the IRS and the California Franchise Tax Board. The type of reporting and tax payments that will be made will depend on which type of SNT is being administered. The main difference will be whether the SNT is considered by the IRS to be a "grantor trust" or "nongrantor trust."

> **Helpful Hint:** In general, a third-party SNT will be a "nongrantor trust" and a first-party SNT will be a "grantor trust." However, it is possible that a third-party SNT could be a "grantor trust" if the parents still have a right to change the terms of the trust. If the SNT trustee is not certain about what type of tax treatment their SNT will receive, it would be best to consult with an SNT attorney or CPA.

For most third-party SNTs, the SNT will be a "nongrantor" trust. The "nongrantor" SNT will file separate federal and state tax returns on behalf of the trust and provide a tax form titled a K-1 to the SNT beneficiary for any SNT income that was distributed on behalf of the SNT beneficiary. Generally, it is best if the "nongrantor" SNT spends any trust income on behalf of the beneficiary. That is because, under IRS rules, trust income that is spent on the beneficiary's behalf is taxed at his or her individual rate, not the trust rate (which will be much higher).

> **Example:** The SNT assets are invested in several funds showing interest earned on the money. For the current year, the interest amounts to $15,000. In the SNT trust accounting, the trustee records that disbursements for the beneficiary's benefit were made out of this income, not the trust principal. When the trust taxes are computed, any money spent from the income for the beneficiary's benefit is taxed at the beneficiary's tax rate. Income that is added to the trust and not disbursed is taxed at the higher trust rate. Thus, it is better tax-wise to distribute income from a "non grantor" SNT.

For the SNT trustee's purpose, the easier tax responsibility is the "grantor trust," or first-party SNT. The IRS income from a first-party SNT is taxed not to the trust, but to the beneficiary with a disability. This is so even if it is retained in the trust.

For a more complete discussion of the SNT trustee's tax responsibilities, see Chapter 17.

WHAT HAPPENS WHEN THE SNT BENEFICIARY DIES OR THE TRUST TERMINATES?

An SNT trustee must continue his or her administration of the trust even though by its terms it has terminated. The three most common events, which result in the termination of an SNT are as follows:

1. Death of the beneficiary
2. Exhaustion of trust assets
3. Failure of purpose—for example, if some SNT provision states that if the beneficiary is able to work and pay for his or her own food, clothing, shelter, and medical care that the trust then terminates and assets distributed to beneficiary, the trust will terminate

Before acting, the trustee must be satisfied that the event has occurred. For example, if death is the triggering event, the trustee should obtain a certified copy of the beneficiary's death certificate.

Upon termination, the trustee's activities are generally divided into three categories:

1. Paying the final expenses of the trust (which may include California's Medi-Cal agency if it is a first-party SNT) and perhaps the expenses of the SNT beneficiary
2. Making a final accounting to the remainder beneficiaries (or the court, if SNT is court supervised)
3. Distributing any remaining assets to the heirs

Before making any payments, the SNT trustee must understand how to prioritize among the claims and debts that may be brought to him or her for payment. As a practical consequence of making the wrong payment, the trustee may be required to pay out of his or her personal assets any claims that were not properly paid from the SNT assets.

> **Critical Pointer:** In order to understand the proper priority among creditors of the SNT, the trustee must first determine whether the SNT is a third-party or first-party SNT. This issue is very important, because if the SNT is a first-party SNT, the trustee must give notice of the SNT termination to California's Medi-Cal agency, the Department of Health Care Services (DHCS). Also, if the beneficiary received Medicaid in other states, notice to those states must be performed. DHCS allows only a few things to be paid from SNT assets before DHCS' Medi-Cal bill must be paid. DHCS' Medi-Cal lien includes all the Medi-Cal payments used by the beneficiary during his or her lifetime. Paying the wrong claims before DHCS' lien is paid can cause the SNT trustee to be responsible for a breach of trust.

If the trust is subject to continuing court supervision, the trustee should prepare a court filing, called a petition, to settle the final account and to distribute the estate. The notice of report and account and petition for distribution will inform the beneficiaries that the trust has terminated. The trustee may also wish to send letters to the beneficiaries, informing them of termination. Preparation of the trustee's final accounting may take a substantial amount of time. The trustee may ask the beneficiaries to waive a final accounting if the beneficiaries have the necessary mental capacity.

For more information on trust termination, see Chapter 18.

CHAPTER 1 SUMMARY

✓ The SNT is a powerful tool that enhances the quality of life of persons with disabilities.

✓ There are two kinds of SNTs (the first-party and third-party SNT), which are treated differently during administration.

✓ Before serving as an SNT trustee, the SNT document should be reviewed by an SNT attorney to make sure it was established correctly.

✓ Being an SNT trustee is both rewarding and difficult, and the SNT trustee should not underestimate the work that goes into being a trustee.

✓ The SNT trustee may always hire attorneys, CPAs, investment advisers, and other professionals to assist in the administration.

✓ There are many rules and responsibilities of being an SNT trustee that are set forth in many different places, including the SNT document, California law, federal law, SSA POMS, DHCS Letters, and case law.

✓ The SNT trustee should know what kind of public benefits the SNT beneficiary receives or may be entitled to.

✓ The two types of public benefits the SNT trustee should understand are SSI and Medi-Cal, although he or she should also have some understanding of IHSS, Regional Centers, SSDI, Social Security, Medicare, Section 8, CalFresh (food stamps), veteran benefits, and other benefits, if his or her beneficiary receives these benefits.

✓ SNT assets can be used in a very broad way to enhance the quality of life of a person with a disability.

✓ An SNT trustee has personal liability for his or her mistakes made while administering an SNT.

✓ An SNT has very specific requirements for record-keeping, accounting, investing, and tax reporting and payment.

✓ An SNT trustee must know what happens when an SNT terminates because of death or for other reason stated in trust document.

CHAPTER 2

Trustee's General Obligations

Serving as trustee is an important job. There are a host of rules that the trustee must follow. Some of these are obvious, like "don't steal trust assets." Others, however, are subtler, like "don't get involved in a conflict of interest," meaning that a trustee cannot lend money to themselves from trust assets even if they intend to pay it back with interest. Violating these rules can cause lots of problems for the trustee and the SNT beneficiary. For example, the trustee has personal liability for any harm caused by him or her, meaning, the trustee can be fined, have to pay damages, be removed as trustee, or even in very extreme cases face criminal charges.

This chapter describes the rules that a trustee must follow, however, to keep it simple, a trustee should continue to repeat the mantra that this is "not my money" and can only be used as described in the trust document. If the trustee keeps this in mind, his or her job will be much easier. An SNT trustee should carefully review Chapters 5 and 7 in setting up procedures that will aid in proper and efficient SNT administration. Also, attached as Appendices A, B, and E to this book are forms that can be reviewed and completed as you go through the following tasks. Appendix A includes the initial fourteen steps an SNT trustee should consider when taking over a new trust; Appendix C is a chart of trustee's duties as spelled out in California law; and Appendix E is a form that is a one-page summary of the type of trust that is being administered that will aid the trustee during administration.

> **Critical Pointer:** The trustee should have no doubts that he or she is correct when making trust decisions. It is strongly

recommended that if there are any doubts, the trustee retain an attorney experienced in assisting with SNT administration. The cost of the attorney will more often than not be much less expensive than trying to correct a mistake by a trustee. See Chapter 20 on how to find a special needs planning attorney who specializes in SNT administration.

WHERE DOES AN SNT TRUSTEE FIND THE RULES ON HIS OR HER DUTIES?

The SNT trustee's legal responsibility is primarily set forth in the trust document. Although, there may be additional rules established by court order (if SNT established by court), trust law, public benefits laws, Program Operations Manuel Systems (commonly called POMS which is the Social Security Administration's book of rules), and sometimes State Medicaid (or in California called Medi-Cal) regulations. These are described in more detail here:

- **Trust document.** The trustee's authority comes first and foremost from the trust document, and his or her duties and powers as described there are the primary instructions. The trustee should read the trust document with care, and from time to time read it again. The trust document may contain specific provisions that take precedence over the general rules that apply to trusts—even the ones mentioned in this book. However, note that there are certain basic rules relating to trusts that will apply no matter what the trust document says. For example, a trust cannot allow or encourage illegal activity on the part of the trustee or the beneficiary.

- **Court Order.** If a court established the trust, then a written court order was issued establishing the SNT. Typically, the order will include specific trustee accounting requirements, bonding requirements, or specific distributions that are allowed or not allowed.

  Critical Pointer: A trustee should never administer a trust without a full copy of the trust document and if established by court order, a copy of the written order. This is the trustee's primary set of instructions.

While the above documents will generally provide all the authority a trustee will need, the trustee should also be aware that the trustee is subject to other rules that may not be spelled out in the trust document. These rules are set forth below:

- **Laws.** The California Probate Code ("Probate Code") provides most of the rules that an SNT trustee will need to know to do his or her job. Various provisions of the Probate Code cover things that are not specifically spelled out in the trust document. The Trustees Powers Act[6], the Uniform Prudent Investor Act[7], and California's Uniform Principal and Income Act (UPAIA)[8] hold particular relevance to all trustees. Other laws may be covered, including contract law, real estate law, and possible litigation. An SNT trustee should always seek legal assistance whenever one of these laws is affected.

- **Case Law.** California court decisions relating to trusts are another source of legal authority for trustees. This is known as the "common law." The common law of California is found primarily in the opinions of California's Supreme Court and the Court of Appeals, but California courts may sometimes follow decisions from other jurisdictions as well.

- **Federal Law.** Certain federal laws, regulations, and case law are also important for the SNT trustee to know. Most public benefits programs the SNT beneficiary is receiving are a result of federal legislation. This includes SSI, SSDI, and the federal Medicaid and Medicare program. The beneficiary may also receive public housing, veteran benefits, or other federal benefits. The Code of Federal Regulations (CFR) is an important tool to know how these federal laws are to be administered.

---

6 Probate Code §§16200-16249.

7 Probate Code §§16045-16054.

8 Probate Code §§16320-16375.

- **POMS**[9] **and DHCS All County Letters.**[10] POMS is an acronym for Program Operation Manuel System and is the Social Security Administration's guide to its own employees on how the agency interprets SSI rules and regulations. The Department of Health Care Services (DHCS) All County Letters is DHCS' guide to its own employees on how the agency interprets Medi-Cal rules and regulations.

An SNT trustee needs to keep all sources of authority in mind as he or she carries out his or her trustee duties.

HOW SHOULD A TRUSTEE APPROACH HIS OR HER DUTIES?

The best Trustee will understand why the trust was created, do their best to meet that intent, and will carefully examine his or her motives during each exercise of discretion.

- **Try to understand why the trust was created.** Understanding the intent behind the SNT will help the trustee fulfill his or her role as trustee. The main reason for creating a SNT is to enhance the quality of life of a person with a disability. An unfortunate reality is that most SNT beneficiaries are unable to work because of their disability, so oftentimes the only money they will have available to them is the money in the SNT and possibly access to public benefits. In order to find as much money as possible to assist the person with a disability, it is important to maximize all sources of revenue for the SNT. In addition to money, the Settlor (or person setting up trust) may have included instructions on other topics, such as paying for beneficiary's advocacy.

- **Trustee should examine his or her motives.** The trustee should be extremely careful that everything he or she does or refrains from doing, as

---

9 POMS can be found by Googling POMS or following the link at https://secure.ssa.gov/apps10/poms.nsf/chapterlist!openview&restricttocategory=05.

10 The DHCS ACWDL can be found by googling All County Welfare Letters or following the link at http://www.dhcs.ca.gov/services/medi-cal/eligibility/Pages/ACWDLbyyear.aspx.

trustee is motivated by the trustee's desire to execute his or her duties faithfully and to the best of his or her ability to the beneficiary. The trustee cannot allow himself or herself to be influenced by his or her personal feelings about an individual beneficiary or his or her own self-interest.

WHAT ARE A TRUSTEE'S LEGAL DUTIES?

Trustees are subject to a variety of duties. The penalty for breaching these duties can result in the trustee having to pay for any resulting damage to the trust out of his or her own pocket. Personal liability—even if the SNT trustee is not paid—is one of the things that go along with being a fiduciary.

> **Helpful Hint:** A list of the California fiduciary duties set forth in the Probate Code is summarized in Appendix C.

1. Duty of Using General Good Sense

The law states that a trustee is required to administer the trust with reasonable care, skill, and caution under the circumstances then prevailing that a prudent person acting in a like capacity would use in the conduct of an enterprise of like character and with like aims to accomplish the purposes of the trust as determined from the trust document.[11]

A trustee is not allowed to manage the money as they might manage their own money. Instead, they must always do everything as a prudent person would under the same set of circumstances. This may sound simple but can actually cause problems for someone not used to administering someone else's money. The question that should be asked every time the trustee is performing a trustee duty is "What would a prudent person do under these circumstances?"

2. Duty Is Greater If Trustees Are (or Hold Themselves Out as) Experts

If a trustee holds him or herself out as an expert in a certain trust duty, that trustee will be held to a higher standard of care than would any other trustee not making those claims. Thus, the standards for judging a trustee's job performance will take

---

11   Probate Code §16040(a).

into account his or her special abilities (whether actual or claimed).[12] Accordingly, a trustee should be very careful when communicating to others about his or her background in serving as trustee.

Generally, a trustee is not required to use any special skills or be held to the same standard as an expert when performing trustee duties. However, if the trustee has—or claims to have—special expertise in connection with any part of trust administration, such as investments, tax preparation, or legal background, the trustee will be held to the same standard of care as that expert.

> **Example:** A trustee claims that they are experts in tax preparation. The trustee then files a tax return that is inaccurate and costs the trust penalties from the IRS. The trustee will be held to a greater standard of care of an expert in tax preparation. Thus, proof of his or her breach of duty will be easier to meet than if a trustee without any special expertise in filing tax documents were to make the same mistake. Note, however, that the trustee who has held out an expertise in tax filings would not also be held to a higher standard under other trustee duties, such as investments.

3. Duty to Carry Out the Terms of the Trust

Under California law, the trustee is under a duty to administer the trust according to its terms.[13] It will be difficult for anyone to find fault with the trustee's performance if everything is done in accordance with the terms of the trust document. If at any time a trustee has a reasonable doubt as to the correct interpretation of the trust document, the trustee should contact an attorney to assist, and if the attorney is unable to determine it as well, the trustee may petition a court for instructions.[14] The trustee should consult with Chapter 20 of this book on finding an appropriate attorney and filing a petition for instructions with the court.

In many SNTs, the parents of the child with a disability may leave something called a memorandum of intent or letter of intent. This document will describe the parents' intent in how they wish to see the SNT assets used for the care of their child

---

12   Probate Code §16014.

13   Probate Code §16000.

14   Probate Code §17200.

with a disability. While the trustee should always review the memorandum, the trustee should remember that this document is not legally binding on the trustee. Many times, the memorandum may recommend distributions that would violate public benefits rules or trust laws. The SNT trustee is free to disregard these suggestions. However, the trustee should also keep in mind that the parents have expressed their intent on how they would like to see the SNT assets used, so a properly serving trustee would take these wishes into account as much as possible.

The only time the trust document should not be followed is if the trust terms are contrary to public policy or there has been a substantial change of circumstances that would mean following the trust terms would cause harm to the SNT beneficiary. The following list includes examples of when the trust terms should not be followed:

- If the trust terms are illegal or are against public policy.[15] An example would be if the trust terms authorized distributions for illegal narcotics or authorized distribution only if the beneficiary divorced his spouse.
- If the trust terms refused to let anyone remove the trustee on any grounds.[16] An example would be if the trustee stopped acting as trustee but refused to resign. If the trust terms stated that the trustee cannot be removed for any reason, this provision will be ignored.
- If an attorney is serving as trustee, he or she cannot be paid as trustee and as attorney for trustee despite any trust terms that allowed this arrangement.[17]
- If the trust terms waive any right for beneficiaries to receive information. This provision must be ignored as invalid.[18]
- If the trust terms waive rights to notice of actions being performed by the trustee. This provision must be ignored as invalid.[19]
- If the trust terms waive (or limit) the trustee's duty to report and account to beneficiaries. A waiver of account is authorized.[20] However, if the trust

---

15 Probate Code §15203.
16 Probate Code §15642.
17 Probate Code §15687.
18 Probate Code §16060.
19 Probate Code §16061.7.
20 Probate Code §16064(a).

provisions do not fully waive an account and report, a trust provision can also limit the time a person has to object to an account.[21]

- If the trust terms limit the trustee's liability.[22] A trustee's liability may be limited up to a certain point. However, a trustee will always be responsible for his or her breach of trust committed intentionally, with gross negligence, in bad faith, or with reckless indifference to the interest of the beneficiary, or for any profit that the trustee derives from a breach of trust.
- If there were changed circumstances. For example, if a required trust investment becomes entirely uneconomic, a court might authorize a substitute investment.[23]

4. Duty of Loyalty/Not to Self-Deal

A trustee cannot engage in any act that puts personal interests in conflict with those of any of the SNT beneficiary.[24] The prohibition against self-dealing applies regardless of the good faith of the trustee.[25] This means that even if the trustee has no intent to harm the trust or the beneficiary, if he or she engages in self-dealing he will be in breach of trust.

A trustee must always act to further the interests of the trust and the beneficiary. The trustee is serving for the benefit of the beneficiary. If any situation should arise in which there is a conflict between the trustee's personal interests and the trust or between the trust and the interests of third parties, the trustee has an obligation to put the interests of the trust first.

A trustee should not personally buy trust property being sold by the trust; because this creates the appearance that the trustee may have taken advantage of the trust. This is true even if the purchase was done at fair market value. A trustee who sells or leases personal assets to the trust likewise breaches his or her fiduciary duty against self-dealing.[26] Similarly, the trustee should never loan trust funds to him or herself or to family members The rules set forth in this paragraph are strictly applied

---

21 Probate Code §16062.
22 Probate Code §16461.
23 Restatement (Second) of Trusts §167 (1959); Restatement (Third) of Trusts §66 (2007).
24 Probate Code §16004(a).
25 *People v Larkin* (ND Cal 1976) 413 F Supp 978.
26 Probate Code §16004(a).

not only to transactions in which the trustee deals directly with him or herself but also to transactions in which the trustee deals with entities (such as partnerships or corporations) in which the trustee is personally interested. These rules apply even though a particular transaction may be scrupulously fair, and even if it is advantageous to the trust.

A trustee will find very little sympathy with a judge or jury if he or she does something that looks like it may be improper, whether or not it really is. If someone questions the trustee's activities, the trustee may find himself or herself having the burden of proving that he or she acted properly. The trustee does not have the advantage of being presumed innocent until he or she is proven guilty. Most of the time, trustees will find the exact opposite to be true.

5. Duty Not to Delegate

Once the trustee has accepted the position of trustee, he or she is responsible for the administration of the trust and should not turn over the administration of the trust to others.[27] This does not mean that the trustee must actually perform all of the administrative work. The trustee may employ agents to advise or assist the trustee in the performance of administrative duties, including accountants, attorneys, auditors, investment advisers, appraisers, or other agents.[28] However, the responsibility for the administration of the trust always remains with the trustee. While the trustee may hire agents to assist, he or she cannot blindly follow their advice. The trustee should seek advice when in doubt but make all final decisions after he or she has independently analyzed the matter. The trustee's reliance on the advice of a competent and qualified professional can be a defense to a claim that he or she breached his or her fiduciary duty to the plaintiff.

The trustee may delegate investment and management functions if prudent under the circumstances.[29] The trustee is required to exercise prudence in selecting an agent and in establishing the scope and terms of the delegation. The trustee is also required to exercise prudence by periodically reviewing the agent's overall performance and compliance with the terms of the delegation. See Chapter 9 for a further discussion of the delegation of investment duties.

---

27   Probate Code §16012.

28   Probate Code §16247.

29   Probate Code §16052(a).

Example: A trustee may hire an investment advisor to assist with the trust financial portfolio. However, a trustee should never delegate decisions on discretionary distributions to a third party, because courts assume that the person setting up the trust appointed that particular trustee because of his or her individual judgment concerning such matters.

If there is more than one trustee, each trustee cannot rely on the other trustees to administer the trust. Unless the trust agreement provides otherwise, all cotrustees must take an active role in administering the trust.[30] A cotrustee's failure to participate in trust administration could constitute unlawful delegation. However, ministerial acts (meaning those not requiring the exercise of personal judgment) can be delegated. In addition, investment and management functions may be delegated to one cotrustee, just as delegation may be made to an investment advisor.

To avoid unlawful delegation and provide for effective management of the trust, the cotrustees should agree in writing on a management method that will involve all cotrustees in active management and appropriately allocate ministerial duties. If one of the trustees acts improperly with respect to trust matters, the other trustee has an obligation to correct the situation. The trustee has an obligation to be aware of what other trustees are doing on behalf of the trust. Each trustee is responsible to the beneficiary for the misconduct and breaches of duty of the other trustees.

6. Duty to Keep Records

The SNT trustee should keep excellent records. A sample of what should be included, in addition to the accountings, and the backup information upon which the accountings are based should include the following:

- **Notes from regular meeting with the beneficiary or his or her legal representatives.** For each meeting, keep a record of the date, the length of the meeting, and a summary of what was discussed. The trustee should also keep records of all other communications between the trustee and the beneficiary, including such things as copies of all correspondence.

---

30 Probate Code §15620.

- **Beneficiary's income tax returns.** If the trust document grants the trustee's discretion in making distributions to the beneficiary, the income tax returns can provide the trustee a great deal of helpful information. Those returns are signed under penalty for perjury. The beneficiary may be reluctant to share his or her income tax returns with a trustee, but the trustee's request for that kind of information is not unduly intrusive—no more so than a bank asking for the same documentation before deciding whether to loan money.

- **Beneficiary's annual spending plans and spending plans.** Because all SNT trustees have complete discretionary authority with respect to distributions, the trustee should help prepare a spending plan for the beneficiary. This shows that the trustee has carefully considered the beneficiary's needs relative to discretionary distributions. For further discussion of how to set up a spending plan, see Chapter 9.

- **Verification of out-of-pocket expenditures.** Since the trustee is entitled to reimbursement of all reasonable amounts the trustee advances on behalf of the trust, he or she should keep copies of proof of payment, such as canceled checks or receipts. For example, if the trustee is travelling with beneficiary and pays for all bills from a personal account, he or she can be reimbursed from the SNT and it is best practice to keep very careful track of these expenditures.

- **Communications with advisers.** Keep all copies of all correspondence between the trustee and his or her advisers, and always ask them to at least summarize any advice they give in writing.

- **Any and all information upon which any exercise of discretion is based.** These documents may include such things as beneficiary's bank statements, credit card statements, pay stubs, or other employment information, invoices, proposals, and any other information given to you to justify a request for a distribution.

For a further discussion of the record keeping responsibility, see Chapter 8.

7. Duty to Account and Report to the Beneficiary

The trustee has a legal duty to account to the current beneficiary of the trust. The trustee is generally required to account, at least annually, at termination of the trust, and, on a change of trustee, to each beneficiary to whom distributions are being made.[31] The duty to account can be waived either by the trust document or the beneficiary. The type of account that must be provided will depend on whether the trust is court supervised or not court supervised. To determine whether the trust is court supervised or not, look at Chapter 19.

The accounting typically includes information about

- How assets were invested;
- How trust assets were spent;
- What assets and liabilities the trust has;
- An explanation of any unusual disbursements;
- The amount of money the trustee received for services; and
- The amount of money paid to advisers such as attorneys or accountants.

In order to simplify the accounting, it is best if the trustee keeps excellent records throughout the year. It is much easier to create an account with up-to-date records rather than digging through shoeboxes of receipts and trying to recreate what happened in the past year.

For a complete discussion of the accounting requirements for both court supervised and non-court supervised SNTs, see Chapter 8.

8. Duty to Furnish Information to the Beneficiary

The trustee has a duty to keep the beneficiaries of a trust reasonably informed of the trust's administration.[32] Unlike the duty to account and the duty to furnish reports discussed above, this duty to inform cannot be waived. A beneficiary may make a reasonable request for information and the trustee must provide the beneficiary with a report of information about the assets, liabilities, receipts, and disbursements

---

31 Probate Code §16062.
32 Probate Code §16060.

of the trust, the acts of the trustee, and the particulars relating to the trust that are relevant to the beneficiary's interest.[33]

A trustee who wishes to have a smooth administration should communicate on a regular basis with the beneficiary. The most common mistake of trust administration is lack of communication between the trustee and the beneficiary. If the trustee wishes to take an action that the beneficiary may have an issue with, it is typically better to notify that beneficiary and see if there will be a dispute later and try to fix it now.

9. Duty to Keep Trust Assets Separate

A trustee must keep the trust property separate and distinct from the beneficiary's other assets.[34] The beneficiary's SSI and other public benefits should be maintained in a separate bank account and never commingled with trust funds.

The trustee should obtain and use a separate tax identification number for the trust. A separate tax identification number can be obtained online.[35] The trustee should not use the beneficiary's social security number for any trust bank or brokerage account if owned and operated by the trust.

The trustee must also keep the trust property separate from his or her own property. In other words, the trustee should have a separate bank account or accounts for the trust, and the trustee must not put either trust principal or income into his or her personal accounts.

10. Duty to Protect and Preserve Trust Assets

The trustee has a duty to protect and preserve the trust assets, and to insure them whenever practicable.[36] The trustee should be sure to consult a competent insurance agent regarding proper coverage for trust assets. Few things are worse than having a trust asset destroyed through no fault of the trustees and then discovering that the asset was not insured. In that case, the trustee's personal bank account may become the insurance company.

---

33 Probate Code §16061.

34 Probate Code §16009.

35 http://www.irs.gov/businesses/small/article/0,,id=102767,00.html.

36 Probate Code §16049.

For a more complete discussion of the duty to protect and preserve assets, see Chapter 7.

11. Duty to Enforce or Defend Claims

The trustee has a general duty to take reasonable steps to enforce claims of the trust.[37] This does not mean that the trustee must enforce every claim. The standard is whether a prudent trustee would take steps to enforce a claim in such circumstances. The trustee must evaluate such factors as whether there is a likely chance of success and whether a judgment would be collectible.[38] In one recent California case, a trustee was held responsible for breach of trust for prosecuting a claim that netted a much smaller recovery than it cost to obtain it.

The trustee also has a duty to take reasonable steps to defend actions that may result in a loss to the trust.[39] Depending on the circumstances, it may be reasonable to settle an action or suffer a default rather than to defend, but no matter how the case is resolved, a trustee who fails to exercise reasonable judgment faces liability.

12. Duty to Invest Assets and Make Productive

The trustee ordinarily has a duty to invest trust property, preserve it, and make it productive.[40] The duty to invest, however, is not absolute. The trustee's investment powers are usually derived from the trust document. If not, these powers are set by California law and by the circumstances of the trust and its beneficiaries. All of these sources of investment powers are considered in determining whether an investment is proper.

In many SNTs, the trustee must comply with the Prudent Investment Standard.[41] This standard requires the trustee to invest the assets as a prudent person would given the current and future circumstances of the beneficiary. However, if the SNT is court supervised, the trustee may have a very specific investment standard that must be followed. For a more complete discussion of the investment requirements, see Chapter 9.

---

37   Probate Code §16010.
38   *Schwartz v Labow* (2008) 164 Cal, App. 4th 417.
39   Probate Code §16011.
40   Probate Code §§16006-16007.
41   Probate Code §§16045-16054.

WHAT CAN HAPPEN IF AN SNT BREACHES A FIDUCIARY DUTY?

If an SNT trustee breaches a fiduciary duty, the court has broad power to fashion an appropriate remedy. A judge could require the SNT trustee to pay to the SNT any of the following:

- Any loss or depreciation in value of the SNT resulting from the breach of duty, with interest.[42]
- Any profit made by the SNT trustee through breach of duty, with interest.[43]
- Any profit that would have accrued to the SNT if the loss of profit were the result of the breach of duty.[44]

The court also has full discretion to excuse the SNT trustee from liability in whole or in part (including liability for interest) if the trustee acted reasonably and in good faith under the circumstances as known to the trustee and if it would be equitable to do so.[45] This discussion is expanded in Chapter 5.

A judge has additional remedies he or she can award against an SNT trustee that has breached his or her duty. These remedies include

- **Reducing SNT Trustee's Compensation.** An SNT trustee's pay may be used to offset any damage suffered by the SNT, but even if the trustee's breach failed to cause any financial damage, the court may still take away the SNT trustee's pay.[46]

- **Surcharge the SNT Trustee.** If the SNT trustee's breach of duty resulted in financial harm to the SNT, the SNT trustee may have to pay a fine to the SNT from his or her own personal funds.[47]

---

42   Probate Code §16440(a)(1).
43   Probate Code §16440(a)(2).
44   Probate Code §16440(a)(3).
45   See Probate Code §§16440(b), 16441(b).
46   Probate Code §16420(a)(7).
47   Probate Code §16420(a)(3).

- **Removal of SNT Trustee.** An SNT trustee may be removed, even if the trustee's breach never resulted in financial harm to the SNT. A judge has authority to do this to protect the SNT.[48]

- **Contempt.** If an SNT trustee disobeys a lawful court order, the fiduciary may be punished for contempt.[49]

- **Costs.** The court is allowed to award costs against an SNT trustee, "as justice may require."[50]

Not every breach of trust will lead to penalties. In Chapter 5, there is a discussion of defenses and other tools that can be used to protect the SNT trustee in case something has gone wrong.

CHAPTER 2 SUMMARY

✓ The SNT trustee has a great deal of power and responsibility when serving as a trustee for a person with a disability.

✓ The SNT trustee duties are found in a number of sources, primarily the trust document, a court order, California law, and federal law.

✓ Trustee should approach trustee duties by understanding intent of trust and understand his or her own motives in making decision on trust duties.

✓ The trustee has many legal duties, which must be followed. These duties include general prudence, carry out terms of trust, not to self-deal, be loyal to SNT beneficiary, not to delegate responsibility, ask for help if duties are more than trustee can manage, keep records, provide information to SNT beneficiary, account and report to SNT beneficiary, protect trust assets, keep trust assets separate, make trust assets productive and invest trust assets.

---

48 Probate Code §17200. Probate Code §15642(a).

49 Code of Civil Procedure §1209(a)(5).

50 Probate Code §1002.

✓ If an SNT trustee breaches a fiduciary of duty, the court may require the SNT trustee to repay (or surcharge) the SNT for any harm caused, disgorge profits, be removed, and pay costs, among other remedies.

✓ A court also has discretion to waive an SNT trustee's breach of fiduciary duty if the trustee acted in good faith and reasonably under the circumstances.

CHAPTER 3

Public Benefits Basics for Persons with Disabilities

One of the most important aspects of administering a SNT is to make sure that the trustee understands the public benefit program's eligibility rules for each benefit the SNT beneficiary receives. This is important because the SNT trustee may accidentally disqualify the person with a disability from his or her public benefits if he or she administers the SNT without taking into account these rules.

> **Helpful Hint:** It will come as a surprise to many that very few people with disabilities will know exactly what public benefits they receive. It is important that the SNT trustee find out what public benefits the SNT beneficiary receives because the rules on administration will substantially change depending on the type of public benefits the person receives.
>
> To assist in finding out which public benefits the SNT beneficiary receives, please review Mistake Number Three in Chapter 19.

If the SNT trustee does not understand the rules, the SNT beneficiary could lose access to Medi-Cal benefits to pay beneficiary's health care costs or lose Supplemental Security Income (SSI) that pays for the beneficiary's food and shelter. This can be devastating for a person with a disability who needs access to all the supports he or she can receive to live. Many SNT trustees believe they can use good old-fashioned common sense when administering an SNT. Sadly, these SNT trustees will fail miserably, because the public benefit rules oftentimes make no sense whatsoever. For example, an SNT trustee cannot reimburse an SSI recipient for the purchase of a television, because the beneficiary will lose his or her SSI eligibility. If, however, the SNT trustee reimbursed the SSI recipient's best friend who bought the television, there is no penalty. It is arbitrary rules like these that will trip up the well-intentioned trustee who does not wish to learn the rules.

In this chapter, the basic rules for eligibility of the main public benefit rules are discussed. In Chapters 4 and 11 - 16, there is a thorough discussion of how certain kinds of SNT disbursements will affect a person with a disability's public benefits. If the SNT trustee still feels that he or she is not comfortable making these types of decisions, he or she should go to Chapter 20 to find assistance.

Public benefits for persons with disabilities can be broken up into three main categories that are described in more detail below:

- **Needs-based benefits** like SSI, Medi-Cal, and In-Home Supportive Services (IHSS)

- **Entitlement benefits** like Social Security, Social Security Disability Insurance (SSDI), Childhood Disabled Beneficiary (CDB), Regional Center, and Medicare

- **Other benefits** like Section 8 and Veteran Benefits

    Helpful Hint: An excellent starting point when learning about California public benefits programs is the website at https://ca.db101.org. This website provides an easy-to-understand format on all types of California's public benefits. There are lots of other websites that are also useful on specific public benefits programs that are found in Chapter 20.

WHAT ARE NEEDS-BASED PUBLIC BENEFITS?

The following benefits are sometimes called "needs-based" or "means-tested" public benefits, because they have strict income and resource requirements. These are the key public benefits that an SNT is designed to protect and include the following:

- Supplemental Security Income[51] (**"SSI"**). SSI provides monthly cash payment for food and shelter to disabled, blind, or aged (age sixty-five or older) persons.

- **Medi-Cal**[52] (known as Medicaid outside the state of California). Medi-Cal pays for a broad array of medical treatments and is the only government program that pays for long-term nursing home care.

- In-Home Supportive Services **(IHSS),** which provides in-home care for persons with disabilities such as general housekeeping or shopping so the recipient can remain at home rather than having to live in an institution and is paid for by Medi-Cal.

- **Cal-Fresh** (Food Stamps), beginning June 1, 2019, persons eligible for SSI can also receive Cal-Fresh food stamps. Prior to this date a person eligible for SSI was unable to qualify for food stamps. This can add an average of $130 a month to an SSI recipient in order to purchase food.

WHAT ARE ENTITLEMENT PUBLIC BENEFITS AND DOES THE SNT TRUSTEE NEED TO WORRY ABOUT THEM?

The following benefits are generally called "entitlement benefits" because a person may still qualify for them and still have substantial wealth in his or her own name. These benefits were typically paid for with taxes while working by either the person with a disability (or under certain situations) their parents. These include the following:

---

51 Title XVI; 42 U.S.C. §§1381–1383f.
52 Title XIX; 42 U.S.C. §§1396–1396v.

- **Social Security Retirement**.[53] This benefit provides a monthly check for eligible workers who are at least sixty-two years of age and sometimes will pay money for the worker's eligible spouse, ex-spouse, and in some instances the worker's children. To qualify for this benefit, a worker must have worked and paid taxes on wages for at least ten years of work, with the required amount of earnings.

- **Social Security Disability Insurance**[54] **(SSDI)**. To receive disability benefits, the worker must be so severely mentally or physically impaired as to be unable to perform any substantial gainful work, and the impairment must be expected to last (or has lasted) one year or to result in death. Generally, for disability benefits, a worker needs to have worked for several years.

- **Childhood Disabled Beneficiary Benefits (CDB), sometimes called Disabled Adult Child (DAC)**.[55] A parent's child with a disability may receive a percentage of the parent's social security check if that child was disabled before age twenty-two. Payments to the child will begin when the parent is disabled, retires, or dies. Payments are 50% on disability or retirement and 75% on death. If the child remains on the program for two years, he or she is qualified to receive Medicare.

- **Medicare**.[56] Medicare provides health insurance for individuals who are age sixty-five or over, disabled, or has end-stage kidney disease or amyotrophic lateral sclerosis (ALS, also known as Lou Gehrig's disease). Medicare does not have an income or resource requirement. Typically, those eligible for SSDI or Social Security qualify for Medicare. Medicare does not provide complete coverage for all health-care needs. It only covers medically "reasonable and necessary" services. For example, it will not pay for many routine or preventive services, such as annual physical exams, eyeglasses, dental care, hearing aids, or long-term care at home or in a nursing home.

---

53 Title II; 42 U.S.C. §§401–418.
54 Title II; 42 U.S.C. §§401–418.
55 Title II; 42 U.S.C. §402(b)–(h).
56 Title XVII; 42 U.S.C. §§1395–1395hhh.

The good news for SNT trustees is that the administration of the SNT should not interfere with the beneficiary's eligibility for these benefits. Thus, if the only benefits that the SNT beneficiary receives are entitlement benefits and he or she is not receiving any needs-based public benefits, the SNT trustee disbursements will not interfere with the beneficiary's public benefits.

IS THERE A SUMMARY CHART FOR THE PUBLIC BENEFITS MOST COMMONLY RECEIVED BY PERSONS WITH DISABILITIES?

The following chart is a nice summary of how the different public benefit programs are organized between needs-based benefits and entitlement benefits.

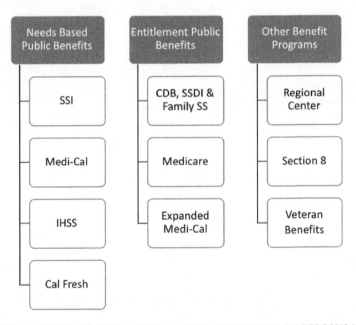

Needs Based Public Benefits	Entitlement Public Benefits	Other Benefit Programs
SSI	CDB, SSDI & Family SS	Regional Center
Medi-Cal	Medicare	Section 8
IHSS	Expanded Medi-Cal	Veteran Benefits
Cal Fresh		

WHAT ARE THE PUBIC BENEFITS MOST COMMONLY RECEIVED BY PERSONS WITH DISABILITIES?

The chart below shows the type of public benefits an SNT trustee would expect to see for different types of persons with disabilities. The main triggers for the different types of benefits are whether person is developmentally disabled, whether they worked prior to disability, the age they were disabled, and the type of care needed.

There are always exceptions to these general rules, but this chart should be a good overview of what benefits are available for different types of persons with disabilities.

Type of Person with a Disability	Effect of Work on Benefits	Financial Benefits	Health Care Benefits	Special Benefits
Developmental disability such as intellectual disability, cerebral palsy, epilepsy, and autism	Person with disability **never worked** or only with substantial assistance	**SSI** **CDB** – if disabled before age 22 and parent paid into system and parent is disabled, retired, or dead	**Medi-Cal** **IHSS** – if need assistance with activities of daily living **Medicare** – but only if receive CDB benefits for two years	**Regional Center** **Cal Fresh** - only if receive SSI or otherwise qualify **Section 8** – if lucky enough to receive due to limited availability
Not a developmental disability, typically mental or physical not considered developmental	Person with disability **never worked** or only with substantial assistance	**SSI** **CDB** – if disabled before age 22 and parent paid into system and is disabled, retired, or dead	**Medi-Cal** **IHSS** – if need assistance with activities of daily living **Medicare** – but only if receive CDB benefits for two years	**Cal Fresh** - only if receive SSI or otherwise qualify **Section 8** – if lucky enough to receive due to limited availability
Developmental disability such as intellectual disability, cerebral palsy, epilepsy, and autism	Person with disability **worked** sufficient time to qualify for SSDI	**SSI** – only if SSDI does not eliminate eligibility **SSDI**	**Medi-Cal** **IHSS** – if qualified for Medi-Cal and need assistance with activities of daily living **Medicare** – after two years of SSDI benefits	**Regional Center** **Cal Fresh** - only if receive SSI or otherwise qualify **Section 8** – if lucky enough to receive due to limited availability

			Medi-Cal	
Not a developmental disability, typically mental or physical not considered developmental	Person with disability **worked** sufficient time to qualify for SSDI	**SSI** – only if SSDI does not eliminate eligibility **SSDI**	**IHSS** – if qualified for Medi-Cal and need assistance with activities of daily living **Medicare** – after two years of SSDI benefits	**Cal Fresh** - only if receive SSI or otherwise qualify **Section 8** – if lucky enough to receive due to limited availability

WHAT PUBLIC BENEFITS REQUIRE SPECIAL SNT ADMINISTRATION KNOWLEDGE?

It is so important to remember that the different public benefit programs have very different eligibility requirements. These eligibility requirements will end up driving the administration of the SNT.

Must Know Rules to Properly Administer SNT	No Effect on SNT Administration	Depends
SSI	SSDI	Section 8 – Read Section
Medi-Cal	CDB / DAC	VA benefits – but does not protect benefits
IHSS	Medicare	
Cal - Fresh	Regional Center	

IF PERSON WITH A DISABILITY IS ELIGIBLE FOR MULTIPLE PUBLIC BENEFITS, WHICH RULES DOES THE SNT TRUSTEE HAVE TO FOLLOW?

If the person with a disability is receiving both SSI and Medi-Cal, then in most cases, the only rules the SNT trustee must follow are those for SSI eligibility. The reason is that in California, as long as the SNT beneficiary is eligible for at least $1 of SSI, he or she is automatically qualified for Medi-Cal.

The SNT beneficiary may only be eligible for Medi-Cal without being eligible for SSI. In these circumstances, the SNT trustee must follow Medi-Cal's rules and not SSI's. In most circumstances, the rules are very similar. However, there are differences.

When these differences exist, an explanation is made in the book of how Medi-Cal will treat that situation.

If the person with a disability is **not** receiving SSI, Medi-Cal, IHSS, or Cal-Fresh, then the SNT trustee must only comply with normal trust administration rules and does not need to learn any special public benefit eligibility rules.

WHAT DOES THE SSI PROGRAM PROVIDE?

The SSI program provides a monthly check to the person with a disability to pay for that person's food and shelter. The maximum amount of SSI an individual can receive in California in year 2020 is $958.63 per month, and $1,582 per month for a couple. These are the numbers most commonly used when administering an SNT. However, as seen in the chart below, the SSI amount can vary depending on the person with a disability's living situation, marital status, and whether the person's disability is blindness.

To determine the correct amount of SSI in California for years after 2020, see www.ssa.gov/pubs/11125.html or Google "SSI in California" and the link to the www.ssa.gov site should direct the trustee to the latest information.

Category	2020 total monthly payment	
Single people	*Disabled*	*Blind*
Independent living status	$958.63	$1,016.04
Nonmedical board and care	$1,213.47	$213.47
Independent living status, no cooking facilities	$1,034.33	N/A
Living in the household of someone else	$689.09	$746.52
Disabled minor child	$849.53	
Disabled minor child in household of another	$591.99	
Disabled couples		
Independent living status	$1,582	
Nonmedical board and care	$2,426.96	
Independent living status, no cooking facilities	$1,764.56	

Living in the household of someone else	$1,202.69
Blind couples	
Independent living status	$1,744.67
Living in the household of someone else	$1,356.16
Non medical out-of-home care	$2,426.96
Blind person with a disabled spouse	
Independent living status	$1,657.65
Living in the household of someone else	$1,281.26
Non medical out-of-home care	$2,388.74
Blind person with a disabled spouse	
Single person	$51.00
Couple	$102.00

To see the annual increase in SSI, here is a chart that shows the maximum amount for an individual with a disability. Each year the SSI amount is adjusted by the cost of living adjustment (COLA). The Social Security Act specifies a formula for determining each COLA. According to the formula, COLAs are based on increases in the Consumer Price Index for Urban Wage Earners and Clerical Workers (CPI-W). CPI-Ws are calculated on a monthly basis by the Bureau of Labor Statistics. Below is a chart showing the last five years of increases for SSI amounts based on the COLA. If there is no increase, then the amount remains the same.

Year	Max SSI Amount for California Individual	Cost of Living Adjustment (COLA)
2020	$958.63	1.6%
2019	$931.72	2.8%
2018	$906.40	2.0%
2017	$891.40	.3%
2016	$889.40	0%
2015	$889.40	1.7%

WHY DOES THE SNT TRUSTEE NEED TO KNOW THE SSI RULES ON RESOURCES AND INCOME?

An SNT trustee must understand the SSI rules on resources or income because distributions from the SNT could create an unexpected loss of SSA. This is because the Social Security Administration (SSA) (the government agency that runs SSI) will count certain types of SNT distributions as a type of SSI income, subject to the SSA's "income rules." Then, if the income is used to buy some kind of asset (or becomes an asset itself, such as money in a bank account), the asset will be subject to separate SSI "resource rules." Either can cause a loss or reduction of SSI, which can then result in loss of Medi-Cal.

In order to be sure that the trust distributions fall into the desired category, the trustee must maintain accurate records of how the trust funds are distributed. These records will be needed if the SSA or other government agency wants verification of the expenditures the trustee has made. It is not unusual for the agencies to make a demand for verification, and the trustee should expect it.

WHAT ARE THE SSI RULES ON RESOURCES?

An otherwise eligible person is not entitled to SSI if the applicant's countable resources and those of the applicant's spouse exceed $3000. For an otherwise eligible single person, the resource limit is $2,000.

COUNTABLE RESOURCES

Generally, an SSI "countable resource" is any asset considered by SSI rules in determining eligibility (therefore a resource is sometimes called a "countable asset"). It could be tangible, like a second automobile, or it could be something like a savings or retirement account.

> **Example:** A single person with a disability has a checking account with $600, a savings account with $500, and an IRA account that is valued at $1,500. This person would not qualify for SSI, because his assets exceed $2,000. If he spent down his assets below the

$2,000 before the first day of the next calendar month he would then qualify for SSI.

EXCLUDED RESOURCES

The beneficiary is allowed to have certain exempt assets, which are excluded from the $2,000 limit. These exempt assets are not counted in determining eligibility, and the beneficiary's ownership of them will not put the SSI benefits at risk. Therefore, the SNT trustee may freely purchase exempt assets for the beneficiary and give them to him or her with no loss in SSI or Medi-Cal.

A complete list of the resource exclusions, more than 40 in all, can be found in POMS SI 01130.050. The more common exempt assets include the following:

- A home of any value, including adjacent land, if the beneficiary lives in it or intends to return to it.
- One automobile of any value.
- Household goods (furniture, furnishings, household equipment, household supplies), personal effects (toiletries, items of personal care), education, clothing, and jewelry (however, giving the beneficiary food is "in-kind support," as explained below).
- Life insurance with a cash surrender value, if its face value is less than $1,500, and all-term life insurance.
- A burial plot, or other burial space, worth any amount.
- A revocable burial fund, worth up to $1,500.

Law specifically exempts all the assets above. The trustee might note that a number of common and useful items are not specifically mentioned as exempt in the SSI regulations, but are not counted because they are included among "personal effects" or are services. These include recreational equipment, games and crafts, books and magazines, telephone, television, computer, Internet or satellite television service and cable service, musical instruments and stereo, travel and education, recreation and entertainment, and some home maintenance, such as gardening. But there are many other items that are listed in the Index under the "No Brainer" guidelines.

WHEN ARE SSI RESOURCES COUNTED?

Resources are counted on the first minute of the first day of each calendar month.[57] If resources meet or exceed $2,000 at that moment, the person is ineligible for SSI for the whole month. Thus, it is possible for the SSI recipient to be over the resource limit during the calendar month but continue to receive the benefit if assets are spent down prior to the first minute of the first day of the calendar month.

> **Example:** An SSI recipient checking account balance is $1,300 and savings account balance is $500 on June 20. The next day, the recipient receives $2,200 from an inheritance. At this point, the SSI recipient's assets exceed the $2,000 limit. However, if the recipient spends his assets to below $2,000 before the end of the day on June 30, he or she will keep SSI eligibility in July.

HOW DO THE SSI RULES DEFINE INCOME?

The SSA treats SNT distributions in one of four ways against the SNT beneficiary as either

1. Unearned income
2. Earned income
3. In-kind support and maintenance (ISM)
4. Not income

Each kind of income is discussed below in order.

> **Critical Pointer:** SSI income that is received during the calendar month is considered "income" throughout the month of receipt, even if it is deposited in a bank account. If, at the end of the month, it is still in the account, it becomes a "resource" in the next month and is then subject to "resource" rules that are discussed above.

---

57   20 C.F.R. §416.1207(a).

Helpful Hint: A common misunderstanding is that "income" for IRS purposes is the same as "income" for SSA purposes. It is not. SSI defines the word "income" differently than what is commonly understood by that term. So, it is important to understand how SSI income will be counted when administering the SNT.

1. Unearned Income

Any money received by the SSI recipient directly (not earned) will be considered "unearned income" and will reduce SSI benefits on a dollar-for-dollar basis. Examples of unearned income include the following:

- Gifts
- Annuities, pensions, and other periodic payments
- Alimony and support payments
- Dividends, interest, and royalties
- Rents
- Prizes and awards

As a result of the penalty, the SNT trustee should avoid making direct payments to the beneficiary, because there will be little advantage from doing so. If the SNT trustee's actions reduce the beneficiary's SSI benefits to zero, then both the beneficiary's SSI and Medi-Cal benefits will be put at risk. The SSA does allow the SNT beneficiary to receive $20 per month of any income with no reduction in benefits.

Example: An SNT beneficiary asks the trustee to provide a monthly allowance of $500 per month to supplement the SSI check of $958.63 per month. If the SNT trustee chooses to authorize this monthly payment, the beneficiary will lose $480 per month of SSI. The net effect is that the beneficiary only receives $20 per month and loses $480 per month from his SNT.

Moreover, if the SNT trustee gives the beneficiary over $912 per month directly from the SNT then the SSI recipient will lose his or her SSI for that month and could ultimately jeopardize his or her eligibility for Medi-Cal as well.

An SNT trustee may not reimburse the beneficiary for purchases he or she has made, even if the purchases are for exempt assets. The payment will simply be counted as direct income. In addition, SSI rules say that if the SNT trustee gives the beneficiary anything that is equivalent to cash, it will also be counted as direct income.

Example: An SNT beneficiary pays $500 for an iPad. The SNT beneficiary asks the SNT trustee to reimburse him for the payment. If the SNT trustee agrees, then the beneficiary will lose $480 from his monthly SSI check because the SSA will treat it as "unearned income." It is critical that payment of money is never made directly to the SNT beneficiary.

If, instead, the SNT trustee had purchased the iPad directly for the beneficiary, then there would have been no loss of SSI benefit. Or, if the SNT trustee had reimbursed a friend of the beneficiary who had bought the iPad for the beneficiary, then that will also result in zero loss of SSI benefit.

2. Earned Income

An SSI recipient will lose eligibility for SSI payments based on earned income. Earned income may be paid in cash or in-kind. If it is in-kind and in exchange for labor, its full current market value is the amount used to determine countable income. Examples of earned income include

- Wages paid
- Net earnings from self-employment
- Payments for participating in a sheltered workshop or work activity center
- Royalties earned in connection with any publication of the individual's work
- Any honorariums received for services rendered

The SSI penalty on earned income is not as strict as it is for unearned income described above. Earned income only reduces a recipient's SSI monthly cash payment by 50 cents for each dollar earned, after taking an earned income exclusion of $65 (or, if the any-income exemption were unused, the total earned income exclusion would be $85).

Example: An SSI recipient earns $900 per month from employment. He is receiving $958.63 per month in SSI. Due to the earned income, his benefits are reduced by $407.50 to $524.22. The reduction is calculated by taking the $65 per month earned income exclusion and the $20 any income exclusion and then dividing the balance of remaining income by half. ($900 - $65 - $20 ÷ 2 = $407.50).

3. In-Kind Support and Maintenance (ISM)

Another kind of income that SSA counts is the receipt of food or shelter by the SSI recipient. Oftentimes, an SNT trustee will pay for the beneficiary's food or shelter. This is called "in-kind support and maintenance" (ISM). In determining ISM, food and shelter is limited to the SSI's recipient's receipt of the following items:

- Food
- Mortgage payments (including property insurance required by the mortgage holder)
- Real property taxes (less any tax rebates or credits)
- Rent
- Heating fuel
- Gas
- Electricity
- Water
- Sewer
- Garbage removal

ISM causes a reduction in the beneficiary's SSI payment, *but not on a dollar-for-dollar basis*, as they are if the SNT trustee were to give the beneficiary cash directly. The theory behind the reduction or elimination is that SSI benefits are specifically intended to pay for a person's food and shelter, so if that person receives those things from another source, then less SSI benefits are needed. As a result, if the SNT trustee pays the beneficiary's grocery bill or rent, the SNT trustee is providing ISM to the beneficiary. In theory, the SSI recipient has less of a need for SSI benefits. Obviously, in reality, this amount of money in California is woefully short of providing even a minimum quality of life, which is why an SNT is so critically important to people with disabilities.

To determine the reduction of SSI, the SNT trustee should understand both the value of the one-third-reduction rule (VTR) and the presumed maximum value (PMV). The difference between VTR and PSM isn't much.

A. Value of One-Third Reduction Rule (VTR)

VTR applies when the benefits recipient lives in another's house throughout a month, receives *both* food and shelter from a person inside the household, and does not meet his or her pro rata share of cost of the food and shelter expenses for the household. This reduction will never be triggered when an SNT trustee pays for shelter items, because it is not a person inside a household. Instead, that reduction is calculated under the Presumed Maximum Value discussed next.

The VTR reduces the SSI benefit by one-third of the portion of the monthly SSI check that the federal government pays for. This is called the federal benefit rate (FBR). In 2020, the reduction to SSI would be $261 (1/3 of $783 (FBR)).

> **Example:** Amir an SSI recipient who receives SSI of $958.63 per month moves in with an uncle who pays for all of Amir's food and shelter costs. Because Amir lives in the same house as his uncle and receives free food and shelter, his SSI check will be reduced by $261. Thus, he will receive $685.63 per month.

B. Presumed Maximum Value (PMV)

The PMV rule applies when an SSI recipient receives either food or shelter from someone not living in the home or if food or shelter is paid while the SSI recipient lives in his or her own house. The reduction for PMV is valued at the lesser of its actual value or at its "presumed" value, which is one-third of the federal benefit portion, plus the $20 general income exclusion.

In 2020, the maximum PMV reduction amount is $281 (1/3 of the 2020 FBR of $783, plus $20). Hence, if the *actual* value of the ISM that the beneficiary receives is below $281, the beneficiary's SSI payment will be reduced to reflect the actual value of the ISM received once the actual value of ISM is proven. Otherwise it is presumed that the value of ISM is $281. If the ISM received has a value greater than the PMV, the beneficiary's SSI benefit will only be reduced by $281.

> **Example:** The SNT trustee distributes $2,200 a month for the beneficiary's rent. This is ISM to the beneficiary each month. If the beneficiary is entitled to receive $958.63 in SSI, the payment of rent will cause a $281 reduction in monthly benefit.

> Thus, as a trustee you have provided a $2,200 apartment for the beneficiary's shelter; the beneficiary still receives $685.63 per month from SSI and the beneficiary is still eligible for Medi-Cal. This is generally a great trade-off—a much nicer apartment with only a modest reduction of SSI.

> **Helpful Hint:** The SNT trustee that has already maxed out the PMV because he or she has paid the SSI recipient's rent can also pay for all of the SSI recipient's food without any further reduction in the SSI check. There is no second PMV reduction for paying food as well as shelter.

> **Helpful Hint:** There is a way to have the SNT trustee fund an ABLE account for an SNT beneficiary that qualifies, pay for shelter items from the ABLE account and have no reduction of SSI check. If the beneficiary qualifies, it increases their monthly cash by $281 per month. Chapter 10 on ABLE accounts discusses this strategy.

4. Not SSI Income

Generally speaking, there is no SSI income triggered at all when an SNT trustee gives the beneficiary something other than money. In most cases, it is safe to provide such "income" to the beneficiary. This is because the value of any noncash item (other than food or shelter) is not counted as income if the item will become an exempt asset when it is retained into the following month. For example, the SNT trustee can distribute to the beneficiary bed or other furniture, which are in-kind income but are not counted by SSI because they are exempt resources. The SNT trustee could also pay for services for the beneficiary that are not counted as income. This can include cable TV, Wi-Fi, internet satellite television, cell phone, or any other type of similar service.

However, if the SNT trustee makes a disbursement for an item that will be counted in the next month as a resource, then the SNT beneficiary may lose his or her eligibility.

> **Example:** An SNT trustee purchases an automobile for $15,500 and the beneficiary takes title to the automobile. However, the SNT beneficiary already owns a motorcycle that is worth $10,000. Because an SSI recipient is only allowed to own one automobile (a motorcycle is counted as an automobile), then the second auto-mobile will be counted as a resource against the SNT beneficiary and he loses eligibility for his SSI, because his recourses exceed the $2,000 resource limit.
>
> If, instead, the SNT trustee had purchased the automobile and kept title in the name of the SNT, the automobile would not be counted as an available asset. (See Chapter 14 on how best to purchase an automobile by an SNT trustee and Appendix T for a sample agreement for purchase of an automobile on behalf of a beneficiary.)

WHAT IS SSI "DEEMING," AND WHY DOES A MINOR OR SPOUSE NOT QUALIFY FOR SSI?

"Deeming" is a type of SSI income and assets that will count against a minor child or spouse. This is typically because the minor is still living with his or her parents and until age eighteen, the parents' assets and income are counted as the minor's for SSI resource purposes. Likewise, an SSI-eligible adult who is living with a spouse: the spouse's assets, and income are counted as part of the SSI-eligible persons for SSI eligibility purposes. This concept is called "deeming.[58]"

---

58   20 C.F.R. §416.1202(b)(1); POMS SI 01330.200.

Generally, the resources of a minor child living with both parents (or a parent and step-parent) are deemed to include the parents' resources in excess of $3,000 (*i.e.*, the resource allowance for a couple), or, if living with one parent, the parent's resources in excess of $2,000. The general resource exclusions apply to the parents' resources for deeming purposes plus the parents' pension funds are exempt.[59]

Generally, if an ineligible spouse and eligible spouse's nonexempt resources exceed $3,000, the SSI-eligible spouse will lose his or her benefits.[60] The SSA counts the value of all resources (money and property), minus certain exempt assets, when determining eligibility. In addition to the general exempt assets such as the home, automobile, and household goods and effects available to any individual, the ineligible spouse's pension funds (e.g., IRAs, 401k) are also exempt.[61]

It does not matter if money is actually provided to the minor or SSI eligible spouse for deeming to apply.[62]

When the minor turns age eighteen, the SSA will only count the minor's assets when determining SSI eligibility. If the SSI eligible spouse moves out, the other spouse's assets will not be counted.

> **Note:** Deeming only applies if the child is living with a parent. If the child is living in an institution or with a grandparent, deeming does not apply.

HOW DOES A BENEFICIARY QUALIFY FOR MEDI-CAL?

There are many ways for a person to be eligible for Medi-Cal. The most common and described briefly below are listed below:

1. **Categorical Eligibility.** People who receive Supplemental Security Income (SSI) or California Work Opportunity and Responsibility to Kids (CalWorks) are categorically eligible to receive Medi-Cal. Thus, even if the SSI recipient receives even $1 of SSI, he or she is automatically receives Medi-Cal.

---

59   20 C.F.R. §416.1202(b); POMS SI 01330.220.

60   20 C.F.R. §416.1205(c).

61   20 C.F.R. §416.1202(a).

62   20 C.F.R. §§416.1160(a), 416.1202.

2. **Expanded Medi-Cal.** Sometimes called Income-based Medi-Cal. If the person's family has income at or below 138% of the Federal Poverty Limit, then qualifies for Medi-Cal. This is true even if the person has assets over the $2,000 resource limit. There is no resource limit for this program. The program is limited to those under age 65.

3. **Aged and Disability Federal Poverty Level** ("A&D FPL"). This program provides free Medi-Cal services for persons with disabilities who meet the income and asset requirements of the A&D FPL program. It covers individuals and couples whose income is slightly higher than the SSI eligibility requirements.

4. **Aged, Blind, and Disabled** (sometimes called "**medically needy**" or "**share of cost Medi-Cal**"). This program provides full-scope Medi-Cal services to aged, blind, or disabled people with income above the eligibility levels of no-cost Medi-Cal programs (such as SSI and A&D FPL). The program usually requires that individuals incur a monthly "share of cost" (which is why it is sometimes referred to as "share-of-cost" Medi-Cal), which functions like a monthly copayment.

5. **250% California Working Disabled**. This program provides full-scope Medi-Cal to persons with disabilities who work and have income that is too high to qualify for other Medi-Cal categories. For this program, the recipient may have up to 250 percent of the federal poverty level in countable income and still receive Medi-Cal benefits. Enrollees pay a monthly, sliding-scale premium for this health coverage.

6. **Pickle Amendment**. The 1976 Pickle Amendment to the Social Security Act requires states to maintain SSI-linked Medi-Cal eligibility for SSI recipients who lose their SSI due to Social Security cost of living allowance. Eligibility extends to those who would have been eligible for SSI in the past, even if they never received it. Thus, the person would be eligible for Medi-Cal but not SSI.

7. **Medi-Cal Waivers.** A Medi-Cal waiver allows the Department of Health Care Services (DHCS) to waive certain Medi-Cal criteria for persons who would not be able to receive Medi-Cal benefits because of too much income or resources. An example is the Home and Community Based Service (HCBS) waivers, which allow community, based Medi-Cal services for certain Medi-Cal beneficiaries to avoid hospitalization or nursing facility placement.

To obtain further information on these different Medi-Cal programs, see https://ca.db101.org/ca/programs/health_coverage/medi_cal/program.htm.

WHAT IS EXPANDED MEDI-CAL?

Expanded Medi-Cal is a way to obtain Medi-Cal for a person with a disability that does not depend on a person's assets. The simplest way to qualify is if the SNT beneficiary:

- Does not qualify for Medicare or has private health insurance, and
- Is a U.S. citizen or a qualifying immigrant.

And is in one of these situations:

- Is a 19-64 years old and the family's income is at or below 138% of the Federal Poverty Level (FPL) (see chart below).
- Is a child 18 or younger and the family's income is at or below 266% of FPL (e.g., in 2019 is $64,495 per year for a family of four).
- Is pregnant, and the family's income is at or below 213% of FPL (e.g., in 2019 is $36,024 if you are single and pregnant with your first child, $54,852 per year for a family of four).

Note: The unborn baby is counted as a member of the pregnant woman's family.

Income-based Expanded Medi-Cal counts most types of earned and unearned income. However, some income is not counted, including SSI benefits and some contributions to retirement accounts. If the SNT beneficiary is in these situations, then there is no limit to how much money or other resources the SNT beneficiary can have and it does not matter whether or not that person is disabled.

An SNT trustee should understand the basics of this program to make sure he or she understands how SNT administration may be affected when a beneficiary is on Expanded Medi-Cal rather than traditional Medi-Cal.

> **Note:** It is important to remember that if an SNT beneficiary is receiving SSI, then they do not qualify for Expanded Medi-Cal and all SSI rules must be followed to preserve eligibility for the public benefit programs. Also, if the SNT beneficiary receives healthcare through Medicare or has private health care insurance, then the SNT beneficiary is receiving traditional Medi-Cal and not Expanded Medi-Cal.

A person is eligible to receive Expanded Medi-Cal if his or her income is below 138% of the Federal Poverty Limit (FPL). To determine this amount, the government looks at the size of the person's family and the person's Modified Adjusted Gross Income (MAGI). The determination of what a person's family is and how the MAGI is calculated is a bit complicated, but the SNT trustee can reference California's website to see if the SNT beneficiary qualifies. See https://www.healthforcalifornia.com/covered-california/income-limits .

In 2020, 138% of the FPL looks like this:

Family Size	138%
1	$17,237
2	$23,336
3	$29,435
4	$35,535
5	$41,635
6	$47,735

WHAT IS IN-HOME SUPPORTIVE SERVICES (IHSS)?

In-Home Supportive Services (IHSS) provides people who have disabilities or are over the age of sixty-five with in-home and personal care services to help them live safely in their own home or maintain an independent living arrangement. It is important for the SNT trustee to maximize as much as possible the IHSS benefits received, because private paying for caregiving services can quickly deplete the assets in an SNT.

IHSS provides the following services:

- Domestic services, such as sweeping, vacuuming, taking out the garbage, wheelchair cleaning and battery recharging, and changing bed linens
- Related services such as meal preparation and cleanup, laundry, and shopping
- Personal care services, such as feeding, bathing, grooming, dressing, bowel and bladder care, and help with medications
- Transportation to medical appointments or alternative sources of services, such as day programs
- Removal and cleanup of yard hazards
- Heavy cleaning
- Protective supervision for cognitively or mentally impaired individuals to safeguard from self-injury or hazard
- Paramedical services, as ordered by a physician such as injections, range of motion exercises, catheter insertion, etc.

WHO IS ELIGIBLE FOR IHSS?

California maintains an excellent website on IHSS eligibility at https://www.cdss.ca.gov/In-Home-Supportive-Services. For a summary of the different types of IHSS eligibility, see the chart at https://ca.db101.org/ca/programs/health_coverage/medi_cal/ihss/program.htm.

CAN AN SNT TRUSTEE JEOPARDIZE A BENEFICIARY'S IHSS ELIGIBILITY?

Yes. IHSS is available to any California resident, living in his or her own home, who is already eligible for Medi-Cal. As discussed above, the five eligibility categories people with disabilities most often use to get on Medi-Cal are as follows:

1. SSI-linked Medi-Cal called categorically eligible Medi-Cal
2. Aged and Disabled Federal Poverty Level Medi-Cal (A & D FPL)
3. California's 250% Working Disabled Program
4. Aged, Blind, and Disabled Medically Needy Medi-Cal (or sometimes called share-of-cost Medi-Cal)
5. Expanded Medi-Cal.

The SNT trustee should make sure that distributions from the SNT do not reduce or eliminate eligibility for IHSS through these programs. For example, if the Medi-Cal were received because the SNT beneficiary has SSI, the loss of SSI would eliminate the recipient's Medi-Cal and linked IHSS service.

Expanded Medi-Cal may not be affected by SNT disbursements. It was added as part of the Affordable Care Act or Obamacare. It is an income-only based program so distributions would only interfere with eligibility for this program if it were counted as the beneficiary's IRS income on a 1040.

See Chapters 15 on making appropriate disbursements to pay for additional services from a good IHSS worker.

CAN AN SNT BENEFICIARY RECEIVE BOTH SSI AND SSDI?

Yes, some SNT beneficiaries are eligible for both SSDI and SSI. This occurs when the claimant's SSDI payments and other benefits do not exceed SSI income and asset limitations.[63] The claimant may also then be eligible for health coverage such as Medicare, Medi-Cal, or private medical insurance coverage.

Many additional benefits programs may be available to an SSDI claimant, depending on his or her work history and the benefits his or her employer had provided. These may include the California State Disability Insurance (CSDI) program and privately sponsored short-term and long-term disability programs.

---

63   42 U.S.C. §402(k)(2)(B).

WHERE CAN THE TRUSTEE FIND A BENEFITS PLANNER?

Because public benefits laws are ever changing and very complex, it might be prudent for the trustee to obtain professional advice on obtaining and keeping public benefits. A list of benefit planners for different cities throughout California is found at https://ca.db101.org.

In addition to these individuals, there are private benefits counselors available who can assist. (One such is James Huyck whose contact information is provided in Chapter 20.)

SHOULD THE TRUSTEE ALSO BE THE BENEFICIARY'S SSI REPRESENTATIVE PAYEE?

Not necessarily. It might make sense if the beneficiary does not have the ability to manage his or her own SSI check and has no trustworthy family or friends able to assist. A Representative Payee is an individual or organization appointed by SSA to receive Social Security or SSI benefits for someone who cannot manage or direct someone else to manage his or her money.

The main responsibilities of a payee are to use the benefits to pay for the current and foreseeable needs of the beneficiary and properly save any benefits not needed to meet current needs. A payee must also keep records of expenses. When SSA requests a report, a payee must provide an accounting to SSA of how benefits were used or saved.

> **Note:** The monthly SSI checks should always be kept separate from the SNT accounts.

To become an SSI Representative Payee, the trustee should contact the SSA office nearest to the beneficiary to apply to be a payee. The trustee then submits an application, SSA Form SSA-11 (Request to be selected as payee) and documents to prove the trustee's identity. To locate a copy of the form with instructions on completing the form, see https://secure.ssa.gov/poms.nsf/lnx/0200502115.[64]

The trustee will need to provide his or her social security number or, if the trustee represents an organization, the organization's employer identification number.

---

64 POMS GN 00502.115.

SSA requires the trustee to complete the payee application in a face-to-face interview (with certain exceptions).[65]

CAN AN SNT BENEFICIARY WORK AND STILL KEEP SSI AND MEDI-CAL?

Yes. There are several SSI and Medi-Cal programs that allow a person to work and remain eligible for public benefits. It is important to remember that each program requires the SNT beneficiary to apply for them. Otherwise, public benefits can still be lost.

The public benefit work programs and incentives include

1. Impairment-Related Work Expense (IRWE)
2. Ticket to Work Program
3. Section 1619(a) and (b) Program
4. Plan for Achieving Self-Support (PASS)
5. 250% California Working Disabled Program (Medi-Cal Only)

A brief description of each program is set forth below

> **Note:** An excellent resource for work programs for persons with disabilities can be found in the SSA's Red Book, at https://www. ssa.gov/redbook/eng/main.htm and https://ca.db101.org/ca/ situations/workandbenefits/.

> **Helpful Hint:** The SSA has a website that provides assistance in finding assistance for a person with a disability to use these programs and to obtain work. See https://choosework.ssa.gov/ findhelp.

---

65 POMS GN 00502.113.

1. Impairment-Related Work Expense (IRWE)

An IRWE is a good tool for the SNT beneficiary who is working and trying to reduce the effect on his SSI or SSDI.[66] The SNT beneficiary can deduct the cost of the IRWE from his or her income, thus reducing (or eliminating) any impact on the SSI benefit.

IRWE's are expenses for services or items related to the person with a disability's impairment that he or she pays in order to support work activities. A payment for a service or item is excludable as an IRWE when

- The individual
  - Is disabled (but not blind); and
  - Is under age 65; or
  - Received SSI as a person with a disability (or received disability payments under a former State plan) for the month before attaining age 65; and
- The severity of the impairment requires the individual to purchase or rent items and services in order to work; and
- The expense is reasonable; and
- The cost is paid in cash by the individual and is not reimbursable from another source (e.g., Medicare, private insurance); and
- The payment is made in a month the individual receives earned income for a month in which he or she both worked and received the services or used the item; or the individual is working but makes a payment before the earned income is received.

Note: The SNT trustee cannot pay directly for IRWEs to receive the deduction; the beneficiary must make the IRWE's payments directly.

Example: George an SNT beneficiary receives $958.63 per month of SSI begins working and earns $600 per month from employment. If there are no other deductions, George will lose $261.50 from his SSI check ($600 earned income - $65 earned income exclusion - $20 general exclusion - ½ of remaining earned income).

---

66   20 C.F.R. §416.976; POMS SI 00820.540(B)(3).

If, however, George is only able to work at all because he paid for transportation by wheelchair van of $100 per month and a one-time fee of $300 for corrective eyewear. George would only lose $57.50 from his SSI check for that month ($600 earned income - $65 earned income exclusion - $20 general exclusion - $400 IRWE - ½ of remaining earned income). This is a savings of $200.

EXAMPLES OF DEDUCTIBLE AND NONDEDUCTIBLE IRWE[67]

TYPE OF EXPENSE	IRWE DEDUCTIBLE	NOT DEDUCTIBLE
Transportation Costs	The cost of structural or operational modifications to your vehicle that you need in order to travel to work, even if you also use the vehicle for nonwork purposes. The cost of driver assistance or taxicabs that is required because of your disability rather than the lack of public transportation. Mileage expenses at a rate determined by us for an approved vehicle and limited to travel to and from employment.	The cost of your vehicle whether modified or not. The costs of modifications to your vehicle that is not directly related to your impairment or critical to the operation of your vehicle, for example, paint or pin striping. Your travel expenses related to obtaining medical items or services.
Attendant Care Services	Services performed in the work setting. Services performed to help you prepare for work, the trip to and from work, and after work; for example, bathing, dressing, cooking, and eating. Services that incidentally also benefit your family, for example, meals shared by you and your family. Services performed by your family member for a cash fee where he/she suffers an economic loss by reducing or ending his/her work in order to help you. This includes your spouse reducing work hours to help you get ready for work.	Services performed on nonworkdays or help with shopping or general housekeeping, for example, cleaning and laundry. Services performed for someone else in your family, for example, babysitting. Services performed by your family member for payment "in-kind", for example, room and board. Services performed by your family member for a cash fee where he/she suffers no economic loss. This includes services provided by your nonworking spouse.

---

67   From SSA's Red Book, see https://www.ssa.gov/redbook/index.html.

Service Animals	Expenses paid in owning a guide dog or other service animal who enables you to overcome functional limitations in order to work Deductible expenses include costs of purchasing the animal, training, food, licenses, and veterinary items and services Other costs directly related to the care of the animal; such as transportation for training and veterinary services	Expenses for non-service animal
Medical Devices	Deductible devices include wheelchairs, dialysis equipment, pacemakers, respirators, traction equipment, and braces.	Any device you do not use for a medical purpose.
Prosthesis	Artificial hip, artificial replacement of an arm, leg, or other parts of the body.	Any prosthetic device that is primarily for cosmetic purpose.
Residential Modifications	*If you are employed outside of home*, modifications to the exterior of your house that permit access to the street or to transportation; for **example:** • Exterior ramps • Railings • Pathways *If you are self-employed at home,* modifications made inside your home in order to create a workspace to accommodate your impairment. This includes enlarging a doorway into an office or workroom and/or modifying office space to accommodate your dexterity challenges	*If you are employed outside of home*, modifications to the interior of your house. *If you are self-employed at home, you cannot deduct any modification-related expenses that will be deducted as a business expense when determining SGA.*

Routine Drugs, Over-the-counter drugs & Medical Services	Regularly prescribed medical treatment or therapy that is necessary to control your disabling condition, even if control is not achieved. This includes: • Anti-convulsant drugs • Anti-depressant medication • Pyschotripic medication • Blood level monitoring • Radiation treatment • Chemotherapy • Corrective surgery for spinal disorders • Counselling, mental health and therapy services • Your physician's fee relating to these services.	Drugs and/or medical services used for your minor physical or mental health problems, for **example:** • Allergy treatments • Routine annual physical examinations • Routine dental examinations • Routine optician services (unrelated to a disabling visual impairment) Prescription drugs that are a violation of Federal law (e g medical marijuana) cannot be deducted as an IRWE, even if allowed by State law
Diagnostic Procedures	Procedures related to the control, treatment, or evaluation of your disabling condition; for example, brain scans, and electroencephalograms.	Procedures not related to your disabling condition, for example, allergy testing.

Nonmedical Appliances & Devices	In unusual circumstances, devices or appliances that are essential for the control of your disabling condition either at home or at work; for example, an electric air cleaner if you have severe respiratory disease. Your physician must verify this need.	Devices you use at home or at the office that are not ordinarily for medical purposes and for which your doctor has not verified a medical work-related need. These include: • Portable room heaters • Air conditioners • Dehumidifiers • Humidifiers
Other Items & Services	Expendable medical supplies; for example, incontinence pads, elastic stockings, and catheters. The cost of a service animal including food, licenses, and veterinary services.	An exercise bicycle or other device you use for physical fitness, unless verified as necessary by your physician. Health insurance premiums.

2. Ticket to Work Program

The Ticket to Work is a federal program designed to help SSI or SSDI recipients, aged eighteen to sixty-four, to obtain, retain, or maintain employment and, eventually, reduce their dependence on cash benefit programs.[68] The recipients will receive a "ticket" that they may use to obtain supportive services, such as vocational rehabilitation, training, referrals, job coaching, and counseling from an approved Employment Network (EN) or State Vocational Rehabilitation agency (VR agency) of their choice.

The program is completely voluntary; there is no penalty if a recipient decides not to participate. If the SSI recipient is making sufficient progress toward his or her employment goal while enrolled in the program, the SSA will suspend medical continuing disability reviews. This is a significant benefit. Under normal circumstances, if the SSA conducts a medical review and determines that the SSI recipient is no longer "disabled" (*i.e.*, working sufficiently to reach SGA, he or she would lose all of his or her benefits. For more information, see http://www.yourtickettowork.com/index.

---

68   20 C.F.R. §411.125. See 42 U.S.C. §1320b-19; 20 C.F.R. §§411.100-411.250; POMS DI 55001.001.

3. Section 1619(a) and (b) Program

These programs allow a disabled or blind SSI recipient to qualify for continued SSI recipient status or to receive Medi-Cal even when working and receiving more than the amount normally allowed from employment.[69] Under §1619(a) of the Social Security Act, an individual may continue to qualify for SSI cash payments even though his or her gross earnings are at or above the work limit allowed (called "Substantial Gainful Activity" by the SSI and SSDI programs) provided all other non-disability requirements (*e.g.*, residency, income, resources) are met.

To be eligible for continued Medi-Cal coverage under §1619(b), an individual cannot have earnings that would be sufficient to replace SSI cash benefits, Medi-Cal benefits, and publicly funded personal or attendant care. The SSA annually determines a threshold amount to measure whether an individual has sufficient earnings to replace these benefits for each state (also called the "chartered threshold"). In 2019, the threshold amount for California is $37,706.[70]

If an individual's earnings exceed the threshold amount, the SSA may still make an individual threshold determination to incorporate specific needs the individual may have. In addition to the applicable threshold requirement, to qualify under §1619(b), a recipient must

- Have used SSI in the previous month;
- Continue to meet medical disability requirements;
- Continue to meet no disability requirements (except for earnings), such as resources, unearned income, and residency; and
- Need Medi-Cal health coverage to continue to work.

4. Plan for Achieving Self-Support (PASS)

The PASS program allows certain people with disabilities to set aside earned or unearned income.[71] Social Security will exempt this income when it is placed into an approved PASS plan and used toward a vocational goal, such as college or a training school. PASS is a SSI program. The beneficiary must meet SSI financial rules to use the program. A detailed application is required. PASS can be a valuable tool for

---

69   42 U.S.C. §1382h(a)-(b); 42 C.F.R. 416.260-416.269; POMS SI 02302.000.

70   POMS SI 02302.200 for latest numbers see https://secure.ssa.gov/poms.nsf/lnx/0502302200.

71   42 U.S.C. §§1382a(B)(4)(A)-(B), 1382b(a)(4); 20 C.F.R. §§416.1180-416.1182; POMS SI 00870.001.

competitive employment. Several factors make PASS an effective tool for someone wanting to work under the SSI program[72]:

- PASS reflects individual choice. Individuals choose their own work goal.
- PASS is self-financed. Individuals use their own funds to pursue the plan. The receipt of, or an increase in, SSI benefits up to the amount of the Federal Benefit Rate (FBR), and any applicable state supplement, replaces some or all of the funds that the individual uses for the PASS.
- PASS is largely self-directed. Individuals decide what goods and services are needed to reach the work goal.

5. California's 250% Working Disabled Program

If the SNT beneficiary is working, disabled, and his or her income is too high to qualify for Medi-Cal, the California 250% Working Disabled Program may allow the SNT beneficiary to receive Medi-Cal by paying a small monthly premium.[73] The SNT beneficiary is allowed when qualifying for this program to earn a fair amount of money and still qualify for public benefits.

To qualify, the SNT beneficiary must

- Meet the medical requirements of Social Security's definition of disability;
- Be working and earning income;
- Have assets worth less than $2,000 for an individual ($3,000 for a couple); the same asset exclusions apply for this program as the ones mentioned above;
- Have countable income less than 250% of the Federal Poverty Level; Disability income does not count for this program; this means that SSDI, Worker's Compensation, California State Disability Insurance, and any federal, state, or private disability benefits are not considered as income for this program; and
- Have countable unearned income less than the appropriate SSI benefit rate.

---

72   POMS SI 00870.001.

73   Welf & I C §14007.9; ACWD Letter No. 00-16 (Mar. 16, 2000).

WHAT OTHER PUBLIC BENEFITS MUST AN SNT TRUSTEE KNOW ABOUT?

There are other public benefits that a person with a disability may have that an SNT trustee should be familiar with:

- **CalFresh** (formerly known as food stamp program). CalFresh is a nutrition program that can help households buy healthy foods. Nationally, the program is called SNAP. It is funded by the federal government. CalFresh benefits are issued on an EBT card that works like a debit card and can be used at most grocery stores and many farmers markets to purchase food. It used to be that persons on SSI were unable to qualify for CalFresh, but as of June 1, 2019, SSI recipients may receive CalFresh which provides extra money for persons with disabilities.

- **Section 8 Housing** (known as "Housing Choice Voucher Program"). Under Section 8, beneficiaries receive a "voucher" or "subsidy" that they can apply to the rental of the housing unit of their choice—as long as the unit meets the Section 8 program requirements. A local Public Housing Agency (PHA) then delivers the subsidy to the landlord under a contract with the US Department of Housing and Urban Development (HUD). The beneficiary pays rent from 30 to 40 percent of their adjusted monthly income, and the PHA subsidy pays the remainder. The program allows very low-income individuals and families to choose where to live (see below for further discussion).

- **Veteran Benefits**. There are many persons with disabilities who became disabled as a result of military service or who previously served in the military. It is important to determine if these individuals can receive additional benefits from the US Department of Veterans Affairs. VA benefits can include compensation (for service-connected disabilities), pensions (for non-service-connected disabilities), and medical and other benefits. Depending on the type of benefit, it may be available to veterans of military service, their dependents, and their survivors (see below for further discussion).

WHAT IS CALFRESH BENEFITS AND DOES AN SSI RECIPIENT QUALIFY?

The CalFresh program is for people with low-income who meet federal income eligibility rules and want additional money to put healthy and nutritious food on the table. Beginning June 1, 2019, recipients of SSI benefits may be eligible for CalFresh Food benefits for the first time. There is no change to the SSI monthly benefit. The amount of CalFresh you get depends on many things, including your household's size, income, and costs. The average CalFresh household gets over $300 each month, but an individual's maximum is $192/month.

To apply as an SSI recipient for CalFresh, click https://www.getcalfresh.org/en/ssi.

WHAT ARE SECTION 8 HOUSING PUBLIC BENEFITS?

The federal Section 8 program began in 1975 as a way to assist people with disabilities, the elderly, and low-income individuals to rent decent, safe, and affordable housing in the community.[74] Section 8 housing assistance programs fall into two general categories: tenant-based assistance (vouchers) and project-based assistance.

- Tenant-based assistance is rental assistance that is not attached to a structure or particular rental unit. A local public housing authority (PHA) administers the program. Under a tenant-based assistance program, tenants are given rental assistance vouchers and then find landlords willing to accept them. The vouchers are "portable" and tenants may move to different rental units owned by landlords willing to accept the vouchers.

- Project-based assistance is linked to a specific federally subsidized apartment. The assistance does not travel with a tenant and, if a tenant moves, it is lost.

---

74 In 1975, when this housing assistance program was established, it was referred to as the "Section 8 " program. In many communities, it is still referred to by this name. However, a federal housing law passed in 1998 gave the program a new name the Housing Choice Voucher Program (HCVP). Because it is more familiar, this book uses the term "Section 8" to refer to the new HCVP.

HOW MUCH RENT DOES A DISABLED TENANT PAY UNDER SECTION 8?

The amount of rent the Section 8 recipient must pay is typically 30 to 40 percent of his or her monthly-adjusted income, with a minimum of $25 per month. Typically, the Section 8 recipient will pay 30 percent of their monthly-adjusted income for his or her share of the rent. To determine the monthly-adjusted income amount, the PHAs conduct a thorough examination of the household's income, including any assets, and calculate an annual adjusted income for that household. The adjustments to the income derive from HUD program regulations, which specify the types and amounts of income and deductions to be included in the calculation of annual and adjusted income. The Section 8 household's share of the rent is called the "total tenant payment."

Section 8 has its own rules on how assets are treated and what counts as income, which differ from other governmental agencies like Social Security or the Internal Revenue Service. The pertinent rules come from HUD and are contained in a Guidebook No. 7420.10G, entitled the "Voucher Program Guidebook, Housing Choice," available on the HUD website (herein the "Guidebook").[75]

Annual income is defined as all earnings, and includes employment wages, public benefits, and disbursements from any investments or pension plans.[76] Annual income includes income earned from assets during the twelve-month period and to which any family member has access.[77] The adjusted annual income is computed by reducing the family's gross annual income by any applicable standard deductions for seniors, persons with disabilities, and dependent children.[78]

Some examples of noncountable income are lump-sum additions to assets (e.g., if the SNT beneficiary receives an inheritance or litigation recovery); any amounts received specifically for, or as reimbursements of, medical expenses; amounts received by an SSI recipient that are disregarded as income by SSI because they are set aside for a PASS; and income received of a live-in aide, such as a personal care attendant, who provides necessary support services for a tenant with disabilities.[79]

---

75 http://www.hud.gov/offices/adm/hudclips/guidebooks/7420.10G/7420g05GUID.pdf.

76 42 USC §1437a(b)(4), 24 CFR §5.609.

77 24 CFR §5.609.

78 24 CFR §5.611(a); Voucher Guidebook 7520.10, §5.5.

79 24 CFR §§5.609(c), 982.316.

DO THE ASSETS OF AN SNT BENEFICIARY COUNT AGAINST SECTION 8 ELIGIBILITY?

Unlike SSI and Medi-Cal, the Section 8 program does not have resource limits. However, resources indirectly affect eligibility because income generated by resources is counted. A portion of an individual's assets will count toward the "annual income" determination. Income from assets is treated differently, depending on the amount of assets on hand.

Assets less than $5,000. If an individual with a disability's net assets are worth less than $5,000, all income derived from the assets is counted toward "annual income."[80]

> **EXAMPLE:** Kirby Rouser holds a Section 8 voucher and pays $150 each month in rent. Last year, his mother passed away and bequeathed him $3,500 in stocks. From these stocks, he earned a $360 end-of-year dividend (equal to $30 per month). Kirby will now have to pay approximately an additional $10 per month toward rent.

Assets greater than $5,000. If an individual with a disability's net assets are worth more than $5,000, the family must count toward annual income the greater of either (1) all income derived from the assets or (2) a percentage of the total value of the assets based on the passbook savings rate, as determined by HUD each year.[81] This is called the imputed income. The PHA will never count the full cash value of the asset toward annual income.

> **Example:** A husband and wife establish a $20,000 trust. Each year, the couple receives a $1,000 disbursement from the trust. The HUD passbook savings rate is 2 percent. The couple's annual income of $1,000 from the trust exceeds $400, which is 2 percent of the total value of the trust. Therefore, the PHA will count $1,000 toward annual income.

---

80 Voucher Guidebook 7520.10, §5.4, Determining Income from Assets.
81 Voucher Guidebook §5.4, Determining Income from Assets.

HOW WOULD AN SNT BENEFICIARY OBTAIN SECTION 8 HOUSING?

An individual applies for a Section 8 voucher with his or her local public housing agency (PHA). Section 8 is not an entitlement benefit, meaning that just because one is eligible to receive it does not mean that he or she will receive it. Because the demand for housing assistance almost always exceeds the number of Section 8 vouchers available, PHAs are usually unable to assist a Section 8 applicant immediately.

Unfortunately, most areas in California have long and growing waiting lists for vouchers; many PHAs have even stopped accepting new applications because of the size of the backlog. Generally, waiting times can vary between several months and several years.

For people with disabilities, there may be special set aside vouchers available. PHAs have several types of available vouchers. The most common would be the "Mainstream Housing Opportunities for Persons with Disabilities" voucher, which allows nonelderly persons with disabilities, who often face difficulties in locating suitable and accessible housing on the private market, to lease affordable private housing of their choice. Recipients of this assistance are selected from the regular waiting list.

Federal fair housing laws require that HUD and PHAs make reasonable accommodations in their policies, procedures, and programs to ensure active participation by people with disabilities. Thus, a person with a disability may request a reasonable accommodation in the PHA's policies for accepting Section 8 applications. Some examples of changes to the application process that can be requested as a reasonable accommodation include the following:

- Allowing additional time to submit an application;
- Allowing applications to be dropped off at the PHA by a friend, family member, advocate, service provider, etc.; and
- Conducting home visits in order to allow an applicant.

PHAs must allow Section 8 vouchers to be used in "special housing types"—including group homes, congregate housing, and shared housing—as a reasonable accommodation for a person with a disability.

CAN THE SPECIAL NEEDS TRUST BE A SECTION 8 LANDLORD?

Yes. If the SNT owns real estate, the trustee can apply to accept Section 8. This is generally a good result, because the SNT is able to generate some income from the home that it would not otherwise be able to receive.

All housing leased through the Section 8 program must meet HUD's housing quality standards and must be physically inspected by the PHA. Further, the SNT trustee must enter into a lease that meets the PHA/HUD requirements. Finally, the housing unit must have rent that is reasonable when compared to similar units in the community. This rule is referred to as "rent reasonableness."

DOES AN SNT PROTECT ELIGIBILITY FOR THE SECTION 8 BENEFICIARY?

Not specifically. This means that there is no statute that specifically allows an SNT to preserve Section 8 eligibility. However, under existing Section 8 rules, an SNT can be used in conjunction with a Section 8 recipient to preserve eligibility for Section 8. The issue is that Section 8 is an income-based program, and resources do not play much of a role in the program. Thus, when an SNT owns assets, the assets themselves are not counted against the Section 8 recipient. However, any income earned from the assets will typically increase the Section 8 recipient's rent payment.

One way that an SNT may be harmful to a Section 8 recipient's eligibility is when income or principal is regularly distributed from an SNT. Some California public housing agencies (PHAs) will count that distribution as Section 8 income, unless a specific exclusion applies.[82] If there is no income distributed from the trust (i.e., it is reinvested in trust assets), then nothing is counted as income. A recent federal court case has held that a PHA that counts distributions from an SNT as income is incorrect.[83]

> **Note:** If a California PHA is counting distributions from the SNT as income for a Section 8 recipient, the trustee should provide the PHA a copy of the *Brookline* case that shows this is against federal law. If the PHA does not acknowledge the case, then the trustee

---

82   Voucher Guidebook 7520.10, §5, Ex. 5-2.

83   *DeCambre v. Brookline Housing Authority* (1st Cir. 2016) 826 F.3d 1.

should contact a local attorney who specializes in these issues to assist. To find such an attorney, see Chapter 20.

The PHAs that count disbursements as income state that a regular recurring distribution from an SNT is included in income.[84] There are numerous categories of distributions that are specifically excluded from being treated as Section 8 income.[85] A few of them include the following:

- Temporary, nonrecurring, or sporadic income (including gifts)
- Lump-sum additions to family assets, such as inheritances, insurance payments (including payments under health and accident insurance and worker's compensation), capital gains, and settlement for personal or property losses
- Amounts received by the family that are specifically for, or in reimbursement of, the cost of medical expenses for any family member
- Income of a live-in aide
- Amounts received by a person with disabilities that are disregarded for a limited time for purposes of Supplemental Security Income eligibility and benefits because they are set aside for use under a Plan to Attain Self-Sufficiency (PASS)
- Amounts received by a participant in other publicly assisted programs which are specifically for or in reimbursement of out-of-pocket expenses incurred (special equipment, clothing, transportation, childcare, etc.) and which are made solely to allow participation in a specific program[86]

Warning: Some California PHAs have taken the position that each and every distribution from an SNT is income to the Section 8 recipient. These PHAs are even counting SNT disbursements that include payments for medical expenses or nonrecurring gifts as income. This practice should be fought. It is not consistent with the law and regulations. In order to find an attorney who can help fights these PHAs, see Chapter 20.

---

84 Voucher Guidebook 7520.10 §5, Ex. 5-2, Income Inclusions, (7).
85 Voucher Guidebook 7520.10 §5, Ex. 5-2, Income Exclusions.
86 Voucher Guidebook 7520.10 §5, Ex. 5-2, Income Exclusions.

Example: Mark Schwartz is a Section 8 recipient beneficiary of an SNT. Mark's SNT trustee makes a one-time payment for a Las Vegas vacation for Mark and is paying Mark's monthly electric bill of $100. There are no other distributions currently being made from the SNT. The one-time payment for the Las Vegas vacation should be exempt as a nonrecurring payment. Under the *Brookline* decision, the $100 a month for the electric bill should also be exempt, but the PHA may still try and count it as income, if it does, then Mark's rent will increase around $30/month.

WHAT SHOULD THE TRUSTEE DO IF THE BENEFICIARY IS ON SECTION 8?

The trustee needs to know whether the local PHA would treat distributions as income. This may be difficult to determine because oftentimes the local PHA does not have a set policy. The author has even had conflicting advice given from the same PHA as to its practice. It may be more prudent to find a local attorney who is familiar with PHA practice and find out from them if the local PHA takes this aggressive position that SNT distributions count as income. At a minimum, the Trustee should be cautious with regular recurring disbursements that do not meet any of the exceptions to being counted as income, and have a plan to defend its spending plan.

The author wishes he had better advice on this issue. The problem is that this is a real gray area in the law. On the one hand the *Brookline* decision would make these disbursements exempt, on the other hand, this decision is limited to the First Circuit Court of Appeals area that does not include California. The reasoning in the opinion is sound and the author has had some success negotiating with local PHAs about its applicability to disbursements.

WHERE CAN AN SNT TRUSTEE FIND MORE INFORMATION ABOUT SECTION 8?

The Technical Assistance Collaborative (TAC) is a national nonprofit organization that advances proven solutions to the housing and community support needs of vulnerable low-income people with significant and long-term disabilities. They issue an excellent publication called Section 8 Made Simple and Priced Out in 2016 among many other publications. Its website is http://www.tacinc.org. You will find plenty of great information there.

WHAT IF THE SNT BENEFICIARY IS A VETERAN?

There are many persons with disabilities who became disabled as a result of military service or who previously served in the military. It is important to determine if these individuals can receive additional benefits from the US Department of Veterans Affairs (VA). For more information on federal benefits, see www.va.gov. For additional California veteran benefits, see http://www.cdva.ca.gov/newhome.aspx.

VA benefits are available to veterans of military service, their dependents, and their survivors but the availability of these benefits depends on the background of the veteran. For an online guide of available federal benefits, see https://www.va.gov/opa/publications/benefits_book.asp.

WHICH VETERANS ARE ELIGIBLE FOR BENEFITS?

Eligibility for most VA benefits is based upon discharge from active military service by other than dishonorable conditions.

Active service means full-time service, other than active duty for training, as a member of the Army, Navy, Air Force, Marine Corps, or Coast Guard, or as a commissioned officer of the Public Health Service, Environmental Science Services Administration or National Oceanic and Atmospheric Administration, or its predecessor, the Coast and Geodetic Survey. Generally, men and women veterans with similar service may be entitled to the same VA benefits.

DOES A SPECIAL NEEDS TRUST PROTECT A VETERAN'S ASSETS WHEN REQUESTING BENEFITS?

There are no rules in the United States Code, the Code of Federal Regulations, or the VA's policy manual regarding VA treatment of trust assets and income or transfers of assets to SNTs. There have been two opinion letters from a VA Office of General Counsel opinion and a Board of Veterans Appeals decision on point.

An opinion by the Portland (Oregon) Regional Counsel of the VA held that assets placed in a SNT were includible in the claimant's net worth for purposes of determining eligibility for a pension.[87] The trust in question was a first party special needs trust prepared on behalf of the surviving spouse of a veteran, with a child serving as trustee.

At present, it appears that an SNT will not preserve eligibility for needs-based VA benefits. Although there are other strategies that can assist a veteran receive services. An SNT trustee should consult with a local veteran organization or seek the services of an attorney who is authorized to practice before the VA.

CHAPTER 3 SUMMARY

✓ Understanding public benefits rules is one of the most important things a SNT trustee will need to understand when administering an SNT.

✓ Using common sense alone without understanding the rules will cause loss of eligibility and other problems for the SNT trustee and the SNT beneficiary.

✓ SSI and Medi-Cal are the two types of benefits a SNT trustee will need to understand very well.

✓ If SNT beneficiary receives Medi-Cal and not SSI then Medi-Cal rules must be followed and not Social Security Rules.

✓ SNT trustee should know if SNT beneficiary is receiving SSI and SSDI and Medi-Cal or Medicare.

✓ SSI and Medi-Cal are needs based benefits meaning that the SNT beneficiary can only have $2,000 in assets and very limited income.

✓ Not all of a SSI recipient's assets are counted; some are exempt, like a home of any value or automobile of any value, plus other assets.

✓ Disbursements from SNT by trustee can be counted as income for SSI eligibility.

✓ Cash given directly to SNT beneficiary will be counted as unearned income and reduce SSI benefit dollar for dollar after first $20.

---

87   1997 VAOPGCPREC Lexis 656 (Aug. 29, 1997).

✓ An SNT trustee paying for food or shelter is counted as in-kind support and maintenance income and will reduce SSI by a modest reduction of $281 in 2020.

✓ There are a variety of ways to obtain eligibility for Medi-Cal, but the primary way for most persons with disabilities is eligibility for SSI.

✓ IHSS is a Medi-Cal paid for program that pays for in home care for persons with disabilities.

✓ SNT beneficiary may receive both needs based benefits like SSI, Medi-Cal, and IHSS and entitlement benefits like Social Security, SSDI, Medicare, and Regional Center all at the same time

✓ SNT trustee cannot screw up entitlement benefits like Social Security, SSDI, Medicare, and Regional Center with disbursements, but can screw up needs based benefits like SSI, Medi-Cal and IHSS.

✓ SSI and Medi-Cal recipient may work and continue to receive benefits through different programs like Impairment Related Work Expenses, Ticket to Work, Section 1619(a) and (b) program, PASS program, and Medi-Cal 250% work program.

✓ SNT trustees should confirm that if the beneficiary is receiving SSI, the beneficiary has also applied for CalFresh food stamps, this was a change in law in 2019 that for first time allows SSI recipient to also receive food stamps.

✓ SSI recipient who has Section 8 should be treated carefully, the SNT trustee should review the local policy in its PHA to determine how disbursements are treated

✓ SNT trustee may wish to consider hiring a VA benefits expert to determine if SNT beneficiary who may be eligible for VA benefits for pension, aid and assistance, and health care.

CHAPTER 4
Understanding the Fundamentals of Making Trust Disbursements

This chapter will discuss the fundamentals of making trust disbursements. Chapters 11 through 16 covers the effect of specific SNT disbursements on a beneficiary's public benefits, however this chapter should be consulted first, before referencing those chapters because if the trustee does not understand the fundamentals, he or she will run afoul of the rules before ever determining the effect that certain specific SNT disbursements will have on public benefits.

Under Probate Code Section 16000, a trustee is bound by the terms of the trust agreement. The performance of his or her duties, especially in making distributions to beneficiaries, must strictly comply with the trust terms. In general, as described below, there are two main kinds of SNT distribution standards, a supplemental distribution standard or a discretionary distribution standard. In both types of distribution standards, the trustee is generally provided some combination of "sole" or "absolute" discretion to make distributions on behalf of the beneficiary.

So how does a trustee exercise this discretion? Is the trustee free to do anything or are there restrictions? Even when a trustee holds sole and absolute discretion over trust distributions, the trustee still must exercise that discretion in a reasonable fashion in good faith. Specifically, the Trustee must balance the competing purposes of the trust. Specifically, the Trustee must weigh his or her responsibility to have assets to distribute against the beneficiary's current and future needs and wants.

Satisfying a beneficiary's immediate and excessive wants will deplete the trust and render the beneficiary helpless in a moment of greater need in the future.

So how does a trustee draw that line? Hopefully the settlor of the trust provided the trustee with a non-binding memorandum of intent or advisory letter describing his or her intent in creating the trust, his or her impressions of the beneficiary with a disability, and his or her opinions on how discretionary distributions should be made. If so, the trustee should closely consult this letter and do his or her best at following its terms. If no such letter was provided, the trustee should do his or her best to recreate this information. The trustee should speak with the settlor's advisors, family, and the beneficiary; but it is important to remember that the trustee should always maintain his or her independence in making the final decision.

All trustees must carefully review the trust's distribution standard, review any limitations described in the document, understand the intent behind the use of trust assets, and follow those instructions to the letter. If there is a deviation, the trustee may be held personally accountable.

WHAT ARE THE SNT TRUSTEE'S LEGAL RIGHTS IN MAKING DECISIONS ABOUT DISTRIBUTIONS?

In the SNT document, the trustee will nearly always be given sole and absolute discretion to make distributions on behalf of the beneficiary. This means the SNT trustee has the right to say yes or no to any distribution request. However, under California law, even when a trust instrument confers "absolute," "sole," or "uncontrolled" discretion, the trustee still must conform to fiduciary principles, which means that the trustee may not act in bad faith and may not disregard the purposes of the trust.[88]

Record keeping The SNT trustee should protect him or herself by keeping a log of all disbursement requests and indicate on the request his or her reasoning in accepting or rejecting each request. The trustee should keep a list of all disbursements on a spreadsheet like Quickbooks or Excel.

> **Examples:** An SNT beneficiary makes a request to purchase cable service. The SNT trustee has full discretion on all distributions.

---

88 Probate Code §16081(a).

The trustee denies the request because he believes the beneficiary watches too much television. The SNT trustee would be protected from being second-guessed by the beneficiary or even a court, even if he were being unreasonable because he is not acting in bad faith or against the purpose of the trust. While the purchase of cable television will not interfere with public benefits and is otherwise an acceptable distribution, the SNT trustee still has discretion to make the decision on whether to buy it or not.

However, assume that the SNT trustee refused to make any distributions at all from the SNT because he does not believe that people with disabilities should be provided any additional items or services not already provided by the government. The SNT trustee would be breaching his fiduciary duty and would be abusing his or her discretion. Because the SNT was established to provide items and services to enhance the quality of life of the beneficiary with a disability, the trustee refusing to make any distributions at all would be violating the whole intent and purpose of the terms of the trust and his or her failure to make any distributions would be considered bad faith.

HOW CAN A TRUSTEE DETERMINE THE SNT'S DISTRIBUTION STANDARD?

In every trust document, the SNT trustee is provided instructions on what his or her authority is in making disbursements on behalf of the beneficiary. This trust provision is often called the "distribution standard." In general, there are two kinds of SNT distribution standards, a supplemental distribution standard or a discretionary distribution standard as described more fully below.

SNTs are written by many different attorneys who create different types of distribution standards. Oftentimes, the provision is unclear because it may begin as a supplemental standard but is later modified to become a discretionary distribution standard.

Practice Tip: If the SNT trustee is unsure of which type of distribution standard he or she is administering, the trustee should contact an attorney experienced in drafting SNTs to review the document and provide an opinion. Failure to understand this essential SNT term will cause the trustee many issues later if his or her actions are questioned.

Note: The authors of this book always prefer the fully discretionary distribution standard. It provides the most flexibility to the SNT trustee to enhance the quality of life of the beneficiary with a disability by allowing the trustee to decide to forego all or a portion of public benefits if it is in the beneficiary's best interests to do so.

The two main types of SNT distribution standards are:

- **The Purely *Supplemental* Distribution Standard:** Some SNTs specifically prohibit the trustee from making any distributions that will reduce or eliminate SSI eligibility for any reason.

  Example: A supplemental distribution standard will often state something like: "The trustee shall not make any distribution that will reduce or eliminate eligibility for public benefits."

The supplemental distribution standard is easier to administer but provides less ability by the trustee to enhance the beneficiary's quality of life. For example, as described in Chapter 12, payments from an SNT for food or shelter will reduce or even eliminate SSI eligibility. Thus, the SNT trustee under a supplemental distribution standard is prohibited from ever making any disbursements from the SNT for beneficiary's food or shelter. This kind of SNT may be easier for a trustee to manage because payments for "food" or "shelter" are prohibited, and therefore do not require the trustee to exercise his or her discretion to pay for these items. However, this type of standard also seriously hampers the ability of the SNT trustee to improve the beneficiary's life by paying rent for a nicer apartment or paying for the beneficiary's food when the beneficiary has little to no money.

It is possible for the SNT trustee to modify the distribution standard to a discretionary distribution standard by modifying the trust document. This will require a petition to a probate court as described in Chapter 5.

- **The *Discretionary* Distribution Standard:** Some SNTs allow distributions even if the disbursement reduces or even eliminates a public benefit, but only if doing so is in the beneficiary's best interest. This type of distribution standard or provision is known as a "discretionary distribution standard." The authors of this book believe all SNTs should have this distribution standard because it provides the trustee with the most discretion to enhance the quality of life of a person with a disability.

> **Example:** A discretionary distribution standard will often look similar to this sample: "The trustee may distribute to or apply for the benefit of Beneficiary such amounts from the principal and income, up to the whole thereof, as the trustee, in the trustee's discretion, considers necessary or advisable to meet Beneficiary's special needs for the remainder of his life. While distributions are supplemental in nature to any public benefits the beneficiary is receiving, our Trustee may make a distribution otherwise covered by public benefits, if it is determined by our Trustee to be in the best interests of the beneficiary to make such distribution."

The discretionary distribution standard requires that the trustee understand how the rules regarding the beneficiary's public benefits are affected by public benefits. For example, as described above, if the beneficiary receives SSI and the trustee pays for food or shelter, the SSA will treat it as a kind of public benefits income called "in-kind support and maintenance."

The effect of the SNT trustee paying food or shelter is the reduction of the SSI check by $281 in 2020. This is generally a good trade-off, because the SNT trustee can then pay beneficiary's rent, utilities, and food, while preserving most of the SSI check and thus improves the beneficiary's standard of living. This is generally the more desirable distribution standard for maximizing the quality of life of the person with a disability.

SHOULD A TRUSTEE SET UP A SYSTEM FOR MAKING DISBURSEMENTS?

Yes. The number one complaint by SNT beneficiaries about an SNT trustee is his or her lack of communication concerning SNT disbursements.

The disbursement procedure should be established very early with the beneficiary (or his or her advocates) to determine how disbursements may be requested. The procedure should explain whether disbursements could be made—for example, only during business hours, on weekdays, or within twenty-four hours from a written request. The procedure should be in writing and given to the beneficiary, any legal guardians, and those friends and family willing to participate. Following these steps will go a long way in eliminating future friction with the beneficiary during the administration.

The trustee can provide a form to the beneficiary in which a written request for disbursement can be made. A sample SNT distribution request form can be found in Appendix G of this book.

The trustee should also clearly communicate his or her decision on each disbursement request. While the trustee has the sole and absolute discretion to make (or not make) a disbursement, a clear communication as to why he or she has refused to make a specific disbursement will be much better for the trustee in the long run.

> **Critical Pointer:** It is a good idea for a trustee to purchase a fax machine, smart phone, or computer for a beneficiary or his or her legal guardian. This way, disbursement requests can be faxed, texted, or emailed directly to the trustee and the trustee will have a written record of what was requested.

WHAT GOODS OR SERVICES CANNOT BE PURCHASED BY A TRUSTEE?

The trustee cannot pay for items forbidden by the trust document.[89] SNT disbursements are limited by the terms of the SNT document. For example, the SNT document may preclude the trustee from making certain specific types of disbursements such as disbursements for liquor, pornography, or cigarettes.

Also, an SNT trustee cannot pay for items that are illegal or against public policy.[90] A common impermissible disbursement would be for illegal drugs.

A common misunderstanding is that an SNT cannot pay for food, clothing, or shelter. This is not true unless the SNT document expressly forbids the disbursement by including a supplemental distribution standard. Clothing can be purchased with no effect on SSI benefits, while the payment for food or shelter may affect the amount of SSI or Medi-Cal a beneficiary may receive, but a trustee may still pay for if the SNT has a discretionary distribution standard. In fact, with a properly drafted SNT, these items are a common distribution from an SNT. For further discussion on paying for food and shelter see Chapter 12.

An example of the broad authority an SNT trustee has in deciding on making disbursements is illustrated by describing how some SNT trustees have participated in authorizing services that are legal in one state and not another. One SNT trustee authorized a distribution for a beneficiary to travel to Nevada, where prostitution and gambling are legal, and were willing to pay for the trip and the services. Others have authorized distributions for marijuana, which is legal under California law, however the federal government has not agreed that medical marijuana is legal. In both circumstances, the trustee made a decision as to whether the requested activity was legal or not. If a trustee is going to make this type of distribution, it would be prudent to have an attorney familiar with criminal law determine if the requested action is a violation of criminal law.

If a SNT trustee refuses to make these types of distributions, he or she would not be abusing her discretion because of the discretion a trustee has in managing the SNT.

---

89 Probate Code §16000.
90 Probate Code §15203.

Critical Pointer: Just because an SNT trustee may make certain types of disbursements does not necessarily mean he or she should. Many SNTs do not preclude an SNT trustee from distributing cash directly to a beneficiary. But an SNT trustee should query whether he or she should make that disbursement. For an SSI recipient, the effect of doing so would be a loss of SSI with little benefit received for the beneficiary. For example, if the SNT trustee makes a $500 per month allowance to the beneficiary, the beneficiary would lose $480 from his or her SSI check. This only allows the beneficiary a modest amount of money ($20 per month) with an accompanying loss of SSI and the inability to invest the SNT assets distributed. This would be a terrible disbursement to make, even though there is no legal prohibition against it.

HOW OFTEN SHOULD THE SNT TRUSTEE REVIEW THE SNT TERMS BEFORE MAKING A DISTRIBUTION?

The SNT trustee should consider reviewing the SNT document every time a new disbursement request is made. An SNT trustee is obligated to administer the trust strictly by the trust document's terms.[91]

There are certain SNT provisions the trustee should know whether the SNT includes (or not):

1. The SNT trustee must know if the SNT has a discretionary or supplemental distribution standard as described above. If a supplemental distribution standard, the SNT trustee cannot pay for anything that will reduce SSI payments, like food or shelter items. If a discretionary distribution standard, the trustee is authorized to make such payments if doing so is in the best interests of the beneficiary.

2. Most SNTs include a list a specific list of items and services that are generally acceptable to purchase. If the item is on that list, the trustee can be comfortable knowing that it is an authorized disbursement. Even when an item is not on the list, the trustee is not prevented from making that

---

91 Probate Code §§16000, 16040(b), 16200.

distribution if the document does not exclude it and it is in best interests of beneficiary.

Critical Pointer: Even though an SNT may authorize a specific distribution, the SNT trustee is not required to make the distribution if, in his or her discretion, the purchase of the item or service is not acceptable for some reason. For example, if the SNT beneficiary wants a home but is requesting a mansion, the SNT trustee can deny this request even though the purchase of principal place of residence would not interfere with public benefit.

Finally, the SNT trustee should review the SNT's terms for items or services specifically not authorized. For example, some parents set up third-party SNTs for children that do not allow disbursements for cigarettes and alcohol, or they limit distributions to times when the beneficiary is drug free. The SNT trustee should be aware of any of these specific limitations in the trust document and must honor them.

CHAPTER 4 SUMMARY

✓ Trustees must exercise their discretion on trust disbursements in good faith

✓ Trustees are required to know what type of distribution standard they are operating under

✓ The Supplemental Distribution Standard does not allow the trustee to make any disbursements that would reduce or eliminate public benefit eligibility

✓ The Discretionary Distribution Standard allows a trustee to make disbursements to enhance the quality of life of a beneficiary with a disability even if it reduces or eliminates public benefits

✓ The trustee should set up a policy on how a beneficiary can request disbursements, proper communication avoids a lot of problems

✓ In most SNTs, the trustee is allowed to make any type of disbursement that enhances the quality of life of the beneficiary

✓ The trustee should review the trust document each time before making a disbursement to ensure he or she is complying with the intent of the person who set up the trust and to make sure that there is no prohibition in the trust document that prevents the trustee from making a distribution

CHAPTER 5
Protecting the SNT Trustee

SNT trustees are subject to so many rules and regulations that it would be the rare trustee who did not commit some kind of breach of trust. A breach of trust is defined as violation of any of a trustee's fiduciary duties as described throughout this book. A trustee's most important protection is knowing when to ask for help. A trustee is always empowered to hire professionals to assist in his or her duties. Chapter 20 offers a variety of options for a trustee who needs assistance.

As is commonly advised to SNT trustees, "common sense" and "doing the right thing" are not the cornerstones of being an excellent SNT trustee. Instead, the trustee must know and comply with the terms of the trust document, plethora of laws governing trustees, and beneficiary's public benefit eligibility rules. Trustees who fail to follow this advice will someday be subject to censure or sanction. Once a trustee commits a breach of trust, the trustee may be personally liable for any harm caused. Trustees should keep this in mind when performing their duties.

In some cases, a trustee's breach may not result in any immediate negative consequences, (*e.g.,* providing cash to beneficiary but no loss of public benefit) so what is the point of changing their actions? What this usually means is that a trustee has not yet been caught in his or her breach. There are no trust police investigating trustee breaches or seeking out trustee negligence or misconduct. Trust laws generally leave it up to the beneficiary, their legal representatives, and the courts to police trustee actions. So, it is possible for a trustee to commit breaches of trust for years before such actions come to light. When they do, it is the rare trustee who escapes unscathed. It may result in years of litigation and possible financial ruin.

There are a number of tools trustees can employ to protect them from breaches of trust. Oftentimes, trustees learn that actions they have taken in good faith were actually in violation of a trust term or in violation of public benefit laws. These trustees are anxious because they have broken the law and imagine swift and terrible justice descending upon them. It is the rare breach of trust that cannot be corrected. Many breaches of trust are not actionable and only need to be corrected to avoid negative outcomes. Also, trust laws provide a trustee the right to seek forgiveness for incorrect actions. Trustees have many tools to avoid breaches of trust by providing accounts and reports, sending out notices to beneficiaries, and seeking court intervention.

This chapter describes a variety of tools and techniques trustees can employ to provide protection and remedy breaches of trust.

HOW DOES AN SNT TRUSTEE GET INTO TROUBLE?

SNT trustee find trouble in many ways. Nearly every SNT trustee that the author has worked with is doing his or her best to help the SNT beneficiary. However, good intentions are not a defense to making mistakes. Most of the mistakes by SNT trustees are not because of bad intentions but rather from not understanding all that is required of an SNT trustee.

Breaches of trust are often uncovered because someone is already unhappy with the trustee for a different reason. This can occur because the trustee is seeking to be paid for services and someone feels the fees requested are too high, after the trustee has rejected a proposed disbursement that the beneficiary or their family thinks is appropriate, when the money in the trust runs out and now the family and beneficiary are closely reviewing all prior services, or when the trustee and beneficiary are not communicating well. The beneficiary, their legal representative, family member or a government agency may then ask to review a trustee's records and breaches (that had nothing to do with the original issue) may come to light. Another way a breach is identified is when the SNT's investments do poorly. The investment turndown is usually just a function of the market, but it opens up a review of the entire trustee's past actions.

To avoid issues, the prudent trustee will ensure that his or her actions are above reproach. If not, even many years later, all of the trustee's actions may be scrutinized. If an action is taken that violates a fiduciary duty, the prudent trustee will take steps to remedy it immediately rather than ignoring it or trying to hide it.

The authors have seen the following SNT trustee's breaches of trust and provide the list so that other SNT trustees can attempt to avoid these situations:

- Due to trustee's lack of knowledge of public benefits, beneficiary was missing out on benefits and trustee refused to call in a case manager who did have the knowledge to maximize benefits and to properly document the matter.
- Trustee failed to document the rationale for expenditures that were not black and white decisions.
- Trustee failed to document that she clearly communicated with the beneficiary's conservator that the current spend rate was going to bankrupt the trust
- Trustee failed to document "sole benefit" rationale for a major expenditure
- Trustee failed to document that family members with a duty of support over beneficiary were contributing appropriately – especially food, clothing and housing
- Trustee failed to document rationale for caregiver salary – can be bigger issue for a family member
- Trustee refused to even attempt to improve communication with conservators and the beneficiary's caregivers because felt they were jerks
- Trustee failed to obtain court order for large, questionable purchases that were in the client's best interest but caused early exhaustion of trust funds
- Trustee failed to spend funds to improve the client's quality of life (because no one asked for anything), made no attempt to communicate with beneficiary
- More generally, trustees get in the most trouble when:
  - Not following the terms of the trust document or court's order
  - Failing to properly communicate with beneficiary or family
  - Not seeking assistance when trustee is unsure of how to handle a situation whether it be legal, tax, or public benefits
  - Losing or reducing beneficiary's public benefit eligibility without understanding consequences
  - Failing to properly account to beneficiary, family members, the court, or government agencies
  - Mishandling of assets

- Self-dealing
- Engaging in acts that create a conflict-of-interest
- Overspending or under spending from trust assets either due to fear of making a mistake or ignorance of what is allowed
- Too conservative investment

Two reported cases from New York describe some issues that may arise when serving as SNT trustee. The two cases highlight the difficulty an SNT trustee in properly exercising authority on making disbursements:

1. In this case,[92] J.P. Morgan Chase Bank and an SNT attorney served as co-trustees of an SNT with over $3,600,000 in assets. The two were held responsible for breach of fiduciary duty by failing to make disbursements on behalf of SNT beneficiary and failing to inform themselves of the beneficiary's needs. The beneficiary was 16 years old when his adoptive mother died in 2005. He was autistic, required constant supervision, non-verbal, and required assistance with all activities of daily living. He was living in a group home where his mother placed him after learning that she was terminally ill. Five years after the mother's death an accounting was filed showing that the trustees received $79,000 in fees. The beneficiary received $3,525 for a part-time care manager. The judge found that no one had visited the beneficiary during the five years from the date of his mother's death to the date of the hearing. The corporate trustee stated that it was responsible for managing the money, not to meet the needs of people with severe disabilities. The court ordered the trustee to hire a care manager who was able to move the beneficiary to a more suitable facility, arranged for a vacation, attend classes, obtain equipment such as computers and iPads to enrich his life, and eventually the beneficiary began to recognize the care manger and even spoke to her. The court held that this case brings into sharp focus the obligations of trustees to beneficiaries of trusts, especially those with disabilities. The court stated:

---

92 *Matter of JP Morgan Chase*, 956 N.Y.S. 856 (Surr. Ct. 2012)

"It is not sufficient for the trustees to simply safeguard the [beneficiary's] trust's assets; instead, the trustees have a duty to [beneficiary] to inquire into his condition and to apply trust income to improving it."

2. In this case,[93] an SNT trustee was held responsible for breach of fiduciary duty by making too many disbursements on behalf of a beneficiary. The trustee was ordered to pay the trust $176,905.99 in damages. Initially, the SNT was funded with $403,000. The trustee expended almost $60,000 per year until there was only $3,253.03 left in trust. The court held that the trustee breached its fiduciary duty by authorizing each and every discretionary disbursement requested by the infant beneficiary's mother. The trustee did not seek public benefits assistance for home health services and transportation needs. For example, the court showed transportation services in excess of $50,000 over four years that possibly could have been covered by public benefits. The trustee spent money on medicine that would have been covered by public benefits. The trustee also made disbursements to mother of $400 a month for food and clothing and failed to take into account the reduction of SSI. The court stated that the trustee made no effort to consult a professional on government benefits or assistance programs as required by the trust document. A trust representative stated, "[i]t was easier to accede to [the mother's] monetary requests than to deny them." It may have been easier, but it was the wrong thing to do.

CAN AN SNT TRUSTEE BE LIABLE FOR ACTIONS OF CO-TRUSTEE?

Yes, the trustee is liable if the trustee:

1. Participates in the cotrustee's breach of trust;
2. Improperly delegates administration of the trust to the cotrustee;
3. Approves, knowingly acquiesces in, or conceals the cotrustee's breach of trust;
4. Negligently enables the cotrustee to breach the trust; or

---

93 *Liranzo v. LI Jewish Education* (NY Sup. Ct., Kings Cty, No. 28863/1996, June 25, 2013)

5. Neglects to take reasonable steps to compel the cotrustee to redress a breach of trust that the trustee knows about or reasonably should have known about.[94]

The authors generally recommend against co-trustees serving as SNT trustees. We are aware of the benefits, typically a check-and-balance, making sure that not one person or entity has full authority to take all trustee actions. However, the potential for unintended liability of an innocent cotrustee, the requirement that each cotrustee participate in administering the trust, take reasonable steps either to prevent a cotrustee from breaching the trust or to compel a cotrustee to redress a breach of trust makes this type of trust difficult to administer.[95] In order to provide the protection and flexibility, the author recommends that a single trustee serve and allow a trust protector or trust advisory committee to have the authority to review trustee actions as a check-and-balance against a poorly serving trustee.

CAN AN SNT TRUSTEE BE LIABLE FOR ACTIONS OF A PREDECESSOR TRUSTEE?

Yes. An SNT trustee could be responsible for a breach of trust committed by a predecessor trustee when the SNT trustee:

- Knows or should have known of the breach of trust and allows it to continue;
- Neglects to take reasonable steps to compel the predecessor to deliver the trust property; or
- Neglects to take reasonable steps to redress the predecessor's breach of trust about which the successor knows or should have known.[96]

In order to avoid this potential, some trust documents include a provision that limits liability on a successor trustee. The SNT trustee should check to see if such a provision exists. If not, the trustee should make sure that he or she is aware of what actions the prior trustee took and take appropriate steps to protect the trustee. This can be problematic if a professional trustee is taking over from a parent or relative

---

94 Probate Code §16402(b).
95 See Probate Code §16013.
96 Probate Code §16403(b).

of the beneficiary who may not have been careful in making sure all trustee actions were properly taken.

ARE ALL TRUSTEE BREACHES ACTIONABLE?

No. It really depends on the circumstances. When the trustee has acted reasonably and in good faith under the circumstances as known to the trustee, the court may excuse the trustee in whole or in part from liability for the breach of trust if it would be equitable to do so.[97]

The trust document may have exculpatory language in it that allows the SNT trustee more latitude in making decisions that would normally be treated as a breach of trust. For example, the prudent person standard (governing trust administration) and the prudent investor standard (governing investment and management functions) may be expanded or restricted by trust provisions.[98] A trustee should be cautious in relying on exculpatory trust provisions because they will be carefully reviewed and strictly construed meaning that if the choice is between protecting the trustee or protecting the beneficiary, the provision will be reviewed to protect the beneficiary over the trustee.[99]

It is possible to exempt a trustee from other certain liabilities. For example, the trust document may exempt a trustee from liability for ordinary negligence. However, no matter how broad the trust provision even if it says the trustee is not liable for any actions taken, for public policy reasons, a trustee can never be exempted from liability for (1) a breach of trust committed intentionally, with gross negligence, in bad faith, or with reckless indifference to the beneficiary's interest or (2) any profit derived from a breach of trust.[100]

An SNT trustee should be aware of several legal doctrines that can protect them. The theory behind these doctrines are that a beneficiary must file a claim against a trustee promptly and not wait to file their claim when it may be more advantageous for them to do so. A defense for a breach of trust is a legal doctrine called laches. The elements of laches are the beneficiary's (1) failure to assert a right,

---

97   Probate Code §16440(b).

98   See Probate Code §§16040(b) and 16045(b).

99   See *Estate of Collins* (1977) 72 Cal. App. 3d 663, 673.

100   Probate Code §16461.

(2) delay in the assertion of the right for some appreciable period, and (3) circumstances that would cause prejudice to an adverse party if assertion of the right is permitted.[101] This protects the SNT trustee from a beneficiary waiting to object to a trustee action for too long. SNT beneficiaries need to know that if he or she is aware of a trustee's breach, the beneficiary needs to file their action promptly without waiting too long or risk losing their rights.

Two other legal doctrines that can be utilized to protect an SNT trustee are called res judicata and collateral estoppel. The idea behind these doctrines is that if an interested party (like a beneficiary) had the opportunity to bring an action against a trustee but chose not to do so, the beneficiary is forever barred from bringing it later. A beneficiary seeking to contest trustee's actions that are identified in a court pleading must bring their claim at the time of the court action. The failure of a beneficiary to raise a claim may bar the beneficiary from ever being able to bring it up later in a court action. This is called res judicata ("a matter judged") or collateral estoppel (an earlier decision rendered by a court in a lawsuit between parties is conclusive as to all issues).[102] The doctrine can be overcome if there is fraud. Fraud occurs when one party unlawfully prevents another from having his day in court, as by failing to provide required notice of the action or the court action does not properly identify the issue that is being contested.

WHAT TOOLS ARE AVAILABLE TO PROTECT AN SNT TRUSTEE?

An SNT trustee has several tools available for protection including:

- **Trustee liability insurance**. Trustee liability insurance provides beneficiary with money for loss resulting from a trustee's improper acts. Consider finding policy that covers the "trust itself; past, present, alternate and future trustees (and their heirs, estates and legal representatives)" One place to check to see if coverage for trustee's actions is with www.dominioninsurance.com. Some trustees make the mistake that a bond (a special type of

---

101 *Getty v Getty* (1986) 187 Cal. App. 3d 1159, 1170 (dismissal of beneficiary's action for fraud affirmed as violating statute of limitations and laches)

102 *Lazzarone v Bank of America* (1986) 181 Cal. App. 3d 581, 589; *Getty v Getty* (1986) 187 Cal. App. 3d 1159, 1173

insurance policy) will protect them in cases of breach of trust. This is not true; a surety bond protects the trust, not the trustee. If an SNT trustee has staff, adding a rider for employee misconduct is also recommended.

- **Timely accountings.** As described in Chapter 8, the trustee can shorten a statute of limitations for claims made against trustee by providing a timely and informative accounting. In general, there is a 3-year statute of limitations to sue a trustee that begins to run when the beneficiary has actual knowledge of a breach or the beneficiary receives an account or report that adequately discloses trustee's acts. It is possible to shorten the time to 180-days in some trusts all as described in more detail in Chapter 8. Typically, the statute of limitations is tolled (meaning does not begin to be counted) if the person is incapacitated. However, for limitations purposes, an incapacitated beneficiary is considered to have received an account or report if received by the beneficiary's legal representative or guardian ad litem, or, in the case of a minor, a guardian or parent who does not have a conflict of interest.[103]

- **Obtaining beneficiary's consent or affirmation.**[104] To give valid consent or affirmance, the beneficiary (1) may not be incapacitated, (2) must know of his or her rights and know of the material facts that the trustee knew or should have known and did not reasonably believe that the beneficiary knew, and (3) must not have been induced to consent by the trustee's improper conduct. In determining whether a beneficiary has been fully and fairly informed of the breach, the courts may look to whether the beneficiary had independent advice.

- **Obtaining beneficiary's release or contract relieving trustee of liability for a breach of trust.**[105] To give valid release or contract, the beneficiary (1) may not be incapacitated, (2) must know of his or her rights and know of the material facts that the trustee knew or should have known and did

103 Probate Code §16460(b).
104 Probate Code §§16463, 16465.
105 Probate Code §16464.

not reasonably believe that the beneficiary knew, (3) must not have been induced to consent by the trustee's improper conduct, and (4) must not have involved an unfair bargain between trustee and beneficiary.

- **Attorney advice.** An SNT trustee is encouraged to obtain an attorney's advice on trust actions. An SNT trustee should be able to consult an attorney to obtain the necessary legal advice on the action that needs to be reviewed. In general, any communications between attorney and client are privileged. However, an SNT trustee should be aware that when consulting an attorney as trustee (in opposed to being their personal attorney), the privilege goes with the trust, not staying with the individual. What this means is that if an attorney provides a written opinion that the trustee breached his or her duty and that document is in the file of either the attorney or the trustee, any successor trustee is entitled to review it and use it against that trustee. If a SNT trustee wants to make sure the privilege stays with the trustee personally, the trustee must hire and pay for the attorney from his or her own assets and ensure that he or she is receiving advice in his or her personal capacity.

CAN AN SNT TRUSTEE OBTAIN PRE-APPROVAL FOR A DECISION THAT PROTECTS A TRUSTEE FROM LIABILITY?

Yes. There are two primary tools. One is called a Notice of Proposed Action (NOPA) and the other is a Petition for Instructions (17200 Petition). The two procedures are discussed below.

- **Utilizing a Notice of Proposed Action (NOPA).** A trustee may wish to consider sending a NOPA to give beneficiaries an opportunity to object before the trustee takes, or does not take, a particular action.[106] If no beneficiary entitled to notice objects, the trustee is not liable to any current or future beneficiary with respect to the action, provided that notice has been given to the guardian or conservator of the estate of any beneficiary

---

106 Probate Code §§16500-16504.

who is a minor or incompetent adult.[107] The NOPA procedure cannot be used in connection with certain actions, such as payment of trustee compensation, settlement of the trustee's accounts, compromise or settlement of claims by or against the trustee, or other specified transactions.[108] A NOPA is still useful because it begins the running of the statute of limitations (the time limit a beneficiary has to sue a trustee for breach of trust) even if the action is not one that it is authorized. A sample NOPA is attached as Appendix X.

- **Utilizing a Petition for Instructions.** Attorneys call this petition a "17200 Petition" based on the statute that authorizes it.[109] Typically, the filing of a 17200 Petition would be done only when there is a significant question that needs answering; such as the trustee is being asked to make a disbursement that may be objectionable by someone. Those individuals and entities that are notified of the 17200 Petition may later be barred from objecting to the trustee's expenditure of funds if they neglect to appear and object to the petition for instructions or even if they do appear, the court overrules their objection and authorizes the trustee to take the action. Many SNT trustees use this petition during administration to authorize a purchase of a home or modified van; to pay for experimental treatments requested by beneficiary or his or her legal representatives; to pay for a lengthy vacation; or to invest in a business. It can be used in just about any situation. However, due to cost, is usually only used for big or controversial expenditures

  Example: Beneficiary's family wants SNT trustee to use trust funds to buy a new primary residence for the beneficiary. The family is looking at a home that costs over $800,000. The SNT trustee may not be willing to make such a large purchase without some assurance that he or she will not be personally liable if someone disagrees with his or her decision later. The SNT trustee hires an attorney to bring a 17200 Petition seeking the court's

---

107   Probate Code §16503(b).
108   Probate Code §16501(d).
109   Probate Code §17200.

instructions on whether trustee should purchase home. Trustee notifies beneficiary, beneficiary's family, all remainder beneficiaries, and the state agencies that run SSI and Medi-Cal of the time and place of the hearing. At the hearing, no one appears to object and the court authorizes the disbursement. For all those properly noticed with the petition, the trustee is protected.

A 17200 Petition can be used in many ways including:
- Determining questions of construction of a trust instrument;
- Determining the validity of a trust provision;
- Settling accounts and passing on the trustee's acts, including the exercise of discretionary powers;
- Instructing the trustee;
- Granting powers to the trustee;
- Fixing or allowing payment of the trustee's compensation or reviewing its reasonableness;
- Appointing or removing a trustee;
- Accepting the resignation of a trustee;
- Compelling redress of a breach of the trust;
- Modifying or terminating the trust; and
- Transferring a supervised testamentary trust between counties[110]

A trustee should retain an experienced attorney to assist with the use of a NOPA or the filing of a 17200 Petition. These matters can be complicated if the trustee is not experienced with the uses and limitations of these procedures.

WHAT CAN HAPPEN TO A TRUSTEE THAT IS FOUND IN BREACH OF TRUST?

If a trustee commits, or threatens to commit, a breach of trust, a beneficiary or co-trustee may commence a proceeding to:
- Compel or enjoin the trustee from breaching the trust;
- Compel the trustee to compensate for a breach;

---

110   Probate Code §17200(b).

- Appoint a receiver or temporary trustee;
- Remove the trustee;
- Set aside acts of the trustee;
- Reduce or deny compensation of the trustee;
- Impose an equitable lien or a constructive trust on trust property; or
- Trace and recover trust property that has been wrongfully disposed of.[111]

These provisions do not preclude any other appropriate remedy provided by statute or common law. For example, the trustee's failure to account or otherwise perform after citation from the judge or court order may be punishable as contempt. Even imprisonment has been used, albeit rarely, to enforce contempt by jailing the trustee until he or she performs his or her duty.

When a breach of trust has caused a loss, a beneficiary or cotrustee may seek damages to redress the loss. The trustee is liable for loss or depreciation resulting from the breach of trust, for profits that the trustee made through the breach of trust, or for any profits that would have accrued to the trust but for the breach of trust.

Under the "American Rule," absent contractual or statutory authorization, attorney fees are not recoverable either as damages or costs and must be borne by the respective parties.[112] However, attorney fees may be awarded to the prevailing party if a beneficiary brings, or a trustee opposes, a contest to the trustee's account without reasonable cause and in bad faith.[113]

A common question is whether the SNT trustee can use trust assets to pay their attorney when defending from a breach of trust lawsuit. Attorney fees and litigation costs incurred in the trustee's successful defense of an action brought by the beneficiary are recoverable from the trust.[114] A successful defense does not necessarily entitle the trustee to reimbursement of all fees that were incurred. The trustee must show that the defense fees were reasonable under the circumstances.[115] When a

---

111 Probate Code §16420.
112 *Estate of Gump* (1982) 128 Cal. App. 3d 111, 118.
113 Probate Code §17211.
114 *Estate of Gump* (1991) 1 Cal. App. 4th 582, 604.
115 *Donahue v Donahue* (2010) 182 Cal. App. 4th 259, 267.

trustee has acted improperly, the court may deny reimbursement of attorney fees.[116] When the trustee successfully defends the majority of claims against him or her and has acted in good faith, the court will award reimbursement for the fees incurred in successfully defending proper actions.[117] When the trustee has been found guilty of a breach of loyalty, however, the court may, in its discretion, deny all fees.[118]

CHAPTER 5 SUMMARY

✓ The SNT trustee will invariably find himself or herself making a mistake at some point while serving.

✓ An SNT trustee is generally liable for actions of a co-trustee and predecessor trust.

✓ Not all SNT breaches of trust are actionable.

✓ The SNT trustee has a number of tools available to limit liability including
  – waiver,
  – notice,
  – statute of limitations,
  – notice of proposed actions, and
  – petition for instructions.

✓ There are a host of remedies the court has available when a trustee is found liable for breach of trust, including
  – removal,
  – surcharge,
  – damages,
  – and in extreme cases, jail time.

---

116 *Estate of Gump* (1991) 1 Cal. App. 4th 582, 605.

117 *Estate of Cassity* (1980) 106 Cal. App. 3d 569, 574.

118 *Estate of Gump* (1991) 1 Cal. App. 4th 582, 609.

CHAPTER 6

Paying SNT Trustees

Trustees have a complicated job in managing SNTs. Many times, the SNT trustee is a non-professional family member or friend who agrees to do the job for free, while other times the trustee is a professional or non-professional who wishes to be paid for their time. In the authors' experience, paying an SNT trustee is proper because of the substantial amount of work and potential personal liability the trustee is exposed to. If deciding to take payment, the SNT trustee must carefully scrutinize the trust document to determine how much the trustee can be paid and if there are any limitations on payment.

It is important that SNT trustees carefully document their decision on how to be paid and keep records of their services. This is an area that beneficiaries and their families will closely review and oftentimes will lead to conflict if a big bill is sprung on the beneficiary without warning and little explanation. If the SNT trustee is billing hourly, a short and concise explanation of the time spent, description of services, and hourly rate should be prepared. In Appendix R is a Trustee's Time Log that can be used to document time. If the SNT is court-supervised trusts, the Trustees' fee generally also must be approved by a Probate judge. This can be difficult in some counties because of different judges and examiners who will scrutinize the time spent and make a decision if it is proper. There may also be maximum hourly rates that can be charged in different counties. In Appendix S is a sample Trustee Declaration for Fees that can be used for trustees who seek a court's approval to be paid.

The authors review the legal authority for obtaining trustee's fees and provide some best practices to aid a trustee in obtaining appropriate fees in this chapter.

HOW DO DIFFERENT TYPES OF TRUSTEE CHARGE FOR THEIR SERVICES?

There are three main types of California trustees, *i.e.*, corporate trustees, private professional trustees, and non-professional trustees. The three different types of trustees charge differently. However, just because a trustee charges a specific fee, that fee may still not be properly paid unless it is legally authorized. The next question in the book describes the amount of the fee that can be legally charged.

In general, the following three types of trustees charge in different ways:

1. *Corporate trustees.* These are banks and corporations that serve as SNT trustees. Corporate trustees generally have a fee schedule that is published on their web site or can be requested by a trust officer. This fee schedule is generally a sliding fee scale based on the amount of investable assets owned by a trust. In a court supervised SNT, a judge does not have to respect the corporate trustee's published fee schedule and can raise or lower a fee based off of the circumstances of a particular matter. In certain circumstances, it is possible to negotiate with corporate trustees to lower their published fee schedule.

   Example, An SNT has $1,500,000 in cash assets, this corporate trustee charge 1.5% of assets up to 1 million and 1.2% of assets from 1 million to 2 million on an annual basis. For this SNT, the annual charge for the trustee would be $21,000, (1.5% x $1,000,000 = $15,000 + 1.2% x $500,000 = $6,000). As assets go up or down, the trustee's fee changes. The benefit of this arrangement for the beneficiary and their family is knowing the amount of fees to be charged.

2. *California licensed private professional fiduciaries.* These are individuals who the State of California licenses through the Bureau of Professional Fiduciaries. See http://www.fiduciary.ca.gov. Private professional fiduciaries generally charge an hourly rate for their services. The rates most typically seen are between $100 per hour to $175 per hour depending on where they are serving and their years of experience. Some fiduciaries also charge a lower rate for their staff in performing ministerial tasks like filing forms or writing checks. Some fiduciaries also will charge on a percentage basis

similar to corporate fiduciaries, but this is rare as most courts will not authorize such a fee without showing the time incurred.

3. *Non-professional trustees.* These individuals are typically family members or friends who agree to serve as SNT trustee. Oftentimes, it may be expected that they will not take a fee. However, as being an SNT trustee can be time-consuming and fraught with potential liability, non-professional trustees should consider being paid for their time. In determining how much a non-professional trustee is to be paid, the typical practice is to use a professional trustee fee as the upper limit on what can be charged. The idea is that these are trained professionals who know what rules need to be followed and have set up systems to handle many trustee responsibilities. It will take a non-professional trustee additional time to handle these tasks due to their unfamiliarity with the tasks required, albeit at a lower rate. However, if the non-professional has expertise in a certain area, like taxes or financial investment, it is possible for them to charge a higher rate. There is no bright line test as to an acceptable rate. In general, it is common to see a non-professional compensated at a rate from $20 per hour all the way up to $150 per hour. It depends on the circumstances of the particular situation.

HOW MUCH CAN AN SNT TRUSTEE BE PAID?

It depends. How much an SNT trustee is paid depends on the language in the trust document and whether the SNT is under ongoing court jurisdiction or court supervision rules. This happens when the SNT was established inside a conservatorship of the estate or with litigation proceeds for a person with a disability who lacks capacity.

Despite a trustee's background (whether professional or not), the actual fee paid is dependent on the following three circumstances:

1. ***If the trust document is silent on trustee compensation***, the trustee is entitled to "reasonable" compensation under the circumstances.[119] This is

---

119   Probate Code §15681.

the most common situation a trustee will typically have to understand, as most trusts do not include a fee provision. When determining what is "reasonable compensation," a court considers the following factors (the importance attributed to the individual factors will vary substantially from case to case):

- The gross income of the trust;
- The success or failure of the trustee's administration, as generally determined, *e.g.*, by the beneficiary continuing to receive public benefits (or if not, the trust was able to provide resources that made beneficiary's life better) or can be things such as absence of disputes or distributions made promptly;
- Any unusual skill, expertise, or experience that the trustee has brought to the position, *e.g.*, knowledge of public benefits, professional trustee, or investment management expertise;
- The "fidelity" or "disloyalty" shown by the trustee, *e.g.*, if trustee is found to have breached his or her duty of loyalty, fees can be eliminated or reduced;[120]
- The amount of risk and responsibility assumed by the trustee (personal liability), as measured, *e.g.*, by negotiating with a public benefits government entity for increase of services provided to beneficiary or running a business owned inside the trust on behalf of a beneficiary with a disability;
- The time that the trustee spent performing trust duties, it is always prudent to keep a time log of time spent and services provided, a sample time log is attached as Appendix R;
- The custom in the community, including the compensation allowed to professional or non-professional trustees by courts and the fees charged by corporate trustees; and
- Whether the work was routine or required more than ordinary skill and judgment, such as paying taxes or operating a business inside the trust.[121]

---

120 Probate Code §16420(a)(7).
121 Cal. Rule of Court 7.776.

If a trustee wishes to be paid a reasonable rate, he or she must keep these factors in mind when setting a "reasonable fee."

> **Example:** An SNT trustee is determining how much of a fee she will charge while serving as trustee of a third-party SNT. The trustee estimates she spent an average of 10 hours a month on trust business, primarily in reviewing investment accounts with a financial advisor, paying bills, checking on the monthly caregiver to make sure services are being provided, issuing reports to the family on care, helping arrange transportation and assisted in paying for a vacation. The trustee did not keep good records of the time spent nor in explaining how she spent her time. The SNT trustee is entitled to her time spent, in reviewing the factors, she believes that a reasonable fee would be $40 per hour for her services. She is paying herself $400 per month for services. While this amount appears reasonable for the services provided, the trustee would be subject to objection because she does not have proper records to support her fees.

2. *If the trust document states a compensation rate for the trustee*, **then that rate will control**, even if it says the trustee is to be paid nothing.[122] It is common that fee clauses call for a formula, fixes a set fee, allows for payment by trustee's existing fee schedule (mostly corporate trustees), or (most commonly) sets fees at a "reasonable rate." If the rate were a reasonable rate, then the factors discussed above would still be relevant in determining what is a "reasonable rate."

The fee provision that states a trustee fee is to cover "ordinary compensation," if the trustee feels that his or her administration as covered extraordinary services, then a trustee should petition a court for greater fees than

---

122   Probate Code §15680, *Thorpe v. Reed* (2012) 211 Cal. App. 4th 1381.

allowed in the trust document.[123] In general, extraordinary compensation is appropriate if trustee manages a litigated matter on behalf of the trust, runs an asset like a closely held businesses or commercial real estate that requires more time, skill, or attention from the trustee. Ordinary services usually include the following:

- Custody of assets;
- Collection and disbursement of income (but not necessarily collections on notes, rentals, or oil interests);
- Investment review of assets;
- Purchases and sales of stocks and bonds;
- Periodic statements to beneficiaries; and
- Preparation of court accountings.

If a trustee wishes to have greater compensation than is allowed in the trust document, a trustee can petition for higher fees in the following circumstances:

- When the trustee's duties are substantially different than contemplated when the trust was created;
- When the compensation in the instrument is inequitable or unreasonably low or high; or
- In extraordinary circumstances calling for equitable relief.[124]

3. *If the SNT was established by court order and the trust is under ongoing court jurisdiction or supervision*, then any fees for the trustee must be fixed and allowed by the court in just and reasonable amounts.[125] The standards for determining a just and reasonable fee are the same as finding fees for a conservator or guardian of the estate.

---

123 *Finkbeiner v Gavid* (2006) 136 Cal. App, 4th 1417
124 Probate Code §15680(b).
125 Rule of Court 7.903(a)(1), (c)(8).

It is important to remember that unless court orders interim fees, a trustee is not entitled to take a fee until a court authorizes it by a court order. The court considers the following nonexclusive factors in determining a trustee's fee:

1. The size and nature of the trust;
2. The benefit to the beneficiary, or his or her trust, of the trustee's services;
3. The necessity for the services performed;
4. The beneficiary's anticipated future needs and income;
5. The time spent by the trustee in the performance of services;
6. Whether the services performed were routine or required more than ordinary skill or judgment;
7. Any unusual skill, expertise, or experience brought to the performance of services;
8. The trustee's estimate of the value of the services performed; and
9. The compensation customarily allowed by the court in the community where the court is located for the management of trusts of similar size and complexity.

No single factor should be the exclusive basis for the court's determination of just and reasonable compensation and there should be no inflexible maximum or minimum compensation or maximum approved hourly rate for a trustee.

Attached as Appendix S are two samples of a type of declaration that trustees have used to obtain fees in a court-supervised SNT, one from a corporate trustee and another from a private professional trustee.

HOW OFTEN CAN A TRUSTEE TAKE A FEE?

Unless the trust document specifies a particular frequency, an SNT trustee in a non-court supervised trust can take fees at any period of time. However, it is most prudent to have fees be paid promptly, *i.e.,* monthly, quarterly or annually. This way, the trustee can ensure that his or her fees are regularly paid, and the beneficiary can see the immediate benefit of the trustee's work. If a trustee takes fees sporadically or waits too long, the trust may run out of money or have so little money left that the months or years of trustee's fees takes such a large percentage of remaining assets that the family, beneficiary, or court will likely challenge the trustee on being paid.

> **Example,** An SNT trustee has worked for five years without taking a fee. The first two years of the administration were difficult because the trustee had to buy a home, evict a tenant, advocate for public benefits, and help the beneficiary obtain much neglected services. The last three years, the trustee's work has been minimal in maintaining investments and paying monthly bills. The SNT trustee's bill for five-years is large (mostly due to the first two-years of service). The beneficiary and his family only remember the last three years of minimal service and fight the trustee on taking his fee. It would have been much easier for this SNT trustee to be paid for her services each year because the family and beneficiary could see the work done by the SNT trustee to justify the fee.

In a court-supervised SNT (one that has been court ordered to comply with California Rule of Court 7.903 rules), the trustee is only allowed to take a fee after a court has reviewed and allowed it. This is typically done during the court accounting that is discussed in detail in Chapter 8. The court account and report is mostly scheduled one-year after the trust is established and every two-years thereafter. This can be a long time to wait for fees. If fees are paid without a court order, the court may disallow all or part of the amount taken and surcharge the trustee or award the trust interest for the loss of use of the funds that were paid out as compensation.[126] A trustee can seek fees on an interim basis, but must seek court permission to do so.[127] This is a common practice for trustees who rely on these fees to make payroll and cover expenses.

---

126   See *Estate of Gilfillan* (1978) 79 Cal App. 3d 429, 437

127   Rule of Court 7.903(c)(8), 7.755, & Probate Code §2643.

WHAT HAPPENS IF THE TRUSTEE WANTS TO INCREASE HOURLY OR PERCENTAGE RATE DURING ADMINISTRATION?

If the SNT trustee wishes to increase his or her fee, it is not as simple as increasing the rate and charging it. The trustee must provide 60-days written notice of the increased fees to all beneficiaries entitled to notice, all beneficiaries who received the trustee's last account, and all beneficiaries who have previously made a written request to the trustee for a notice of increased trustee's fees and have given an address for receiving notice by mail.[128]

This law applies to unsupervised third-party SNTs and first-party SNTs. It is unclear whether it applies to a court supervised first-party SNT, but the better practice would be to imitate its requirements. If within the 60-day period, a beneficiary files a petition for review of the trustee's fee, then the increase in the trustees' fee would not take effect until the petition is dismissed or otherwise ordered by court.[129]

WHAT HAPPENS IF SOMEONE DISPUTES THE TRUSTEE'S FEE?

The SNT trustee and the beneficiary are entitled to petition a court to resolve a fee dispute.[130] The trustee can ask the court to approve the fee (and even if already removed) can ask the successor trustee to pay the fee. This is one of the main reasons it is prudent for a trustee to keep track of his or her time on a spreadsheet in order to justify the fee requested.

In Chapter 5, this book covers the ways a trustee can file a 17200 Petition as a way to protect the trustee.

CAN A TRUSTEE BE REIMBURSED FOR COSTS INCURRED DURING ADMINISTRATION?

Yes. A trustee is entitled to repayment from the trust for costs that were properly incurred during administration.[131] The trustee is also entitled to costs, even if not properly incurred, if the costs benefited the trust.

---

128   Probate Code §15686(b).

129   Probate Code §15686(c).

130   Probate Code §17200(b)(9).

131   Probate Code §15684(a).

If a trustee advances costs on behalf of trust business, the trustee is entitled to an equitable lien on the trust property for the amount of the advance plus interest, if made for the protection of the trust.[132]

ARE THERE ANY PRACTICES A TRUSTEE CAN DO TO MAKE OBTAINING FEES EASIER?

Yes. Here are some suggestions to make obtaining fees easier:

- **Capturing all of trustee's time**. The effect of missing even a small amount of time can be significant. It is a much better practice to try and capture all of the trustee's time.

  Example: If trustee bills at $150 an hour and misses 15 minutes of billable time a day (.2 or .3 of an hour), the trustee loses $37.50 a day, $187.50 a week, $787.50 a month, and $9,450 a year. If the trustee is a professional and doing this consistently with his or her cases, it will have a serious impact on the ability to keep the doors opened.

- **Keeping contemporaneous time records**. Some trustees try to recreate time when billing at a much later date; typically, at the end of the month or even years have gone by. The trustee will certainly lose many of the .2 and .3 of an hour tasks that do add up as described above. When trying to recreate time, the explanation of services will often not be descriptive enough because of the lack of time between performing the service and billing for it. It takes much longer to recreate time than it does to spend the minute or two before and after each task to tap a timer or log your time. There are many practice management software systems available to capture time as tasks are performed. Some include stopwatches that the trustee can click on and off as work is performed that allow the trustee to capture all of the time incurred. For example, Time & Chaos, Clio, Quickbooks are some

---

132 Probate Code §15685.

of the software programs. Another benefit is that they are cloud-based, have apps for smart phones, and can be accessed even when away from the office.

- **Billing consistently.** As described above, beneficiaries and their families do not like to receive multiple months of bills at one time. It creates an additional risk of fee disputes. Plus, if the trust is running out of money, a court will often protect the beneficiary at the expense of the trustee's fee. It is much better to bill regularly.

- **Complying with local rules**. Many Probate Courts have local rules and practices for trustee's fees. It is important to check these rules before submitting a request for fees. Local rules are available on the Probate Court's website. The typical rules will include certain services that must be charged at a lower rate, cannot be charged, or set a maximum hourly trustee rate.

- **Provide thorough explanation of services provided.** It is important to properly describe time spent on a matter. The explanation should describe how the service benefitted the beneficiary and the SNT. The trustee should use complete sentences because it creates a better impression to court and to the beneficiary. It can be helpful to tell the reader a complete story of what services the trustee performed on behalf of client. A few examples are in the table below.

- **Do not use the time log as a daily diary.** While it is important to provide a thorough explanation of benefits, being overly inclusive will also have a negative impact on the reader of the bill. It is a good idea to edit the explanation to the minimum of words that shows the benefit of the services provided.

- **Use active language not passive language.** Arrange, Appeared at, Conference with, Letter to, Telephone call to/from, Teleconference with, Travel to/from. This provides the reader with knowledge of the tasks provided and the active participation the trustee engages in to warrant his or her fee. For example, "Review caregiving contract of B. Boore concerning in-home caregiving needs and confirming letter prepared to B. Boore."

- **Do not include tasks that may not warrant the trustee's billing rate.** Courts and clients are sensitive to paying for tasks that may not require a professional. These tasks are necessary and should be billed so it is better if the trustee included a more thorough description. Here are some examples:

Example	Suggestion
Open mail	Review utility and therapy bills and correspondence from SNT attorney
Write checks	Review and pay bills for physical therapy not paid for by Medi-Cal
Trip to home or Driving time	Travel to beneficiary's residence to inspect living situation. Travel from hospital after visiting beneficiary to ensure has sufficient care
Send e-mail	Prepare correspondence to government agency in response to its inquiry on distributions
Set up file	Initial meeting with beneficiary and complete intake process

- **Do not include attorney-client privileged communications in time log.** A trustee's communications with his or her attorney are privileged. Too often, trustees will include these communications in their time log. This has the effect of waiving the attorney-client privilege and can be used against the trustee if there is future litigation.

- **Bill for all trustee's time, even for the time that the trustee may not charge.** There are times when a trustee will make a mistake and must correct that mistake. Billing for these services may not be advisable. A trustee should be transparent on what services will be billed and which will not. However, it is still good practice to include the time spent and then state that there will be "No Charge" for services. This can happen if the trustee is correcting an easily avoidable error. It informs the reader of the bill that the trustee is not charging for everything and shows the services that have already been deducted from the bill.

- **Proofread the trustee's bills.** It is always a good idea to review the bills prior to sending it out. It sounds obvious, but if the trustee has multiple accounts then it may be difficult to do so. Yet, this is the one action that may end up saving the trustee the most money because it may show time that was missed, identify duplicate charges, show attorney-client privileged information, or indicate a charge that was in a bill that was supposed to be for another client. A trustee's credibility will be harmed if the bill includes these errors.

A sample time log is attached as Appendix R.

When completing a time log, there are some additional considerations the trustee should keep in mind. The trustee should anticipate showing the time log to those who will review the bill. Is it the court, the beneficiary, or someone else? Write to the audience and make sure that the bill explains what services were provided. If there is a large task, sometimes it makes sense to break it up. For example, instead of saying "Sale of home" say "Remove and safeguard beneficiary's tangible personal property, discard years of accumulated trash, inspect home for habitability, hire and supervise contractor, and hire and supervise realtor." It provides a more thorough and honest description of services.

The trustee should also avoid using words that make it sound like the trustee is inefficient. For example, instead of saying "review file" state "reviewed contract for caregiving services." Some other examples are here:

Don't	Do
Telephone call w/bene	Telephone call with beneficiary concerning distribution for caregiving services
Pay Bill	Pay beneficiary's caregiver and gardener. Submit request for gardening service for upcoming year
Open Mail	Discard junk mail; submit bills for prompt payment

CHAPTER 6 SUMMARY

✓ Trustees charge a variety of ways, generally individuals charge per hour and corporate fiduciaries charge a percentage rate.

✓ A trustee can be paid a total amount of their "reasonable" fee or a fee set in the trust document.

✓ A trustee must check the trust document to see if there is a limitation on trustee's fee.

✓ A trustee can take their fee depending on what type of SNT is being administered, if under ongoing court jurisdiction/supervision when a court authorizes it, if not under court jurisdiction/supervision, then at any time (unless the trust document states differently).

✓ If a trustee wants to increase the rate, must provide adequate notice in writing before a trustee can take the fee.

✓ There are a variety of ways a trustee's fee can be challenged, but typically it is done by a 17200 Petition.

✓ A trustee is entitled to all out-of-pocket costs during administration

✓ A trustee should keep a current time log that properly explains the fees that are being charged to make obtaining fees easier.

CHAPTER 7

A Professional Trustee's Guide to Setting Up Systems for Successful SNT Administration

By Herb Thomas, Kevin Urbatsch, and Michele Fuller

The successful SNT trustee will have excellent systems and procedures to meet the many trustee duties described in this book. This chapter provides a roadmap on setting up needed systems and procedures designed by a professional trustee who has managed hundreds of SNTs.

The SNT trustee will need to develop systems and procedures to focus on the following areas of administration, including:

1. Preparing for administration:
   A. Reading and understanding the trust document
   B. Identifying the beneficiary and other interested parties
   C. Documenting the distribution standard
   D. Setting up successful onboarding of the beneficiary
2. Administration processes:
   A. Setting up a spending plan
   B. Setting up disbursement procedures
   C. Setting up recordkeeping procedures
   D. Scheduling investments review

> E. Preparing accountings and reports
> F. Planning for tax filings
> G. Developing protection procedures for the trustee
3. Post-administration process:
> A. Determining type of SNT termination
> B. Planning checklist for finalizing administration process

WHEN SETTING UP A PROFESSIONAL TRUSTEE'S OFFICE, SHOULD THE TRUSTEE PREPARE A BUSINESS PLAN?

Yes, especially if the trustee is going to manage multiple SNTs. It is easier to design systems now before the press of business becomes too much to do it later. The professional trustee's business plan should include:

1. Managing and finding appropriately trained and motivated staff to assist the trustee in maintaining those mechanisms and requirements and generally enabling the trustee to perform all required responsibilities skillfully and faithfully;
2. A secure and efficient arrangement for the safekeeping of trust assets;
3. An accurate and efficient means of accounting for the flow of funds and assets into and from the trustee's possession;
4. An accurate and efficient means of reporting the accounting results to beneficiaries and others entitled to the information;
5. Adequately skilled tax advice and fiduciary tax return preparation services;
6. Retention of competent counsel on all other compliance matters, including obligations to courts having jurisdiction over the trust administration;
7. Competent and diligent advice as to the investment of trust assets; and
8. Appropriate professional liability insurance coverage, bonding or both.

WHAT ARE THE SNT TRUSTEE'S INITIAL DUTIES?

The idea of taking on the trusteeship of an SNT may be overwhelming at first. However, if the trustee breaks up the trust duties into smaller parts, it will be much easier to manage. The trustee can review the 14-Step Summary in Appendix A and have it printed out and reviewed prior to taking on any SNT administration.

When an individual or entity begins to serve as an SNT trustee, certain tasks should be completed immediately. Initially, the trustee should:

1. **Evaluate the beneficiary's living and personal care situation, determine whether there are unmet needs, identify steps to be taken, and create deadlines.** For example, a person with a disability may require drug therapy each month. If a parent or caregiver, who is no longer available, administered the drugs to his or her child or took the child to a clinic for that treatment, a replacement needs to be located immediately. The individual needs to be willing to help and acceptable to the beneficiary. The beneficiary's living and personal care situation should be reevaluated at least yearly.

2. **Determine which type of public benefits the beneficiary is receiving or may be eligible for.** It is important to know what benefits the beneficiary is receiving because the type of benefits will determine how the SNT will be administered. The SNT trustee should be asking a series of questions, such as: what is the beneficiary's current income level for any program for which the beneficiary receives a cash benefit? If the beneficiary is receiving Medicaid, is the benefit linked to SSI or is the beneficiary receiving Medicaid under Expanded Medicaid, the share of cost, or no share of cost program? Is the beneficiary receiving subsidized housing? If so, under what program? Is the beneficiary receiving Community Living Support hours (CLS)? If so, what are the terms of those services and who is providing them? Does the beneficiary have a parent who will retire soon? If so, what is the effect on the beneficiary's current benefits and spending plan? Then, the SNT trustee should review the income and resource rules for those benefit programs. For a more complete discussion of these public benefits see Chapter 3. In order to ensure that the trustee has the proper information, the trustee should have documentation in their file, such as copies of beneficiary's identification, health care cards, and SSA letters regarding the type and amount of public benefits. The trustee should check the claimant number on the SSA letter. This is helpful if the SNT beneficiary is unsure of

what benefits he or she receives. It also helps the trustee identify possible gaps in public benefit coverage.

3. **Read the trust document**. The SNT trustee must understand the terms of the trust they are administering. If there is any doubt, the trustee should consult an experienced SNT attorney to review the trust and receive advice on the trust terms. Of utmost importance, the trustee should understand the distribution standard of the SNT. Does it authorize distributions that could cause a loss or reduction in benefits? What are the requirements for bond or for accountings? Does the trust, or order establishing the trust, limit allowable investments? Does the trust require the trustee to report to Social Security for distributions that affect entitlement, or does it require the trustee to pursue all benefit programs for which the beneficiary may be entitled? Does the trust contain improper terms—for instance, authorizing distributions for "support" of the beneficiary, or direct the trustee to pay income to the beneficiary? The trustee should understand the limits of his or her authority when conducting trust business. An experienced SNT attorney may be able to help modify terms that are too restrictive or not in compliance with the law and changing government policies. If there are additional questions, the trustee can reach out to an experienced special needs planning attorney. The Academy of Special Needs Planners has a national list of such experts and is searchable by geography at https://specialneedsanswers.com.

4. **Determine whether the trust in question is a first-party or a third-party SNT**. The administration of each type of SNT will be very similar, but there are significant differences. For example, a third-party SNT may have multiple beneficiaries whereas the first-party SNT must be drafted and administered to benefit only the one primary beneficiary during his or her lifetime. In a first-party SNT, on the death of the beneficiary, remainder beneficiaries cannot be paid until after the Medicaid agency is paid. To distinguish between the two types of trusts, an explanation is set forth in Chapter 1. If a trustee is not sure of the type of SNT that is being administered, an experienced SNT attorney can help determine the type.

5. **Determine whether the SNT is under court supervision.** Typically, a court supervised SNT is one that is a first-party SNT established by a court. Finding out whether the SNT is court supervised will let the trustee know the type of rules the trustee must follow. Generally, it is much easier to administer a trust that is not court supervised. It is critical to know what the court will allow and how to comply with all court rules and deadlines. Often, experienced counsel is necessary to be able to do so and will help insulate the SNT trustee from running of court requirements.

6. **Meet with the beneficiary, the trust advisory committee members, and the trust protector, if any**. The trustee should meet with all parties named in the trust. A group meeting will help set appropriate standards and expectations from the start that may avoid disappointments and errors down the line. If the trustee is unclear as to how to manage the meeting, the trustee should consult with an attorney experienced in administering SNTs to either chair the meeting or to prepare an appropriate agenda. At the meeting, the trustee be ready to handle commonly asked questions such as:

A. How to contact the trustee to request distributions;

B. Review the information needed to properly set up the spending plan and why it is necessary;

C. How trustee decisions are made when making distributions, including an overview of the rules the SNT trustee must abide by in order to allow the beneficiary to remain eligible for benefits;

D. The turnaround time necessary for making a disbursement, e.g., beneficiary must provide bill more than the day before it is due;

E. How distributions are made, whether directly to the service provider, payment of a credit card charge, reimbursement to a third party, etc.;

F. How trust assets will be invested;

G. What information will and will not be provided to beneficiary, including accountings, investment statements, etc.; and

H. How trustee is paid.

9. **Prepare a spending plan for the distribution of SNT assets**. The trustee should work with the beneficiary and a financial advisor to develop a realistic spending plan or what is sometimes referred to as an expenditure plan or spending plan, for the SNT beneficiary. The term "spending plan" is preferable to a "spending plan," as it describes a positive experience for the beneficiary, versus the perceived restrictiveness of a spending plan, like describing a nutrition plan versus a diet. The spending plan should be shared with the beneficiary, the trust protector, trust committee, and any key advisers. See below for assistance in setting up the spending plan.

8. **Determine who is responsible for the care and advocacy of the beneficiary.** An SNT beneficiary may lack capacity to manage his or her own personal care or support needs. Sometimes, the SNT trustee will be the same person who has this legal responsibility. However, the SNT beneficiary may have others who have the legal duty to care for, or oversee the care of, the beneficiary. The trustee will often be working with these individuals when making disbursements. A list of these fiduciaries includes a guardian or conservator, SSA representative payee, authorized representative, or agent under a power of attorney. The extent and limits of the authority for each and the scope of the trustee's responsibility in relation to the other fiduciaries is typically set up in the document or court order establishing the role. The SNT trustee should seek copies of all documents giving them their authority to manage the beneficiary's care and understand how they all work together to act in the best interests of the beneficiary.

WHAT SHOULD THE TRUSTEE BE LOOKING FOR WHEN REVIEWING TRUST DOCUMENT?

Before making any attempt to administer the trust it is important that you read the entire trust document more than once and that you take notes or use a form to keep notes. Here are some of the important points to look for and notate:

1. It is a first-party or third-party trust?
2. Is the beneficiary on public benefits? If so, which benefits?

3. Is there a trust protector or a trust advisory group? What is the scope of their authority?
4. Is the trust court supervised (reviewed by the court on an ongoing basis)?
5. What are the distribution standards (supplemental or discretionary)?
6. Is there a memorandum of intent?
7. Is there a successor trustee?
8. Who are the remainder beneficiaries?

The trustee should document this information. A sample form for tracking this information can be found in Appendix E (SNT Summary Sheet). This document is referred to when the trustee has a question about what is allowed during administration or must reply to the beneficiary or public agencies.

WHAT RECOMMENDATIONS ARE THERE WHEN WORKING WITH THE BENEFICIARY AND OTHERS?

Success in most endeavors involves working well with people. In SNT administration, the beneficiary is the most important person that the trustee needs to consider. The trustee's primary duty is to ensure that trust assets are being protected and are utilized for the primary benefit of the beneficiary. The trustee needs to properly set expectations by effectively communicating with the beneficiary. However, an effective administration will include proper communication with everyone on the Beneficiary's team of caregivers, advisors, agents, and advocates.

In order to comply with the trustee's duty, the trustee should know who is responsible for the beneficiary's care and what other professionals are involved in the beneficiary's life and trust operations. The trustee must be able to track these people, so it is imperative to have contact information for each of the individuals involved in the trust and have a way to periodically update this contact information. There is nothing more frustrating than needing to talk to someone on an emergency basis and find out that the contact information is old or does not exist.

The following is a list of people who the trustee should obtain contact information:

- Beneficiary;
- Beneficiary's legal representatives like Representative Payee, Agents for health care and finances, conservator, and case manager;
- Family members who are actively involved (significant other, parents, etc.)
- Trust Protector (if nominated in the document)
- Trust Advisor Committee members (if nominated in the document)
- Successor trustees;
- Remainder beneficiaries (this may be difficult to maintain, but super helpful when the trust terminates);
- Beneficiary's health care providers;
- Care Manager;
- Caregiver or caregiver agency;
- County court information where trust is being administered;
- Attorney for trustee, beneficiary and others;
- Bond agent;
- Financial advisor;
- Tax professional;
- Case workers;
- SSA office or DHHS office;

If the trustee is only managing a few trusts, it may be fine to use a program like Microsoft Outlook, or an Excel spreadsheet. However, professional trust administrators who manage many trusts will find it prudent to invest in some type of Customer Relations Management or practice software. In addition to being used to keep contacts up to date, the programs can be used to keep case notes, track billable time, and calendar important matters for thousands of matters with a simplified interface. Cloud-based software is recommended because it allows a trustee access to information anywhere there is internet access and is often available across different devices.

It is also important to periodically update contact information. Some trustees will check every time someone calls to see if contact information has changed and others will review this information during the annual accounting period. Regardless of the system, a prudent trustee will set up a system to avoid losing contact with important persons during administration.

HOW CAN A TRUSTEE DOCUMENT THE DISTRIBUTION STANDARD?

In a well-drafted trust document, the SNT trustee is provided instructions on what his or her authority is in making disbursements on behalf of the beneficiary. This trust provision is often called the "distribution standard." In general, there are two kinds of SNT distribution standards, a supplemental standard or a discretionary standard, as described more fully below.

A trustee managing numerous trusts should identify the distribution standard and document it, so it is easy for the trustee to locate during administration. SNTs are written by many different attorneys who create different types of distribution standards. Identifying the proper distribution standard during administration can be time-consuming if the trustee has to find it within the trust document before making every distribution. The prudent trustee will check the appropriate box on Appendix E as to which distribution standard applies. This way, when determining whether a distribution can be made, the trustee will have a quick reference to make sure he or she is in compliance with the trust document, or whether it should be amended in order to best meet the needs of the beneficiary.

The two types of distribution standards common to SNTs are:

- **The Purely *Supplemental* Distribution Standard:** Some SNTs specifically prohibit the trustee from making any distributions that will reduce or eliminate SSI eligibility for any reason. As described in Chapter 12, payments for food or shelter will reduce or even eliminate SSI eligibility. Thus, the SNT trustee is prohibited from making any disbursements that will reduce the beneficiary's SSI income. This kind of SNT may be easier for a trustee to manage because payments for "food" or "shelter" are prohibited, and therefore do not require the trustee to determine the impact of these distributions on the beneficiary's public benefits. However, this type of standard also seriously hampers the ability of the SNT trustee to improve the beneficiary's life by paying rent for a nicer apartment or paying for the beneficiary's food. If this type of provision exists and the SNT trustee determines such expenditures would be in the best interests of the beneficiary, an SNT can be modified to allow a discretionary distribution standard. Depending on the trust terms, modification may require a probate court petition as described in Chapter 5.

135

> **Example:** A supplemental distribution standard will often look like this sample: "The trustee shall not make any distribution that will reduce or eliminate eligibility for public benefits."

- **The *Discretionary* Distribution Standard**: Some SNTs will allow distributions even if they reduce or even eliminate a public benefit if doing so is in the beneficiary's best interest. This type of distribution standard or provision is known as a "discretionary distribution standard." This standard requires that the trustee carefully examine how the rules regarding SSI "in-kind support and maintenance" (referred to as ISM) will be applied. The beneficiary's SSI benefits will be reduced or eliminated if he or she receives distributions for food or shelter (SSA treats these as ISM). The trade-off, however, is that the well-being and standard of living of the beneficiary may be enhanced, even after the SSI reduction is imposed. This is generally the more desirable distribution standard for maximizing the quality of life of the person with a disability.

> **Example:** A discretionary distribution standard will often look similar to this sample: "The trustee may distribute to or apply for the benefit of Beneficiary such amounts from the principal and income, up to the whole thereof, as the trustee, in the trustee's discretion, considers necessary or advisable to meet Beneficiary's special needs for the remainder of his life. While distributions are supplemental in nature to any public benefits the beneficiary is receiving, our Trustee may make a distribution otherwise covered by public benefits, if it is determined by our Trustee to be in the best interests of the beneficiary to make such distribution."

> **Note:** If the SNT trustee is unsure of which type of distribution standard, the trustee should contact an attorney experienced in drafting SNTs to review the document.

The authors of this book always prefer the fully discretionary distribution standard. It provides the most flexibility to the SNT trustee to enhance the quality of life of the beneficiary with a disability by allowing the trustee to decide to forego all or a portion of public benefits if it is in the beneficiary's best interests to do so.

WHY SHOULD A TRUSTEE SET UP A SPENDING PLAN?

Prior to making any distributions, the SNT trustee should work with the beneficiary (or other supports and fiduciaries) to develop a spending plan. The plan should take into consideration the beneficiary's income, the sources of income, anticipated gains on the investments, the expenses of the beneficiary, any unmet needs, regular administrative expenses, and any anticipated large expenses. Utilizing the services of other professionals, such as financial and tax advisors, are of great help in creating the spending plan.

Whenever possible, have the beneficiary review and agree to the proposed spending plan. Reviewing the spending plan helps illustrate the impact of spending on the life of the trust, and can help both the Beneficiary, or their legal representative, and the SNT trustee make educated spending decisions. Appendix F is a spending planning worksheet to help create the spending plan. There are also numerous spending planning worksheets online or some are imbedded in software programs like QuickBooks.

A trustee has many important duties that he or she must keep in mind while serving as trustee. These include following the terms of the trust, acting in the best interests of the beneficiary, properly investing trust assets, keeping great records, paying taxes, and providing accounts when requested. All of this is made easier by setting up a spending plan, establishing good procedures as outlined in this book, and consistently following them.

SHOULD A TRUSTEE HIRE SOMEONE TO EVALUATE THE BENEFICIARY'S NEEDS?

In many cases, yes, this is typically not a legal duty of the SNT trustee. However, some trust documents require this be done annually to protect the beneficiary and ensure their needs are being met.

> **Helpful Hint:** The trustee should review the trust documents to see if a Memorandum of Intent was prepared. This may have valuable information on the beneficiary and his or her condition. A Memorandum of Intent is usually drafted by parents as part of their estate plan and should be updated regularly.

The trustee should generally do the evaluation in person or hire a professional. If he or she does not understand how the beneficiary's disability affects the beneficiary's life, then it is best to do an "in person" meeting which can eliminate many future communication problems. The impact of a disability can be difficult to describe in writing or over the phone. Simply reviewing medical documents or a list of conditions may not let the trustee understand how the disabilities affect the beneficiary's ability to function on a daily basis, meet short and long-term goals, and communicate their needs.

If the trustee does not feel comfortable doing the evaluation, he or she can hire a professional to do it. The type of professional chosen to perform the evaluation may depend on examining a particular aspect of the Beneficiary's life or health. For example, if it is mental health related, a psychiatrist or neuropsychologist can assist. All of these evaluations can be paid for from the trust assets.

An evaluation of the beneficiary may include the following areas:
- Contact with family and whether continuing and facilitating such contact is part of the trustee's responsibility, or to determine what degree of contact is recommended;
- An evaluation of the beneficiary's physical and mental condition;
- Rehabilitation and training programs in which he or she participates (or should be participating);
- Current living situation and whether it is still appropriate, including (when appropriate) an evaluation of the caregivers for the beneficiary;

- Financial condition, including available government benefits, to determine the beneficiary's needs and the effect of distributions from the SNT on the beneficiary's eligibility for public assistance;
- Identifying any unmet needs and if additional benefits should be sought and by whom;
- Exercise of his or her civil rights. For example, is the beneficiary receiving a fair wage for work performed or being denied his or her right to vote or marry? Is the guardianship unnecessarily restrictive and the guardian's powers need to be revisited?
- Current and future educational needs and programs;
- Recreational activities, leisure time, and social needs, and the appropriateness of existing program services.

After the initial evaluation, the evaluation should be repeated at least yearly, or when a major change occurs in the beneficiary's life, such as a move or marriage.

HOW DOES A TRUSTEE CREATE A SPENDING PLAN FOR AN SNT BENEFICIARY?

The easiest way to create a spending plan is to do it in five steps:
- list monthly income;
- identify and list all current and future expenses;
- compare income and expenses;
- consider likely return on the investment of funds; and
- review regularly and make appropriate changes.

Ideally, setting up a spending plan should be done by having discussions with the beneficiary (and his or her advocates, friends, and family) regarding how the SNT assets should be used to enhance the beneficiary's quality of life.

> **Helpful Hint:** Use the list at the end of Chapter 9 and Appendix O. Review it with the beneficiary (and with those who know the beneficiary well) to see what kinds of goods and services he or she expects the trust to pay for on a monthly basis and those items he or she may desire. Some trustees have reported that with certain

beneficiaries, this may not be prudent. These beneficiaries look at the list as a shopping list and seek all kinds of items they will not use or need. Further, if the assets in the SNT are limited, it may be better to limit the beneficiary's options to the needs they identify themselves without looking at the list.

These discussions will aid the Beneficiary in understanding what the expectations are for use of the funds and the impact disbursements have on the life of the trust. It will also allow the trustee to set appropriate expectations from the outset. The trust document should also be read (and any memorandum of intent reviewed) to see how the person setting up the trust intended for trust assets to be used to enhance the quality of life of the beneficiary. Regardless of the amount held in trust, the trustee will protect him or herself by sticking with a spending plan but staying flexible when circumstances change.

Example: SNT trustee of a first-party trust meets with beneficiary and his girlfriend to discuss a spending plan. The beneficiary wants to use the funds to buy a car for him and one for his girlfriend, pay for rent on a two-bedroom apartment where he and his girlfriend will live, buy furniture, a home gym, and a computer, supply a monthly allowance of $1,000, and in a couple of years, pay for college.

The trustee can immediately set the proper expectations. The trustee can explain that because this is a first-party SNT, the trustee is not allowed to use any funds for the girlfriend. Distributions are only allowed for beneficiary's primary benefit. Payment of rent will reduce the amount of SSI the beneficiary will receive (which may or may not be in his best interest). Cash allowance directly to the beneficiary is not allowed, as it will eliminate SSI and increase share of cost for Medicaid. They should then discuss whether it is realistic to buy all these items immediately, given that the beneficiary wants to pay for school. The planning meeting allows the trustee to set the whole tone of the administration. It is best done at the beginning of administration so a beneficiary does not get frustrated if he or she expects to receive things and keeps getting rejected without explanation.

The spending plan itself requires the trustee to delve into the entire financial background of the beneficiary. Depending on the cooperation of the beneficiary, this can be quite simple or very frustrating. If the beneficiary is not cooperative and does not have friends or family who will support them, the trustee may be able to obtain information from the beneficiary's school records, such as an Independent Education Plan (IEP). It may be difficult for the trustee to obtain these reports, but if there is a caseworker or care manager for the beneficiary, it may be possible to request them.

If the SNT assets came from a litigation recovery, the beneficiary's personal injury attorney may have obtained a "Life Care Plan" as part of the litigation. These plans are an excellent way to obtain information about the care and services the beneficiary will require throughout his or her life.

The trustee can only do as much as he or she can with the information at hand. It would still be a good idea to establish a spending plan even if the beneficiary does not cooperate. It will provide direction when deciding on making distributions and preserving assets for expected future disbursements.

To aid the SNT trustee, a worksheet is set forth in Appendix F of this book. Also, there are software programs that can assist and are widely available, such as QuickBooks or Quicken. The worksheet provides a list of commonly addressed income and expense items that should be reviewed. It is recommended that this spending plan be reviewed periodically (perhaps once a year while doing the accounting) to make any changes and updates to it, especially prior to any major purchase (such as a home or auto purchase) or consistent fairly large disbursements (such as caregiving fees).

Helpful Hint: For further assistance, several companies have online financial calculators that will give an estimate of the estimated costs of taking care of a person with a disability. Merrill Lynch provides such a calculator at http://specialneedscalc.ml.com/?_ga =1.160389949.1278225624.1463326399.

The calculators are of limited use but do provide a ballpark figure to begin calculations.

IS THERE A SYSTEMATIC WAY TO MAKE APPROPRIATE SNT DISTRIBUTIONS?

At the onset of administration, the beneficiary and his or her advocates and representatives should be provided with written disbursement procedure guidelines. This documented method of how disbursements are made and when they are made (*e.g.*, on weekdays, twice a month, or for urgent matters) can reduce the frustration that some beneficiaries can experience when they want impulse purchases by the SNT trustee. In order to help the trustee determine what is an acceptable SNT distribution, Appendix H is a decision tree that assists in determining whether a distribution will affect public benefits.

> **Note:** Built into the checklist at Appendix H is the presumption that the SNT trustee understands what SSI considers unearned income, in-kind support and maintenance (ISM), available resource, food, shelter; "primary benefit," and other important public benefit considerations. Thus, it is important that the SNT trustee use this checklist with a firm understanding of these various terms, which are discussed in Chapter 3.

WHAT DISTRIBUTION SYSTEM SHOULD BE IMPLEMENTED?

The SNT trustee should have a written disbursement request form that is used for all beneficiary disbursement requests. It is best to use a form that the beneficiary or the beneficiary's advocate can fill out, sign and either fax or email to the trustee. The form set forth in Appendix G can be used for single requests. It can also be adapted to include more than one item or service. It is important to explain how the trustee will acknowledge receipt each request. It is probably best to email an acknowledgement as this will preserve a written record of trustee actions. For the technology minded, some trustees have used an app on a smartphone that allows for disbursement requests to be made to the trustee.

Developing a process for disbursement requests, like one outlined here, is critical to the SNT trustee whether they administer one trust or several. By requiring a written request, the trustee has written documentation that the beneficiary, or their legal representative, has requested a disbursement, identified who the disbursement should be paid to, verified the amount to be disbursed and why. The form in Appendix G also helps the trustee verify that the request was checked for compliance with the beneficiary's stream of benefits, the disbursement standard in the trust agreement, and within the beneficiary's spending plan. The form also documents when the request is outside of those parameters as well and what factors influenced the trustee's decision. This type of documentation is important to insulate the trustee from liability if their administrative decisions are ever called into question. It is also a practice that lends itself to create accountability for those that administer trusts on a professional level. It may seem a bit overzealous for the family member trustee, but this type of process is like insurance. You never know when you will need it, and you are always glad you have it when something goes wrong. Documenting the basis for a decision at the time it is made is vital, as it is incredibly difficult to remember why a certain action was taken if it is called into question years later.

Whatever distribution system is put in place, the SNT trustee must include a procedure for what documentation will be required before a distribution is made. For example, the trustee should require written documentation supporting a request, such as a doctor bill, quote for services, or an invoice. If the trustee is paying a credit card bill, the beneficiary should also provide a receipt from the vendor or service provider. This is important in the event a disbursement is ever questioned by a government agency or the court.

If there is a large disbursement, the trustee can be protected by obtaining permission from the court for making that disbursement. The trustee should determine when he or she would go to court, *e.g.*, obtaining authority for a large disbursement like a home or car. If the disbursement is questionable, a court petition may also be recommended, *e.g.*, if the trust does not have a lot of money and the beneficiary requests a therapy pool. While technically a therapy pool would be allowable, the trustee may be concerned with the large percentage of trust assets being used to comply with request. It may be prudent (if the trustee agrees the therapy pool is in the best interest of the beneficiary) to document the file with a letter from a medical professional explaining how the pool will benefit the beneficiary and obtain court agreement with the disbursement.

It is also important for the trustee to remember that the reviewers of trustee's actions like the SSA or the court will look at SNT disbursements with a critical eye. SSA eligibility workers or the court may question SNT disbursements that are valid but may appear to be excessive. For example, while a riding lawn mower would be an acceptable SNT disbursement, in one case the SSA worker believed it was excessive due to the beneficiary's relatively small yard and was trying to count it as SSI income. The SNT trustee in that case obtained a doctor's letter stating that the beneficiary needed a riding lawn mower due to the beneficiary's physical limitations prior to making the disbursement and had it in their file. The SNT trustee provided the documentation as to why the riding lawn mower was purchased and the doctor's letter to SSA, and it then withdrew its objection. Thus, even for disbursement that are valid, the prudent SNT trustee will provide as much documentation to support of each disbursement made as possible.

WHAT RECORDKEEPING SYSTEM SHOULD BE IMPLEMENTED?

Document everything! It is extremely important that a trustee keep excellent records. Not only should a trustee document activity by the trustee but also document conversations made with the beneficiary, his advocate, care providers, and other third parties. The software packages mentioned above are excellent ways to document activities and conversations. Most fiduciaries find it beneficial to document activities and conversations immediately after they occur. A lot of the CRM programs also include billing components, so if the trustee is charging for hourly services it is a way to ensure that your time is being accurately recorded.

A sample of what should be included, in addition to the accountings, and the backup information upon which the accountings are based should include the following:

- **Notes from regular meeting with the beneficiary or his or her legal representatives.** For each meeting, keep a record of the date, the length of the meeting, and a summary of what was discussed. The trustee should also keep records of all other communications between the trustee and the beneficiary, including such things as copies of all correspondence.

- **Beneficiary's income tax returns.** If the trust document grants the trustee's discretion in making distributions to the beneficiary, the income tax returns can provide the trustee a great deal of helpful information. Those returns are signed under penalty for perjury. The beneficiary may be reluctant to share his or her income tax returns with a trustee, but the trustee's request for that kind of information is not unduly intrusive—no more so than a bank asking for the same documentation before deciding whether to loan money.

- **Beneficiary's annual spending plan or spending plan.** Because SNT trustees typically have complete discretionary authority with respect to distributions, the trustee should help prepare a spending plan for the beneficiary. This shows that the trustee has carefully considered the beneficiary's needs relative to discretionary distributions. For further discussion of how to set up a spending plan, see above.

- **Verification of out-of-pocket expenditures.** Since the trustee, or beneficiary's legal representative, is entitled to reimbursement of all reasonable amounts the trustee advances on behalf of the trust, he or she should keep copies of proof of payment, such as canceled checks or receipts. For example, if someone is travelling with beneficiary and pays for all bills from a personal account, he or she can be reimbursed from the SNT and it is best practice to keep very careful track of these expenditures.

- **Communications with advisers.** Keep all copies of all correspondence between the trustee and his or her advisers, and always ask them to at least summarize any advice they give in writing.

- **Any and all information upon which any exercise of discretion is based.** These documents may include such things as beneficiary's bank statements, credit card statements, pay stubs, or other employment information, invoices, proposals, and any other information given to you to justify a request for a distribution.

HOW SHOULD A TRUSTEE KEEP TRACK OF TRUST ASSETS?

A trustee must have a procedure for tracking trust assets. Trust assets typically include cash, investment accounts, bank accounts, jewelry, real property, collectible items, artwork, etc. Software programs like Quicken, QuickBooks or Excel are ideal for tracking these items. Once the SNT is established the assets should be included onto the appropriate spreadsheet.

On an ongoing basis, financial account statements should be reviewed when received and the information input (reconciled) into your software program so that your accounting takes less time. Bank accounts should be reviewed and reconciled monthly. Many banks have opted out of paper statements but have them available for download for a period of time. Those statements should be saved and maintained by the trustee. Cloud based systems, like Dropbox, Box, and One Drive, are just some of the methods used to store large amounts of data. The advantage to these cloud-based systems is that the information is available on almost any device where internet is available, and readily accessible to the trustee.

WHEN SHOULD A TRUSTEE KEEP TRACK OF TRUST INVESTMENTS?

Always. It is axiomatic that once an investment strategy has been implemented, it will almost immediately begin to fluctuate with market events. Some asset classes will rise in value, while others fall and still others move sideways. These movements are natural and, given that there is price momentum associated with most capital markets, they are not cause for alarm. However, if a trustee allows the portfolio to drift too far from its target, the trustee is in effect making a decision to change, sometimes radically, the risk/reward structure of the portfolio. Rather than allow such implicit decisions to occur, the trustee will need to review the asset allocation structure of the trust investments immediately. The trustee will use its discretion to (i) rebalance back to the minimum or maximum exposure, (ii) rebalance back to the target exposure, or (iii) determine that the costs (especially taxes) associated with rebalancing make the exercise unwise.

If a trustee is not experienced in financial management (and as discussed elsewhere in this book), this is a duty that can be delegated to a financial advisor. A trustee should consider setting up at least a quarterly review procedure to review investment performance and to make sure the investments are working as intended. This book is devoted to providing information to individual trustees. Corporate trustees (typically banks) are subject to all the same rules and laws that are described in this book. However, they have an additional level of scrutiny from the federal banking authorities. It is illustrative to review what the federal government requires when reviewing a corporate trustee's investments. The following requirements are part of the FDIC's review of a corporate trustee:

Investment Review

If the bank has discretion over the account's assets, sufficient information should be provided to the reviewing authority to enable it to make informed and intelligent decisions. At a minimum, information considered necessary to perform an investment review includes:

- Investment powers authorized by the trust instrument and/or governing law,
- Investment objective of the account (income, growth, etc.),
- Listing of account assets, reflecting cost and market values,
- Projected yields on individual assets,
- Projected income of the overall account, and
- Amount of principal and income cash on hand.

An investment review may include, but is not limited to, the following items:

- Investment objectives - Are they consistent with the objectives of the trust? Are assets held consistent with the chosen investment objectives and/or asset allocation models?
- Diversification of discretionary investments - Is the account properly diversified consistent with either the Prudent Investor Act or Prudent Man Rule, as applicable?
- Concentrations - Are there any undue concentrations, either within a type of security, industry, or specific obligation?

147

- Own-bank or affiliate obligations - Is the purchase appropriate, yield adequate, and authorization documented?
- Investments in companies related to, or loans made to, bank insiders - Are there any conflict of interest or self-dealing concerns?
- Approved hold, buy, and sell lists - Is the account in compliance?
- Maturity of assets - Are there excess funds invested in short-term (lower yielding) investments? Is there adequate liquidity?
- Asset valuations - Are assets including real estate, limited partnerships, closely held businesses, real estate syndications, and derivatives valued accurately?
- Insurance coverage - Is it adequate?
- Environmental risk factors - Are there any environmental risk concerns?
- Complaints - Are complaints by grantors, beneficiaries, plan administrators, etc. being reviewed? Have previous complaints been resolved?
- Criticisms - Is corrective action being taken with regard to criticisms noted by internal and external auditors and regulatory authorities?

All of the items listed above will not necessarily be included in every trust department's account review program. Therefore, examiners must exercise discretion in assessing the adequacy of account reviews. An assessment should be made after giving consideration to the department's overall account review program, fiduciary responsibilities, committee minutes, file documentation, account officer expertise, and account sampling. Some trust departments may believe that completion of an investment review satisfies the account review requirement for discretionary accounts. Examiners should remind management that fulfilling account administrative duties (*i.e.*, timely mailing of customer statements, income distributions, fee calculations, etc.) is also a fiduciary responsibility that should be reviewed to reduce exposure to liability.

If the account review program is materially deficient, the Report of Examination should contain criticisms of management. The examiner-in-charge should obtain management's response and plan for corrective action.

WHAT TYPE OF REVIEW SHOULD A TRUSTEE DO IF THEY ARE CONCERNED ABOUT CURRENT FINANCIAL ADVISOR'S TRUST INVESTMENTS?

If the trustee is concerned that an existing financial advisor is not doing a suitable job, he or she should consider doing a tiered type of review with a new financial advisor. A tier review might include the following:

I. Tier One Review would flag areas of concern for follow up by the trustees and typically will include the following:
- Review of the last four quarterly investment statements;
- Ensure that there is an existing investment policy; and
- Review existing fee schedule charged by investment advisor

II. Tier Two Review - If areas of concern have been identified by a Tier One review, the trustee may wish to know more. At the end of a Tier Two review, the Trustee should receive an action plan that helps them overcome any issues and demonstrates they are complying with their duty of care. A tier two review typically includes the following:
- Meetings with the portfolio manager to go through the account statements; and
- Review of all underlying fund reports and other investment information with the portfolio manager.

III. Tier Three Review would determine after a Tier One and Tier Two review that an account should be significantly restructured. An investment advisor should then:
- Rewrite the Investment Policy Statement to reflect the current situation;
- Assist the Trustees to renegotiate the fee structure of the account if it is not appropriate;
- Reanalyze the asset allocation and restructure it to reflect the Trustee's current plans;
- Reorganize the account to include appropriate performance reporting so that the Trustees are able to better track the account. This includes adding benchmarks for all investments; and

- Replace the existing investment manager if the Trustees are no longer comfortable with the investment arrangements.

SHOULD A TRUSTEE HAVE AN INVESTMENT POLICY STATEMENT?

One of the best things that trustees can do is to create an Investment Policy Statement. Some trustees may provide non-specific mandates to investment managers, *e.g.*, "manage the assets of the trust in a prudent manner." However, this type of mandate is not measurable, and a trustee will want to hold investment managers accountable as required by their duty of care. Trustees should insist on a measurable investment policy statement. Areas where measurable standards can be added include:

- The asset allocation of the account;
- The maximum position sizes of investments;
- The minimum credit rating on bonds;
- The rating of mutual funds;
- The deviation of performance from benchmarks; and
- The maximum loss allowed by a manager or position

Scott MacDonald and Daniel Cutter of Merrill Lynch provide an excellent SNT Investment Policy Statement at Appendix P. In addition, below is a sample Investment Policy Statement for an SNT:

SPECIAL NEEDS TRUST
OBSERVATIONS AND RECOMMENDATION SUMMARY

OBJECTIVES TO CONSIDER:
- Definition of the specific needs of the client

SUMMARY OF OBSERVATIONS:
- Overview of current situation
- Balance Sheet
- Income Statement

SUMMARY OF RECOMMENDATIONS:

- Analysis and overview of proposed allocation to fulfill specific needs

METHODOLOGY:

- Disclosure of fees, tax issues, court approval language

SUMMARY OF BENEFITS:

- Details of the customized investment strategy

HOW SHOULD A TRUSTEE SET UP AN ACCOUNTING AND REPORT PROCEDURE?

A trustee is required to account to beneficiaries on trust activities that show assets on hand, assets received, assets distributed and trust liabilities. It is best to record the accounting due date on the Trust Summary Sheet as set forth in Appendix E and in the trustee's calendar.

Be sure to schedule ample time to prepare the accounting before it is due because it can be time consuming. To make the accounting easier, the trustee may want to make monthly entries into an Excel spreadsheet when the trustee reviews and reconciles the financial statements. It is also a good time to review the trust document two months before submitting the accounting to ensure the trustee is preforming all fiduciaries duties or requirements. This will allow the trustee to correct or address any issues.

If the SNT being administered is not court-supervised, the account requirement is generally required once a year. However, the trust document may waive the account requirement or make it more frequent but remember the trust can never waive the requirement to keep a beneficiary reasonably informed of trust activities. So, it is generally recommended to provide an account and report even if the trust document waives the requirement. These accountings will include investment information, bank holdings, the value of collectibles, real property, etc. See Chapter 8 for a full description of what is required in an accounting.

HOW DOES AN SNT TRUSTEE PREPARE FOR FILING TAX RETURNS?

As noted in Chapter 17, a major responsibility of the trustee is to make sure that all applicable tax returns are filed, and taxes are paid. The trustee will primarily be concerned about trust income. However, there may be instances where the SNT has to deal with real property and employment taxes. Unless a trustee has specialized training in income tax preparation, it is best to gather and forward all income tax documents to a tax professional, such as an Enrolled Agent (EA) or a Certified Public Accountant (CPA).

Because most tax related information is issued by the end of January up until early March, this documentation can be collected and provided to the tax professional to do the preparation work. It is best to contact the tax professional by October of the tax year (*i.e.,* October 2020 when preparing for year 2020) to ensure the preparer can complete and file the tax returns without the need for filing an extension. The tax professional will most likely provide a list of documents to retain and submit to prepare the returns. For trustees unfamiliar with reviewing tax returns, the early meeting is also a good time to ask the preparer to show the trustee how to review the returns for first-party and third-party SNTs.

A convenient way to gather tax documents is to set aside all "information returns" (*e.g.,* 1099s, 1098s) in a folder upon receipt. Some tax preparers will have online portals where the trustee can email scanned documents to them; others may want to meet with in person to review documents.

Once a draft tax return is provided, it is paramount that the trustee begins to review the tax document quickly to be able to file or forward the returns in a timely manner. For first-party SNTs, the grantor letter must be sent out to the trust beneficiary as quickly as possible so that he or she may use that information to prepare his or her own personal return. For third-party SNTs, the trustee may have to pay taxes due with that return and gather funds for future estimated quarterly payments.

WHAT OTHER PROTECTIVE PROCEDURES CAN A TRUSTEE IMPLEMENT?

There are at least six keys areas of protection that the fiduciary should consider:

1. Computer or cyber security;
2. Access to client funds;
3. Insurance;

4. Documentation and recordkeeping;

5. Personal safety; and

6. Billing

Cyber Security - Volumes have been written on the importance of securing data on computers, creating hard to break passwords, and backing up data. However, most cyber security experts say there is no way to completely secure data. Nonetheless, for the protection of trust information and resources, the SNT trustee must take steps to secure data.

For securing computers, the easiest thing is to set up a hard-to-guess password that is different from other passwords. The SNT trustee will also need a good "firewall" to protect the system when searching the Internet. For financial and online storage websites, it is a good idea to use unique and different password for each online institution you visit (*e.g.*, Wells Fargo, Merrill Lynch, Schwab, etc..). Secure passwords will consist of a combination of capital letters, numerals, and special characters. Software containing client information like demographic data that resides on your personal computer or in the cloud, financial information should be password protected. Backing up your data to an online cloud storage location like Carbonite is a good way to protect data in the event of a disaster at your office location.

Access to client funds - The SNT trustee is entrusted to make sure trust funds are safe. Are the funds really safe if someone who is not the appointed authority has access to monies? Unless the SNT trustee is working with a trusted business partner who shares the same liability for each matter, no one else should have unfettered access to client funds. This includes transferring money or directing financial advisors to use funds to make payments. If an employee or even a "trusted" person has the authority to move funds, the trustee increases the possibility of misappropriation of the funds.

There are "view-only" options for staff persons, tax professionals, beneficiaries, and other persons to view accounts without providing them authority to access the money. Beneficiaries and their representatives can also receive copies of monthly financial statements. But, the SNT trustee should make sure that only the trustee is able to access trust funds.

Insurance – "If you wait long enough the improbable is bound to happen. —John M. Cowden.

A professional fiduciary (trustee) should have **Errors and Omissions (E&O) insurance**. This protects the trustee in case of a trustee's mistake or negligence. The most organized and efficient person still makes mistakes. If something does go wrong, it may not be the trustee's fault, but just because there is a trustee, the trustee can still be named in a lawsuit. Even with E&O, an SNT trustee will likely be paying a deductible to defend the trustee in a lawsuit but it is much less expensive than covering the whole loss.

A trustee should obtain **Umbrella Coverage** as extra liability insurance. This coverage is designed to help protect a trustee from major claims and lawsuits and as a result it helps protects the trustee's assets. It also provides additional liability coverage above the limits of auto and homeowners, policies. Coverage is also provided should a trustee be sued for:

- Slander – injurious spoken statement
- Libel – injurious written statements
- Malicious prosecution
- Shock/mental anguish
- Other personal liability situations

A trustee should also buy basic **business insurance** to cover office equipment and protects the trustee in case visitors are injured while visiting the trustee's office. A trustee should also consider a rider on their coverage for **Employee Theft Insurance** to cover the trustee in case a trustee's staff person embezzles funds from the business or from a trust account.

Personal Safety – Trustees must take into consideration their personal physical safety. Some SNT beneficiaries, their families, or others with bad intentions may not be pleased that a trustee has been appointed to handle the funds of a person with a disability. These individuals will seek out the trustee for confrontation. If that place is the trustee's home, then it is best not to use the trustee's home address on printed material, or have it listed as the trustee's place of business on a website. Commonly, private professional fiduciaries in California will use a P.O. Box or a UPS Store as a business address and will either meet with clients in the field or by invitation to their unlisted office location.

Documentation and recordkeeping. Document everything! That is the simplest advice anyone can give a trustee. It is the trustee's best support on why a certain decision was made if challenged. It has the added benefit of showing the beneficiary and their family that their concerns were noted and documented.

There are software systems that make keeping documents and records much easier. Practice management software like Amicus Attorney, Smokeball, or Clio, can maintain customer data, record your notes with sequential dates, and can be used as your filing and billing system. For smaller offices, MyCase, Practice Panther, and Time Matters, may be cost effective alternatives.

The trustee will need to retain written letters, emails and text messages. For de-livered mail, the trustee may want to have physical file cabinets to retain important documents like letters, legal papers, financial statements and nursing home bills. The trustee can also scan these documents and save them on a cloud-based com-puter system so that they are easily accessed when the trustee is away from the of-fice and needs to review information. There are electronic document programs that can be password protected and set up to resemble a filing system similar to physical filing cabinets. Document management programs identified below not only allow the trustee to securely store and email documents but can save the files to the cloud for remote access.

- eFileCabinet, http://www.efilecabinet.com
- PinPoint, http://www.lsspdocs.com
- Kofax   PaperPort
  https://www.kofax.com/Products/paperport?utm_source=google&utm_medium=cpc&utm_campaign=dr&gclid=EAIaIQobChMIqZn99LyV5gIVi ddkCh2mng-VEAAYAiAAEgJpCPD_BwE
- Processing programs like Microsoft Word can also be set up to resemble a physical file cabinet but the documents will be available to anyone who can access the system and may not be safe, also it is easier to have files erased when saved as Word documents.

Billing for Services – Billing the trust for services is sometimes a source of frustration for the beneficiary and the trustee. The beneficiary can sometimes be overwhelmed by the amount of the bill, especially for Court supervised matters where the bill is not presented a year or more after services have been performed. For the trustee, it can be can all a different matter, because after summoning his intellect, searching for and creating successful outcomes, overcoming obstacles, risking trustee's personal assets, sometimes enduring verbal and physical animosity, to then have a court (that spent little to no time reviewing your time records) reduce the fee, it can be disheartening. It is often not possible to have the court appreciate the work a trustee is subjected to on a daily basis, there are ways to protect the trustee by documenting the work performed and present it in a manner that succinctly details all of the efforts expended.

A trustee's invoice should include the following items:
- Date of service;
- Category of Service (e.g., banking, bill paying, bookkeeping, financial review, meeting w/client, etc.);
- Detailed description of service;
- Initials for person performing service (if others help you);
- Amount of time to perform activity;
- Billing rate for service; and
- Cost of a particular service.

There is a more complete description of completing billing requests in Chapter 6 and Appendices R and S.

WHAT SYSTEMS CAN AN SNT TRUSTEE UTILIZE WHEN THE TRUSTEE WILL NO LONGER BE THE TRUSTEE?

There are many reasons why an SNT trustee will no longer be serving as trustee (*e.g.*, the trustee resigns, becomes incapacitated, trust funds are exhausted, a successor trustee is chosen, the beneficiary is able to return to the workforce and no longer needs the SNT, or the beneficiary dies). When a beneficiary dies, the procedures set forth in Chapter 18 should be followed.

The process for winding down your administration is dependent on the circumstances, and whether the trust is a first party or third party SNT. The steps required to properly terminate administration for each type of SNT are outlined below.

Asked to resign or removal by authorized party – An SNT trustee may be removed or asked to resign. An SNT trustee may be asked to resign for many reasons. Serving as SNT trustee is a very personal service and like any relationship, may come to an end or require a change. If there is a request for resignation or possible removal, it would be prudent to find out if the situation is because of something the trustee did, if so see if the situation can be rectified without formal removal. If the trustee is being removed, the trustee should ask if he or she could resign instead. This is important when responding to inquiries by governing entities or insurers as to whether a trustee has been removed or resigned. The trustee must be diligent in assisting in the transition process. Depending on whether the successor is a professional or a non-professional, the successor trustee may need assistance in the process of transfer by following the checklist below.

Voluntary resignation - If the trustee is resigning, the trust document should provide the trustee with the directions for resigning. Normally this requires a thirty-day written notice to the beneficiary, or his or her legal guardian, and Trust Protector or Trust Advisory Committee if applicable. An SNT trustee should follow the checklist below to make sure all steps are taken in wrapping up their administration and transitioning to a successor trustee:

- Communicate early with the beneficiary and other parties on logistics of resignation and replacement;
- Obtain a successor trustee. Work with an attorney and other parties to select a successor. Sometimes a successor trustee is already named in the document, along with the procedures for the successor to begin the administration. If so, then the transition can be worked out between the two trustees. It will be important for the named successor trustee to review the trust document to ascertain if he or she is able to execute the directions laid out in the trust. Once that is affirmed, then a notarized document signed by the resigning trustee along with the consent of the successor

trustee to act is all that is needed to start under the new trusteeship for non-court supervised trusts;

- Provide a written copy of the signed trust to successor trustee;
- Prepare required written notices for resignation (usually 30-days);
- Prepare a final accounting and report for the trust for all services performed since the last account;
- Ascertain how the successor trustee would like to receive liquid assets (including investments). This may mean re-titling accounts, writing a check for assets in bank accounts, or wiring funds to the new accounts established by the successor trustee. Be sure to withhold enough funds (a reserve) to pay the final legal fees, tax advisor fees, administrative fees and cover any checks that have not cleared. Provide documentation identifying the trust's real property and personal assets (*e.g.*, raw land, developed property, art, coins, and other collectibles);
- Provide demographic information about the beneficiary (SSN, DOB, address, phone, medical insurance plans, and information about trust income and the beneficiary's personal income). Include the names, roles, and contact information for important parties such as trust protectors, investment advisors, tax professionals, advisory committee members, caregivers, care managers, etc.
- Obtain a receipt for trust assets from the successor trustee. This receipt should be kept providing evidence that the transfers took place and that the new trustee has acknowledged acceptance and responsibility for the assets.
- Additionally, copies of the trust files, including legal documents, financial statements, correspondence, bookkeeping related files (Quicken files or Excel), and insurance records should be copied and sent to the successor trustee (depending on the technological capabilities of the new trustee, electronic files for everything but the original trust should be sufficient).

Incapacity (or death) of the trustee. An SNT trustee should be prepared for his or her own incapacity or death. The trustee should have a succession plan that takes into account what happens if they cannot continue to serve. A lifetime of excellent service may be wiped out by everything crumbling after the trustee is no longer there to manage the trust. This is one reason why it is important to maintain good contemporaneous records so that the successor can step in and begin the administration as quickly as possible.

For professional trustees with business partners or support staff members, the transition will not be as difficult as it is with a sole practitioner or for non-professional trustee. For the trusts that name a successor trustee, the transition would be the similar to a resignation except that the trustee may not be able to sign resignation documents. A copy of the trust and a certification of trust naming the new trustee, along with a death certificate or letter regarding the current trustee's incapacity may be enough to convince some financial institutions to acknowledge the new trusteeship. For court supervised SNTs, a petition will need to be filed to appoint a new trustee. Once that appointment is approved the court order should be enough to take control of the assets. For third-party SNTs, a well-drafted trust should nominate a successor trustee and outline the process for their appointment. If the third-party trust does not name a successor, it may direct the trust protector of the advisory committee to select a trustee. If the trust document fails to provide direction as to whom and how a successor trustee is appointed, any interested party may petition a court of competent jurisdiction to fill the vacancy.

When trust funds are exhausted - Trust funds can be exhausted while the beneficiary is still alive. While it is always desirable to make the trust funds "last as long as possible" the funding may have reached its limit. As discussed above, the importance of establishing a spending plan is important. When making a spending plan, the trustee can forecast the trust running out of money. A frank discussion with the beneficiary and his or her advisors about the money running out should be performed as soon as it is apparent when funds will be gone. This discussion should also be confirmed in writing to the beneficiary and his or her legal representatives.

A trustee should also determine how much in fees he or she could be paid. Oftentimes, the money will run out and the trustee still has a legal duty to complete the trust termination process. This may end up being pro bono if the trustee has not prepared payment of a proper fee. The beneficiary should also be prepared to know when money will run out and what will happen to them when the SNT money is no longer available. While yearly accountings should be sent to the beneficiary and his representatives, one year prior to the ending of the SNT, it is advisable to send a letter to the beneficiary team informing them that trust assets are declining and providing them with a timeline for the depletion of funds. A follow up call should be made to the beneficiary to discuss the letter and timeline.

When the beneficiary no longer needs an SNT – On a rare occasion, an SNT beneficiary will be able to return to the workforce, is no longer in need of public benefits or protections afforded by an SNT, and makes the decision that he or she would like to terminate the trust and receive all the assets outright. This is a very difficult decision for an SNT trustee, as he or she must weigh many factors and impact on the beneficiary prior to termination of the SNT. The trust document itself may not authorize disbursement in this circumstance to the beneficiary. Pursuant to federal statutes and policy, early termination of a first-party SNT triggers an immediate reimbursement to the states and is best done with legal guidance and careful consideration. See Chapter 18 for a discussion on the proper procedure for terminating a first-party SNT and the checklist in Appendix N.

Third-party SNTs may provide direction for terminating the trust in the event the beneficiary enters or re-enters the workforce. Some of the language in the trust may require that the beneficiary work for two years without an assistance from the trust and that the beneficiary submits two statements from either medical doctors or psychologists stating that the beneficiary is able to handle his or her own finances. Once that has been determined, the trustee should consult with an attorney about the process of winding down the trust.

A few things the SNT trustee should keep in mind are that there will be fees and costs when doing an early SNT termination, *e.g.* final taxes and administrative costs. The trustee should see if the beneficiary has an investment advisor to receive invested funds so that capital gains taxes are avoided in the transfer of assets. The trustee should also make sure the beneficiary is able to receive all other assets, like real estate and cash.

CHAPTER 7 SUMMARY

The chapter provides:

- ✓ A professional trustee's overview of a trustee's duties during SNT administration.

✓ A step-by-step process in reviewing a trust document for what duties a trustee has when administering the trust.

✓ Recommendations for working with beneficiaries and their families.

✓ Documenting the trust distribution standard.

✓ Systems for setting up a spending plan.

✓ Creating systems for making appropriate distributions.

✓ Creating proper recordkeeping systems.

✓ Systems for keeping track of trust assets.

✓ Timelines for reviewing trust investments.

✓ Setting up accounting procedures.

✓ When to prepare for filing tax returns.

✓ Sample of common protection procedures a trustee should implement including insurance and managing money policies.

✓ Transferring trusteeship procedures and protections.

CHAPTER 8

Keeping Records, Preparing Accountings, and Providing Notice To Government Agencies

This chapter will describe the SNT trustee's obligation to keep records of trust transactions and when (and to whom) the trustee will be required to account and report. The trustee's responsibility to account will increase depending on whether the SNT is under continuing court jurisdiction. The final part of the chapter will discuss the notice requirements the trustee must meet.

> **Note:** Most SNTs are not under court jurisdiction. The ones that are generally include those first-party SNTs established by a court for a beneficiary who lacks capacity. If not sure what type of SNT is being administered, the SNT trustee should consult Chapter 2 for a discussion of the different types of SNTs or review Chapter 20 to find a special needs planning attorney who can assist in making this determination.

There are two different account and report requirements, depending on whether the SNT is under court jurisdiction:

- A trust under court jurisdiction will require an accounting be prepared in a very formal way as set forth in the Probate Code, reviewed by court staff (often called examiners), and then reviewed again by a judge. Depending on the county, court examiners and judges may not understand how an SNT is supposed to operate. Oftentimes, this will lead to trustees being very reluctant to make appropriate disbursements in fear of a court finding them at fault. It is important that SNT trustees and the attorneys that represent them understand what is allowed and properly educate these courts on how to properly administer an SNT.

- A trust not under court jurisdiction will typically require an accounting at least once a year. However, an SNT document may waive this requirement. Regardless of the waiver, an SNT trustee may decide to prepare an account to begin the running of the statute of limitation. Further, an SNT trustee will have a duty to keep beneficiaries reasonably informed and this duty may require much of the information that would be required in an account.

WHAT IS THE TRUSTEE RECORD KEEPING RESPONSIBILITIES?

Trustees have a legal duty to maintain accurate records of all trust business.[133] Records should be thorough, legible, and easily accessible and should provide a full description of the trustee's administration. Keeping detailed and accurate records ensures that the trustee can fulfill his or her duties to provide information, file tax returns, and submit complete accounts and reports. For example, an SNT trustee may be asked to provide information to the Social Security administration if the beneficiary is on SSI. The SNT trustee must be able to determine whether distributions from the SNT are considered SSI income, not income, in-kind income or in-kind support and maintenance. To be certain that SNT distributions from the trust fall into the desired category, the trustee should include a short description of the purpose of each distribution.

---

133 See Probate Code §§16060, 16062, and 16064.

Keeping good records also provides the best means of protecting trustees against liability in case a beneficiary questions the propriety of an administrative act. If proper records are not kept at the same time as the actions taken, it can be incredibly difficult to go back and recreate records months (or even years) later. Waiting to try and recreate records is more costly and will cause a trustee numerous headaches and problems.

The record-keeping requirement is relatively easy for a naturally organized person. However, if this is not an accurate description of trustee, then the trustee should hire someone to assist in keeping records—oftentimes a bookkeeper can serve that role.

WHAT INFORMATION SHOULD BE RECORDED?

In general, the trustee should set up a system that keeps the following information available:

- Cash and assets received. Cash amounts spent. Plus, the allocation of the assets between principal, income, or both.
- Inventory of all trust assets, including,
  1. Current valuation of trust assets;
  2. Cost basis (the amount paid for an asset, e.g., if person paid $50,000 for a home, the cost basis in real property is $50,000 even if its value has increased to $100,000);
  3. Periodic market valuations of securities; and
  4. Gains and losses incurred on sale of assets and other dispositions.

- Records of all transactions must be retained and organized so as to reflect their connection to the above data, e.g.,
  1. Canceled checks, paid invoices, and receipts;
  2. Bank statements;
  3. Explanation of each disbursement made;
  4. Trust and beneficiary income tax returns (sometimes called fiduciary tax returns); and
  5. Tax audit reports.

- Other documents that should be maintained:
    1. Investment policy statement and ongoing updates
    2. Quarterly investment reviews
    3. Updates to health records and care plans
    4. Trustee annotations of conversations with professional advisers and interested third parties
    5. Pertinent e-mails and letters related to trust activity
    6. Court documents and orders

WHAT IS THE PROCEDURE FOR KEEPING RECORDS?

There is no one way to keep records. Whatever procedure is selected, the trustee should keep a record of each disbursement, as it is made, keep the receipt for the disbursement, and review the records monthly. The trustee should review the records monthly, and again at the end of each year.

The individual trustee may maintain trust records with a system of folders. A separate folder is maintained for each of the following categories:

1. A copy of the trust agreement and all amendments
2. A copy of the beneficiary's public benefit program eligibility letters and notices
3. Notices sent by trustees to beneficiaries and others
4. Cost-basis information
5. Completed discretionary action forms and information regarding to whom and why the discretionary payments were made, or why the transfer between principal and income was made
6. Information evidencing compliance with the Prudent Investor Rule
7. Bank statements and canceled checks
8. Deposit slips and other income items
9. Paid bills
10. Copies of tax returns
11. Status of assets (or, depending on their number and complexity, one folder for each asset), including confirmations of purchases and sales
12. Transactions of any business operated by the trust
13. Correspondence and memoranda of a routine nature

14. All correspondence and memoranda in connection with the above or other actions of the trustee that might be called into question later

> **Helpful Hint:** Because most SNTs last for years, it would also be prudent for a trustee to purchase a software accounting system like *Quicken* or *QuickBooks* to keep track of the ongoing trust transactions. This will aid the trustee greatly when he or she is preparing end-of-the-year accountings. The cost of the software and any training programs the trustee wishes to take can be paid for from trust assets. Keeping documents in a cloud-based system like Dropbox, Box, or Google Drive is a good way to securely store and organize documents. Be sure to properly dispose of any sensitive information or documents that may contain account information, social security numbers, or medical documentation.

WHAT HAPPENS IF A TRUSTEE FAILS TO KEEP PROPER RECORDS?

If an SNT trustee fails to keep appropriate records, he or she will be unable to provide an accurate account of trustee actions to the beneficiary, public benefit agencies, to a court, and to other government agencies, like the IRS.

A trustee can be removed if he or she fails to keep proper records, because a court may find that a trustee who fails to keep adequate records is unfit for the office.[134] Further, trustees who fail to keep proper records can also be held liable for breach of fiduciary duty, contempt, damages, and, where appropriate, attorney fees.[135] It also means that if a trustee is questioned in court and has failed to keep proper records, all presumptions will be made against the trustee and all doubts arising from the failure to keep records will be resolved against the trustee.

> **Example:** A trustee has been using trust cash each month for beneficiary's acupuncture treatments. The trustee fails to make a note of the transactions, obtains no invoices, and gets no cash

---

134 See Probate Code §§15642, 16420, 17200(b)(10).
135 See Probate Code §§16060, 17200(b)(7), 17211(b); Code Civil Procedure §1209(a)(5).

receipts. Two years later, the trustee's actions are being questioned in court. If the trustee is unable to provide accurate records of these transactions, he or she will be presumed to have misused the funds and could be required to pay back the trust money from his or her own personal funds, called a surcharge.

WHO IS ENTITLED TO REVIEW TRUST RECORDS?

The trustee has an affirmative duty to keep the beneficiaries of a trust reasonably informed of the trust and its administration.[136] A trustee is required to provide the beneficiary with a report of information about the assets, liabilities, receipts, and disbursements of the trust, the acts of the trustee, and the particulars relating to the trust that are relevant to the beneficiary's interest.[137] This duty cannot be waived.[138] This duty is in addition to any duty to account as described later in this chapter.

The obligation to disclose information to a beneficiary also includes the beneficiary's legal representative (like an attorney, conservator, or agent under power of attorney) if their legal authority covers that request. A major exception to this rule is matters subject to an attorney-client or attorney–work-product privilege. Thus, any document that includes communications between the SNT trustee and his or her attorney should not be disclosed.

If the beneficiary (or his or her legal representative) wants to review records, the beneficiary must give sufficient notice to the trustee. It would be prudent for the SNT trustee to be present when the beneficiary is reviewing the files to make sure nothing is taken and that all files have been provided. If the beneficiary wants copies of trust records, trust assets can be used to pay for it.[139]

The SNT trustee may also be required to show government agencies (e.g., the Social Security Administration or the Department of Health Care Services—the agencies that run SSI or Medi-Cal) copies of trust records to show that administration of the SNT has been appropriate. If the SNT trustee refuses, the beneficiary could lose eligibility for these programs.

---

136 Probate Code §16060.
137 Probate Code §§16061, 17200(b)(7).
138 Probate Code §16068.
139 See Probate Code §15684.

WHO IS NOT ENTITLED TO REVIEW TRUST RECORDS?

As part of a trustee's duty of confidentiality, he or she has a duty to not disclose to any third parties any information acquired as trustee when the trustee should know that the effect of the disclosure will be detrimental to the beneficiary's interest.

There are exceptions to this duty to not disclose. One is if a trustee is a party to litigation, the civil litigation rules override the basic duty of confidentiality.[140] However, even if there is a pending litigation, documents protected by the attorney-client privilege are protected.

Another exception is if a government regulation to which the trust is subject suspends the duty of confidentiality. For example, if the beneficiary is receiving SSI and the Social Security Administrations wants to review the trust to see if it meets the legal requirements of being a trust, the trustee will be required to give a copy to the agency to make sure it complies with its internal rules. Failure to provide the trust or trust records will jeopardize the beneficiary's eligibility for public benefits.

Another common exception is when a specific statute requires the disclosure. For example, many first-party SNTs are established by court order, including ongoing court jurisdiction over the trust. The trustee will be obligated to provide records to the court during court accountings.

> **Helpful Hint:** It is important that a trustee know when it is appropriate to disclose confidential trust information and when it is not. Whether the trustee is allowed to do this depends on the terms of the trust, which is asking for the information, why they are seeking the information, and whether there is some legal requirement for disclosure. If the trustee is uncertain, he or she should see an attorney experienced in trust administration to make sure that valuable privacy rights are not lost by improper disclosure. See Chapter 20 on where to go for help.

---

140   See *Coberly v Superior Court* (1965) 231 Cal. App. 2d 685.

WHAT ARE THE TRUSTEE'S GENERAL ACCOUNTING REQUIREMENTS?

SNT trustees have a general duty to account to beneficiaries and to maintain and provide them with information about the trustee's administrative decisions and acts.[141] The type of account the trustee must provide depends on whether the SNT is under continuing court jurisdiction or is not being supervised by the court.

- Non–court supervised SNTs generally include all third-party SNTs and some first-party SNTs. The first-party SNTs that are not court supervised generally include those established for beneficiaries who are disabled but still have mental capacity to manage their own affairs.

- Court-supervised SNTs are generally first-party SNTs established through a conservatorship or with the beneficiary's litigation proceeds for those beneficiaries who are disabled and lack the mental capacity to manage their own legal affairs.

However, these are generalities; the trustee should make sure he or she knows if the SNT is under continuing court jurisdiction or not, because it makes a big difference on what type of accounting is required.

> **Critical Pointer:** Not all court-established first-party SNTs are court supervised. A first-party SNT may be court established and not require court-supervised accountings. It is imperative that the trustee reviews the trust document and the court's order establishing the first-party SNT for direction on whether the trust must file accounts and reports for court approval. If the trustee does not feel comfortable making that decision, he or she should review Chapter 20 to find an attorney to see if the SNT requires a court supervised account.

---

141   Probate Code §§16060, 16062, and 16064.

WHAT ARE THE ACCOUNTING REQUIREMENTS FOR A NON–COURT SUPERVISED SNT?

An SNT trustee of an SNT that is not under court supervision typically must account at least once a year to each beneficiary to whom distributions are authorized to be currently distributed.[142] This is typically only to the SNT beneficiary. The terms of an SNT may waive the account requirement for the SNT trustee.[143] The trustee should check the terms of the trust to see what is required. For example, some SNTs may include a trust advisory committee or trust protector are also entitled to an account.

> **Note:** Even if there is a waiver of account, the SNT trustee must still comply with the duty to keep a beneficiary reasonably informed of trust actions. Because an SNT beneficiary is entitled to receive disbursements based on the trustee's discretion, it could be argued that the trustee has an obligation to disclose much of the information that would typically be included in an account regardless of a waiver of account. The better practice would be to do regular accountings and be transparent about trustee services.

As described below, the typical accounting format is very informal. However, any SNT trustee may submit a more formal accounting to the court.[144] In such a case, the accounting must be submitted to the court in a specific format. See discussion on filing court-supervised account for the format and form of a court accounting later in this chapter. The benefit of petitioning a court for approval is to limit the period of time during which a beneficiary may legally challenge the actions of the trustee.

The beneficiary may also compel the trustee to account if the trustee has failed to submit a required or requested report or account within sixty days after written request of the beneficiary, and no report or account has been made within six months preceding the request.[145]

---

142 Probate Code §16062.
143 Probate Code §16064(a).
144 Probate Code §17200(b)(5).
145 Probate Code §17200(b)(7).

WHO SHOULD PREPARE NON–COURT SUPERVISED ACCOUNTINGS?

The trustee has the overall duty to prepare the account.[146] Many SNT trustees will prepare the account personally. This process can be simplified if the SNT trustee uses an accounting software program, such as *Quicken* or *QuickBooks*, which can generate a year-end report that can be included with the account.

If the account will be complicated or the SNT trustee does not wish to prepare it, the trustee is authorized to hire someone to assist in preparation of the account. In locating someone to assist, the SNT trustee should make sure that person has experience in preparing a trust account, because it can be different than doing most other types of financial accounting. Professionals who can assist the SNT trustee with the account generally include an attorney, a paralegal, and a CPA. However, if there are relatively few transactions, hiring a bookkeeper may be less expensive.

Remember that if the trustee hires a professional to assist with the account, the responsibility of the account remains with the SNT trustee.[147]

What Must an Accounting in a Non–Court Supervised Account Include?

In general, there is a cover letter that will state that the SNT trustee is providing this account to a beneficiary. There is certain language in this cover letter that an SNT trustee will wish to include to shorten the statute of limitations on trustee actions. See **Appendix J** for a sample of such a cover letter.

Either in the cover letter, or as part of an attachment, the account should contain the following information. It is recommended that the SNT trustee put each one on a separate schedule, on a separate page:

---

146   Probate Code §16062(a).
147   Probate Code §16012.

1. A statement of receipts of principal and income that have occurred during the last year of the trust, or since the last account;

SNT RECEIPTS		AMOUNT	
Fremont Bank, Checking Account #123456789			
1/10/2010	Marathon Oil Dividend	$1.00	
4/23/2010	Myers Note Payment	$100.00	
5/23/2010	Myers Note Payment	$150.04	
6/23/2010	Myers Note Payment	$150.04	
12/23/2010	Marathon Oil Dividend	$50.00	
	Total Receipts		$400.08

2. A statement of disbursements made of principal and income that have occurred during the last year of the trust, or since the last account;

SNT DISBURSEMENTS			
Fremont Bank, Checking Account #123456789		Amount	
1/9/2010	Rent - Petaluma Estates	$2,500.00	
2/23/2010	Atty Fees: Urbatsch	$600.00	
3/23/2010	Telephone	$100.00	
4/26/2010	Caregiver Exp.	$300.00	
5/26/2010	Best Buy - Television	$1,620.00	
6/30/2010	Bus Pass	$50.00	
7/28/2010	AT&T cell phone	$180.00	
12/26/2010	MOMA (Year Pass)	$550.00	
	Total Disbursements		$5,900.00

3. A beginning statement of the assets on hand of SNT;

BEGINNING SNT ASSETS ON HAND	
Asset Description	Value as of January 1, 2016
Fremont Bank, Checking Account #123456789	$50,000
Myers Note	$10,000
Marathon Oil Stock	$10,000
Total Assets	$70,000

4. An ending statement of the assets on hand as of the end of the period covered by the account;

ENDING SNT ASSETS ON HAND	
Asset Description	Value as of January 1, 2016
Fremont Bank, Checking Account #123456789	$47,000
Myers Note	$8,000
Marathon Oil Stock	$10,000
Total Assets	$65,000

5. The trustee's compensation for the last complete fiscal year of the trust or since the last account;

SNT Trustee Compensation		
Fremont Bank, Checking Account #123456789		Amount
1/9/2010	Trustee Fees	$500.00
2/23/2010	Atty Fees: Urbatsch	$500.00
3/23/2010	Telephone	$500.00
4/26/2010	Caregiver Exp.	$500.00
5/26/2010	Best Buy - Television	$500.00
6/30/2010	Bus Pass	$500.00
7/28/2010	AT&T cell phone	$500.00
12/26/2010	MOMA (Year Pass)	$500.00
	Total Disbursements	$4,000.00

6. The agents hired by the trustee, their relationship to the trustee (a sample of this statement is typically placed in cover letter, See **Appendix J**), if any, and their compensation, for the last complete fiscal year of the trust or since the last account;

SNT Compensation of Agents Hired By Trustee		Amount
1/9/2010	Atty Fees: Urbatsch	$500.00
2/23/2010	Atty Fees: Urbatsch	$600.00
3/23/2010	Cons.: Huyck	$100.00
4/26/2010	EA Fes: Kosnik	$300.00
7/28/2010	Atty Fees: Urbatsch	$550.00
	Total Disbursements	$2,0500.00

7. A statement that the recipient of the account may petition the court under Probate Code §17200 to obtain court review of the account and the trustee's acts (a sample of this statement is typically placed in cover letter; see **Appendix J**);

8. A statement that claims against the trustee for breach of trust may not be made after the expiration of three years from the date the beneficiary receives an account or report disclosing facts giving rise to the claim (a sample of this statement is typically placed in cover letter, See **Appendix J**);[148] and

9. A statement of the names and last-known addresses of all contingent beneficiaries.[149]

WHAT TYPE OF FORMAT MUST THE ACCOUNTING BE IN?

As long as the items in the previous question are present, the accounting does not have to be in any specified format. This makes it easier to attach receipts and disbursement schedules produced by financial management programs, such as *QuickBooks* or *Quicken*.

Attached in **Appendix J** there is a sample accounting cover letter to an SNT beneficiary covers the needed information.

HOW CAN A TRUSTEE SHORTEN THE LENGTH OF TIME HE OR SHE IS LIABLE FOR HIS OR HER ACTIONS AS TRUSTEE?

A concern that many trustees have (or should have) is shortening the amount of time they can be sued for actions made as a trustee. If no accounts are delivered to trustees, then trustees can be responsible for their actions as long as they are alive. This means that a trustee could have been negligent in year 2012, and because the beneficiary did not discover it until 2031, that beneficiary could still sue the trustee. Imagine how difficult it would be for a trustee to file a good defense—especially if that person was no longer serving as trustee and had thrown away or lost trust

---

148   Probate Code §16063(a).

149   Rules of Court 7.902.

records. Remember, if the trustee does not have records, all presumptions are made against the trustee, presuming he or she did something wrong.

A primary reason for doing annual accountings is the triggering of the statute of limitations. In general, if the trustee provides an accurate account that adequately disclose any item in the account or report, a beneficiary can only file a lawsuit on those actions for the next three years.[150] The three-year statute can only be started for an incapacitated adult and minor beneficiaries by service of the account on the legal representative, guardian, or parents.[151]

To start the three-year period running, the account or report must include a prescribed form of notice, in twelve-point boldface type, informing the beneficiaries of their right to object within the specified time, the manner in which to object, and the commencement of the three-year period:[152]

> **You are entitled, under Probate Code §17200, to petition the court to obtain a court review of the account and of the acts of the trustee. Claims against the trustee for breach of trust may not be made after the expiration of three years from the date you received an account or report disclosing facts giving rise to the claim.**

> **Helpful Hint:** Attached as **Appendix J** is a cover letter to beneficiaries that complies with the legal requirements of a non–court supervised accounting that will trigger the three-year statute of limitations.

There is a chance that the terms of the SNT will shorten the three-year statute of limitations even further. If the SNT document contains language relieving the trustee of liability for a breach of trust when a beneficiary fails to object to a trustee's account within a specified period of time (the law says it cannot be shorter than 180 days), then that is allowed.[153] However, even if the trust instrument contains a

---

150 Probate Code §16460(a)(1).
151 Probate Code §16460(b).
152 Probate Code §16461(c)(3).
153 Probate Code §16461.

waiver, a court may require an accounting if there is a showing that it is reasonably likely that a material breach of trust has occurred.[154]

> **Example:** A sample SNT provision limiting liability might state something like, "If a beneficiary has received an interim or final account in writing, or other written report, that adequately discloses the existence of a claim against the trustee, the claim is barred with respect to that beneficiary unless the beneficiary delivers a written objection to the trustee within 180 days after receipt of the account or report by the beneficiary."

A trustee is not protected from an SNT waiver of liability (no matter how broadly stated) if his or her own actions for breach of trust were committed intentionally, with gross negligence, in bad faith, with reckless indifference to the beneficiary's interest, or for any profit the trustee derived from a breach of trust.[155]

WHO SHOULD GET A COPY OF THE NON—COURT SUPERVISED ACCOUNT?

The SNT beneficiary should receive a copy of the accounting. If he or she is a minor or lacks capacity and has a legal representative, such as a conservator, guardian or custodial parent, they should each receive a copy of the accounting.

Generally, these are all the people who are legally required to receive an account. However, if the trustee is concerned that the people named as a remainder or contingent beneficiaries may later complain about trustee actions, he or she may provide a copy to these beneficiaries to trigger the statute of limitations against them, just as described for the primary beneficiary in the previous question.

> **Helpful Hint:** The trustee should have the beneficiary, if competent, sign approvals of the annual accountings as they are delivered. If beneficiary does not have capacity, consider having the legal guardian or conservator sign on behalf of the beneficiary.

---

154 Probate Code §16064(a).
155 Probate Code §16461(b).

The trustee has the option of asking a court to review and approve the accountings if the beneficiary does not approve them.

CAN A BENEFICIARY WAIVE A TRUSTEE'S ACCOUNT REQUIREMENT?

Yes. An SNT beneficiary may waive (in writing) the right to a report or account that is not under court jurisdiction from the trustee.[156] However, the beneficiary can withdraw this written waiver at any time "as to the most recent account and future accounts."[157] A beneficiary's waiver of account would not begin the statute of limitations on actions taken by trustee. Finally, a beneficiary's waiver has no effect on the beneficiary's right to petition for a report or account under Probate Code §17200. See Chapter 5 for a discussion of petitions under Probate Code §17200.

> **Helpful Hint:** Because a beneficiary has the right to withdraw his or her waiver, the statute of limitations does not begin to run, and the cost and expense of an account is not overly burdensome, it would probably be best for an SNT trustee to do an accounting rather than seek a waiver.

WHAT IS A COURT-SUPERVISED ACCOUNT?

A court account is a filing with the probate court that has jurisdiction over the SNT; it includes detailed financial information about the SNT for a specified period. Court accountings are very different from what most people think of as accountings. Instead of tracking assets by their tax cost basis, a court account tracks the "carry value" of assets from the last accounting period. Carry value is the value of an asset at the beginning of the trustee's relationship with that asset.

Court accounts must comply with a strict set of rules set forth in Probate Code. Thus, it is important that the trustee either be very familiar with these rules or hire someone to assist in the preparation of these accounts.

---

156   Probate Code §16064(b).
157   Probate Code §16064(b).

The effect of a court order approving an account is conclusive on all persons, assuming proper notice has been given, actions were properly disclosed by trustee, there was no fraud, and the order so finds.[158] Thus, it is important that the SNT trustee provide a thorough description of trustee matters to

> **Helpful Hint:** Costs related to preparing court accountings can be dramatically reduced by minimizing the volume of individual security transactions in the trust's investment portfolio. This is because each individual transaction must be separately identified in the account.

WHAT TYPE OF SNT MUST FILE A COURT ACCOUNT?

Typically, only an SNT under continuing court jurisdiction is required to file a court account. This type of SNT is generally a first-party SNT that has been established through a court petition for a beneficiary who lacks the capacity to manage his or her own affairs. Mostly, these SNTs are established from a litigation recovery[159] or through the beneficiary's conservatorship from an inheritance or the existing assets of the beneficiary.[160]

A trustee should know if the SNT is under ongoing court jurisdiction. It would be the rare trustee who agreed to serve in an SNT, under ongoing court jurisdiction, who had not been appointed through a court petition. If unsure, the trustee should contact an attorney to see if there is such a requirement.

An SNT trustee may still be required to file a court account in a non court-supervised trust, if ordered to by the court, or may choose to do so to shorten any statute of limitations period.[161]

---

158 Probate Code §1260(c).
159 Probate Code §§3600-3613.
160 Probate Code §2580.
161 Probate Code §17200(b)(5).

WHO SHOULD FILE A COURT-SUPERVISED ACCOUNT?

The SNT trustee is responsible for filing an account. A court account can be complex and very challenging. It is strongly recommended that an attorney experienced in administering SNTs and filing fiduciary accounts with the court represent the trustee. A CPA may be of assistance in preparing the court authorized accounting schedules, but very few CPAs do this type of work. It is very different from preparing other types of accounts, and it is recommended that, just as with attorneys, the trustee find a CPA experienced in preparing just these types of account schedules. Chapter 20 provides information on locating such an attorney.

WHAT ARE THE LEGAL REQUIREMENTS FOR A COURT-SUPERVISED ACCOUNT?

Generally, the trustee must account one year after the trust is established and every two years thereafter, unless the court orders a different timeframe.[162] All accounts filed with the court under the Probate Code must include a financial statement and a report of administration as provided in the law[163] and also the names and addresses of beneficiaries.[164] Further, the account must state the period covered[165] and contain a summary showing all of the following, to the extent applicable):

- Property on hand at the beginning of the period covered by the account (all inventories);
- Assets received during the accounting period, excluding property listed in an inventory;
- Receipts, excluding items listed under items (1) and (2) or receipts from a trade or business;
- Net income from a trade or business;
- Gains on sales;
- Disbursements, excluding disbursements for a trade or business or distributions;
- Loss on sales;
- Net loss from a trade or business;

---

162   Probate Code §2620(a).
163   Probate Code §§1060-1064.
164   Cal Rules of Court 7.902.
165   Cal Rules of Ct 7.901(a).

- Distributions to beneficiaries, the ward, or conservatee; and
- Property on hand at the end of the accounting period, stated at its carry value (fiduciary acquisition value).[166]

The accounts must be in very a specific format, set forth by statute, including a series of schedules that are attached to the account. These schedules (as described below) primarily come from the Judicial Council of California forms.

The Probate Code defines the two types of accounts as either a "standard accountings" or "simplified accountings."[167] The difference between the two is that a standard accounting lists receipts and disbursements by subject-matter category, with each receipt and disbursement category subtotaled, whereas a simplified accounting lists receipts and disbursements chronologically, by receipt or payment date, without subject-matter categorization.

> **Note:** Unless the court account is rather simple, nearly all court accounts are done under the standard format.

A SNT trustee must use a standard accounting if
1. The SNT assets contains income real property;
2. The SNT assets contains a whole or partial interest in a trade or business;
3. The appraised value of the SNT assets is $500,000 or more, exclusive of the beneficiary's personal residence;
4. Either the receipts schedule or the disbursements schedule prepared in simplified accounting format is more than five pages long, in which case the excessively long schedule must be prepared in standard accounting format, although the balance of the accounting can be prepared as a simplified accounting; or
5. The court directs that a standard accounting be filed.[168]

If the SNT contains none of these items, the trustee can prepare a simplified accounting. In many cases, even an experienced preparer might choose the simplified

---

166 Probate Code §1061(a).
167 Probate Code §2620(a); Cal Rules of Court 7.575.
168 Cal Rules of Court 7.575(b).

accounting in an appropriate case, *e.g.,* if there are very few different expense categories and if it is possible to automate the transfer of totals from the schedules to the summary form. To do so, however, the person preparing the accounting must use the mandatory Judicial Council account forms, as described in the next question.

WHAT ARE THE JUDICIAL COUNCIL FORMS?

The Judicial Council of California is the policymaking body of the California courts. Among its several duties is promulgating rules of court administration, practice, and procedure. As part of this responsibility, the Judicial Council has come up with sample forms that are sometimes mandatory and sometimes optional. A complete list of all these forms can be found at https://www.courts.ca.gov/forms.htm.

For court-supervised accounts, the Judicial Council has created thirty-four forms and one worksheet to be used for standard (categorized) accounts and simplified (chronological) accounts. These specific forms can be found at https://www. courts.ca.gov/forms.htm?filter=GC. Once at that page, the trustee will need to scroll down to the forms that begin at Judicial Council Form GC-400 and proceed through Judicial Council Form GC-405.

> **Note:** The forms are titled under Guardianship and Conservatorships but still must be used for SNTs under continuing court jurisdiction.

WHAT JUDICIAL COUNCIL FORMS MUST BE USED IN A COURT-SUPERVISED ACCOUNTING?

Only one form, Summary of Account—Standard and Simplified Accounts (Judicial Council Form GC-400(SUM)/GC-405(SUM)), is mandatory for a simplified or standard accounting. (For a copy of the form, see https://www.courts.ca.gov/documents/gc400sum.pdf.)

If the trustee wishes to use the simplified accounts (chronological) method, he or she must use some of the Judicial Council forms. The following Judicial Council forms are mandatory for simplified accounts and may be used in standard accounts at the SNT trustee's option:

- GC-400(PH)(1)/GC-405(PH)(1): Cash Assets on Hand at Beginning of Account Period
- GC-400(PH)(2)/GC-405(PH)(2): Noncash Assets on Hand at Beginning of Account Period*
- GC-400(AP)/GC-405(AP): Additional Property Received During Period of Account*
- GC-400(B)/GC-405(B): Gains on Sales*
- GC-400(OCH)/GC-405(OCH): Other Charges*
- GC-400(D)/GC405(D): Losses on Sales*
- GC-400(DIST)/GC-405(DIST): Distributions to Conservatee*
- GC-400(OCR)/GC405(OCR): Other Credits*
- GC-400(E)(1)/GC-405(E)(1): Cash Assets on Hand at End of Account Period
- GC-400(E)(2)/GC-405(E)(2): Noncash Assets on Hand at End of Account Period*
- GC-400(F)/GC-405(F): Changes in Form of Assets*
- GC-400(G)/GC-405(G): Liabilities at End of Account Period*
- GC-405(A) Receipts—Simplified Account; and
- GC-405(C) Disbursements—Simplified Account

Of the forms listed above, those marked with asterisks may be omitted if the accounting has no information for those forms.

In addition to those forms above, the following optional forms may be used only in standard accounts and cannot be used in a simple account:

- GC-400(A)(1) through (A)(6): Receipts
  - (A)(1): Dividends
  - (A)(2): Interest
  - (A)(3): Pensions, annuities, and other regular periodic payments
  - (A)(4): Rent
  - (A)(5): Social Security, veteran benefits, other public benefits
  - (A)(6): Other receipts
- GC-400(C)(1) through (C)(11): Disbursements
  - (C)(1): Conservatee's caregiver expenses
  - (C)(2): Conservatee's residential or long-term care facility expenses
  - [(C)(3) is for guardians only: minor's education expenses]

- – (C)(4): Fiduciary and attorney fees
- – (C)(5): General administration expenses
- – (C)(6): Investment expenses
- – (C)(7): Living expenses
- – (C)(8): Medical expenses
- – (C)(9): Property sales expenses
- – (C)(10): Rental property expenses
- – (C)(11): Other expenses
- GC-400(NI): Net income from trade or business
- GC-400(NL): Net loss from trade or business
- GC-400(A)(C): Receipts and disbursements worksheet (do not file)

Experienced trustees may have already developed their own forms prior to the Judicial Council releasing these accounting forms. These trustees are allowed to continue to use their forms as long as their forms provide the same information as required by the Judicial Council forms and as long as they [169]

- provide state receipts and disbursements in the subject-matter categories specified in the optional Judicial Council forms for receipts and disbursements schedules;

- provide the same information about any asset, property, transaction, receipt, disbursement, or other matter that is required by the applicable Judicial Council accounting form; and

- provide the information in the same general layout as the applicable Judicial Council accounting form, except that instructional material contained in the form and material contained or requested in the form's header and footer need not be provided.

Obviously, if a trustee were doing his or her first account, it would be best to use the judicial council forms, as they are already established.

---

169   Cal Rules of Court 7.575(e)(2).

WHAT OTHER INFORMATION MUST BE PROVIDED IN A COURT ACCOUNT?

In addition to the Judicial Council forms that are included as attachments to the court petition, the court petition itself must include certain information during the court accounting. These include

1. **Description of Financial Transactions**. The trustee should inform the court of the financial activities of the SNT that are not readily understood from the schedules described above.[170] This includes any problems encountered with investments or any changes made in the overall investment plan of the trust.

2. **Explanation of Unusual Items**. The trustee should explain any usual items in the account.[171] It is common that after a year (or two years) some transactions may look unusual in retrospect. These can include payments of cash, disbursements to third parties for reimbursements of different transactions, or payments to professionals for services that may appear unusual without an explanation.

3. **Disclosure of Family Relationships**. The trustee is required to disclose any family or affiliate relationships of any trust transactions. Family is defined very broadly to include a relationship created by blood or marriage. Affiliate is defined as an entity that directly or indirectly through one or more intermediary's controls, is controlled by, or is under common control with the trustee.[172] For example, if the trustee hired his brother to make modifications to real estate owned by the trust. The trustee must disclose this relationship to the court. While not improper, the court will review these transactions more closely to make sure that these transactions are reasonable and are not disguised gifts to family members.

4. **Allegations of Cash Investments**. This is a simple statement that all cash has either been invested or maintained in interest-bearing accounts, except for an amount of cash that is reasonably necessary for the orderly administration of the SNT.[173]

---

170   Probate Code §1064(a)(1).
171   Probate Code §1064(a).
172   Probate Code §1064(c).
173   Probate Code §1064(a)(5).

5. **Requests for Compensation**. The petition should disclose any compensation paid from SNT assets during the accounting period to the trustee, the advisory committee members (if there is one), or the trustee's attorney allowed under a prior court order for periodic payments on account, and the citation to the authority that authorized the payment (e.g., a prior court order).[174] This is a requirement because oftentimes an SNT under continuing court jurisdiction does not allow the trustee, his attorney, or any member of the trust advisory committee to receive compensation without a court order. To obtain compensation, it is best that the trustee and his attorney complete a declaration that shows all the hours that were spent on the trust administration during the accounting period.

Note: A sample petition for first account and report is attached as **Appendix Q.**

In addition to the petition, with each court account, the trustee must also provide some of the original financial statements of accounts held as part of the trust estate. The statement must show the account balance as of the close of the accounting period and, in the case of an account that closes during the accounting period, the closing statement of each such account as well as the opening statement of any new accounts. With the first account filed by the trustee, he or she must also provide the original statements showing the balance immediately preceding the date of appointment.

A private professional trustee must file all original account statements for all periods of the accounting.[175] This requires the filing of all original statements received during the accounting period and not just at the end or beginning of the accounting. While the statute speaks of conservators, it would be prudent for a private professional trustee to comply with this rule also. If a statement contains confidential information, it must be filed with a separate affidavit describing the character of the statement, captioned "CONFIDENTIAL FINANCIAL STATEMENT" in uppercase letters.

---

174   Cal Rules of Court 7.755, 7.903(8).
175   Probate Code §2620(c)(3).

The accounting petition will also generally require that a proposed court order be filed with the paperwork. Different counties will have different rules about this, so the trustee should check the local rules to see what a proposed order should include. For example, some will require that the order include all factual statements made in the petition, while some will only want all rulings issued by the court.

HOW DOES SNT TRUSTEE FILE COURT ACCOUNT?

The person filing the paperwork should bring copies of all documents. All documents typically include

- Petition for Account and Report (with all attached schedules)
- Notice of Hearing
- Declarations of Attorney (or sometimes trustee) in support of fees
- Proposed Order Approving Account

> **Note:** The Judicial Council has a form that can be used to provide notice to all parties called: Notice of Hearing—Probate (Judicial Council Form DE-120) a copy of which can be found at https://www.courts.ca.gov/documents/de120.pdf.

Typically (some counties may differ), the court will provide a hearing date. The original will be filed with the court, but the filing clerk will file stamp the papers to show the date they were filed with the court. Some counties will allow the person filing the paperwork to select the hearing date. It is important to keep these documents as part of the SNT trustee's file.

There is a filing fee that can be paid for from the trust. Currently, the filing fee for trust accountings for SNTs established through court petitions is $200.[176] Most counties are not aware of this exception for these types of SNTs and will attempt to charge the full filing fee of $435.

Once the case is filed, the SNT trustee will be given a Notice of Hearing. This Notice must be served on all parties as described in the next question.

---

176 Government Code §70652(d).

HOW MUST NOTICE BE GIVEN BY THE TRUSTEE OF THE COURT-SUPERVISED ACCOUNT?

At least thirty days before the date of the hearing, the trustee must provide notice of the time and place of the hearing to all those who are entitled to notice.[177]

Notice is required to be provided to all nonpetitioning trustees, all nonpetitioning beneficiaries who are entitled to notice, and any person who requested special notice.[178] The trustee should consider providing notice to the State Director of Health Care Services, the Director of Mental Health, and the Director of Developmental Services. This may already be required by law if the SNT was established with litigation proceeds.

Typically, the only document that is served is a copy of the Notice of Hearing and not a copy of the Petition or other filed documents.

WHAT HAPPENS AT THE COURT HEARING?

In most counties, a probate examiner will review the paperwork a few days before the hearing to see if all of the technical requirements have been followed in submitting the accounting. The examiner will review the paperwork to see if all schedules are there, notice was sent, and all information is included. Some counties will let their examiners also ask questions about the substance of the account. The examiner will then inform the trustee (or his or her attorney) of any technical defects in the accounting submission and if there are any questions about the petition.

The attorney or trustee at this time has the opportunity to respond to the examiners' notes. This may require a continuance of the hearing date. Once the notes are cleared, the hearing may be pregranted, or the attorney or trustee may have to address an issue with the probate judge and a hearing will take place. At the hearing, the judge will ask the trustee or the trustee's attorney questions on any issues that have arisen because of the account. The judge will then issue a ruling on the petition and the account.

---

177 Probate Code §17203(a).
178 Probate Code §17203(a).

Helpful Hint: It may be surprising to learn that many judges and court examiners have little understanding of SNTs and will ask questions or issue rulings that bear no relation to the law. Some judges believe that the SNT is to be very narrowly construed and can only pay for certain things, like medical equipment. One judge refused to allow a trustee to buy a fax machine for the beneficiary to make disbursement requests from the trust and made the trustee pay back the cost of the fax machine to the trust. Thus, it is a good idea to find out by talking to local attorneys how a judge is likely to rule on a certain case.

It is important that the trustee and his or her attorney do not let these misperceptions interfere with the purpose of these trusts and educate these judges about how the trust should work. Many judges will second-guess the trustee on disbursements made or not, investments made, and other actions by the trustee. Judges legally do not have the right to second-guess the trustee of an SNT unless the trustee acts in bad faith or in disregard of the purposes of the trust.[179] This being said, it is still important to remember that court hearings are expensive and fights with the court are counterproductive for the beneficiary, so it may be best to limit the fights the trustee will make with the court to only those that are important.

WHAT IS THE EFFECT OF SOMEONE OBJECTING TO TRUSTEE'S ACCOUNT?

Once an account has been furnished, a beneficiary may object to the account for a number of reasons, including:

- Incomplete, inaccurate, false or fraudulent trust accounting information;
- Mismanagement of trust assets;
- Waste of trust assets;
- Theft of trust assets;
- Failure to fully account for trust assets; and/or
- Failure to make trust assets productive.

---

179 *Estate of Genung* (1958) 161 Cal. App. 2d 507; Probate Code §16081(a).

In many cases, accounting disputes can be resolved informally by providing additional information and explanation. It is oftentimes a lack of communication or appropriate records that can be exchanged that solves the issue. However, if the beneficiary feels the errors are serious, the beneficiary will file a written objection or petition for breach of fiduciary duty to initiate a formal process to have their concerns remedied. Once the objection to the accounting has been filed, the burden of proof is on the trustee to prove each and every item described is true and accurate, and not in violation of their duties as trustee.[180] Once the trustee substantiates the account and report by substantial evidence, the burden of proof shifts to a challenger to show that the item in question is wrong.[181] This will increase the legal fees incurred by the trust.

This does not mean that the beneficiary has a blank check to object to every item in a trust accounting. Just the opposite, if the beneficiary objects to the accounting without reasonable cause and in bad faith, the court may award costs and expenses of litigation to the trustee and take it out of the beneficiary's share of the trust.[182] However, this rule also goes the opposite direction if the trustee's opposition to the objection is without reasonable cause and in bad faith, the court may award costs and expenses of litigation to the beneficiary from trustee's personal assets.[183]

WHAT IS THE EFFECT OF THE COURT SIGNING AN ORDER ON A COURT-SUPERVISED ACCOUNT?

Once a judge has signed the order approving and settling the accounting, the order is conclusive against everyone who has been given notice. This means that those persons can no longer sue the trustee for any acts disclosed in the accounting.[184]

If the trustee does nothing with the order, the order is final after 180 days after the date of entry of the order. However, if the trustee feels that it is important to cut

---

180 *Purdy v. Johnson* (1917) 174 Cal. 521.
181 See *Neel v Barnard* (1944) 24 Cal. 2d 406, 420.
182 Probate Code § 17211.
183 Probate Code § 17211(b).
184 Probate Code §1260(c).

off the right to appeal sooner, he or she can provide notice of entry of judgment, which cuts off the time to appeal at sixty days.[185]

HOW CAN THE TRUSTEE RECEIVE SSA AND DHCS NOTIFICATIONS AND OTHERWISE KEEP INFORMED OF BENEFICIARY'S SSI AND MEDI-CAL ELIGIBILITY?

In order to receive notifications and keep informed, the trustee must make sure that the appropriate Social Security Administration (SSA) agency and Department of Health Care Services (DHCS) agency has the trustee's address and the beneficiary's address. Further, the SNT should request that he or she receive copies of all communications affecting the beneficiary's benefits.

The trustee should also instruct the beneficiary to be sure to let the beneficiary know promptly of receipt of any SSA notices.

The SNT trustee might find it helpful to be named an authorized representative for SSI and Medi-Cal purposes. If the trustee chooses to do this, he or she is then taking on the legal responsibility of maintaining the beneficiary's eligibility for public benefits. This is a duty the SNT trustee typically does not have unless there is specific wording in the SNT document requiring the trustee to keep the beneficiary eligible.

- To become an authorized representative for an SSI recipient, the trustee must sign and submit to SSA a written statement appointing him or her to represent the SNT beneficiary in their dealings with SSA. The trustee will need to complete Form SSA-1696 (Appointment of Representative) for this purpose. The form can be found here: http://www.ssa.gov/online/ssa-1696.pdf.

- To become an authorized representative for Medi-Cal, the trustee should complete and sign a MC 306 Appointment of Representative, which can be found at http://www.dhcs.ca.gov/formsandpubs/forms/Pages/MCEDFormsMC300.aspx.

---

185 Probate Code §1300(b); Cal Rules of Court 8.104(a).

Note: Keep in mind that an authorized representative for an SSI recipient is not the same thing as an SSI Representative Payee. An authorized representative is allowed to communicate with SSI and represent the beneficiary before the Social Security Administration. A Representative Payee is appointed by the SSA to receive monthly checks that are then spent on the recipient's behalf.

DOES THE SNT TRUSTEE HAVE TO REGULARLY REPORT TO THE SOCIAL SECURITY ADMINISTRATION (SSA)?

Generally, no. If the SNT document does not require the trustee to maintain the beneficiary's eligibility for benefits, there is no legal requirement that the trustee provide ongoing reports to the SSA. It is up to the SNT beneficiary or his or her Representative Payee to make the reports to the SSA.

However, in some SNT trust documents, the trustee may be required to make all necessary reports to appropriate public benefit agencies or may be required to maintain the beneficiary's eligibility for all public benefits. If the trust document includes such a term, then the trustee is responsible for making a report to the SSA. To see what is required in an SSA report, see next question and answer.

However, even if the SNT document does not require the SNT trustee to maintain benefits, the SSA has the right to audit SNT records. In that case, the SNT trustee would need to comply with SSA's reasonable requests.

> **Note:** Regardless of whether the SNT trustee is required to maintain benefits, the SNT trustee may want to send the reports anyway if he or she does not believe the beneficiary is providing them. The SNT trustee will eventually have to deal with the potential loss of future public benefits so it may just be easier to send the reports now so there is not a later SSA overpayment request and loss of benefits.

WHAT TYPES OF THINGS MUST BE REPORTED TO SSA?

The SSI program requires periodic reports from all SSI recipients.[186] If the SSI recipient has a Representative Payee, the payee is obligated to make the report. These reports must be completed for eligibility to continue. Reports are required if the following changes occur in the life of the SSI recipient:

- Moves or changes of address (COA)
- Persons moving in or out of the household
- Death of a household member
- Changes in income and resources for recipients and individuals involved in deeming cases. These individuals are:
  - Ineligible spouses and ineligible children living with recipients,
  - Parents living with eligible children,
  - Essential persons,
  - Sponsors of aliens and living-with spouses of sponsors, and
  - Eligible aliens with the same sponsor.
- Changes in help with living expenses
- Entering or leaving an institution
- Marriage, separation, or divorce
- Leaving the United States for more than thirty days in a row
- Changes in school attendance (if under age twenty-two)
- Death of the recipient or individuals involved in deeming cases
- Fugitive felons status (fleeing prosecution, unsatisfied warrants, probation and parole violation)

The report is due within ten days after the end of the month in which the event took place. Thus, if the SSI recipient moved in July, the report would be due by August 10.

The report may be brief, but it should be in writing to the SSA and it should include the beneficiary's name and Social Security number, a description of the event that triggered the report, and the date of the event.

The SNT trustee should keep a copy of all reports sent to the SSA.

---

186   POMS SI 02301.005.

Critical Pointer: All communications to the SSA should be done by certified mail. The SSA is notorious for losing correspondence and claiming they never received notice.

The effect of failing to make a required report on time, the SSI program is entitled to reimbursement for all SSI benefits incorrectly paid to the beneficiary and SSI can assess a penalty of up to $100, depending on the lateness of the report.[187] In **Appendix D**, a description of the reporting requirements for both SSA and DHCS is fully described.

WHAT IF THE BENEFICIARY WORKS, WHAT NEEDS TO BE REPORTED TO SSA?

If the beneficiary is on SSI and not SSDI, they have to report any earnings monthly to SSA, by the 10th of the month following the month in which they worked, or did not work if they had been working and then quit. SSA then recalculates their SSI check automatically and adjusts it up or down for the check issued the month following the recalculation. The process is called "Retrospective Monthly Accounting," and is probably best shown by **example:**

> **Example:** Beneficiary has been receiving $783 SSI check until January. In February, client earns $200. On or before March 10th, the client reports to SSA that they earned $200 in February. SSA does the calculations and reduces the SSI payment down for the month of April. Thus, the beneficiary's SSA check is based on earnings two months' back.

Reporting to SSA triggers all the calculations automatically, either up or down, and no attorney is required. However, whoever is doing the reporting should always make sure the report is in writing and to keep a copy.

---

187   POMS SI 02301.100.

HOW DOES A TRUSTEE FIND THE BENEFICIARY'S LOCAL SSA OFFICE?

If the SNT trustee is not sure which office the report should be sent to, the trustee should go to http://www.socialsecurity.gov/locator/ and use the beneficiary's zip code to find the local office.

WHAT NEEDS TO BE REPORTED TO DHCS IF THE BENEFICIARY RECEIVES ONLY MEDI-CAL?

When a person accepts a Medi-Cal card, that person (or his or her representative) must report all changes in either income or resources that could affect his or her eligibility. These changes should be reported to the Medi-Cal regional office that serves his or her home county. Calling, writing, or visiting the Medi-Cal regional office may make these changes. All changes *must* be reported within ten days after the change happens (or within ten days after the beneficiary realizes the change has taken place.)[188] Failure to report a change may result in the beneficiary receiving the wrong Medicaid benefits.

Changes to report include the following:

- **Living Arrangements or Change of Address.** Any change in where a beneficiary or his or her spouse lives and/or gets mail must be reported. (This includes if the beneficiary moves in or out of someone's household, enters a hospital or nursing home, leaves a hospital or nursing home, or moves from one medical facility to another.)

- **Income Changes.** Any increase or decrease in the amount of money or change in the source of money that a beneficiary or his or her spouse receives must be reported. (Income includes all earned or unearned income, gifts, or any type of money that belongs to the beneficiary.) If a beneficiary applies and is approved for benefits for which he or she is entitled, he or she must report this change within ten days.

---

188   Cal.C.C. §50185(a)(4).

- **Resource Changes.** Any change in what a person owns must be reported. This means that the beneficiary buys, sells, gives away, or receives any asset (thing of value) or any part of an asset, he or she must report the change to the Medi-Cal regional office. (Resources or assets include any property the recipient owns or has interest in; money in banks, credit unions, etc.; stocks; bonds; life insurance policies and any other items of value.)

- **Family Size.** Any change in the family size must be reported. (This includes the death of a beneficiary, the death of a spouse, the moving of a beneficiary's child under the age of eighteen out of the beneficiary's household.)

- **Change in Health Care Coverage.** Any change in a beneficiary's health-care coverage.

In **Appendix D**, a description of the reporting requirements for both SSA and DHCS is more fully described.

IF SSA NOTICE IS RECEIVED DENYING OR REDUCING BENEFICIARY'S SSI, WHAT SHOULD TRUSTEE/BENEFICIARY DO?

Unless the SNT document requires it or if the trustee is also the SSA Representative Payee for the beneficiary, the trustee does not have the legal responsibility to do anything. However, it is generally better practice for a trustee to assist the beneficiary if the beneficiary is unable or unwilling to appeal to preserve SSI eligibility. In order to make sure that the SNT trustee obtains all relevant SSA communications, see question and answer above on how to become an SSA authorized representative.

If the SSA sends notice that it intends to reduce or eliminate the beneficiary's SSI, an appeal should be filed immediately. SSI recipients generally have sixty days from the time they receive notice from the SSA to file appeals.[189] The letter from SSA will typically set forth the sixty-day right. The SSA presumes that an individual

---

189   See, 20 C.F.R. §§416.1409, 416.1433.

receives the notice five days after the date of the letter unless the individual can show that he or she received it later.[190]

> **Critical Pointer:** It is the better practice to appeal within ten days of receipt of the notice. If the appeal is filed within ten days, any SSI payments currently being made will continue until a decision is made, often called "aid paid pending."[191] If made after the ten days, SSI payments will be discontinued pending the appeal. If the recipient loses the appeal, benefits received may have to be paid back. Typically, the SSA will not inform the SSI recipient of this right.

Unless it is an obvious mistake that can easily be corrected, the SNT trustee should contact an attorney to assist with the appeal. To locate an SSA appeals attorney, see Chapter 20.

CHAPTER 8 SUMMARY

- ✓ The trustee is legally obligated to keep records of the trust administration that are clear and concise.
- ✓ If a trustee fails to keep good records, he or she may be liable for damages, costs, fines or sanctions, removal as trustee and (if serious) possibly held in contempt of court.
- ✓ The trustee should keep records for practical reasons, because to do so will allow an easier and cheaper administration when preparing tax documents and preparing accountings.
- ✓ Excellent trust records will also protect a trustee if someone sues him or her, because a failure to have records will be held against the trustee.
- ✓ Trust records are private documents and only certain people, or entities are entitled to review them.

---

190   20 C.F.R. §1401.
191   20 CFR §416.1336(b).

✓ Trustee is legally obligated to account and provide information about trust administration.

✓ A trustee's legal obligation to account will depend on whether the SNT is under continuing court jurisdiction.

✓ If SNT is *not* under ongoing court jurisdiction, the trustee is generally required to account at least once a year, unless waived by trust document.

✓ A trustee account is the responsibility of trustee, but he or she may delegate it to a professional if needed.

✓ The trustee's account for non-court supervised trusts should include all transactions made, amounts held in trust, agents hired by the trustee, investment, compensation received, and any issues that have arisen in the past year.

✓ The trustee's account for non-court supervised trusts does not need to be made in any specific format; however, certain disclosures do need to be made in account concerning right to object.

✓ The trustee's account for non-court supervised trusts can trigger statute of limitations for all person receiving copy of account, which, depending on terms of trust, can vary from three years to 180 days.

✓ Trustees of first-party SNTs under continuing court jurisdiction have a much more comprehensive accounting requirement.

✓ Trustees of court-supervised SNT must account to the court one year after establishment of the trust and every two years thereafter.

✓ The trustee has to follow a very specific format for the account schedules, which can be found under the Judicial Council Forms.

✓ The trustee can use either a standard accounting or simplified accounting, depending on a variety of factors, although most trustees use the standard accounting.

✓ In addition to accounting schedules of financial transactions, the trustee must account to the court on a variety of transactions, including unusual disbursements, hiring of family or affiliates, financial transactions, investment of cash, and compensation of trustee and attorney.

✓ A court hearing will be held where a judge will review account schedules and report of trustee and issue ruling.

✓   A beneficiary may object to an accounting and it is up to trustee to provide proof that everything was done correctly.

✓   If a beneficiary or trustee objects or defends an account without reasonable cause, they can be held responsible for the other party's fees and costs.

✓   Once court issues ruling on court accounting, it is conclusive on all parties at least 180 days after the issuance, or 60 days after a notice of entry of judgment has been served.

CHAPTER 9

Establishing Beneficiary's Spending Plan and Managing SNT Investments

This chapter will cover the trustee's duty to invest and manage trust assets. It begins with the general rules concerning the trustee's duty to invest trust assets, then discusses investment standards based on the type of SNT the trustee is managing, provides a summary of the types of proper asset classes for an SNT, discusses the use of professional money advisers to assist the trustee, and answers common questions that arise when hiring a professional money advisor, and ends with a discussion on how to monitor ongoing investments.

Investing trust assets is a challenge for those with little investment or financial background. In its simplest sense, investment involves allocation of SNT assets among existing asset classes of the trust (which may be nontraditional), bonds, equities and cash equivalents. The nature of the allocation depends on risk tolerance, economic and market conditions, time horizon (short term or long term), income needs, liquidity requirements, and tax and legal issues (investments only in certain types of investments). Aside from assets that may already be a part of the SNT (e.g., a family business, home, or existing real estate), the three general types of investments are as follows:

- **Cash:** Cash provides for immediate or short-term needs and is available for scheduled distributions or any unplanned emergency that may arise. Penalty-free certificates of deposit, money market accounts, treasury bills, and savings accounts are examples of investments that are considered to be "cash" or "cash equivalents."

- **Fixed Income:** Investments in this category feature predetermined returns that may or may not be taxable depending on the entity issuing the bonds. Investment vehicles in this category may include (but are not limited to) bonds, notes, certificates of deposit, and annuity benefits. These types of investments are most often utilized to provide for predictable future needs or to protect against market volatility.

- **Equities:** This category may include stocks, mutual funds, real estate, or other investments purchased with the intension of a later sale at higher price. Equities are most appropriate to be purchased as a long-term investment and can be held for five to ten years or more.

A trustee should always remember that he or she will be held to a higher standard of care and fidelity than if the trustee were investing his or her own funds. Thus, the trustee cannot be overly aggressive in investing the trust's assets. Not surprisingly, courts often over-reward conservative investment styles. When in doubt, less risk, even at some sacrifice to return, would be less likely to be challenged by a beneficiary or their representative. As a result of this fear of court challenge, most people believe that trust investments should be made conservatively; however, do not make this mistake: investing only in safe and conservative (but low yielding) investments is also a challengeable act. The problem with investing too conservatively for a trust that is supposed to last a long time is that the investment income will not cover the annual cost-of-living increases over that period, and the trustee will not have enough money to provide for the future special needs of the beneficiary.

The discussion in this chapter on trustee investment and management only scratches the surface of the variety of situations that may arise during a trustee's administration. It is nearly always prudent to hire a professional to assist in the trustee's investment of trust assets.

WHY SHOULD A TRUSTEE SET UP A BUDGET OR SPENDING PLAN?

A trustee has many important duties that he or she must keep in mind while serving as trustee. These include following the terms of the trust, acting in the best interests of the beneficiary, properly investing trust assets, keeping great records, paying taxes, and providing accounts when requested. Setting up a spending plan makes all of this easier.

> **Note:** This book uses the term "spending plan" rather than the more commonly understood term "budget" when describing this process. This is more a matter of perception rather than any real difference in the process. In the authors' experience, when discussing a "budget" with an SNT beneficiary, he or she would immediately become defensive because the term budget was oftentimes associated with cutting back on spending. If the term spending plan is replaced with "spending plan" the beneficiary and his or her family were much more responsive and willing to work with the SNT trustee in developing a plan.

HOW DOES A TRUSTEE SET A SPENDING PLAN FOR AN SNT BENEFICIARY?

The easiest way to set a spending plan is to do it in four steps:
1. list monthly income;
2. identify and list all expenses;
3. compare income and expenses; and
4. be ready to make appropriate changes.

Setting up a spending plan should be done by having discussions with the beneficiary (and his or her advocates, friends, and family) on how the SNT assets should be used to enhance the beneficiary's quality of life.

> **Helpful Hint:** Use the list at Appendix O and go over it with the beneficiary (and with those who know the beneficiary well) to see what kinds of items and services he or she expects the trust to pay for on a monthly basis and those items he or she may desire. Some

trustees have reported that with certain beneficiaries, this may not be prudent. These beneficiaries look at the list as a shopping list and seek all kinds of items they will not use or need. Further, if the assets in the SNT are limited, it may be better to limit the beneficiary's options and simply ask the beneficiary about their needs and wants.

These discussions will aid the trustee in understanding what the expectations are for use of the funds. It will also allow the trustee to set appropriate expectations. If there are unrealistic expectations, they should be corrected immediately. The trust document should also be read (and any memorandum of intent reviewed) to see how the person setting up the trust intended for trust assets to be used to enhance the quality of life of the beneficiary. Regardless of the amount held in trust, the trustee will protect him or herself by setting up a spending plan, sticking to it, and, if circumstances change, having the flexibility to modify it.

> **Example:** SNT trustee meets with beneficiary and his girlfriend to discuss a spending plan. The beneficiary wants to use the funds to buy an automobile for him and one for his girlfriend, pay for rent on a two-bedroom apartment where he and his girlfriend will live, buy furniture, a home gym, and a computer, supply a monthly allowance of $1,000, and in a couple of years pay for school.

The trustee can immediately set the proper expectations. The trustee can explain that because this is a first-party SNT, the trustee is not allowed to use any funds for the girlfriend, because distributions are only allowed for beneficiary's sole benefit, that payment of rent will reduce the amount of SSI the beneficiary will receive (which may or may not be in his best interest), and that a cash allowance directly to the beneficiary is not allowed, as it will eliminate SSI and increase share of cost for Medi-Cal. They should then discuss whether it is realistic to buy all these items immediately, given that the beneficiary wants to pay for school. The spending plan meeting allows the trustee to set the whole tone of the administration and get the beneficiary's buy-in. The spending plan also helps illustrate the effect of purchases, particularly large ones, on the life of the trust. Creating a spending plan is best done at the start of administration.

The spending plan itself requires the trustee to delve into the entire financial background of the beneficiary. Depending on the cooperation of the beneficiary, this can be quite simple or very frustrating.

If the beneficiary is not cooperative and may not have friends or family who will support the person with a disability, the trustee may be able to obtain information from the beneficiary's school records, such as an Independent Education Plan (IEP), or from the Regional Center's Individual Program Plan (IPP). It may be difficult for the trustee to obtain these reports, but if there is a caseworker or care manager for the beneficiary, it may be easier to obtain.

If the SNT assets came from a litigation recovery, the beneficiary's personal injury attorney may have obtained a "Life Care Plan" as part of the litigation. These plans are an excellent way to obtain information about the care and services the beneficiary will require throughout his or her life.

The trustee can only do as much as he or she can with the information at hand. It would still be a good idea to set a spending plan even if the beneficiary does not cooperate. It will provide direction when deciding on making distributions and preserving assets for expected future disbursements.

To aid the trustee, a worksheet is set forth in Appendix F of this book. The worksheet provides a list of commonly addressed income and expense items that should be reviewed. It is recommended that this spending plan be reviewed periodically (perhaps once a year while doing the accounting) to make any changes and updates to it.

> **Helpful Hint:** For further assistance, several companies have online financial calculators that will give an estimate of the estimated costs of taking care of a person with a disability. Merrill Lynch provides such a calculator at http://specialneedscalc.ml.com.

WHAT IS THE TRUSTEE'S GENERAL DUTY WHEN INVESTING AND MANAGING TRUST ASSETS?

In general, a trustee has a duty to invest trust property, preserve trust assets, and make the assets productive.[192] This means that a trustee has a legal obligation to gather the trust assets that are (or should be) owned by the trust, review the asset composition in order to develop an investment plan, provide protection for the trust assets, and make the assets productive, typically by investing cash or renting out real property.

> **Warning:** Some trustees believe that if the trustee such as a family member does not take a fee, the trustee will not be held responsible for his or her negligent acts. This is wrong. A trustee's duty of care remains whether or not he or she receives a fee.[193] This means that if the trustee breaches one of the following duties, he or she will be held *personally* responsible even if the trustee never got paid.

A number of trustee responsibilities arise when investing and managing assets:

1. Duty to Review Assets and Make Productive.

When a trustee takes control of an SNT, he or she must, within a reasonable time, review the trust assets and make decisions concerning the assets so that the assets are protected and productive.[194] The trustee must review whether each asset should be retained or disposed of to comply with the purposes, terms, distribution requirements, and circumstances of the trust.[195]

This means that a trustee is not allowed to hold cash or assets without investing them or making them productive in some way. Thus, keeping all of the assets in a non–interest bearing checking account or owning a home that is vacant and habitable without trying to rent it out would be violating the trustee's duty.

192　Probate Code §§16006-16007.

193　Probate Code §16041.

194　Probate Code §16007.

195　Probate Code §16049.

The trust may contain language that alters this duty—for example, if the trust language permits investment in specific unproductive assets appropriate for a situation (like a vacation home), then the trustee would be allowed to do so without necessarily maximizing the yield from that asset.

2. Duty to Consider Beneficiaries' Needs.

The trustee must consider the interests and needs of all of the beneficiaries in making investment decisions within the terms of the trust instrument.[196] "Impartially" does not necessarily mean "equally." People who set up trusts frequently express intent to favor one beneficiary (e.g., the person with a disability) over another (e.g., the remainder beneficiaries, or those who would inherit if the person with a disability died). In such cases, the terms of the trust control and one beneficiary can have priority over another.[197]

In nearly every SNT administration, the only beneficiary's interest that must be considered is the person with a disability, who is the primary beneficiary. The trustee should understand what assets would be needed to care for the person with a disability and invest accordingly. A few trusts may require that investment decisions also consider remainder beneficiaries. If that is the case, investment decisions must take into account the interests of these remainder beneficiaries, which may alter some of the investment strategies of the trustee. If the trustee is not sure of which type of beneficiary should have priority over another type of beneficiary, the trustee should contact an attorney. See Chapter 20 for a discussion on how to find assistance from a special needs planning attorney.

3. Duty to Diversify.

A trustee has a general duty to diversify the investments of the trust unless, under the particular circumstances surrounding the administrations, it would not be prudent to do so.[198] For example, the trustee is probably not under a duty to diversify if the trust is extremely small, if it will only be around a short time, or if general economic conditions are so unstable that the trustee would be wise to invest all the

---

196 Probate Code §16003.
197 Probate Code §16000.
198 Probate Code §16048.

trust funds in a single safe-asset class (*e.g.*, fixed-income government securities from solvent government entities).

The idea of diversification is to spread risk among various types of investments and to provide a rate of return without incurring undue risk. For example, if the trust assets are heavily weighted or exclusively invested in fixed investments (such as bonds), it may be prudent to balance the portfolio through the purchase of securities to provide a greater chance of a higher rate of return.

Upon becoming an SNT trustee, the trustee need not *immediately* diversity the trust assets if other factors would prove harmful to the trust. For example, large capital gain positions, if sold, might cause large tax liabilities. A plan to diversify assets over multiple tax years—if property documented and approved by the court—should satisfy the trustee's duty to diversify.

> **Note:** It is important for the trustee to review the trust document. The duty to diversify can be expanded, restricted, eliminated, or altered by a statement in the trust.[199] Thus, if the trust document allows it, a trustee can invest in an undiversified portfolio.

4. Duty to Keep Beneficiaries Informed.

As described in Chapter 8, the trustee must keep the beneficiaries "reasonably informed of the trust and its administration."[200] This generally includes providing a report on investments made and how well the investments performed. When there is a duty to disclose, the disclosure must be full and complete, and any material concealment or misrepresentation will amount to fraud sufficient to entitle the injured party to bring an action against the trustee.[201]

5. Duty to Keep Trust Assets Separate.

The trustee has a duty to keep trust assets separate from the trustee's own property and properly identified.[202] This means that the trustee should not mix his or her own

---

199 Probate Code §16046(b).

200 Probate Code §16060.

201 *Werschkull v United Cal. Bank* (1978) 85 Cal. App. 3d 981.

202 Probate Code §16009.

personal assets with the beneficiary. Doing so would be a breach of trust and lead to consequences for the trustee.

Further, because assets are held in an SNT, the trustee should make sure that the person with a disability's own assets (typically from SSI or SSDI) are not commingled with the trust's assets. This can be a problem if the trustee is also serving as the Representative Payee for the beneficiary. If these assets are commingled, it could jeopardize continued public benefits eligibility.

6. Duty to Avoid Self-Dealing, Impropriety, and Conflicts of Interest.

If an investment may benefit trustee personally, or if the trustee wishes to invest in property in which the beneficiary has an ownership interest (or that the trustee already owns), a conflict of interest may be created. Situations in which the trustee participates with the beneficiaries or self-deals inherently call into question a trustee's duty of loyalty. Some of these situations are discussed below:

- **When a trustee buys an asset or sells an asset to the beneficiary.** For example, self-dealing can occur if the SNT trustee is asked to buy the beneficiary's automobile so that he can receive a new one. It is not absolutely improper for the trustee to buy from or sell to a trust beneficiary.[203] However, a trustee may be challenged if there is a dispute over the proper value of the asset. To protect him or herself, the trustee should employ a professional, disinterested professional to set the market value. Further, the trustee could petition a court for instructions[204] and obtain permission for the particular transaction as described in Chapter 5. This would be the safest thing a trustee could do to protect him or herself from later second-guessing.

- **When a trustee is asked to participate on the trust's behalf in an investment with the beneficiary.** An SNT trustee may, for example, be asked to help the beneficiary buy real estate with the beneficiary. If the trustee makes an independent evaluation that the investment is proper,

---

203 Probate Code §16004.
204 See Probate Code §17200.

there is nothing wrong with this.[205] In this case, it is good practice to disclose the investment and the beneficiary's interest to all other interested parties. If the trust is subject to continuing court supervision, the court should be advised. This type of disclosure will protect the trustee from possible breaches of duty if the investment does not perform as planned.

- **When a trustee is asked to delegate decision-making authority to a beneficiary on investment and asset management.** The fact that the trust and a beneficiary share ownership of an asset does not give the trustee a right to delegate ultimate decision-making authority over the asset to the beneficiary or to anyone else.[206] In such situations, the trustee and beneficiary should negotiate an arm's-length, written management agreement, as if they were co-trustees. If such an agreement cannot be reached, the trustee can sell the trust's share to the beneficiary, purchase the beneficiary's share, or, by agreement, put the property on the market. This can happen sometimes during an SNT administration when the beneficiary and the SNT trustee co-owns the home that is the beneficiary's primary residence.

- **When a trustee profits from the use of trust property or obtains some benefit from transactions using trust property.** A trustee may be held responsible when the trustee profits from the use of trust property, participates in transactions adverse to the beneficiary, or attempts to enforce a claim against trust property that the trustee purchased after appointment as trustee.[207] If the trustee moves into a home owned by the SNT or exclusively uses an automobile purchased for the beneficiary, this could violate the trustee's duties.

---

205 Probate Code §§16002, 16012.
206 Probate Code §16012.
207 See Probate Code §16004(a)-(b).

ARE THERE ANY EXCEPTIONS TO THE TRUSTEE'S GENERAL DUTY TO INVEST AND MANAGE ASSETS?

Yes. If the trust document limits the trustee's duty to invest and manage assets, then the trustee may rely on the trust document to negate these duties. Thus, if the trust document says that all investments must be in a certain stock portfolio or that real estate may stay vacant, then the trustee may follow that advice without getting in trouble, but only up to a point.

A trustee cannot blindly follow the trust document's terms and be completely free from potential liability. If there is significant loss in the assets because the trustee blindly follows the trust instrument's instructions, he or she could still be found liable if he or she could have done something to stop the losses. There is no bright line test to say when a trustee should do something, but if there are significant losses, the trustee should do something. Preferably, the trustee would petition a court for instructions on what to do. Once a court rules on the issue, the trustee would be protected.

SHOULD A TRUSTEE BUY AND MAINTAIN INSURANCE ON TRUST ASSETS?

Yes. It is vitally important to insure against the risks of owning property. The trustee has a duty to protect trust assets. Insurance is the primary way to do this. It is obvious that all real property, automobiles, and other trust assets must be insured. If the beneficiary is renting an apartment, the trustee should also consider renter's insurance.

The trustee should make sure that there is sufficient liability insurance to protect the trust assets from a lawsuit. This should be one of the first items a trustee will consider if, for example, a residence is held for the use of a beneficiary, an automobile has been purchased for the beneficiary's use, or a business is being run inside the trust.

WHAT SHOULD A TRUSTEE DO TO PROTECT BENEFICIARY'S PERSONAL PROPERTY?

A trustee is also responsible for any tangible personal property in the trustee's possession.[208] As describe above, the trustee should insure against any loss of personal property.

If a beneficiary goes into a board and care or some type of skilled nursing facility, the trustee should safely store the beneficiary's belongings. The appropriate type of storage depends on the asset: furniture may be stored in a warehouse; paintings and stamps require specialized storage to prevent deterioration; jewelry, coins, and other small valuables should be stored in a safe deposit box. The name on the account should be, "[name of trustee], trustee of the [name of beneficiary] special needs trust.".

The storage facility should be inspected occasionally to ensure that it is secure and meets the trustee's storage requirements. The trustee should maintain a written record of these inspections, noting the inspection date, the trustee's impressions of the property's condition, and any other considerations affecting a decision to retain or dispose of the property. These reports should be kept in the appropriate asset file. Additional insurance should be purchased to insure the contents of the storage unit, especially if there are items of particular value. If an individual is residing in a home or facility with other people, personal items should be labeled and secured.

IS A TRUSTEE ALLOWED TO INVEST TRUST PROPERTY ANY WAY HE OR SHE WANTS?

No. There is always a limitation on how trust property may be invested. The standard of investment will depend on a couple of factors (described more fully below):

- If the SNT is a court supervised first-party SNT, then the trust will generally be required to invest in a limited way, as set forth in the Probate Code and as described in the next question and answer.
- If the SNT is not court supervised, then the trustee will invest trust assets in one of two ways: (1) if the SNT document is silent or if it states that the trustee shall invest as authorized by California law, then the default investment standard will be the prudent investor rule; or (2) if the SNT document

---

208   Probate Code §16047.

sets forth an investment standard, that standard is what will be used when investing assets.[209]

WHAT CAN A TRUSTEE INVEST IN WITH A COURT SUPERVISED FIRST-PARTY SNT?

There is a special investment standard for first-party SNTs. An SNT under ongoing court jurisdiction is generally one that was established for a beneficiary that has lost capacity. These are mostly SNTs that are established through a conservatorship or with litigation proceeds. See Chapter 1 and 19 to learn how to distinguish these types of trusts.

Unless good cause is shown, such a trust must allow only the following type of investments:[210]

1. Direct obligations of the United States, or of the State of California, maturing not later than five years from the date of making the investment.

2. United States Treasury bonds redeemable at par value on the death of the holder for payment of federal estate taxes, regardless of maturity date.

3. Securities listed on an established stock or bond exchange in the United States that are purchased on the exchange.

4. Eligible securities for the investment of surplus state moneys as provided for in Government Code §16430 (*i.e.*, generally most California municipal bonds, notes, and some commercial papers).

5. An interest in a money market mutual fund registered under the Investment Company Act of 1940[211] or common trust funds under 12 C.F.R. §9.18, the portfolios of which are limited to United States government obligations maturing not later than five years from the date of investment and to repurchase agreements fully collateralized by United States government obligations.

6. Units of a common trust fund described in Financial Code §1564, which fund has as its objective investment primarily in short-term fixed income obligations and will be permitted to value investments at cost under regulations of the appropriate regulatory authority.

---

209 Probate Code §16200(a).
210 Probate Code §2614.
211 15 U.S.C. §§80a-1—80a-64.

The trustee can expand the available investments for good cause by obtaining court permission. Petitioning the court is generally a good use of trust funds if the trust has significant assets because of the very peculiar (and narrow) choice of authorized investments.

> **Critical Pointer:** There is some concern among attorneys that the above-authorized investments do not allow investment in traditional mutual funds (a type of investment that builds in diversity of investment and increased rates of return). Other attorneys believe that because the permitted investments authorize investments into individual securities, this by implication also authorizes investments in mutual funds. It is surprising how little some judges understand even basic investment concepts, such as using such funds to decrease risk and increase returns. Nevertheless, the safest course in many instances is to petition the court to expand the trustee's investment authority to include investment in mutual funds. See Chapter 5 for a discussion on petitioning the court.

> **Warning:** It may be that the trustee has been a trustee of a court-supervised SNT for many years and has been investing in things that are not authorized in the acceptable investment list (in technical violation of the California Probate Code). If the trustee is unsure of the SNTs investment standard, he or she should visit an estate-planning attorney to discuss the matter. See Chapter 20 for a discussion on how to find an attorney.

WHAT CAN A TRUSTEE INVEST IN WITH NON–COURT SUPERVISED SNTS?

Many SNTs do not include an overall investment standard; the ones that do typically state that the trustee is obligated to follow California law. If that is the case, then the general rule for trusts is that the trustee must invest under the prudent investor rule.[212] The California prudent investor rule states,

---

212   Probate Code §16046(a).

1. A trustee shall invest and manage trust assets as a prudent investor would, by considering the purposes, terms, distribution requirements, and other circumstances of the trust. In satisfying this standard, the trustee shall exercise reasonable care, skill, and caution.

2. A trustee's investment and management decisions respecting individual assets and courses of action must be evaluated not in isolation but in the context of the trust portfolio as a whole and as a part of an overall investment strategy having risk and return objectives reasonably suited to the trust.[213]

The prudent investor rule superseded the old law that some investments are improper *per se* and permits a trustee to invest in any kind of property or type of investment, as long as the trustee exercises reasonable care, skill, and caution.[214] In determining whether or not a trustee is in compliance with the prudent investor rule, a number of factors are relevant. The court will evaluate compliance with the following duties:

- Duty to select risk and return objectives reasonably suited to the particular SNT;[215]
- Duty to diversify;[216]
- Duty to investigate facts relevant to investing and managing assets;[217]
- Duty to evaluate investments in the context of the portfolio as a whole;[218]
- Duty to avoid unreasonable or inappropriate costs;[219] and
- Duty to consider tax consequences.[220]

In general, a trustee should not place all the trust's eggs in one basket. For example, if all of the trust assets are invested in an airline stock and there is a terrorist

---

213 Probate Code §§16045-16054.
214 Probate Code §16047(a).
215 Probate Code §16047(b).
216 Probate Code §16048.
217 Probate Code §16047(d).
218 Probate Code §16047(b).
219 Probate Code §16050.
220 Probate Code §16047(c)(3).

attack that results in huge losses for the airline industry, the value of the trust assets would be compromised. Thus, a trustee needs to diversify the trust assets and minimize the risk that the trust could be impoverished by a downturn in any one stock or any one-market sector.

However, when a court is determining whether a trustee has followed the prudent investor rule, such a determination is made in light of the facts and circumstances existing when a trustee made his or her investment decisions.[221] This is important, because the trustee will not want to be judged in hindsight. For example, if trustee invested in an airline stock (as part of a larger portfolio) and that stock suffered a decline due to an unanticipated strike, then the trustee will not be held responsible for that particular loss in value of the stock—if the overall investment strategy is done prudently. Thus, a trustee may lose money in investments from time to time and nevertheless be complying with the prudent investor rule.

If a trustee lacks the knowledge or experience to carry out his or her duties, prudent investing may require the trustee to delegate investment decisions to (or at least receive advice from) an investment expert.[222] Assuming delegation is done prudently with respect to costs, selection of the expert, terms of the delegation, and periodic review, the trustee will not be liable for the expert's actions.[223] In the questions below, there is a discussion on selecting an appropriate investment advisor.

WHAT IF THE TRUST DOCUMENT OR A COURT ORDER SPECIFIES HOW A TRUSTEE SHOULD INVEST IN A WAY THAT CONTRADICTS THE PRUDENT INVESTOR RULE?

There are two situations when a trustee is not required to follow the general prudent investor rule.

1. where the trust document modifies the investment standard then the trustee can comply with the trust description of how investments should be managed;[224] or

2. where a court order requires a different duty of investment, the trustee must follow the court order. This can happen in SNTs when a court

---

221 Probate Code §16051.

222 Probate Code §16052(a).

223 Probate Code §16052(c), See also Probate Code §16401.

224 Probate Code §§16000, 16046(b).

establishes a first-party SNT for a person with a disability who also lacks capacity.[225] In this case, the permitted investments are very narrow, and any expansion of investment authority must be done by court permission, as described in the previous question and answer.

A trustee is not liable to a beneficiary for the trustee's good faith reliance on the trust's express provisions.[226] Thus, if the trust document states that investments are authorized that otherwise would not be approved if the trustee were required to follow the prudent investment standard, the trustee may invest that way.

> **Example:** If the trust document stated that the trustee shall invest 20 percent of the assets in the trust in Fabrinet stock. Generally, investing 20 percent of trust assets in the stock of one company would be a violation of the prudent investor rule. However, if the trust document specifically authorizes such an investment (and it would not be really dumb to do it), a trustee may do so without worrying about being sued for violating the investment standard.

However, even if a trust document allows a trustee to invest in a particular way, if it would be stupid to do so, the trustee can still be sued for following the terms of the trust.

> **Example:** If the trust document stated that the trustee shall invest all trust assets with ABC Corporation and ABC Corporation had, due to factors within the reasonable knowledge of the trustee, lost 50 percent of its value each of the last three years, a trustee could be sued for continuing to invest trust assets with ABC Corporation, provided that factors within the reasonable knowledge of the trustee suggested a different course of action. In this case, the trustee would be better served investing the money elsewhere.

---

225   California Rules of Court 7.903(c)(4).
226   Probate Code §16046(b).

The safest course for the trustee in this situation would be a petition for instructions. See Chapter 5 on how to do this.

WHAT ARE THE CONSIDERATIONS IN DEVELOPING AN OVERALL SNT INVESTMENT STRATEGY?

Regardless of the investment standard of the trust, a trustee will need to develop an investment strategy. An appropriate investment strategy will take into account specific circumstances of the trust and its beneficiaries, the factors listed in the Prudent Investor Act, and the costs of various investments. The factors that should be considered are

1. General economic conditions
2. The possible effect of inflation or deflation
3. The expected tax consequences of investment decisions or strategies
4. The role that each investment or course of action plays within the overall trust portfolio
5. The expected total return from income and the appreciation of capital
6. Other resources of the beneficiaries known to the trustee as determined from information provided by the beneficiaries
7. Needs for liquidity, regularity of income, and preservation or appreciation of capital
8. An asset's special relationship or special value, if any, to the purposes of the trust or to one or more of the beneficiaries[227]

A full analysis of all factors relevant to developing investment strategies is beyond the scope of this book. Indeed, such an analysis would likely fill many books. The appropriate strategy will likely depend on the intended level of current distributions and the expected duration of the trust.

The factors in developing an investment strategy include consideration of and balancing the beneficiary's future as well as current needs. For instance, a $1 million trust account seems like a large amount of money to most people. However, a beneficiary with a disability may need to depend on that fund for a lifetime—the

---

227   Probate Code §16047(c).

balance of which could well be eighty years. Even a withdrawal of $50,000 a year will mean that the size of the fund will likely decline over the years in terms of purchasing power. If the withdrawals are limited to $30,000 a year in the first few years, the trust fund could be expected keep up with inflation. To see how that works out, let's do the math:

Let's assume that (1) the trust will have an average annual return of 7 percent, including interest, dividends and capital appreciation, (2) trustee fees and other expenses will be 1 percent a year, and (3) inflation will average 3 percent per year. Different assumptions will, of course, lead to different results. Any distribution policy can reflect actual returns and costs after several years. But here are the results after ten, twenty, and thirty years given distributions of $50,000 a year in the first example and of $30,000 a year growing with the growth of the trust fund in the second **example:**

	Example 1	Example 2
Year 1		
Trust fund	$1 million	$1 million
Annual distributions	$50,000	$30,000
Year 10		
Trust fund	$1.1 million	$1.3 million
Annual distributions	$50,000	$39,000
Year 20		
Trust fund	$1.2 million	$1.75 million
Annual distributions	$50,000	$52,000
Year 30		
Trust fund	$1.45 million	$3.3 million
Annual distributions	$50,000	$99,000

Belt-tightening in the first several years of a trust can reap some significant results for the trust and for the beneficiary's later years. However, this must be balanced against the beneficiary's likely lifespan, likely future needs, and potential benefit of current spending. For instance, there is little need to preserve capital in a trust whose primary beneficiary has a terminal illness. Similarly, it is a dilemma for a young client where extra tutoring may help a child achieve educational success that may make the difference between learning an employable skill in later life and having to depend on the trust for support. Of course, the future is not clear, but if the expenditure were reasonably likely to produce the desired result, one would not withhold payment in such case, even if it would mean exceeding the normal safe threshold for trust expenditures.

The foregoing example illustrates that the SNT trustee must make financial decisions based on the beneficiary's personal needs. Often the best results require professional and family member co-trustees, or trust advisers and trust protectors, to reach a consensus based on both financial and a careful assessment of the beneficiary's current and future needs and current and potential future resources, as opposed to a blanket standard for all SNTs in all situations.

If the persons who receive trust income (known as current income beneficiaries) are different from those who will receive the principal when the trust terminates (known as remainder beneficiaries), trust records should classify all receipts and disbursements as either income or principal. In most cases, there will be no difficulty with this. Things like rent, ordinary dividends, and interest are clearly income; generally, proceeds from the sale of an asset are principal.

WHAT STEPS CAN A TRUSTEE DO TO DEVELOP AN INVESTMENT STRATEGY?

When developing an investment strategy for an SNT, it is imperative to focus on the short- and long-term needs and goals of the SNT beneficiary. The determination begins by taking an inventory of the current and future needs of the client and ranking them by priority. Such a "Wish List" can aid the trustee and financial advisor in evaluating what is probable, possible, or unattainable for the SNT beneficiary. The next step is allocating the assets to provide the best possible chance of earning the income needed to accommodate the beneficiary's ongoing special needs. Finally, there needs to be a system to review the ongoing investment strategy so changes can be made on changes in the beneficiary's circumstances or changes in the market.

While this task might seem daunting, there is legal shelter for trustees under the law governing trust investments, known as the Uniform Prudent Investment Act. The essence of the UPIA is that risk can be legally viewed in totality for the portfolio, rather than on each invested security. It therefore allows for prudent diversification of the client's investment assets. The UPIA's focus is on the *process* of how investments are determined and implemented, not the result of independent investments.

As an SNT trustee, it is central to compliance with the UPIA to draft an investment policy statement (IPS) for the trust. An IPS outlines the client issues, risk level, restrictions, parameters, and goals for the SNT related to investments. The IPS serves as the "game plan" for the SNT investments and expenditures. In Appendix P, there is a sample IPS that was established in a different matter.

In order to develop the investment strategy, a trustee should follow the following steps:

- **Setting the Spending plan:** The first step is to develop a spending plan for the client. Obviously, the amount being used to fund the SNT will generally serve as a barrier to pay for the beneficiary's entire spending plan. Thus, it is important to manage client expectations in regard to what is a feasible, sustainable annual spending plan. In order to manage expectations, some trustees do not distribute a list, like the "no-brainer" list in Appendix O to the beneficiary. Instead, some trustees simply ask the beneficiary to create a "Wish List," and try to separate needs from wants. It is up to the individual trustee's discretion to decide how much, if at all, the beneficiary participates in developing the spending plan.

Some common examples of typical SNT beneficiary needs are:
- Home/personal residence purchase (and ongoing expenses related to home maintenance)
- Home adaptations related to disability access
- Adaptive automobile

221

- Adaptive disability equipment, e.g., wheelchairs, telephone equipment, lavatory, speech
- Related physical therapies, clinics, providers, etc.
- Caregivers, paid family caregivers
- Prosthetics, catheters, etc.
- Parental respite care
- Clothing
- Benefits disqualifying distributions—primarily rent

Some common examples of typical SNT beneficiary wants are:
- Computer and video equipment and software
- Travel expenditures
- Companion Travel expenses
- Clothing and specialized wear, shoes, etc.
- Educational expenses
- Internet or cell phone expenses
- Furniture
- Social activity and hobby expenses

Helpful Hint: In some first-party SNT cases where the funds came from a litigation recovery, the personal injury attorney may have paid for a Life Care Plan for the SNT beneficiary. The Life Care Plan goes over all the future needs and costs of the beneficiary. It can be a good starting point for determining client needs.

- **Testing the Likelihood of Earning Enough to Meet Spending plan:** The trustee will want to use financial software that uses probabilistic modeling so the spending plan can be tested. It is important to increase the costs of providing equipment and services with inflation over time. The trustee must account for this in the analysis if the trustee is to continue to maintain the client's lifestyle in the future. In addition, taxation of earnings and benefits must also be accounted for, as well as variability and uncertainty of future investment returns. Once there is a target spending plan determination, it is crucial to create forward-looking financial planning projections to "test" the likelihood of attaining the proposed spending plan. The probabilistic financial software will help you determine how likely the spending plan is to last over the beneficiary's life. There may be times when the trustee is having a difficult time creating the spending plan. When this arises, the probabilistic software can help determine how much can be spent annually without running out of money. As a reminder, special needs planning is not a one-time event, it is a process that will change over time. Therefore, the trustee will have to update and adjust this spending plan process many times over the life of the beneficiary.

Note: There are special needs planning calculator programs freely available on the Internet to aid in developing a spending plan and financial forecasting, such as the Merrill Lynch Special Needs at http://specialneedscalc.ml.com. While these can be a great starting point, it is generally preferable to employ a financial professional with experience and expertise related directly to beneficiaries with disability cases to evaluate and prepare the client's spending plan. In order to locate such a financial professional, please review Chapter 20.

• **Investing and Allocating Assets:** The next step is properly investing the available SNT assets. Obviously, the needs, circumstances, age, and financial risk tolerance of the beneficiary will determine the appropriate risk level of the client's SNT investments. This concept is the basis of the prudent investment laws related to investing as an SNT trustee.

As risk and return are inherently related, it is ultimately a trade-off between stable, low-risk investments (a low "fear factor") and achieving a higher annual spending plan to improve the beneficiary's lifestyle and combat the effects of inflation (a reasonable return on investment assets). Most practical investment solutions will combine safety and surety for short-term needs with higher yielding investments dedicated to achieving long-term goals.

Example: A first-party SNT may be the recipient of a structured settlement annuity that pays a guaranteed monthly amount into the SNT. An investment advisor may include short-term bonds and high-quality stocks to provide a comprehensive investment program to achieve the beneficiary's lifetime goals. This allocation between bonds, annuities, and stocks provides the basis for a prudent investment plan. It is best to have an independent financial advisor run analysis prior to investing in a structured settlement.

Using the financial planning projection systems discussed earlier, the SNT trustee can test various spending plan scenarios involving a multitude of investment risk levels. Each will provide insight as to how likely the proposed spending plan is to be attained over the life expectancy of the beneficiary. An annual spending plan can then be adopted based upon the most likely scenario with the least amount of risk. This directly determines the risk level for the SNT assets and allows the SNT trustee to implement an investment program, which matches the client's need to their necessary risk matrix.

For some first-party SNTs (as discussed in prior question/answers), certain state laws under the Probate Code limit allowable SNT investments. If an SNT is created by a court (as in most personal injury claims or through a conservatorship of the estate), California Rule of Court 7.903 requires that investments in the SNT comply with the more stringent standards of California Probate Code §2574. The practical implications of these regulations are that these SNT's may not invest in

- Traditional mutual funds or unit investment trusts
- US Treasury bonds greater than five years in maturity
- Corporate bonds of any type or maturity
- Insurance or annuity products
- OTC stocks
- And many other "risky" investments

Note: If the SNT trustee wishes to expand investment authority even for these types of first party SNTs, he or she is allowed to do so with court permission. A special needs planning attorney can assist with the filing of a petition to probate court. See Chapter 16 to find a special needs planning attorney.

- **Plan for Ongoing Review of Investments.** The final step of any investment strategy is to develop a plan for reviewing the investment strategy implemented. Beneficiaries are human beings who undergo myriad changes over time. Markets and investments are continuously evolving due to volatile economic conditions. The trustee should continually monitor and adjust the IPS and investments based upon changes in

  - Actual vs. projected trust expenditures
  - Health changes of the SNT beneficiary
  - Aging of the beneficiary, particularly attainment of majority age
  - Parental caregiver aging or incapacitation
  - Changes to the living situation of the beneficiary
  - Investment performance
  - Additional caregiver expenses
  - Health-care adjustments
  - Change in the Beneficiary's benefits
  - Social Security Administration and Medicaid or Medicare policy changes
  - Any large anticipated expenses, such as a home purchase

Brokerage account statements should be audited for transactions and reconciled monthly. Care should be taken to conduct investment performance reviews of the trust accounts at least quarterly.

Ongoing investment management of the SNT assets requires periodic review of transactions and investment performance. Brokerage account statements should be audited for transactions and reconciled monthly. Care should be taken to conduct investment performance reviews of the trust accounts at least quarterly. In evaluating the trust performance, the trustee might utilize the following data:

- Basic performance measures showing market gain or loss, dividends and interest received.

- Relative performance comparisons to market indices, such as the Standard and Poor's 500 Index or the Blackrock Aggregate Bond Index, or a combination of these.

Proper record keeping, quarterly investment reviews and annual IPS and financial plan updates are imperative to maintain compliance with the UPIA.

CAN THE TRUSTEE DELEGATE THE INVESTMENT RESPONSIBILITIES TO ANOTHER?

Yes, a trustee is allowed to delegate investment and management functions as prudent under the circumstances.[228] This is contrary to the general rule. Other than investment and management functions, a trustee cannot delegate his or her other responsibilities to others.[229] For a trustee who has little to no experience in investing or managing assets, it would likely be a breach of that trustee's duty to not consult with investment counselors, real estate brokers, accountants, tax attorneys, and other specialists as necessary in managing trust assets.[230]

If a trustee decides to delegate investment or management responsibilities, the trustee must still exercise prudence in (1) selecting the agent, (2) establishing the scope and terms of the delegation of authority, and (3) periodically reviewing the agent's overall performance and his or her compliance with the terms of the delegation.

---

228 Probate Code §16052(a).
229 Probate Code §16012.
230 Estate of Gump (1991) 1 Cal. App. 4th 582, 595.

WHAT PRINCIPLES SHOULD A TRUSTEE UNDERSTAND WHEN HIRING A FINANCIAL PROFESSIONAL?

Hiring a financial professional for the special needs trust should not be done haphazardly. It is important that the trustee find the right person to help the special needs beneficiary meet their expected future goals. Thus, it is imperative that the financial planner not only have the experience in managing assets, and in particular, experience in managing assets for a person with a disability.

The United States Department of Labor (DOL) undertook a multi-year regulatory project to address the problems with conflicts of interest in investment advice. The Department's conflict of interest final rule and related exemptions aim to protect investors by requiring all who provide retirement investment advice to plans, plan fiduciaries and IRAs to abide by a "fiduciary" standard—putting their clients' best interest before their own profits. This rule, adopted in April 2017, was ultimately vacated by the US Fifth Circuit court of Appeals in March of 2018.

The current rules for investment standards are encapsulated in the Securities and Exchange Commission's Regulation Best Interest, which was approved in June, 2019. Regulation BI, which takes full effect as of June 30, 2020, seeks to "... enhance the broker-dealer standard of conduct beyond existing suitability obligations and make it clear that a broker-dealer may not put its financial interests ahead of the interests of a retail customer when making recommendations." Further information is available on the SEC site: https://www.sec.gov/info/smallbus/secg/regulation-best-interest

Consumer watchdog groups have been critical of Regulation BI, claiming that it contains much weaker protections for investors than the DOL rule. In any event, an SNT Trustee should fully understand what standard of investment they have consented to in the agreement they sign with their chosen financial firm:

Suitability Standard of Investing:

- Financial Professionals and their firms are only required to make suitable (reasonable) recommendations
- Advisors are regulated by FINRA
- Brokers are not required to put client's interest first
- Brokers/Insurance Agents are not obligated to disclose conflicts of interest
- Commissions charged are only loosely regulated and need not be reasonable

Fiduciary Standard of Investing:

- Financial Advisors are regulated by FINRA and/or the SEC
- Advisors are required to put client's best interest first
- Financial Advisors must disclose conflicts of interest
- Binds Advisor + Firm as a Fiduciary to the client
- Averts any "Material Conflict of Interest"
- Must charge fees which are "reasonable"

The basis of a Trustee's relationship with a financial firm is governed exclusively by the contract which is signed when opening the account. In order to receive some modicum of liability protection for investment decisions, the Trustee should ensure that the contract provides that the firm and the advisor are held as fiduciaries on the account and not held to any type of lower standard of care.

Below is a very brief summary of who the financial players are:

1. Types of Financial Professionals

There are generally three types of financial professionals that can be hired to assist a trustee:

- **Investment advisor** refers to any individual or firm providing investment advice for compensation as part of a regular business of giving investment advice. An investment advisor must register with the Securities and Exchange Commission (SEC) or appropriate state securities agencies as an investment advisor, unless specifically exempted from registration. Investment advisers may recommend stocks, bonds, mutual funds, partnerships, or other SEC-registered investments for clients. To register, an applicant must file a Form ADV (Advisor) detailing educational and professional experience with either the SEC or the state(s), stating the basis for their compensation and disclosing whether he or she has ever been the subject of disciplinary action. This form or its equivalent must be shown to potential clients prior to the commencement of a professional engagement.

- **Financial advisor** is a generic term used broadly by consumers and financial services professionals to describe an individual engaged in providing financial advice, services, or products to a client for compensation. The term "financial advisor" covers a broad spectrum of financial professionals, including financial planners, insurance agents, registered representatives, money managers, investment advisers, and individuals who sell, or advise people on, financial products.

- **Broker/Dealer** is a term used to describe an individual or a company that is licensed to buy and sell investment products for or to clients. Some broker/dealers are large companies that sell securities that they own (thus, the term "dealer"), while others are firms that only buy and sell securities on behalf of investors (thus, the term "broker"). To be in the US securities business, an individual or a company must be a broker/dealer or an individual must be affiliated with a broker/dealer as a registered representative. There are different types of brokers, including full service firms like Merrill Lynch and discount brokers like Charles Schwab.

2. How Financial Professionals Are Paid

Investment advisers and financial planners can be compensated in a number of ways:
- An hourly rate
- A flat fee to complete a specified project
- A quarterly or annual retainer fee
- A fee charged as a percentage of assets that the financial professional manages (Typically anywhere from 0.50% per year to 2.00% per year. The more assets, the lower the fee.)
- Commissions paid to the financial professional from financial or insurance products sold
- A combination of fees and commissions

3. Types of Financial Professional Designations

There are a whole host of designations for financial advisers. Some are well recognized and respected, while others are merely made up to aid in marketing products, like selling annuities to seniors. The designation pecking order includes the CFP

229

(certified financial planner) designation. Other designations, like the ChFC (chartered financial consultant) and CLU (chartered life underwriter), are focused on specific segments of the financial advisory field. Below are a few of the most respected designations that a SNT trustee may want to see from a financial professional being hired:

1. CERTIFIED FINANCIAL PLANNER™ (CFP®)

This is perhaps the most widely recognized credential in the financial planning industry. The academic requirement consists of eight Principal knowledge topic categories covering professional conduct and regulation, general principles of financial planning, education planning, risk management and insurance planning, investment planning, tax planning, retirement savings and income planning and estate planning. Once that is complete, students must sit for the board exam. The CFP® Exam is offered in a computer-based format during an 8-day testing window. The exam is administered on one day for two 3-hour testing sessions, separated by a scheduled 40-minute break. Once a passing grade has been achieved, prospective certificants must also complete at least 6,000 hours of professional experience plus a bachelor's degree in order to obtain the CFP designation. To find a CFP in your community, go to, http://www.cfp.net/search. Certified financial planners owe their clients a fiduciary duty—the highest duty in the law, and similar to the duty a trustee owes to a beneficiary.

2. Chartered Financial Analyst (CFA)

This designation is generally considered to be one of the most difficult and prestigious credentials in the financial industry, at least in terms of investment management. The academic requirements for this designation are second only to those for CPAs. Three years of coursework must be completed, covering a range of topics and disciplines, such as technical and fundamental analysis, financial accounting, and portfolio theory and analysis. Those who earn this designation often become portfolio managers or analysts for various types of financial institutions. However, such a designation does not necessarily impose a fiduciary duty upon individual investors.

3. Chartered Financial Consultant (ChFC)

This designation is used by financial professionals—including accountants, attorneys, bankers, insurance agents and brokers, and securities representatives—who have earned the ChFC designation by completing the American College's eight-course education program, met experience requirements, and agreed to uphold a code of ethics.

4. Registered Investment Advisor (RIA)

This designation applies to those who have taken and passed a test and filed a Form ADV IV with the SEC. Generally, RIAs owe to their clients a fiduciary duty. An individual who works with a registered investment advisor is sometimes called an investment advisory representative (IAR).

5. Registered Representative

A registered representative is a designation given to stockbrokers who represent a broker/dealer. Their duty is circumstantial to a specific case; thus they do not necessarily owe their clients a fiduciary duty.

6. Insurance Agent

Many life insurance agents hold themselves out to be "financial advisers." Life insurance agents owe a duty of reasonable care—the care commonly exercised by others in their industry. As such, it is generally acknowledged that insurance agents have the lowest hurdle with regard to the duty they owe to their clients. Some insurance agents are extraordinary, and one should not judge a specific professional based solely upon his or her particular license.

7. Agencies in Charge of Financial Advisor Oversight

The trustee should review any financial advisers' background through on-line access to the agencies that oversee them. The following is a list of useful websites of these agencies:

- The Securities and Exchange Commission (SEC) provides useful information to research advisor licensing. Their main page is http://www.sec.gov. On the SEC homepage, look for "Investor Information—Check Out Brokers and Advisers," at http://www.sec.gov/investor/brokers.htm.
- The Financial Industry Regulatory Authority (FINRA), formerly known as the National Association of Securities Dealer, Inc. (NASD), has a separate system for monitoring securities dealers. Go to http://www.finra.org/Investors/ToolsCalculators/BrokerCheck.
- In addition, the CFA Institute http://www.cfainstitute.org (formerly the Association for Investment Management and Research, or AIMR) provides background about the roles of securities analysts and brokers.
- You can find more information on licensing at the state level on state government websites. To find state securities regulators, go to the North American Securities Administrators Association, Inc. (NASAA) website at http://www.nasaa.org , and select "Find a Regulator" on the left panel.
- To find state insurance regulators, go to the National Association of Insurance Commissioners (NAIC) at http://www.naic.org. The NAIC provides an interactive map of "State Insurance Department Web Sites" at http://www.naic.org/state_web_map.htm.

WHAT STEPS SHOULD A TRUSTEE TAKE WHEN HIRING A FINANCIAL ADVISOR?

The trustee should be in control in the selection process. It is acceptable to obtain the advice of the beneficiary and the family of the beneficiary, but the trustee has the ultimate responsibility (and liability) in the selection process.

Screening several advisers may appear to be a lot of effort, but remember that a trustee will be legally required to engage the services of a competent professional; meeting with just one (unless the trustee has worked with them before and has previously made comparisons) will not allow the trustee the opportunity to compare services.

4.   Before Meeting with Financial Advisor

A trustee should do as much online research as possible on the prospective advisor. Reviewing their website is a good first step, but the trustee should dig a bit deeper. There are ways to get information on the investors' references and credentials.

According to the SEC's website:

> Most investment advisers must fill out a form called "Form ADV." They must file their Form ADVs with either the SEC or the state securities agency in the state where they have their principal place of business, depending on the amount of assets they manage.
>
> Form ADV consists of two parts. Part 1 contains information about the advisor's business and whether they've had problems with regulators or clients. Part 2 outlines the advisor's services, fees, and strategies. Before you hire someone to be your investment advisor, always ask for, and carefully read, both parts of Form ADV.
>
> You can get copies of Form ADV from the investment advisor, your state securities regulator or the SEC, depending on the size of the advisor. You can find out how to get in touch with your state securities regulator through the North American Securities Administrators Association, Inc.'s (NASAA) website or by calling (202) 737-0900. Ask your state securities regulator whether they've had any complaints about the advisor, and ask them to check the CRD (Central Registration Depository).

If the SEC registers the investment advisor, you can get a copy of the Form ADV by accessing How to Request Public Documents. In addition, at the SEC's headquarters, you can visit our Public Reference Room from 10:00 a.m. to 3:00 p.m. to obtain copies of SEC records and documents.[231]

There are also websites to check the background of the financial advisor. The California website that helps to locate these websites for California financial advisers is https://dbo.ca.gov. The trustee may also check out the SEC website at http://www.sec.gov/investor/brokers.htm. Some other agencies that collect information on financial advisers include

1. Certified Financial Planner Board of Standards, Inc.
   888-237-6275 - www.CFP.net
2. North American Securities Administrators Association
   202-737-0900 - www.nasaa.org
3. National Association of Insurance Commissioners
   816-842-3600 - www.naic.org
4. Financial Industry Regulatory Authority (FINRA)
   800-289-9999 - www.finra.org
5. National Fraud Exchange (fee involved)
   800-822-0416

5. The Initial Meeting

Most advisers will meet personally with the trustee at no charge for between one half hour to one hour. The primary purpose of an initial meeting is introduction and mutual assessment. The trustee should make the most of this meeting.

Attached as Appendix I is a list of questions a trustee should ask during this meeting with space for providing answers. In the alternative, a trustee can use the form provided by the SEC at http://www.sec.gov/complaint/callform.htm.

Critical Pointer: When the trustee asks questions, make sure to use the forms provided to write down the answers he or she

---

231 http://www.sec.gov/investor/pubs/invadvisers.htm.

receives from the prospective advisor and the basis of the decision the trustee made. Also, let the prospective financial professional know that you are taking notes so that it will keep them honest.

The trustee should not expect an initial meeting to result in any specific recommendations from the prospective advisor about how to handle trust assets. A good advisor must do extensive investigation of the beneficiary's situation before making any specific recommendations. Even if a prospective financial advisor seems to meet all of the beneficiary's needs, the trustee should not discount his or her gut reaction to meeting with the person. If the trustee does not feel comfortable with the financial advisor, then he or she should not hire the advisor.

6. Preparing and Signing the Agreement

The terms of the agreement with the financial advisor should be in writing.

> **Critical Pointer:** The first consideration for establishing a relationship with a financial firm is to verify that the account will be governed by the "Fiduciary Standard of Investment" which bars conflict of interest, self-dealing and exorbitant fees of the broker/financial advisor. (See "Principles to Understand" section of this chapter.) The trustee should ask to see the clause in the investment contract which specifically confirms this, as well as the declaration of the actual stated fee to be charged to the account (including hidden internal fees of investment products).

In establishing the scope and terms of the delegation, the trustee and the investment agent should prepare written guidelines that include

- a summary profile of the trust and its purposes;
- the investment objectives for the assets delegated to the agent, including a statement of risk tolerance;
- asset allocation targets;
- a description of acceptable asset class characteristics;
- a description of how performance will be measured;
- income and/or cash flow requirements for the beneficiaries;

- investment time horizon;
- other liquidity needs for the trust for payment of taxes, fees, or other expenses;
- a description of the tax status of the trust; how taxes are allocated, and whether there are (or should be) any special restrictions on trust investments as a result of the trust's tax status;
- an agreement of how transactions will be reported to the trustee; and, ideally,
- a summary description of how communications will be transacted between the agent and the trustee and how investment transactions will be approved.

CAN A TRUSTEE STILL BE HELD RESPONSIBLE FOR BREACHES IF HE OR SHE DELEGATES THE DUTY OF INVESTMENT TO A PROFESSIONAL?

Yes. As already discussed, the trustee may delegate the financial and management functions of the trustee's job to a professional. However, this does not end the trustee's responsibility. He or she must still monitor the ongoing performance of the financial advisor.[232]

If the trustee fails to continue monitoring the advisor's performance and the advisor is not performing his or her job appropriately, the trustee may still be held liable.[233] Further, a trustee found liable for the acts or omissions of an agent is liable for any loss or other adverse consequences affecting trust property as a result of the act or omission of the agent, if that act or omission would be a breach of the trust if committed by the trustee.[234] Thus, if the financial advisor is not following the appropriate investment standard set forth in the trust document, both the financial advisor and the trustee will be held liable.

---

232 Probate Code §§16052(a)(1) and (a)(3).
233 Probate Code §§16401, 16052.
234 Probate Code §16401(b).

WHAT TYPE OF MONITORING OF THE FINANCIAL ADVISOR SHOULD A TRUSTEE DO?

As described in the previous question and answer, the failure to review the financial advisor's performance can lead to the trustee being sued if the advisor has done something wrong. Thus, it is critically important to continually review the investment advisor's performance. The trustee should review investment performance no less frequently than quarterly.

At a minimum, the trustee should have a copy of the investment strategy that was decided upon and regularly receive the advisor's financial statements.

> **Practice Pointer:** If the trustee does not have experience in reading these types of statements, the SEC has provided a Beginners' Guide to Financial Statements at http://www.sec.gov/investor/pubs/begfinstmtguide.htm.

WHAT SHOULD A TRUSTEE DO IF HE OR SHE SUSPECTS WRONGDOING BY A FINANCIAL ADVISOR?

It is imperative that the trustee acts promptly.[235] Depending on the type of wrongdoing suspected, the trustee should take reasonable steps in solving the issue. This can include immediate termination, reporting to appropriate entities (courts and financial oversight groups) and possibly (in more serious matters) filing a lawsuit against the advisor.

If there is only a suspicion of wrongdoing, then a suggested course of action that may solve the problem:

1. Talk to the financial professional and explain the problem. Where is the fault? Were communications clear? Refer to the trustee's notes. What did the financial professional tell the trustee?

2. If the financial professional cannot resolve the problem, then talk to the financial professional's supervisor (which, for brokers, is often the firm's branch manager).

3. If the problem is still not resolved, write to the compliance department at the firm's main office. Explain the problem clearly, and how it should be

---

235 Probate Code §16401(b)(6).

resolved. Ask the compliance office to respond within thirty days. If trustee is still not satisfied, contact the appropriate regulatory agencies and file a complaint. For example, if the SEC is the appropriate agency, the trustee can file a complaint at

Office of Investor Education and Advocacy

US Securities & Exchange Commission

100 F Street, NE

Washington D.C. 20549-0213

Fax: (202) 772-9295

http://www.sec.gov/complaint.shtml

If there is more than suspicion of wrongdoing, then the following course of action may solve the problem:

1. Fire the financial professional.
2. If court supervised, immediately bring the wrongdoing to the court's attention.
3. Report the financial professional to appropriate regulatory agencies and file a complaint. For example, if the SEC is the appropriate agency, the trustee can file a complaint at

   Office of Investor Education and Advocacy

   US Securities & Exchange Commission

   100 F Street, NE

   Washington D.C. 20549-0213

   Fax: (202) 772-9295

   http://www.sec.gov/complaint.shtml

HOW DOES A CALIFORNIA LICENSED PRIVATE PROFESSIONAL TRUSTEE FOLLOW THE TERMS OF THE TRUST WHILE PROTECTING HIS OR HER FIDUCIARY PRACTICE?

As noted throughout this book, a trustee is obligated to follow the terms of the trust and owes many duties to the beneficiary. A private professional fiduciary trustee not only has to make difficult decisions for the beneficiary but must balance these decisions with protecting his or her own fiduciary practice from personal liability. A California Licensed Professional Fiduciary (CLPF) serving as trustee is usually a small business owner hired to administer an SNT. The trustee is at risk if he or she does something wrong or if it is alleged that he or she does something wrong. The fiduciary can protect themselves with Errors and Omissions Insurance, a surety bond and a *thoroughly defined repeatable fiduciary process.*

The most comprehensive way for a CLPF to protect his or her practice is to follow the outlined process defined below. It is a process used by many institutions and boards of director to ensure compliance and fiduciary oversight. This process will provide a protective shield for the CLPF to use if he or she is ever the defendant of an action brought against them. This thoroughly defined repeatable process was developed by the Special Needs Team, Scott MacDonald and Daniel Cutter, at Merrill Lynch. The process covers the Five D's CLPF should follow to protect themselves from liability and is described in detail in response to the next question.

WHAT ARE THE FIVE D'S AND HOW CAN FOLLOWING THEM PROTECT AN SNT TRUSTEE?

As noted in the prior question, the Merrill Lynch Special Needs Team of Scott MacDonald and Daniel Cutter developed a defined repeatable process they call the Five D's that when followed will protect an SNT trustee when administering an SNT.

4. Due Diligence:

The first D is for *Due Diligence*. The trustee will either be investing the assets by themselves or working with an investment professional to invest the assets. If the trustee is investing the assets by themselves, then it is best to understand who is giving the trustee advice. Is the trustee making investment decisions by themselves or are they receiving advice from someone else? If it is someone else, who is it and are they qualified to be giving advice?

If the trustee is working with an investment professional, then it is best to start the due diligence process by learning about the investment professional. To begin, the fiduciary should find out the company and the type of investment professional they are working with. This will help the fiduciary learn if investment professional works as an independent professional or for an investment firm and the type of firm. Some firms come with an 800 number where advice is given by a different professional each time and therefore has no continuity of advice and guidance for the trustee or beneficiary. It is important to understand who the investment professional is and where the investment professional works. Once this information is obtained it is best to lookup the record of the investment professional through the regulatory agencies FINRA (https://brokercheck.finra.org) and the SEC (http://www.sec.gov/investor/brokers.htm).

Next, the trustee will want to understand how the investment professional is paid. Is the professional being paid by commission or by fee or a combination of both? Can the trustee delegate investment management to the investment professional? If the investment professional is being paid by commission, then the trustee can NOT delegate investment management to the investment professional. If they are getting paid a fee, then the trustee will want to know the rate and how it is paid. Is it a monthly, quarterly or yearly fee and are there any other costs related to the products or services the investment professional is providing?

Finally, the trustee will want to learn if the investment professional has any professional designations to see their focus of work. Many people can call themselves investment professionals, but the trustee should seek the professional that focuses on a relationship as opposed to a product or transaction. The professional designation will help the trustee understand if the investment professional is focused on a product or relationship. The designation will also help the trustee understand if the investment professional is held to a suitability standard (lower standard) or a fiduciary standard (higher standard). This will help the trustee determine the general standard of care of the investment professional.

Investment professionals working for a brokerage firm like Merrill Lynch, Morgan Stanley, Wells Fargo, UBS, etc. are held to a suitability standard whereas independent Registered Investment Advisors (RIA's) are held to the higher fiduciary standard. Investment professionals at brokerage firms will be held to a fiduciary standard if they have a CFP® or if the trustee signs a delegation investment contract. It is recommended to ask for a fiduciary delegation contract when working with professionals at a brokerage firm.

When a trustee is administering a SNT, there will be many people looking over his or her shoulder. There may be other family, friends, professionals or even a trust advisory committee watching his or her every move. It is highly recommended to work with a professional financial team that focuses their investment practice on Special Needs Planning and to introduce this team of investment professionals to the trustee's attorney, benefits coordinator, accountant, care planner, etc. This will ensure that everybody is working together and collaborating for the benefit of the beneficiary. In addition, each professional will be a second set of eyes for each other to make sure that the beneficiary is being served properly.

A list of questions is set forth in Appendix I to use when interviewing a financial professional that should elicit the important information.

5. Depletion Analysis:

The second D is for *Depletion Analysis*. Once the due diligence is completed and the investment professional is hired, the next step is to begin the depletion analysis. The depletion analysis is an analysis that shows how long the assets will last based on the beneficiaries' current spending plan. The depletion analysis can also be used to show how much money can be spent over the life of the beneficiary. It is a very flexible tool and can be customized to the exact needs of the beneficiary.

It is important to understand industry best practices. When it comes to running the depletion analysis, the trustee should check the technology being used to ensure the most accurate outcome. The main technology used in the depletion analysis is called Monte Carlo Simulation. Monte Carlo Simulation is used to model the probability of different outcomes in a process that cannot easily be predicted due to the intervention of random variables. It is a technique used to understand the impact of risk and uncertainty in forecasting models. It gives a probability of success of different outcomes. It is superior to spreadsheets and present value, future value (deterministic) calculations because it calculates thousands of scenarios instead of just one scenario. It provides the trustee with a much more comprehensive view of what may happen and how likely it is to occur.

Another reason why the trustee should not rely on a deterministic or a fixed approach is because it doesn't always take inflation into account. Inflation causes the prices of goods and services to increase annually. This increase tends to be a higher increase for special needs families due to the higher costs increases of the goods and services they access. For example, the cost of healthcare has increased more than the rate of inflation over the past decade and is expected to continue to increase for years to come. Special needs individuals who are accessing government benefits not only have higher rates of inflation for the goods and service they are accessing but they are not receiving as high of annual increases to their income. Therefore, their purchasing power is being compressed at a higher rate than non-special needs beneficiaries.

It is recommended to collect the best most up to date data for this step. If the data is off the results will be off too. It is well known that the best plans can get off track due to unexpected situations. Life does not move in a linear direction, there are ups and downs, emergencies and unexpected changes. Probabilistic modeling will help the trustee solve for these unknown outcomes by assign a probability of achieving each outcome. It is best to err on the side of caution by preparing for the worst-case scenario but hoping for the best-case scenario. That is why the trustee should work with a professional who is aware of the most up to date tools in the industry.

6. Decision Framework:

The third D is for *Decision Framework*. The depletion analysis gives the trustee an opportunity to perform a financial analysis to determine the best outcome for the beneficiary in a risk-free environment. Multiple independent scenarios can be run to determine the best outcome for beneficiary. It is important to develop a decision framework for which to make major decisions about the beneficiary that is backed up by quantitative and qualitative metrics. Institutions do a great job of developing decision frameworks through a set of pre-determined rules and regulations. Think of how corporations use a board resolution. A board resolution is a way of documenting a decision made by a Corporation's Board of Directors on behalf of the Corporation. A resolution is an action taken by the board of directors which applies to a single act. Major decisions in corporations are formally voted on, approved and documented. Corporations typically require resolutions for any actions with major financial implications, changes in procedures or changes in authority. Resolutions are added to the corporate and become a permanent part of the corporate record. Think of the decision framework as a tool to help develop the board resolution or Investment Policy Statement (IPS), a sample of which is included in this book at **Appendix P.**

The outcome of the decision framework is used to create the Investment Policy Statement. The Investment Policy Statement is similar to a Board Resolution and should be used to document the decision the advisor and the trustee agree on to care for the beneficiary. The first part of the statement includes the beneficiary's broad investing goals and objectives. The next part discusses the path that the investment professional, in collaboration with the trustee, follow to reach a set of goals.

The decision framework also helps show a court or Trust Advisory Committee that the trustee is acting in a prudent manner by testing multiple outcomes to determine the best choice for the beneficiary. Like it or not, the United States is a litigious country and the trustee must protect themselves from people who question their decisions. If a trustee can show a history of using information provided by third party professionals to help the trustee make big decisions throughout the life of the beneficiary, then it should satisfy the trustee's "duty of care."

This is not a tool that should only be used to create the initial plan. It is a tool that can be used when there is a material change in the life of the beneficiary. There are many reasons that would warrant developing a new depletion analysis. For example, if the parents of the beneficiary die or become incapacitated, or if the beneficiary needs to move, or if the cost of care for the beneficiary changes would all warrant creating a new depletion analysis. When the next big change happens, because it will, simply follow the same protocol to ensure the decision is backed up by sound reasoning and a documented process.

7. Delegate Investment Management:

The fourth D is for *Delegating Investment Management*. It is recommended to delegate investment management to the investment professional. The trustee has a duty to prudently invest the assets on behalf of the beneficiary and to periodically monitor the performance of the investment professional. Simply delegating investment management alone will not insulate the trustee from liability. The trustee is obligated to monitor the activities of the investment professional at least annually. However, it is recommended for the trustee to meet with their investment professional more than once a year. Delegating investment management to a financial professional will do three things for the trustee.

First, delegating investment management will place the financial advisor into a fiduciary standard of care. The fiduciary higher standard of care says that investment professionals must place the needs of the client over their own needs. It is particularly important to understand the difference when working with brokerage firms, like Merrill Lynch, Morgan Stanley, Wells Fargo or UBS. Brokerage firm investment professionals are held to the lower suitability standard of care which says that investment professionals' recommendation must be suitable for the clients' needs. The Department of Labor created a Fiduciary Rule for all investment professionals including brokerage firms to be held to the fiduciary standard. It was supposed to be phased in April 10, 2017 but was overturned by the Fifth Circuit Court of Appeals. However, according to language from the Department of Labor Secretary, Alexander Acosta, the DOL is working with the SEC resurrect the fiduciary rule. It is important to note that investment professionals at brokerage firms have a much more rigorous compliance oversight since the 2008 Great Recession and the initiation of the original DOL Fiduciary Rule.

Second, delegating investment management to an agent will provide the trustee with additional protection from the Uniform Prudent Investment Advisor Act (UPIA). The Uniform Prudent Investor Act (UPIA) is a uniform statute that sets out guidelines for trustees to follow when investing trust assets. It is an update to the previous prudent man standards intended to reflect the changes that have occurred in investment practice since the late 1960s. Specifically, the Uniform Prudent Investor Act reflects a modern portfolio theory (MPT) and total return approach to the exercise of fiduciary investment discretion. The UPIA says the trustee is not liable to the beneficiary of any wrongdoing because the trustee delegated investment management to a professional. By delegating investment management, the trustee will be protected from decisions by the investment professional on the investments in the portfolio. This will reduce the liability on the trustee because the trustee is delegating their investment decision to an investment professional acting as an agent for the trustee.

Third, it gives the investment professional the ability to make trades in your portfolio without contacting the trustee. This could alarm some trustees, but keep in mind the advisor will be getting paid a fee for his or her service so the trustee does not have to worry about churning because the advisor will not be getting paid a commission on each trade. Rather, the advisor will be getting paid a fee for service. An additional benefit to the trustee is time saving which leads to cost savings for the beneficiary. The investment professional does not have to get in touch with the trustee for each trade. The more conversations the financial professional and the trustee have, the more charges to the beneficiary. This will allow the investment professional to execute trades more quickly without having to contact the trustee which will lead to cost savings for the beneficiary. Some trustees may be alarmed at giving discretion because they think the advisor can change the entire portfolio. The advisor can change the stocks and bonds within the portfolio, but they cannot change the risk profile of the portfolio. The advisor can buy and sell stocks and bonds within the portfolio, but they cannot change the risk profile from a conservative allocation to an aggressive asset allocation or vice versa. Therefore, it is recommended that trustees delegate investment management to their investment professional so that they are better protected in case of litigation.

8. Document, Document, Document:

The fifth D is for *Documenting*. Trustees have a duty to monitor, that is, the trustees continued responsibility for oversight of the suitability of investments already made as well as the trustee's decisions respecting new investments. Many trustees believe they are protected from liability when they delegate investment management to an agent, but they are not fully protected unless they monitor the choices and investments of that agent. They must periodically review the choices and the performance of the account with the agent. The trustee must document the discussions they have with the agent and the agent must document the discussions they have with the trustee. It is especially important to include any material changes to the beneficiary that would impact the current investment policy.

It is recommended for the trustee to view themselves as a board of directors overseeing an institution when they administer a trust. A Board of Directors has a fiduciary duty to the corporation and shareholders much like a trustee has a fiduciary duty to the trust and its beneficiary. It is best to document the decisions of the trustee and their agents with regard to the trust. The notes should be similar to meeting minutes from a board of directors. The trustee should prepare their notes as if they are going to be read on the front page of the Wall Street Journal. The notes should be worded in a clear and concise manner to accurately convey the meaning of the action taken. The words should contain enough detail to make them useful if they are ever needed for reference or used as evidence that an action was taken.

While it is not necessary (nor recommended) to record everything that was said at the meeting, there are some things that should always be recorded such as the date, time and location of the meeting. The meeting notes should include who attended and whether it was a special meeting or regular meeting. The meeting notes should also include what was discussed, such as the advice and guidance from the professionals involved, whether that guidance was followed and what actions were taken by the trustee. The notes should include key points from the discussion and how they plan to move forward.

If there is a material change, the trustee would repeat the steps of the Five D's starting at step two with the depletion analysis. An example of a material change might be whether to move a beneficiary from their home into a facility or keep the beneficiary in their home with extra care. The trustee would start by working through the depletion analysis, defining the decision framework and developing the plan of action. The trustee would document this with notes similar to a board resolution and have the investment professional update investment policy statement with the new recommendation. Once the plan is implemented, the trustee would document any additional communication with the beneficiary and set up a time to review the plan with investment professional every three months. The greatest thing about a process is that it is repeatable. It can help the trustee make the best decision for the beneficiary while protecting the trustee from litigation as long as they continue to follow this *thoroughly defined repeatable fiduciary process.*

CHAPTER 9 SUMMARY

✓ The trustee has a duty to invest trust property, preserve trust assets, and make the assets productive.

✓ Part of the trustee's responsibility when taking over a trust is to invest assets within a reasonable time and protect them, diversify assets, keep trust assets separate from personal assets, consider beneficiary's interests, keep beneficiary reasonably informed of trust actions, and avoid conflicts of interest, impropriety, and self-dealing.

✓ Review the trust document: it may set up specific requirements for managing and investing assets and may be relied upon by the trustee.

✓ The trustee should make sure all trust assets are insured typically with homeowners, renters, automobile, and general umbrella policy.

✓ The trustee should be prepared to examine surety bond requirements and to post bond.

✓ The trustee should not forget to purchase liability insurance if caregivers, drivers, or related activities are operating under the auspices of trust business.

✓ The trustee must also store trust personal property if beneficiary is moved from home.

✓ The trustee is not allowed to invest trust assets anyway he or she wants; rather, the type of investment standard will be determined by a variety of factors: whether trust is court supervised and whether the trust document specifies the investment standard (if silent, the trustee must follow the Prudent Investor Act).

✓ If the SNT is court supervised, the trustee has very limited investment options; however, the trustee may petition the court to increase options for good cause.

✓ If the SNT is not court supervised, then the trustee should check the SNT document to see if it sets forth the investment standards and follow those terms.

✓ If the SNT is not court supervised and if the SNT document is silent or states those investments shall be made under California law, then the trustee must follow the Prudent Investor Rule.

✓ The Prudent Investor Rule allows the trustee to invest as a prudent person would and looks at overall performance rather than reviewing individual investments.

✓ The trustee should develop an investment strategy that takes into account a variety of factors, including assets available, beneficiary's present and future needs, and the length of time assets may be needed.

✓ It is prudent (if possible) to limit trust expenditures during the establishment of the trust, because long-term investing will allow for better distributions later and preserve more capital, so the beneficiary does not outlive the trust assets.

✓ Trustees who have little or no investment or asset management experience should delegate these functions to a professional money advisor. Proper delegation is an acceptable way to manage trust assets.

✓ The trustee should control the selection process and interview several candidates before selecting a financial advisor.

✓ Appendix I has a list of questions that can be asked of a prospective financial advisor.

✓ The trustee should write prospective advisor's answers next to questions and keep responses as part of trust records.

✓ The trustee should do a background check of the financial advisor,

✓ The trustee should enter into a comprehensive agreement with financial advisor which clearly outlines the terms of the relationship.

✓ The trustee must still review financial advisor's ongoing performance or be held responsible if the advisor does something wrong.

✓ The trustee will best be protected if they follow the Five D's – Due Diligence; Depletion Analysis; Decision Framework; Delegation of Investment Management; and Document, Document, Document.

CHAPTER 10

Understanding and Using ABLE Accounts

By: Kevin Urbatsch, Michele Fuller, and Jessica Farinas

ABLE accounts are a special type of investment designed to allow persons with disabilities to control and grow money in a tax-free environment without jeopardizing their eligibility for public benefits like Supplemental Security Income ("SSI"), Medi-Cal, Section 8 ("HUD housing"), CalFresh (food stamps), and all other federal public benefit programs with a financial eligibility test.

ABLE accounts are a huge boon for persons with disabilities. Because of many public benefit resource limitations, persons with disabilities have historically been limited to less than $2,000 in resources or risk losing essential public benefits. The authors have been advising person with disabilities and their families on the advantages of using ABLE accounts along with advising special needs trust ("SNT") trustees on funding ABLE accounts to enhance the quality of life of SNT beneficiaries.

In order to understand when to implement an ABLE account strategy for an SNT beneficiary, it is important to understand ABLE account requirements and limitations. As described in more detail below, the main ABLE account limitations are:

- A person must have been disabled prior to age 26 to utilize the account;
- A person can only have one account that can only be funded with cash;
- The account can only be funded annually up to the annual gift exemption amount (in year 2020 - $15,000 in total, not per person);
- The account can grow up to $100,000 and not disqualify the SSI recipient or if person with a disability is only qualified to receive Medi-Cal, the

account can grow up to the State 529-Plan limit (in California $529,000) and not be disqualifying;

- The account disbursements must only be for "Qualified Disability Expenses" (or risk triggering a penalty); and
- In most state ABLE programs, on the death of the person with a disability any remaining funds in the account must be paid back to the State Medicaid program for any services paid since the opening of the account.

There are a host of benefits to ABLE accounts for persons with disabilities. If the person with a disability has capacity, he or she can control his or her own account and utilize it to save for bigger purchases like vehicles, education, and related items that were unattainable before ABLE was available. Moreover, for the special needs trustee there are multiple planning opportunities in using ABLE accounts including paying for a person's food or shelter from ABLE account so it does not reduce the monthly check from SSI or transferring funds into ABLE to allow persons with disabilities to manage their own money.

ABLE accounts are managed by the States and only States that have created a program have ABLE accounts that an eligible person can join. California's ABLE program opened on December 18, 2018 and is called CalABLE (https://calable.ca.gov). Californians interested in utilizing an ABLE account may use programs in other states if those states allow out-of-state residents to join, which nearly all of them do. In addition, California residents who already have an account opened in another state can have their out-of-state ABLE account balance transferred to the CalABLE program if they wish to do so. In order to advise persons with disabilities, it is important to know how to evaluate the different programs.

The best way to stay current on ABLE programs is to use the website for the ABLE National Resource Center at www.ABLEnrc.org. This website provides a wealth of information on the current status of legislation, states implementation of ABLE programs, and provides some tools on evaluating different programs but another comparison tool provides a more substantive evaluation and can be found at https://oakwealth.com/special-needs-resources.

WHAT IS AN ABLE ACCOUNT?

An ABLE account is an IRS tax-favored, public benefits safe-harbor allowing needs-based federal benefits for individuals with disabilities to continue or begin. It was part of a federal statute titled Achieving a Better Life Experience "ABLE" Act of 2014, enacted Dec. 19, 2014.

The legislation was designed to allow individuals with disabilities a way to save and accumulate money in a tax-favored manner without interfering with their needs-based public benefits like SSI or Medi-Cal.[236] ABLE protects all needs-based federal programs, including food stamps, Section 8, and other federal means-tested programs.[237]

DO ALL PERSONS WITH DISABILITIES QUALIFY TO USE AN ABLE ACCOUNT?

No. A person must have a disabling "condition that began prior to reaching age 26."[238] This does not mean that the person must be under age 26 to establish an ABLE account, but that the person had a disabling condition that existed prior to age 26.

> **Note:** There is a bill currently pending, the ABLE Age Adjustment Act (HR 4813 / S 2704, introduced into Senate as S.651, as of March 2019, referred to the Committee on Finance), if passed, would increase the age of onset of disability to 46, half way to full retirement age 66. Readers should check http://ablenrc.org/ to see if that age limit has changed.

The designated beneficiary can establish disability in one of two ways:

1. By showing he or she is currently eligible for Social Security Disability Insurance (SSDI) or SSI benefits, based on a disability that began before age 26 or

2. By certifying, or having a parent or guardian certify that the individual has a medically determinable impairment "which results in marked and severe

236 Sections 101(1) and (2) of the Act; 26 U.S.C. §529A.
237 ABLE Act, Section 103(a).
238 26 USC § 529A(b)(1)(B) and 26 CFR § 1.529A-1(b)(4).

functional limitations" that has lasted or is expected to last for 12 consecutive months, or is likely to result in death, with the disability or blindness occurring before age 26.[239]

"Disabled" means the person must either already be receiving Social Security benefits based on his or her disability or otherwise qualify as "disabled" by the Social Security Administration. This test is typically different if the person is an adult versus a child; however, the ABLE regulations[240] use the child definition regardless of age as defined here:

"Disability" for an individual under the age of 18 is defined as "a medically determinable physical or mental impairment or combination of impairments that causes marked and severe functional limitations, and that can be expected to cause death or that has lasted or can be expected to last for a continuous period of not less than 12 months."[241]

CAN PERSON WITH DISABILITY CONTROL HIS OR HER OWN ABLE ACCOUNT?

Yes. Unlike with SNTs, the designated beneficiary of an ABLE account can control his or her ABLE account. For example, the individual may use the account to purchase items at his or her own discretion like saving for a vehicle, trip, or pay tuition at school. Depending on the state program, access to the funds includes debit cards, setting up direct pay to service providers, and having ABLE funds direct deposited into another related bank account. In addition, a minor designated beneficiary may take control over the account upon reaching age 18.

This is one of the best reasons for an SNT trustee to fund an ABLE account for a beneficiary. If the beneficiary has capacity to manage his or her own financial affairs, providing them the ability to manage, save, and spend some of their own money is one way to greatly enhance the beneficiary's quality of life.

CalABLE has stated that it will offer such a debit card, though as of November 22, 2019 it has not yet been rolled out. "Extended Fact Sheet, "available at https://www.treasurer.ca.gov/able/resources/factsheets/factsheet-extensive-en-us.pdf. This

---

239 26 USC § 529A.

240 IRS Regs §1.529A-2(e)((1)(A) and defined in IRS Regs §1.529A-2(e)((2).

241 20 C.F.R. §416.906.

allows the individual to exercise financial independence without first asking permission from his or her trustee.

WHO CAN FUND AN ABLE?

Any "person" can contribute to an individual's ABLE account, including the person with a disability.[242] A "person" is defined to include a trust or estate.[243] The contribution to an ABLE account is also deemed a completed gift for gift tax purposes.[244]

There is no effect on public benefits of an SNT trustee funding a beneficiary's ABLE account. The SSA has stated:

> A third-party contribution is not income to the designated beneficiary. ... A transfer of funds from a trust, of which the designated beneficiary is the beneficiary and which is not considered a resource to him or her [an SNT], to the designated beneficiary's ABLE account generally will be considered a third party contribution for ABLE purposes because the contribution is made by a person or entity other than the designated beneficiary (namely, the trustee) and because the designated beneficiary does not legally own the trust.[245]

This means that as long as the SNT document does not preclude funding an ABLE account, an SNT trustee will have no issue in doing so. Use of an ABLE account can be a fantastic tool for an SNT trustee to allow for ease of purchase of goods and services for the beneficiary. It is a great place to place assets which are problematic, like holiday and birthday gifts, for a beneficiary on SSI.

---

242   26 USC § 529A(b)(1)(A); 26 CFR § 1.529A-2(a)(4).

243   26 USC § 7701(a)(1) (defines ⊠person⊠ to include an individual, trust, estate, partnership, or corporation); POMS SI 01330.740.B.2; CMS SMD #7-002 (note 1), p. 4.

244   26 CFR § 1.529A-3(b)(2); 26 CFR § 1.529A-4(a)(1).

245   POMS SI 01130.740(C)(1)(b).

HOW MANY ABLE ACCOUNTS CAN A PERSON WITH A DISABILITY HAVE?

One. A designated beneficiary is permitted to have only one ABLE account.[246] If more than one account is opened, the subsequent account is countable by the public benefit agency and provides no tax benefit to the person with a disability.[247] However, if all contributed amounts are returned in a timely fashion, then it is treated as if the account had never been opened.[248]

DO ABLE ACCOUNTS NEED TO BE ESTABLISHED IN STATE OF RESIDENCE?

No. The original federal ABLE law required individuals to open ABLE accounts in their home state. However, the US Congress amended ABLE and eliminated this state residency requirement. Therefore, an individual will be able to open an ABLE account in any State.

The following website, http://ablenrc.org, has a current list of states which sponsor ABLE accounts. Some states restrict access to residents. Be aware that most states' provision for what happens upon the death of the beneficiary is that remaining assets are used to reimburse the state's Medicaid agency up to the amount of benefits paid on behalf of a beneficiary. A small number of states, including California, Illinois, and Oregon, have opted to have any remaining funds at the time of death of the beneficiary be paid to the person's estate, and not reimburse the state. Be a good consumer and compare the state programs and requirements carefully, including how the funds are invested, ease of use by the beneficiary, costs, etc.

HOW MUCH CAN BE FUNDED INTO AN ABLE ACCOUNT?

An ABLE account is only allowed to be funded with a single annual federal gift tax exclusion amount (as set forth in IRC § 2504(b)), which is currently $15,000.[249] This annual limitation applies to the total annual amount contributed to the account, on an aggregate basis. As a result, caution should be taken when there are multiple contributors to the accounts.

---

246   26 USC § 529A(b)(1)(B).
247   26 USC § 529A(c)(4).
248   26 CFR § 1.529A-2(c)(2)(ii).
249   26 USC § 529A(b)(2)(B); 26 CFR § 1.529A-2(g)(2).

The funding of the account does not need to occur all at once. An account contributor may fund it any way they wish as long as total contributions do not exceed the annual gift tax exemption amount. For example, an ABLE account could be funded monthly up to $1,250 per month ($15,000 over 12 months). This way, an account contributor, like an SNT trustee may fund the account to determine if the beneficiary is able to manage the funds and resist predators.

If a contributor funds an amount with more than the federal gift tax exclusion, the program is to return the excess amounts to the contributor, including any income associated with it, on a last-in, first-out basis.[250] The due date to return the funds is the time when the designated beneficiary's tax return, for the year in which the contributions are made, is due. Id. A 6-percent excise tax is applied to excess contributions if not returned.[251]

Under the 2018 Tax Cut and Jobs Act, an ABLE account can now be funded with a rollover from the funds in the same person's 529 Plan into an ABLE account.[252] This rollover counts towards the $15,000 funding limit so care should be made not to over fund the ABLE account. In addition, the new law allows an employed ABLE beneficiary to contribute to their ABLE account above the annual maximum limit (currently $15,000), up to the Federal Poverty Limit for a one-person household (in 2019 is $12,140) for a maximum annual contribution of $27,140.[253] Finally, the new tax law allows ABLE account owners who contribute to their own account, may be eligible to take advantage of the Retirement Savings Contributions Tax Credit that provides a special tax break to low- and moderate-income taxpayers who are saving for retirement.[254]

HOW BIG CAN AN ABLE ACCOUNT BE BEFORE JEOPARDIZING PUBLIC BENEFIT ELIGIBILITY?

An ABLE account benefits the designated beneficiary by allowing savings over the resource requirements of the federal public benefit programs, typically no more

---

250   26 CFR § 1.529A-2(g)(4).

251   26 USC § 4973(a)(6). 26 USC § 529A-3(e).

252   Pub. L. No. 115-97, Sec 11025.

253   Pub. L. No. 115-97, Sec 11024(a).

254   Pub. L. No. 115-97, Sec 11024(b).

than $2,000. However, there are limits on how large an ABLE account can grow. The limits are contingent on which needs-based public benefits the designated beneficiary is receiving.

If the designated beneficiary receives SSI, the ABLE account may grow up to $100,000 and will not be counted as a resource for SSI eligibility.[255] If the account grows to over $100,000, the designated beneficiary's SSI benefits are not terminated. Rather, the SSI benefits are suspended until the ABLE account balance drops below $100,000, at which point the SSI benefits resume.[256]

> **SSA's Example:** Paul is the designated beneficiary of an ABLE account with a balance as of the first of the month of $101,000. Paul's only other countable resource is a checking account with a balance of $1,500. Paul's countable resources are $2,500 and therefore exceed the SSI resource limit. However, since Paul's ABLE account balance is causing him to exceed the resource limit (*i.e.*, his countable resources other than the ABLE account are less than $2,000), Paul's SSI eligibility is suspended and his cash benefits stop, but he retains eligibility for Medicaid.

If a person receives SSI, he or she automatically receives Medi-Cal under the categorically eligible program. A suspension of SSI benefits due to too much money in an ABLE account does not mean an immediate loss of Medi-Cal benefits.[257] Medi-Cal eligibility and benefits will continue uninterrupted.

If a person is qualified for Medi-Cal under any Medi-Cal program other than SSI categorical eligibility, a California designated beneficiary's ABLE account can have up to $529,000 without jeopardizing Medi-Cal eligibility. This is because under the ABLE Act, if the designated beneficiary is receiving only Medi-Cal, the ABLE account may grow up to the State's limit under its "Qualified State Tuition Program," *i.e.*, 529 Plan.[258] In California, the 529 Plan limit is currently $529,000. See, www.scholarshare529.com .

---

255 POMS SI 01130.740.C.3.
256 POMS SI 01130.740.D.1.a.
257 Section 103(b)(2), ABLE Act of 2014; POMS SI 01130.740.D.1.a.
258 26 CFR § 1.529A-2(g)(3).

HOW IS AN ABLE ACCOUNT TAXED?

Income earned inside an ABLE account grows income tax free.[259] Distributions from ABLE accounts, that are for "Qualified Disability Expenses" (QDE) are also not taxed.[260] QDE's are defined in the next question.

There is a penalty if an ABLE account recipient makes a distribution for non-QDEs. Distributions for non-QDEs will be includible as gross income and subject to a 10% penalty.[261] There are a few exceptions to incurring the penalty.

- ① It does not apply to any distribution made from the ABLE account on or after the death of the designated beneficiary to the estate of the designated beneficiary, to an heir or legatee of the designated beneficiary, or to a creditor.[262]

- ② It also will not apply if the ABLE account refunds exceed contributions that were made into the account.[263]

The SSA in its POMS clarified how distributions would be treated for SSI. If a disbursement is made for a non-housing QDE and retained by the recipient after the month of disbursement, the amount will remain exempt so long as the QDE purchase is made later.[264] SSA looks to the intent behind the disbursement. If that intent changes, the risk is that the disbursement will become a countable resource. As stated in the POMS SI 01130.740(D)(3)(c):

> In June, Jennifer takes a $7,000 distribution from her ABLE account to pay an educational expense that is a QDE. Her educational expense is due in September. In August, Jennifer gets a job offer and decides not to return to school. The $7,000 becomes a countable resource in September because she no longer intends

---

259 26 USC § 529A(a).
260 26 USC § 529A(c)(1)(B); 26 CFR § 1-529A-3(a).
261 26 USC section 529A(c)(3)(A); 26 CFR § 1-529A-3(a), (d)(1).
262 26 CFR § 1-529A-3(d)(2)(i).
263 26 CFR § 1-529A-3(d)(2)(ii).
264 POMS SI 01130.740(C)(5).

to use it for an educational expense that is a QDE, unless Jennifer re-designates it for another QDE or returns the funds to her ABLE account prior to September.

The SNT trustee should understand how these rules work because if a distribution is made with the intent to avoid penalties and the beneficiary ends up being hit with a public benefit reduction or increased taxes, it may be a breach of fiduciary duty by the trustee.

WHAT ARE "QUALIFIED DISABILITY EXPENSES"?

As noted above, distributions from ABLE accounts, that are for "Qualified Disability Expenses" (QDE) are not taxed.[265] The ABLE Act defines QDEs as "expenses related to the eligible individual's blindness or disability which are made for the benefit of an eligible individual who is the designated beneficiary."[266] It then lists a range of categories of potential uses for funds set aside in ABLE accounts, including the following:

Types of QDEs

> Education, housing, transportation, employment training and support, assistive technology and personal support services, health, prevention and wellness, financial management and administrative services, legal fees, expenses for oversight and monitoring, funeral and burial expenses, and other expenses, which are approved by the Secretary under regulations and consistent with the purposes of this section.[267]

The IRS has stated that QDEs should be "broadly construed to permit. . . basic living expenses and should not be limited to expenses for which there is a medical necessity or which provide no benefits to others. . . ." and should include any benefit related to the designated beneficiary "in maintaining or improving his or her health, independence, or quality of life."[268] As an example, the regulations specify

---

265 26 USC § 529A(c)(1)(B); 26 CFR § 1-529A-3(a).
266 26 USC § 529A(e)(5).
267 Id.
268 26 CFR § 1.529A-2(h)(1).

that a smart phone could qualify as a covered expense, provided that it serves as "effective and safe communication or navigation aid for a child with autism."[269] "Qualified Disability Expenses" are expenses related to the blindness or disability of the beneficiary and that are for the benefit of the beneficiary.[270] "Qualified Disability Expenses" should "be broadly construed to permit inclusion of basic living expenses" and "should not be limited to expenses for items for which there is a medical necessity or which provide no benefits to others in addition to the benefit to the eligible individual."

> IRS Example. B, an individual, has a medically determined mental impairment that causes marked and severe limitations on her ability to navigate and communicate. A smart phone would enable B to navigate and communicate more safely and effectively, thereby helping her to maintain her independence and to improve her quality of life. Therefore, the expense of buying, using, and maintaining a smart phone that is used by B would be considered a qualified disability expense.[271]

IS THERE A BENEFIT FOR PAYING FOOD AND SHELTER EXPENSES FROM AN ABLE ACCOUNT RATHER THAN AN SNT?

Yes. The ABLE Act specifically states that distributions for housing expenses "shall not be so disregarded."[272] The SSA clarified in its POMS that ABLE account housing expenses are the same as "shelter" expenses under the Social Security rules.[273]

This could have been a big issue for SSI recipients who used ABLE accounts to pay for housing expenses because the Social Security Administration (SSA) treats certain types of shelter expenses as a type of "income" called "in-kind support and maintenance" (ISM) that triggers a penalty. As described in Chapter 3, the SSA treats the following shelter expenses as ISM if someone else (including an SNT trustee) pays

---

269   26 CFR § 1.529A-2(h)(2).

270   IRC §529A(3)(5)

271   IRS Regs §1.529A-1(h)(2).

272   Section 103(a)(1), ABLE Act of 2014.

273   POMS SI 01130.740(B)(8).

for it: mortgages, real estate taxes, rent, heating fuel, gas, electricity, water, sewer, or garbage removal.[274] The penalty for paying for shelter items is a reduction in the SSI recipient's monthly check.[275] The reduction in benefits is determined by either the one-third-reduction rule (VTR)[276] or the presumed maximum value (PMV)[277] depending on the SSI recipient's living situation. In general, the penalty for someone else paying for ISM is a reduction (in year 2020) in the monthly SSI check of either $261 if VTR or $281 if PMV depending on which reduction methodology is used.[278]

The good news for SSI recipients is that the SSA expressly exempted distributions from ABLE accounts as being treated as ISM.[279] This means that an ABLE account can be used to pay shelter items and keep the extra $261 or $281 per month. It must be remembered that a disbursement made for a housing QDE is exempt only in the month made, but a countable resource if retained beyond the month of disbursement, even if the housing expense is later made.[280] Thus, there is no penalty when making housing disbursements from ABLE accounts as long as payment is made in the same month as withdrawal.

Retention of distributions over multiple months can cause multiple SSI penalties. An example is set forth in the article Nancy S. Germany, Disability, Poverty and the Policy Behind the ABLE Act, NAELA Journal, Volume 14, Issue 2 (Fall 2018):

> If....the ABLE account distributes $2,000 to pay for rent and utilities in March, and the SSI recipient uses $1,000 to pay rent and utilities in April, the entire $2,000 will be counted as the SSI recipient's resource for the month of April (thus disqualifying the SSI recipient from April's SSI check). If the SSI recipient uses the remaining $1,000 to pay for May's rent and utilities, the $1,000 will be counted as the SSI recipient's resources for May and if the person's other countable resources add up to more than $2,000,

---

274 20 CFR § 416.1133(c); POMS SI 00835.465(D)(1).
275 20 CFR § 416.1102.
276 20 CFR § 416.1131(a)
277 20 CFR § 416.1140(a)(1)
278 POMS SI 00835.901.K.
279 POMS SI 01130.740(C)(4).
280 POMS SI 001130.740(D)(2).

he or she will lose May's SSI check. The lesson here is that if the SSI recipient had used the entire $2,000 in the month of March, there would have been no loss of SSI. It is important that disbursements from an ABLE account for housing expenses be made for those housing expenses in the same calendar month.

WHAT HAPPENS TO FUNDS IN AN ABLE ACCOUNT ON DEATH OF PERSON WITH A DISABILITY?

The ABLE Act requires that when the designated beneficiary dies any assets remaining in his or her ABLE account shall be subject to "pay back" from any state Medicaid plan, up to the value of Medicaid services provided to the beneficiary, from the time the account was opened to the filing of a claim by the State.[281] The State is considered a creditor of the ABLE account and not a beneficiary.[282]

The payback amount is calculated after:[283]

- all outstanding qualified disability expenses (QDE) are paid,
- after any funeral and burial expenses for the designated beneficiary are paid, and
- any Medicaid premiums paid by the beneficiary are subtracted.[284]

Several States have included in their ABLE enacting statute, that it will not seek payback from an ABLE account on the death of a designated beneficiary. California's CalABLE program is one of those States.[285]

WHY SHOULD AN SNT TRUSTEE CONSIDER FUNDING AN ABLE ACCOUNT?

There are several benefits to allowing an individual with a disability to maintain an ABLE account. The most profound benefit for many SNT beneficiaries is to provide the beneficiary with the self-determination of managing his or her own money. The

---

281   26 USC § 529A(f).

282   *Id.*

283   26 CFR § 1.529A-2(p); 26 CFR § 1.529A-3(b)(4).

284   IRS Regs §1.529A-2(p).

285   See, Welfare and Institutions Code § 4885(b).

SNT beneficiary will be able to purchase items without having to ask permission from an SNT trustee. This can be particularly galling for SNT beneficiaries who have complete capacity to manage their own affairs.

An additional benefit is the payment of food or shelter expenses that will not be treated as ISM. This means that the SNT beneficiary who is an SSI recipient will receive all housing payments made from the ABLE account without an SSI reduction. The value of avoiding the ISM deduction is equivalent to $3,000 more in tax-free payments from the SSA annually.

WHAT CONCERNS SHOULD AN SNT TRUSTEE IN DETERMINING WHETHER TO MAKE A DISTRIBUTION TO FUND AN ABLE ACCOUNT?

There are possible issues with the funding of an ABLE account for the benefit of a person with a disability. The main concern is whether the person with a disability (or their legal guardian) can properly manage the account. This may be of a primary concern when the person with a disability lacks capacity or has diminished capacity. It may also be a concern if the person has never had to manage an account before. If this is the case, then proper education before funding the account may be prudent. A concern for an individual with a disability who has not managed funds before is the possibility of being subject to fraud, undue influence or exploitation. There are people who specialize in finding such persons and taking advantage of them.

The ongoing requirements that distributions must be made for "Qualified Disability Expenses" means that if the person with a disability is not maintaining perfect records of how disbursements are being made, it may subject the account to excessive tax penalties and loss of SSI or Medi-Cal.

If the SNT being administered is a third-party SNT, the funding of an ABLE account will subject any unused funds at the time of the beneficiary's death to a Medicaid payback (in States other than California) that would not otherwise occur if the funds stayed in the third-party SNT. So, a prudent trustee of this type of SNT should be careful not to over-fund an ABLE.

A CHART COMPARING ABLE ACCOUNTS WITH DIFFERENT TYPES OF SNT?

Below is a chart that highlights the difference between ABLE and SNTs.

Issue	(d)(4)(A) SNT	Pooled SNT	Third-Party SNT	ABLE Account
Purpose of Establishment	Enhances quality of life of person with a disability by paying for goods and services without the loss of SSI or Medicaid	Enhances quality of life of person with a disability by paying for goods and services without the loss of SSI or Medicaid	Enhances quality of life of person with a disability by paying for goods and services without the loss of SSI or Medicaid	Allows individuals with disabilities to have a cash account to save money and pay for certain expenses without loss of SSI or Medicaid or any other federal benefit program
Primary Beneficiary	Person with a disability	Person with a disability	Person with a disability, but can be others	Person with a disability
Settlor/Maker	Person with a disability, his or her parent, grandparent, legal guardian or the court	Person with a disability, his or her parent, grandparent, legal guardian or the court	Any person or entity except the person with a disability	Person with a disability or their agents, guardians, SNT trustees, and maybe others
Trustee/ Owner	Any individual or professional but not person with a disability	A non-profit agency but may outsource trusteeship to a professional	Any individual or professional but not the person with a disability	Any individual, including person with a disability
Number of Trusts/ Accounts Allowed to have	Unlimited	Unlimited	Unlimited	One
Source of Funding	Person with a disability's assets	Person with a disability's assets	Assets of anyone but the person with a disability	Assets of anyone

Issue	(d)(4)(A) SNT	Pooled SNT	Third-Party SNT	ABLE Account
Purpose of Establishment	Enhances quality of life of person with a disability by paying for goods and services without the loss of SSI or Medicaid	Enhances quality of life of person with a disability by paying for goods and services without the loss of SSI or Medicaid	Enhances quality of life of person with a disability by paying for goods and services without the loss of SSI or Medicaid	Allows individuals with disabilities to have a cash account to save money and pay for certain expenses without loss of SSI or Medicaid or any other federal benefit program
Amount Allowed to Be Funded into Trust/Account	Unlimited, but no additional funding after age 65	Unlimited, but may incur SSI/Medicaid penalty if funded after age 65	Unlimited	Limited to annual gift tax exemption from all sources (currently $15,000 per year) plus wages up to $12,140
Amount Trust/Account is allowed to hold	Unlimited, but no additional funding after age 65	Unlimited, but may incur penalty if funded after age 65	Unlimited	Currently $100,000 for SSI recipients and up to state's 529-plan amount currently $560,000
Use of Funds	Must be for "sole benefit" of person with a disability and certain disbursements may reduce or eliminate SSI or Medicaid eligibility	Must be for "sole benefit" of person with a disability and certain disbursements may reduce or eliminate SSI or Medicaid eligibility	No limitation, except for certain disbursements may reduce or eliminate SSI or Medicaid eligibility	Only "qualified disability expenses" as defined by the IRS code and regulations, otherwise tax penalty
Effect of Paying for Food or Shelter	Implementation of SSI ISM penalty	Implementation of SSI ISM penalty	Implementation of SSI ISM penalty	Implementation of SSI ISM penalty (but not for food or shelter items)

Issue	(d)(4)(A) SNT	Pooled SNT	Third-Party SNT	ABLE Account
Purpose of Establishment	Enhances quality of life of person with a disability by paying for goods and services without the loss of SSI or Medicaid	Enhances quality of life of person with a disability by paying for goods and services without the loss of SSI or Medicaid	Enhances quality of life of person with a disability by paying for goods and services without the loss of SSI or Medicaid	Allows individuals with disabilities to have a cash account to save money and pay for certain expenses without loss of SSI or Medicaid or any other federal benefit program
Taxation of funds	Taxed as a grantor trust at person with a disability's tax rate	Taxed as a grantor trust at person with a disability's tax rate	Taxed as a non-grantor trust except to the extent funds are used on behalf of the beneficiary	No income tax on growth but gross income plus a 10% penalty for non-qualified distributions
Receiver of assets from trust/account on death of person with a disability	Medi-Cal first, then can go to heirs or whomever is named in document	Medi-Cal first, then can go to heirs or whomever is named in document	Heirs or whomever is named in document	Medi-Cal first, (except when using CalABLE account) then can go to heirs

CHAPTER 10 SUMMARY

✓ ABLE accounts allow people with disabilities to save and control money in excess of the SSI resource limitations of $2,000

✓ ABLE accounts can only be used by people who were disabled prior to age 26 under Social Security Administration's definition of disability for a minor

✓ ABLE accounts are joined by opening an account in an active State program

✓ ABLE accounts are to be controlled by the person with a disability, unless that person is unable to manage his or her own financial affairs

✓ ABLE accounts can be funded by any person, including an SNT trustee

✓ A person can only have one ABLE account

✓ A person can join an ABLE account in any State as long as that State accepts out-of-state residents

✓ There are tools available to review the different ABLE programs, there are differences in investment opportunities, usage of debit cards, and ease of use

✓ An ABLE account can only be funded with the annual gift tax exemption amount, currently $15,000 a year in total from all sources, except of a person with a disability who works who is allowed to fund ABLE with earnings of an amount based on the Federal Poverty Limit currently $12,140

✓ An ABLE account can grow up to $100,000 before SSI is suspended, if person is not qualified to receive SSI, then account can grow up to the State's 529 plan limit, in California $560,000, before it affects Medi-Cal eligibility

✓ The earnings inside an ABLE account grow income tax free and when distributions are made for Qualified Disability Expenses (QDE) they are distributed income tax free, if distributed for non-QDE, then there is a 10-percent penalty on top of the tax assessed

✓ QDE's are to be broadly construed to permit basic living expenses and should not be limited to expenses for which there is a medical necessity or which provide no benefits to others and specifically includes: Education, housing, transportation, employment training and support, assistive technology and personal support services, health, prevention and wellness, financial management and administrative services, legal fees, expenses for oversight and monitoring, funeral and burial expenses

✓ A benefit of using an ABLE account to pay for person with a disability's food or shelter items is that it does not trigger the In Kind Support and Maintenance (ISM) penalty for SSI eligibility, saving up to $3,372 a year for persons with disabilities

✓ On the death of person with a disability, the assets inside an ABLE account are subject to pay back to the State Medi-Cal office, although California's DHCS has stated it will not enforce this rule based on a California law that exempts CalABLE from recovery

✓ The benefits for an SNT trustee of funding an ABLE account is to take advantage of the fact that the ISM penalty for paying for food and shelter is not charged against an ABLE account like it is with an SNT, allows for a person with a disability to manage and save the money in an ABLE account and provides self-determination, and makes it easier for SNT trustee to provide flexibility for person with a disability to spend his or her own money

✓ The concerns an SNT trustee may have in funding an ABLE account is whether person with a disability may be subject to undue influence, not maintain proper records, or will spend money so frivolously that the trustee may be held responsible for the person with a disability's actions

✓ A chart comparing the different types of SNTs with an ABLE account is included at end of chapter

CHAPTER 11

Effect of SNT Disbursements on Public Benefits

The primary purpose of an SNT is to enhance the quality of life of an SNT beneficiary. The best way to do this is to pay for goods and services that improves the beneficiary's life better without jeopardizing the beneficiary's public benefits eligibility. However, the trustee should also understand what the exact services public benefits provide for the beneficiary and be able to determine whether it is better for the beneficiary to pay for goods or services even if there is a reduction or even elimination of the beneficiary's public benefits.

This chapter provides important guidelines on how certain SNT distributions will affect public benefits. Because some disbursements are so critical to the beneficiary's life, there are separate chapters devoted to some of the most common disbursements such as Chapter 12 on paying for beneficiary's food, clothing, and shelter, Chapter 13 on buying and managing a beneficiary's home, Chapter 14 on buying and managing beneficiary's transportation needs, and Chapter 15 on evaluating and paying for beneficiary's caregivers.

Once the decision has been made to make a disbursement, the next step will be to make the disbursement in the best way possible. This is a critical decision because not only does the type of disbursement affect public benefits eligibility, but the way a disbursement is made can also affect public benefit eligibility. Chapter 16 describes the different ways a trustee can make a disbursement that will not only reduce the impact on the beneficiary's public benefit eligibility but also makes it easier to provide the goods and services to the beneficiary in an efficient manner. For example, as described in that chapter, the trustee should consider utilizing a True Link card, paying the beneficiary's credit card, paying for good or service directly, or reimbursing a third party who purchased the good or service for beneficiary.

> **Critical Pointer:** A common misconception of SNTs is that the trust can only pay for a small number of items and services for the person with a disability. This is untrue. The SNT is designed to enhance the quality of life of the person with a disability. Thus, it can pay for any item or service that will do so. This includes everything on the planet that humans have come up with to make our lives easier or better. Given the large number of items and services out there, the SNT is really a wonderful tool that greatly improves the overall quality of life of a person with disabilities.

The universe of available SNT distributions is extraordinarily large and this chapter will not be able to cover every possible scenario. In order to assist the trustee, there are a host of questions and answers in this chapter on the effect of different types of disbursements will have on beneficiary's public benefits. In addition, attached as Appendix H is a decision-making tree that will provide a step-by-step analysis to determine whether a disbursement will interfere with public benefits. Moreover, attached as Appendix O, is a list of SNT permissible distributions of items and services that will not interfere with SSI or Medi-Cal—the so-called No-Brainer List.

However, the trustee should always remember that just because a disbursement will not interfere with public benefits does not mean the trustee can simply make it. The trustee should remember to carefully review the terms of the trust and the stated intent of the SNT document (and possibly a memorandum of intent) because it may include other advice or prohibitions that would limit what a trustee can pay. It is always important to remember that the trustee must act in the beneficiary's best interests and depending on the terms of the document and could mean considering not only the immediate needs of the beneficiary but his or her future needs. See Chapter 4 for a review of the general fiduciary rules a trustee must consider on trust disbursements.

DO DISTRIBUTIONS FROM SNT AFFECT A BENEFICIARY'S ELIGIBILITY FOR PUBLIC BENEFITS?

It depends on what is being purchased and what public benefits the beneficiary is receiving.

- If the beneficiary is receiving needs-based benefits like SSI, Medi-Cal, IHSS, or Section 8 (housing benefits), certain SNT disbursements may affect eligibility in a variety of ways depending on the type of public benefits the beneficiary receives, what is purchased, and how it is purchased.

- If the beneficiary is receiving only entitlement benefits like SSDI, CDB, Medicare, or Regional Center Services, SNT disbursements will likely have no effect on benefits.

It is critical that the trustee know what benefits the beneficiary is receiving prior to making any disbursements. If the trustee fails to determine this essential information, he or she will not be able to properly administer an SNT.

> **Note:** It is common that beneficiaries will not know which public benefits they receive. The programs are run by the same government agencies and the services appear identical. Do not trust what the beneficiary says about the benefits they receive; the trustee should find out themselves. If the trustee is not sure how to do this, he or she should hire an attorney or find a public benefits consultant. Check with Chapter 20 to find a professional to help.

The authors have had SNT trustee refuse to make perfectly acceptable disbursements because they thought it would jeopardize the beneficiary's public benefits, only to find out the beneficiary was eligible for SSDI benefits that would not be impacted by any type of SNT disbursement. This error meant that an SNT beneficiary was not provided services to enhance his quality of life and the trustee to breach his fiduciary duty. In other cases, the beneficiary was receiving SSDI benefits, but also Medi-Cal. Because the trustee believed that disbursements would not impact SSDI benefits, his disbursements causes the beneficiary to trigger a share-of-cost for his Medi-Cal benefits, meaning the beneficiary had to pay money to obtain healthcare that he would not have had to do if the SNT had been properly administered. Again, the trustee did not understand what public benefits the beneficiary was receiving, so failed in its duty to properly manage the trust.

This book provides a laundry list of disbursements that have no impact on benefits, distributions that will impact benefits (and how), and techniques in how a trustee can determine when public benefits will be impacted. Once a trustee understands how disbursement may affect (or not affect) the beneficiary's eligibility for public benefits, disbursements can be made that will enhance the beneficiary's quality of life.

WHAT DOES "SOLE BENEFIT" MEAN FOR FIRST-PARTY SNT DISTRIBUTIONS AND HOW DOES IT AFFECT DISBURSEMENTS?

Every disbursement from a first-party SNT must be for the beneficiary's "sole benefit." If it is not, then the SNT administration may cause a disqualification of the beneficiary's SSI and Medi-Cal benefits.

Before we discuss this important concept, the SNT trustee must know what type of SNT they are administering. In short, a first-party SNT is one that was created using the beneficiary's own assets. A third-party SNT is one that was created using anyone else on the planet's assets (other than SNT beneficiary's). For more information on the distinction between first- and third-party SNTs, see Chapter 19.

> **Note:** The "sole benefit" rule does not typically apply to third-party SNTs. However, some third-party SNTs may also include this limitation, either by design or by ignorance. If a third-party SNT includes a "sole benefit" limitation, the SNT trustee must honor it.

One of the legal requirements for a qualifying first party SNT is that it be for the "sole benefit" of the beneficiary.[286] This phrase has been historically difficult to understand due to changing or differing attitudes on what it meant. However, in 2018,

---

286 POMS SI 01120.201(F)(1)-(4).

the SSA modified its interpretation of the "sole benefit" standard to make it easier to understand. It used to be that distributions for "sole benefit" meant that distributions had to provide a direct benefit to the beneficiary and no one else. In the new POMS, the SSA substantially relaxed its policy, modifying the "sole benefit" rule by allowing SNT distributions to be made under a more reasonable "primary benefit" standard. The revised POMS states:

> The key to evaluating [the "sole benefit" requirement] is that, when the trust makes a payment to a third party for goods or services, **the goods or services must be for the primary benefit of the trust beneficiary. You should not read this so strictly as to prevent any collateral benefit to anyone else**. For example, if the trust buys a house for the beneficiary to live in, that does not mean that no one else can live there, or if the trust purchases a television, that no one else can watch it. On the other hand, it would violate the sole benefit rule if the trust purchased an automobile for the beneficiary's grandson to take her to her doctor's appointments twice a month, but he was also driving it to work every day.[287]

The new "primary benefit" interpretation of "sole benefit" expressly allows other people to benefit from an SNT disbursement as long as the beneficiary receives the primary benefit of the distribution. Under the new POMS, as long as a SNT disbursement can be justified as primarily benefitting the beneficiary, it meets the "sole benefit" criterion, even if it also conveys collateral benefits (*e.g.*, a non-beneficiary's living with the beneficiary in a trust-purchased house). There is still a limitation on what can be distributed under the new standard. For example, a disbursement may violate the "sole benefit" rule if the purchased good or service is used disproportionately by non-beneficiaries, as shown by example of the automobile purchased by the trust "for grandma" but used most often for grandson's work commute.

---

287 POMS SI 01120.201F.3.a. (emphasis added).

KEVIN URBATSCH AND MICHELE FULLER-URBATSCH

Example: An SNT makes a distribution for the purchase of a salt-water spa for a beneficiary who has cerebral palsy. The beneficiary lives with his parents. While the spa may benefit the parents, who may use it in the future, it is of primary benefit for the beneficiary and would meet the definition of sole benefit.

Example: A first-party SNT trustee is asked by beneficiary's mother to purchase a treadmill for her son, the beneficiary. Her son used a wheelchair for mobility and was unable to walk. Mother said her son was like Christopher Reeves and that it was part of his therapy. The SNT trustee asked for a prescription from a medical professional that authorized this treatment. The mother could not provide the prescription, so the SNT trustee refused, because such a distribution would violate the "sole benefit" terms of the SNT.

EVEN IF AN SNT TRUSTEE MAKES A DISBURSEMENT THAT WILL NOT INTERFERE WITH PUBLIC BENEFITS, SHOULD THE DISTRIBUTION BE MADE?

Not always. Just because a distribution will not interfere with public benefits, does not mean that it should automatically be made. The SNT trustee still has a fiduciary duty to comply with the terms of the trust and maintain trust assets for the special needs of the beneficiary. The trustee must consider whether the payment for this item or service meets with the overall spending plan for the beneficiary and is in the beneficiary's best interest.

Example: The SNT trustee is funded with $150,000. The beneficiary asks for an automobile to provide. The beneficiary has found his dream automobile, the Porsche 911 Turbo, with a price tag of $122,000. While the purchase of the automobile would not interfere with the beneficiary's public benefits (because one automobile of any value is an exempt resource), it may not be prudent to make such a disbursement, especially if the beneficiary has numerous other needed expenditures. Although, under the terms of the SNT and the public benefit eligibility requirements, technically, the SNT trustee would be in his legal rights to make this distribution without breaching his fiduciary duty. The trustee's decision may be different if the beneficiary has only months to live and has always dreamed of owning this type of Porsche.

Although, an experienced SNT attorney once stated that to avoid problems with the Social Security Administration, an SNT beneficiary who is an SSI recipient should not drive a nicer automobile than the SSA representative who is reviewing their case for SSI eligibility.

IS THERE A SYSTEMATIC WAY TO DECIDE IF AN SNT DISTRIBUTION WILL INTERFERE WITH SSI OR MEDI-CAL ELIGIBILITY?

In order to help the trustee determine what is an acceptable SNT distribution, the authors have provided a checklist in Appendix H that provides assistance in determining whether a distribution will affect public benefits.

> **Note:** Built into the checklist is the presumption that the SNT trustee understands what SSI considers unearned income, in-kind support and maintenance (ISM), available resource, food, shelter; "sole benefit," and other important public benefit considerations. Thus, it is important that the SNT trustee use this checklist with a firm understanding of these various terms, which are discussed in Chapter 3.

WHAT IS THE EFFECT OF A TRUSTEE BUYING EXEMPT ASSETS, GOODS, OR RESOURCES FOR BENEFICIARY?

There is no effect on public benefits when an SNT purchases an exempt asset for a beneficiary.

An SNT beneficiary is allowed to have certain exempt resources, which are excluded from the SSI and Medi-Cal resource limits of $2,000 for an individual and

$3,000 for an eligible couple.[288] These exempt assets are not counted in determining eligibility, and the beneficiary's ownership of them will not jeopardize his or her SSI benefits. Therefore, the trustee may purchase exempt assets for an SNT beneficiary, and they can own these items in his or her own name without interfering with benefits.

The following assets are exempt by law:

- If the beneficiary is eligible for SSI, the beneficiary's home, including the land on which the home stands and other buildings on that land, if the beneficiary lives in it or intends to return to it.[289] If the beneficiary does not receive SSI but does receive Medi-Cal, the home's assessed value may be limited to $750,000 (plus annual Consumer Price Index increases). Thus, the applicable home equity limit for 2019 would be $878,000. However, because California has not, as of October 2019, enacted regulations implementing the statutory dollar cap, an individual's principal residence of any value is still exempt.[290]

- Household goods (which include, but are not limited to, furniture, appliances, electronic equipment such as personal computers and television sets, carpets, cooking and eating utensils, and dishes) and personal effects (which include, but are not limited to, personal jewelry including wedding and engagement rings, personal care items, prosthetic devices, wheelchairs, and educational or recreational items such as books and musical instruments) regardless of value.[291] The rules now defines household goods as items of personal property, found in or near a home, that are used on a regular basis, or items needed by the homeowner for maintenance, use, and occupancy of the home and defines personal items as items of personal property that ordinarily are worn or carried by the individual, or are things that otherwise have an intimate relation to the individual.

---

288   20 C.F.R. §416.1205(c).
289   20 C.F.R. §416.1212.
290   See Welf & Inst. Code §14006(b); 22 Cal Code Regs §50425; 20 C.F.R. §416.1212(b).
291   POMS SI 01130.430; 20 C.F.R. §416.1216.

- One automobile (or other vehicle) of unlimited value if used for transportation for the individual or a member of the individual's household.[292]

- Life insurance with a cash surrender value, if its face value is less than $1500, and all term life insurance.[293]

- A burial plot, or other burial space, of any value.[294]

- A revocable burial fund, worth up to $1500.[295]

- Up to $100,000 in an ABLE account. See Chapter 10.

- Unlimited amounts held in a qualifying special needs trust.

There are some other resources that the SSA does not count including:
- Property essential to self-support (See the SSI Spotlight on Property You Need for Self-Support);
- Resources that a blind or disabled person needs for an approved plan for achieving self-support (PASS). (See the SSI Spotlight on Plans to Achieve Self-Support);
- Money saved in an Individual Development Account (IDA) (See the SSI Spotlight on IDAs);
- Support and maintenance assistance and home energy assistance that we do not count as income;
- Cash received for medical or social services that we do not count as income is not a resource for 1 month. (EXCEPTION: Cash reimbursements of expenses already paid for by the person are evaluated under the regular income and resources rules);

---

292 20 C.F.R. §416.1218. Regulations effective March 9, 2005 eliminated the dollar value limit of an automobile. See 70 Fed Reg 6344; 20 C.F.R. §416.1102. It had previously been limited in value to $4500.

293 20 C.F.R. §416.1230.

294 20 C.F.R. §416.1231.

295 20 C.F.R. §416.1231(b).

- Health flexible spending arrangements (FSAs);
- State or local relocation assistance payments are not counted for 12 months;
- Crime victim's assistance is not counted for 9 months;
- Earned income tax credit payments are not counted for 9 months;
- Dedicated accounts for disabled or blind children;
- Disaster relief assistance that we do not count as income;
- Cash received for the purpose of replacing an excluded resource (for example, a house) that is lost, damaged, or stolen is not counted for 9 months;
- All Federal tax refunds and advanced tax credits received on or after January 1, 2010 are not counted for 12 months; and
- The first $2,000 of compensation received per calendar year for participating in certain clinical trials.

WHAT IS THE EFFECT OF A TRUSTEE PAYING FOR ASSETS, GOODS, OR RESOURCES NOT IDENTIFIED AS EXEMPT ASSETS?

It depends. If the trustee buys the item and distributes it to the beneficiary who owns it, he or she may lose eligibility for SSI or Medi-Cal depending on value of item. If instead, the trustee purchases this type of item and owns it in the SNT's name, it will not affect eligibility for public benefits.

> **Example:** SNT trustee is asked to purchase an automobile for the beneficiary, who is receiving SSI and Medi-Cal. The beneficiary already owns one automobile in his name. The SNT trustee may still purchase a second automobile for the beneficiary, but the title must be in the name of the SNT. The beneficiary is only allowed to own one automobile in his name without interfering with his SSI and Medi-Cal. A second automobile owned by the SNT will not count as the beneficiary's resource or asset for public benefit eligibility purposes.

WHAT IS THE EFFECT OF PAYING FOR SERVICES FOR THE BENEFICIARY?

It depends. If the trustee pays the service vendors directly for services (that are not considered food or shelter), the distribution will have no impact on public benefit eligibility.[296] Some examples of these services include telephone, cable, Internet access, recreation, vehicle costs (maintenance, insurance, and registration if SNT includes an automobile), hair care, pet care, and many others.

> **Example:** SNT trustee is asked to pay for the beneficiary's cable, phone, internet, house cleaning, and lawn care. The SNT trustee may purchase all of these services by paying the vendors directly. None of these items will impact the beneficiary's eligibility for SSI or Medi-Cal, because they cannot be used to offset his or her need for food or shelter and are not medical care costs covered by Medi-Cal.

> **Note:** See Appendix O for a more complete list of available items and services that may be purchased without interfering with beneficiary's public benefits—the "No-Brainer" list.

> **Warning:** As described in Chapter 16, SNT trustee should not reimburse beneficiary directly for services the beneficiary paid for, even if those services would have been considered exempt if paid by the SNT trustee. If the SNT trustee reimburses the SSI recipient/beneficiary, the amount of SSI will be reduce the SSI check dollar-for-dollar as "unearned income."

WHAT IS THE EFFECT OF PAYING FOR A BENEFICIARY'S MEDICAL NEEDS?

It depends. The trustee is authorized to pay for beneficiary's medical needs that are not already being paid for by Medi-Cal or other public benefit programs. This

---

296   POMS SI 00815.400.

disbursement will always be exempt from consideration as income under the SSI program and most other public programs.[297]

As a result, the purchase of any good or medical service for the SNT beneficiary not already available through Medi-Cal or another public benefit program that can be justified by a medical authority's order will not cause a reduction in SSI benefit levels. The term "medical authority" is broadly interpreted and includes, in addition to medical doctors, many other health-care providers, such as podiatrists, chiropractors, physical therapists, and psychologists. Other common distributions that can be made include dental work, acupuncture, and massage expenses.

> **Example:** SNT trustee is asked to pay for the beneficiary's monthly massage. The SNT trustee may purchase this service by paying the vendor directly. This item items will have no effect on the beneficiary's eligibility for SSI or Medi-Cal, because Medi-Cal does not pay for this service.

> **Example:** SNT trustee is asked to pay for the beneficiary's mental health treatment. The SNT trustee may pay for these treatments but only after determining that Medi-Cal will not pay for it. This can be done by submitting the treatment to Medi-Cal for payment, if the services requested exceed what Medi-Cal will pay, the SNT trustee may pay for it with no loss of benefits.

WHAT IS THE EFFECT OF PREPAYING FOR THE BENEFICIARY'S FUNERAL?

This will depend on how the pre-need funeral is owned.

- If SNT trustee prepays for a funeral and attendant costs and distributes the ownership of the prepaid funeral to the beneficiary, the entire value of the prepaid funeral is exempt, except for revocable set asides money, which

---

297   See 20 C.F.R. §416.1103(b).

can add up to only $1,500. Anything over that amount will be counted as an available resource for SSI and Medi-Cal eligibility purposes.[298]

• If the SNT trustee prepays for funeral and attendant costs and the SNT owns all the contracts and burial plots and insurance, the entire amount is exempt and will have no effect on the beneficiary's public benefits.

> **Critical Pointer:** An SNT trustee of a first-party SNT should consider prepaying a beneficiary's funeral. The reason is that there may be no money left in the trust after the beneficiary dies. As described in Chapter 18, on first-party SNT termination, under SSI rules, an SNT trustee can only use trust funds to pay for the beneficiary's funeral it the trustee has already paid back Medi-Cal back for all the services it supplied to beneficiary. This means that if the government's recovery right is greater than the amount remaining in trust, there will be no money to pay for the beneficiary's funeral. If the beneficiary has no friends or family members with the ability to pay for the burial, the beneficiary will likely be cremated by the county as an indigent. An ignoble end to a meaningful life.

The trustee should always make sure that the beneficiary has a plan for funeral. The trustee should offer to pay for a pre-paid funeral and own the contract in the SNT. If the beneficiary (or his or her legal representative) does not wish to the purchase, it would be prudent to have them sign a waiver of purchase of a pre-paid funeral contract. A sample form is attached as Appendix W to this book.

> **Note:** Under California's Medi-Cal rules, the rules are different than SSI's rules noted above, because it would allow the SNT trustee to pay for the beneficiary's funeral before it seeks payback for all services it paid during beneficiary's lifetime.[299] The SNT

---

298 20 C.F.R. §416.1230(b)(8); 20 C.F.R. §416.1230. 20 C.F.R. §416.1231(b); 20 C.F.R. §416.1231(a) (SSI) and 22 Cal Code Regs §50477; ACWD Letter No. 93-71 (Oct. 4, 1993); Welf & I C §11158; 22 Cal Code Regs §50479 (Medi-Cal).

299 See: Medi-Cal Eligibility Procedures Manual, Art 9J, §VII(C)(1), at p 9J-75).

trustee may still pay for beneficiary's funeral if he or she obtains permission from the Department of Health Care Services (DHCS) in advance.

WHAT IS THE EFFECT OF AN SNT INVESTING IN A BUSINESS?

The investment by the SNT trustee in a business should have no impact on beneficiary's public benefits.

If the SNT trustee may be asked to invest in a business, it can either be as a simple investment or it may be part of a strategy to have the business hire the beneficiary to work to provide private health insurance benefits through employment, rather than relying solely on Medi-Cal. If the business were owned by the SNT, it would have no effect on the beneficiary's public benefits.

> **Warning:** In a first-party SNT that is under court jurisdiction, the investment in a business must be approved through a court.[300]

There are however numerous considerations that must be made when doing this type of investment. Any investment in a business must comply with the investment standard of the trust. If the SNT is under the Uniform Prudent Investment Act (as described in Chapter 9), investment in the business must comply with that rule. Moreover, the management of the business may greatly increase the number of hours and overall commitment of the trustee. A trustee should carefully evaluate if he or she is interested in owning and operating a business. If the SNT trustee is attempting to do this, he or she should seek assistance from an experienced special needs planner that can be located in Chapter 20.

WHAT IS THE EFFECT OF BUYING A BUSINESS AND DISTRIBUTING IT TO THE BENEFICIARY?

It depends. The SNT trustee may be asked to invest in a business that is owned by the beneficiary. While certain resources of a business may be owned by the

---

300   Cal Rules of Court 7.903(c)(4); Probate Code §2614.

beneficiary in his or her name without interfering with public benefits because they are otherwise exempt, there is not an unlimited exemption for property used in a trade or business under both SSI and Medi-Cal.[301]

The business exemption can apply to real property, motor vehicles, and cash (on hand or in checking accounts, but not savings accounts), as well as equipment, inventory, licenses, and materials.[302] For example, all the limousines in a limousine service can be excluded from the applicant's countable assets. Property used in a trade or business is excluded from resources regardless of the value or rate of return as long as it is in current use or, if not in use for reasons beyond the individual's control, as long as there is a reasonable expectation that the use will resume.[303]

A separate issue will be the income earned from the business. It will still be counted against a beneficiary for public benefits eligibility purposes. If beneficiary receives SSI, the income will be counted as earned income (or possibly unearned income) and reduce or eliminate SSI eligibility, and if the beneficiary receives only Medi-Cal (and not SSI), the income may add or increase a "share of cost" to keep or maintain Medi-Cal.

> **Critical Pointer:** The SNT trustee should understand the effect a business's property and income will have on the beneficiary's public benefits. Purchasing and managing a business is fraught with technical details; if the SNT trustee is attempting to do this, he or she should seek assistance from an experienced special needs planner as set forth in Chapter 20.

WHAT IS THE EFFECT OF MAKING PAYMENTS ON BEHALF OF THE BENEFICIARY'S MINOR CHILD OR SPOUSE?

The answer will depend on the type of SNT that is being administered.

If it is a third-party SNT, the terms in the trust document will determine if assets can be used to make payments for the beneficiary's minor child or spouse. There

---

301 42 U.S.C. §1382b(a)(3); POMS SI 01130.500-01130.504; ACWD Letter Nos. 91-28 (Mar. 22, 1991), 95-22 (Apr. 3, 1995).

302 20 C.F.R. §416.1220; 22 Cal Code Regs §50485.

303 See POMS SI 01130.501; ACWD Letter No. 91-28 (Mar. 22, 1991).

is no effect on beneficiary's SSI or Medi-Cal benefits if such distributions are made pursuant to terms of document. Further, if the beneficiary is divorced and there is a valid child support order, the trustee can be compelled to pay for the beneficiary's child support even if it violates the terms of the trust.[304]

If it is a first-party SNT, there is not an easy answer. The difficulty is because an SNT disbursement for a beneficiary's minor child or spouse may be considered a violation of the first party SNT's "sole benefit" requirement that is discussed in more detail in Chapter 16. There is no written law, regulation, or policy that would state this type of disbursement is a violation of the "sole benefit" rule. However, several SSA officials have stated at various times orally that it believes payments for a beneficiary's minor child or spouse is a violation of the "sole benefit" rule. The best advice is to petition the court and ask the court for direction on whether such disbursements can be made. (See Chapter 5 on how to petition court to make request.) The court order may not be valid against the SSA (because it is a federal agency) but would be valid against Medi-Cal that is a state-run agency.

> **Example:** The first-party SNT trustee is asked to pay for the ben-
> eficiary's minor child's food and shelter. If the SNT trustee pays for
> the minor child's support, the beneficiary's first-party SNT could
> be subject to attack from the SSA or DHCS, because it may no
> longer be counted as for the "sole benefit" of the beneficiary. The
> SNT trustee could argue that paying the legal support obligations
> of the beneficiary is for the beneficiary's "sole benefit." At this
> time, there is no definitive guidance if this distribution would be
> authorized.

This issue has been controversial. Experienced Florida special needs attorney David Lillesand makes a compelling argument that paying these expenses would not violate the "sole benefit" rule because there is no federal regulation or even a POMS provision that addresses the use of first-party SNT funds to pay for a person with a disability's spouse or children. Public policy and state law criminal statutes indicate that withholding support for spouses or minor children would violate the

---

304 *Ventura County Dep't of Child Support Servs. v Brown* (2004) 117 Cal.App.4th 144.

law. Because first-party SNTs are self-settled trusts and not safe from the claims of legitimate creditors, it would seem not only right, but also proper, that trust funds be used to support the beneficiary's legal dependents. Plus, if there is an existing spousal or child support order in place against the beneficiary, then failure to comply could lead to the beneficiary going to jail. In this case the trustee is certainly authorized to pay for the valid debts and judgments against the beneficiary. Thus, keeping a beneficiary out of jail would certainly be in the "sole benefit" of the beneficiary.

WHAT IS THE EFFECT ON A BENEFICIARY'S SECTION 8 ELIGIBILITY WHEN MAKING SNT DISBURSEMENTS?

There should be no impact, but there are certain local Public Housing Agencies (PHAs) that take the position that a disbursement will be treated as Section 8 income and could either increase the beneficiary's rent or disqualify him or her from the program.

This became an issue that was resolved in a federal appellate decision that says Section 8 should not be impacted by distributions from an SNT.[305] However, certain PHAs may still trigger a penalty from SNT disbursements. If this is the case, the SNT trustee should consider retaining counsel to challenge the PHA on this issue.

To understand the impact, it is important for the trustee to understand some basics of how Section 8 works. Under Section 8, recipients receive a "voucher" or "subsidy" that they can apply to the rental of the housing unit of their choice—as long as the unit meets the Section 8 program requirements. A local PHA then delivers the subsidy to the landlord under a contract with the US Department of Housing and Urban Development (HUD). The recipient pays a portion of the monthly rent called the Total Tenant Payment (generally 30% of the beneficiary's adjusted income) and the PHA subsidy pays the remainder.

To learn more about Section 8, the trustee can download a wonderful guide called Section 8 Made Simple published by the Technical Assistance Collaborative.[306]

---

305 *DeCambre v. Brookline Housing Authority* (1st Cir. 2016) 826 F. 3d 1.

306 http://www.tacinc.org/knowledge-resources/publications/e-books/section-8-made-simple.

Critical Pointer: Often PHAs will be unfamiliar with SNTs and these rules and have not (and in many cases are still not) enforcing them. For many years, special needs attorneys reported little to no interference with Section 8 when establishing and administering SNTs. Recently, however, a few county PHAs throughout California are taking the position that every distribution from a first-party SNT will be counted as a Section 8 recipient's income. A SNT trustee should check with local special needs attorneys to see if the county where the beneficiary resides is enforcing these rules and, if so, should review Chapter 20 to find an advocate to fight this position.

WHAT IS THE EFFECT OF MAKING A DISTRIBUTION THAT EXHAUSTS TRUST ASSETS?

Unless the trust document states otherwise, a distribution that takes all the money in the SNT will not interfere with public benefits. Whether the complete exhaustion of SNT assets is intentional or unintentional, the result is the termination of the trust, because there can be no trust without a corpus.[307]

If the SNT is a first-party SNT, notice of the termination must be provided to the SSA and DHCS. This may also trigger a request from the SSA or DHCS for an accounting of how assets in the trust were spent. See Chapter 8 concerning the requirements to prepare an account and Chapter 18 for more information on terminating an SNT.

> **Helpful Hint:** A first-party SNT trustee may want to consider the possibility of retaining a nominal amount of assets to avoid termination. This might be prudent if the beneficiary remains disabled and continues to receive public benefits, because there is always the possibility that he or she may receive additional assets in the future—whether from an unplanned inheritance, a personal injury settlement, or some other source. The existing first-party SNT

---

307   Probate Code §15202.

could remain in existence indefinitely to serve as a potential re-pository for those assets, thus avoiding the delay and expense of establishing a new SNT.

WHAT IS THE EFFECT OF THE SNT TRUSTEE LENDING TRUST MONEY TO THE BENEFICIARY?

If done properly, there should be no impact on public benefits.

A beneficiary may receive cash as a loan from the SNT trustee, if it is bona fide and made in good faith. The receipt of the cash will not be treated as income.[308] However, if, on the first day of the next calendar month from the receipt of the loan, the loan proceeds have not been spent, the cash will be counted as an SSI re-source.[309] If the balance of the unpaid proceeds from the loan is over $2,000 for on the first day of the next calendar month, the individual beneficiary will lose eligibil-ity for SSI and Medi-Cal until it is spent down to below $2,000 for an individual or $3,000 for a couple.

The loan must be a bona fide loan. In order for the SNT trustee to make a loan, the loan must be bona fide, which means the loan agreement must be valid under California law, in effect at time of transaction, an acknowledgment that cash will be repaid, a repayment plan, and repayment plan must be feasible.[310] Because of these restrictions, it is difficult to envision many situations when a loan to a beneficiary would be in the best interests of the beneficiary. A sample loan document is at-tached as Appendix U to be used for an SSI recipient who has lost SSI benefits during an appeal to recover benefits.

> **Example:** An SNT beneficiary asks for a loan to pay for his or her food shelter of $900 per month while awaiting a determination on his application for SSI and Medi-Cal. Repayment will be made when the SSA repays for the months it took to determine SSI eli-gibility. The SNT trustee and beneficiary enter into a loan trans-action. For six months, the SNT trustee lends the beneficiary the

---

308 POMS SI 00815.350.
309 POMS SI 01120.220(D)(3)(a).
310 POMS SI 01120.220(C).

money. On the sixth month, the SSA approves eligibility for SSI and pays a lump-sum amount to the beneficiary for the six-month wait. The beneficiary repays the SNT the amount that was loaned. There is no effect on SSI for this transaction.

Example: The SNT trustee has been distributing $500 per month to the beneficiary for a year. The SSA was never informed. The beneficiary during his annual review tells the SSA worker that he has been receiving this money. The SSA seeks an overpayment reimbursement from the beneficiary of $5,760 ($480 x 12) for the unearned income. In defending the request, the beneficiary suggests that trustee should characterize disbursement as a loan. This will not work, because the loan is not bona fide. While it is possible to enter into an oral contract valid under California law, the loan was not entered into at the time the money was spent. Also, it would be difficult to show a feasible repayment plan.

WHAT IS THE EFFECT OF PAYING FOR ALCOHOL, COFFEE, OR CIGARETTES?

Some SNT beneficiaries will make requests for the purchase of alcohol, coffee, or cigarettes. The authors' advice is that distributions for these items are acceptable.

Cigarettes will be okay because in no way can a cigarette be considered food. An overzealous SSA eligibility worker, however, could consider alcohol and coffee, food. This is an issue that is really debatable, as alcohol and coffee offer little to no nutritional value. Sadly, the SSA instructions do not give us a strict definition of what is "food." Is it only items that are eaten that offer some nutritional value, or is it anything that is consumed?

However, even if alcohol or coffee were considered food, paying for them would be treated as SSI in-kind support and maintenance (ISM) and valued at no more than the presumed maximum value (PMV), meaning that the SSI check would only be reduced by $281 per month in 2020 or the value of the purchase, whichever is less. Thus, in general, if the beneficiary seeks payment for these items, it should not be a problem.

> **Critical Pointer:** A trustee should carefully review the trust document. Some people who set up SNTs for people with disabilities will have prohibited distributions for the purchase of alcohol or cigarettes.

WHAT IS THE EFFECT OF PAYING FOR BENEFICIARY'S MARIJUANA?

The effect on public benefits would be non-existent. It would not be treated as income or a resource by SSI or Medi-Cal. Marijuana is legal under State law; however, the federal government has not legalized it. It is unlikely that the existing federal-state conflict concerning the legality of marijuana will be resolved any time soon. For products that include hemp-derived CBD oil which there would be little concern for the distribution for these items.

> **Warning:** If the SNT beneficiary is the recipient of Section 8 benefits, the Public Housing Agencies follow federal regulations and do not allow marijuana by their recipients. Plus, many group homes, assisted living facilities, and nursing facilities have prohibitions against use. The trustee should evaluate the consequences to beneficiaries if they lose their living situation because of their use of marijuana.

An SNT trustee should be cautious about using trust assets in a way that may be permissible under state law but illegal under current federal law. A trustee who expends funds in a SNT to purchase marijuana for the beneficiary, even when state law authorizes this use, assumes some risk that the trust distribution will be regarded by federal law enforcement officials as violating federal drug laws. Yet, in many circumstances, the beneficiary uses marijuana medically as medicine. It would not be right to deprive a beneficiary of a needed medication.

In order to make the distribution, it may take some doing because most marijuana dispensaries only operate on a cash basis. An SNT trustee may decide to fund an ABLE account (see Chapter 10 to see if beneficiary qualifies to use an ABLE account). The beneficiary can then decide whether to use the ABLE account for the purchase of marijuana. The trustee may decide to reimburse a friend or relative for purchase from a dispensary but should obtain proof of payment and receipt of the goods. As further described in Chapter 16, the trustee could use a TrueLink card. However, according to TrueLink representatives, it will be treated as a "cashless ATM purchase." This could have an impact on SSI because it will show up as a cash disbursement. Moreover, if the SNT trustee has stated that "cash" disbursements are not allowed, it would not work. Perhaps, if the trustee temporarily allowed the TrueLink to use cash, the beneficiary uses it to purchase the marijuana, requires receipts for the purchase, and then turns on the prohibition against cash disbursements.

WHAT IS THE EFFECT OF PAYING FOR DATING OR ROMANCE?

The effect of paying for these services will have no effect on the beneficiary's public benefits and hopefully will greatly enhance the beneficiary's quality of life.

Common requests to an SNT trustee include online dating services, birth control (not paid for by Medi-Cal), the beneficiary's share of a movie or other type of date (except dinner), sex toys and aids, the beneficiary's wedding ring, the beneficiary's share of wedding costs, and the beneficiary's share of honeymoon costs, including hotel and restaurant meals.

> **Warning:** If the trustee's SNT is a first-party SNT, then an issue can arise if the trustee pays not only for the beneficiary but also the beneficiary's partner. This would be a violation of the "sole benefit" rule on disbursements. So, it is important that the trustee only pay for the beneficiary's share.

Common requests to a third-party SNT trustee that generally will not interfere with public benefits if authorized by the document include gifts, flowers, shows, engagement rings, and wedding rings.

WHAT IS THE EFFECT OF PAYING FOR PORNOGRAPHY AND EROTIC MATERIAL?

There is no effect on public benefits if the trustee pays for the beneficiary's pornography or erotic material. Many SNT trustees have a difficult time agreeing to pay for the beneficiary's review of legal pornography (whether online, in movies, or in print).

The issue is generally not with public benefits eligibility (as there is no effect on beneficiary's public benefits in making such distributions) but rather the salacious content of the materials. Many SNT trustees seem to have a hard time handling these requests. Trustees are human; prone to biases and prejudices tempered by their own life experience. As such, every trustee must to be aware of their own bias in making a decision, especially when it comes to controversial issues. A trustee can also easily slip into a paternalistic position of approving or denying a request simply on what they think is best. However, the trustee has a duty of impartiality to separate their own personal partiality from the decision-making process.

There is no right or wrong answer to this issue, but the SNT trustee is there to make SNT distributions that will enhance the quality of life of the beneficiary, not to sit in judgment of other people's lifestyles. If the SNT trustee agrees to the distribution, it is probably best to set boundaries early and let the beneficiary know exactly what types of disbursements will be acceptable to the SNT trustee.

WHAT IS THE EFFECT OF PAYING FOR THE BENEFICIARY'S PETS?

The distribution for a beneficiary's pet will have no effect on a beneficiary's SSI or Medi-Cal. Payment for pet supplies is not counted as in-kind support or maintenance. It also is counted as for the "sole benefit" of the beneficiary if he or she is beneficiary of a first party SNT. Common requests that are authorized include pet supplies, veterinarian services, pet food, pet toys, grooming, dog walker, pet sitter, and anything else related to the care of pets.

CAN SNT TRUSTEE MAKE GIFTS TO BENEFICIARY'S FRIENDS OR FAMILY OR DONATIONS TO CHURCH OR CHARITIES?

The answer depends on which type of SNT is being administered.

- For first-party SNTs the answer is always no. Gifts to friends or families and donations to charities are strictly prohibited, because these distributions are not made for the "sole benefit" of the beneficiary. If the first-party SNT authorizes these disbursements, it would not be a valid SNT.[311]

- For third-party SNTs, the answer is maybe. It will depend on the terms of the trust document. If the SNT's terms allow gifts or donations to be made, then these distributions can be made without interfering with public benefits eligibility.

CHAPTER 11 SUMMARY

✓ SNT distributions may have an impact on eligibility for needs-based public benefits like SSI, Medicaid, Home Health services, and Section 8.

✓ SNT distributions will not have an impact on eligibility for entitlement public benefits like SSDI, CDB, and Medicare.

✓ If trustee is administering a first party SNT, the trustee must make sure that all distributions are for beneficiary's "sole benefit" as defined by the Social Security Administration (SSA).

✓ Just because an SNT disbursement does not interfere with public benefits mean the trustee should make it, there are still other considerations that should be considered before making the disbursement.

✓ An SNT trustee can purchase any exempt assets, goods or resources with no impact on needs based public benefits.

✓ An SNT trustee can purchase non-exempt assets, goods or resources with no impact on needs based public benefits, but needs to be careful in how they are owned.

✓ An SNT trustee can pay for beneficiary's services without impact on public benefits as long as the trustee pays for services correctly.

✓ An SNT trustee can pay for beneficiary's medical needs without impact on public benefits as long as Medicaid will not pay for this particular need.

✓ An SNT trustee should pre-pay for beneficiary's funeral, especially if administering a first party SNT, because the Medicaid payback is paid prior to the ability to pay for funeral.

---

311 42 U.S.C. §1382b(c)(1)(C)(ii)(IV); POMS SI 01120.203(B)(1)(e).

- ✓ An SNT trustee can invest in a business but should only do so with assistance to determine the effect it will have on the beneficiary
- ✓ An SNT trustee can pay for a beneficiary's minor child or spouse from a third party SNT, but if the SNT is a first-party SNT, then the trustee should be cautious in doing so to not run afoul of the "sole benefit" requirement.
- ✓ An SNT trustee should be able to make trust disbursements with no impact on Section 8 eligibility but be cautious of some Public Housing Agencies that do not understand the law.
- ✓ An SNT trustee can use all of the money in the SNT without jeopardizing public benefits eligibility.
- ✓ An SNT trustee may lend money to the beneficiary without impacting needs based public benefits, but the loan must be "bona fide" as required by the Social Security Administration.
- ✓ An SNT trustee can pay for beneficiary's alcohol, coffee, or cigarettes with no impact on needs-based public benefits.
- ✓ An SNT trustee can pay for beneficiary's marijuana use with no impact on needs-based public benefits but should tread cautiously because marijuana is still illegal under federal law.
- ✓ An SNT can make payments for beneficiary's dating, romance, or pornography needs with no impact on public benefits, but if the SNT is a first party, all disbursements must be for the beneficiary's "sole benefit."
- ✓ An SNT trustee can make gifts to beneficiary's friends, family, or donations to church and charities from a third party SNT but would violate the "sole benefit" requirement from a first-party SNT.
- ✓ An SNT trustee can make payments for the beneficiary's pet with no impact on needs based public benefits.

CHAPTER 12

Effect on Public Benefits of Paying for Beneficiary's Food, Clothing, Utilities, Shelter, and Vacations

The request for payment of food, clothing, utilities, and shelter is one of the most commonly misunderstood SNT disbursement requests. There is a lot of misinformation about this type of disbursement with many people having the understanding that an SNT can never pay for food, clothing, utilities, or shelter. This is generally not true and failing to understand the rules around this type of disbursement request will cause the beneficiary a lot of unnecessary hardship. This will be discussed in more detail in this chapter, but in order to understand the effect on the beneficiary's public benefits for these types of disbursements, the trustee must know the SNT's distribution standard and what public benefits the beneficiary is receiving. This is discussed in this chapter but is also discussed in Chapter 4, 7, and 19.

> **Note:** There is no public benefits penalty at all for an SNT trustee to pay for a beneficiary's clothing. There used to be a reduction on benefits for clothing, like food or shelter, but it was removed from the list. So, clothing is allowed with no effect on public benefits.

In general, if the SNT has a "discretionary distribution standard" and the person is receiving SSI, there may be a small reduction in the SSI check for payments of beneficiary's food, utilities, or shelter, but this is one situation when a reduction in public benefits is generally preferable because the SNT trustee can greatly enhance the quality of life of the beneficiary by paying for more food and a better living situation to a much greater extent than public benefits can provide. As described below, the authors generally recommend that SNT trustee trigger this penalty because then the trustee can pay for all of beneficiary's food, rent, mortgage, or utilities with only a small reduction in beneficiary's SSI check.

There is an exception to this general rule when the SNT has a "supplemental distribution standard." This type of distribution standard means that the trustee is prohibited from making any disbursement that reduces the beneficiary's eligibility for public benefits. If the beneficiary receives SSI, then this SNT trustee will not be able to distribute trust assets for beneficiary's food and shelter. Again, the rule is different if the beneficiary does not receive SSI at all but is receiving Medi-Cal, then the SNT trustee may make this distribution without a problem (as long as the trustee does not pay for the beneficiary's entire amount of need).

> Practice Tip: One of the benefits of using an ABLE account for payment of beneficiary's food and shelter is that it causes no reduction in public benefits. If the beneficiary qualifies for use of an ABLE account, the trustee may funnel funds from the SNT through the ABLE account to pay for beneficiary's food and shelter. This will cause no reduction in public benefits and can be used no matter the SNT's distribution standard. This is discussed in more detail in Chapter 10.

WHAT IS THE EFFECT ON BENEFICIARY'S SSI WHEN PAYING FOR A BENEFICIARY'S FOOD, SHELTER, AND UTILITIES?

It depends. If the SNT trustee pays for the SSI recipient's food or shelter, the beneficiary's monthly SSI benefit will be reduced (or possibly eliminated). The calculation of the penalty is a little complicated to explain, but in general, if the SNT trustee pays for the beneficiary's food or shelter, then the SSA will reduce the beneficiary's SSI check by $281 per month (in 2020).

Note: SSI defines the term "shelter" to include the following payments made by SNT trustees on behalf of a beneficiary:

1. mortgage payments (including property insurance required by the mortgage holder);
2. real property taxes (less any tax rebates or credits);
3. rent;
4. heating fuel;
5. gas;
6. electricity;
7. water;
8. sewer; and
9. garbage removal.[312]

The technical application of the penalty is that if an SSI recipient receives food or shelter from a third party (like an SNT trustee), the SSA treats this as a type of SSI income called In-Kind Support and Maintenance (ISM).[313] If the SNT trustee then pays for the beneficiary's ISM (*e.g.* beneficiary's food or shelter), then the SSI recipient is penalized under the SSA's Presumed Maximum Value (PMV) rule.[314] The PMV penalty is the reduction of SSI benefits by the lesser of one-third of the Federal Benefit Rate (FBR) (amount of SSI check paid for by federal government) plus the $20 general income exclusion or the actual value of what was received.

In 2020, the FBR is $783 per month. SSA presumes that ISM payments cover 1/3 of the FBR, so it reduces the overall SSI check by one-third and then SSA adds the $20 any income disregard. So, the math goes $783 divided by 3 plus $20 (any income disregard) that equals $281 per month.

Note: The FBR and PMV numbers change each year due to the cost of living adjustment. For the latest FBR and PMV amounts,

---

312   20 C.F.R. §416.1133(c); POMS SI 00835.465(D)(1).
313   20 C.F.R. §416.1102.
314   20 C.F.R. §416.1140; POMS SI 01120.200(E)(1)(b).

see POMS SI 00835.901 (available on the SSA's POMS website, scroll to the bottom of the page for current figures).

Once the penalty is assessed, the SNT trustee can pay for all the beneficiary's food and shelter needs with no further reduction in benefits.

> **Example:** A beneficiary is receiving $958.63 of SSI per month and has been paying for all of his food or shelter from his SSI check. He wants to move to a safer neighborhood but to do so his rent will increase to $1,200 per month. It is obvious he cannot afford to pay it from his SSI check and asks the SNT trustee to pay the rent. The payment of rent by the SNT will be counted as ISM. ISM reduces the beneficiary's SSI check by the PMV rule. This rule would reduce the beneficiary's SSI check by a maximum of $281 per month in year 2020. Meaning, the beneficiary will continue to receive $685.63 per month from SSI, pay no rent, live in a safe apartment in a nice neighborhood, and the trustee can also pay for beneficiary's utilities and food with no additional loss of benefits. This is a good result.

However, if the beneficiary had been receiving SSI in the amount of $220 per month before receiving payment of food and shelter from the SNT, then the trustee's payment of rent would completely eliminate the beneficiary's SSI eligibility under the PMV rules. This is because the deduction of $281 for PMV applies in full and would reduce the SSI check to zero. This means that the loss of SSI will also cause a loss of SSI eligible Medi-Cal[315] and that paying food or shelter may not be in the beneficiary's best interest in this scenario.

---

315 It is possible that the beneficiary could receive another type of Medi-Cal, so even paying food or shelter here may be appropriate. It is best to review these types of situations with a special needs planning attorney or benefits counselor.

WILL SNT TRUSTEE BE ABLE TO MAKE DISBURSEMENT FOR FOOD OR SHELTER IF THERE IS A REDUCTION OF SSI BENEFITS?

The ability to pay for a beneficiary's food or shelter if it triggers an SSI reduction of benefits will depend on the SNT's distribution standard. If the distribution standard is discretionary, meaning distributions can be made that may reduce or even eliminate public benefits, and the beneficiary is on SSI, then it is possible for the trustee to make a distribution for food or shelter. If the distribution standard is supplemental, meaning a distribution cannot reduce or eliminate public benefit eligibility and the beneficiary is on SSI, then the trustee cannot make such a distribution.

> **Example:** A beneficiary is receiving $958.63 of SSI per month and has been paying for all his food or shelter from his SSI check. He wants to move to a safer neighborhood, but to do so will increase his rent $1,200 per month. It is obvious he cannot afford to pay it from his SSI check and asks the SNT trustee to pay the rent. The SNT trustee reviews the SNT distribution standard and determines it is a supplemental standard, meaning that the trustee is prevented from making any distributions that would reduce or eliminate public benefit eligibility. Because the payment of rent would reduce or eliminate SSI, the trustee is prohibited from making this distribution. If living in a safer neighborhood is of great importance, the SNT trustee may wish to petition a court to modify the distribution standard to allow a discretionary distribution standard. A description of this procedure is described in Chapter 5.

In every trust document the trustee of the trust is given instructions on what he or she can and cannot spend money on. This trust provision is often called the "distribution standard." In general, there are two kinds of distribution standards, a purely supplemental standard or a fully discretionary standard as described below:

- **The Purely *Supplemental* Distribution Standard:** Some SNTs specifically prohibit the trustee from making any distributions that will reduce or eliminate eligibility for SSI for any reason. As described above, payments for food or shelter will reduce or even eliminate SSI eligibility. Thus, the SNT trustee is prohibited from making any disbursements that will reduce the SSI check. This kind of SNT may be easier for a trustee to manage, as distributions or payments for "food" or "shelter" are prohibited and therefore do not require the trustee to determine the impact of these distributions on the beneficiary's public benefits. However, this type of standard also seriously hampers the ability of the SNT trustee to improve the beneficiary's life by paying rent on a nicer apartment or paying for the beneficiary's food. It is possible for the SNT trustee to modify the distribution standard by modifying the trust document. This will require a petition to a probate court as described in Chapter 5.

Example: A supplemental distribution standard provision will often look like this sample: "The trustee shall not make any distribution that will reduce or eliminate eligibility for public benefits."

- **The *Discretionary* Distribution Standard:** Some SNTs will allow distributions that can be made even if they reduce the amount of benefit or even eliminate public benefit eligibility. This type of distribution pattern is known as a "discretionary distribution standard." This requires that the trustee carefully examine how the rules regarding SSI "in-kind support and maintenance" will be applied. The beneficiary's SSI benefits will be reduced or eliminated if he or she receives ISM. The trade-off, however, is that the well-being and standard of living of the beneficiary may be enhanced, even after the SSI reduction is imposed. This is generally the more acceptable distribution standard for maximizing the quality of life of the person with a disability.

Example: A discretionary distribution standard will often look similar to this sample: "The trustee may distribute to or apply for the benefit of Beneficiary such amounts from the principal and income, up to the whole thereof, as the trustee, in the trustee's discretion, considers necessary or advisable to meet Beneficiary's special needs for the remainder of his life. While distributions are supplemental in nature to any public benefits the beneficiary is receiving, our Trustee may make a distribution otherwise covered by public benefits, if it is determined by our Trustee to be in the best interests of the beneficiary to make such distribution."

Note: The authors of this book always prefer the fully discretionary distribution standard. It provides the most flexibility to the SNT trustee to enhance the quality of life of the beneficiary with a disability by allowing the trustee to decide to forego all or a portion of public benefits if it is in the beneficiary's best interests to do so.

WHAT HAPPENS IF THE BENEFICIARY'S SSI CHECK IS LESS THAN THE PMV PENALTY AMOUNT?

There are times when an SNT beneficiary receives only a few hundred dollars of SSI because the SSI recipient may have other sources of income. If the SSI recipient receives less than $281 per month in SSI (in 2020) and the SNT trustee makes a payment for food and shelter as ISM, the SSI recipient will lose his or her SSI payment and categorical eligibility for Medi-Cal if the ISM amount is greater than the SSI recipient's SSI check.

> **Example:** An SNT beneficiary who is receiving SSI of $200 is also receiving retirement benefits of $700 per month. The SNT beneficiary wants the trustee to pay for his rent and utilities that total $900 per month. The effect of the SNT trustee making this payment is that the beneficiary will lose up to $281 of his SSI check. Because the beneficiary is only receiving $200, the entire amount of the SSI check is lost. This will eliminate the beneficiary's categorical eligibility for Medi-Cal. The loss of SSI is usually not a big issue, but the loss of Medi-Cal can be devastating.

> **Note:** In the prior example, even if the SNT beneficiary will lose his categorical eligibility for Medi-Cal because he lost his SSI check, the

SNT trustee should determine if the beneficiary could otherwise qualify for Medi-Cal. There are other ways for an SNT beneficiary to qualify for Medi-Cal. The SNT trustee should know whether the beneficiary could qualify for Medi-Cal under Expanded Medi-Cal, medically needy Medi-Cal, share-of-cost Medi-Cal or under a waiver program. A further description of the other types of Medi-Cal programs is discussed in this chapter.

[If the SNT trustee is uncertain of the beneficiary's ability to qualify for Medi-Cal, he or she should hire a public benefits consultant.] To find a public benefits consultant, see Chapter 20. It is possible to hire a special needs planning attorney to assist, but it is usually not cost effective to have an attorney provide these types of services at their hourly rate versus the typically lower rate of the public benefits expert.

WHAT IS THE EFFECT OF PAYING FOR A BENEFICIARY'S CLOTHES IF THE BENEFICIARY IS RECEIVING EITHER SSI OR MEDI-CAL?

Paying for the beneficiary's clothing has no effect on SSI eligibility. This is a change from prior law. Before 2005, paying for clothing was considered the same as paying for food or shelter and treated as "in-kind support and maintenance" (ISM) income, but these rules changed and clothing was taken off the list.[316] Thus, the trustee can purchase all the clothing the beneficiary could need without interfering with SSI eligibility. However, if the SNT beneficiary receives Medi-Cal only (and not SSI) then the purchase of beneficiary's clothes may result in an increase in the share-of-cost to receive Medi-Cal.[317] However, as long as the SNT trustee did not pay for *all* of the beneficiary's clothing, the purchase of clothes would not impact Medi-Cal eligibility at all.

---

316 Regulations effective March 9, 2005, eliminated "clothing" from the definition of income and from the definition of in-kind support and maintenance. See 20 C.F.R. §416.1102.

317 22 C.C.R. §50509.

IF THE SNT BENEFICIARY ONLY RECEIVES MEDI-CAL AND NOT SSI, CAN SNT TRUSTEE PAY FOR FOOD, HOUSING, OR UTILITIES?

Yes. However, the SSI PMV rules do not apply to Medi-Cal or IHSS benefits. Instead, the SNT trustee may pay for some percentage of the beneficiary's food, clothing, shelter, and utilities without interfering with Medi-Cal eligibility. If the SNT trustee pays for the entire amount of these items, the Medi-Cal recipient will have income that may increase the beneficiary's Medi-Cal share-of-cost or even loss of Medi-Cal.[318]

Practitioners differ in their advice on how much of an item of need should be paid for, *for example* whether the trustee should pay 75 percent of the cost up to 99.99 percent of the cost. In the author's opinion, it is probably safer to pay something more significant than 1 percent of the item of need.

> **Example:** SNT beneficiary is on Medi-Cal (but not SSI) and wants the SNT trustee to pay for his food and rent. The cost of the food is $500 per month and the rent $2,000 per month. If the SNT trustee were to pay the entire $2,500 amount, then the beneficiary would have an additional $2,500 in countable income for Medi-Cal eligibility. Instead, if the SNT trustee paid only $400 per month for food and $2,400 per month for rent and the SNT beneficiary paid the remaining $200 per month for the balance of the food and shelter, then the beneficiary would continue to receive all Medi-Cal.

WHAT IS THE EFFECT OF PAYING FOR A RESTAURANT MEAL?

A common request from an SNT beneficiary is for purchase of a restaurant meal. The Social Security Administration (SSA) will count the entire meal as "food." This is questionable. While the food that forms the part of the meal is certainly food, the payment for the tip, service, and part of the bill that constitutes the restaurant's overhead is certainly not food. Thus, an SNT trustee should be able to pay for nearly the entire meal and characterize these payments as waiter and food preparation

---

318   22 C.C.R. §50509.

service. The beneficiary could pay the balance directly or the trustee could distribute $20 per month to the beneficiary for his or her share of the meal.

The balance of the payment of the restaurant meal would be treated as in-kind support and maintenance (ISM) and valued at no more than the presumed maximum value (PMV), meaning that the SSI check would only be reduced by $281 per month in 2020 or the value of the meal whichever is less. In one example in the POMS, the SSA states that the entire restaurant meal would be counted as ISM. However, it appears that this did not set SSA policy but was used without consideration of the factors identified above.[319]

> **Note:** If the trustee has already triggered the full PMV penalty for payment of beneficiary's food and shelter, then the trustee can pay for restaurant meals with no further penalty.

> **Critical Pointer:** A restaurant meal paid for while the beneficiary is on vacation is not counted as ISM. See next question on paying for vacations.

WHAT IS THE EFFECT OF PAYING FOR VACATION COSTS, INCLUDING HOTEL AND RESTAURANT MEALS?

An SNT beneficiary may take a vacation and maintain his or her benefits. When an SNT beneficiary is temporarily absent from a permanent living arrangement, in-kind support and maintenance (ISM) continues to be valued based on the beneficiary's permanent living arrangement.[320] The SSA does not count ISM the beneficiary receives during his or her temporary absence. This is true even if the SNT pays for food (e.g., restaurant meals) or shelter (e.g., hotels) during the absence.

An SNT trustee should be aware that SSI benefits would be terminated if a benefits recipient were out of the country for more than thirty days.[321] There are

---

319   POMS SI 01120.201(I)(1)(d).
320   POMS SI 00835.040.
321   See POMS SI 00501.410.

exceptions for certain blind or disabled children of military parents stationed over-seas and students who are temporarily abroad for study purposes.[322]

> **Example:** The SNT beneficiary wishes to visit his family in New Orleans. The trustee is asked to pay for the beneficiary's hotel bills, restaurant meals, and other travel costs for the trip. The SNT trustee is authorized to pay for all of these items without any re-duction of the beneficiary's eligibility for public benefits.

An issue may come up where the beneficiary wants to pay for a friend or family member to come with him or her. In order to pay for a companion, see Chapter 15.

CHAPTER 12 SUMMARY

✓ SNT trustee may make disbursements for food, shelter, utilities, and shelter as long as the trust document allows it and the trustee understands the rules.

✓ SNT trustee must know if the document includes a supplemental distri-bution standard or a discretionary distribution standard, if supplemental trustee may not pay for food or shelter items for an SSI recipient if discre-tionary distribution standard, because there is only a modest reduction on the SSI check and trustee can make disbursement.

✓ The penalty for someone else (like an SNT trustee) paying for an SSI recipi-ent's food or shelter is a one-third reduction of the federal portion of the SSI check plus $20, which in 2020 is a $281 reduction.

✓ SNT trustee will generally want to trigger the SSI penalty and pay for benefi-ciary's food or shelter needs because it is a greater benefit for beneficiaries.

✓ SNT trustee may want to consider using an ABLE account to pay for ben-eficiary's food or shelter because it can be done with no reduction in the SSI check.

✓ SNT trustee may pay for beneficiary's clothing with no reduction of SSI or Medi-Cal.

---

322 See instructions in POMS SI 00501.415 for blind or disabled children of military parents stationed overseas and POMS SI 00501.411 for students temporarily abroad.

- ✓ SNT trustee may pay for food, clothing, utilities, and shelter for a beneficiary who only receives Medi-Cal (and not SSI) as long as the trustee does not pay for the entire amount of the beneficiary's needs.
- ✓ Restaurant meals are treated as "food" by SSA and may trigger an ISM and PSM penalty.
- ✓ SNT trustee may pay for beneficiary's food or shelter needs while the beneficiary is on vacation, so it is okay to pay for restaurant and hotels with no reduction in benefits.

CHAPTER 13

Buying, Managing, and Selling Beneficiary's Home

One of the best ways to enhance the quality of life of a person with a disability is for the SNT trustee to buy and maintain a home where the beneficiary can live rent free. This has the benefit of providing a safe, clean and controlled living situation for the beneficiary. It can also be a prudent investment to diversify trust assets into real estate. Housing for persons with disabilities is an ongoing struggle. There is no housing market in the United States where a person with a disability whose sole source of income is SSI can afford a safe, decent rental unit. See TAC's report titled Priced Out in the United States.[323] According to this study, this is worse in California where there are approximately 590,000 SSI recipients and the *average* cost of a 1-bedroom apartment is 138-percent of the total SSI check and for a studio efficiency apartment 117-percent of the total SSI check. In order to live, many people with disabilities are living in group situations in dangerous and unsafe neighborhoods or living homeless in the streets.

One primary benefit of home ownership is that if the home is the SNT beneficiary's principal place of residence it is an exempt resource for SSI and Medi-Cal eligibility purposes (meaning it does not count against the $2,000 resource limitation for an individual).[324] For public benefit purposes, "[a]n individual's home is property in which he or she has an ownership interest and that serves as his or her principal place of residence. It can include:

---

323 http://www.tacinc.org/knowledge-resources/priced-out-v2.
324 POMS SI 01130.100(B)(1) and ACWD Letter No. 96–55 (Sept. 20, 1996).

- the shelter in which he or she lives;
- the land on which the shelter is located; and
- related buildings on such land."[325]

Because of the obvious benefits, many SNT trustees will work towards finding an appropriate living situation by paying beneficiary rent (See Chapter 12) or buying a home. However, the SNT trustee must do a proper evaluation to determine on a case by case basis if a home purchase is something the trustee should do. A short list of some of the considerations include:

- Does the trustee have legal authority to buy a home?
- Are there sufficient assets in the trust to buy and maintain a home, such as utilities, insurance, repairs, property taxes, and other maintenance costs?
- What are the public benefit consequences in purchasing and owning a home?
- Should purchase of home be outright or by mortgage?
- Who should own the home, the individual beneficiary, the trustee, or should it be co-owned with other parties?
- If co-owned, how will expenses be prorated?
- What happens if a co-owner dies or defaults on obligations?
- What type of home modifications can be paid for by SNT trustee to assist the beneficiary?
- How will trustee handle all the responsibilities a trustee has in owning a home?
- Who will live in the home and should everyone pay rent to live there?
- Will trustee be able to respond to unexpected issues with owning the home, such as residents deciding to create and run a meth lab, set up and run a brothel, allow transients to crash in home, trashing home or simply refuse to pay rent (each of these examples are based on real life examples)?
- What happens if the trustee needs to sell the property?

Given the various expenses associated with owning a residence and paying for the beneficiary's other care needs, an SNT trustee should carefully consider the

---

325 POMS SI 01130.100(A)(1).

wisdom of investing special needs trust assets in the purchase and maintenance of a home for the beneficiary. If there are suitable rental units available for an individual with special needs, it may be prudent to encourage a beneficiary to rent accessible homes or apartments. Without sufficient housing options in the rental market, however, SNT trustee are oftentimes persuaded to purchase a home and make modifications to suit the beneficiary's needs. The downside of a trustee investing in real estate is the potential financial crisis of depleting the trust's cash to carry the residence over time and being forced to sell the home in favor of a less accessible rental arrangement. The distress for both the trustee and the beneficiary is palpable when faced with a SNT having a steadily declining balance, beneficiary's other needs still needing to be met, and the unfortunate need to sell the home. These are choices that ultimately satisfy no one.

> **Note:** A checklist that trustee can use when buying real estate that will allow the trustee to discuss and obtain buy in from the beneficiary concerning all these issues is attached as Appendix Y.

DOES THE SNT TRUSTEE HAVE LEGAL AUTHORITY TO PURCHASE A HOME USING SNT ASSETS OR SELL A HOME OWNED BY THE SNT?

The purchase of a home by the SNT trustee may be the biggest purchase an SNT trustee will make. Trustees have the legal power to acquire property.[326] "Property" is defined to include both real and personal property.[327] The SNT trustee should, however, check the trust document to see if there is an express prohibition against the purchase of real estate. If there is, the SNT trustee cannot make the purchase absent a court order.

Unless the trust terms require it, no court approval for purchase of a home is required for a third party SNT. Likewise, many first party SNTs do not require court approval. However, with respect to first party SNTs that are established and funded through the court some local rules require court approval for the purchase of a home.[328] The trustee should determine whether the local probate court would

---

326 Probate Code §16226.
327 Probate Code §62.
328 See, e.g., Los Angeles Ct R 4.116(b)(2).

require a court order to purchase the home. It would be prudent for a trustee to seek a local attorney to assist in determining whether court authorization is required. See Chapter 20 on how to find legal assistance for SNTs.

A trustee has the power to sell trust assets unless expressly prohibited from doing so by the trust instrument.[329] A trustee must follow the prudent investor rule and exercise care and prudence in deciding whether to sell real property owned by the trust.[330] Factors to consider include whether the property has become an inappropriate trust investment, tax considerations, costs of sale, and the suitability of the property as a home for the beneficiary. The sale of a home owned by an SNT will not affect the beneficiary's eligibility for public benefits. However, see question below on effect of public benefits when a beneficiary owned home is sold.

> **Critical Pointer:** A petition for instructions (as described in Chapter 5) authorizing the purchase or sell of a home by a trustee may be prudent whether it is legally required or not. The cost of homes in California is high enough that a trustee has a great deal of liability exposure in the event a judge, SNT beneficiary, Department of Health Care Services, or remainder beneficiary questions the trustee's exercise of his or her discretion in the purchase or sell of a home. With appropriate notice, a hearing, and a court's order, the trustee should be protected from potential future liability.

ARE THERE SUFFICIENT ASSETS IN THE TRUST TO PURCHASE A HOME FOR BENEFICIARY?

This is one of the more difficult calculations an SNT trustee will need to undertake. It is advised that the trust consult with a knowledgeable real estate broker and financial advisor to determine the up-front and long-term costs of managing a home. Having reviewed hundreds of SNTs that managed real estate for the beneficiary, the lifetime costs of managing real estate is a lot more money than many SNT trustees

---

329   Probate Code §16226; *Church v Church* (1940) 40 Cal. App.2d 696.
330   Probate Code §16047.

understand. In addition, if a difficult housing situation arises, it can take an inordinate amount of the SNT trustee's time to manage. It is advised that the SNT trustee take the time to really understand the transaction before agreeing to the purchase of a home.

The next question in the book goes into details on what costs are associated with home purchase and maintenance. However, the SNT trustee has additional concerns. In general, SNT trustees should understand that an SNT will not be able to use a traditional mortgage to purchase a home. Banks and other traditional mortgage lenders will not loan money to a trust no matter how fiscally sound. The only available lender may be private money lenders who will charge a lot more in interest. Thus, the SNT trustee may need to determine if the SNT can pay for the entire home in cash or enter into a co-ownership arrangement.

> **Example:** SNT receives funds of $800,000 and beneficiary wants the SNT trustee to use assets to buy home. SNT beneficiary and family come to the trustee with homes in the $750,000 to $800,000 range. The beneficiary and family believe the trustee can purchase home with a 10 or 20-percent down and the balance with a mortgage. Unfortunately, that is not available to SNTs, and the trustee has to inform the family that such a purchase is impossible. The next question from the beneficiary and family is asking for the SNT trustee to make the down payment and the family to obtain a mortgage for the balance of the purchase.

The SNT trustee may make this disbursement but has a fiduciary duty to ensure it is the right decision for the beneficiary. Initially, does the family qualify for the mortgage. Then, are there still sufficient funds in the SNT to pay the down payment and take care of the beneficiary's other special needs? If the SNT trustee agrees to the purchase, should the SNT trustee own that percentage of the property as an asset of the SNT or distribute it out to beneficiary. A beneficiary may not be able to accept property because of age or lack of capacity. If the trustee agrees to own the percentage of property, the next determination is what happens if the family defaults on the mortgage, is there protection for the SNT? How will ongoing expenses of insurance, property taxes, maintenance, or utilities be paid, pro-rata or will family or SNT trustee pay all of them?

The trustee then needs to know who will live in home. If the trust owns the home, it must make that property productive. This means charging rent for the persons who live in the home. This can be awkward for family members who may not understand the legal rules the SNT trustee must meet. The SNT trustee will then want to make sure that it can afford any modifications to make the home accessible for a beneficiary with mobility issues. The SNT trustee may make the decision that the beneficiary would be better off renting an accessible apartment then spending such a significant percentage of trust assets on a home. Or, the SNT trustee could make the decision that it will pay $160,000 for a down payment on home, maintain a 20-percent interest in home, agree to a pro rata split of expenses with family living in home, allow the beneficiary to live rent free, but have the family members living in the home (and who do not have ownership interest) agree to pay rent at fair market value. The SNT trustee has done the financial analysis that this situation provides the best opportunity for beneficiary to have a clean and safe place to live, enough money to pay for other expected special needs, and provide for the long-term protection of beneficiary and the trust assets.

If the SNT is court supervised, the SNT trustee should confirm with the court that it will authorize payment for the home. Some local Probate Courts have unstated minimums that must remain in the SNT. For example, if the SNT has $500,000 in assets, the trustee can only use up to 50% of trust assets to buy a home. Other county Probate Courts require that an SNT under ongoing court jurisdiction or supervision are required to obtain court approval.

Even if the SNT is not court supervised, the SNT trustee may want to confirm the purchase of the real property with a Probate Court by doing a voluntary petition for instructions. This has the benefit of protecting the SNT trustee in case he or she is later second guessed for the purchase. See Chapter 5 and 20 to find the procedure to do this.

The other issue that can come up for the SNT trustee is buying a home for a minor SNT beneficiary when the beneficiary's parents are still alive. Because a parent owes a duty of support to a minor, an SNT trustee must make sure that the parent is paying his or her fair share to support the minor. In this case, it is strongly recommended that the SNT trustee petition the Probate Court to allow for the purchase of a home. See Chapter 5 on how to utilize Probate Code §17200 petitions for instructions.

HOW MUCH DOES IT COST TO BUY AND MANAGE A HOME FOR SNT BENEFICIARY?

When people think of how much it will cost to buy a home, they tend to think of the purchase price. However, there is a lot more to the cost than the purchase price, including:

- **Property tax**. California property tax rates average .77% but can fall between 1.1 percent to 1.6 percent of the home's assessed value.

- **Homeowners insurance premiums**. SNT trustees have a legal duty to protect trust assets from being by such things as fire, flood, earthquake, vandals, or other unpleasant surprises. Depending on coverage and other factors, the average homeowner's policy in California is estimated at $974 per month.

- **Accessibility modifications**. One of the initial considerations for the beneficiary is whether the home is accessible for beneficiary's needs. Common accessibility modifications would be building a ramp, widening doorways and hallways, making bathroom accessible, and possible additions of other items such as a Hoyer lift.

- **Ongoing home repairs and maintenance**. One popular method for calculating home repair cost says that 1% of the purchase price of the home should be set aside each year for ongoing maintenance. For example, if the home cost $300,000, a spending plan of $3,000 per year for maintenance. A general rule is the spending plan should be $1 per square foot per year for maintenance and repair costs. If the home is 2,000-square-foot home, for example, spending plan $2,000 a year for maintenance and repairs. Since there is no universal application that governs how much should be set aside for home maintenance and repairs—and factors like age and local weather can be significant factors—it makes sense to take a more holistic approach to estimate the cost of home maintenance:

- First, take the average of the 1% rule and the square foot rule. If 1% of the purchase price equals $3,000, and the square foot rule equals $2,000, then the average is $2,500.
- Next, add 10% for each factor (weather, condition, age, location, type) that adversely affects the home. If it is an older home, in a floodplain, or in an area that experiences freezing temperatures, increase the total by 30%: $2,500 x 1.3 = $3,250 (or $270.83 per month).[331]

- **Utility costs.** As described in Chapter 12, paying utilities will cause a reduction of benefits for an SSI recipient, but this penalty is oftentimes intentionally triggered to provide the SNT beneficiary a better quality of living. The SNT trustee should consider the ongoing costs of utilities in maintaining the home over the beneficiary's lifetime.

- **Cleaning costs.** The person with a disability may be able to clean home on own, but not always. The SNT trustee should consider the ongoing costs of a cleaning service that will regularly service the home.

- **Crime prevention** that may include installing an alarm system or providing stronger locks and floodlights.

- **Landscaping** which may include watering, gardening, snow removal, and associated costs with maintaining the grounds.

- **Home furnishings.** Many times, the person with a disability has little to no furniture and needs to furnish the new home that may include dining room, living room, bedroom, bathrooms, etc. This can easily cost in the tens of thousands of dollars.

---

331 See article by Paula Pant titled "How Much You Should Spending plan for Home Maintenance" at https://www.thebalance.com/home-maintenance-spending plan-453820.

- If a condominium is purchased, there are also **homeowner's association dues** that must be paid that can be hundreds of dollars a month.

[In addition to the costs of purchase and accessibility modifications, the SNT trustee should consider the costs of replacing various home components and whether the trust will have sufficient assets to make these repairs] Here's what the National Association of Home Builders estimates as the life span for various housing components:

- Roof: Typically, 20 to 30 years, depending on material, although slate, copper, clay or concrete roofs have an expected life span of more than 50 years.
- Flooring: Carpets last eight to 10 years, linoleum 25, vinyl up to 50; wood, marble, slate and granite can last 100 years.
- Decks: About 20 years "under ideal conditions."

Consumer Reports, meanwhile, says to expect the following life spans:
- Oil furnace: 20 years.
- Gas furnace: 18 years.
- Electric furnace: 15 years.
- Central air conditioner: 15 years.
- Gas range: 15 years.
- Electric range: 13 years.
- Refrigerator: 13 years.
- Dryer: 13 years.
- Freezer: 11 years.
- Washing machine: 10 years.
- Dishwasher: 9 years.

WHO SHOULD OWN THE HOME, THE SNT OR THE BENEFICIARY?

If the trust terms authorize it, a third party SNT or first party SNT trustee may purchase a home and make an outright distribution of the home to the beneficiary (*i.e.,* title to the home will be held by the beneficiary). There are both practical and legal issues that should be considered by the trustee in making this decision. From the "needs-based" public benefits perspective, a home, including adjacent land, is an exempt asset and will not be counted against the beneficiary for eligibility purposes provided that the beneficiary lives at the home or intends to return. This is true even if title were to be taken in the beneficiary's name instead of in the name of the trustee.[332] The trustee should review the following advantages and disadvantages below and determine which is best in his or her situation.

Advantages of direct home ownership by the SNT beneficiary:

- Self-determination by the beneficiary with a disability to own and control a valuable asset.
- The ability to create an estate plan leaving the home to the heirs of the beneficiary's choice.
- A step-up in basis on the value of the home at the death of the beneficiary with a disability. This benefit applies only if the SNT that makes the distribution is not a grantor trust (see Chapter 17, on taxation, which describes grantor trust status).
- Providing equity for collateral to a loan for the beneficiary with a disability.
- Minimizing the recovery claim by the Department of Health Care Service (DHCS) in a first-party SNT if the beneficiary places the home in a revocable living trust.[333] See Chapter 18 on Medi-Cal recovery claims for first-party SNTs.

Disadvantages of direct home ownership by the SNT beneficiary:

- If the beneficiary is unable to manage his or her own financial affairs, a conservatorship of the estate may need to be opened to manage the home, but that home should still be placed in a revocable living trust to avoid estate recovery claims.
- The beneficiary will be required to manage all home ownership issues, such as insurance, maintenance, and general upkeep. This may be an issue for some beneficiaries due to their disabilities or lack of experience in managing a home.
- If the beneficiary is vulnerable to predators, he or she might be persuaded to sign the house over to someone else.

---

332   20 C.F.R. §416.1212 (SSI); 22 Cal Code Regs §50425 (Medi-Cal).

333   Welfare & Institutions Code §14009.5.

- If the distribution is to a minor, then law limits many of the minor's dealings with the property. A minor cannot delegate a power or enter into a contract relating to an interest in real property and may disaffirm most other contracts. Therefore, brokers, transfer agents, title companies, and others will not knowingly deal with a minor, and unless the minor is emancipated, a guardian may have to be appointed to deal effectively with a minor's property.
- The home will be subject to the personal creditors of the beneficiary. If the home were owned by a third-party SNT, it would be protected from most of the beneficiary's creditors.
- If the beneficiary sells the home, he or she will have only three months to purchase a new home without an SSI penalty.[334] If the beneficiary does not find a new home or, if after the purchase of a new home, there are assets in excess of $2,000, the beneficiary will lose SSI and Medi-Cal due to excess resources, unless those assets are transferred to a first party SNT. If the home in the SNT were sold, the sales proceeds would not be counted against the beneficiary.
- If home is rented, the rental income will count against the beneficiary's SSI and Medi-Cal eligibility.

Warning: There may be an issue with making a distribution of a home from a first-party SNT to a beneficiary. While the SSA has specifically authorized such a distribution, DHCS may challenge this distribution as circumventing the Medi-Cal payback requirement. This may invite a DHCS lawsuit against the trustee. To alleviate this concern, a notice of proposed action or Petition for Instructions should be prepared and served on DHCS. This should provide the trustee with protection from liability.

Advantages of home ownership by the trustee of the SNT:

---

334 POMS SI 01130.110(A)(1).

- The trustee can control the ownership of the home, meaning that the trustee is assured that taxes are paid, insurance is paid, and the home remains in repair.
- The trustee can diversify trust investments to include real property.
- The trustee can rent the home without any effect on beneficiary's SSI or Medi-Cal.
- The trustee can protect the home from the beneficiary's creditors in certain circumstances. Generally, much better protection in a third-party SNT.
- The trustee can own the property on behalf of a minor or adult who lacks capacity without having to obtain a guardianship or conservatorship.
- The trustee can control what persons are allowed to live in the home with the SNT beneficiary and protect the beneficiary from predators who would attempt to take advantage of the beneficiary.
- The trustee can sell the home without it interfering with the beneficiary's public benefits.

Disadvantages of home ownership by the trustee of the SNT:

- The trustee must make sure that all property taxes are paid.
- The trustee must make sure all fire, earthquake, and homeowners' insurance is paid.

   Note: Trustee should have regular appraisals done on property to make sure insurance coverage is adequate.

- The trustee must make regular inspections of property and make sure all maintenance and repairs are being made.
- The trustee must collect rental payments and enter into rental agreements with others living in the property. This also means that if rental payments are not made, eviction proceeds may need to be instituted.
- The home may not receive a basis step-up on the death of the beneficiary if it is owned by a nongrantor trust, like third-party SNT.
- The home becomes part of the first-party SNT property for payback recovery by DHCS during trust termination. See Chapter 18 for discussion of first-party SNT payback.

WHAT ARE SNT TRUSTEE'S LEGAL RESPONSIBILITIES IF SNT OWNS HOME?

The SNT trustee has various fiduciary duties when the SNT owns real estate. The trustee is responsible for maintaining sufficient casualty and liability insurance.[335] The SNT trustee should obtain appraisals of the property at routine intervals to obtain adequate insurance protection. The trustee should also consider the need for flood, fire, or earthquake insurance. This decision depends on the location of the property, the types of structures, the ability of the trust estate to bear an uninsured loss, the cost of premiums, and the commercial availability of the desired coverage. If these problems are beyond the trustee's level of expertise, an insurance specialist should be consulted. Check Chapter 20 for a discussion in finding appropriate professionals to assist.

The SNT trustee also must perform ongoing maintenance and inspection. If the property has tenants, the trustee may engage on-site management or professional property managers to handle day-to-day management and maintenance. Property owners, particularly landlords, have a duty to inspect premises for defects and to correct any defects found.

DO SNT TRUSTEES HAVE TO CHARGE RENT TO PERSONS LIVING IN SNT OWNED HOME?

Yes. One of the most basic tenets of a trustee's fiduciary duty is to protect trust assets and make them productive. The SNT trustee has an obligation to collect rent and is liable for failing to do so without adequate reason.[336]

Family members or the trust beneficiary cannot use trust-owned property as a personal asset and live in trust rental property rent-free. However, SNT trustees may not need to charge the SNT beneficiary "rent" to live in the trust owned home because it can be treated as a "special needs" distribution. The purpose of the SNT is to enhance the quality of life of the beneficiary and providing a safe, clean place to live would seem to be one of the biggest needs a beneficiary with a disability has so providing it free of rent would be an appropriate distribution.

---

335 See Restatement (Third) of Trusts §76, Comment d (2007); Restatement (Second) of Trusts §176, Comment b (1959).

336 *Purdy v Johnson* (1917) 174 Cal. 521.

However, other people that live in the home (including relatives) would either need to pay rent or reach alternate arrangements with the SNT trustee. Oftentimes, the person the SNT trustee has to ask to pay rent is a parent or relative who is providing the care for the person with a disability. This can be quite a shock to family members who do not understand why they have to pay rent to live with their loved one. It could also be that this family member has given up their job or career to stay home and care for person with a disability and has little to no income to pay such an obligation. In this instance, the SNT trustee can enter into an arrangement for the person to continue to provide caregiving services in lieu of rent.

It is recommended that any persons (other than beneficiary if not charging rent) allowed to live on premises have a written lease or agreement with the SNT trustee to avoid any future disputes as to the extent of the right to live in the SNT owned home. Trustees should investigate relevant market rent levels to determine fair market rent before entering negotiations for a lease extension or for a new lease. A skilled real property broker or manager can be helpful in this area. The trustee may also want to engage on-site management or professional property managers to handle day-to-day management and maintenance. Property owners, particularly landlords, have a duty to inspect premises for defects and to correct any defects found.

If a tenant fails to pay, the trustee may need to file an unlawful detainer action to evict the tenant. If a tenant is damaging the home or otherwise illegally running a business or harming the home in any way, the SNT trustee must file appropriate legal action. This can be problematic when the persons causing the harm are also the relatives providing care for the SNT beneficiary. The SNT trustee may become involved in a protracted legal dispute with dangerous people. The SNT trustee is cautioned to take immediate and appropriate action and should bring in the proper authorities as quickly as possible including Adult/Child Protective Services, or even the police or sheriff.

WHAT IS THE EFFECT ON SSI OR MEDI-CAL OF PURCHASING A HOME OUTRIGHT WITH TRUST ASSETS?

There is only a small impact on beneficiary's SSI payment if a home is purchased outright for the beneficiary as his or her principal residence when using an SNT's assets. The SNT trustee buying a home for an SSI recipient is considered a type of SSI income called in-kind support and maintenance (ISM). However, it is only treated as ISM in the month of purchase. Thus, the beneficiary only loses $281 (in 2020) from SSI in the month of purchase. There is no further penalty.

> **Note:** See effect on SSI if the home is purchased with a mortgage in the next question.

If this is a first party SNT, the SSA requires that title to the home be held in the name of the beneficiary or in the name of the SNT.[337] If this is a third party SNT, the title of the home would likely remain in the name of the SNT unless the trust document authorized distribution of the home to the beneficiary.

If the home is purchased outright in the name of the beneficiary, after the first month of ISM, owning the home has no effect on the beneficiary's public benefits as long as it remains the beneficiary's principal residence. This is because a principal place of residence is an exempt asset for SSI and Medi-Cal eligibility purposes.[338]

> **Example:** The SNT trustee pays $600,000 for a home in August 2020 and distributes title in the name of the beneficiary. The beneficiary would lose $281 (the 2020 PMV amount) of SSI in August 2020 as ISM. Going forward, the SNT beneficiary may live in the home without any further reduction of SSI.

If the home is purchased outright and title is held in the name of the SNT, the SSA considers the SNT beneficiary to have an "equitable ownership under a trust."[339] This means that the home purchase would be considered ISM income in the month of purchase only, or a one-month SSI reduction of $281 (in 2020). After the initial month, the SNT beneficiary may live in the home rent-free without it being considered ISM.[340]

---

337   POMS SI 01120.201(F)(3).
338   20 C.F.R. §§416.1210(a), 416.1212.
339   POMS SI 01120.200(F)(1).
340   POMS SI 01120.200(F)(2).

> **Example:** If the SNT trustee purchases a home for $500,000, the SNT beneficiary would lose $281 (the 2020 PMV amount) of SSI in the month of purchase as ISM. Going forward, the SNT beneficiary may live in the home rent-free without any further reduction of SSI.

There is no parallel provision to "equitable ownership under a trust" in the Medi-Cal rules, so the treatment is uncertain. However, Medi-Cal rules do provide that it will not count third party contributions of shelter unless the third party pays "the entire item of need" for a calendar month.[341] Accordingly, it may be possible to avoid having Medi-Cal count the beneficiary's use of the trust's property as ISM by either charging a nominal monthly rent to the beneficiary.

WHAT IS THE EFFECT ON SSI OF PURCHASING A HOME WITH A MORTGAGE?

If the home is purchased with a mortgage and title is held in the name of the SNT, the payment of the mortgage will be treated as in-kind support and maintenance (ISM) in the form of shelter in the month of the purchase.[342] The subsequent monthly mortgage payments will also result in the receipt of income in the form of ISM, each valued at no more than the presumed maximum value (PMV) of $281 (the 2020 PMV amount).[343]

> **Example:** If the SNT trustee purchases a home for $500,000 with a down payment and a mortgage and monthly payments of $1,800 for twenty years, the SNT beneficiary would lose $281 (the 2020 PMV amount) of SSI in the month of purchase as ISM. Going forward, each and every month the mortgage is paid, the SNT beneficiary would lose $281 each month as ISM (or that year's current PMV rate).

---

341   22 Cal Code Regs §50509
342   POMS SI 01120.200(F)(3)(b).
343   POMS SI 01120.200(F)(3)(b).

WARNING: It is nearly impossible to find a lender who will provide a mortgage to a trust. The only available lenders are generally private moneylenders, who will charge a very high rate of interest, which makes it uneconomical to purchase a home from an SNT with a mortgage.

WHAT IS THE EFFECT ON SSI OF SELLING A BENEFICIARY'S HOME?

If the principal residence of the beneficiary is sold and title is held by the SNT (either first party or third party), then there is no effect on SSI. The assets will still be held in the exempt SNT and not affect the beneficiary's SSI eligibility.[344]

However, if the beneficiary sells the principal residence when title is held in his or her name, the proceeds of the home sale will be an available resource if not spent within three month on a new primary residence.[345] The proceeds can be used on a down payment, settlement costs, loan processing fees and points, moving expenses, necessary repairs to or replacement of the new home's structure or fixtures (*e.g.*, roof, furnace, plumbing, built in appliances) that are documented prior to occupancy, and mortgage payments.[346] If there are remaining assets from the purchase of a new primary residence, the beneficiary can then either fund the assets to a first party SNT or spend down these asset to below $2,000 for an individual or $3,000 for a couple.

Example: Beneficiary has been residing in home owned in beneficiary's name as her primary residence. She decides to sell the home to buy a smaller one. She nets $500,000 from the sale. She buys a new home within two months for $200,000. The $300,000 will be counted as an available resource for SSI purposes (going back to the sale date) unless otherwise spent down or transferred to a first party SNT.

---

344   POMS SI 01120.200(F)(1).
345   POMS SI 01130.110.
346   POMS SI 01130.110(B)(2).

WHAT IS THE EFFECT ON SSI AND MEDI-CAL OF RENTING OUT ROOMS IN THE BENEFICIARY'S PRINCIPAL RESIDENCE?

The effect of renting out rooms in the beneficiary's principal residence will depend on who owns the property.

- If the SNT owns the primary residence, then rental income will have no effect on the beneficiary's public benefits. The SNT is an exempt asset—and that includes any income earned from trust assets.[347]

- If the beneficiary owns his or her own residence, the rental income will count as unearned income.[348] This means that for every dollar of rent received after the first $20 will reduce the SSI check dollar for dollar.

If the beneficiary owns the home, the beneficiary may deduct certain expenses (up to the pro-rata share of home rented) to reduce the effect the rent will have on the beneficiary's SSI for the following:

- Interest and escrow portions of a mortgage payment (at the point the payment is made to the mortgage holder);
- Real estate insurance
- Repairs (i.e., minor correction to an existing structure);
- Property taxes;
- Lawn care;
- Snow removal;
- Advertising for tenants; and
- Utilities.[349]

There are also certain nondeductible expenses:

- Principle portion of a mortgage payment; and
- Capital expenditures (i.e., an expense for an addition or increase in the value of property which is subject to depreciation for income tax purposes).[350]

---

347   POMS SI 01120.200(G)(1)(a).
348   POMS SI 00830.505(A)(4).
349   POMS SI 00830.505(A)(11).
350   POMS SI 00830.505(A)(12).

Example: The SNT beneficiary owns a primary residence with six rooms. He rents to his cousin one room for $1,500 per month. The total allowable expense deduction for the rental is $300 per month. However, because the renter only rents 1/6 of the home, the deduction is reduced to 1/6 of the expense deduction, or $50. Thus, the SNT beneficiary will lose $1,430 from his or her SSI each month during the rental. The calculation is $1,500 rent - $50 allowable deduction - $20 one-time exclusion = $1,430. Because in year 2020, the maximum SSI authorized for an individual is $958.63 per month, this SNT beneficiary would lose his or her SSI and will then lose his or her categorical eligibility for Medi-Cal. However, that person may still qualify for Expanded Medi-Cal.

If the beneficiary is a Medi-Cal–only recipient and the home is owned in the name of the beneficiary, the beneficiary who has income from real property may deduct certain expenses from gross rents. These deductions include property taxes and assessments, mortgage interest payments, insurance, utilities, and upkeep and repairs.[351] The principal on a mortgage is not deductible.[352]

WHAT IS THE PUBLIC BENEFITS EFFECT OF MAKING HOME MODIFICATIONS OWNED BY A BENEFICIARY OR SNT?

Making modifications to the beneficiary's principal place of residence will have no impact on a beneficiary's public benefits. When SNT pays for improvements or renovations to the beneficiary's principal place of residence, the beneficiary does not receive income, even if the home is in the name of the beneficiary. The SSA states in its policy manual:

> If the trust pays for repairs, maintenance, improvements, or renovations to the home, such as renovations to the bathroom to make it handicapped accessible, installation of a wheelchair ramp

---

351 22 Cal Code Regs §50508.
352 22 Cal Code Regs §50508(a)(1)(B).

or assistive devices, or replacement of a roof, the trust beneficiary does not receive income. Disbursements from the trust for improvements increase the value of the resource and, unlike household operating expenses, do not provide ISM.[353]

Moreover, making home modifications to a home owned by the SNT will have no impact on public benefits. It merely increases the value of an asset owned in a qualifying SNT.

> **Example:** SNT trustee pays $45,000 for renovations to the beneficiary's bathroom to make it handicap accessible, to install a wheelchair ramp for accessibility, and to fix the roof. There is no effect on the beneficiary's SSI benefits. The home modifications are not considered income or ISM and as a result will not reduce the beneficiary's SSI check.

WHAT IS THE PUBLIC BENEFITS EFFECT OF MAKING HOME MODIFICATIONS TO A HOME OWNED BY SOMEONE ELSE?

If the trustee of either a first party or third party SNT is asked to make a modification to a home not owned by the trustee, the trustee is generally allowed to do so if it is in the best interests of the beneficiary. If the SNT trustee makes this disbursement, there should be no effect on SSI or Medi-Cal when modifying a home owned by someone other than beneficiary or the SNT as long as the primary benefit of the modification is to benefit the beneficiary. This may be more of an issue if the disbursement is made from a first-party SNT and the disbursement could be considered not for the "sole benefit" of the beneficiary. The distinctions between acceptable purchases and those that may trigger a penalty can be quite narrow, and different facts will have different results. It is strongly recommended that the trustee consult an experienced special needs practitioner in making this type of determination.

---

353 POMS SI 01120.200(F)(3)(c).

Typically, the type of modifications requested is for accessibility to a bathroom, adding a ramp, adding an elevator, or widening doorways or hallways. However, it could be something less obvious, such as adding a therapy room, a pool, or a sauna to the home. In general, adding ramps, widening doors to accommodate wheelchairs, and installing disability modifications to a bathroom add little significant value to the home. However, modifications that add several hundred square feet to a bedroom, a therapy room, a swimming pool, or a bathroom may add significant value.

> **Example:** The beneficiary is renting property. He had some mobility issues but was able to remain mobile until recently and now needs a wheelchair for all mobility needs. The beneficiary has permission from the landlord to make the bathroom accessible. He asks trustee to make the requested modifications at a cost of $8,000. The SNT trustee may make the modifications without any effect to beneficiary's SSI or Medi-Cal.

The SNT trustee will need to carefully consider approving a modification if there are no protections in place if, for example, the homeowner either evicts the beneficiary, sells the property, dies and heirs may evict or sell home, lose the property through foreclosure, or has future creditor issues. The SNT trustee will need to be careful in making a significant disbursement if any of the above concerns arise.

> **Example:** Same facts as prior example, but as soon as the modifications are done the landlord evicts the beneficiary. The SNT trustee has no recourse for the $8,000 distribution.

The trustee should find a way to protect the disbursements that do add substantial value to the home or are a large disbursement of trust assets. In order to make the SNT disbursement better protected, the trustee should make sure there are protections in place to preserve beneficiary's rights. For example, the homeowner could later sell the property, die, and heirs may evict beneficiary or sell the home, lose the property through foreclosure, have future creditor issues, or simply evict the beneficiary. Some protections could include the beneficiary receiving a life estate in the home, an occupancy agreement binding on owner and heirs, co-ownership, or recharacterize distribution as loan to property owner with secured interest in home. Before making such a distribution, the trustee should consult an attorney to make sure these protections are included to protect trust assets.

> **Example:** The trustee is asked to make expenditures of $50,000 in the residence of the beneficiary to make accessibility modifications to bathroom and add a saltwater sauna. The beneficiary's brother owns the home. The trustee believes that the beneficiary will benefit from accessibility modifications so he can use the bathroom. Plus, a doctor has given a recommendation that a sauna will ease the beneficiary's pain to his limbs and provide therapy to beneficiary's body. The trustee agrees to make distribution but will only do so if brother deeds 20 percent interest in home, which is valued at $250,000, to protect the disbursement

> **Example:** First-party SNT trustee is asked to pay for a new roof to the beneficiary's parents' home, where the beneficiary lives. The modification, while likely required for the beneficiary's safety, is not truly for the beneficiary's "sole benefit," because a roof repair is typically for the benefit of the property's owners. In this case, it is likely the distribution would not be treated as for the sole benefit of beneficiary. However, if the trustee agreed to make disbursement in exchange for a percentage ownership in home equal to the disbursement amount in relation to overall value of property, then it should qualify as an acceptable disbursement as an investment of the SNT.

DOES THE SNT TRUSTEE HAVE TO HIRE A LICENSED CONTRACTOR TO DO MODIFICATIONS TO SNT OWNED PROPERTY?

Generally, yes. A SNT trustee may be asked to allow a family member or other third party who is not a licensed contractor to do the modifications to the trust owned home. The SNT trustee is strongly cautioned to not allow this even though it will "save money." If something goes wrong, the SNT trustee may be personally liable for any thing not done to code, done incorrectly, could be liable for damage to third parties, and could hurt the property value if not done with proper permits. The advice would be to hire a licensed contractor. Plus, if the SNT is court supervised, the court reviewing the trustee's actions will likely consider the hiring of an unlicensed contractor as a breach of the trustee's fiduciary duty, especially if any harm results.

No matter who is hired, the SNT trustee's ability to shield themselves from liability for the acts of an agent is limited, assuming the trustee (1) uses reasonable prudence in selecting an agent, (2) periodically reviews the agent's overall performance and compliance with the terms of delegation, and (3) takes reasonable steps to redress any wrongs on learning of an agent's act or omission.[354] Under California law, a trustee is not liable for the acts or omissions of an agent employed by the trustee in the administration of the trust unless the trustee:

- Has the power to direct the act of the agent;
- Delegates to the agent the authority to perform an act that the trustee is under a duty not to delegate;
- Fails to use reasonable prudence in the selection or retention of the agent;
- Fails to periodically review the agent's overall performance and compliance with the terms of the delegation;
- Conceals the act of the agent; or
- Fails to take reasonable steps to compel the agent to redress the wrong when the trustee knows of the agent's acts or omissions.[355]

This protection excludes situations in which the trustee knows of the agent's acts or omissions and either conceals them or neglects to take reasonable steps to correct any wrongdoing.

SHOULD AN SNT TRUSTEE CONSIDER JOINTLY OWNING REAL PROPERTY?

It depends. An SNT trustee may be asked to jointly own real property when the beneficiary has an existing home, has sold it, and wants to buy a new home but does

---

354 Probate Code §16401.

355 Probate Code §16401(b).

not have enough money to do so or a parent (or other relative) wishes to buy a home for the person with a disability but needs more money to do so.

As long as the SNT trustee has the authority to purchase real estate, the trustee can use SNT assets to jointly own property. To protect the beneficial interest in the distribution, an SNT trustees will often make sure that the SNT (or the beneficiary) takes title to the pro-rata amount of the contribution. As described above, the ownership of the real property (as long as for the beneficiary's principal place of residence) is an exempt asset for both SSI and Medicaid purposes.

The real problems that arise with joint ownership are practical ones. For example, the trustee is often at the mercy of the joint owner, who stops making mortgage, insurance, or maintenance payments because of financial hardship, the joint owner dies, or the joint owner decides to sell and begins a partition action (a legal proceeding to force a sale of the home). It is important that the trustee come up with a plan (in advance) to solve any of these problems that may arise.

> **Example:** SNT trustee is asked to contribute $200,000 for the outright purchase of principal residence for beneficiary. The beneficiary's parent will contribute the remaining $100,000. The SNT trustee and parent execute a deed with SNT owning two thirds of property and the parent owing one third of property. A separate agreement is entered into so that all expenses are shared pro rata, based on percentage ownership. After several years, while the beneficiary is residing in the home, the parent had paid all the expenses and the beneficiary was well taken care of. However, in year seven, the parent dies. In the parent's estate plan, he left his share of the home to his nondisabled child, the beneficiary's sibling. The sibling decides that she does not want to own the property and wants to sell. The SNT does not have enough money to buy the sibling out and refuses to sell. The sibling could force a sale through a partition action, and when sold, the beneficiary would need to move from the home.

WHAT ARE THE TAX CONSEQUENCES IF A HOME IS TRANSFERRED INTO SNT?

In order to respond, the SNT trustee needs to be familiar with the tax consequences of home ownership by an SNT. Under Proposition 13, real property may be reassessed at its current market value when ownership of the property changes.[356] The general rule is that transfer of real property into a trust constitutes a change in ownership, unless an exception applies. For property tax purposes, the trust beneficiary is generally treated as the owner of real property held in trust.[357] Moreover, the trustee is never viewed as the "owner" of the trust property, even though the trustee has legal title to the property and the power to sell it.[358]

However, in nearly all circumstances, there will be no reassessment when transferring a home into an SNT because exceptions apply to the two most common factual situations that arise:

When a parent or grandparent wishes to transfer his or her home into a third party SNT. A transfer by parents of their principal residence or other real property with assessed value up to $1 million to an SNT for a child is treated as a transfer to the child, and a claim for the parent-child exclusion from reassessment should be filed.[359] Similarly, a claim for exclusion can be filed with respect to a transfer from a grandparent to a grandchild, or to an SNT for the benefit of a grandchild if all of the parents of the grandchild who qualify as children of the grandparent are deceased as of the date of transfer.[360]

When a person with a disability wishes to transfer his or her own home into a (d)(4)(A) SNT. A transfer by a person with a disability into his or her own first party SNT will not present a change of

---

356 Cal Const art XIIIA.

357 See, e.g., *Reilly v City & County of San Francisco* (2006) 142 Cal. App 4th 480.

358 18 Cal Code Regs §§462.160, 462.240.

359 Cal. Rev & Tax Code §63.1(a)(1), (c)(9).

360 Cal. Rev & Tax C §63.1(a)(3), (c)(2), (c)(9).

ownership triggering reassessment as long as the settlor-transfer-or is the sole present-interest beneficiary of the trust.[361]

WHAT ARE THE TAX CONSEQUENCES IF THE SNT HOME IS SOLD?

The sale of a home can result in a capital gains tax on the sales proceeds if the home has appreciated in value since its purchase. When a trust owns the home, the capital gains tax rules are different depending upon whether the trust is a first-party or a third-party special needs trust. Internal Revenue Code §121 provides that $250,000 of capital gain from the sale or exchange of real property can be excluded from the taxpayer's gross income if, during the 5-year period ending on the date of the sale or exchange, the real property had been owned and used by the taxpayer as the taxpayer's principal residence for periods aggregating 2 years or more.

The beneficiary of a first party SNT trust is considered the owner of the trust, and thereby qualifies in his or her individual capacity for the capital gain tax exclusion if the SNT meets any of the grantor trust rule criteria in IRC §§671–679; the capital gain is reported on the beneficiary's income tax return. Most (d)(4)(A) SNTs are considered grantor trusts under the IRC, but not all of them. On the grantor trust rules, see Chapter 17.

The capital gains exclusion is not available for a third party SNT, which will always have been funded with someone else's property and will never be a grantor trust for income tax purposes.

CAN THE SNT TRUSTEE BECOME A SECTION 8 LANDLORD AND RENT TRUST OWNED HOME TO BENEFICIARY WITH A SECTION 8 VOUCHER?

Yes, an SNT can be a Section 8 landlord. Section 8 is a housing program administered by the United Department of Housing and Urban Development (HUD). See Chapter 3 for a lengthier description of the Section 8 program. In general, the Section 8 program provides a rental subsidy to private landlords. Practically speaking, the beneficiary/tenant applies for a housing subsidy to the local Public Housing Authority (PHA). The PHA is the entity that manages the local Section 8 vouchers.

---

361 Cal. Rev & Tax C §62(d); 18 Cal Code Regs §462.160(b)(1)(A).

The trustee/landlord is like any private landlord who agrees to participate in the Section 8 program with a PHA. The three parties (the SNT trustee, the PHA, and the SNT beneficiary) enter into a lease agreement under which the tenant pays a portion of his or her income (generally 30 percent), and the PHA pays the rest directly to the landlord.[362] The advantage of this arrangement over the usual beneficiary/tenant agreement with an independent landlord and the PHA is that the trust receives a steady stream of income.[363]

CHAPTER 13 SUMMARY

✓ SNT trustee have authority to buy and sell real estate, as long as the trust document does not expressly prevent it.

✓ SNT trustees should do extensive due diligence when purchasing a home and analyze all costs associated including property taxes, homeowners insurance, maintenance, utilities, cleaning, safety, landscaping, home furnishings, and homeowners association dues to make sure there are sufficient assets in the trust to manage the home and the beneficiary's other special needs.

✓ The SNT trustee should carefully consider who should own the home, the trust or the beneficiary, there are both advantages and disadvantages that should be considered.

✓ The effect on an SSI recipient's public benefits eligibility from the outright purchase of a home is small, in the month of purchase, the SSI check will be reduced by $281 as a 2020 PMV penalty, but then there is no further reduction.

✓ The effect on an SSI recipient's public benefits eligibility from the purchase of a home by mortgage is larger, in the month of purchase, the SSI check will be reduced by $281 as a 2020 PMV penalty and then each month after that, there is an additional PMV reduction until the mortgage is paid off.

✓ If the SNT owns the home, there is no effect if the home is sold and the assets held in the trust; however, if the beneficiary owns the home, he or

---

362   42 U.S.C. §§1437a(a)(1)(A), 1437f(o).
363   24 C.F.R. §982.306(d).

she has 3-months to buy a new home without penalty, but if fails to do so, those assets are countable against his or her SSI eligibility.

✓ If the SNT owns a home and rents out rooms to others, the receipt of rental income has no effect on SSI eligibility; however, if the beneficiary owns the home, the receipt of rental income is treated as SSI "unearned income" and will create a dollar-for-dollar reduction of benefits, after taking into account certain allowable deductions.

✓ The SNT trustee can make home modifications on home owned by trust, by beneficiary, or even a third party without any effect on SSI eligibility; however, if it is a first party SNT, the home modifications must primarily benefit the beneficiary to not be counted.

✓ The SNT trustee can jointly own real estate with other parties, but practically, this could have many issues if the co-owners default, die, or decide to sell.

✓ The transfer of a home to an SNT should not trigger reassessment because the most common scenarios have exceptions to reassessment, but the SNT trustee should consult with an expert to make sure his or her situation meets the proper exception.

✓ The sale of a home by an SNT can trigger capital gains taxes, if the SNT is a third-party, there is no exclusion for capital gains tax; if the SNT is a first-party (and a grantor trust), as long as beneficiary resided in home 2 or more years in the past 5, he or she can take a $250,000 capital gain exclusion.

✓ The SNT trustee can become a Section 8 landlord and rent to a beneficiary with a Section 8 voucher; this provides a steady stream of income for the SNT to help pay for beneficiary's other special needs.

CHAPTER 14

Managing Beneficiary's Transportation Needs

Persons with disabilities need a safe and reliable means of transportation. Oftentimes, this is done by purchasing an automobile. Due to the cost of a new automobile, many persons with disabilities and their families are unable to afford such a vehicle and make do with a high mileage, older vehicle without all of the modern safety features. Moreover, if the person with a disability has mobility issues, the costs of a vehicle adapted for use of persons with disabilities can easily exceed $75,000.

Because of these high costs, the SNT trustee may be asked to distribute SNT funds for the purchase of an automobile. Often, this request includes a specific automobile or specific adaptations that the beneficiary needs. The SNT trustee must consider a variety of factors in exercising his or her discretion to pay for an automobile. As always, the SNT trustee should review the trust document to see if it has any limitations on the purchase of an automobile and determine if the purchase of an automobile fits within the SNT's spending plan. But, specifically for an automobile, the trustee must determine:

- What is effect on public benefits like SSI and Medi-Cal?
- If this is a first party SNT, is the purchase of a vehicle for the "sole benefit" of the beneficiary?
- Who should own the vehicle?
- Who will pay for maintenance, gas, insurance, and related costs?

Attached as Appendix T is Motor Vehicle Ownership and Maintenance Contract that can be entered into with the family concerning the use of an SNT purchased and owned automobile. The advice in this chapter is that the SNT not own the automobile, but rather have a lien on it. There are certain times when the trust may need to own the automobile, so this agreement can be of assistance. Also, even if only a lienholder, the SNT trustee may want to ensure that the car will be used for the primary benefit of the beneficiary.

WHAT IS THE EFFECT ON SSI OR MEDI-CAL OF BUYING AN AUTOMOBILE, MOTORCYCLE, BOAT, SNOWMOBILE, OR ANIMALS USED FOR TRANSPORTATION?

The purchase of an automobile (and even distribution of title to the automobile to the SNT beneficiary) will not affect public benefits eligibility as long as it is the beneficiary's only automobile, because one automobile of any value is an exempt resource.[364]

There is a broad definition of the term "automobile." The SSA defines it to mean any registered or unregistered vehicle used for transportation. Vehicles used for transportation include but are not limited to cars, trucks, motorcycles, boats, snowmobiles, animal-drawn vehicles, and even animals.[365] However, the primary purpose of the "automobile" must be for transportation and not pleasure. The following vehicles do not meet the definition of an automobile:

- A vehicle that has been junked
- A vehicle that is used only as a recreational vehicle (*e.g.,* a boat used on weekends for pleasure)[366]

Thus, if the beneficiary does not own a vehicle, the trustee could purchase one and distribute it to the beneficiary, who could own it in his or her name.

> **Warning:** The limitation of one vehicle is strict. It is important for the SNT trustee to know if the beneficiary and his countable family already have one vehicle. If a second is purchased, then one

---

364 20 C.F.R. §§416.1210(c), 416.1218; 22 Cal Code Regs §50461(a).
365 POMS SI 01130.200(B)(1).
366 POMS SI 01130.200(C)(3).

vehicle will be counted as an available resource. For example, if the SNT beneficiary is a minor, but receiving SSI, and the family owns one vehicle, that is exempt, but if the SNT trustee buys a second for the beneficiary's use (as long as beneficiary is a minor), then that second vehicle counts against the limitation if owned by family. The same issue arises if the SNT beneficiary is married, a spouse's vehicle will count as the one vehicle.

Also, beware of the motorcycle in the garage or the automobile that no one drives. Many families do not consider these as countable because no one uses them and does not let SNT trustee know about them. The SSI will count these as an automobile and if there are more than one, it will start counting them as resources. It is important to obtain a proper inventory. A temporarily broken-down vehicle normally used for transportation also meets the definition of an automobile, so make sure to ask about vehicles not in use and then review POMS on limitations.[367]

WHO SHOULD HOLD TITLE TO THE AUTOMOBILE?

It is recommended that if the SNT trustee purchases an automobile, that it distributes the automobile ownership to the beneficiary or to a responsible third party (typically a parent) but the SNT trustee should hold a lien on the vehicle to make sure the beneficiary or third party does not sell or encumber the automobile.

If the SNT beneficiary is an adult, has capacity, is able to safely drive, and there is little concern over predators, it is best if the individual owns the automobile. If there is a concern with the beneficiary owning the vehicle, another responsible third party should own the vehicle. The SNT trustee should not be the owner. Otherwise, the trustee and the assets of the trust may be liable if the beneficiary or a third-party driver is negligent and causes an accident. The SNT trustee on behalf of the SNT could then be a defendant in a lawsuit and the assets of the trust subject to

---

367   POMS SI 01130.200(F)(1).

the driver's creditors. If the individual is the owner, then SNT assets would not be subject to these creditors.

> **Example:** The SNT trustee purchases a modified van for benefi-
> ciary's use. The SNT is the owner of the vehicle. The main driver is
> beneficiary's parent. While driving the beneficiary to school, the
> parent is momentarily distracted and runs into a line of children
> causing lots of harm. Because the SNT owns the vehicle, it can be
> a defendant in any lawsuit brought by the parents of the children
> injured, thus subjecting all of the SNT assets to pay for the injured
> children and not to be used for the beneficiary with a disability.

The trustee of the SNT should still be named as a lienholder on the automobile so that the individual with ownership cannot sell or borrow against the vehicle without the permission of the SNT trustee. This lien protects the value of the vehicle for the sole benefit of the beneficiary, consistent with the SNT's terms and the requirements of the SSI and Medi-Cal programs.

In first party SNT, the SSA has authorized this procedure in its POMS as follows:

> Purchased goods that require registration or titling, for example
> an automobile or real property, must be titled or registered in the
> name of the beneficiary or the trust(ee) unless State law does not
> permit it. For example, State law may not allow an automobile
> to be registered to the beneficiary, or may require a co-owner, if
> the beneficiary is a minor or an individual without a valid driver's
> license. Some State Medicaid agencies may permit an automobile
> to be titled in a third party's name if the trustee holds a lien on the
> automobile. A lien guarantees that the trust receives the value of
> the automobile if it is sold and prevents the purchase from being
> considered a transfer of resources.[368]

---

368   POMS SI 01120.201(F)(3)(a).

IF AN AUTOMOBILE IS BEING PURCHASED BY A FIRST PARTY SNT TRUSTEE, HOW SHOULD THE PURCHASE OF THE AUTOMOBILE MEET THE SOLE BENEFIT REQUIREMENT?

Because the first party SNT must be for the beneficiary's sole-benefit, the trustee must ensure the vehicle is to be used for the primary benefit of the beneficiary. As noted in the POMS, [e]ven if a person or entity other than the beneficiary or the trust(ee) is listed on the title of the purchased good, it must still be used for the sole benefit of the trust beneficiary."[369]

This does not mean that no one else can ever use the automobile, but the primary benefit of the use of the automobile must be for the beneficiary. The SSA describes this requirement in its POMS as follows:

> The key to evaluating this [sole benefit] provision is that, when the trust makes a payment to a third party for goods or services, the goods or services must be for the primary benefit of the trust beneficiary. You should not read this so strictly as to prevent any collateral benefit to anyone else. For example, if the trust buys a house for the beneficiary to live in, that does not mean that no one else can live there, or if the trust purchases a television, that no one else can watch it. On the other hand, it would violate the sole benefit rule if the trust purchased an automobile for the beneficiary's grandson to take her to her doctor's appointments twice a month, but he was also driving it to work every day.[370] (emphasis added)

The first-party SNT trustee should ensure that the primary benefit of the automobile will go to the SNT beneficiary and not towards anyone else. In Appendix T, the Motor Vehicle Maintenance Agreement can be modified to make it clear that the purchase of the automobile is dependent on it being used for the primary benefit of the beneficiary.

---

369   POMS SI 01120.201(F)(3)(a).
370   POMS SI 01120.201(F)(3)(a).

WHAT IF SNT BENEFICIARY NEEDS A SECOND AUTOMOBILE OR WISHES TO BUY A BOAT OR RECREATIONAL VEHICLE?

If the SNT trustee wants to purchase a boat to be used for pleasure or purchase a second automobile, motorcycle, truck, snowmobile, etc., the trustee can do so even if the beneficiary already owns one vehicle. The effect on SSI eligibility is not good if the beneficiary already owns one automobile and title for the second vehicle is also placed into the name of beneficiary. The SSA will exempt the vehicle with the greatest equity value and count the other vehicle.[371]

In order to not have any vehicle count, the SNT trustee should hold title to the second vehicle in the name of the SNT. As described above, this may expose SNT assets to potential liability, so depending on the situation, a separate SNT may be established that only holds title to the additional vehicles.

> **Example:** SNT trustee has purchased a modified van for beneficiary. The beneficiary owns the van in his name. There is no effect on SSI of having distributed the modified van to the beneficiary. Now the beneficiary would like to purchase a boat to be used for fishing on the weekends. The trustee can purchase the boat but title must be held in the name of the SNT. A distribution of the boat to the beneficiary in his name would be counted as an available resource.

> **Helpful Hint:** If an SNT beneficiary requires more than one automobile, the SNT can purchase and retain ownership of any additional automobiles and maintain SSI and Medi-Cal eligibility. Remember, these programs allow beneficiary to own only one vehicle. In these circumstances, it may be prudent to establish a separate SNT to hold title to any additional automobiles. This way, if the automobile is involved in an accident, the trust that holds the beneficiary's other assets is not subject to any accident victim creditors.

---

371 POMS SI 01130.200(F)(1).

HOW ARE ONGOING MAINTENANCE, GAS, INSURANCE, REPAIRS, AND RELATED COSTS PAID BY SNT TRUSTEE?

An SNT trustee can normally pay for beneficiary's share of any ongoing automobile maintenance, gas, insurance, repairs, and related costs without issue. However, if the SNT trustee is aware that other family members are using the automobile for their personal use then expenses should be done in a pro-rata fashion.

This is even more important in court-supervised SNTs. Courts will generally require the spouse or parents, who will be driving the vehicle, to contribute a pro rata share to the cost of gasoline and routine maintenance. The trustee can require the family member driving the automobile to maintain a mileage log so that payments from the SNT are only made for the portion of time the family is using the automobile for the benefit of the beneficiary.

ARE THERE ANY SPECIAL REQUIREMENTS FOR INSURANCE FOR A SNT PURCHASED AUTOMOBILE?

Yes, in addition to the normal automobile policy requirements, make sure that the SNT is an added named insured and loss payee if the automobile is owned by the SNT beneficiary or third party. This way, if the SNT purchased vehicle is in an accident, and the insurance company pays off, the money does not go to the beneficiary (and causes a public benefits issue) or to a third-party and they use it on themselves. Instead, the SNT trustee would receive the funds that can be used to purchase another vehicle.

> **Example:** The SNT trustee purchases a Honda Pilot for the transportation needs of the beneficiary. The SNT trustee places ownership of vehicle in name of beneficiary's father. For two months, the automobile is consistently used solely for the benefit of beneficiary. In the third month, the father is in an accident and the Honda Pilot is totaled. The insurance company pays $30,000 to cover damage but because the SNT trustee failed to make sure the SNT was an additional named insured or loss payee, the $30,000 goes directly to beneficiary's father who used it for himself. The beneficiary is asking the SNT trustee to purchase another

automobile because he requires transportation. The SNT trustee will either have to pay another full amount for purchase of the automobile or fail to be able to do so if the SNT does not have sufficient funds. It is possible, this could be grounds for a breach of fiduciary duty claim.

Also, if purchasing insurance for a modified van, make sure the insurance coverage includes the van's accessibility modifications. The general automobile insurance policy will not cover the accessibility modifications (because the insurance company will consider the modifications as "highly modified") but only cover the vehicle. The SNT trustee should make sure that an insurance rider is included that covers accessibility modifications. An insurance rider provides additional coverage for something not specifically covered with your primary policy. Though insurance riders cost extra, having them on your account will help offset costs during an accident.

Example: A modified van is being driven by beneficiary's primary caregiver. While driving, the caregiver is distracted, runs off the road, and the van is totaled. The SNT trustee seeks reimbursement from the insurance company and is shocked to learn it will cover cost of van of $35,000 but will not cover the $30,000 of accessibility modifications. Had the SNT trustee had an insurance rider, the loss would have been covered.

WHAT KIND OF VEHICLE SHOULD BE PURCHASED BY AN SNT TRUSTEE?

An SNT trustee can purchase any type of vehicle as long as it meets the intent of the trust document. An automobile of any value is exempt for SSI and Medi-Cal purposes as long as it is used for the beneficiary's transportation needs. However, the SNT trustee must always consider the SNT's spending plan and determine how much the SNT can really afford.

The reality is that many beneficiaries and their families will want an automobile that the SNT cannot afford. The SNT trustee will have to exercise their discretion in saying no to the Escalade and yes to the more reasonably priced vehicle. If the SNT trustee is asked to purchase a modified van, the cost of a new one can easily exceed

$75,000. There are multiple dealers that sell used modified vans in excellent condition for less than $35,000. It can save considerable funds for the SNT to consider a used vehicle. Of course, the unique situation of the beneficiary is going to drive the SNT trustee's discretion.

CHAPTER 14 SUMMARY

- ✓ SSI and Medi-Cal recipients are entitled to own one automobile for transportation purposes that does not count against their $2,000 resource limitation.
- ✓ The SSA counts boats, snowmobiles, animals used for transportation in its definition of what is an automobile.
- ✓ Title of the automobile should not be held by SNT trustee but instead in the name of the beneficiary or a third party to avoid the SNT being liable for harm caused by automobile's driver.
- ✓ The SNT trustee should obtain a lien on the automobile to avoid the owner from selling or encumbering the vehicle without the SNT trustee's permission.
- ✓ If a first party SNT trustee is purchasing a vehicle, the trustee must make sure the automobile is being primarily used by the beneficiary and not other third parties.
- ✓ If the beneficiary wishes a second automobile, the SNT trustee can accommodate this desire by holding title to the second automobile in the SNT, but should be cautioned that doing so will expose other trust assets to potential liability, it may be prudent to have a separate SNT established that only holds additional automobiles.
- ✓ The SNT trustee can pay for the beneficiary's share of the ongoing maintenance fees, gas, insurance, repairs and related costs, but if others are using the automobile, they should pay their pro rata share of expenses.
- ✓ The SNT trustee should make sure the SNT is named as an additional insured and loss payee for the automobile if owned by third party to make sure that it receives money back if automobile is damaged.
- ✓ If the automobile is a modified van, the SNT trustee should make sure that insurance covers not only the vehicle, but also the accessibility

modifications – many policies do not cover these, so SNT trustee must ask for an insurance rider.

✓ The SNT trustee should carefully consider the cost of the automobile with the SNT's overall spending plan, if purchasing a modified van, it may be prudent to check the used car market to save tens of thousands on cost.

CHAPTER 15

Evaluating and Paying for Caregiving and Companion Services

By Robert Nuddleman and Kevin Urbatsch

Hiring caregivers is one of the more difficult tasks an SNT trustee will be asked to perform. The beneficiary's caregiver will have a profound impact on the well-being and comfort of the beneficiary. The caregiver will oftentimes be in charge of making sure the beneficiary's ongoing healthcare and comfort needs are being taken care of and will have a tremendous amount of personal contact with the beneficiary. The caregiver needs to be trained, supervised, honest, and dependable. Not only is finding such a caregiver difficult to do, it is also an area rife with employment legal obligations and tremendous expense. It is into these waters that the authors wade into to provide some clarity on how best to hire a caregiver, what the effect of paying a caregiver may be, a summary of who should be the employer for a caregiver, and many other issues the SNT trustee must be ready to understand when finding a caregiver for the beneficiary.

In addition to caregivers, the SSA has long had an issue with a first party SNT trustee paying for companions for persons with disabilities, oftentimes creating different policies for family member companions, limiting the types of services companions can do, or strictly limiting when such companionship services can be paid. In 2018, the SSA significantly changed the policies in authorizing companionship and made it much easier for the SNT trustee to make such disbursements as described in this chapter.

CAN AN SNT TRUSTEE HIRE A CAREGIVER FOR BENEFICIARY?

Yes. Hiring a caregiver is often the most important service an SNT trustee can provide to a person with a disability. A caregiver can allow a beneficiary to remain at home or simply provide services to enhance the beneficiary's life.

It is never a good idea to hire someone casually to help with caregiving services for the beneficiary. When a person is hired, many trustees assume they can simply pay an hourly wage directly to the caregiver and that is all that is required. This assumption is far too simplistic. Many trustees will get into trouble for failing to recognize that what he or she thought was a simple arrangement was instead a legal employer/employee relationship. The result could be that the trustee is personally responsible for failing to comply with a host of employment laws and incur significant liability for a caregiver's injuries and unpaid taxes. Hiring a caregiver without following the correct steps could result in significant liability for the SNT Trustee.

The issues involved in hiring caregivers can be deceptively difficult. The following are the types of questions the trustee must be able to answer:

- Is the caregiver status as employee or independent contractor correct and clearly understood and documented?
- Is the proposed caregiver someone who can be hired, *e.g.*, someone who does not have a criminal record or has proper United States documentation to work?
- Is the compensation reasonable given the assets available to the trustee?
- Does the proposed pay structure (*i.e.*, salary, hourly, per shift, etc.) comply with the law?
- Is the proposed caregiver trained and capable of providing the required level of care?

Helpful Hint: A rich source of data on all aspects of caregiver hiring, training, and selection is found at www.caregiver.org. Any trustee considering hiring a caregiver should review this website.

Warning: The hiring of a caregiver will greatly increase the potential for abuse by the caregiver. The caregiver will oftentimes have the most unfettered personal contact with the beneficiary, which can lead to serious issues later. The SNT trustee should consider all aspects of protecting the beneficiary from abuse during the caregiver hire and while managing the caregiver.

WHAT IS THE EFFECT ON SSI OF PAYING FOR CAREGIVERS OR COMPANIONS FOR THE SNT BENEFICIARY?[372]

The Social Security Administration (SSA) has long had issues with first party SNTs that included provisions for paying for companion and caregiver expenses. SSA representatives often approached these distributions with skepticism, objecting to them outright or imposing additional requirements that varied between field offices. In response to this uncertainty, SNT trustees often were conservative when evaluating and approving requests for companions and caregivers.

The 2018 revised POMS directly address this issue by including in the third-party payment exception the right of SNT trustees to make distributions for caregiving and companion care. The revised POMS notes that "[p]ayment for companion services can be a valid expense[,]"providing the example of an Alzheimer's patient who cannot be left alone and requires a sitter.[373] Incidental expenses incurred by the companion in the course of providing the service also can be paid by the trust. "For example, if the [SNT trustee] pays a companion to take the beneficiary to a museum, the trust can pay for the admission of the companion to the museum, as this cost is part of providing the service."[374]

The revised POMS also include express directions to field offices limiting review of payments for caregivers. Under the revised POMS, when evaluating the propriety of trust disbursements for caregivers, field offices are directed:

---

372 Certain portions of the responses to these questions were strongly influenced by the excellent article by attorney Anna Sappington titled: *The Social Security Administrations' Policy Overhaul: A Practitioners Guide to the 2018 Special Needs Trust POMS Revisions*, published by the NAELA Journal

373 POMS SI 01120.201(F)(3)(a).

374 *Id.*

- Not to request evidence of medical training or certification of family members paid by the trust to provide care;
- Not to request income tax information "or similar evidence" to establish a business relationship;
- Not routinely to question the reasonableness of the compensation paid to service providers by the trust. If there is a reason to question the reasonableness of compensation, field offices are directed to consider the time and effort involved in providing the service and the "prevailing rate of compensation" for similar services in the beneficiary's geographic area.[375]

The SSA has struggled for years to decide whether distributions from a SNT to the beneficiary's family in payment for caregiving services violated the "sole benefit" rule. This has been emphatically resolved in the revised POMS, which states that while "[f]amily members may normally [provide care] without compensation, ... that does not prohibit the trust paying for these services."[376] The POMS also specifies that the policy allowing payments for caregiving should be applied uniformly regardless of who provides caregiving services. As stated in the POMS, "[a] third party service provider can be a family member, a non-family member, or a professional services company. The policy is the same for all."[377]

> **Helpful Hint:** Even though the SSA no longer requires a medical determination that caregiving or companions are needed for beneficiary's medical reasons, it is still a good idea to obtain a letter from the beneficiary's physician documenting a need for a caregiver or companion. It is not only the SSA that is interested in why such disbursements are made, but also the local Probate Court judge who may question this type of disbursement. Having the letter from a doctor or independent evaluator, (like National Care Advisors identified in Chapter 20) can provide the support needed to protect the trustee from attacks on the exercise of his or her discretion.

---

375 Id.
376 Id.
377 Id.

Family caregivers are often the most likely candidates to be caregivers or companions. They are aware of the needs of the person with a disability, often provide better care, and may cost less than a third party hired through an agency. SSA's prior policies in this regard were intrusive and unnecessary and likely resulted in many SNT trustees paying more money for third parties that provided worse care. SSA's new policy is pragmatic, reasonable, and better serves the interests of SNT beneficiaries. Caregiving and companions significantly enhances the quality of life for persons with disabilities. It provides beneficiaries assistance with activities of daily living, supplies companionship, increases comfort, and offers additional opportunities for a beneficiary's community involvement. The revised POMS' policy authorizing caregiving expenses provides SNT trustees with confidence that is acceptable to pay caregivers, even if they are family members.

WHAT IS THE EFFECT ON SSI OF PAYING FOR TRAVEL COMPANIONS FOR BENEFICIARY?

Oftentimes, an SNT beneficiary is unable to attend events or go on vacations without assistance. In these situations, the SNT trustee may be asked to pay for someone (or several people) to assist the beneficiary in enjoying these activities.

The SSA's prior policy in the old POMS regarding travel expenses for persons other than the SNT beneficiary was very restrictive. Although a SNT trustee could pay for the beneficiary's travel expenses, the trustee could pay for a non-beneficiary to accompany the beneficiary only when the beneficiary traveled for the purpose of obtaining medical treatment.[378] This was true even if the beneficiary required the assistance of others to travel safely. The effect of SSA's policy was harsh. In some cases, the SNT beneficiary was unable to travel or was forced to travel in an unsafe manner. It also was unfair: forcing non-beneficiaries to pay out-of-pocket meant that SNT beneficiaries who required support were less able to travel than those fortunate enough to be able to travel alone.

The revised POMS reverse this unsafe and unfair policy. SNT trustees are allowed to pay travel expenses of third parties who accompany and provide services or assistance necessary due to the beneficiary's medical condition, disability, or

---

378   Former POMS SI 01120.201F.2.b.

age.[379] Services necessary due to the beneficiary's age "means that the beneficiary is a minor and cannot travel unaccompanied."[380] Travel expenses are defined the same way as the Internal Revenue Service defines them, to include SNT beneficiary's transportation, lodging, and food.[381] The revised POMS' guidance also discourages undue scrutiny or second-guessing of such payments:

> Absent evidence to the contrary, accept a statement from the trustee that the service or assistance provided is necessary to permit the trust beneficiary to travel. Do not request a physician statement concerning medical necessity. You should not request evidence of medical training or certification for the person accompanying the trust beneficiary.[382]

Field offices are to review an SNT trustee's determination that assistance is necessary only when they have evidence indicating it is not. Field offices also should not require persons accompanying the beneficiary to have received official medical training or certification.

The SNT trustee is limited in how many companions it can pay to accompany a beneficiary. In evaluating the number of people necessary to provide support, SSA field offices are to use a reasonableness test.[383] The POMS provide an example of a SNT trustee paying for "other individuals, such as parents or caretakers," to provide supervision and assistance to a minor child with a disability on vacation, noting, "[t]ravel without this support would not be possible."[384] However, in order for an SNT trustee to pay a third party's expenses, the companion must actually provide services to the beneficiary necessary in order for the beneficiary to travel.[385] For example, a SNT trustee cannot pay for a third party to travel in order that *another* third party

---

379 POMS SI 01120.201F.3.b.
380 *Id.*
381 *Id.*
382 *Id.*
383 POMS SI 01120.201F.3.b.
384 *Id.*
385 *Id.*

also can accompany.[386] This request often arises in the context of parents requesting that a SNT trustee pay for the beneficiary's siblings to accompany them on the trip, on the basis that the parents cannot leave the nonbeneficiary children home alone and they cannot afford to privately pay for them. The SSA has expressly noted "the fact that ... parents or caretakers cannot afford to pay for the other children's trip, or cannot leave them at home, is not a consideration relevant to the sole-benefit requirement."[387] The SSA's new POMS policy on paying for companion travel is another example of the SSA creating a more reasonable standard for SNT trustees and beneficiaries to follow.

> **Example:** A first-party SNT beneficiary who has cerebral palsy would like to go on a cruise. The beneficiary is able to do some things for herself but requires assistance with bathing, dressing, eating, and transportation. Her doctor has made a written recommendation that she not go on a cruise without assistance. The SNT trustee is asked to pay for an assistant to help the beneficiary while on the cruise. The SNT trustee can pay for the attendant's full costs during the cruise and pay reasonable salary for her services. There is no effect on public benefits in paying for the companion.

> **Example:** A first-party SNT beneficiary has schizophrenia but with medication is able to manage all of his personal care. The beneficiary asks the trustee to pay for his friend to assist him on his trip to Hawaii. The beneficiary is unable to get a doctor to agree that he requires any assistance with his any of his needs. The SNT trustee should refuse this distribution because it would not be for the "sole benefit" of the beneficiary.

---

386 *Id.*
387 *Id* in NOTE.

WHAT IS THE EFFECT ON SSI OF PAYING FOR THIRD PARTIES TO VISIT THE BENEFICIARY?

SSA's old policies strictly limited the first party SNT trustee's ability to pay for non-beneficiaries' travel when not accompanying the beneficiary. Third party travel expenses were limited to travel to visit the beneficiary "for the purpose of ensuring the [beneficiary's] safety and/or medical well-being[.]"[388] In order to qualify for this exception to the "sole benefit" rule, the beneficiary had to live in a "long-term care facility ... or other supported living arrangement in which a non-family member or entity is being paid to provide or oversee the [beneficiary's] living arrangement."[389] This was a strict limitation because SNT trustees could not pay for third parties to visit to ensure the safety or medical well-being of a beneficiary living independently.

The new POMS incorporate the prior exception, but expand it by allowing certain travel to visit a SNT beneficiary living independently:

c. Payment of third party travel expenses to visit a trust beneficiary

The following travel expenses to ensure the safety or medical well-being of the trust beneficiary are allowable and do not violate the sole-benefit rule:

- Travel for a service provider to oversee the trust beneficiary's living arrangements when the beneficiary resides in an institution, nursing home, other long-term care facility (for example, group homes and assisted living facilities), or other supported living arrangements.
- Travel for a trustee, trust advisor named in the trust, or successor to exercise his or her fiduciary duties or to ensure the well-being of the beneficiary when the beneficiary does not reside in an institution.

NOTE: A third party can be a family member, non-family person, or another entity. If you have questions about whether a

---

388 Former POMS SI 01120.201F.2.b.

389 *Id.*

disbursement is permissible, please request assistance from your regional office.[390]

This new SSA policy expands the types of services the SNT trustee can pay for third parties to visit a beneficiary.

WHAT IS THE EFFECT OF HIRING AN IHSS WORKER AS A CAREGIVER?

The In-Home Supportive Services (IHSS) program provides in-home and nonmedical personal care services to persons with disabilities to enable them to remain in their homes. In general, IHSS provides personal care services, which include assistance with ambulation, bathing, oral hygiene, grooming, and dressing; care and assistance with prosthetic devices; bowel, bladder, and menstrual care; skin care; repositioning, range-of-motion exercises, and transfers; feeding and assurance of adequate fluid intake; respiration; paramedical services; and assistance with self-administration of medications.[391] In addition to the personal care services described above, ancillary services, such as meal preparation and cleanup, laundry, food and other shopping, and domestic services, are available as long as they are subordinate to personal care services.[392] Persons can receive transportation, yard abatement, heavy cleaning, protective supervision, and certain paramedical services. For a further discussion of the IHSS program see Chapter 3.

Because IHSS caregivers have no job security and usually receive minimal (or very low) wages, it is difficult to attract and retain individuals to this type of employment. Recent changes to federal overtime laws resulted in the State of California refusing to authorize more than 40 hours of IHSS work per week, further limiting those willing to work for IHSS. When a good IHSS caregiver is working for the beneficiary, the beneficiary may ask the SNT trustee to supplement this low pay to retain the services of the IHSS worker. Or, the SNT trustee may be asked to hire the IHSS caregiver to provide additional services because the caregiver already understands beneficiary's needs and may be less expensive than hiring agency caregivers.

---

390 POMS SI 01120.201F.3.c. (emphasis in original).
391 Welfare & Institutions Code §14132.95(d)(1).
392 Welfare & Institutions Code §14132.95(d)(2).

For most persons receiving IHSS, the IHSS caregiver's salary from the state cannot be supplemented.[393] For example, if IHSS will pay a caregiver for 10 hours a month at $12 an hour, a trustee cannot augment the worker's salary by paying an additional $5 hour on top of the $12. However, the trustee can hire the IHSS caregiver for additional hours and pay a premium wage for those hours.

Further, the IHSS worker cannot be hired to supplement services already contracted for through the IHSS program. For example, if the IHSS worker is contracted to do laundry for five hours a month, the SNT trustee cannot pay the IHSS worker to perform an additional five hours of laundry. In order to properly structure the pay for an IHSS worker, the SNT trustee should know what services the IHSS worker has been hired to provide and how many hours a month are being paid for by the government.

> **Example:** If IHSS is paying a caregiver $12 an hour for ten hours a month, a trustee cannot augment the worker's salary by paying an additional $5 hour on top of the $12. However, the trustee can hire the IHSS caregiver for additional hours and pay a premium wage for those hours. For example, if the IHSS worker is being paid $12/ hour for ten hours, the SNT can pay $20 an hour for an additional ten hours helping the beneficiary, which brings the IHSS's worker's average pay up to $17.50 an hour for all the work provided.

> Note, however, that the services provided during the hours paid by the trustee must be different from the services authorized by IHSS. If the services are the same, the hours provided by IHSS may be reduced. For example, if IHSS pays for two baths a week and the trustee agrees to pay for five baths a week, then IHSS will cease paying for the two baths a week, because it sees a need for only two.

---

393   42 C.F.R. §447.1; MPP Regs §30-767.4.

HOW SHOULD A TRUSTEE HIRE A CAREGIVER?

There are really three basic ways to hire a caregiver.

1. The trustee contracts with a care management, professional employment, or health care agency which employs the caregivers.
2. The trustee uses a referral registry of available help and selects a caregiver.
3. The trustee hires the caregiver himself or herself.

In order for the trustee to better understand the available options, below is a summary description of the various types of caregiving services:

- **Home Care Agency/Organization**

The term home care agency is very broad. Most often it indicates that a home care provider is certified or licensed by the state or federal government. However, in some instances, certification or licensing is not a legal requirement. Thus, it is important for the trustee to understand what the home health agency's credentials are in deciding whether to use them.

Home health agencies usually provide a plethora of skilled and unskilled caregivers. For example, some agencies provide services through physicians, nurses, therapists, social workers, homemakers, durable medical equipment and supply dealers, and volunteers. Home health agencies recruit and supervise their own personnel. As a result, the home health agency will assume liability for all care and employment matters.

In general, this is the most expensive option, but is usually the safest for the trustee if care is taken in selecting an appropriate agency. Some benefits of using a home health agency are:

- Agencies are responsible for ensuring all applicable state and federal labor, health, and safety laws and regulations, including payroll tax and social security withholding requirements are followed.
- Agencies generally have rigorous screening procedures and provide training for their employees.
- Agencies can usually provide a caregiver on short notice in an emergency, or they can provide several candidates to choose from.
- If the caregiver hired through the agency does not work out, the agency will provide someone else.
- Agencies will typically provide caregiver supervision 24/7 for any crisis.

- Agencies may also include on staff professional certified care managers that can help an SNT trustee.

• Employment Services Organization

An Employment Service Organization is a company that partners with a trustee, beneficiary, or family to hire a caregiver that is selected by the trustee, beneficiary or family and referred to the Organization. The Organization then becomes the sole employer of record for the caregiver and handles all of the administrative aspects of employment, including payroll processing, tax reporting, and human resources support. It also assumes all of the employment liability.

• Referral Registry

Most communities have attendant registries that are a good resource for finding in-home help. These registries usually are not licensed or regulated by government. When calling an attendant registry, it is important to inquire about their particular screening process or training requirements. The trustee should also inquire about the fees charged. Fees for using a registry can vary greatly, from free to thousands of dollars.

There are also nonprofit community agencies that maintain lists of individuals available to perform all kinds of household tasks, from cleaning and laundry to repairs and gardening. It is a good idea to shop around and obtain the best service for the lowest fee.

The trustee will select and supervise the work of a registry-referred provider. The trustee must also pay the caregiver and comply with all applicable state and federal labor, health, and safety laws and regulations, including workers' compensation, payroll tax, and social security withholding requirements as described below. The referral registry is usually not the employer, and therefore the SNT, the care recipient or the SNT Trustee may be held as the responsible employer.

• Individual selected by trustee

A trustee can directly hire an individual to be the beneficiary's caregiver. The screening process is generally easier if the trustee uses a registry, but using one is not necessary. Caregivers can be anyone the trustee can find, including friends, family, nurses, therapists, aides, homemakers, or privately employed chore workers.

The trustee will select and supervise the work of the caregiver. The trustee must also pay the caregiver and comply with all applicable state and federal labor, health, and safety laws and regulations, including payroll tax and social security withholding requirements, as described below.

Some benefits of using an individual:

- Can hire a trusted family member or friend of the beneficiary who knows the beneficiary and who the beneficiary trusts
- Generally costs less to hire someone directly

The biggest drawback to hiring a caregiver directly is that the care recipient, the SNT and possibly the SNT trustee will be considered the caregiver's employer. The SNT trustee is then personally responsible for adhering to the oftentimes confusing employment laws and this can be daunting. Failure to follow the law can have significant financial repercussions.

> **Helpful Hint:** A sample caregiving contract is attached as Appendix L to this book. It can be used as a reference when the SNT trustee is hiring a caregiver directly but is not a substitute for obtaining the advice of trusted counsel. Employment laws change quite frequently, and different situations require different strategies.

SHOULD A TRUSTEE USE A HOME CARE AGENCY OR HIRE A PRIVATE INDIVIDUAL?

It depends. The real goal is to find the right person for the job. Thus, each situation will be different, depending on the

- Level of care required;
- Availability of a trusted individual to serve;
- Amount of SNT's assets to pay for services; and
- Ability to manage either an individual or agency.

In general, if the assets justify it, hiring a home care agency is often the preferred method for an SNT trustee. It is better because the trustee will not have to be involved in the day-to-day administration of the caregiver and will generally be protected against liability as long as appropriate steps were taken in the selection and periodic review of the agency. In selecting an agency, it is important that the trustee make sure that the agency is licensed, bonded, and insured. Plus, home health agencies costs vary widely. A trustee should check around to see if he or she could find the one that provides the best expertise with a good reputation at the best price.

However, if the trustee only has limited trust assets to work with, then directly hiring an individual may be the only affordable option. If there is no family member or friend available to serve, then it may be prudent to review a local registry of available workers as described in the previous question. You can also look within the caregiving circles of people who have a family member with a similar disability as the SNT beneficiary, or ask the beneficiary's doctor, physical therapist, hospital or nursing home personnel, church members, and not-for-profits that serve the community of persons with disabilities. It is very important that the trustee does an adequate background check and reasonably reviews the qualifications of a potential caregiver. Failure to do so can result in a trustee being sued and may place the beneficiary in a very dangerous situation.

See, Appendix K for a checklist for hiring and managing a caregiver and Appendix L for a sample caregiving agreement.

CAN A TRUSTEE HIRE A PROFESSIONAL CARE MANAGER INSTEAD OF A HOME CARE AGENCY?

Instead of hiring a home care agency or personally supervising the caregiver, a SNT trustee can hire a professional case manager to supervise the privately hired caregiver. However, the care manager is usually not the employer, which means the SNT beneficiary or SNT trustee may still be the employer of record and responsible for all the legal employment requirements of being an employer.

A professional care manager can assist the SNT trustee as well as the beneficiary and his or her family by providing a plethora of services that the SNT trustee may not be competent to provide. Care managers are professionals—trained to evaluate and recommend care for persons with disabilities. A care manager might be a nurse, social worker, psychologist, or public benefits expert who specializes in assessing the abilities and needs of persons with disabilities.

Care managers can assist the trustee and serve in any of a number of functions. For example, a care manager may

- Assess the level and type of care needed and develop a care plan
- Take steps to start the care plan and keep it functioning
- Make sure care is in a safe and disability-friendly environment
- Resolve family conflicts and other issues with long term care
- Become an advocate for the care recipient and the caregiver
- Manage care for a loved one for out-of-town families
- Conduct ongoing assessments to implement changes in care
- Oversee and direct care provided at home
- Coordinate the efforts of key support systems
- Provide personal counseling
- Help with Medi-Cal qualification and application
- Arrange for services of legal and financial advisers
- Provide placement in assisted living facilities or nursing homes
- Monitor the care received in a nursing home or in assisted living
- Assist with the monitoring of medications
- Find appropriate solutions to avoid a crisis
- Coordinate medical appointments and medical information
- Provide transportation to medical appointments
- Assist families in positive decision making
- Develop care plans for older loved ones not now needing care

The services offered will depend on the educational and professional background of the care manager, but most are qualified to cover items in the list above or can recommend a professional who can. Fees may vary. There is often an initial consultation fee that is followed by hourly fees for services. The hiring of a case manager is an appropriate expenditure of an SNT.

WHAT QUESTIONS SHOULD BE ASKED OF A POTENTIAL HOME CARE AGENCY?

Not all home care agencies are equal. The SNT trustee should assess which agency is best for his or her beneficiary. If the SNT trustee is uncertain how best to match an agency with the beneficiary, the trustee should hire a professional care manager to assist in matching an appropriate agency with the beneficiary. The following is a list of issues that should be considered by the trustee when hiring a care agency:

- When discussing hiring an agency, the trustee should be very clear about the beneficiary's care needs, emotional needs, personality traits, cognitive status, and nonpersonal needs (such as travel) for improved screening.
- The trustee should be very specific about dates and times when care will be needed.
- The trustee should seek a full description of agency caregiver screening and employment process. The more sophisticated the agency, the more sophisticated the screening process the agency will employ. Care agencies are supposed to conduct criminal background checks and proof of US employment eligibility. Many also conduct DMV checks with regular review, fingerprinting, skills testing and thorough reference checks.
- The trustee should seek a written explanation of all of the agency's services and fee structure.
- The trustee should ask the agency to assess the beneficiary's needs in person and create a plan of care with written caregiver instructions that will be updated as needed.
- The trustee should ask if the agency hires the caregivers as employees or independent contractors. Since one of the main benefits of using an agency is that it will handle the employment issues, if the agency hires caregivers as independent contractors, it is safer to look for a different agency.
- Ask the agency if it complies with all state, federal and local laws. When the agency's employee says, "yes," ask that person to put that in the contract.
- Be aware that some agencies have referral fees or otherwise prohibit beneficiaries from hiring caregivers directly. Read these provisions carefully in the caregiver contract or the SNT trustee could find it bound to pay high prices even if the caregiver is receiving relatively low wages.

WHAT SHOULD THE SNT TRUSTEE BE CONCERNED ABOUT WHEN DIRECTLY HIRING CAREGIVERS

Hiring caregivers directly, as opposed to using a care agency or other third party employer, requires careful consideration and planning. Most caregivers are not independent contractors, which means the caregiver will most likely be an employee of the SNT beneficiary or the SNT trustee or both.

Understanding the duties imposed on employers, and how the laws apply to caregivers, will help the SNT trustee minimize liability to the SNT, the beneficiary and the trustee.

WHAT QUESTIONS SHOULD BE ASKED OF A POTENTIAL CAREGIVER?

In selecting an appropriate caregiver, a trustee should create a job description for the type of care that the SNT beneficiary will require, as well as information about the hours and wages. The trustee will then have a good idea of what questions should be asked based on the needs of the beneficiary.

Example: Sample Job Description

Position: Home care worker for person with disability

Reports to: SNT trustee

Hours: Monday through Friday, 9:00 a.m.–1:00 p.m.

Minimum Requirements: 1–2 years of experience in home care, good interpersonal skills, ability to occasionally carry up to 25 pounds and help lift 150 pounds, may require frequent bending, torqueing, and kneeling, ability to read, write and communicate in English.

Responsibilities: 1. Assist with dressing, 2. Bathing, 3. Preparing lunch, 4. Shopping

When preparing for the caregiving interview, the trustee should have a list of questions pertinent to the job description and a sample work contract ready for the applicant to read. A sample caregiving agreement is attached as Appendix L to this book. The following are some suggested questions for the interview:

- Why are you interested in this job?
- Where have you worked before?
- Why did you leave?
- What were your duties?
- How do you feel about caring for a person with a disability?
- What do you find to be the most difficult part of working in home care?
- How do you handle people who are angry, stubborn, or fearful?
- Tell me about a time your client did not want to comply with medical orders?
- What would you do if your client started yelling or screaming at you?
- What would you do in case of an emergency such as _____?
- Do you have a driver's license?
- Do you have an automobile?
- Would you be able to transfer someone from a wheelchair into an automobile or onto a bed?
- Is there anything in the job description that you are uncomfortable doing?
- What time commitment is you willing to make to stay on the job?
- Can you give one personal reference and me two work-related?

Immediately after the interview, it is important for the trustee to write down first impressions and, if possible, discuss these with another family member or friend. It also would be best before hiring the person for the person with a disability to meet with them.

The trustee should also check the references of at least two final applicants. If the offer is accepted, the caregiver and the in-home helper should set a date to sign the contract and begin work. Both employer and employee should keep a copy of the contract.

> **Helpful Hint:** It is always prudent to run a background check when hiring individuals to assist a person with a disability. One service, for around $100, will provide criminal searches, identity verification, reference check, and several qualification confirmations. See, http://www.choicetrust.com. Another option is to utilize a professional screening company. Some additional resources

on how to safely screen, hire, and check on new employees is located at www.esrcheck.com. Certain laws limit the types of background checks you can perform, and, in most cases, there must be written authorization to perform the background check. For example, in California, you are not allowed to conduct a financial background check (e.g., credit check) unless the person will have access to certain specified financial and personal information.

WILL THE CAREGIVER HIRED BE AN EMPLOYEE OR INDEPENDENT CONTRACTOR?

In general, no matter how careful an SNT trustee is, the caregiver will nearly always be an employee. The distinctions between the two are as follows:

- For federal payroll tax purposes, an employee is "any individual who, under the usual common law rules applicable in determining the employer-employee relationship, has the status of employee."[394] The federal employment tax regulations set out these common law rules.[395] In general, an employer-employee relationship will exist when the person for whom the services are performed has the right to control and direct the worker who performs the services.[396] This is called the "control test" and is set forth in more detail below. For California's workers' compensation matters, employee is defined as "every person in the service of an employer under any appointment or contract of hire or apprenticeship, express or implied, oral or written, whether lawfully or unlawfully employed."[397] For wage and hour purposes, an employer is anyone who directly or indirectly "employs or exercises control over the wages, hours or working conditions of any person."[398]

---

394 Internal Revenue Code ("I.R.C.") § 3121(d)(2).
395 See Treasury Regs. §§ 31.3121(d)-1, 31.3306(i)-1, and 31.3401(c)-1.
396 Treasury. Reg. § 31.3121(d)-1(c)(2).
397 Cal. Labor Code§3351.
398 8 Cal. Code Regs. §11150, subsection 2(H)

- The presumption is that the relationship is one of employer/employee. It is up to the trustee to prove that the relationship is that of an independent contractor, and caregivers are rarely properly classified as independent contractors.

One of the primary factors the IRS and California EDD consider in determining whether a worker is an employee (as opposed to an independent contractor) is whether the employer has the right to control the manner in which services are performed. A good overview of these factors is found in U.S. Wage and Hour Division Administrator's Interpretation No. 2015-1 titled "The Application of the Fair Labor Standards Act's 'Suffer or Permit' Standard in the Identification of Employees Who Are Misclassified as Independent Contractors."[399] In the memo, the Wage and Hour Division Administrator David Weil focusses on the "economic realities" test. Other factors that the IRS considers in determining whether a worker is an employee are discussed in IRS Publication 15-A. Other factors that the EDD considers in determining whether a worker is an employee are discussed in EDD Publication DE-44. If the worker meets many of the following factors, the IRS will find an employer/employee relationship exists between the SNT trustee and the caregiver:

1. The worker is required to comply with the employing entity's instructions.
2. The employing entity or another must train the worker.
3. The employing entity integrates the worker's services into its business operations.
4. The worker must render his or her services to the employing entity personally.
5. The employing entity hires, supervises, and pays any assistants to the worker.
6. There is a continuing relationship between the worker and the employing entity.
7. The worker must devote substantially full time to the employing entity's care.
8. The worker does not work for more than one employer at a time.
9. The worker performs work on the employing entity's premises.

---

399 See, https://www.dol.gov/whd/workers/misclassification/ai-2015_1.htm

10. The worker must perform services in the order or sequence that the employing entity sets.
11. The worker must submit oral or written reports to the employing entity.
12. The employing entity pays the worker by the hour, week, or month.
13. The employing entity pays the worker's business and/or traveling expenses.
14. The employing entity furnishes significant tools, materials, and other equipment to the worker.
15. The employing entity invests in facilities that he or she uses in his work.
16. The worker does not realize a profit or suffer a loss because of his or her services.
17. The worker does not make his or her services available to the public on a regular and consistent basis.
18. The employment entity has the right to discharge the worker.
19. The worker does not have the right to end his or her care relationship with the employing entity at any time he or she wishes without incurring liability.

Some examples where the IRS determined there was an employee/employer relationship:

- A worker managed the convalescent's personal needs; entertained the "convalescent," lived in the convalescent home, accompanied the convalescent on trips, and provided any other services necessary for the comfort or well-being of the convalescent.[400]

- A brother engaged his sister, who is independent of his financial support, to act as his housekeeper and companion and to perform minor nursing services for him in his home during regular hours and according to his instructions.[401]

---

400 Revenue Ruling 56-109, 1956-1 C.B. 467.
401 Revenue Ruling 54-572, 1954-2 C.B. 341.

- Relatives were retained to provide personal care in the home of a family member and were paid, in part, by a welfare agency.[402]

- A hospital resident retained a private attendant to perform services of a domestic nature for the resident where the resident hired that attendant from a list provided by the hospital.[403]

The most common ways that trustees get into trouble is when the caregiver files a wage and hour claim as an employee, when the caregiver is injured while working, and when there is an IRS audit. In these instances, if the SNT trustee has not complied with the myriad tax reporting and employment laws, he or she will be subject to serious penalties.

> **Warning:** Some trustees illegally pay the caregiver cash without reporting the employment to anyone. An SNT trustee will be subject to severe penalties, and large fines will arise if taxes go unpaid or if wage and hour laws and workers' compensation requirements are ignored. The SNT trustee will likely have to pay these fines from his or her own pocket. It makes little sense for a trustee to put himself or herself in such jeopardy.

WHAT EMPLOYMENT ISSUES MUST THE SNT TRUSTEE UNDERSTAND?

It depends on whether the SNT trustee hired a home care agency or hired an individual from a registry or an individual.

1. If the SNT trustee uses a home care agency or employment services organization, the agency or employment services organization should be the caregiver's employer and should manage all employment related issues.

2. If the SNT trustee uses a registry or hires an independent care manager, the SNT or the SNT trustee may the employer and must address a number of issues, including wage and hour laws, notice and recordkeeping

---

402   Private Letter Ruling 9309026 (December 4, 1992).
403   Revenue Ruling 74-388, 1974-2 C.B. 325.

requirements, safety, liability, immigration laws, insurance issues, and withholding procedures, which are described below.

As described in the previous answer, caregivers are hired as either employees or independent contractors. The legal distinction between the two is enormous, but the practical difference can be miniscule. However, nearly all caregivers hired to take care of an individual with a disability will be employees.

When a SNT becomes an employer, the trustee must register with the California Employment Development Department within fifteen days. A regular employer should use EDD Form DE1. A household employer should use EDD Form DE1-HW. The SNT will be assigned a state employer identification number.

A newly hired caregiver should be asked to complete IRS Form W-4, "Employee's Withholding Allowance Certificate," and US Citizenship and Immigration Services (USCIS) Form I-9, "Employment Eligibility Verification." The SNT trustee also must verify that the caregiver may legally work in the United States. Employees in California must also receive a Labor Code 2810.5 Notice to Employee, specifying the employees' pay rates, the name of the employer, the pay dates, workers' compensation insurance information and other data.

The following is a list of the most common (but not nearly all) employment issues that must be resolved by an SNT trustee who has hired a caregiver:

- **Liability.** When home care is provided, the SNT trustee must protect the SNT assets and himself or herself from liability resulting from injury of the caregiver or losses from caregiver theft. A trustee should examine existing homeowner's liability and casualty insurance to see if adequate caregiver coverage is provided. If not, insurance should be purchased. Further, liability may attach to an SNT trustee as employer under a legal doctrine called *respondeat superior* for injuries caused by an employee's negligent or wrongful operation while acting within the scope of the employment.[404] For example, if the caregiver causes an automobile accident on the way to the store to pick up groceries for the SNT beneficiary, the SNT trustee, as

---

404 Civil Code §2338.

employer may be liable. An insurance broker should be consulted for each policy to confirm caregiver coverage.

- **Workers' Compensation.** In California, policies providing comprehensive personal liability coverage must include workers' compensation benefits for household employees, unless the benefits are otherwise covered or the employee's services are performed in connection with a trade, business, or occupation.[405] There are some exceptions. For example, an employee injured on the first day of work may not be covered by the homeowner's policy. It is almost always a smart decision to obtain a workers' compensation rider on the homeowner's policy. The SNT trustee should consult with his or her insurance broker to make sure that workers' compensation is provided.

- **Minimum Wage/Overtime.** The minimum wage and overtime laws are very complex and differ depending on the nature of the work. Caregivers should never be paid a salary or on a "per shift" basis, because a salary does not compensate the employee for any overtime hours worked. Since January 1, 2014, California's Domestic Workers Bill of Rights requires most caregivers to receive at least one and one-half times the employee's regular hourly rate for all hours worked in excess of 9 hours per day or in excess of 45 hours per week. Recent changes to the federal "companion" exemption may require overtime after 40-hours in a week. If the caregiver does not qualify as a "personal attendant" under the Domestic Workers Bill of Rights, the overtime requirements differ depending on whether the employee is a "live-in" or not. Each worker's situation must be examined for proper compliance.

- **Social Security/Medicare Withholding.** The SNT trustee will be required to withhold Social Security and Medicare (commonly called FICA) on wages for domestic help hired to provide care if the worker is paid more than

---

405 Insurance Code §§11590-11593.

specific limits.[406] Generally, 7.65 percent of the paycheck is withheld, and the employer pays another 7.65 percent on the employee's behalf.[407]

- **Unemployment.** An SNT trustee must pay unemployment tax (commonly called FUTA). Withholding is required if a care worker is paid compensation above specific limits during any quarter of the current or preceding calendar year.[408] There are also state unemployment, disability insurance, and employment training taxes to be considered.

  Helpful Hint: Unless the SNT trustee is very experienced in employment issues, it is strongly recommended that the trustee hire a payroll service to pay appropriate taxes. Some companies, such as Paychex (http://www.paychex.com), ADP (https://www.adp.com), and BenefitMall (https://www.benefitmall.com) may provide limited HR support in the employee/employer relationship.

WHO SHOULD BE THE CAREGIVER'S EMPLOYER?

An "employer" is anyone who "employs or exercises control over the wages, hours or working conditions of any person."[409] While many caregivers and families may want to treat the caregiver as an independent contractor, most government agencies will classify caregivers as employees. Incorrectly classifying a caregiver as an independent contractor can result in significant penalties and the failure to correctly pay the worker, creating significant liabilities.

The caregiver needs to be employed by someone, and oftentimes will have "joint employers." Since an employer is anyone who controls the hours, wages or working conditions, family members who hire the caregiver or direct the caregiver regarding the services to provide can be considered a joint employer. The SNT trustee who decides when and how to pay the caregiver, or who has control over whether to pay the caregiver, can be considered a joint employer. If the beneficiary directs the work

---

406   I.R.C. §§3102(a), 3121.
407   I.R.C. §§3101, 3111.
408   I.R.C. §3306.
409   8 Cal. Code Regs. §11150, subsection 2(H)

the caregiver performs, the beneficiary can be considered a joint employer. A conservator of the person of the beneficiary or a care manager that oversees the work to ensure the beneficiary is receiving proper care can be considered a joint employer.

Identifying a specific person or trust as the employer can help direct the inquiry to a specific person. Since the beneficiary will almost always be considered an "employer," the employment agreement or offer letter, and other employment documents will oftentimes identify the beneficiary as the employer. There may be reasons to have the SNT designated as the employer. SNT trustees should consult with their counsel before identifying the SNT as the employer.

Because the SNT trustee must necessarily perform many of the duties of an "employer," the SNT trustee should always identify the context in which the SNT trustee is performing services. For example, if the SNT trustee is going to sign an employment agreement, the agreement should state he or she is signing as the SNT trustee and not in their individual capacity.

Because an employer is anyone who exercises control over the hours, wages or working conditions, communication with caregivers regarding the work should be limited to whoever is going to be the employer, or the employer's designee. If three different family members are scheduling and directing the caregivers regarding the work to be performed, all three could be considered an "employer." When communicating with the caregiver about work tasks, persons that are not the employer should be clear that they are presenting the "employer's" ideas and concerns.

HOW SHOULD THE TRUSTEE HANDLE CAREGIVER AND OTHER SNT EMPLOYEES' TAXES?

Under federal and state tax laws, almost all caregivers are treated as employees subject to payroll tax, rather than as independent contractors. This is true whether the caregiver works full time or part time, and whether the caregiver is hired on a permanent or temporary basis. The caregiver may ask to be treated as an independent contractor rather than an employee, and the trustee may prefer to treat the caregiver as an independent contractor. However, the preferences of the caregiver and the trustee in this regard are not the controlling factor.

A caregiver who is hired through an agency may be an employee of the agency, rather than the SNT, where the trustee makes ongoing payments to the agency for the caregiver's services. The trustee should ascertain that the agency does in fact treat the caregiver as an employee for tax purposes and that the agency carries a workers' compensation insurance policy.

Payroll tax rules are complex and confusing. Federal and state rules are not consistent with each other. The penalties for failing to pay required payroll taxes are severe. The authors recommend that the trustee utilize a payroll service or hire a tax professional who is familiar with payroll taxes.

A newly hired caregiver should be asked to complete IRS Form W-4, "Employee's Withholding Allowance Certificate," and US Citizenship and Immigration Services (USCIS) Form I-9, "Employment Eligibility Verification." The SNT trustee must verify that the caregiver may legally work in the United States. The employer can also verify citizenship status by using E-Verify located at https://www.uscis.gov/e-verify.

Federal and state laws distinguish between "regular" and "household" employees. Different payroll requirements apply to these two types of employees. Federal and state rules are different; an employee may be considered a regular employee by one government entity and a household employee by the other. Federal law defines a household employee as a worker who performs domestic services in the private home of the employer.[410] Examples include private nurses and health aides.

When the employer is a nongrantor trust (typically a third-party SNT), the employee cannot be a household employee because the employer trust does not have a home. However, when the employer is a grantor trust (typically a first-party SNT), it is theoretically possible for the trust to have a household employee, because the grantor trust is generally ignored for tax purposes.

> **Critical Pointer:** Even in the case of a grantor trust, caregivers should never be treated as household employees for federal tax purposes. This is because payroll taxes are computed on the employer (beneficiary's) personal income tax returns, and the payroll taxes are paid as part of the beneficiary's personal tax liability. The trustee usually has no control over the preparation and filing of this return. In addition, the payroll tax liability may give rise to an estimated tax requirement. If there is a tax overpayment, it is

---

410   IRC §3510(c).

possible that the SNT beneficiary will receive a tax refund in his or her personal name. It is far better to treat all caregivers as regular employees for federal tax purposes so that the trustee retains control of the payroll tax reporting and payments.

When a SNT becomes an employer, the trustee must register with the California Employment Development Department within fifteen days. A regular employer should use EDD Form DE1. A household employer should use EDD Form DE1-HW. The SNT will be assigned a state employer identification number.

Some employment taxes must be withheld from an employee's pay. These include the employee's share of social security and Medicare taxes and the California state disability tax. The employer must pay other taxes. These include the employer's share of social security and Medicare taxes and the federal and California unemployment taxes. In addition, regular employers must withhold federal and state income taxes.

Household employers must withhold income taxes only if the employer and employee agree that the employer will do so. There are various exceptions to these requirements when the employer and employer are related.

The minimum wage and overtime laws are very complex and differ depending on the nature of the work. Each worker's situation must be examined for proper compliance.

HOW MUCH SHOULD A CAREGIVER BE PAID?

A home care agency will have its own fee schedule. The amount of fees will depend greatly on the type of services needed. An individual caregiver is generally paid an amount equal to the prevailing wage for similar services performed in the community where the services will be performed. Thus, if the caregiver is only providing home cleaning services, shopping, and preparing meals, the pay should equal what it would generally cost to hire someone to perform these tasks. One way to determine these costs is to check Craigslist to see what similar services are being offered in the beneficiary's community. Thus, a trustee should have a good idea what others in the area charge for similar services.

The minimum wage and overtime laws are very complex and differ depending on the nature of the work and the location. Recent changes in the law also require all employees to receive paid sick leave and other paid or unpaid time off. Which laws apply may depend on how many workers are employed.

> **Warning:** Sometimes an SNT trustee is asked to pay a premium to the beneficiary's family members or friends to provide caregiving services. A trustee is breaching his legal duty if he or she pays more than those services are worth. Further, if a trustee hires his own family, he or she could be liable for self-dealing and be liable for breach of fiduciary duty unless the trust document authorizes this type of hiring or there is a court order authorizing this expenditure.

DOES THE TYPE OF CARE ALTER THE OVERTIME REQUIREMENTS?

Yes. Federal law and California law treat caregivers differently depending on the type of work performed. Under California law, a caregiver that meets the "personal attendant" exemption is someone who primarily dresses, feeds and supervises a person who by reason of age or disability needs assistance. The employee cannot spend more than 20% of his or her time performing duties other than dressing, feeding and supervising the care recipient (*e.g.*, house cleaning, gardening, etc.).

In 2005, the California Labor Commission said that "Supervision" would necessarily include certain efforts that are essential for independent living other than feeding and dressing (including isolated instances where assistance with medications is provided). According to the Labor Commissioner, "supervising" may also include assistance in obtaining medical care, preparing meals, managing money, shopping for groceries or personal items, using a telephone or performing housework when such activities are related to the independent living of the person and cannot be performed by him or herself alone due to health or age limitation. The Labor Commissioner specifically referenced duties included by U.S. Department of Health and Human Services National Center for Health Statistics' definitions for activities of daily living which include bathing, showering, getting in or out of a bed or chair and using toilet. Therefore, providing "care" is considered part of a personal attendant's duties.

For specifics regarding when to pay overtime, see the discussion below. When hiring a caregiver, it is important to determine whether the care recipient requires just fellowship and protection, or also requires assistance with the activities of daily living. It is also important to determine how much time the worker will spend performing non-personal attendant duties.

DOES IT MATTER IF THE WORK IS PERFORMED IN THE HOME OR AT A FACILITY?

Yes. In California, the location of the work can alter which wage order applies. Different wage orders have different overtime rules. Wage Order 15 and the Domestic Workers Bill of Rights apply to household workers. Wage Order 5 applies to residential care facilities, assisted living facilities and other places providing board and lodging.

If the work is performed at a residential care facility or an assisted living facility, the personal attendant exemption and the Domestic Workers Bill of Rights do not apply. This means the employee will be entitled to overtime after 8 hours in a day, after 40 hours in a week and for the first 8 hours on the 7th consecutive day worked. The employee will also be entitled to double time when the employee works more than 12 hours in a day or more than 8 hours on the 7th consecutive day worked.

CAN AN SNT TRUSTEE PAY A CAREGIVER A "DAILY" OR "WEEKLY" RATE?

Yes, but the trustee should not do so. A daily or weekly rate is a salary. Even if the trustee agrees that the salary will cover all hours worked, the law says that a salary only compensates an employee for the "regular non-overtime hours" worked. For a personal attendant, this means the first 9 hours in a day or the first 45 hours in a week. For a companion, this means the first 40 hours in a week. If the trustee pays a worker a daily or weekly salary, the trustee is not paying the employee for any overtime hours. All caregivers should be paid by the hour and should be paid for all hours worked.

Helpful Hint: It is essential that all caregivers complete and submit time records. A trustee should have a way of maintaining these time records in case there is later a need to substantiate to a court or government agency.

WHAT IS THE MINIMUM WAGE FOR CAREGIVERS

At the time of the writing of this book, all employees must receive the federal minimum wage of $7.25 per hour. California employees must receive at least the state minimum wage. California's minimum wage laws do not cover any individual who is the parent, spouse, child, or legally adopted child of the employer. Those same family members are also exempt from federal minimum wage as long as the family members are the only "regular" employees. [411]

California's minimum wage is set to increase to $15.00 per hour over the next several years:

$13.00, effective January 1, 2020

$14.00, effective January 1, 2021

$15.00, effective January 1, 2022

Several cities have adopted their own minimum wage obligations. Employees performing work within the city limits are usually entitled to the higher city-required minimum wage obligations. The SNT trustee should check with the relevant city and county to determine if there have been changes to the minimum wage in that particular locale.

WHEN IS THE CAREGIVER ENTITLED TO OVERTIME?

The answer to this question is complicated and can change depending on a variety of very small factors. It is prudent to retain an employment attorney to review these issues prior to running afoul of these rules.

In answer to the question, if a worker meets California's personal attendant exemption (see "Does The Type of Care Alter the Overtime Requirements?)" above,

---

411   29 U.S.C. §203(s)(2)

the employee is entitled to overtime when he or she works more than 9 hours in a day or more than 45 hours in a workweek, regardless of whether he or she is a "live-in" or not. If the employee does not meet the personal attendant exemption, the employee is entitled to overtime when the employee works more than 8 hours in a day, or more than 40 hours in a week, and for the first 8 hours on the 7th consecutive day worked in a workweek. The non-personal attendant is also entitled to double time when the employee works more than 12 hours in day or more than 8 hours on the 7th consecutive day worked in a workweek.

If the non-personal attendant employee is a "live-in," the employee is entitled to overtime after working a 12-hour span, but the employee must receive at least 3 hours of non-work time during the 12-hour span. Non-personal attendant live-in employees receive double time after the first 9 hours on the 6th and 7th consecutive day worked.

In contrast, federal regulations, revised on January 1, 2015, only exempt persons employed by a member of the family who perform "companionship services." Companions working for a third party care agency are never exempt from federal overtime laws. Under the revised regulations, effective January 1, 2015, the term "companionship services" means the provision of fellowship and protection for an elderly person or a person with an illness, injury, or disability who requires assistance in caring for himself or herself. The term "companionship services" includes the provision of care, when the care is provided attendant to and in conjunction with the provision of fellowship and protection, and does not exceed 20 percent of the total hours worked per consumer and per workweek. In other words, if the companion spends more than 20 percent of his or her time assisting the elderly or disabled person with the normal activities of daily living, the worker is entitled to overtime under federal law.

If the employee does not meet the federal companion exemption, the worker must receive overtime when the employee works more than 40 hours in a week. There are no daily overtime requirements under federal law.

Employers in California must comply with federal and state law. When the two laws differ, the employer must apply the law that most benefits the employee. For example, if the employee is a "personal attendant" but not a "companion" employed by the family, the employee must receive overtime when he or she works more than 9 hours in a day or more than 40 hours in a week.

DOES THE EMPLOYER HAVE TO PAY FOR ALL HOURS THE CAREGIVER IS IN THE HOME?

It depends. An employer has to pay the employee for all "hours worked." For household occupations, "hours worked" is defined as "the time during which an employee is subject to the control of the employer, and includes all time the employee is suffered or permitted to work, whether or not required to do so."[412] So, if the SNT trustee requires the caregiver to be in a specific location, even if the caregiver is able to spend the time in purely personal pursuits, the employee is subject to the trustee's control and must be paid for his or her time.

Depending on the circumstances, there may be significant periods of time when the caregiver is not required to perform any duties. If the caregiver is free to leave the premises and engage in personal pursuits, then that time is not compensable even if the caregiver decides to remain on the premises. It is important to clearly identify when the caregiver is relieved of duties and free to leave the premises, so the caregiver knows and understands he or she is free to leave. If possible, the specific schedule should be in writing and should state whether the caregiver is required to remain on the premises or not.

DOES THE EMPLOYER HAVE TO PAY THE CAREGIVER WHEN THE CAREGIVER IS SLEEPING?

Under California law, if the caregiver is required to remain on the premises, the employer is obligated to pay the caregiver even if he or she is sleeping. Under federal law, there are provisions allowing employers to deduct sleep time in some circumstances, but because California employers have to comply with state and federal law, employers must pay employees whenever they are subject to the control of the employer.

The SNT Trustee should be cautious about allowing caregivers to spend the night when the care recipient does not require overnight care. If the caregiver believes he or she is required to spend the night, then the employee may be entitled to compensation for the sleep time. If the SNT trustee is going to allow the caregiver to remain on the premises even though no work is required, the employment

---

412   8 Cal. Code Regs. §11150(2)(H).

agreement should specifically state that the caregiver is free to leave the premises even though the caregiver may choose to remain on the premises once the shift is completed.

HOW MANY REST AND MEAL BREAKS DOES THE EMPLOYER HAVE TO PROVIDE?

Almost all California employees are entitled to a 10-minute paid rest break for every 4 hours worked, or major portion thereof, whenever the employee works at least 3.5 hours. That means, if the employee works 3.5 hours, the employee is entitled to a duty-free rest period of at least 10 minutes. If the employee works 6 hours or more, the employee is entitled to a second duty-free rest period. If the employee works 10 hours or more, the employee is entitled to a third duty-free rest period. And, so on.

The employee does not need to "clock out" for the 10-minue rest breaks, but the employee should have uninterrupted time for the rest breaks. Whenever possible, the rest break should occur in the middle of each 4-hour block. The employer does not have to relinquish "all" control, but the employee must be relieved of all duties. For example, the employer can require the caregiver to remain on the premises, but the employee should be free to use the time as he or she sees fit.

Employers are also required to provide an unpaid 30-minute meal break whenever the employee works more than 5 hours in a workday. If the employee works more than 10 hours in a workday, the employee is entitled to a second meal break. Unlike rest breaks, employees must be free to leave the premises for the entire meal period, and the employee must clock in and out showing when the meal periods begin and end.

Failure to provide rest or meal breaks can result in significant penalties (1 hour's pay for each day the employee does not get all required meal break and 1 hour's pay for each day the employee does not get all required rest breaks).

Because caregivers oftentimes cannot leave their charges unattended for significant lengths of time, employers and employees can agree to an "on-duty" meal period. This means the employee will not be free to leave the premises and the employer will pay the employee for time worked. If the employer and employee have a written on-duty meal agreement, the employer can avoid the meal period penalties (but the employer must still pay the employee for the time worked during the meal period). The on-duty meal agreement must be in writing and it must specifically state that the employee can revoke the on-duty meal agreement at any time.

> **Note:** A sample on-duty meal agreement is included in the sample caregiver agreement attached to Appendix L. On-duty meal agreements are not allowed in every situation, so speak with your attorney to ensure an on-duty meal agreement is appropriate.

CAN THE EMPLOYER DEDUCT THE VALUE OF FOOD AND LODGING FROM THE CAREGIVER'S WAGES?

Yes, but an employer can only use meal and lodging actually provided, and the amounts an employer can deduct are limited.

The lodging deductions range from about $52 per week for a shared room to approximately $675 per month for an apartment. Meals range from about $4 to $8 depending on whether the employee receives breakfast, lunch or dinner. The specific amounts are set forth in the wage order.[413] Any deductions must also be reflected on the employee's pay stubs. Using food or lodging as "compensation" can also have tax consequences for the employer and the employee. If the employer is going to use the meal or lodging as a credit against the employer's minimum wage obligation, the employer must have a written agreement allowing the deduction.

DOES THE EMPLOYER HAVE TO PROVIDE PAID TIME OFF?

Employers do not have to provide paid vacation or paid holidays, but employers are required to provide at least 3 days or 24 hours of Paid Sick Leave. Some cities and counties require greater paid sick leave hours. The Paid Sick Leave can be used for (and should only be used for) specified reasons, including the employee's own illness or a family member's illness, or for the care or prevention of the employee's own health condition or a family member's own health condition, or for certain absences related to domestic violence. Employers can choose to provide the full amount of Paid Sick Leave each year, or have the employee accrue the Paid Sick Leave over time

---

413   8 Cal. Code Regs. §11150(10).

at the rate of 1 hour of Paid Sick Leave for every 30 hours worked. The accrued and used paid sick leave must be provided to the employee with every pay stub.

The Healthy Families Health Workplaces Act says the employer must provide 3 days or 24 hours of paid sick leave but does not address what happens if the employee typically works more or less than a standard 8-hour workday. The Labor Commissioner takes the position that the employer must provide the greater of the two. For example, if an employee normally works 5 hours a day, the employer must provide 24 hours of paid sick leave. If the employee normally works 12 hours a day, the employer must provide three 12-hour days (*e.g.*, 36 hours) of paid sick leave.

Employers are required to post a notice regarding Paid Sick Leave in the workplace. Allowing an employee to use Paid Sick Leave for reasons unrelated to illness or injury may unintentionally create a paid time off or paid vacation policy. Paid time off and vacation are different from paid sick leave because paid time off and vacation is considered a wage and must be paid out at the end of the employment relationship. Paid sick leave is not a wage and does not have to be paid out at the time of termination.

If an employer offers paid vacation, the employer cannot have a "use it or lose it" policy. Once an employee earns the paid vacation, the employee must be allowed to use the vacation or be paid the vacation at the end of the employment. Employees must be allowed to carry over any unused vacation time, and the employee must be allowed to continue to accrue vacation even after the employee has earned his or her yearly allotment. Employers can put a "cap" on the accruable vacation, but the cap should be at least 1.75 to 2 times the amount the employee can accrue in any given year.

The employment agreement should specify whether, and under what circumstances, the employee will be entitled to paid time off.

> **Helpful Hint:** The employer should check to see if a city has implemented additional requirements for paid sick leave. For example, the City of Los Angeles mandates up to 45 hours of paid sick leave.

WHAT FORMS AND POSTERS WILL THE TRUSTEE NEED IF THE TRUSTEE IS THE EMPLOYER OF THE CAREGIVER?

Every employer is required to have certain documentation when hiring and employing workers. Other documents are highly recommended. The following is a short list of documents employers should complete and/or provide to the employee when hiring the employee:

Require	Recommended
Labor Code 2810.5 Notice to Employee	Employment Agreement (including job description, at-will statement, pay rates, etc.)
W-4 Form: Employee Withholding	Background Check Authorization (if going to conduct background check)
DE 4 – CA Withholding certificate	Anti-Harassment Policy
I-9 Form: Employment Eligibility Verification	Emergency Contact Information (for worker)
Workers' Compensation Brochure	Confidentiality Agreement
Form DE 2515: Disability Insurance Pamphlet	
Form DE 2511: Paid Family Leave Pamphlet	
New Employee(s) Report: Form DE-34	

Many of these forms can be obtained from a payroll processing company. Others can be found online or in stationary stores. Employers are also required to have certain notices posted in the workplace. A trustee can purchase large laminated posters containing most of the required postings from payroll companies, HR companies, office supply stores and some big box stores. The large laminated posters are nice because most of the required posters are in a single place. Unfortunately, most families do not have wall space for such a large poster, and the posters tend to be "one-size fits all," which may not work well for the SNT trustee's purposes. The large laminated posters do not include the Wage Order or city or county specific posters, which must also be posted in the workplace.

The following is a list of required state and federal posters, and where they can be downloaded. City and counties may have additional posters that must be included. Household employers may find it easier to print out the required postings and place them in a binder labeled: Workplace Posters.

CALIFORNIA POSTING REQUIREMENTS
HOUSEHOLD OCCUPATIONS

Posting	Information	Source
Industrial Welfare Commission (IWC) Wage Order 15-2001	IWC Wage Order 15-2001 (Household Occupations) applies to all persons employed in household occupations whether paid on a time, piece rate, commission, or other basis. https://www.dir.ca.gov/iwc/IWCArticle15.pdf	IWC FORM 1115 Rev. 07-2014 CLC § 1183(d)
2015 California Minimum Wage	Sets forth California's minimum wage. http://www.dir.ca.gov/iwc/MW-2014.pdf	AB10, Stats of 2013, amending CLC § 1182
Paid Sick Leave	Provides information about paid sick leave entitlement and usage (Assembly Bill 1522). https://www.dir.ca.gov/DLSE/Publications/Paid Sick Days Poster Template (11 2014).pdf	DLSE Paid Sick Leave Posting 11/2014
Payday Notice	Must specify the regular paydays and the time and place of payment. An employer-developed notice is permitted. http://www.dir.ca.gov/dlse/paydaynotice.pdf	DLSE 8 Rev. 06-02 CLC § 207
Safety and health protection on the job	Contains pertinent information regarding safety rules and regulations. https://www.dir.ca.gov/dosh/dosh publications/shpstreng012000.pdf	CLC §6328

Emergency phone numbers	Lists emergency responders' phone numbers. https://www.dir.ca.gov/dosh/dosh_publications/s500pstr.pdf	Title 8, CA Code of Regulations §1512(e); March 1990 S-500
Notice to employees— injuries caused by work	Advise employees of workers' compensation benefits. http://www.dir.ca.gov/dwc/noticeposter.pdf	Title 8, CA Code of Regs § 9881; DWC 7(6/10)
Notice of workers' compensation carrier and coverage	States the name of the employer's current compensation insurance carrier, or the fact that the employer is self-insured. Obtained from the employer's worker's compensation insurance carrier.	CLC § 1102.8
Whistleblower protections	Must be prominently displayed in lettering larger than size 14 type and include a list of employee rights and responsibilities under the whistleblower laws, including the telephone number hotline maintained by the office of the California Attorney General. (Employers can develop their own post) https://www.dir.ca.gov/dlse/WhistleblowersNotice.pdf	CLC § 1102.8(a)
No smoking language	Signage must be posted designating where smoking is prohibited/permitted in a place of employment. This law is enforced by local law enforcement agencies.	CLC § 6405(c)(1)
Discrimination & Harassment in Employment are Prohibited by Law	The California Department of Fair Employment and Housing (DFEH) enforced laws that protect from illegal discrimination and harassment in employment. http://www.dfeh.ca.gov/res/docs/Publications/DFEH-162.pdf.pdf	Fair Employment and Housing Act, Gov't Code § 12900 et seq.

Pregnancy disability leave	Employers of five to 49 employees must post. "Notice A" – CA law protects employees against discrimination or harassment because of an employee's pregnancy, childbirth or any related medical condition. http://www.dfeh.ca.gov/res/docs/Publications/NOTICE%20A.pdf	Title 2, CA Code of Regulations § 7291.16(e); DFEH-100-20
Notice to employees: Unemployment, disability, and family leave	Advises employees of potential unemployment insurance and paid family leave insurance benefits. http://www.edd.ca.gov/pdf_pub_ctr/de1857a.pdf	DE 1857A Rev. 42(11-13)
Notice to employees: unemployment insurance benefits	Notice that employer is reporting wage credits that are being accumulated for an employee to use as a basis for unemployment insurance benefit. http://www.edd.ca.gov/pdf_pub_ctr/de1857d.pdf	DE 1857D Rev. 17(5-11)
Notice to employees: time off to vote	Not less than 10 days before every statewide election, every employer shall keep posted conspicuously at the place of work, if practicable, or elsewhere where it can bee seen as employees come or go to their place of work, a notice setting forth the provisions of section 14000. https://www.sos.ca.gov/elections/tov_final.pdf	Elections Code Section 14001 et seq.
Notice: Employee Polygraph Protection Act	Employers are generally prohibited from requiring or requesting an employee or job applicant to take a lie detector test, and from discharging, disciplining, or discriminating against an employee or prospective employee for refusing to take a test or for exercising other rights under the Act. http://www.dol.gov/whd/regs/compliance/posters/eppabw.pdf	WH 1462 Rev. Jan 2012

FEDERAL POSTING REQUIREMENTS

Posting	Information	Source
Federal Minimum Wage	The Fair Labor Standards Act sets forth the Federal Minimum Wage for hours worked. http://www.dol.gov/whd/regs/compliance/posters/minwage.pdf	WHD 1088 Rev. July 2009
USERRA – Uniformed Services Employment and Reemployment Rights Act	Applies to all employers with one or more employees. Employees have the right to be reemployed in their civilian job if they leave to perform service in the uniformed service. http://www.dol.gov/vets/programs/userra/USERRA_Private.pdf	DOL Publication July 2008
OSHA – Occupational Safety and Health Administration	Employers must provide employees a workplace free from recognized hazards. It is illegal to retaliate against an employee for using any of their rights under the law, or reporting a work-related injury or illness. https://www.osha.gov/Publications/osha3165.pdf	OSHA Publication 3165
IRS Tax Withholding Notice	Employers must notify employees that have worked at any time during the year from whom no income tax was withheld. Such employees may be eligible for an Earned Income Credit http://www.irs.gov/pub/irs-pdf/n1036.pdf	Notice 1015 Rev. 12-2014
Equal Employment Opportunity is the Law	Applicants to and employees of most private employers, state and local governments, educational institutions, employment agencies and labor organizations are protected under Federal law from discrimination. http://www1.eeoc.gov/employers/upload/eeoc_self_print_poster.pdf	EEOC-P/E-1 Rev. 11/09

WHAT CAN AN SNT TRUSTEE DO TO REDUCE CAREGIVING COSTS?

Home health care can be very expensive. It is the rare SNT that has sufficient assets to pay for all of a beneficiary's needed caregiving services throughout his or her lifetime. Thus, many trustees struggle to make sure that assets will stretch out as far as possible. Here are some suggestions for stretching out the dollars for caregiving:

1. **Check for Long Term Care Insurance.** While rare, a beneficiary of an SNT may be eligible to have long term care insurance pay for a home care agency.

2. **Negotiate the rate.** If the trustee has hired a home care agency, it can often find more affordable ways to meet the SNT's spending plan by using less expensive caregivers. For example, an expensive RN should not be handling services an unskilled worker can manage.

3. **Cutback hours.** The trustee can sometimes reduce hours without jeopardizing care. It is important to continually assess the beneficiary's needs to determine if a cutback in hours can provide an almost equal level of care. A trustee should also be wary of agencies that continually "suggest" that more hours are needed. Before agreeing, make sure that more hours are truly needed.

4. **Discuss with doctor.** The beneficiary's doctor may know of less expensive resources for nonmedical care.

5. **Discuss with place of worship.** A beneficiary's place of worship, or the trustee's, may sometimes know volunteers willing to help people with disabilities in the community.

6. **Discuss with beneficiary's family and friends.** The trustee may be able to reduce fees by having family or friends taking over some of the duties that the trustee has to pay for, like cleaning or shopping.

7. **Visit disability centered not-for-profits.** There are many not-for-profits that assist persons with disabilities. For example, the Centers for Independent Living have centers all around the state that can help.

8. **Seek other nonprofit resources.** For example, Family Caregiver Alliance (www.caregiver.org) provides grants to those needing respite (family caregiver relief) care, which can offset some of the costs.

9. **Apply for government resources**. California Medi-Cal provides In-Home Support Services (IHSS), which can provide funds to pay for, or at least supplement, nonmedical caregiving services.

10. **Shop separate services around**. If both medical care and personal care are needed, make sure that if one agency is handling both that a less expensive personal care agency is not available to pay for the personal care. Oftentimes, if one agency handles both, the personal care is much more expensive.

11. **VA Benefits**. If the beneficiary is a veteran, he or she may qualify for aid and attendance benefit. Check with a local VA agency to see if beneficiary qualifies.

WHAT OTHER RESOURCES CAN AN SNT TRUSTEE REVIEW TO ASSIST IN HIRING CAREGIVERS?

The following books will help a trustee understand the incredible pressures and difficulties that many caregivers face and provide solutions that will assist both the SNT trustee and those providing care.

D. Jeanne Roberts. *Taking Care of Caregivers*. San Mateo: Bull Publishing Company, 1991.

James R. Sherman. *The Caregiver Survival Series*. Golden Valley: Pathway Books, 1994.

Helping Yourself Help Others: A Book for Caregivers. New York: Times Books, 1994.

Nancy Mace and Peter Rabbins. *The 36-Hour Day*. Baltimore: The Johns Hopkins University Press, 1991 edition.

Angela Heath. *Long-Distance Caregiving*. Lakewood: American Source Books, 1993.

The following websites can help trustees manage a caregiver.

AARP's website has a caregiver resource center that provides exceptional assistance in hiring, training, and retaining a caregiver at http://www.aarp.org/relationships/caregiving-resource-center.

Eldercare Services' website and blog has information, education, and caregiver services at www.eldercareanswers.com.

Family Caregiver Alliance's website provides information and education on a variety of caregiver issues at www.caregiver.org.

H.E.L.P.'s website offers some wonderful caregiving tools. H.E.L.P. also provides classes for those who are helping the elderly and disabled. http://www.help4srs.org/healthcare/caregiving.

Legally Nanny's website offers advice to individuals hiring elder care providers on legal and tax advice. For a fee, they will assist in handling the legal and tax requirements of hiring an at home caregiver. http://www.legallynanny.com.

CAN THE SNT TRUSTEE HIRE THE BENEFICIARY'S PARENTS TO SERVE AS CAREGIVER?

Generally, yes, but certain issues must be resolved by the SNT trustee before agreeing to pay a parent. It often makes sense to hire a parent to be the beneficiary's caregiver, and many of the employment laws (including minimum wage and overtime) do not apply when a parent is "employed by" the care recipient. Parents are aware of their child's needs, often provide better care, and typically cost less than a third party. Further, the parent may have given up a job to care for their child and may need the funds to allow them to continue to provide care. The SNT trustee may need to address the following issues:

- If a minor child beneficiary is receiving SSI, the payment of caregiving income to the parent may reduce or eliminate the child's eligibility for SSI under a concept called SSI deeming.[414] This concept is discussed in Chapter 3 more fully, but the basic idea is that a parent must use his or her income to support those dependent on them. The SNT trustee must make sure that any payments to a parent will not interfere with the child/SNT beneficiary's SSI eligibility.

- If the parents are trustees, they may have a conflict of interest in hiring themselves as employees of the trust that they administer. If the SNT document does not expressly allow them to hire themselves as caregiver, then court instruction should be obtained through a court petition to approve the hiring and setting the amount of their compensation. This petition is further discussed in Chapter 5.

- If the beneficiary is a minor, the parents have an existing duty to pay for that child's support that the SNT's assets cannot be used to offset. Parents have a general obligation to support their minor children "in the manner suitable to the child's circumstances."[415] Parents also have equal responsibility to support "to the extent of their ability, a child of whatever age who is incapacitated from earning a living and without sufficient means."[416] The parents' duty of support does not necessarily end with the furnishing of mere necessities. A minor child is entitled to be maintained in a style and condition consonant with his or her parents' position in society, and this duty of support continues even if the child is "possessed of ample means" of his or her own.[417] Because of their general duty of support, parents will be expected to provide some level of care for the beneficiary without compensation or reimbursement. However, SNT trustees have been successful in allowing trust assets to pay for items that go beyond the mere duty

---

414 20 C.F.R. §416.1160 for the rules about how a parent's income is "deemed" to be that of a minor child for SSI eligibility purposes.

415 Family Code §3900.

416 Family Code §3910.

417 *Chapin v Superior Court* (1966) 239 Cal.App.2d 851.

of support and constitute exceptional needs. SNT trustees have also been successful in paying for items when the parents are unable to afford these items due to unemployment as described below.

There is an exception to this general rule. When the parents are unable to afford basic support, a child's assets can be used to pay for the support or, in certain circumstances, supplement the parents' basic support to provide a higher standard of living for the child:

> … that a parent possessing adequate financial resources has a duty to provide his or her child with basic support regardless of the child's independent resources. Such a rule serves the dual purposes of assuring that a child's independent income is preserved for use of the child during his or her adult years, and at the same time permitting, in an appropriate case, such income to be used to supplement the parents' contribution so that the child might enjoy a higher standard of living during minority than the parents could otherwise afford. In the absence of a clear contrary trust purpose or the inability of the parents reasonably to provide any support, we conclude that this approach both respects the parents' statutory obligations of support mandated by Civil Code sections 242, 243, and maintains the flexibility authorized to trial courts by Civil Code section 246 and Probate Code section 1504.[418]

> **Example:** Jonathan is the trustee of his adult friend Simon's first-party SNT. Simon's mother, Alene, has been taking care of Simon since the accident that caused his disability. Alene asks Jonathan to pay a monthly amount to provide caregiving to Simon. Jonathan may authorize such payments as long as the fee is reasonable. Jonathan checks with area caregivers and provides a salary commensurate with that of the city they live in. Jonathan

---

418   *Armstrong v Armstrong* (1976) 15 Cal 3d 942, 949.

further will have to comply with all employment obligations, so he hires Paychex to do all employment withholding. He further consults with his insurance broker to make sure that all insurance is in place to protect the SNT.

Example: Father is the trustee of a first-party SNT that is under ongoing court jurisdiction for his minor son. He has quit his job to take care of his son and is living on a very limited income. Son is receiving SSI and Medi-Cal due to Father's limited resources and income. Father would like to pay himself as son's caregiver. Father must file a petition with court to determine whether he will be able to make these disbursements. The court petition will need to address the issue of his legal duty of support, his earning capacity, and the amount of the compensation. If court agrees, he can pay himself for these services. However, Father must be careful to not pay himself too much income, because doing so would eliminate his son's SSI due to SSI deeming to a minor child. See Chapter 4 for further discussion on deeming.

CAN A TRUSTEE HIRE OTHER FAMILY MEMBERS TO PROVIDE CAREGIVING SERVICES?

There are special exemptions from California overtime laws for personal attendants employed by the "parent, grandparent, spouse, sibling, child, or legally adopted child of the domestic work employer." The wage orders, including the minimum wage order, specifically exclude "any individual who is the parent, spouse, child, or legally adopted child of the employer." Therefore, it may be less expensive to hire a relative to provide the care.

It is unclear whether the exemptions apply to in-laws (*e.g.*, daughter-in-law), but the likely answer is that the exemption does not apply to in-laws. However, there is no reason that the son could not employ his wife to take care of the husband's mother. This would make the son the domestic work employer and the wife exempt from California's overtime laws under the Domestic Workers Bill of Rights.

The family may still be required to comply with the federal overtime laws depending on the type of work performed (see question Does The Type of Care Alter the Overtime Requirements?). The trustee must also consider other ramifications of hiring a relative, such as whether the family care provider will make subsequent claims against the trust, increased opportunities for potential elder abuse, and potential familial strife.

CAN A TRUSTEE HIRE AN UNDOCUMENTED WORKER AS CAREGIVER?

It is not advisable to hire an undocumented worker. The trustee could be subject to civil fines and criminal penalties (when there is a pattern or practice of violations). Criminal penalties can range from $375 up to $3,200 per worker for knowingly hiring an undocumented worker, $110 for each form up to $1,100 for each form for failing to comply with Form I-9 requirements can range from $375 up to $3,200 for each worker for committing or participating in document fraud, amongst additional civil penalties.[419]

WHAT HAPPENS IF THE TRUSTEE FAILS TO COMPLY WITH EMPLOYMENT LAWS?

In general, the SNT trustee will be responsible to pay the taxes and will be subject to penalties. The SNT will be responsible for all unpaid income, FICA, and FUTA taxes.[420] The federal tax penalty for failure to withhold income taxes is 1/5 percent (3 percent if no informational returns were filed) of the wages subject to income tax withholding. The social security tax penalty is 20 percent (40 percent where no informational returns were filed) of the social security taxes required to be withheld.[421] The trust will also be responsible for interest on unpaid taxes at the statutory rate.[422]

There may also be fines assessed to the trustee for failing to withhold and penalties may be sought for failure to file a tax return.[423]

---

419 INA §274 (Immigration and Nationality Act)
420 I.R.C. §§3304, 3102, 3301.
421 I.R.C. §3509.
422 I.R.C. §6601.
423 I.R.C. §6651.

> **Warning:** If it is found that the trustee willfully failed to collect and pay taxes, the trustee may be personally liable for the total amount of the uncollected tax under the "100% penalty provisions of the Internal Revenue Code.[424]

There may be ways to alleviate some of these penalties and fines by showing that the employer relied on existing practice. However, the findings must be in good faith with reliance on long-standing employment practices.

California may add additional penalties beyond the IRS California imposed liability for unpaid personal income, unemployment insurance, and state disability insurance taxes. In addition, California imposes a 10 percent penalty on any employer that, without good cause, fails to pay any contribution required of it or its employees.[425] If the Employment Development Department of California (EDD) determines that the employer willfully engaged in fraud in misclassifying its workers, instead of a 10 percent penalty, the EDD has discretion to issue a 50 percent penalty.[426] Plus, the EDD can issue a personal liability tax assessment against the trustee that failed to make payment. California will also require interest be paid on any unpaid contributions.[427] Unpaid personal income tax is generally assessed at a rate of 6 percent of wages subject to withholding.

Again, California has some opportunities to find relief from these penalties and fines on findings that the employer innocently and honestly believed that workers were independent contractors and not employees.

ONCE A CAREGIVER IS HIRED, WHAT SHOULD THE TRUSTEE DO TO MONITOR THE CAREGIVER?

The SNT trustee should do the following to make sure that the caregiving arrangement continues to be in the best interest of the beneficiary:

- Make sure that there is a personal care agreement with the caregiver specifying the name of the employer, the workers' duties, the compensation

---

424 I.R.C. §6672.

425 Cal. Unempl. Ins. Code §1112.

426 Cal. Unempl. Ins. Code §1128(a).

427 Cal. Unempl. Ins. Code §1113.

arrangement and the "at-will" nature of the employment. An example of a caregiver agreement is set forth in Appendix L.

• Make sure that there is a written care plan or caregiver instructions that identify the trustee's expectations for care, the beneficiary's specific needs, and the caregiver's roles and tasks to resolve those needs.

• Make sure there is a communication log or notebook where caregivers will document beneficiary care follow up and communicate with each other (if there is more than one caregiver).

• Make sure that the caregivers can communicate with each other if the notebook/log is insufficient by providing needed numbers to all caregivers.

• Make unannounced visits to ensure that caregiver is providing needed care.

• Communicate immediately with caregiver if expected needs are not being met.

• Provide ongoing training and professional support for caregiver as needed.

• If the trustee suspects a problem, be sure to investigate before taking disciplinary action, unless the beneficiary's safety is at issue.

Note. There is no caregiver that cannot be replaced (even family members). It is the beneficiary's safety and quality of life that must be maintained.

CHAPTER 15 SUMMARY

✓ The trustee can make disbursement for caregivers and companions for the beneficiary that may be the most important distribution that can be made but is also fraught with potential liability if not done correctly.

✓ The Social Security Administration (SSA) recently modified its policy on payments by first party SNT trustees to authorize the hiring, including family members

✓ The SSA also will not challenge the payment for travel companions for beneficiary necessary to provide services or assistance necessary duet to beneficiary's medical condition, disability, or age

✓ The SSA will still determine if the SNT is paying for too many companions, e.g., trustee can pay for mom and dad for minor disabled beneficiary, but likely not be able to pay for other minor brothers and sisters even if the parents cannot afford to take them

✓ The SSA authorizes spending trust funds for others to travel to visit the beneficiary to ensure the safety or medical well-being of the trust beneficiary

✓ The Trustee cannot supplement the pay of the IHSS caregiver, but may be able to hire for other services

✓ Trustee should hire an entity that is familiar with caregiving tax requirements.

✓ A caregiver can be hired several different ways, by private agency, using a referral registry or hiring one directly

✓ The SNT trustee should carefully evaluate the best way to hire a caregiver based on level of care, trust of person hired, amount of money it will cost, and ability to manage the situation

✓ The chapter provides numerous options for evaluating the best option for hiring caregivers, including evaluating and questions that should be asked

✓ A caregiver will almost always be an employee and not an independent contractor

✓ There are a host of local employment requirements for a caregiver that the trustee must be aware including: appropriate forms and posters that must be displayed, liability for accidents during work, workers' compensation, minimum wage/overtime, and payroll withholdings

✓ There are options for lowering ongoing caregiving costs, including checking for insurance, negotiating the rate, reducing hours, discussing with doctors, checking places of worship, families and friends, checking with local charities, confirming government resources, shopping around for services, and checking with VA if beneficiary or parent was in the military

✓ A parent can be hired as caregiver, but care should be taken to not pay a parent who already owes a duty to support a minor child or adult with a disability.

✓ A parent serving as trustee should file a separate petition to the court to determine if it is ok to hire himself or herself as caregiver

✓ A caregiver must not be undocumented worker and knowingly hiring an undocumented worker could lead to penalties

- ✓ If employment taxes were not properly paid, the trustee may be subject to draconian civil and criminal penalties
- ✓ Once an employee is hired, the SNT trustee should ensure there are procedures and policies to monitor that caregiver

CHAPTER 16

Proper Methods for Making SNT Distributions

For SNT trustees, the way an SNT distribution is made is just as important as knowing the effect the purchase of a specific good or service has on the beneficiary's public benefits. In earlier chapters, there is a discussion on how different types of SNT disbursements (such as for beneficiary's food or vacations) has on the beneficiary's eligibility for public benefits. Once the SNT trustee understands the effect the good or service has on eligibility, it is still imperative for the trustee to know how to properly make that distribution. Failing to understand the proper methods of making SNT disbursements can also lead to loss of public benefits, even when the underlying good or service is exempt.

> **Example:** SNT beneficiary wants a new television. The SNT trust-
> ee agrees to purchase it because she correctly determines it is
> an exempt asset for SSI eligibility purposes. The beneficiary uses
> his own money to buy the television and asks the SNT trustee to
> reimburse him the $600 it cost. The SNT trustee reimburses the
> beneficiary the $600. The effect of this distribution is the benefi-
> ciary loses $580 from his SSI check. This is because the disburse-
> ment of cash directly from the SNT to the beneficiary is treated by
> the Social Security Administration (SSA) as SSI unearned income,
> even when used for an exempt asset. The penalty to the benefi-
> ciary for unearned income is a dollar-for-dollar reduction of SSI
> after the first $20 of any income disregard.

The better way to have handled this situation is to have the trustee purchase the television directly, reimburse a third party for their purchase of the television, provide the beneficiary with a True Link card and pay for it using the card, or have beneficiary use a credit card and the trustee pay the credit card bill. These are all acceptable methods for making SNT disbursements that would not have interfered with the beneficiary's public benefits. These methods are discussed in more detail in this chapter.

HOW DOES AN SNT TRUSTEE MAKE APPROPRIATE DISBURSEMENTS?

There are several ways for an SNT trustee to make disbursements that will not interfere with the beneficiary's public benefit eligibility. The following list is a summary of the appropriate methods of SNT distributions and each are discussed in more detail later in this chapter.

1. **Pay for good or service directly.**[428] The trustee can pay for a computer and personally deliver it to the beneficiary, buy kitchen appliances online (like at Amazon.com or Overstock.com) and have the item delivered to beneficiary, or pay directly for beneficiary's cell phone or lawn service.

2. **Reimburse a third party for purchase.**[429] The trustee can reimburse a friend or relative who pays for the good or service. For example, the beneficiary's best friend purchases tickets to a baseball game for $50. The trustee can reimburse the friend the $50 for beneficiary's ticket.

3. **Purchase a gift card or certificate for the beneficiary.**[430] If the Trustee carefully follows the rules, he or she can purchase a gift card or gift certificate and provide it to beneficiary. However, a gift card or certificate must meet certain very specific requirements as described later in this chapter.

   Warning: This method of distribution is not recommended. As discussed later in this chapter, the authors are uncertain if any gift cards exist that meets the SSA's rules. There are better methods

---

428 20 C.F.R. §416.1103(g); POMS SI 00815.400; POMS SI 00815.550; POMS SI 01120.203(I)(1)(c).

429 POMS SI 01120.200(E)(1)(d); POMS SI 01120.203(I)(1)(g).

430 POMS SI 01120.203(I)(1)(f).

of distribution that are less dangerous than using the gift card exception.

4. **Pay the beneficiary's credit card bills.**[431] The beneficiary can charge items to a credit card and the trustee can pay the bill. The trustee must continue to exercise his or her discretion over each charge made—for example, if the trustee pays the whole bill and certain items were for food or shelter purchases, then in-kind support and maintenance (ISM) may be triggered.

5. **Using an Administrator Prepaid Card.**[432] The trustee can utilize a restricted debit card that can be customized to block the cardholder's access to cash, specific merchants, or entire categories of spending. This is a relatively new method of distribution that was created in the latest SSA's POMS update. It is important that the trustee own the card and not the beneficiary.

6. **Fund an ABLE account.**[433] The trustee can distribute funds to an ABLE account and the beneficiary can then choose to use the funds for his or her own Qualified Disability Expenses. See Chapter 10 on the eligibility requirements for using ABLE accounts.

WHEN SHOULD AN SNT TRUSTEE PAY FOR A GOOD OR SERVICE DIRECTLY?

The trustee should utilize this distribution method when paying beneficiary's monthly bills or for specific requested goods. For example, if the trustee has agreed to pay for the beneficiary's monthly cell phone bill, gym membership, and internet costs, the trustee can place the payment of the bills on auto pay from trust accounts each month. If the beneficiary asks for trustee to pay for his or her Amazon purchases, the SNT trustee can pay Amazon directly and have the goods shipped directly to beneficiary.

If the SNT trustee pays for food or shelter items directly for an SSI recipient, those disbursements will still be treated as In Kind Support and Maintenance (ISM) and the Presumed Maximum Value (PMV) one-third reduction of the SSI check will

---

431 POMS SI 01120.203(I)(1)(d).

432 POMS SI 01120.203(I)(1)(e).

433 POMS SI 01120.203(I)(1)(c), (h).

still apply even if trustee pays for the food or shelter directly. See Chapter 12 for effect on paying for food or shelter.

Similarly, if the trustee purchases a good or service that is not exempt, it will still be counted as a resource even if paid for directly. For example, if the trustee purchases a second vehicle for the beneficiary and distributes it to the beneficiary in the beneficiary's name, that vehicle will be counted as a resource because only one vehicle is exempt for SSI eligibility purchases. See Chapter 14 for a description of the vehicle exception.

WHEN SHOULD AN SNT TRUSTEE REIMBURSE THIRD PARTIES FOR PURCHASES?

The trustee can utilize this distribution method whenever any third party pays for a beneficiary's good or service. The trustee can even pay the third party's credit card bill directly for the beneficiary's goods are services paid for by the friend or relative. For example, if the beneficiary's sister purchased a new refrigerator for the beneficiary, the trustee can pay the sister back directly or pay the credit card bill.

However, just as with paying for things directly in the prior question, if the third party has paid for food or shelter treated as ISM, then the penalty still applies. Or, if the third party purchased a countable asset and the beneficiary owns it, it will still count against the beneficiary's eligibility even though the SNT trustee merely reimbursed the third party.

SHOULD AN SNT TRUSTEE USE A GIFT CARD OR GIFT CERTIFICATE FOR AN SNT BENEFICIARY?

The author's experience is that SNT trustees should not try and utilize this method of distribution. The SSA allows it but in order for it to work, the gift card or certificate must meet two very important requirements:[434]

> The gift card or gift certificate cannot be able to be used to buy
> food or shelter. It does not matter if food or shelter was actually
> purchased. It only matters if the card or certificate holder has the

---

434 POMS SI 00830.522.

ability to purchase food or shelter items. For example, a gift card or certificate for a restaurant, grocery store, Wal-Mart—which sells food—or Visa gift card would not meet the exception because the holder has the ability to buy food. Generally, gift cards or certificates for stores such as Macy's, clothing stores, bookstores, or electronics stores could meet this first requirement because it cannot be used to buy food or shelter items.

The gift card or gift certificate also must include a legally enforceable prohibition against selling the card for cash. The SSA states that absent evidence to the contrary, presume a gift card or certificate can be resold. For example, evidence to the contrary may include a legally enforceable prohibition on resale or transfer of the card imposed by the card issuer merchant printed on the card. The author has not yet found a commonly sold gift card that has this prohibition in it.

The penalty for providing a gift card or certificate to the beneficiary that either can be used to buy food or shelter or can be resold is unearned income. It is commonly misunderstood that if a gift card or gift certificate pays for food or shelter items, it will be treated as ISM income. This is wrong. It is treated as SSI "unearned income" and will reduce the SSI payment "dollar-for-dollar" after the first $20.[435] Any amount not spent for a disqualifying gift card will also be treated as a resource on the first day of the next calendar month.

Because of the draconian penalty and the lack of any gift card or certificate that meets both requirements, plus the availability of other methods of distribution, this method of disbursement is not recommended.

> **Example:** Trustee distributes a Best Buy gift card worth $2,500 to the beneficiary. There is a restriction on the resale of the gift card. In the month of distribution, there is no effect on beneficiary's public benefits. Best Buy does not sell food or shelter items, so it

---

435   20 C.F.R. §416.1124(c)(12); POMS SI 00810.420, 01120.200(E)(1)(a).

will not be treated as unearned income. However, if the value of the card were not spent down so that all the beneficiary's resources are below $2,000 by the first day of the next calendar month, he or she would lose SSI in the next calendar month and for each month thereafter until done so.

Example: Trustee distributes a Wal-Mart gift card worth $2,500 to the beneficiary, who receives SSI in the amount of $958.63 per month. There is a restriction on the resale of the gift card. However, Wal-Mart stores sell groceries. SSA will treat the gift card at its face value as unearned income in the month it is received, meaning that the beneficiary's SSI will be lost in the month of distribution (after first $20 reduction of dollar for dollar on benefits).

If the beneficiary only spends $500 in the month of receipt, then the $2,000 balance will be counted as a resource on the first day of the next calendar month. Any remaining value on the card is a resource beginning the month following the month the gift card was received, meaning that if the card is not spent down so that all the beneficiary's resources are below $2,000, he or she would lose SSI in the next calendar month and the following months until done so

SHOULD AN SNT TRUSTEE PAY THE BENEFICIARY'S CREDIT CARD BILLS?

Yes, this is a method of disbursement that surprises many SNT trustees given some of the other restrictions the SNT trustee must follow. The reason it works is that the trustee is directly paying a valid debt of the beneficiary. A trustee still must exercise his or her discretion over each item in the credit card bill and consider the possible negative consequences of having a beneficiary buying things without oversight, but for many trustees and beneficiaries this is a great way to provide a SNT beneficiary with some control over their own life.

Example: Paul Parry, an SNT beneficiary uses his credit card to buy a cell phone for $100, appliances for $40, concert tickets for $60, and groceries for $50. The SNT trustee can pay for the cell phone, appliances, and concert tickets, but if he or she pays the $50 for groceries, that portion of the bill will be counted as ISM against the beneficiary. If ISM were not an issue because the trustee is already paying Paul's rent, then it would be okay to pay for the food as well without any further reduction from his SSI check.

It is also important to know if the SNT beneficiary is a first-party SNT, the trustee must make sure that each payment is made for the sole benefit of the beneficiary. In the above example, if the concert tickets were for Paul Parry and a friend, the trustee could only pay for Paul's share of the ticket price. The other ticket would have to be paid from either Paul's public benefits money or by his friend.

The SNT trustee should remind the beneficiary that the SNT is not a blank check and that the SNT trustee is not simply paying for everything on the credit card bill. While the SNT trustee can make payments on the credit card, the trustee still has a fiduciary duty to make sure that such disbursements are in the best interest of the beneficiary. Thus, it is important to communicate with the beneficiary about the types and amounts of disbursements that will be approved.

Example: Mitch Schroeder, an SNT beneficiary, uses his credit card to buy a scooter for $3,500, buys hundreds of dollars of clothing each month, . The purchase of the scooter would cause Mitch to lose his SSI because it is a second vehicle and countable. (See Chapter 14 on Vehicles.) The SNT trustee refuses to pay for it. Mitch cannot afford to pay even the minimum balance of the credit card bill from his monthly SSI check. Mitch goes into default, loses his credit card, and loses his credit. In a worst-case scenario, he could have to declare bankruptcy and lose SSI until he sold the scooter. Depending on the circumstances, this may not be the worst thing to happen in this case.

Another issue arises if the beneficiary takes a cash advance on the credit card. The cash will not be counted as income in the month of receipt. This is because it will be treated as a loan.[436] However, if the beneficiary holds onto the cash until the first day of the next calendar month, it will be treated as a resource and could jeopardize eligibility if the loan is over $2,000 (for individual) or $3,000 (for couple).[437]

SHOULD THE SNT TRUSTEE USE AN ADMINISTRATOR PREPAID CARD (LIKE TRUE LINK) FOR THE BENEFICIARY?

Trustees of special needs trusts are increasingly relying on "administrator-managed prepaid debit cards," such as True Link cards, when disbursing funds to beneficiaries. These cards offer trust beneficiaries greater independence and the ability to get what they need more quickly. But such cards existed in a regulatory gray area as far as the Social Security Administration (SSA) was concerned. That is no longer the case. The SSA created a new policy in 2018 that expressly authorized the use of these cards, and even mentioned True Link by name.[438]

Because the cards can be managed online, trustees are able to link the trust funds to checking and similar accounts and quickly transfer funds to beneficiaries for their use. Along with ongoing monitoring and the ability to print off regular reports, the cards allow trustees to block purchases that my run afoul of SSA's rules, and thus jeopardize the beneficiary's continued eligibility for public benefits. Each True Link card, for example, can be customized to block transactions that might negatively affect benefits, such as purchases at grocery stores, restaurants, and bars. Administrators can also set up the card to work only at specific, authorized merchants -- and nowhere else.

The SNT, not the beneficiary, must be the account owner and administrator. The card should not be used to take out cash or then the amount will be considered cash income, which can jeopardize SSI benefits if the cash is not spent in the month of receipt. The card should not be used to buy food or shelter (if trustee does not want to trigger the In-Kind Support and Maintenance (ISM)), as then this would be counted by SSA as ISM, which can reduce the amount of your SSI benefit by the

---

436   POMS SI 00815.350.

437   POMS SI 01120.220(D)(3)(a).

438   POMS SI 01120.203(I)(1)(e).

one-third penalty. If the card is used at places that sell food or shelter, like Walmart, Target, or drugstores, receipts should be collected for all purchases to show that food was not purchased.

> **Helpful Hint:** An SNT trustee should go to www.truelinkfinan-cial.com to set up a True Link card for beneficiary if the trustee believes it is a good option for the beneficiary.

SHOULD THE SNT TRUSTEE FUND AN ABLE ACCOUNT FOR THE SNT BENEFICIARY?

The trustee should consider making a disbursement to an ABLE account for the beneficiary. The trustee should review Chapter 10 in detail to determine if an ABLE account will work in their particular situation. The benefit of this method of distribution is that the trustee allows the beneficiary to manage the money in a tax preferred account without affecting his or her benefits.

There are benefits to funding an ABLE account. For example, if the trustee funds the ABLE account and the beneficiary pays for his or her food or shelter from the ABLE account, it does not trigger an In Kind Support and Maintenance (ISM) penalty against the beneficiary. This provides more available funds to allow the beneficiary with enough money from his or her SSI check. There are other benefits such as allowing beneficiaries to manage and save their own money to achieve their own personal goals. It can be empowering for them who have had to allow others to manage their own financial affairs so long.

It is not for all beneficiaries, but for those with capacity, it can be a real benefit to them. The SNT trustee should make sure that the beneficiary is someone who can manage his or her own funds and would not be subject to undue influence. Plus, at this time, it is uncertain if the trustee may be held responsible for the beneficiary's actions in managing his or her own account. For example, what if the trustee funded the account each year for five years at $15,000 a year and then the beneficiary simply gives the money away. Would the trustee be responsible for making sure disbursements were not made to a beneficiary who would not spend the money well? It may be prudent for the trustee to perform some due diligence prior to making such a disbursement to a beneficiary.

WHAT IS EFFECT OF DISBURSING CASH TO AN SNT BENEFICIARY WHO RECEIVES SSI OR MEDI-CAL?

The disbursement of cash to an SNT beneficiary (even from the SNT trustee[439]) will reduce the amount of the monthly check from SSI or create (or increase) a share-of-cost for Medi-Cal, depending on whether the SNT beneficiary receives SSI or only Medi-Cal.

For the SNT beneficiary who is receiving SSI, providing cash of over $20 per month to an SSI beneficiary is nearly always a bad idea. If the beneficiary is on SSI, any cash provided to the beneficiary will be treated as SSI unearned income and reduce the SSI check dollar-for-dollar after the first $20 given.[440]

> **Example:** The SNT beneficiary is receiving $958.63 per month from SSI. The SNT trustee decides to give the beneficiary $500 per month as an allowance to supplement the SSI. The effect of the monthly cash disbursement is a loss of SSI of $480. Thus, the beneficiary only receives an extra $20 per month of spending cash but has lost $480 per month from his SNT that could have been used to pay for acceptable items and services.

For the beneficiary who does not receive SSI, but still receives Medi-Cal, distributing cash directly to the beneficiary will increase the beneficiary's Medi-Cal share-of-cost.[441]

> **Example:** The SNT beneficiary is receiving Medi-Cal as a medically needy person, but not SSI. The SNT trustee decides to give the beneficiary $500 per month as an allowance. The effect of the monthly cash disbursement is that the $500 per month will be counted as Medi-Cal income and will be calculated as part of the beneficiary's share-of-cost requirement. Thus, the beneficiary (depending on his other income) may have to pay an additional $500

---

439   POMS SI 01120.203(I)(1)(a).
440   POMS SI 00810.420, 01120.200(E)(1)(a).
441   22 Cal Code Regs §§50503, 50507.

406

per month toward his medical care before Medi-Cal will cover his or her medical costs.

WARNING: The SNT trustee should never distribute cash directly to a beneficiary who is an SSI or Medi-Cal recipient. This includes adding funds to beneficiary's debit card.[442] The effect will be the same even if the case disbursement is to reimburse the beneficiary for the purchase of an exempt item.

CAN THE TRUSTEE GIVE CASH (OR AN ALLOWANCE) TO THE BENEFICIARY OR REIMBURSE THE BENEFICIARY?

If the beneficiary receives cash, it will either be counted as unearned income for SSI purposes and reduce the beneficiary's SSI check dollar-for-dollar after the first $20 SSI any income exclusion or if the beneficiary is a Medi-Cal recipient, it will increase the beneficiary's share-of-cost.

For SSI and Medi-Cal recipients, the trustee distributing cash to the beneficiary is not a good idea.

Example: Sarah Van Pelt an SNT beneficiary wishes to receive $250 to buy a television set and asks for an ongoing monthly allowance of $600 for living expenses. If the trustee agrees to do so, Sarah will lose $830 from her SSI check in the first month of receipt as unearned income ($850 in the first month - $20 any income exclusion), if she is only a Medi-Cal recipient, will owe an additional $830 as a share-of-cost before Medi-Cal will begin to pay her medical expenses. For every month thereafter, if Sarah is an SSI recipient, she will lose $580 from her SSI check ($600 unearned income less $20 any income exclusion), and if a Medi-Cal–only recipient will have an increased $600 share-of-cost for Medi-Cal.

---

442   POMS SI 01120.200(I)(1)(a).

The Medi-Cal share of cost calculations are more complicated than stated in these examples but are to provide the basics of the effects on Medi-Cal when cash is provided to a Medi-Cal recipient.

This is true even if the beneficiary is only seeking reimbursement for purchases made, which will also be treated as SSI unearned income regardless if the reimbursement was for items that are exempt or not counted by SSI.

Example: George Borges, an SNT beneficiary, purchased San Francisco Giants baseball tickets for $200. He asks the trustee to reimburse him for the tickets. If the trustee agrees to do so, George will lose $180 from his SSI check or, if he is a Medi-Cal–only recipient, will owe an additional $200 as a share-of-cost before Medi-Cal will begin to pay his medical expenses. This is true even though purchasing baseball tickets would be an acceptable distribution if made directly by the trustee.

This may be the hardest rule to follow for many trustees, especially if prior trustees (often family members) were providing such an allowance to the beneficiary. The prior trustee may have been able to get away with the improper disbursement, but it will only be a matter of time before the agencies that run the public benefit programs catch on and seek an SSI "overpayment" of benefits paid or deny Medi-Cal eligibility. Thus, a prior trustee's violation of the rules is no excuse for a current trustee to fail to refuse to follow existing rules.

Example: The SNT trustee has been distributing $500 per month to the beneficiary for a year. The SSA was never informed. The beneficiary during his annual review tells the SSA worker that he has been receiving this money. The SSA seeks an overpayment reimbursement from the beneficiary of $5,760 ($480 x 12) for the unearned income.

CAN THE TRUSTEE GIVE THE BENEFICIARY A BANK DEBIT CARD FROM AN SNT ACCOUNT?

No. If this happens, it is treated as if the beneficiary receives a resource of the amount of cash held in the bank account. This situation is different from a credit card, described in the prior question, because it simply provides unfettered access to all the cash in the bank account. This would then be a countable resource to the beneficiary and would likely eliminate eligibility for both SSI and Medi-Cal.

CHAPTER 16 SUMMARY

✓ The trustee must know how to make a proper disbursement from an SNT, because if done incorrectly it can reduce or eliminate public benefits eligibility.

✓ The methods to make a proper SNT disbursement are for the trustee to:
- Pay for goods or services directly
- Reimburse third parties for purchases
- Pay the beneficiary's credit card bills
- Use an Administrator Managed Prepaid Card (like True Link)
- Fund an ABLE account.

✓ The use of gift cards or gift certificates is authorized but the authors recommend not using this method of distribution.

✓ The trustee still needs to use discretion in using these different methods and in certain circumstances may still trigger penalties if for example, if the SNT trustee paid the beneficiary's credit card debit and some of the charges were for food, this would trigger an ISM penalty.

✓ The Administrator Managed Prepaid Card must be owned by the SNT and not the beneficiary.

✓ The trustee should never give cash directly to the SNT beneficiary or reimburse the beneficiary for purchases he or she makes, even if for exempt items as it will be treated as unearned income.

✓ The trustee should not allow the beneficiary to have a debit card from the trust accounts.

CHAPTER 17

SNT Taxation

By Courtney Kosnik, EA, Kevin Urbatsch and Michele Fuller

One of the trustee's primary responsibilities is making sure that all applicable taxes are paid, and proper tax returns are filed.[443] The SNT trustee is typically only concerned with income taxation, but there may also be potential estate, gift, employment, and property tax issues and filing requirements to consider. If the SNT owns a business or rental property, city or county business taxes may also apply.

> **Warning:** Tax law is complex and full of exceptions to general rules. Tax laws change frequently. This chapter is intended only as a basic introduction to the most common SNT tax filing requirements and related tax issues that may apply. It is not intended to be a substitute for professional advice related to a particular tax issue. Dollar amounts and other figures cited in this chapter are current as of the publication date but should not be relied upon without consulting one of the websites listed below.

The Internal Revenue Service (IRS), California's Franchise Tax Board (FTB), Employment Development Department (state employment taxes), the State Board of Equalization (real estate taxes) have many useful publications available for free on their websites. These can be downloaded or ordered by mail. The websites are

---

443   I.R.C. §§6012(b)(4); Treas Reg §1.641(b)-2(a); Revenue & Tax Code §18508(a); 18 Cal Code Regs §18505-1.

IRS www.irs.gov
FTB www.ftb.ca.gov
Employment Development Department www.edd.ca.gov
State Board of Equalization www.boe.ca.gov

> **Helpful Hint:** To avoid any argument that notices were not ac-
> tually sent, all notices to both the IRS and Franchise Tax Board
> should be sent by certified mail, return receipt requested. The
> trustee should also request that a copy be sent back and provide
> a self-addressed stamped envelope.

SHOULD THE SNT TRUSTEE HIRE A TAX PROFESSIONAL TO HELP?

The trustee is strongly advised to hire a tax professional who is familiar with the taxation of trusts to handle the SNT's taxes. The trustee can use SNT funds to pay the tax professional. Rather than waiting until tax returns are due, the authors recommend that the trustee notify the trustee's tax professional when a new SNT is established, or when the trustee becomes the successor trustee of a preexisting SNT. The trustee should provide the tax professional with a copy of the trust document, federal tax id number, and at least two years prior years return (if available).

A tax professional that has an understanding of the beneficiary's needs and family situation, as well as some familiarity with the trust's income, expenses, and assets, can identify potential tax problems and help in planning future transactions to minimize their tax impact.

Even if a tax professional is hired, the trustee should remember that he or she is still responsible for any errors on the return that result in underpayment of tax and for any penalties for failure to file on time.[444] It is important that the trustee carefully screen the tax professional, review all tax documents before they are filed, and review this chapter to make sure that all applicable taxes are reported and paid.

In this chapter, we discuss the considerations in hiring a tax professional. Further, in Chapter 20, there are suggestions on how to locate an appropriate tax professional.

---

444   I.R.C. §§6901(a)(1)(B), (b); Revenue & Tax Code §§19071-19072, 19512.

WHAT KIND OF TAX PROFESSIONALS SHOULD BE HIRED TO ASSIST THE SNT TRUSTEE?

An SNT trustee is allowed to hire an accountant or other professional to assist the SNT trustee.[445] However, the SNT trustee must use reasonable prudence in selecting the tax professional and periodically review the professional's performance.[446] If the SNT trustee fails to use reasonable prudence, he or she will be legally responsible for mistakes made by the accounting or tax professional.

Typically, the SNT chooses to hire an attorney, a certified public accountant (CPA), an enrolled agent (EA), or a California Tax Education Council (CTEC) tax preparer. An attorney's practice may include tax return preparation and planning. Attorneys are typically hired if there is a complex tax issue requiring a legal opinion or litigation in court. CPAs are qualified in all areas of public accounting, including taxation and auditing, and can assist in overall tax planning. EAs specialize only in taxation, specifically in tax law and tax code. They can assist in overall tax planning just as a CPA would and can assist in all levels of tax representation. A CTEC tax preparer is limited to filing a tax return and answering questions from the IRS on returns they filed. In addition to these tax professionals, there are payroll services that prepare employment tax returns and bookkeepers that specialize in the preparation of court accountings.

The most important factor in selecting a tax professional is that person's familiarity and experience with fiduciary taxation, and with the tax issues affecting SNTs in particular. Some tax professionals may limit their practice to preparing personal income tax returns or may specialize in business taxation and have little or no experience with fiduciary tax matters. A tax professional's practice may or may not include bookkeeping or the preparation of court accountings. The trustee might hire more than one tax professional to assist with the same SNT. For example, the trustee might hire an enrolled agent to prepare the SNT's fiduciary income tax returns, and a payroll service to prepare employment tax returns.

The main difference (although there are others) between an Attorney, CPA, an EA and a CTEC Tax preparer is their education and exams.

---

445   Probate Code §16247.
446   Probate Code §16401.

- Licensed California attorneys can legally prepare tax returns and assist a client with tax matters. An attorney in California must be licensed through the State Bar of California. To obtain a license, an individual must pass the two-day California bar exam and ethics exam. There are ongoing continuing legal education requirements. Most attorneys also received a JD degree from a law school. While attorneys are allowed to prepare such returns, not many attorneys are competent to do so. The two types of attorneys who generally will prepare returns are tax attorneys or estate and trust attorneys. Typically, an attorney is the most expensive option. One real benefit in working with an attorney is that all communications between the attorney and SNT trustee are protected by attorney-client privilege.

- To earn the CPA designation in California, accountants must earn a four-year college or university degree with specific course requirements at a school recognized by the California State Board of Accountancy, successfully complete a rigorous, standardized uniform national examination, complete an ethics examination, and acquire two years of public accounting experience to meet the stringent licensing requirements of the State of California. To assure that they stay current on developments in the field and maintain their licenses in California, CPAs are required to complete a minimum of forty hours of continuing education each year. In addition, members of the California Society of CPAs are obliged to adhere to a code of professional ethics.

- An individual can become an EA in two ways. An individual can become an EA if he has worked for the IRS for five years and has held a position that regularly engaged in applying and interpreting the provisions of the Internal Revenue Code, or if he has taken the Special Enrollment Examination, which consists of three parts. The first part consists of questions on tax code for individuals, the second part on tax code for business entities, and the last part is on Representation, Practice and Procedures. An EA must also pass a Federal background check. To maintain this license continuing education is also required with a minimum of seventy-two hours every three years, including two hours of ethics each year.

- An individual can become a CTEC registered tax preparer by obtaining a license issued by the California Tax Education Council. The license requirements are to pass a sixty-hour course on tax preparation, including a final exam. The class covers most issues commonly found on an individual's tax return. The course does not cover partnerships, corporations, trusts, nonprofits, etc. (It generally does cover briefly sole proprietorships.) Furthermore, in order to renew this license, the preparer must complete a minimum of twenty hours each year of continuing education on tax issues. (Generally the requirement for completing these courses is attendance, not demonstrated proficiency.)

To verify that an individual has the appropriate license:
- Attorneys, contact the State Bar of California www.calbar.ca.gov
- CPAs, contact the California Board of Accountancy www.dca.ca.gov/cba
- CRTPs, contact the California Tax Education Council www.ctec.org
- EAs, call the IRS Office of Professional Responsibility at (313) 234-1280.

HOW DOES AN SNT TRUSTEE FIND AND HIRE A TAX PROFESSIONAL?

There is no one place that is a clearinghouse for finding the best type of tax professional. One of the best ways to find a professional is to seek the advice of a special needs planning attorney. Oftentimes, the attorney has a relationship with one or more tax professionals who are familiar with the needs of an SNT trustee.

Below is a list of accountant associations that can provide some leads for an SNT trustee:
- AAA Association for Accounting Administration (http://www.cpaadmin.org/)
- AGNI Accountants Global Network International (http://www.agn.org/)
- AGN - North America (http://www.agn-na.org/)
- AICPA American Institute of CPAs (http://www.aicpa.org/)
- BBB The Better Business Bureau (www.bbb.com)
- BKR International (http://www.bkr.com/)
- CBA California Board of Accountancy (http://www.cba.ca.gov/)
- CPAAI CPA Associates International (http://www.cpaai.com/)
- CSEA California Society of Enrolled Agents (http://www.csea.org/)
- Diamond Certified (www.diamondcertified.org)

- IAAER International Association for Accounting Education and Research (http://www.iaaer.org/)
- IGAF International Group of Accounting Firms (http://www.igaf.org/)
- IRS US Internal Revenue Service (http://www.irs.gov/)
- NAEA National Association of Enrolled Agents (http://www.naea.org/)
- Polaris International (http://www.polarisinternational.org/)

Questions that should be asked of any tax professional:
- What is their operating credential?
- How many years have they worked in taxation?
- What is their educational background?
- Do they specialize in any areas of taxation?
- What accounting experience do they have with special needs trusts?
- Do they guarantee their work?
- What is the hourly billing rate?
- Do they have references?

IS ADDING TO (OR FUNDING) AN SNT BY GIFT OR INHERITANCE A TAXABLE EVENT?

Generally, no. The assets that are placed into an SNT typically come from an inheritance, gift, or similar type arrangement. In nearly every case, any tax owed would already have been paid by whoever was placing assets into the SNT. However, if a SNT receives a distribution or a series of distributions, from a deceased person's retirement plan, IRA, or annuity, the SNT will usually be subject to income tax on those distributions.

> **Example 1:** In her living trust, a mother left her entire estate to her daughter's third-party SNT. The entire net estate (after paying mother's final expenses) is valued at $300,000. The receipt of $300,000 from the mother's living trust by the daughter's third-party SNT is not a taxable event for the SNT. Thus, the entire $300,000 would be owned by the SNT and no tax would be immediately owed.

Example 2: Assume the same facts in Example 1. The daughter's uncle names the SNT as the beneficiary of his IRA. After the uncle's death, the SNT begins to receive annual distributions from the uncle's IRA. The SNT must report these distributions as income and pay any income tax due as a result of receiving the distributions.

Critical Pointer: Anyone naming a SNT as the beneficiary of a retirement plan or annuity should consult with an estate-planning attorney to ensure that the trust is properly drafted.

There could be a tax owed if persons or entities failed to pay all applicable taxes prior to transferring the assets to the SNT.

Example: A mother in her living trust left her entire estate to her daughter's third-party SNT. Mother died in 2019. Her entire estate is worth $12 million, after paying mother's final expenses of $100,000 other than the federal estate tax. The trustee of the mother's living trust transferred the full $11.9 million to daughter's third-party SNT. In 2019, an estate with a net worth of more than $11.4 million must pay a federal estate tax. The IRS could seek payment of the estate tax from either the mother's trustee or the third-party SNT assets.

If real property is transferred to the SNT, the property will be reassessed for property tax purposes unless exclusion applies. See discussion below about real property taxes.

If a trustee is uncertain whether all appropriate taxes were paid, he or she should consult with a tax professional. See Chapter 20 for a discussion on finding appropriate tax professionals.

IS FUNDING AN SNT WITH A LITIGATION RECOVERY A TAXABLE EVENT?

Generally, no. Any tax owed would already have been paid by whoever was placing assets into the SNT.

> **Example:** A person with a disability was injured in an automobile accident. He received a net settlement of $300,000 for his physical personal injuries after paying his attorney's fees and court costs. The entire $300,000 would be added into his first-party SNT, and no tax would be immediately owed.

> However, if the litigation recovery is taxable and taxes were not paid, then the SNT trustee may be responsible for the taxes.

> **Example:** A person with a disability was injured in an automobile accident. He received a net settlement of $200,000 for his physical personal injuries and $100,000 for lost wages. The entire $300,000 was added into his first-party SNT and no taxes were paid. The $100,000 for lost wages is taxable. If the funds were transferred to the SNT without paying the taxes, the IRS could seek payment for those taxes from the SNTs assets.

A first-party SNT is often funded with the proceeds of a personal injury award or settlement. A litigation settlement or judgment compensating an individual for physical injury or sickness is not income,[447] the subsequent earnings (usually interest or dividends) derived from the initial award may be taxable.

> **Example:** An injured person receives a $3 million settlement, which is paid directly to her first party SNT. The funds are invested and earn $150,000 per year in dividends. The $3 million is not taxable income, but the $150,000 must be reported as income.

---

447 I.R.C. §104(a)(2).

One issue that may arise in a first-party SNT is with a particular type of investment. Personal injury awards and settlements are often paid, at least in part, in the form of an annuity (often called a structured settlement annuity), so that the first-party SNT receives payments over a period of time rather than in a lump sum. These annuity payments will generally be nontaxable.[448] Thus, the SNT trustee should not worry about including these payments as part of the SNTs taxable income.

Often the SNT beneficiary because of his or her disability, will have tax-deductible medical expenses that can seriously reduce the taxes for an SNT. However, if the SNT beneficiary is under the age of twenty-four, his or her income may be subject to the "kiddie tax," which can have the effect of limiting available medical expense deductions.

It should also be noted that no medical expense deduction is allowed for payments to a caregiver who is a relative (spouse, parent or other ancestor, lineal descendant, brother or sister) of the disabled beneficiary, unless the relative has an appropriate professional license.[449]

WHAT TAX IDENTIFICATION NUMBER SHOULD A TRUSTEE USE FOR THE SNT?

Every SNT should have a tax identification number (TIN). A tax identification number may also be referred to as an employer identification number (EIN) or federal employer identification number (FEIN). This number, rather than the beneficiary's social security number, should be used on all SNT accounts. Keeping the SNT's taxable income separate from the beneficiary's taxable income will help the trustee when dealing with government employees who administer the public benefits programs.

It is possible the SNT already has a TIN. Either, the attorney who drafted the SNT will have already applied for at TIN, or an earlier trustee will have obtained one. The trustee should make sure that the trust does not already have a TIN before obtaining one. A successor trustee for an SNT that already has a TIN should not obtain a new one but should use the existing TIN.

---

448 I.R.C. §104(a).
449 I.R.C. §§152(d)(2), 213(d)(11).

The TIN is relatively easy to obtain online. Go to www.irs.gov and search for online EIN. The trustee can then click "Apply for an Employer Identification Number (EIN) Online." There will be a series of questions. Most of which are self-explanatory. In going through the online application process, the trustee should do the following:

1. Click on "irrevocable trust" when it asks which type of entity the trustee is seeking to obtain an identification number for.

2. The grantor of the trust will depend on whether or not it is a first- or third-party trust. If first party, the grantor is the beneficiary and if third party, the grantor is the person(s) putting assets into the trust, typically a parent or grandparent.

3. A social security number of the grantor will then be needed.

4. There are then questions on the trustee, including the trustee's address. It is important that the trustee keep address information current as this is the address the IRS will use to communicate with the trustee on tax issues.

As an alternative, the trustee can also use IRS form SS-4 to apply for a tax identification number for the SNT by telephone, fax, or mail. If not already done, the trustee should let all financial institutions know the TIN number for all trust assets.

SHOULD A TRUSTEE (OR SUCCESSOR TRUSTEE) NOTIFY THE IRS OR CALIFORNIA FRANCHISE TAX BOARD WHEN HE OR SHE BECOMES TRUSTEE?

Yes. The trustee (or when a successor trustee takes control) should notify the IRS and California Franchise Tax Board that the trustee is taking control of the SNT.[450] This is done by filing a completed IRS Form 56 (Notice Concerning Fiduciary Relationship) for both the IRS and Franchise Tax Board.

To obtain a copy of the form, you can go to www.irs.gov and search for Form 56. Completing the form is fairly straightforward:

Part I: Name the person for whom trustee is acting. For a third-party SNT, the trustee is acting on behalf of the SNT. Thus, trustee should use the TIN number obtained as described in

---

450   See I.R.C. §§6903, 7701(a)(6); Treas Reg §301.6903-1

previous question. Then trustee enters his or her name and address information.

Part II: Check box C stating trustee is acting pursuant to valid trust instrument

Part III: On line 2, state income. On line 3, state 1041. On line 4, state date taken over as trustee going forward. On line 5, check box. On line 6, leave blank.

Part IV: Use these sections only if trustee is notifying IRS that he or she is no longer serving as trustee.

Part V: Leave blank

Part VI: Sign under Fiduciary's Signature, add title as "Trustee," and date form.

The trustee should send the form to the local IRS office. If unknown by the trustee, check on www.irs.gov and search for local offices. Enter the zip code where trustee is located.

While the California Franchise Tax Board does not have a similar form, it will accept a signed original IRS Form 56. The trustee should mail it to

Franchise Tax Board
PO Box 942840
Sacramento, CA 94240-0040

SHOULD A TRUSTEE NOTIFY THE IRS OR FRANCHISE TAX BOARD WHEN HE OR SHE IS NO LONGER SNT TRUSTEE?

Yes. The Form 56 should be filed again. However, the former trustee should complete Part V describing when his or her services ended on the SNT.

HOW DOES INCOME TAX APPLY TO TRUSTS?

For income tax purposes, trusts are considered to be either "grantor" or "nongrantor" trusts. It is very important to understand the distinction between the two types of trusts. Whether a SNT is considered a "grantor" or a "nongrantor" trust determines how it is taxed and what federal and state income tax forms must be filed for the trust.

A trust is considered to be a grantor trust if certain benefits or powers are held by the grantor, the trustee, or a third person. The term "grantor" is generally synonymous with the terms "settlor" or "trustor," meaning the person who creates a trust. A trust may be considered a grantor trust if the trust income can be used to benefit the individual who funded the trust. Nearly every first-party SNT—that is, a SNT funded with the disabled beneficiary's own assets (usually money received as a result of litigation or a settlement, or an outright inheritance)—is taxed as a grantor trust because the income may be distributed to or used for the benefit of the person who funded the trust.[451] The difference between a first-party SNT and a third-party SNT are discussed in Chapter 2.

A summary of the difference in tax treatment between a "grantor trust" and "nongrantor trust" is as follows:

A. Grantor Trusts

A grantor trust is *not* considered a separate entity for income tax purposes. This means that a SNT that is a grantor trust does not pay its own income tax. The trustee still has tax return filing requirements, as discussed below. Instead, the person who is treated as the owner of the trust (the beneficiary with a disability in the case of a first-party SNT) will report the trust's income, deductions, and credits on his or her personal income tax returns and pay any income tax attributable to the trust income.

In many cases, it is advantageous for a SNT to be taxed as a grantor trust, because the beneficiary is likely to be in a lower income tax bracket than the trust would be if the trust were taxed as a separate entity.

---

451 I.R.C. §677.

B. Nongrantor Trusts

Any trust that is not a grantor trust is a separate entity for income tax purposes and is called a nongrantor trust. The nongrantor trust must pay any income tax due on its net taxable income. Like an individual, a nongrantor trust must file annual federal and California income tax returns, called "fiduciary income tax returns," to report the trust's income, deductions, and credits. A trust's taxable income is computed in much the same way as that of an individual.[452]

No standard deduction is available to a trust, unlike an individual; a trust must itemize its deductions. Federal tax law allows most trusts a very small personal exemption—$300 in the case of a "simple trust"[453] or $100 in the case of a "complex trust."

Because of public benefit eligibility requirements, no SNT will ever be a simple trust. Any nongrantor trust that does not come within the definition of a simple trust is a complex trust—therefore, a nongrantor SNT will be treated as a complex trust for income tax purposes.[454]

WHAT ARE A FIRST-PARTY SNT TRUSTEE'S REPORTING REQUIREMENTS?

As described above, if the first-party SNT is considered a "grantor trust," the income earned by the SNT assets is taxed to the SNT beneficiary.[455] Thus, for all practical purposes, the first-party SNT is invisible. All income is treated as the beneficiary's. This is so even if the income it is retained in the trust and never distributed for the benefit of the beneficiary.

> **Note:** The beneficiary is often the preferred taxpayer because his or her income tax brackets are usually much lower than the trust's tax brackets. In 2019, an individual will pay the highest income tax rate of 37 percent (federal) on taxable income over $510,300,

---

452 I.R.C. §641(b).

453 A simple trust is one that is required by the trust document to distribute all of its current income.

454 I.R.C. §642(b).

455 I.R.C. §671; Treas Reg §1.671-4.

while trusts (third-party SNTs with undistributed income) pay the highest income tax rate on taxable income over $12,750.[456]

The SNT trustee is required to report information to the beneficiary. The standard method for doing this is by completing only the part of IRS Form 1041 and FTB Form 541 that includes identifying information (name, address, and tax identification number), with an attachment listing items of SNT income, gain, loss, deduction, and credit that will flow through to the SNT beneficiary's personal income tax returns (IRS Form 1040 and FTB Form 540).[457] This is filed with the IRS and the FTB. The trustee must give a copy of this attachment, referred to as a "grantor letter," to the beneficiary.[458]

> **Note:** In preparing the "grantor letter," the trustee should list tax-deductible medical expenses paid on behalf of the SNT beneficiary so that the beneficiary can deduct these.

In lieu of the above method of tax reporting for a grantor trust, the IRS provides three optional methods. These optional reporting methods are discussed in the instructions to IRS Form 1041. In the author's opinion, the standard method described above is the simplest of the various reporting methods.

In order to minimize or eliminate the financial burden on the beneficiary, the SNT trustee can pay for the preparation of the trust's and the beneficiary's tax returns and can pay any tax that is due on the beneficiary's behalf.

WHAT ARE A THIRD-PARTY SNT TRUSTEE'S REPORTING REQUIREMENTS?

A third-party SNT is typically a nongrantor trust. This means that the third-party SNT trustee reports the SNT's income on the trusts own income tax return and pays, from trust income or principal, the taxes on its income.[459] A nongrantor third-party SNT is subject to the maximum tax rates at a lower threshold than an

---

456   IR-2018-222, November 15, 2018.
457   I.R.C. §6034A(a); Treas Reg §1.671-4(b)(2).
458   I.R.C. §671. Revenue & Tax Code §17731.
459   I.R.C. §671.

individual, so it will generally pay a greater tax on income than would a beneficiary under a grantor trust. However, as discussed in more detail below, there is a way to significantly reduce the overall taxes paid by utilizing the trust's deduction for distributions made for the benefit of the trust beneficiary.

> **Note:** In 2019, an individual will pay the highest income tax rate of 37 percent (federal) for taxable income over $510,300 while for trusts (third-party SNTs retained income) pay the highest income tax rate for taxable income over $12,750.[460]

Because the undistributed income of a nongrantor trust will typically result in higher taxes, many trustees will look for a way to reduce the trust's tax burden. One significant way to do so is by distributing income to the beneficiary (or on the beneficiary's behalf). If this is done, the trustee may take a deduction against the trust income, and taxes will be paid at the beneficiary's (often much lower) tax rate. The distribution deduction may not exceed the smaller of (1) the actual amount distributed; or (2) the trust's "distributable net income" (DNI).[461] Thus, most third-party SNT trustees attempt to make sure that all income is distributed each year.

> **Example:** An SNT has $40,000 of dividend and interest income. The trust has $5,000 of tax-deductible administration expenses. Its net income is $35,000. If it distributes $50,000 to or for the benefit of the beneficiary, its distribution deduction will be limited to $35,000 (the lower of the actual distributions of $50,000 or the DNI of $35,000). If, instead, it distributes $10,000 for the benefit of the beneficiary, its distribution deduction will be limited to $10,000 (again the lower of the actual distribution of $10,000 compared with the DNI of $35,000). The additional $25,000 of income will be taxed at the (often higher) trust tax rate. (Note that although this example uses a simple fact situation for illustrative

---

460   Revenue Procedures 2015-53.
461   I.R.C. §§651, 661.

purposes, DNI is not always the same amount as the trust's net income after deductions.)

Warning: It is possible that a third-party can be taxed as a grantor trust—for example, when a parent has established a revocable third-party SNT while the parent is still living. Because the parent can still change the SNT's terms and provisions, the taxation of the SNT will be identical to the first-party SNT discussed in the prior question, except that the parent, rather than the beneficiary, will be treated as the grantor for income tax purposes. If the trustee is not certain if his or her SNT is a grantor or nongrantor trust, the trustee should consult with an attorney. See Chapter 20 for instructions on locating an attorney.

When appropriate, distributions made on behalf of the SNT beneficiary can be used to reduce the overall income tax.

Example: A third-party SNT earns $25,000 of net income during 2019. As noted above, if this income were retained in the trust and no disbursements were made on the beneficiary's behalf, the trust would be paying income tax of 37 percent on net income over $12,750. However, if the third-party SNT trustee had made disbursements of trust income throughout the year of $25,000 on the beneficiary's behalf, the top tax rate paid would only be 12 percent ($25,000 pass through income less standard deduction of $12,200 equals net income of $12,800), assuming the beneficiary had no other taxable income.[462]

Critical Pointer: If it is appropriate, the third-party SNT trustee at the end of the year should make sure that all income was distributed, but if not, the trustee may make a tax election to make disbursements in the first sixty-five days of the following year and

---

462 See Revenue Procedures IR-2018-222.

have those disbursements counted as being made in the prior taxable year.[463] Obviously, distributions should not always be made solely for tax purposes. However, if there are distributions that will enhance the quality of life of the beneficiary, and saves on taxes, it should be considered.

The taxable income of a nongrantor trust is computed in much the same manner as taxable income for individuals. There are specific differences, however, with respect to computing the taxable income of trusts. For example,

- the exemption is $100 for a complex trust, whereas an individual does not have any exemption after 2017 under the Tax Cuts and Jobs Act(TCJA).[464] However, as discussed below, a third-party SNT may qualify as a "qualified disability trust" and obtain a higher exemption,[465]

- expenses that would be miscellaneous itemized deductions for an individual taxpayer but that would not have been incurred absent the trust (*i.e.*, trustee fees and attorney fees related to trust tax matters) may be deducted and are not subject to the 2-percent adjusted gross income floor;[466] these deductions are no longer allowed for individual taxpayers under TCJA, and

- if the income is distributed in a given year (or if an election is made sixty-five days into the next year[467]) to the SNT beneficiary (or for his or her benefit), then the SNT receives a deduction and the beneficiary will be responsible to pay the tax on that income.

The trustee reports the beneficiary's share of a nongrantor trust's income, deductions, and credits on Schedule K-1, which is filed with the IRS and FTB as part of the trust's fiduciary income tax return. The trustee must provide copies of the

---

463   I.R.C. §661(a); I.R.C. §663(b).

464   The term "complex" does not refer to the level of difficulty involved in trust administration. Rather, a "complex trust" is defined as any nongrantor trust that does not come within the definition of a "simple trust." A "simple trust" is required by the trust document to distribute all of its current income. All qualifying third party SNTs give the trustee discretion regarding distributions of income and principal, and are therefore complex trusts.

465   I.R.C. §642(b).

466   I.R.C. §67(e).

467   I.R.C. §661(a); I.R.C. §663(b).

federal and California Schedules K-1 to the beneficiary for use in preparing the ben-eficiary's personal income tax returns.

A detailed discussion of trust income taxation far exceeds the scope of this book. If an SNT trustee is unfamiliar with these rules, he or she is strongly encour-aged to hire a tax professional familiar with filing fiduciary income tax returns. See Chapter 20 for instruction on finding a competent tax professional.

WHAT IS A QUALIFIED DISABILITY TRUST?

As noted in the previous question, a third-party SNT as a nongrantor, complex trust only has a $100 personal exemption. A trust may increase its personal exemption if it qualifies as a qualified disability trust (QDT). To be characterized as a QDT, the trust must be irrevocable and established for the sole benefit of a person under the age of sixty-five who is disabled, as defined by the SSI programs.[468] If the trust meets these requirements, a QDT is entitled to an exemption that was based on the personal exemption. Under TCJA suspended personal exemptions until 2026, IRS has main-tained the exemption for QDTs[469] ($4,200 for 2019[470]). Distributions from a qualified disability trust are not subject to the "kiddie tax."

> **Note:** Some third-party SNTs are not set up to be for the "sole benefit" of a beneficiary under age sixty-five, because they in-clude provisions for a beneficiary's non-disabled children or sib-lings. The trustee should carefully review the SNT's terms to see if it qualifies. If unsure, the trustee should meet with an attorney or tax professional to see if the trust complies with the QDT re-quirements. To find such an attorney or tax professional, check Chapter 20 of this book.

---

468 I.R.C. §642(b)(2)(C)(ii); 42 U.S.C. §1396p(c)(2)(B)(iv).

469 Section 11041 of The Tax Cuts and Jobs Act of 2017, P.L. 115-97, suspended personal exemptions for tax years 2018 through 2025 under IRC 151. However, Qualified Disability Trusts are allowed an exemption during 2018 through 2025 under IRC 642. For tax year 2018, the exemption amount for a Qualified Disability Trust is $4,150. This amount is allowed in full and is not subject to phaseout. Therefore, do not use the Exemption Worksheet for Qualified Disability Trusts in the 2018 Form 1041-ES Instructions to phaseout any amount of the exemption.

470 See Revenue Procedures 2016-12, IRB 2016-2 (12/23/2010).

HOW MUCH INCOME IS REQUIRED BEFORE A THIRD-PARTY SNT TRUSTEE HAS TO FILE A TAX RETURN? WHAT TAX FORMS NEED TO BE FILED? IS THERE A TIME LIMIT WHEN THE FORMS NEED TO BE FILED?

In general, the filing of tax forms by the trustee is similar to filing tax returns for an individual. Tax returns must generally be filed prior to April 15 of each year.[471]

- **Federal Requirement:** The third-party SNT trustee must file an **IRS Form 1041** (US Income Tax Return for Estates and Trusts) if there is any taxable income for the tax year,[472] or if there is gross income of $600 or more, regardless of the amount of taxable income.[473]

- **California Requirement:** The third-party SNT trustee must file **FTB Form 541** (California Fiduciary Income Tax Return) if there is net taxable income of over $100; if the gross income exceeds $10,000, regardless of the net taxable income; or if the trust has alternative minimum tax liability (see Instructions for FTB Form 541 (General Information—Who Must File).[474] As a practical matter, a California fiduciary income tax return should be filed if there is a federal filing requirement.

  Note: It is possible that the SNT trustee would be required to file FTB Form 541 and not an IRS Form 1041 depending on the amount of income. It is sometimes advisable to file even when filing is not required, as when the SNT has a loss that can be carried forward to a future tax year.

CAN A THIRD-PARTY SNT TRUSTEE SEEK AN EXTENSION OF TIME TO FILE RETURNS AND PAY TAXES?

Yes, for an extension of time to file and Yes (for good cause) for an extension of time to pay taxes. A trustee may request an extension of time to file both federal and

---

471 I.R.C. §6072(a); Treas Reg §1.6072-1(a); Revenue & Tax Code §18566.

472 I.R.C. §6012(a)(4).

473 I.R.C. §6012(a)(4).

474 Revenue & Tax Code §18505(e)-(f)).

California tax returns. However, as described below, this does not extend the time to pay the tax.

For federal IRS purposes, to receive an automatic six-month extension to file the federal (Form 1041) tax form, the trustee must

- Submit IRS Form 7004 (Application for Automatic 6-Month Extension of Time to File Certain Business Income Tax, Information and Other Returns) or an application in any other manner prescribed by the commissioner;
- File the application on or before the date prescribed for filing the return with the appropriate IRS office; and
- Show on the application the properly estimated tax amount for the taxable year.

For California FTB purposes, to receive an automatic six-month extension to file the California (Form 541) tax form, the trustee does not need to file a written application.[475] Even though no form is required, the trustee should use FTB Form 3563 to make an extension payment if it is estimated that there will be a state income tax balance due.

An extension of time for filing the tax return is not an extension of time for payment of either the federal or California tax due.[476] The trustee may request an extension of time to pay the trust's federal taxes by filing IRS Form 1127 (Application for Extension of Time for Payment of Tax).

In rare cases, the IRS or FTB may grant an extension of time to pay the income tax. Granting an extension of time for payment is discretionary with the IRS[477] and ordinarily is allowed only in cases of undue hardship.[478] For California purposes, the trustee may make a request to the FTB for a reasonable extension for payment of tax. However, the FTB will only grant if there is a very good reason the tax cannot be immediately paid.[479]

---

475   18 Cal Code Regs §18567(a).

476   Treas Reg §1.6081-1(a), Revenue & Tax Code §18567(b).

477   I.R.C. §6161.

478   Undue hardship is described in Treasury Regulations §1.6161-1(b)).

479   Revenue & Tax Code §18567(c).

Critical Pointer: The trustee should always make the best possible estimate of the trust's income tax liability and pay that amount on or before the original due date. If possible, the trustee should inform the beneficiary of the approximate amount of trust income that must be reported on the beneficiary's personal income tax returns, so that the beneficiary can calculate his or her personal income tax liability as accurately as possible. If the trust files on extension, the beneficiary should obtain an extension of time to file his or her personal income tax returns. If the beneficiary files before receiving a Schedule K-1 or grantor letter (discussed above) from the trust, he or she will likely have to file amended returns after receiving the trust's information.

IS THERE A PENALTY FOR FAILURE TO FILE AND PAY TAXES?

Yes. A late filing penalty will be imposed if the trustee fails to file a required tax return. In general, for both federal and California purposes the penalty for late filing of a tax return is 5 percent of the tax due each month that the return is late, up to a maximum of 25 percent.[480] This penalty can be avoided completely as long as the trustee files an extension in a timely manner or files the tax return by the due date. There may be exceptions if there was reasonable cause for delay, such as the death or serious illness of the responsible person. Penalties may be increased if the failure to file was intentional. A late payment penalty may be imposed if less than the full amount is paid on time. The federal penalty for late payment of tax is described as follows:

- 0.5 percent of the net tax due for each month (or fraction of a month) the tax remains unpaid. This is calculated from the date the tax is due; the maximum penalty is 25 percent.[481]
- That penalty is doubled to 1 percent if payment is not made within 10 days after the IRS gives notice.[482]

---

480   I.R.C. §665, Revenue & Tax Code §19131.
481   I.R.C. §6651(a)(2).
482   I.R.C. §6651(d).

The California penalty for late payment of tax is 5 percent of the total unpaid tax plus .5 percent of the remaining tax for each month the tax remains unpaid, to a maximum of forty months.[483] The total penalty may not exceed 25 percent of the total unpaid tax.[484]

As with the penalty for late filing, the penalty for late payment may be abated if reasonable cause for the delay can be shown.[485]

DOES A THIRD-PARTY SNT NEED TO PAY AN ESTIMATED TAX?

Yes. As a general rule, third-party SNTs which are nongrantor trusts are required to pay quarterly estimated taxes for federal and California taxes.[486] As described in the previous questions on third-party SNT taxation, nearly all third-party SNTs are nongrantor trusts.

For federal purposes, SNTs that did not have a tax liability in the prior year or will have a tax less than $1,000 in the current year are exempt from paying estimated taxes.[487] In all other cases, the third-party SNT must make four equal estimated tax payments each year.

> **Example 1.** The trustee expects that the SNT's total income tax for the current year will be $3,300. The trustee expects that there will be about $2,500 of federal income tax withholding, leaving a balance due of $800. No federal estimated tax payments are required. If the withholding amount were less than $2,300, estimated tax payments would be required in this example.

> **Example 2.** The trustee expects that the SNT's total income tax for the current year will be $1,100. There is no withholding. Federal estimated tax payments are required.

---

483 Revenue & Tax Code §19132(a)(2).

484 Revenue & Tax Code §19132(a)(3).

485 I.R.C. §6651(a)(2); Revenue & Tax Code §19132(a)(1).

486 I.R.C. §6654(l)(1); Revenue & Tax Code §19136(a).

487 I.R.C. §6654(e).

The estimated tax payment must be calculated as follows:

- For trusts with adjusted gross income of $150,000 or less[488] in the preceding tax year, the required annual payment is the lesser of (i) 90 percent of the tax for the current taxable year or (ii) 100 percent of the tax for the preceding taxable year, if it was a taxable year of twelve months and a return was filed.[489]

- For trusts with adjusted gross income in excess of $150,000[490] in the preceding tax year, the required annual payment is the lesser of (i) 90 percent of the tax for the current taxable year or (ii) 110 percent of the tax for the preceding taxable year, if it was a taxable year of twelve months and a return was filed.[491]

The third-party SNT trustee computes federal estimated taxes on IRS Form 1041-ES, which contains detailed instructions regarding payment dates and filing an early return, rather than paying a fourth installment of estimated tax. Payments are made with estimated tax voucher forms.

California trusts are required to make estimated tax payments in the same manner as individual taxpayers. However, a California estimated tax is not required if the prior year's tax was less than $500 or the current year's tax will be less than $500.[492] The third-party trustee calculates estimated taxes on FTB Form 541-ES, which contains detailed instructions regarding payment dates and filing an early return rather than paying a fourth installment of estimated taxes. Payments are made with estimated tax voucher forms.

Penalties for underpayment of estimated tax are imposed unless the estimated tax paid is more than the smaller of (1) 100 percent of the prior year's tax liability (110 percent if the SNT's adjusted gross income for the prior year was more than $150,000); or (2) 90 percent of the current year's tax liability.[493]

---

488   As determined under I.R.C. §67(e).
489   I.R.C. §6654(d)(1)(B).
490   As determined under I.R.C. §67(e).
491   I.R.C. §6654(d)(1)(C).
492   Revenue & Tax Code §19136(c).
493   I.R.C. §6654(a), (e)(1); Revenue & Tax Code §19136.

HOW IS A SNT BENEFICIARY TAXED?

It will depend on whether the individual with a disability is a beneficiary of a first-party SNT or a third-party SNT. If the trustee is unsure of the type of SNT that is being administered, a discussion of the differences is discussed in Chapter 1.

Because a first-party SNT is generally taxed as a grantor trust, the trust is not treated as a separate entity for tax purposes. The beneficiary should report the trust's income, deductions, and credits on the beneficiary's personal tax return as if the trust did not exist.

Because a third-party SNT is generally taxed as a nongrantor trust, the trustee must provide the beneficiary with a Schedule K-1 showing the amounts of trust income, deductions, and credits that the beneficiary must report on his or her personal income tax returns.

Trust distributions to or for the benefit of the beneficiary are considered income of the beneficiary only to the extent of the trust's "distributable net income" (DNI). Distributions that exceed the trust's DNI are considered distributions of principal and are not taxed as income.

> **Example:** A SNT has $30,000 of interest income. The trust has $10,000 of tax-deductible administrative expenses, leaving it a DNI of $20,000. If the trust distributes $25,000 on behalf of the beneficiary, $20,000 will be taxed as income to the beneficiary. The remaining $5,000 will be considered a nontaxable distribution of trust principal.

Income has the same "character" in the hands of the beneficiary that it had in the hands of the trust. "Character" refers to the type of income and affects how that income is taxed. For example, distributions to a beneficiary may include interest, which is taxed as ordinary income, and qualified dividends, which are taxed at a lower rate.

> **Note:** An issue that confuses many people when discussing the word "income" is that it may have different meanings depending on the situation. In this chapter, income is discussed as the IRS and FTB define it in the context of taxation. In most other parts

of the book, public benefit programs, such as SSI, Medi-Cal, or Section 8, define "income". These public benefit programs define the word "income" much differently than does the IRS or FTB. For example, the Social Security Administration treats the receipt of food or shelter by the SSI recipient as a type of "income." The IRS or FTB would not do so. Thus, the trustee should remain diligent in knowing how the word "income" is being used in this book.

Often, distributions are made from a third-party SNT to pay the beneficiary's medical expenses that are not covered by public benefit programs. This can create a tax problem for the beneficiary if the amounts involved are large, because the beneficiary may not take a medical expense deduction for amounts paid by the nongrantor trust.

> **Example:** Suppose an SNT has $80,000 of "distributable net income" and the trustee employs a caregiver at a cost of $75,000 per year. The entire $75,000 is deductible by the trust and reportable as income by the beneficiary. Although the entire $75,000 was spent for a caregiver and would have been deductible as a medical expense if the beneficiary had paid the caregiver directly, the beneficiary may not take this deduction. Thus, the beneficiary would need to pay tax on the full $75,000 of "income."

> **Critical Pointer:** Regardless of who pays, there is no medical expense deduction allowed for a caregiver who is a relative (spouse, parent or other ancestor, lineal descendant, brother or sister) of the beneficiary with a disability, unless the relative has an appropriate professional license.[494]

Another issue that may arise is when the SNT beneficiary is young and applies regardless of the child being claimed as a dependent on his or her parent's tax return. Distributions to the beneficiary may subject the beneficiary to the "kiddie tax."

---

494   I.R.C. §§152(d)(2), 213(d)(11).

This tax applies to the "unearned income" (income that does not represent compensation for working) of a child under age nineteen, or aged twenty-four in the case of a student, unless the child's earned income equals at least half of his or her support. When the "kiddie tax" applies, under the new TCJA, the child is taxed at the same rate as trusts and estates, which as we've seen climb to the highest tax rate of 37-percent quickly. A child's unearned income that exceeds $2,200 for 2019 triggers kiddie tax rules. Keep in mind if the Trust is a QDT, then this will not apply.[495]

> **Note:** If the SNT distributions and other income payments to the child amount to more than half of the support of the child, the parents will not be able to claim the child as a dependent for federal or California income tax purposes.

HOW ARE TRUSTEE'S FEES TAXED?

Fees earned by a trustee are taxable as income. How the trustee's fees are reported and taxed depends upon whether the trustee is considered a professional fiduciary under tax law.

In general, an individual (usually a family member or friend) who serves as a trustee on a single occasion is not considered a professional fiduciary. Someone who is in the business of serving as a trustee, executor, or conservator and does this kind of work on an ongoing basis is considered a professional fiduciary for federal tax purposes, regardless of whether or not he or she is licensed under applicable state law.

A nonprofessional trustee should report his or her trustee fees as miscellaneous income on Schedule 1, line 21 of his or her federal income tax return (IRS Form 1040). Fees earned by nonprofessional trustees are not subject to self-employment tax.

The fees earned by a professional trustee are considered business income and must be reported on Schedule C of the trustee's personal income tax return. A professional trustee's net business income is subject to self-employment tax.[496]

---

495   I.R.C. §1(g), also see IRS Pub 929.
496   Rev. Rul. 58-5, 1958-1 CB 322.

HOW SHOULD THE TRUSTEE HANDLE CAREGIVER AND OTHER SNT EMPLOYEES' TAXES?

Under federal and state tax laws, almost all caregivers are treated as employees subject to payroll tax, rather than as independent contractors. This is true whether the caregiver works full time or part time, and whether the caregiver is hired on a permanent or temporary basis. The caregiver may ask to be treated as an independent contractor rather than an employee, and the trustee may prefer to treat the caregiver as an independent contractor, however, the preferences of the caregiver and the trustee in this regard are not the controlling factor. For a thorough discussion on the factors in determining whether a caregiver is an employee or independent contractor, see discussion in Chapter 15.

A caregiver who is hired through an agency may be an employee of the agency, rather than the SNT, where the trustee makes ongoing payments to the agency for the caregiver's services. The trustee should ascertain that the agency does in fact treat the caregiver as an employee for tax purposes and that the agency carries a workers' compensation insurance policy.

Payroll tax rules are complex and confusing. Federal and state rules are not consistent with each other. The penalties for failing to pay required payroll taxes are severe. The authors recommend that the trustee utilize a payroll service or hire a tax professional who is familiar with payroll taxes.

A newly hired caregiver should be asked to complete IRS Form W-4, "Employee's Withholding Allowance Certificate," and US Citizenship and Immigration Services (USCIS) Form I-9, "Employment Eligibility Verification." The SNT trustee must verify that the caregiver may legally work in the United States and should retain the I-9 for three years after the date of hire or one year after the date employment ends, whichever is later. These forms must be stored separately from other personnel files.

Federal and state laws distinguish between "regular" and "household" employees. Different payroll requirements apply to these two types of employees. Federal and state rules are different; an employee may be considered a regular employee by one government entity and a household employee by the other. Federal law defines a household employee as a worker who performs domestic services in the private home of the employer.[497] Examples include private nurses and health aides.

---

497 IRC §3510(c).

When the employer is a nongrantor trust (typically a third-party SNT), the employee cannot be a household employee because the employer trust does not have a home. However, when the employer is a grantor trust (typically a first-party SNT), it is theoretically possible for the trust to have a household employee, because the grantor trust is generally ignored for tax purposes.

> **Critical Pointer:** Even in the case of a grantor trust, caregivers should never be treated as household employees for federal tax purposes. This is because payroll taxes are computed on the employer (beneficiary's) personal income tax returns, and the payroll taxes are paid as part of the beneficiary's personal tax liability. The trustee usually has no control over the preparation and filing of this return. In addition, the payroll tax liability may give rise to an estimated tax requirement. If there is a tax overpayment, it is possible that the SNT beneficiary will receive a tax refund in his or her personal name. It is far better to treat all caregivers as regular employees for federal tax purposes so that the trustee retains control of the payroll tax reporting and payments.

When a SNT becomes an employer, the trustee must register with the California Employment Development Department within fifteen days. A regular employer should use EDD Form DE1. A household employer should use EDD Form DE1-HW. The SNT will be assigned a state employer identification number.

Some employment taxes must be withheld from an employee's pay. These include the employee's share of social security and Medicare taxes and the California state disability tax. The employer must pay other taxes. These include the employer's share of social security and Medicare taxes and the federal and California unemployment taxes. In addition, regular employers must withhold federal and state income taxes.

Household employers must withhold income taxes only if the employer and employee agree that the employer will do so. There are various exceptions to these requirements when the employer and employer are related.

The minimum wage and overtime laws are very complex and differ depending on the nature of the work. Generally, a live-in employee must be paid one and one-half times the regular rate for all hours worked over twelve hours (rather than over eight hours) in one workday (for five workdays; on the sixth and seventh day, the overtime rate for time worked in excess of nine hours per day is double the regular pay).[498] Special exemptions apply to domestic companions for the aged or infirm.[499] However, each worker's situation must be examined for proper compliance.

WHEN WOULD AN SNT BE SUBJECT TO AN ESTATE TAX?

As already discussed, the initial funding of an SNT from an estate should not require payment of any estate tax, unless the SNT was somehow funded from a taxable estate that failed to pay the tax.

An estate tax may be owed after the death of a first-party SNT beneficiary.[500] The taxable estate is calculated by subtracting certain deductions from the decedent's "gross estate."[501] This rarely happens, however, because the SNT would have to be funded with significant assets before an estate tax would be assessed.

Under current law in 2019, an estate tax will only be imposed on estates over $11.40 million. Be sure to verify with a legal or tax professional whether the law has changed. If the SNT beneficiary's estate is over the applicable exclusion amount, the beneficiary's trustee or executor must file an estate tax return (IRS Form 706) within nine months after the date of the beneficiary's death, unless an extension is obtained.[502]

> **NOTE:** California repealed its inheritance tax in 1982.[503] Thus, there is no separate estate tax for California.

---

498 Wage Order No. 15-2001(3)(A)-(B) (8 Cal Code Regs §11150(3)(A)-(B)).

499 29 U.S.C. §213(a)(15).

500 I.R.C. §2001(a).

501 I.R.C. §2051.

502 I.R.C. §6075(a).

503 Revenue & Tax Code 13301.

WHEN WOULD AN SNT BE SUBJECT TO THE FEDERAL GIFT TAX?

A gift tax is imposed on lifetime transfers of property for less than full and adequate consideration.[504] The transfer of property constitutes a completed gift, and thus is subject to tax, to the extent that the donor has parted with dominion and control of the property so as to leave the donor no power to change its disposition.[505] The gift tax is imposed on the donor (the person or entity making the gift) rather than the recipient of the gift.

There are two main exceptions to the application of the gift tax. Under the gift tax laws, the first $15,000 of gifts to any person made during a calendar year is not included in the total amount of gifts made during such year.[506] In addition, there is a lifetime gift tax exemption amount that can be given away to any number of people that will be free from gift taxes, but will reduce the amount that can be given away by the taxpayer tax-free on his or her death. In other words, the lifetime gift tax exemption is tied directly to the federal estate tax exemption. If an individual gifts away any amount of his or her lifetime gift tax exemption, then this amount will be subtracted from his or her estate tax exemption on death. For 2020, the lifetime gift tax exemption is $11,580,000, which is the same as the federal estate tax exemption discussed in the previous question.

The transfer of assets to a first-party SNT should not be subject to the federal gift tax. This is because the assets used to fund the SNT already belonged to the beneficiary before they were transferred to the SNT. The first-party SNT trustee is not allowed to make gifts to anyone. However, if a first-party SNT trustee breaches the terms of the trust and does make a gift to someone other than the beneficiary, a gift tax may be imposed. In this case, the trustee will be personally liable for any gift tax.

The transfer of assets to a third-party SNT may be subject to the federal gift tax. A transfer to an irrevocable trust is generally treated as a gift to the income beneficiary. In most cases, a transfer to a third-party SNT would not be eligible for the $15,000 annual exclusion. This is because the exclusion does not apply unless the trustee is required to distribute all income to the beneficiary currently, which would be inappropriate in the case of an SNT.

---

504 I.R.C. §§2501(a), 2512(b).

505 Treasury Regs §25.2511-2(b).

506 I.R.C. §2503(b), Rev Proc 2015-53.

In the unlikely event that an SNT is subject to a gift tax, the trustee must file a gift tax return (IRS Form 709) no later than April 15 of the year after the calendar year in which the gift was made, unless an extension is granted.[507]

WHEN WOULD THE SNT TRUSTEE NEED TO BE CONCERNED WITH PROPERTY TAXES?

If the SNT holds real estate, the trustee is required to pay applicable property taxes during trust administration. California values real property for tax purposes at the lower of (1) fair market value on the date of the year in question, or (2) a base-year value determined under Proposition 13 guidelines, adjusted for inflation. The property tax rate is generally 1 percent of assessed value.[508] The assessed value cannot be increased by more than 2 percent per year.[509]

Real property is generally reassessed when there is a change of ownership. A change of ownership can occur by sale, gift, or inheritance.[510] Thus, when real estate is transferred into a SNT, or purchased by a SNT, it will generally be reassessed as of the transfer date. This may result in a property tax increase.

Certain transfers are excluded from reassessment. In the context of SNTs, the exclusion most likely to apply is the parent-child exclusion. This exclusion applies to transfers of a principal residence, plus a maximum of $1 million (assessed value, not market value) of other real property.[511] When a parent transfers real estate to a SNT for the benefit of a disabled child (regardless of the child's age), the transfer may qualify for this exclusion.[512] The trustee must claim this exclusion by filing the appropriate forms with the Assessor's office in the county where the real property is located.

---

507 I.R.C. §§6019, 6075(b)(1).

508 Cal Const art XIIIA; Revenue & Tax Code §§50-51, 93, 110.

509 Revenue & Tax Code §51(a)(1)(D).

510 Revenue & Tax Code §60.

511 Revenue & Tax Code §63.1.

512 Revenue & Tax Code §63.1(a)(1), (c)(9).

CHAPTER 17 SUMMARY

- ✓ The SNT trustee should be prudent in selecting and hiring a tax professional.
- ✓ Typically, the funding of an SNT is a nontaxable event.
- ✓ Trustee should obtain a tax identification number from the IRS for the SNT.
- ✓ The SNT trustee should complete and file IRS Form 56 when taking over control of SNT and then file one when he or she is no longer serving as trustee.
- ✓ The SNT trustee is required to provide tax information to beneficiary of SNT.
- ✓ There is a significant difference in treatment of taxes for trusts treated as grantor trusts versus nongrantor trusts.
- ✓ A first-party SNT is often treated as a "grantor trust," and the SNT beneficiary at his or her tax rate pays taxes.
- ✓ A third-party SNT is often treated as a "nongrantor trust," and taxes are paid at the more expensive trust tax rates; however, an SNT trustee may reduce the tax amount owed by distributing taxable income for the use of the beneficiary, and then taxes will be owed at his or her tax rate.
- ✓ A qualified disability trust may increase its personal exemption from $100 to an individual personal exemption amount, which is much higher (in 2019, $4,200). Of use only for third-party SNTs who meet certain requirements.
- ✓ A third-party SNT must file an IRS form 1041 and FTB from 541 if there is taxable income owed.
- ✓ A third-party SNT can seek an extension of time to file tax returns; however, the payment of tax should be made on time to avoid penalties and interest.
- ✓ There are fairly significant penalties assessed for failure to pay a timely tax that increase significantly the longer the tax remains unpaid.
- ✓ A third-party SNT will need to pay estimated taxes the second year of its existence if its income is over a modest amount.
- ✓ The SNT beneficiary's taxes will depend on the type of SNT. The beneficiary may have some adverse tax consequences if caregivers are hired and paid for in a third-party SNT, or the beneficiary may be subject to kiddie tax in a third-party SNT if the beneficiary is young.

✓ Trustee fees will be taxed differently between professional and nonprofessional trustees.

✓ Employment taxes will need to be paid on any employees the SNT trustee hires to assist the beneficiary.

✓ Estate taxes are generally not an issue, unless there is a fairly significant amount of assets held in trust on the death of the beneficiary in a first-party SNT.

✓ Gift taxes are not an issue in a properly administered first-party SNT.

✓ Real property taxes will need to be paid on any real property owned by the trust.

CHAPTER 18

Terminating The SNT

An SNT will end or terminate for several reasons. The most common events that result in SNT termination are the:

1. Death of the beneficiary;
2. Triggering of termination event described in trust (for example, trust may terminate if beneficiary is able to work);
3. SNT assets are few or uneconomical to administer; or
4. Failure of trust purpose (for example, beneficiary is no longer disabled).

On termination, the SNT trustee has an obligation to wrap up the affairs of the trust. This obligation includes the normal trustee responsibilities of doing final accounts, paying taxes, paying creditors, and making final distributions. However, this process is drastically different between a first-party SNT and a third-party SNT.

The biggest difference is that a first-party SNT includes a payback to all State's Medicaid agencies, including California's Medi-Cal agency, the Department of Health Care Services (DHCS) for all Medi-Cal services received by the SNT beneficiary. This can be problematic if there is not enough money left in the SNT to pay the Medi-Cal amount. A third-party SNT has no such payback requirement to DHCS and is terminated like most trusts referring to basic rules.

> **Warning:** The SSA has specific requirements for "early termination provisions" in first-party SNTs. Early termination means an SNT terminates prior to the beneficiary's death typically because the beneficiary is no longer disabled or there is very little money left in the trust. This rule only applies to first-party SNTs and not

to third-party SNTs. The SSA requires that first-party SNTs that include an early termination provision must include the payback provision to the State Medicaid agency and any funds that remain must go to the beneficiary.[513] While first-party SNTs that include these provisions are now not considered exempt for SSI eligibility purposes, it does not mean that the beneficiary will immediately lose his or her SSI if an SNT includes a nonqualifying early termination provision. Once the SSA discovers that a first-party SNT includes a nonqualifying early termination provision, it will issue a notice to the beneficiary that the SNT is no longer valid and provide a 90-day right for the beneficiary or trustee to amend the SNT to remove the disqualifying provision. If an SNT trustee or beneficiary receives such a notice, he or she should contact a special needs attorney immediately to assist with this procedure.[514]

The chapter will go into the specific requirements of terminating a first-party SNT and a third-party SNT. See Appendix N for a checklist on things that should be considered on the death of the SNT beneficiary.

WHAT ARE SNT TRUSTEE'S LEGAL RESPONSIBILITIES ON SNT TERMINATION?

A trustee must continue his or her administration of an SNT even though the trust has terminated.[515] This means that even though a beneficiary has died, or the money has run out, the trustee still has a legal obligation to wrap up the final affairs of the trust. As funds are depleted, it is important that the SNT trustee monitor funds closely, so they have at least a minimum level of funds to be able to pay for final expenses as detailed below. Before acting, the trustee should be satisfied that the terminating event has occurred. For example, if death is the triggering event, the trustee should obtain a certified copy of the death certificate for the beneficiary.

On termination, the trustee's activities are generally divided into three categories

---

513   POMS SI 01120.199
514   See Chapter 14 on instructions on how to find a special needs planning attorney.
515   Probate Code §15407(b).

1. Paying the final expenses of the trust and perhaps the expenses of the beneficiary or his or her estate;
2. Making a final accounting to the remainder beneficiaries (or the court if SNT is court supervised); and
3. Distributing any remaining assets to the appropriate people or entities.

Before making any payments from the SNT, the trustee must understand which claims and debts should be paid first. The consequences of making the wrong payment is that the trustee may be required to pay out of his or her personal assets any claims that were not properly paid from the trust. Likewise, if the trustee pays creditors who were not authorized to be paid, the trustee may have to reimburse that payment to the beneficiary who would have received it. Thus, it is important that the SNT trustee know the proper priority before making any payments from the trust.

In order to understand the proper priority among creditors of the SNT, the trustee must first determine whether the SNT is a third-party or a first-party SNT. This issue is very important, because a first-party SNT requires that any assets remaining in the trust upon the death of the beneficiary be used to pay back the state before third-party debts can be paid from trust assets.

If the trust is subject to continuing court jurisdiction, the trustee should prepare a final accounting on termination of the trust, and his or her attorney should prepare a petition to settle the final account and to distribute the estate. The notice of report and account and petition for distribution will inform the beneficiaries that the trust has terminated. The trustee may also wish to send letters to the beneficiaries informing them of termination. Preparation of the trustee's final accounting may take a substantial amount of time. These issues are discussed in more detail later in this chapter.

WHAT ARE THE SNT TRUSTEE'S RESPONSIBILITIES IN TERMINATING A FIRST-PARTY SNT?

The legal obligations upon termination of a trust of any trustee is to pay creditors and claims of the SNT, pay any taxes, prepare account, and make any final distributions to remainder beneficiaries. In the case of a first-party SNT, determining the priority of payment of debts and claims is critically important due to the Medi-Cal payback provision. Improperly paying a debt prior to Medi-Cal receiving its claim may lead to a claim against the SNT trustee by the state for the amount owed.

> **Note:** The only first-party SNT payback requirement is for Medi-Cal (or other state's Medicaid). There is no payback required for SSI, SSDI, Social Security, Medicare, HUD ("Section 8") housing programs, or other similar type governmental programs.

Below are the basic steps necessary for terminating a first-party SNT:

Step One: Send notice to government agencies and remainder beneficiaries

Step Two: Review documents from State Agencies detailing benefits paid on behalf of beneficiary, also called a lien

Step Three: Check to see if exceptions to Medi-Cal payback apply

Step Four: Determine priority of authorized creditors

Step Five: Pay allowable funeral expenses

Step Six: Pay authorized creditors

Step Seven: Prepare or arrange for filing final tax return

Step Eight: Make final distributions

Step Nine: Prepare and distribute final accounting

STEP ONE: SEND NOTICE TO GOVERNMENT AGENCIES AND REMAINDER BENEFICIARIES

When the SNT terminates, the trustee must notify all state agencies that provided Medi-Cal (or in other states called Medicaid) assistance to the beneficiary in order to obtain a detailed report of expenses paid on behalf of the beneficiary during that individual's lifetime. The trustee should also check to determine whether the beneficiary received, or might have received, Medicaid services out of state. If so, then notice should also be sent to the other states' Medicaid agency to determine if there is a potential claim against the first-party SNT.[516]

Notice to state agencies should be sent as soon as possible after the SNT terminates to start the claims period running. DHCS must reply within four months of the date the SNT trustee provided notice to it with a claim for payback.[517] If it fails to do so, it may not make a claim for recovery.[518] If the SNT trustee fails to provide appropriate notice, DHCS has three years to make a claim for recovery.[519]

Notice should be sent to the following California agencies as well as to any other state agencies where the beneficiary may have received medical services and to any agency that has filed a request for notice.

Office of Director
Department of State Hospitals
1600 9th Street
Sacramento, CA 95814

Department of Developmental Services, Director's Office
1600 9th Street
Sacramento, CA 95814

Department of Health Care Services
Third-Party Liability and Recovery Division
Estate Recovery Section—MS 4720

---

516   A trust is obliged to reimburse any state that provided medical assistance, and for any period of time, including assistance received before the trust was created. POMS SI 01120.203(B)(1)(h).

517   Probate Code §§3605(a), 9202, and see *Shewry v Wooten* (2009) 172 Cal App 4th 741.

518   Probate Code §9201.

519   Code of Civil Proc §338; *Shewry v. Begil* Cal App 4th 639.

PO Box 997425

Sacramento, CA 95899-7425

Practice Tip: The SNT trustee can complete an on-line notice to DHCS of the beneficiary's death and the termination of the SNT termination at https://apps.dhcs.ca.gov/AutoForm2/Page/ AutoForm2.aspx.

The SNT trustee also has a duty to keep the beneficiaries[520] reasonably informed of the trust and its administration.[521] The SNT trustee should consider sending out a notice of SNT termination to the remainder beneficiaries. The SNT trustee may (or may not) have to provide a copy of the trust and an account to the remainder beneficiaries. However, because the SNT trustee has an obligation to provide both information[522] and a copy[523] of the trust on request of a beneficiary, he or she may want to provide them at the outset to avoid any later issues.

STEP TWO: REVIEW PAYBACK REPORT FROM STATE AGENCIES

If DHCS or other Medicaid agency provides a timely response, the trustee should carefully review the report it receives to determine the accuracy of the services and costs for which the agency is claiming reimbursement. If the trustee does not have sufficient expertise or information about the beneficiary's circumstances to personally conduct this review, then members of the beneficiary's family as well as a care manger should be consulted to go over the itemized bills in detail. Billing errors are frequent. Oftentimes there are duplicate entries, entries for services never provided or even entries that show a payment that was made at times when the beneficiary was not even alive.

---

520 A "beneficiary" of a trust refers to any person who has any present or future interest, vested or contingent. Probate Code §24(c). This would include the people who would inherit the trust funds after the death of the SNT beneficiary.

521 Probate Code §16060.

522 Probate Code §16061.

523 Probate Code §16060.7.

Practice Pointer: There are professionals who can be hired to review Medi-Cal's bills to determine if the report provides an accurate summary of expenditures. See Chapter 20 on finding a public benefits expert.

The cost of conducting the review, whether conducted internally or by an outside expert, is an "administrative expense," which is paid before the Medi-Cal reimbursement. (See Step Four for description of priority of payments.) The amount of the reimbursement must be approved by the state Medicaid agency. If the SNT was funded with the proceeds of a personal injury settlement, the claims report may identify expenses that were already reimbursed by an insurer or were the subject of a lien waiver at the time of the settlement. Therefore, the trustee should make sure they are not paying twice for the same claim.

If there are sufficient errors and DHCS refuses to negotiate the payback amount down, the SNT trustee should consider filing a Probate Code §17200 petition as described in Chapter 5.

STEP THREE: CHECK TO SEE IF EXCEPTIONS TO MEDI-CAL PAYBACK APPLY

There is a split in California legal authority on whether exceptions to recovery apply on the termination of an SNT. One appellate court has stated that no payback to DHCS for Medi-Cal services paid an SNT beneficiary of a first-party SNT is required in certain circumstances.[524] DHCS has no right to a payback of Medi-Cal services if the first-party SNT terminates and

- the SNT beneficiary has a surviving spouse;
- the SNT beneficiary has a disabled child;
- the SNT beneficiary has a child under age twenty-one; or
- the SNT beneficiary was under age fifty-five when non long-term Medi-Cal services were received.[525]

---

524 *Shewry v Arnold* (2004) 125 Cal.App.4th 186.
525 42 U.S.C. §1396p(b)(1)(B), (b)(2)(A); Welfare & Institutions Code §14009.5.

> **Note:** Before relying on these exceptions, the SNT trustee should check the author's website to see if this exception still applies. DHCS has attempted to change this law by legislation. Thus far it has been unsuccessful, but this may change in the future. To make sure that the exceptions still apply, review www.UrbLaw.com.

In the case that described the exception, the first-party SNT beneficiary died but left a child with a disability. In analyzing whether exceptions apply to Medi-Cal's right of recovery in this situation, the court stated that all the recovery exceptions (described above) apply regardless of whether assets were held in a first-party SNT or not. DHCS does not agree with this decision. Since this decision came out, two other cases were issued that held these exceptions do not apply. So, it is prudent for the SNT trustee to petition a court to determine if exceptions apply.[526]

Thus, if the trustee runs into a situation where there may not be a payback because the beneficiary only received community based Medi-Cal services while under the age of fifty-five or the beneficiary leaves a minor child, child with a disability, or spouse, he or she should consult with an attorney to assist in negotiating with DHCS on the Medi-Cal recovery. See Chapter 20 on how to find special needs planning attorney's help during SNT administration.

If an exception applies, the trustee can skip Steps Four and Five and go right to Step Six.

STEP FOUR: DETERMINE PRIORITY OF AUTHORIZED CREDITORS

If no Medi-Cal payback exception applies (see Step Three), there are only a few things that may be paid from a first-party SNT prior to paying Medi-Cal's recovery claim. In order to better understand the authorized disbursements prior to Medi-Cal's recovery, it is necessary to understand where the rules on Medi-Cal recovery come from.

There are two different government public benefit programs that are typically associated with first-party SNT planning, Supplemental Security Income (SSI), and Medi-Cal. Both SSI and Medi-Cal agree that a first-party SNT is entitled to pay

---

526 *Herting v.* California *DHCS,* (2015) 235 Cal.App.4th 607; *Gonzalez v. City National Bank, et al.* (2019) 2019 WL 2576537.

certain expenses from the SNT's assets before paying the Medi-Cal recovery claim. The problem that arises is that SSI and Medi-Cal's rules are in conflict over the categories of payments that are allowed.

The SSI program allows the SNT trustee to pay the following two types of items prior to the Medi-Cal payback:

- Taxes due from the trust to the State or Federal government because of the death of the beneficiary
- Reasonable fees for administration of the trust estate such as an accounting of the trust to the court, completion and filing of documents, or other required actions associated with termination and wrapping up of the trust[527]

The SSI program specifically excludes the following things from being paid by the SNT trustee before the Medi-Cal payback:

- Taxes due from the estate of the beneficiary, other than those arising from inclusion of the trust in the estate
- Inheritance taxes due for residual beneficiaries
- Payment of debts owed to third parties
- Funeral expenses
- Payments to residual beneficiaries[528]

The Medi-Cal program allows the SNT trustee to pay the following two types of items prior to the Medi-Cal payback:

- The cost of the individual's remaining management and investment fees
- Outstanding bills for the benefit of the disabled individual or spouse that fall within the terms of the trust; or burial/funeral expenses of the disabled individual or disabled spouse[529]

Reasonable fees for administration of the SNT include fees for the following:

- Trustee, attorney, or public benefit expert who reviews the Medi-Cal claims
- Cost of accounting

---

527 POMS SI 01120.203(B)(3)(a).
528 POMS SI 01120.203(B)(3)(b).
529 Medi-Cal Eligibility Procedures Manual Letter No. 192, p 9J-75.

- Completion and filing of documents in connection with wrapping up of the SNT including tax returns and appropriate notices

The SSI rules expressly prohibit two common kinds of expenditures expressly permitted by Medi-Cal's rules: debts owed to third parties and funeral expenses.[530] What makes this unusual is that the rules for SSI are far more restrictive than those for Medi-Cal, but there is only a recovery for Medi-Cal and not one for SSI. It would typically be expected that the agency receiving the funds would set the rules, not an agency that receives nothing. As a result, to have a qualifying first-party SNT that qualifies for SSI purposes, a California SNT must preclude paying for things that would otherwise be allowed.

Because of the difference in rules, the SNT trustee is left in a bit of a quandary to pay for remaining third-party creditor claims or to pay for a funeral. It is not uncommon for an SNT beneficiary to have no assets (other than an SNT) to pay for a funeral. The good news is that in California, the Department of Health Care Service (DHCS), the agency that administers Medi-Cal in California, will let an SNT trustee pay for a funeral even if there is not enough money left in the SNT to pay all of Medi-Cal's lien. See Step Five for procedure in getting a funeral paid from trust assets.

> **Example:** An SNT beneficiary dies at age eighty-five and his trust has $100,000. After the SNT beneficiary's death, the SNT trustee is presented with a bill of $3,000 for a wheelchair, a bill of $2,000 from the SNT trustee's attorney for trust administrative expenses, federal and state income taxes of $1,000. The remainder beneficiaries of the SNT are the SNT beneficiary's two adult children aged forty-five and forty-eight.

The SNT trustee sends notice to DHCS of the death of the beneficiary. DHCS sends a timely notice to trustee requesting $300,000 as the payback amount. The SNT trustee reviews the Medi-Cal bills and determines that it is valid.

---

530   (SSI) POMS SI 01120.203(B)(3)(b); (Medi-Cal) Medi-Cal Eligibility Procedures Manual Letter No. 192, p 9J-75.

The SNT trustee may pay the $2,000 bill for the attorneys' expenses in wrapping up trust estate and the $1,000 for taxes. However, the SNT trustee may not pay the $3,000 bill for wheelchair expenses, and the two children will receive nothing. The rest of the trust estate goes to DHCS.

> **Practice Pointer:** The SNT trustee should never make disbursements to family members before knowing whether there are sufficient assets to pay back the state Medicaid agencies. Doing so may result in the SNT trustee being responsible for paying the Medi-Cal payback out of his or her own assets if the distributes do not have sufficient assets to pay back Medi-Cal.

STEP FIVE: PAY ALLOWABLE FUNERAL EXPENSES

A common SNT termination event is the death of the SNT beneficiary. Within days of the death of an SNT beneficiary, the beneficiary's family or friends may call the trustee to ask whether funeral expenses can be paid from the first-party SNT. Until a determination is made on whether there are sufficient assets to pay the Medi-Cal recovery claim, the general rule is that funeral expenses cannot be paid. This is because the SSI rules only allow the trustee to pay funeral expenses for an SNT beneficiary after the Medi-Cal reimbursement is paid. See explanation in Step Four. If there is no money left after the Medi-Cal payback, then no funeral expenses can be paid.

> **Note:** SSI's prohibition against paying funeral expenses has been strongly criticized by a number of commentators, and has famously been described as the "stinking dead body rule" by Florida social security and special needs attorney David L. Lillesand. He has often suggested that if there is no money to bury the person with a disability to have the body delivered to the local Social Security office for disposition.

However, in California, the DHCS agency is much more lenient probably because Medi-Cal rules expressly authorize payments for a funeral prior to Medi-Cal's payback. Remember that even though SSI has these more restrictive rules, it is not receiving any payback money from the SNT. Thus, on the SNT beneficiary's death, it is common to contact DHCS to seek permission to pay the deceased beneficiary's funeral expenses even when the Medi-Cal payback is greater than the assets remaining in the first-party SNT.

In the author's experience, the DHCS worker will allow the disbursement as long as the expenses are "reasonable." The author has taken this to mean that expenses can be paid for the funeral but not a large party for family, friends, or caregivers.

> **Practice Pointer:** If the first-party SNT document expressly disallows funeral expenses to be paid because of SSI reasons, the SNT trustee may wish to request instructions through a Probate Code §17200 petition to authorize the disbursement for funeral expenses despite the plain language of the SNT. Courts will generally authorize this disbursement despite the trust's language because DHCS will consent to the distribution and often there is no one else left in the SNT beneficiary's life to pay for the burial. For more information about utilizing a Probate Code §17200 petition, see Chapter 5.

> **Practice Pointer:** Because the SSA rules state that funeral expense do not have priority over the Medi-Cal lien, it is good practice to have the SNT trustee fund a prepaid burial plan or an irrevocable burial trust for the beneficiary during the individual's lifetime. There is no prohibition against the SNT trustee paying for such a funeral. See Chapters 11 on how to pay for a prepaid funeral. If the beneficiary does not consent to the purchase of a prepaid funeral, it would be prudent to have the beneficiary (or his or her legal representative) sign the waiver set forth in Appendix W.

STEP SIX: PAY AUTHORIZED CREDITORS

After all allowable SSI and Medi-Cal fees and expenses have been paid and the Medi-Cal payback has been paid as described in Step One through Step Five, the first-party SNT trustee may pay any remaining debts of the trust. Trust debts may include expenses incurred for case management, services for the beneficiary, investment advice, legal advice, or tax preparation that remain unpaid when the beneficiary died.

> **Example:** After the SNT beneficiary death, the SNT trustee paid all taxes, allowable debts, and the Medi-Cal payback amount. There still remains $80,000 in trust assets. The SNT trustee has received bills of $3,000 for wheelchair expenses, $5,000 in remaining care giving expenses, and $2,500 for public benefit advocacy work. The SNT trustee is authorized to pay these expenses from the funds.

STEP SEVEN: PREPARE A FINAL TAX RETURN

One of the last steps required to properly wrap up SNT administration is the preparation and filing of the final tax return. Depending on the timing of the trust termination, the return may not be filed for many months. The SNT trustee should contact an experienced tax preparer to finalize this important step of administration, as well as set aside funds for any anticipated taxes to be paid. Otherwise, the SNT trustee may have to pay for tax preparation and any taxes owed out of their own personal funds. This process is explained in detail in Chapter 17.

STEP EIGHT: MAKING FINAL DISTRIBUTIONS

If there are funds remaining in the SNT after the payment of all administrative expenses, taxes, and valid Medi-Cal reimbursements, the remainder should be distributed according to the terms of the SNT. Generally, the document will specify who should receive the funds after payment of all expenses.

> **Example:** The SNT trustee has paid all taxes, expenses, and the Medi-Cal payback provision. There remains $200,000 in trust. The SNT document says that all remaining assets will go to the beneficiary's then living children. On the death of the beneficiary, he had four surviving children. The SNT trustee will make disbursements

to all four children. It is a good idea to have each child sign a receipt showing they received their disbursement.

The SNT trustee should carefully review the SNT document to see if the beneficiary was left with something called a power of appointment. An example of a type of power of appointment is as follows:

> Sample Power of Appointment: The trustee shall distribute the undistributed balance of the trust estate as the beneficiary may direct by exercise of a special power of appointment to any one or more persons or entities, or trusts for their benefit, other than the beneficiary's estate, the beneficiary's creditors, or creditors of the beneficiary's estate.

If there is a power of appointment, the SNT trustee should check to see if, while the beneficiary had legal capacity, he or she executed a separate will, a living trust, or a writing that exercised the power of appointment. In this case, the assets would no longer be distributed as set forth in the SNT document but rather by the document the SNT beneficiary executed. If the SNT trustee is unsure whether such a power of appointment exists or if one was properly exercised, he or she should check with an experienced estate-planning attorney. See Chapter 20 on locating an experienced special needs attorney.

> **Example:** The SNT states that the remaining trust assets shall be distributed to the SNT beneficiary's then living children. The SNT beneficiary has two living children at the time of his death. The SNT has $500,000 in assets after all expenses and taxes were paid. However, the SNT also states that the beneficiary has a power of appointment to alter distribution through a valid will.

The SNT trustee finds a document that purports to be the last Will and Testament of the beneficiary leaving all the assets to a charity. The SNT trustee should determine if the power of appointment was validly executed (for example, making sure beneficiary had legal capacity when he signed the document and the will meets California legal requirements). If the power of appointment were validly executed, the SNT trustee would distribute the $500,000 to the selected charity.

STEP NINE: PREPARE A FINAL ACCOUNTING

Once the correct expenditures have been determined and made, the SNT trustee should prepare a final accounting. (See Chapter 8 for the form of account.) If the SNT has been under court jurisdiction, a final accounting and report will need to be filed and set for hearing in the local probate court. A court account must be filed in a very specific format that is discussed in more detail in Chapter 8.

If the SNT has not been court supervised, the trustee will generally not need to file an account with the court. However, he or she may still want to provide a final accounting to all interested parties, including the remainder beneficiaries and DHCS to begin the running of the time that these parties could file a lawsuit against the trustee. See Step Two above for addresses to send account to DHCS.

> **Note:** Some SNTs will waive the accounting requirement. Even if it does, it may still be prudent to send one so that the running of the statute of limitations begins immediately.

WHAT ARE THE SNT TRUSTEE'S RESPONSIBILITIES IN TERMINATING A THIRD-PARTY SNT?

While third-party SNT administration is typically not done with court oversight and is managed privately by the SNT trustee, it is still a good idea to formally wrap up the SNT. Unlike the first-party SNT, the third-party SNT does not have a Medi-Cal payback requirement on trust termination which makes termination that much simpler for the trustee.

Many SNT document will provide written instructions on what is required when the trust terminates. If it does not, then the SNT trustee must utilize the California Probate Code that provides authority for wrapping up the trust. Typically, this includes paying final expenses including last illness, burial, and administrative expenses, and taxes. If the trustee is uncertain or unfamiliar with trust termination, he or she may wish to hire an experienced estate-planning attorney. In order to find such a qualified attorney, see Chapter 20.

STEP ONE: PAYMENT OF FEES AND EXPENSES

In most well drafted third-party SNTs, the trust document may authorize, *but not require*, payments of fees and expenses. The trust should specifically state that any payment made for fees and expenses is within the discretion of the trustee so that an outside third-party cannot enforce a claim or right against the trust. Expenses typically include payment of any expenses of last illness, funeral, and burial or cremation, including memorials and memorial services. Thus, the trustee has the option of paying most of the bills of the beneficiary or not.

> **Note:** The SNT trustee should check the trust language to make sure that the SNT does not require payments of these bills. The trust may have been drafted without the benefit of an attorney's advice and the trust would require payment of these bills by trustee.

The SNT trustee must still pay those expenses that he or she entered into as trustee of the SNT. For example, caregiver expenses, attorney's expenses, CPA expenses, or other service providers. Below is a summary of the types of expenses the SNT trustee will generally be expected to pay:

- **Professionals' Fees**. Professional fees are generally those for persons who provide advice and assistance to the trustee. They include fees for legal advice, accounting and tax advice, and other professional services needed to properly administer the trust.

- **Funeral Expenses**. An SNT beneficiary will generally not have sufficient resources to pay for a funeral. It is appropriate to authorize, but not require, payment of burial or cremation and other funeral expenses—including removal, transportation and disposition of remains, memorials, and memorial services.

- **Debts**. One of the most important differences between third-party and first-party SNT is creditor rights. If the third-party SNT is properly drafted the beneficiary's creditors will have no claim to trust corpus. Creditors only have a claims against funds distributed outright to the SNT beneficiary. Thus, it will be up to the SNT trustee's discretion to pay for the beneficiary's bills he or she incurred personally.

- **Taxes**. During the lifetime of the SNT beneficiary, the third-party SNT should authorize the trustee to prepare and file returns and arrange for payment of all taxes applicable to the trust, including all local, state, federal and foreign taxes incident to the trust agreement. Upon death, the trustee should make sure that tax payments are current or reserved for prior to distribution of the remaining trust estate to beneficiaries. The third-party SNT may or may not be included in the beneficiary's estate. The trustee should work with a tax professional to determine what state and federal taxes are due because of the death of the special needs beneficiary.

STEP TWO: FINAL DISTRIBUTION

Upon the termination of the SNT, the third-party trust should provide for distribution of the remaining trust estate. Since there is no payback requirement and a clause for payback should not be part of the third-party special needs trust, distribution can be made to any individual(s), or charity chosen as set forth in the trust document.

The SNT trustee can prepare a spreadsheet that will make sure that all assets were properly distributed. The document will cover the following:

- Distribution provisions (as governed by the trust). This will generally be set up in the SNT. If not, or if left to "heirs" the SNT trustee may need to determine who the beneficiary's "heirs" are. This usually requires an understanding of the California Probate Code. If the trustee is unsure, he or she should retain an experienced estate-planning attorney.
- Date of distribution. The dates the SNT trustee provides assets to beneficiaries should be documented so if questions arise later, the trustee will have the information ready to answer the questions.

- Preliminary distributions. The trustee may have some outstanding issues to resolve that may take time. He or she may allow an early distribution so beneficiaries can receive some distributions pending the resolution of other issues.
- Consent to distribution by beneficiaries. If there is some question as to who should receive what, the trustee may prepare a consent of distribution to be signed by all beneficiaries. This way, the trustee is protected if later questions arise as to the advisability of certain disbursements.
- Waiver of accounting. In the next step, the trustee can provide an account to beneficiaries. Instead, the trustee may seek a waiver of the accounting requirement.
- Reserve amounts. The trustee may decide to keep a reserve. This is an amount of money left in the trust after all disbursements are made. This is in case there are later tax or debt claims that will need to be paid. Typically, a reserve is maintained for less than a year.

STEP THREE: FINAL ACCOUNT

While a final account is not necessarily required for a third-party SNT administration, it is often a good idea to prepare one so the statute of limitations period will begin to run on trustee's activities.

Ordinarily, an action for breach of trust has a four-year statute of limitations from the date the "cause of action shall have accrued."[531] If an adult beneficiary with capacity who receives a trust accounting[532] wishes to pursue a claim against the trustee for breach of trust, the claim must be filed within three years after receipt of the account or report.[533] This shortened three-year statute of limitations may also apply to incapacitated adult and minor beneficiaries if the account is served on the legal representative, guardian, or parents.[534] For a more complete discussion of the accounting requirement, see Chapter 8.

---

531 Code Civil Procedure §343.

532 Probate Code §16063.

533 Probate Code §16460(a)(1); *Noggle v Bank of America* (1999) 70 Cal App 4th 853.

534 Probate Code §16460(b).

CHAPTER 18 SUMMARY

The chapter provides:

- ✓ A checklist of things to do on behalf of the SNT beneficiary after his death
- ✓ A general discussion of the SNT trustee's legal responsibilities on trust termination (paying all valid debts and taxes, doing a final account, and making final distribution)
- ✓ Steps to terminating a first-party SNT:
    - Send Notice to Medi-Cal and Medicaid agencies.
    - Review timely claims (four months) from Medi-Cal and Medicaid agencies.
    - Determine if exception to first-party SNT applies (SNT beneficiary leaves child with a disability, child under age twenty-one, surviving spouse, or only community-based Medi-Cal received prior to age fifty-five).
    - Understand priority of creditor claims for first-party SNT.
        - * Taxes may be paid before Medi-Cal payback.
        - * Administrative expenses may be paid before Medi-Cal payback.
    - Funeral expenses may be paid if permission received from DHCS.
    - Pay off remaining debts.
    - Make final disbursements (watch out for power of appointment provisions).
    - Do a final accounting.
- ✓ Steps to terminate a third-party SNT:
    - Termination is much easier than first-party SNT because there is no payback to DHCS for Medi-Cal payments.
    - SNT trustee typically has discretion to pay (or not pay) the beneficiary's final debts.
    - SNT trustee must pay remaining trust expenses and taxes.
    - Make final disbursements.
    - Should do final accounting.

CHAPTER 19

Avoiding Common SNT Trustee Mistakes

Because the administration of a special needs trust is a difficult task, mistakes are often made. This chapter will go over some of the more common mistakes that arise during special needs trust (SNT) administration.

If an SNT trustee uses common sense during SNT administration, that trustee is destined to fail. The reason that common sense fails is the disheartening uncertainty of the laws that govern SNT administration and the ever-shifting policy changes made by governmental agencies. Sometimes, something that appears to be in the best interest of the person with a disability, which the trustee thinks he or she should have no problem paying, may actually cause the *loss* of public benefits. Frustratingly, even if in one year it is okay to spend money on something, that same item may be forbidden the next year by a change in law or policy. The best an SNT trustee can do is comply with the law or policy as written at the time such a distribution is being made and to remain vigilant as to changes in laws or policies that may change how a trustee is to do his or her job.

In order to understand the areas where SNT trustees make the most mistakes, an overview of the top mistakes and how to avoid them are summarized below.

MISTAKE NUMBER ONE: NOT READING THE SNT DOCUMENT

All too often, the SNT trustee will invest assets, make disbursements, or perform other tasks when administering the SNT that are specifically forbidden by the trust document. Some of the advice in this book or described in this chapter that would otherwise be acceptable for the trustee to perform is not acceptable if the SNT document states that the trustee cannot do it.

The SNT document is always the first place that the SNT trustee should look to determine if he or she is able to perform a certain task. If the SNT document is silent on the issue, then it may be best to see if there is any prohibition in California law or in the public benefits laws that might prevent such a distribution.

A deviation from the trust terms without a sufficient excuse is a breach of trust and can open up a trustee to a claim for removal, sanctions, or damages.[535] To comply with trust terms, the trustee has to understand them. This is not always easy to do. The trustee must interpret the terms of a trust as the person who set up the trust intended them. If it is still unclear as some words or different people can interpret phrases differently and the effect of the different interpretations would cause potential harm, the trustee should file a Petition for Instructions with the court to see if the trustee's interpretation is correct. This can be done as set forth in Chapter 5.

However, if there has been a substantial change in circumstances from the time the trust was drafted, the trustee is not shielded from liability by slavishly comply with the terms of the trust. Doing so could still constitute a breach of trust. For example, if the trust required the trustee to maintain an investment that was no longer economical, the trustee would not be shielded from liability by continuing to invest in that asset. If the trustee is unclear on taking a certain action, the trustee should file a Petition for Instructions with the court. This can be done as forth in Chapter 5.

> **Example:** An SNT trustee wishes to purchase a home to be owned by the SNT for the use of the SNT beneficiary. Under California law and the public benefit laws, this is a perfectly acceptable way to spend the money in an SNT. However, this particular SNT document specifically forbids the SNT trustee from purchasing real estate. If the SNT trustee goes ahead and buys the property, he or she is in breach of trust and could be subject to removal as trustee, fines (called a surcharge), and any damages incurred.

---

535   See Probate Code §16000 and *Estate of Gilmaker* (1962) 57 Cal. 2d 627.

MISTAKE NUMBER TWO: FAILING TO KEEP CURRENT ON SPECIAL NEEDS TRUST LAWS

An SNT trustee should have a system to alert him or herself of changes in the laws on SNT administration and public benefits eligibility, or secure experienced special needs counsel to help advise them. Chapter 7 outlines recommended systems for the SNT trustee to incorporate that will assist in maintaining a current understanding of any changes in law or policy. Chapter 20 also lists some websites that will enable a trustee to keep current on these laws. At a minimum, the SNT trustee should go to the website www.UrbLaw.com and sign up for the Special Needs News. There we offer a monthly e-mail newsletter that identifies any significant changes in the laws and regulations concerning special needs administration.

The other website that should be regularly reviewed concerns California public benefits programs and is located at https://ca.db101.org. This website does an excellent job of providing simple explanations of the various California public benefits programs.

MISTAKE NUMBER THREE: CONFUSING THE PUBLIC BENEFIT PROGRAMS

Public benefits recipients, their families, and even many attorneys often confuse the type of public benefits being received by a SNT beneficiary. Confusion is quite common between Supplemental Security Income (SSI) and Social Security Disability Insurance (SSDI) because the monthly cash payments come from the same place, the Social Security Administration (SSA). Also, many SNT beneficiaries do not keep correspondence from the SSA, and the SSA will not communicate with an SNT trustee unless he or she has the permission of the public benefits recipient (or the recipient's SSA-appointed Representative Payee), which may be difficult to obtain. This means knowing which benefits are being received can be problematic. For a more thorough discussion of the different types of public benefits, see Chapter 3.

The trustee needs to know what public benefits the SNT beneficiary is receiving because the administration differs drastically depending on the type of benefits involved. If the only benefits involved are, SSDI, Social Security (SS), and Medicare, which have no income or resource limits, the administration is much simpler. These programs do not have special rules where SNT disbursements affect ongoing eligibility. Thus, the SNT trustee need follow only the terms of the trust document as to what disbursements are acceptable. If the SNT beneficiary is receiving SSI or Medicaid, the SNT trustee must follow strict rules during administration, as these benefits have both income and asset limits. As a result, disbursements must be made carefully so as not to impact eligibility. To make matters slightly more difficult, an SNT beneficiary could be receiving a combination of benefits, such as SSI, SSDI, Medicare, and Medicaid.

Because the SNT beneficiary and their family may not know exactly what public benefits are being received, it will be up to the SNT trustee to find out. One way to determine if the beneficiary is receiving SSI is to find out how much money the beneficiary is receiving. In 2020, the maximum federal SSI an individual can receive in California is $958.63.[536] Thus, an SNT beneficiary who is receiving less than that is likely to be receiving SSI. To find the latest maximum monthly benefit for a person on SSI in California, see www.ssa.gov/pubs/11125.html or Google "SSI in California."

Another option for identifying the right benefit is for the SNT trustee to determine when the checks arrive:

- SSI checks arrive on the first of each month.
- SSDI checks typically arrive on the third of the month or may arrive on the Wednesday closest to the recipient's birthday.
- If however, the person receives both SSI and SSDI, the checks arrive on the third of the month.

Once the SNT trustee knows the type of public benefits involved, the trustee needs to identify which public benefit laws to follow during administration. In most cases, the SNT beneficiary is receiving SSI and Medi-Cal. Under this scenario, the trustee is responsible for following only the SSI rules and regulations. Much of the time, the trustee only needs to worry about the rules set forth in the SSA's Program Operation Manual System (POMS). In some cases, the SNT beneficiary does not receive SSI but still receives Medi-Cal under a different eligibility program. In this situation, the trustee must follow the Medi-Cal rules and regulations, which are found in each state's Medicaid plan and state policies.

---

536 An SSI recipient who is blind or who lives in an apartment without a kitchen, however, could receive a larger monthly check so it is important to know these other factors before relying solely on the amount of the check being received.

In addition to SSI and Medicaid, the SNT trustee should get a complete picture of other public benefits the beneficiary is receiving, like Section 8 or Veteran Benefits. An SNT trustee should understand how the administration of the SNT might affect these benefits. The rules may be unclear, however, or the benefits may be treated differently throughout each state by the different local agencies. Thus, a thorough understanding of the public benefit programs requirements and policies is essential knowledge for the SNT trustee.

A quick overview of the most common SNT beneficiary scenarios is as follows:

- **SSI and Medi-Cal Recipient:** In many cases, the SNT beneficiary will be receiving SSI and Medi-Cal, because in California, if the SSI beneficiary receives any amount—even one dollar of SSI—he or she automatically receives Medi-Cal. Under this scenario, the trustee is responsible only for following the SSI rules and regulations, which are generally found in the Program Operation Manuel System (commonly called the POMS), the SSA's internal guidelines on how to administer the SSI program. The POMS rules can be found on their website, which is set forth in Chapter 20.

- **Medi-Cal–Only Recipient:** In some cases, the SNT beneficiary does not receive SSI but still receives Medi-Cal under a different eligibility program. If this is the case, the trustee does not need to follow the SSI rules but must follow the Medi-Cal rules and regulations, which are found in the California Welfare and Institutions Code, California regulations, and All County Welfare Director's Letters. These rules can all be found on their respective websites, which are set forth in Chapter 17.

  Note: Generally, these rules are very similar to SSI's rules. However, there are some distinctions. In this book, we make note if the Medi-Cal rules are different from those for SSI. Further, Medi-Cal has one program called "Expanded Medi-Cal" that has drastically different rules than traditional Medi-Cal. These rules are discussed in depth in Chapter 3.

- **SSDI, Social Security, and Medicare Only:** These public benefit programs are generally the easiest ones to manage by the SNT trustee, because these programs do not have income or resource limitations. As a result, SNT disbursements will have any effect on ongoing eligibility. Thus, the SNT trustee need only follow the terms of the trust document with respect to acceptable disbursements.

  Warning: The SNT trustee should make very sure that the beneficiary receives only these benefits and not SSI or Medi-Cal. It is possible for a beneficiary to have SSI and SSDI or both Medi-Cal and Medicare. If this is the case, the SNT trustee must follow the rules of either SSI or Medi-Cal during administration.

- **Other Benefits, Such as Veteran Benefits, Section 8, Food Stamps, and CalWorks:** The SNT trustee should get a complete picture of the public benefits. An SNT trustee should understand how an SNT might affect these benefits if the SNT beneficiary is eligible. The difficulty with many of these benefits is that in some cases the rules are unclear and in other cases they are treated differently throughout California by the different agencies. We will do our best to highlight when these uncertainties arise and how different agencies may be treating different issues.

MISTAKE NUMBER FOUR: CONFUSING THE DIFFERENT TYPES OF SPECIAL NEEDS TRUSTS

It is critically important to determine, at the outset, what type of special needs trust is being administered. SNTs fall into two basic categories: (1) the third-party SNT and (2) the first-party SNT. If it is a first-party SNT, the trustee must then also determine if it is a court-supervised SNT or not.

An SNT trustee has nearly identical duties in administering first-party SNT and third-party SNT. However, there are critical distinctions between the two that will cause the trustee problems if he or she does not understand the particular rules for each. To determine whether the trust is a first-party SNT or a third-party SNT the trustee must understand that:

- A first-party SNT is funded with the person with a disability's money or assets. That's it. If the money being transferred to the trusts is the person with a disability's own assets, then the trust must be a first-party SNT to work. This type of SNT typically arises when the beneficiary with a disability has received a litigation recovery or the beneficiary receives an inheritance or gift in his or her own name and transfers the property to an SNT. However, if a person with a disability has existing assets and wishes to transfer them, he or she is allowed to do that as well.
- A third-party SNT is funded with money or assets that belong to a third person that is not the person with a disability. This is typically done through a parent or grandparent's estate plan or it could be part of a Go Fund Me promotion. However, anyone but the person with a disability can put money or assets into the trust.

Ownership of assets can be confusing. There may be legal issues, like community property issues or rights to an inheritance, that can be confusing to those not used to making these types of determinations. One question that often arises is whether the assets are the person with a disability's if they never actually receive it but instead the money goes directly to a trust. In this scenario, can the trust be a third-party SNT rather than a first-party SNT? The answer is no. If the person with a disability has legal ownership of the money or assets, those assets belong to him or her whether the assets were ever actually in the name of the person with a disability.

> **Example:** Peter, a person with a disability who is an SSI recipient, receives an inheritance of $50,000 as part of his Uncle Paul's will. Uncle Paul's estate is being probated in court, and his executor, Mary, wishes to give Peter his money but recognizes that by giving the money directly to him, he will lose his SSI and Medi-Cal. Mary suggests writing the check directly to Peter's third-party special needs trust, which had been previously set up and funded by Peter's parents. Mary believes that if Peter never touches the money, it was never his, so it preserves his SSI eligibility.

471

This is incorrect. Peter has a legal right to his inheritance even if he never actually receives it. Thus, the only way to preserve this money and keep SSI and Medi-Cal is to have the money transferred to a properly established first-party SNT. If Mary places Peter's inheritance into the third-party SNT, it would make the third-party SNT invalid for public benefit purposes and Peter would lose his eligibility for both SSI and Medi-Cal. However, if the funds were left to Peter through Uncle Paul's trust, careful review of the trust document by an experienced special needs planning attorney to examine all available options is strongly recommended.

In order to understand the primary differences between the different types of special needs trusts, the SNT trustee should know the legal rules that must be followed in setting up the two types of trust.

The rules that make a third-party SNT legal are relatively easy to meet. For SSI purposes, the Social Security Administration ("SSA") defines a third-party trust as "a trust established by someone other than the beneficiary as grantor."[537] The SSA defines a grantor as "the individual who provides the trust principal (or corpus)."[538] The regulations impose basically two requirements for third-party SNTs:

1. The beneficiary cannot have authority to revoke the trust; and
2. The beneficiary cannot direct the use of trust assets for his or her support and maintenance under the terms of the trust.[539]

Generally, a third-party SNT is the best method for bequeathing or gifting assets to a person with a disability. This is the most common use of third-party SNTs. While the legal rules for setting up a third-party SNT are relatively easy to meet, this type of SNT also provides quite a bit of flexibility. As a result, these types of third-party SNTs may require more work to administer, because the trust document may require the SNT trustee to also provide lifetime care and advocacy for the person with a disability and may also include multiple beneficiaries.

---

537 POMS SI 01120.200(B)(17).
538 POMS SI 01120.200(B)(2).
539 42 U.S.C. §1382b(e)(3)(A), 20 C.F.R. §416.1201(a)(1); POMS SI 01120.200(D)(2).

The rules that make a first-party SNT legal are a bit more complicated. A first-party SNT is a federally authorized safe harbor trust that allows an individual with a disability to transfer his or her own assets into the trust without being penalized by needs-based public benefits programs. As long as the statutory requirements are met, an individual with a disability can transfer his or her assets into a first-party SNT without penalty. All other transfers to a non–first party SNT will trigger some type of penalty; usually a period of time that the public benefits recipient is ineligible for benefits.

The type of first-party SNT that an individual trustee would be responsible for is often called a (d)(4)(A) SNT, Litigation SNT, or Payback SNT. The rules for this type of first-party SNT are as follows:

- Beneficiary must be disabled under Social Security Administration's rules;
- Person must be under age 65 when trust is established;
- Trust must be established by the individual, a parent, grandparent, legal guardian or the court;
- Trust must be for the "sole benefit" of the person with a disability; and
- Trust must include a provision that all Medi-Cal (or Medicaid from other States) will be paid back on the death of the beneficiary.[540]

The (d)(4)(A) SNT can be complicated to establish. If the SNT trustee is not sure that the SNT was set up correctly, the trustee should contact an experienced special needs planning attorney to make sure it was done properly. The above list will make the (d)(4)(A) SNT legal for Social Security purposes, but the State of California and the California regulations have some additional requirements.

If the (d)(4)(A) SNT is established by a court for a person with a disability who also lacks capacity to manage his or her own person affairs, then the (d)(4)(A) SNT must also have the following requirements:

1. A "no contest" provision which is a provision that penalizes someone if they file a lawsuit against the trust is not allowed;
2. Prohibit any changes to the SNT without court approval;
3. Clearly identify the SNT trustee and any other person with authority to direct the trustee to make disbursements;

---

540   42 U.S.C. §1396p(d)(4)(A).

4. Prohibit investments by the SNT trustee other than those permitted under the California laws of conservatorship;

5. Require SNT trustees to post bond (at the expense of the trust) which is a type of insurance policy that the trustee will not steal the money in the trust;

6. Require the SNT trustee to file court accounts and reports for court approval subject to very specific court rules one year after the trust is established and every two years thereafter;

7. Require court approval of changes in SNT trustees and a court order appointing any successor trustee;

8. Require compensation of the SNT trustee, the members of any advisory committee, or the attorney for the SNT trustee to be in just and reasonable amounts that must be fixed and allowed by the court.[541]

Warning: A court-supervised (d)(4)(A) SNT is much more difficult and expensive to administer. It is strongly recommended that a special needs planning attorney be hired to assist in the administration. The rules are tricky and many California probate courts are far too harsh on SNT trustees who make simple mistakes during administration.

If the SNT trustee is asked to administer the (d)(4)(A) SNT, he or she should ask for a copy of the court's order establishing the trust. The court's order may have additional requirements that the SNT trustee must follow.

Note: A common misconception among many people including SSA eligibility workers is that every (d)(4)(A) SNT must be established by a court. This is wrong. There are many (d)(4)(A) SNTs that are established by the individual. Prior to 2016, an individual could not establish his or her own (d)(4)(A) SNT, but because of the Special Needs Trust Fairness Act, an individual can now do so. In addition, a parent or grandparent can establish a (d)(4)(A) SNT

---

541   California Rules of Court 7.903(c).

on behalf of their child/grandchild. The SSA POMS refer to these trusts as "Seed Trusts."[542] A (d)(4)(A) SNT that is a "Seed Trust" does not need to follow the eight rules set forth above.

There are two other types of first-party SNTs that an individual SNT trustee in California will not be asked to administer. These two types of first-party SNTs are known as

1. The Miller Trust. Not in use in California. The Miller Trust is a trust that is composed only of pension, Social Security, and other income in a state that does not allow an income "spend down."[543] It is aptly named a Miller Trust due to the Colorado case *Miller v Ibarra* (D Colo 1990) 746 F Supp 19; and

2. The Pooled SNT. An individual SNT trustee will not be the trustee of this type of SNT because it is administered by a nonprofit. The pooled SNT is a trust that contains the assets of an individual with a disability if (a) the trust is established and managed by a nonprofit corporation and uses separate accounts of pooled assets; (b) the accounts are established by the individual beneficiary, a parent, a grandparent, a legal guardian, or the court; and (c) the state will, on the beneficiary's death, receive all amounts remaining in the beneficiary's account (unless the account is retained in the trust) up to the amount of Medi-Cal benefits paid.[544]

MISTAKE NUMBER FIVE: SNT TRUSTEE FAILS TO ESTABLISH A SYSTEM TO REQUEST DISBURSEMENTS

The number one beneficiary complaint about an SNT trustee is his or her lack of communication concerning disbursements on behalf of the person with a disability. The easiest way to avoid this complaint is to set up a procedure on how to request disbursements and the procedure for approving or not approving disbursement requests and have a process for sharing this information with the beneficiary or their legal representative.

---

542   POMS SI 01120.203(B)(1)(f).
543   42 U.S.C. §1396p(d)(4)(B).
544   42 U.S.C. §1396p(d)(4)(C).

The trustee should meet with the beneficiary, any legal guardians, and those friends and family willing to participate. A spending plan should be established from this meeting so that monthly expenses may be paid without constant requests.

The disbursement procedure should determine whether disbursements could be made only during business hours, on weekdays, or after twenty-four hours from a written request. It is in the trustee's best interest to clearly communicate these policies to the beneficiary. This will go a long way in eliminating friction during the administration.

> **Helpful Hint:** In order to have a clear record of all disbursements, a good suggestion is for the SNT trustee to purchase a fax machine or document scanner for a beneficiary or his or her caregiver. In this way, disbursement requests can be faxed or scanned and e-mailed directly to the trustee's office and the trustee will have a written record of all requests.

See Chapter 7 for a thorough discussion on how to set up a disbursement procedure. See Chapters 11 - 15 for how SNT distributions affect public benefits, and Chapter 16 for a discussion on the proper method for making SNT distributions.

MISTAKE NUMBER SIX: SNT TRUSTEE MAKES DISTRIBUTIONS FOR PERSONS OTHER THAN PERSON WITH A DISABILITY

The SNT trustee's ability to make distributions to persons other than the beneficiary of an SNT will depend on the type of SNT that is being administered and whether the document authorizes it.

- **Third-Party SNT, May Be Authorized:** A third-party SNT trustee may make distributions to third parties but only if the trust terms allow gifts or distributions to others. Sometimes, a third-party SNT will allow disbursements for a spouse or child of the beneficiary with a disability. A third-party SNT may also authorize gifts to recognize the beneficiary's family and friends on their birthdays or during holidays. It is not improper to include such provisions and to make such payments in a third-party SNT when authorized. Also, a third-party SNT may be established so that there are multiple beneficiaries. This means that the person with a disability could be only one beneficiary under the trust.

- **First-Party SNT, Not Authorized.** A first-party SNT must only be used for the sole benefit" of the primary beneficiary during his or her lifetime. If there is a distribution that provides some benefit to the beneficiary, it will be considered for the beneficiary's sole benefit.[545] The disqualification for failing to meet this requirement will cost the beneficiary his or her SSI and linked Medi-Cal benefits. If the beneficiary is only receiving Medi-Cal, the SNT must still be solely for the beneficiary's benefit.[546] If a distribution is made as a gift to a third party or charity, it will not be for the sole benefit of the beneficiary. The harder question is paying for the minor children or spouse of the person with a disability. See Chapter 2 for a more complete discussion of "sole benefit."

  > **Example:** An SNT beneficiary would benefit from having a pool installed at his home. His doctor has said he requires exercise and in a pool is the only safe place for this person with a disability. Public or other private pools will not let him attend because of liability concerns surrounding his disability. The family requests that the SNT trustee purchase a pool at the family home. This type of distribution would be authorized, even though other family members may enjoy the pool. The primary benefit and purpose of the pool is for the beneficiary. In this example, the SNT trustee may want to place a lien on the home or take a percentage ownership of the home for the purchase price of the pool to protect the beneficiary if the family decides to move later.

---

545   42 U.S.C. §1382b(c)(1)(C)(ii)(IV).
546   42 U.S.C. §1396p(c)(2)(B)(iv).

MISTAKE NUMBER SEVEN: DISTRIBUTING MORE THAN TWENTY DOLLARS PER MONTH DIRECTLY TO SNT BENEFICIARY

The interplay of SNT distributions and continuing eligibility for public benefits programs, such as Supplemental Security Income (SSI), makes being an SNT trustee very complicated. In Chapters 11 through 15, there is a thorough discussion of how different types of distributions will affect the person with a disability's public benefits.

One common mistake that many trustees make is giving money directly to the SNT beneficiary. Any money the trustee gives to the beneficiary directly will be considered by the Social Security Administration (SSA) as "unearned income" to the beneficiary under the SSI rules, and after a set-aside of the first $20 each month (general income exclusion), will reduce the SSI recipient's benefits on a dollar-for-dollar basis.[547] In other words, the trustee should never distribute cash directly to a beneficiary who is receiving SSI. The correct procedure is to pay vendors directly for goods and services in order to avoid the dollar-for-dollar reduction. There are also ways to utilize credit cards to make payments easier. See Chapter 16 for a thorough discussion of the proper ways to make SNT disbursements.

> **Example:** Kirby, an SNT beneficiary, is receiving $958.63 per month of SSI payments. Kirby asks for a $500 per month allowance from the SNT because the amount of SSI is insufficient to pay for his monthly expenses. The SNT trustee agrees and begins providing $500 per month to Kirby. The legal effect of this disbursement is that Kirby loses $480 from his monthly SSI check and nets only $20 from his SNT.

The better practice would be to take some of the monthly expenses that are being paid for with Kirby's SSI check and have the SNT pay them directly, this way Kirby has more available cash. Another solution is if Kirby qualifies for a credit card, he can use the credit card and send the bill to the SNT trustee to pay or he could utilize a True Link card that allows the trustee to fund a card with money from the trust and allows the beneficiary to use it. See Chapter 16 for a more thorough discussion on the different methods for making a disbursement.

---

547   20 C.F.R. §416.1124(c)(12); POMS SI 00810.420, 01120.200(E)(1)(a).

Warning: The SNT trustee should be careful when there is a request to provide cash directly to an SSI recipient. Many SSI recipients have been receiving cash directly from other sources and still receive their full SSI check. The SNT beneficiary may insist that it is okay to provide the cash because he or she has received it for many years with no penalty. All that has happened is that the SSA has not yet caught up to this SSI recipient. Sometimes, the SSA will not find out for months (or even years). When it does find out (and the SSA is good at discovering these things), it will seek to have the money paid back. The SSA calls this an "overpayment." If the SSI recipient does not have the money, the SSA will reduce the monthly SSI check until the overpayment is repaid or may deny eligibility for SSI. Further, the SSA may (in extreme cases) allege fraud against the SSI recipient or those that provided those funds. It is simply not worth it to provide cash directly to an SSI recipient.

Another similar issue is where the SNT trustee reimburses the person with a disability for items he or she has purchased, even if the person with a disability purchased items that are exempt from being counted by public benefit agencies. This type of disbursement will also be treated as "unearned income" for SSI eligibility.

Example: Jody, an SNT beneficiary, uses her own money to pay for a $200 cell phone. She asks the SNT trustee to reimburse her for this payment. If the SNT trustee reimburses Jody for the phone, Jody will lose $180 per month of SSI (after the $20 set-aside amount). If, instead, the SNT trustee purchased the cell phone directly, there would be no reduction. Likewise, if Jody's friend purchased the cell phone and the SNT trustee reimbursed the friend, there would be no SSI reduction. See Chapter 16 for a more thorough discussion.

SSI rules also provide that if the trustee distributes anything to the beneficiary that is equivalent to cash, it will be counted as SSI "unearned income."

Example: If an SNT trustee gives Richard an SNT beneficiary a gift card (or gift certificate) worth $500 that he can use to buy food or shelter directly, such as to a Wal-Mart, Target, restaurant, grocery store, or Visa gift card, it will be counted as SSI "unearned income" and will reduce Richard's SSI check by $480.[548] If the store does not sell food or shelter items, as in the case of Macy's, clothing stores (such as the Gap), bookstores, or electronics store, it will not be counted against the beneficiary. However, the gift card must also include a legally enforceable prohibition on selling the card for cash. If it fails to have this prohibition, it will still be considered as SSI "unearned income" in the month of receipt. See Chapter 16 for a more thorough discussion.

Warning: A common misunderstanding is that a gift card that can pay for food or shelter will be treated as in-kind support and maintenance (ISM) (see Chapter 3 for a full discussion of ISM) or only a $281 (in year 2020) reduction in SSI. This is wrong. It is treated as "unearned income," which results in a dollar-for-dollar reduction after the first $20. Thus, the SNT trustee should only use gift cards if they understand the legal consequences of doing so. See Chapter 16 for a discussion of these requirements.

MISTAKE NUMBER EIGHT: A SNT TRUSTEE WHO REFUSES TO MAKE DISTRIBUTIONS FOR THE SNT BENEFICIARY

Too often, SNT trustees become overly concerned about the SSI and Medi-Cal rules and stop making distributions that could benefit the SNT beneficiary, even those that are perfectly acceptable. The primary purpose of any SNT is to improve the overall quality of life of the person with a disability. The trustee is asked to perform a balancing act between making distributions that do not violate the rules of the applicable benefit program (typically SSI and Medi-Cal) and providing the beneficiary with goods and services so that he or she does not have to live at the poverty level.

---

548   POMS SI 00830.522.

The most difficult balancing task an SNT trustee is required to perform is deciding whether a distribution that will reduce (or even eliminate) a beneficiary's government benefits is in the beneficiary's best interest. See Chapters 11-15 for a full discussion of acceptable distributions that will not interfere with public benefit eligibility.

In order to properly decide how and when to make payments from an SNT, the trustee must be familiar with the SSI rules on "income" and "resources." See Chapter 3 for a more complete discussion of the public benefit rules. In general, the trustee should pay careful attention to the following issues when making distributions:

- **Resources.** An SSI and traditional Medi-Cal recipient is entitled to only $2,000 in countable resources and an eligible couple, $3,000.[549] Thus, the trustee should not purchase items that are considered countable resources that will cause the beneficiary to exceed the applicable resource limitation. For example, the SNT trustee should not buy in the name of the SSI recipient a second automobile or vacation home.

- **Income.** The SSA will count a distribution of cash to a SSI benefits recipient by an SNT trustee as unearned income. The trustee should not provide money directly to the beneficiary (or reimburse the beneficiary for money he or she has spent), because after the first $20 (general income exclusion), each dollar so given will be considered to be "unearned income" and reduce the beneficiary's SSI payment dollar-for-dollar. See Mistake Number Seven above on the effect of providing cash directly to an SNT beneficiary.

- **In-kind support and maintenance.** A trustee should be extremely careful in providing "food" or "shelter" items to an SNT beneficiary. SSI benefits are intended to pay for a person's food and shelter. Hence, if the beneficiary receives food or shelter as a result of payments by the trustee, it is considered by the SSA as "in-kind support and maintenance" (ISM) and will result in a reduction (or possible elimination) of the beneficiary's SSI payments. However, the SNT trustee who understands this rule can provide a real benefit to the SNT beneficiary. See Mistake Number Nine for discussion of

---

549   20 C.F.R. §416.1205(c).

when making payments for food and shelter is acceptable. However, a careful reading of the trust document is necessary, as some trusts specifically prohibit disbursements which diminish or reduce benefits.

MISTAKE NUMBER NINE: FAILING TO DISTRIBUTE FOR BENEFICIARY'S FOOD OR SHELTER WHEN IT IS ACCEPTABLE

A common misunderstanding is that an SNT trustee can never make distributions for the beneficiary's food or shelter needs. This is incorrect. If the SNT beneficiary is an SSI recipient, then payment of food or shelter costs may cause a small reduction in the overall SSI check. This is usually okay, because the cost of food and shelter in California is so much higher than the highest SSI monthly payment.

As described below, even if the SNT beneficiary is a Medi-Cal–only recipient, then a substantial portion of the recipient's food and shelter costs can still be made from the SNT without any loss or reduction of Medi-Cal.

How SSI treats payments of food or shelter. An SSI recipient is expected to pay for all of his or her food and shelter costs out of the monthly SSI check.

> **Note:** Under SSI rules, "shelter" includes room, rent, mortgage payments, real property taxes, heating fuel, gas, electricity, water, sewerage, and garbage collection services.[550] Food does not include many things bought in a grocery store, such as paper products, soap, personal toiletries, and pet food.

An SSI recipient in California as of 2020 is entitled to receive $958.63 per month. The federal government in the amount of $783 pays a portion of this and the balance is paid by the state of California.[551] The monthly SSI check is reduced if the SSI recipient receives income. As Chapter 3 explains in detail, "income" is defined by the SSA and is not defined the same as how "income" is defined by the IRS for income tax purposes.

---

550   20 C.F.R. §416.1130(b).

551   This monthly amount can change each year. Check the Myers Urbatsch, PC website at www. UrbLaw.com to learn if these amounts have changed.

One type of SSA "income" is defined as when someone else, including an SNT trustee, provides food or shelter to the SSI recipient. This type of SSI income is called "in-kind support and maintenance" (ISM).[552] If the SNT trustee provides ISM to the beneficiary, the beneficiary's SSI benefits will be reduced, but not on a dollar-for-dollar basis as with "unearned income." Instead, there are two different formulas that the Social Security Administration uses to reduce the SSI benefits for a person who receives ISM. Which formula is used depends on the household and living arrangements of the SSI recipient.

The two formulas that are used to place a value on ISM are the value of the one-third-reduction rule (VTR) and the presumed maximum value rule (PMV). It is more common for an SNT trustee to be concerned with PMV because that is the rule where a third party (like an SNT) provides food or shelter to an SSI recipient.

- **Value of One-Third Reduction Rule** (VTR): The VTR applies when the benefits recipient lives in another's house throughout a month, receives both food and shelter from inside the household, and does not meet his or her pro rata share of cost of the food and shelter expenses for the household. VTR reduces the SSI benefit by one third of the SSI federal benefit rate (FBR), or $261 (one third of $783 in 2020).[553] The VTR applies in full or not at all.[554]

  Note: When an individual lives alone, the VTR will not apply, because there are no other household members from whom the individual can receive ISM. In this case, any ISM received from outside the household is counted using the PMV rule described below.

  Example: Robert, an SSI recipient, lives in a home with three other people. His SSI benefit amount is $958.63 per month. Food and shelter expenses total $2,400 for the household. His pro rata share of the food and shelter expenses are $600. If the SSI recipient only

---

552   20 C.F.R. §§416.1102, 1130; POMS SI 01120.200(E)(1)(b).
553   20 C.F.R. §§416.1131, 416.1133.
554   20 C.F.R. §416.1131(b).

pays $540 toward expenses, he is not meeting his pro rata share of costs. The SSA will reduce his SSI check by $261 (in the year 2020). If the VTR applies, even if the difference between what he paid and his pro rata share is only $60, Robert is still subject to the full one-third reduction.

- **Presumed Maximum Value Rule (PMV)**: The PMV applies whenever the VTR (see above) does not apply.[555] The PMV rule applies when an SNT trustee (or any third party) pays a SSI recipient's food or shelter costs.[556] The effect of these distributions are that the person's SSI benefits will be reduced by the lesser of one-third of the federal benefit rate plus the $20 general income exclusion or the actual value of what was received.[557] In 2020, the PMV is $281 (one third of the federal benefit rate is $261 plus the $20 general income exclusion).

Example: Beth, an SNT beneficiary and SSI recipient, lives with three roommates and has been able to afford her share of the rent from her SSI check. She wishes to live alone and asks the SNT trustee to pay rent at a new apartment. Her SSI benefit is $958.63 per month in 2020. The SNT trustee agrees to pay for a new apartment that costs $2,000/month. The effect of this payment is that Beth's SSI check will be reduced by $281 to $677.63 per month.

Warning: The loss of $281 from an SSI check is usually an acceptable loss if the SSI recipient will receive a nice, clean, and safe place to live and only lose a small portion of the SSI check. However, if the SSI recipient is receiving only $281 per month or less in SSI, paying for food or shelter will eliminate eligibility for SSI altogether. It is important that the SNT trustee knows exactly how much of the SNT beneficiary's monthly check comes from SSI. Further, the amount of the loss will change each year, so the SSI trustee

---

555   20 C.F.R. §416.1140.
556   POMS SI 01120.200(E)(1)(b).
557   20 C.F.R. §416.1140.

should check to make sure he or she knows exactly what the amount of the PMV loss would be.

If the SNT beneficiary is a Medi-Cal–only recipient, the SNT trustee can make disbursements for food or shelter from the SNT but not for all of it.[558] The SNT trustee can come up with a percentage of the overall cost of food and shelter and pay that from the SNT, while the Medi-Cal recipient must pay the balance.

> **Example:** Rhonda is an SNT beneficiary. She receives only Medi-Cal and not SSI, because she receives a monthly annuity payment of $1,000 per month. Rhonda's rent and utilities are $2,000 per month and her food cost is $500 per month. The SNT trustee could pay for a certain percentage of Rhonda's food and shelter costs without jeopardizing her benefits. Thus, the SNT trustee could pay 90 percent of the costs of $2,250 for food, shelter, and utilities, and Rhonda would pay the balance without any loss of her Medi-Cal.

MISTAKE NUMBER TEN: FAILING TO MAINTAIN EXCELLENT RECORDS AND FAILING TO PROPERLY ACCOUNT FOR TRUSTEE ACTIONS

All SNT trustees must keep accurate records of their SNT transactions. It is very important to have complete records when the SNT trustee makes his or her annual report to the SNT beneficiary, makes a report to a court when required, files annual income tax returns with the IRS, and makes necessary reports to agencies providing public benefits.

It would be prudent for the SNT trustee to use a computer program, such as Quicken, to keep track of disbursements. The SNT trustee should keep receipts of all disbursements as well. This is one reason why requiring a beneficiary or his or her legal representatives to make a written request for disbursements is preferred as described in Mistake Number Five in this Chapter.

---

558   22 Cal Code Regs §50509.

Warning: Recently, the Social Security Administration (SSA) (the agency that manages SSI) has been demanding that SNT trustees provide several years of records of SNT disbursement requests. In one case, it asked for over twenty-one years of records. If the SNT trustee is unable to provide these records, it will be presumed that the disbursements were made inappropriately and the SNT beneficiary will lose his or her eligibility for SSI or be charged with an SSI overpayment. For example, SNT trustees may distribute cash to themselves or to others, such as guardians, to use for the SNT beneficiary. There may be no problem with the use of the funds, but the inability to explain the expenditures can create future difficulties for both the beneficiary and trustee.

All SNTs have accounting requirements. If the SNT is not court supervised, the account must be done on a yearly basis and can be provided in a summary fashion. If the SNT is court supervised, the account is a very formal court filing in which it is strongly encouraged that you retain an attorney or a fiduciary experienced in court accountings to assist.

For further discussion of the requirement to maintain records and issue accounts, see Chapter 8.

MISTAKE NUMBER ELEVEN: TERMINATION OF FIRST-PARTY (D)(4)(A) SNT— MAKING INAPPROPRIATE DISBURSEMENTS PRIOR TO MEDI-CAL RECOVERY

When a first-party SNT terminates, a first-party SNT must pay back Medi-Cal (and Medicaid in other states if the SNT beneficiary received services in another state) before disbursements can be made to the SNT's remainder beneficiaries. Thus, the SNT trustee has to be very careful about how money in the SNT is spent prior to Medi-Cal being paid back.

The Medi-Cal agency in California (the Department of Health Care Services (DHCS) must be paid back from assets held in the first-party SNT. If an SNT trustee makes an inappropriate disbursement, he or she will be liable for breach of trust. In California, there is some discrepancy between what the Social Security Administration (SSA), the agency that runs SSI, says that the SNT trustee can pay and what the DHCS says that the SNT trustee can pay prior to the payback to DHCS. Oddly, even though there is no payback to SSA for SSI paid, the SSA has set some very strict rules (more strict than those of the DHCS) on what can be paid prior to the Medi-Cal recovery.

- **Priority under Medi-Cal Program.** Under DHCS' guidelines, the SNT may retain funds to pay the following expenses before paying the Medi-Cal reimbursement claims:

  - The cost of the individual's remaining investment fees and management fees, such as attorney's fees, trustee's fees;
  - Outstanding bills for the benefit of the disabled individual or spouse that fall within the terms of the trust; or
  - Burial/funeral expenses of the disabled individual or disabled spouse.[559]

- **Priority under SSI Program.** The Social Security Administration's rules on what can be paid before payment of Medi-Cal recovery claims are strict. Only the following administrative expenses may be paid before reimbursement of Medi-Cal payments:

  - State and federal taxes due from the trust because of the death of the beneficiary or termination of the trust and transfer of trust assets to the remainder beneficiaries
  - Reasonable fees for administration of the trust estate, such as an accounting of the trust to a court, completion and filing of documents, or other required actions associated with termination and wrapping up of the trust[560]

The following disbursements are expressly prohibited from being paid before reimbursement of Medi-Cal's payments:

---

559 Medi-Cal Eligibility Procedures Manual Letter No. 192, p 9J-75.
560 POMS SI 01120.203(B)(3)(a).

- Taxes due from the estate of the beneficiary other than those arising from inclusion of the trust in the estate;
- Inheritance taxes due for residual beneficiaries;
- Payment of debts owed to third parties;
- Funeral expenses; and
- Payments to residual beneficiaries.[561]

In California, the SSI rules expressly prohibit two kinds of expenditures expressly permitted by California's Medi-Cal rules: debts owed to third parties and funeral expenses. For practical purposes, when terminating a first-party SNT, the SSI rules must be followed if the beneficiary receives SSI (as is often the case), even if they were disregarded when drafting the SNT document.

> **Helpful Hint:** Within days of the death of an SNT beneficiary, the beneficiary's family or friends may call the trustee to ask whether funeral expenses can be paid from the trust. As indicated above, the SSI rules allow the trustee to pay funeral expenses for the deceased beneficiary only after the Medi-Cal reimbursement is paid. If Medi-Cal's recovery claims exceed the remainder of trust assets, it is best to contact DHCS and seek approval for funeral payments before payment of the Medi-Cal claims. It is also prudent to confirm this agreement by a letter to the DHCS representative.

The best practice however is to prepay funeral and burial expenses before the death of the beneficiary. The trustee is authorized to make these distributions during the lifetime of the beneficiary.[562]

For more discussion of how Medi-Cal's recovery is handled after SNT termination, see Chapter 18.

---

561 POMS SI 01120.203(B)(3)(b).
562 POMS SI 01120.203(B)(3)(c).

CHAPTER 19 SUMMARY

The Top Mistakes Made by SNT Trustees

- ✓ Fails to read the trust document
- ✓ Fails to keep current on changes in the laws for special needs trusts and public benefits
- ✓ Confuses the different types of public benefits programs
- ✓ Confuses the different types of special needs trusts
- ✓ Fails to set up system to request disbursements
- ✓ Wrongfully makes distributions to persons other than SNT beneficiary
- ✓ Wrongfully gives cash directly to SNT beneficiary
- ✓ Wrongfully refuses to make appropriate distributions to SNT beneficiary
- ✓ Fails to make distributions of food and shelter when appropriate
- ✓ Fails to maintain records and failing to properly account for trustee actions
- ✓ Wrongfully makes distributions of first-party SNT assets on termination prior to Medi-Cal's recovery rights

CHAPTER 20

Finding Help Administering SNT

As this book highlights, the job of being an SNT trustee is more difficult and more complex than most trusts. Acting as SNT trustee involves working in compliance with ever-changing federal and state laws and policies, public benefit rules, meticulous record keeping, and emotional intelligence. There are many opportunities to make mistakes which have a lasting impact on the beneficiary's well-being. Thus, it is important that an SNT trustee know where to find help when needed.

This chapter will guide the trustee in locating the appropriate person, entity or court procedure to obtain assistance with different aspects of administration.

WHERE CAN AN SNT TRUSTEE FIND A SPECIAL NEEDS PLANNING ATTORNEY FOR ADVICE?

The best sources of help for SNT trustees are attorneys who specialize in this area of law. Not every attorney can provide the advice that a special needs trustee will need. The trustee should make sure that the attorney he or she seeks assistance from truly understands special needs planning. The attorney should really understand the public benefit issues that arise when administering an SNT. Not every estate-planning attorney will understand these issues; even ones who help set up SNTs may not understand all the unique public benefit issues.

The following websites can help you find a special needs planning attorney and allows you to join the author's special needs news monthly brochure:

- **The Urbatsch Law Firm, P.C.** is the law firm of Kevin Urbatsch, the author of this publication. It is recommended that the readers of this publication review the website for any updates to this book. It also includes general information about special needs trust administration and a trustee can sign up to receive the Special Needs News, which provides a monthly e-mail update on information and services available to persons with disabilities. The website also includes Kevin Urbatsch's upcoming seminar schedule on many special needs issues. The Urbatsch Law Firm, P.C.'s website is https://www.urblaw.com.

- **Academy of Special Needs Planners** (ASNP) is a nationwide attorney organization dedicated to special needs planning. It has general information for nonmembers, including a list of California attorneys who specialize in special needs planning. ASNP's website is https://specialneedsanswers.com.

- **California Advocates for Nursing Home Reform** (CANHR) is a statewide organization that includes attorneys who can assist with special needs planning. Its primary focus is assisting elders obtain eligibility for nursing home eligibility; however, there are lots of special needs planners who belong to the organization. CANHR website is http://www.canhr.org.

- **Professional Fiduciary Association of California** (PFAC) is not an attorney organization but rather a statewide trade association for the state's private professional fiduciaries. The website has lots of great information on how to be a trustee of a trust. PFAC's website is http://www.pfac-pro.org.

WHERE CAN AN SNT TRUSTEE FIND GENERAL INFORMATION ABOUT CALIFORNIA'S PUBLIC BENEFIT PROGRAMS?

An SNT trustee who wishes to become more familiar with California's laws and regulations concerning public benefit programs can do so through the following websites:

- **Disability Benefits 101** offers easy-to-understand, practical information on California public and private benefits (including SSI, SSDI, Medi-Cal and Medicare), employment services (different right to work programs), and other programs (food stamps or CalWorks). See https://ca.db101.org.

- **Program Operations Manual System (POMS)** consists of the internal rules used by the Social Security Administration to process Supplemental Security Income (SSI) claims. Once familiar with the format of these rules, an SNT trustee can find lots of valuable information on SSI and how SNTs are evaluated by the Social Security Administration. The POMS is available for free online at https://secure.ssa.gov/apps10/poms.nsf/partlist!OpenView.

- **All County Welfare Director Letters** (ACWDLs) are letters issued by the Department of Health Care Services (DHCS) to its staff with its interpretation of California Medi-Cal laws, rules, and regulations. These are not organized in a particularly easy to understand format, but a careful, diligent search can provide plenty of information on how California's Medi-Cal rules are interpreted by DHCS. For online access to the ACWDLs, see DHCS' website at https://www.dhcs.ca.gov/services/medi-cal/eligibility/Pages/ACWDLMasterIndex.aspx.

- **Technical Assistance Collaborative** (TAC) has helpful information on Section 8 housing for individuals with disabilities, including a thorough and informative free guide entitled "Section 8 Made Simple." See http://www.tacinc.org.

- The **California Probate Code** and the **Welfare and Institutions Code** are the two most commonly used codes for special needs administration. The California codes are available for free online at https://leginfo.legislature.ca.gov/faces/codes.xhtml.

- **California Code of Regulations** includes the regulations for various public benefit programs in California and California's authority for special needs trusts. The state regulations are available online for free at http://ccr.oal. ca.gov/linkedslice/default.asp?SP=CCR-1000&Action=Welcome.

- **Code of Federal Regulations** (CFR) includes the regulations on various federal public benefit programs such as SSI and Section 8 that are important when planning for persons with disabilities. The CFR is available online at https://www.law.cornell.edu/cfr/text.

WHERE CAN AN SNT TRUSTEE FIND INFORMATION ON NOT-FOR-PROFIT AGENCIES THAT PROVIDE SERVICES AND RESOURCES TO PERSONS WITH A DISABILITY?

There are many nonprofit organizations that provide services and resources to enhance a person with a disability's life. Below (in alphabetical order) is a small sample of some of the ones that the author has worked with, or whose services he has great respect for:

- The **Arc of California** is a not-for-profit group dedicated to advocacy for individuals with disabilities. This advocacy includes providing employment opportunities for persons with disabilities, securing appropriate housing and leisure activities, and numerous other items of support for both family of persons with disabilities and the persons themselves. See http://www. arccalifornia.org.

- **California Disability Community Action Network** (CDCAN) by Marty Omoto provides cutting-edge information on legislative action that affects individuals with disabilities. The website also offers periodic e-mail updates. See http://cdcan.us.

- **California Foundation for Independent Living Centers** (CFILC) is a statewide organization of twenty-five independent living centers that promote independent living by individuals with disabilities. The centers provide counseling on public benefits, housing, and access to services. See http:// cfilc.org.

- **Californians for Disability Rights, Inc**. is a longstanding advocacy group representing the rights of persons with disabilities. See http://www.disability rights-cdr.org.

- **Disability Rights Education & Defense Fund** (DREDF) provides advocacy on behalf of individuals with disabilities. See http://www.dredf.org .

- **Janet Pomeroy Center** provides recreational, vocational, and educational opportunities for people with disabilities through programs and services that encourage self-expression, promote personal achievement, and lead to greater independence. Their website is https://www.prrcsf.org.

- **Matrix Parent Network & Resource Center.** Matrix was founded upon the belief that parents can and must be the primary managers and advocates on behalf of their child with special needs. Parent-to-parent support and networking is central to the Matrix philosophy. It is powerful, effective, and allows us to continue expanding our services in the community, particularly to populations who are historically underserved. See http://www.matrixparents.org.

- **National Alliance on Mental Illness** (NAMI) is a national nonprofit association that provides information and assistance to individuals with mental illness. There are NAMI organizations throughout the country. See http://www.nami.org.

- **Star Academy** is a school that provides an intensive, individualized education program for students with disabilities. Their website is http://www.staracademy.org.

- **Support for Families** is a San Francisco–based organization to ensure that families of children with any kind of disability or special health-care need have the knowledge and support to make informed choices that enhance their children's development and well-being. Through fostering partnership among families, professionals and the community our children can flourish. There are numerous resource fairs and seminars to help understand how to help a person with a disability. The website is https://www.supportforfamilies.org.

WHAT GOVERNMENT AGENCIES ARE THERE ASSISTING PERSONS WITH DISABILITIES?

A list of the most common government agencies that provide services and support to persons with disabilities is provided below:

- **California Department of Developmental Services** (DDS) is the state agency providing services and support to children and adults with developmental disabilities. These disabilities include mental retardation, cerebral palsy, epilepsy, autism, and related conditions. See https://www.dds.ca.gov.

- **California Department of Health Care Services** (DHCS), formerly known as DHS, was reorganized in 2007. This agency administers Medi-Cal. See http://www.dhcs.ca.gov/Pages/default.aspx .

- **California Department of Mental Health** (DMH) provides information on services available in California for individuals with mental health issues. See https://www.dhcs.ca.gov.

- **Centers for Medicare and Medicaid Services** (CMS) is the Department of Health and Human Services website, which provides information on the federal government's participation in providing health care. See http://www.cms.hhs.gov.

- **Social Security Administration** includes helpful and plentiful information on the federal government assistance programs for individuals with disabilities. See http://www.ssa.gov.

- **Department of Veterans Affairs**' website includes information on benefits available to veterans with disabilities. See http://www.va.gov.

WHO CAN AN SNT TRUSTEE HIRE TO ASSIST WITH EVALUATING A BENEFICIARY'S HEALTH CARE COVERAGE AND NEEDS?

There are private organizations which will assist in case management, needs assessment, and benefits. Once such organization which the authors consistently rely upon is National Care Advisors. See www.nationalcareadvisors.com.

WHO CAN AN SNT TRUSTEE HIRE TO ASSIST WITH PUBLIC BENEFIT ELIGIBILITY FOR PERSONS WITH DISABILITIES?

There are certain individuals who will provide advocacy and advice any time a person with a disability's public benefits are cut and advocacy is needed. Here is one person who the author frequently refers clients to for public benefits advice:

James Huyck is a consultant/advocate to trustees, families, consumers, attorneys, organizations, and others in successfully "navigating the regional center system" and other state agency services, which can be difficult and frustrating at times. He currently assists families with disabled members and all professionals who administer special needs trusts in accessing services from California's Regional Centers for the Developmentally Disabled and other government benefits programs. This includes assistance dealing with issues related to both eligibility and/or the receipt of needed services. He can be contacted at jfhuyck@yahoo.com or (916) 529-5300.

WHO CAN AN SNT TRUSTEE HIRE TO ASSIST WITH FINANCIAL PLANNING FOR A PERSON WITH A DISABILITY?

There are a host of financial advisers who will claim they have specialized knowledge in helping persons with disabilities. However, the SNT trustee should make sure that the selected financial advisor truly understands the unique planning needs of persons with disabilities. Chapter 9 describes in detail how to find an appropriate financial advisor. Below are the names of two financial advisers the author has worked with.

Scott MacDonald of Merrill Lynch. Scott MacDonald is a first vice president and certified special needs advisor. He has over twenty-four years of industry experience, joining Merrill Lynch in 1987. Mr. MacDonald has been featured in a variety of publications on serving clients with disabilities, including the *Oakland*

Tribune and a cover story in *On Wall Street* magazine. He was a special consultant of Special Needs Trusts: Planning, Drafting, and Administration through the California Continuing Education of the Bar and has lectured extensively for various Bar and Consumer Attorney Associations, the Special Needs Alliance, the National Guardianship Association and the Professional Fiduciary Association of California. Scott MacDonald can be contacted at scott_m_macdonald@ML.COM or (800) 260-2919.

Daniel Cutter of Merrill Lynch. Daniel Cutter is a certified special needs advisor at Merrill Lynch and a partner of a group focused on serving special needs families. Daniel has been in the financial industry since 1999. He earned his MBA in Finance from the University of San Francisco. Daniel is a special consultant of Special Needs Trusts: Planning, Drafting, and Administration through the California Continuing Education of the Bar (CEB). He serves on the board of the YMCA in Berkeley. Daniel lives in Berkeley with his wife, Heather, and their two boys. Daniel Cutter can be reached at daniel_cutter@ml.com or (415) 955-3902.

Scott and Daniel provide customized financial planning and asset management for families with special needs loved ones, including special needs trusts, pooled special needs trusts, conservatorships, guardianships, charitable trusts, generational skipping trusts, and a variety of family trusts.

WHO CAN AN SNT TRUSTEE HIRE TO ASSIST WITH TAX FILING AND PLANNING FOR A PERSON WITH A DISABILITY?

In order to select an appropriate tax advisor, the SNT trustee should make sure that the professional understands fiduciary income tax. Chapter 11 discusses the different types of licenses that a tax professional can obtain. The author recommends two tax professionals whom he has referred clients to in the past:

Courtney Kosnik. Courtney assisted with Chapter 17 discussing taxes for this edition. She has many years of experience in public accounting specializing in trust and estate tax, tax planning for high net worth individuals, mid to upper level executives and closely held business owners. While she is located in Michigan, she can assist with tax returns all over the country. Courtney can be contacted at (586) 276-0720 or courtney@betterbiztax.com. Her website is https://www.bbtainc.com.

WHO CAN AN SNT TRUSTEE HIRE TO ASSIST WITH EMPLOYING A CAREGIVER FOR THE SNT BENEFICIARY?

In order to comply with the myriad of employment related issues discussed in Chapter 15, the author recommends TEAM, Risk Management Strategies. With TEAM, trustees, beneficiary, or a family refer workers for hire, meaning they can pick people they know and trust to provide care for their loved ones. Once a worker is identified, TEAM will perform the necessary employment verification, process hiring paperwork, and manage all employee administration, ensuring that the trustee stays informed – and that the beneficiary receives the best care. TEAM can be found at http://team-risk.com.

About the Authors

Kevin Urbatsch is a nationally recognized attorney in special needs planning and settlement planning for persons with disabilities. He is a principal of The Urbatsch Law Firm P.C. located in California. Kevin also serves as National Director of the Academy of Special Needs Planners (ASNP), a national organization of special needs and settlement planning professionals. Kevin is a Certified Specialist in Estate Planning, Trust, and Probate Law by the California State Bar Board of Legal Specialization and a Fellow of the American College of Trust and Estate Counsel (ACTEC). Kevin serves as counsel for CPT Institute, a national Pooled Special Needs Trust program.

Kevin is a frequent lecturer to other attorneys, financial professionals, and families of loved ones with special needs. He has lectured before the Academy of Special Needs Planners, National Academy of Elder Law Attorneys, American Association of Justice, Professional Fiduciary Association of California, numerous California bar associations, and not-for-profit groups.

Kevin is the author (or co-author) of the following books and treatises including:

- *Administering the California Special Needs Trust* (1st and 2nd Edition) published by IUniverse;
- *Drafting the World's Greatest Special Needs Trust* available as part of ASNP membership;
- *Special Needs Trusts: Protecting Your Child's Financial Future* (4th through 8th Edition) published by Nolo Press.
- Original Attorney-Editor and co-author of CEB's award winning publication titled *Special Needs Trusts – Planning, Drafting, and Administration* and author of several chapters

In 2013, *Parenting Magazine* named Kevin as one of the nation's Top Child Advocates for his work in fighting for the rights of children with special needs. In

May 2011, Kevin was presented the NAELA's Presidential Recognition Award for his work in special needs planning. In each year from 2010 to 2020, Kevin was named a *Northern California Superlawyer*. In 2009, Kevin was named KRON-TV's Best of the Bay estate-planning attorney for Northern California.

Michele P. Fuller is the founder of Michigan Law Center, P.L.L.C, and President of Advocacy, Inc., a non-profit organization. Her law practice focuses on advocacy, protection, and asset preservation for persons with disabilities, including working in the following areas of law: elder law, special needs planning, special needs trust administration, and settlement planning.

Michele was recently appointed Special Assistant Attorney General to assist in settlement planning for the Flint Water claimants. She is the former Chair of the Elder Law and Disability Rights Section (ELDRS) of the State Bar of Michigan and has leadership positions in several national organizations: Advisory Board Member of the Academy of Special Needs Planners (ASNP) and Michigan Chapter of NAELA Board of Directors. She is also active in the National Academy of Elder Law Attorneys (NAELA), the Michigan Association for Justice, and a regular contributor for the Institute for Continuing Legal Education (ICLE).

Michele is honored to have received the 2018 State Bar of Michigan UnSung Hero Award, given annually to an attorney demonstrating dedication in their practice for the betterment of others. She has also been nominated to the Super Lawyers list for the last several years. Other awards she has received include: American Institute of Legal Counsel 10 Best Elder Law Attorneys 2016-2019, and Distinguished Lawyers 2016-2019 by The Expert Network, given to the top 3% of attorneys in the nation. She was also named the Women-in-Law Elder Law and Special Needs Planning Attorney of the Year by Lawyer's Monthly Magazine in 2016. Parenting Magazine also named Michele the Top Special Needs Child Advocate in 2013.

Michele and her award-winning special needs attorney and spouse, Kevin Urbatsch, frequently write together. Their publications include: *Administering the Michigan Special Needs Trust;* the 2nd and 3rd editions of *Administering the California Special Needs Trust;* and *Special Needs Trusts: Protect Your Child's Financial Future,* 6th and 7th Editions, NOLO Press. She is also the author of *Saving Grace,* an elder law client's experience, and *Finding Peace: a guide for caregivers,* to be published in 2020.

Michele and Kevin have also co-authored several nationally published articles, including *Traps for the Unwary During Special Needs Trust Administration,* in Estates and Trusts Magazine, *the Future of Planning for Persons with Disabilities* which was published in the Fall 2013 edition of the NAELA Journal, and *Pooled Trusts: An Approach to Special Needs Planning for Families of Modest Means*, published in the May-June 2013 edition of BiFocal, a Journal of the ABA Commission on Law and Aging. Michele has also contributed to Michigan Bar Journal, *Planning for a Person with Disabilities, Considerations when Settling a Lawsuit for an Individual Lacking Capacity or a Minor,* and *Divorce and Disability: Identifying and Resolving the Unique Issues of a Spouse with Disabilities.* In addition to the Michigan State Bar Journal, Michele has contributed to the MAJ Journal, Elder Law Answers, NAELA news, and other publications.

Michele is a frequent presenter for various national and statewide organizations such as ElderCounsel, MassMutual, the American Bar Association, American Association for Justice, Michigan Association for Justice, the Institute of Continuing Legal Education, Michigan Brain Injury Association of Michigan and the Michigan Guardianship Association, among others. She is of council for several non-profit organizations, national and statewide, which administers pooled special needs trusts.

Michele graduated with Honors as a member of the James Madison College at Michigan State University with a Bachelor of Arts in International Relations. Michele then attended American University International Law Master's program and obtained her Juris Doctor from the University of Detroit Mercy School of Law.

CONTRIBUTING AUTHORS

Jessica Farinas is an attorney at the special needs and settlement planning law firm, The Urbatsch Law Firm P.C. located in California. She co-authored an article in Volume 24, Issue 1 of the 2018 California Trusts and Estates Quarterly entitled *Achieving a Better Life Experience (ABLE) Accounts: A New Planning Tool for Persons with Disabilities* and another article for CEB's Estate Planning Reporter titled *Achieving a Better Life Experience (ABLE) Accounts: Understanding Them, Evaluating Them, and Using Them* Vol. 41, No. 1, August 2019.

Jessica is a member of the Academy of Special Needs Planners (ASNP) and served on the Planning Committee for their 2018 National Meeting in Las Vegas, Nevada. She is also a member of East Bay Trusts and Estates Lawyers (EBTEL). Jessica has been a member of the California Bar since 2016. She earned her law degree from Golden Gate University School of Law in 2015 and undergraduate degree in Politics from University of California, Santa Cruz in 2011. As a law student, Jessica won a place on the Moot Court Board, founded and chaired the Estate Planning Society, and worked as an Extern with the Honorable Sandra K. Bean in Alameda Superior Court's probate division.

Courtney Kosnik has worked in public accounting since 1996 and as an IRS Enrolled Agent since 2001. Before opening her own accounting firm, Courtney worked as an accountant for several small businesses, as a senior accountant for CPA firm Melican & Associates, and as a Trust Tax Specialist for National City Bank. Courtney opened Better Business Tax & Accounting in 2001 and has grown the firm to service over a thousand individual and business clients across the country. Her firm specializes in tax accounting for estates and trusts and services trustees and law firms nationwide.

In 2013 Courtney completed her three-year fellowship with National Tax Practice Institute. Following her passion, which is all things related to the tax code, Courtney teaches continuing education with the NTPI fellowship at their annual conference. She is involved in the Michigan and National chapters of the National Association of Enrolled Agents and has participated in FLY-IN DAY, joining other IRS Enrolled Agents in Washington DC to meet with members of Congress to educate them about how taxpayers are affected by tax code changes. Courtney has four children and lives in Ann Arbor, Michigan.

Robert Nuddleman is the owner and primary attorney at the Nuddleman Law Firm, P.C. He represents individuals and companies in federal and state court and various administrative agencies such as the California Department of Industrial Relations (Labor Commissioner), Equal Employment Opportunity Commission, Department of Fair Employment and Housing, and Unemployment Insurance Appeals Board. A significant focus of Mr. Nuddleman's practice relates to wage and hour claims, breach of contract, trade secret protection, claims of sex, race, age, and pregnancy discrimination or harassment and accommodating persons with disabilities.

Mr. Nuddleman advises and represents business clients in employment and business matters in an attempt to avoid litigation and reduce potential exposure to claims of all kinds in light of developing law. A particular focus of Mr. Nuddleman's practice includes advising caregiver agencies, trustees, conservators, families, residential care facilities, care homes and others regarding wage and hour and employment laws in the elder care industry. Mr. Nuddleman frequently presents seminars and workshops regarding workplace disputes and compliance with federal, state and local employment laws.

Herb Thomas is a California licensed Private Professional Fiduciary #85 and the principal fiduciary for Kairos Fiduciary Services, which focuses on Special Needs Trust and Settlement Trusts throughout California and nationally. Herb has extensive experience serving families with SNTs and Settlement Trust Administration, Medi-Cal and Social Security advocacy, and estate settlement.

Herb is the co-author of chapter 7 "A Professional Trustee's Guide to Setting Up Systems for Successful SNT Administration." He is a frequent speaker at various industry and trade conferences. These include the Academy of Special Needs Planners (ASNP), The Bar Association of San Francisco, Estate Planning Councils of Fresno and Diablo Valley, The Professional Fiduciary Association of California (PFAC) and the San Francisco Jewish Business Leadership Council.

Before starting his private fiduciary practice in 2004, Herb served as the Benefits Advocate for Kaiser Permanente's (KP) first Community Benefits Advocacy program. As part of the program, he worked through the complex web of public and private benefits including Medi-Cal, COBRA, and VA to subsidize cost of member care, and later implemented this program across several bay area hospitals. Herb's previous work experience includes a seven-year stint with the Internal Revenue Service as taxpayer delinquency investigator. In this position he located taxpayers who had not filed federal income tax returns and assisted them with becoming compliant with federal regulations.

Herb holds a BS in Health Sciences and has served on boards of various not for profit organizations such as BIA4Autism, PFAC and Legal Assistance for Seniors. He is married with three children. His youngest child is a vibrant and clever boy, who was diagnosed with autism at the age of 3.5. As a family, they enjoy traveling to destinations like Russia, Brazil, Tanzania, Western Europe and to any beach in Hawaii. In his leisure time Herb enjoys tinkering with devices and repairing gadgets.

APPENDIX A

SUMMARY: Fourteen-Steps to Begin SNT Trust Administration

STEP ONE – OBTAIN THE ENTIRE TRUST DOCUMENT AND RELATED DOCUMENTS

Before taking on an SNT administration, ensure that the trustee has all documents related to the trust. This will always include a complete and signed copy of the trust agreement. The trustee should check to see if there were any amendments to the trust document, because those documents will change the original trust's terms. Other documents that the trustee may need are a Memorandum (or Letter) of Intent or a Court Order Establishing the Trust. It may be that these documents were not prepared for this administration, but the trustee should ensure that he or she has a complete copy of all trust documents. If the trustee is taking over from a prior trustee, the new trustee should obtain all trust records, including bank statements, tax returns, documents on discretionary distributions and any related trust records.

STEP TWO – READ THE ENTIRE TRUST DOCUMENT AND RELATED DOCUMENTS

Read the entire trust agreement thoroughly to become familiar with the terms of the SNT and to determine if there are any immediate tasks that need to be accomplished. Some parents or other loved ones also draft a Memorandum of Intent that provide further instructions that can assist in the administration. Also, many first party SNTs are created by Court Order and this order may require additional legal responsibilities the trustee must meet. The surest way for a trustee to get in trouble is to not read the trust agreement and to unintentionally violate the terms of the trust which is an absolute breach of trust.

STEP THREE - DETERMINE TYPE OF SPECIAL NEEDS TRUST

Determine whether this is a first party SNT or third party SNT because administration will be different depending on the type of SNT. In Chapter 1 and 19, there is a full description to determine the differences between the two types of SNTs.

In short, a first party SNT is funded with the beneficiary's property and is sometimes referred to as a "self-settled" trust. This type of SNT typically arises when the beneficiary with a disability has had an accident and received a civil settlement or judgment or the beneficiary receives an inheritance or gift in his or her own name and transfers the property to an SNT. There are legal requirements to this trust that require different steps for a trustee to follow that are described in this book.

A third-party SNT is funded with property that belongs to a third person that is not the beneficiary. This is typically done by a parent or grandparent's estate plan. However, a third party SNT can be established with anyone else's money, so can be established in lots of different situations. In general, this is an easier trust to administer because the additional first party SNT rules on administration do not apply.

STEP FOUR - COMPLETE TRUST SUMMARY FORM

A Trust Summary Form should be completed and placed in the front of the file for the trust. It is recommended that a different color paper is used so it can be immediately reviewed. The form should be a quick reference guide to the type of trust, distribution standard, type of public benefits, and related information.

A sample form for both a first and third-party SNT is included in this book at Appendix E.

STEP FIVE – EVALUATE BENEFICIARY'S CONDITION

Evaluate the beneficiary's living and personal care situation and determine whether any immediate action needs to be taken. This is more important for SNT trustees because oftentimes the SNT beneficiary requires substantial assistance with all aspects of daily living. For example, a person with a disability may require drug therapy each month. If the parent gave the drugs to his or her child but is now deceased, a replacement needs to be located immediately who is willing and able to help.

It is recommended that an evaluation of the beneficiary be conducted at least once a year. This allows the trustee to properly set up a spending plan and to adjust payments for the care needed by the beneficiary. The evaluation should include (at least) the following items:

- An evaluation of the beneficiary's contact with family members and whether continuing and facilitating such contact is part of the trustee's responsibility.

- An evaluation of the beneficiary's disability, including an evaluation of the beneficiary's physical and mental condition.

- An evaluation of the beneficiary's rehabilitation and training programs in which he or she participates (or should be participating).

- An evaluation of the beneficiary's current living situation and whether it is still appropriate, including (when appropriate) an evaluation of the caregivers for the beneficiary.

- An evaluation of the beneficiary's financial condition, including available government benefits, to determine the beneficiary's needs and the effect of distributions from the SNT on the beneficiary's eligibility for public assistance.

- An evaluation of the beneficiary's exercise of his or her civil rights. For example, is the beneficiary receiving a fair wage for work performed or being denied his or her right to vote or marry?

- An evaluation of the beneficiary's current and future educational needs and programs.

- An evaluation of the beneficiary's recreational activities, leisure time, and social needs, and the appropriateness of existing program services.

STEP SIX – DETERMINE BENEFICIARY'S PUBLIC BENEFITS

The beneficiary's public benefits will drive the administration. It is important to know whether the beneficiary is receiving (or may receive) Supplemental Security Income (SSI), Social Security Disability Insurance (SSDI), Medicare, Medicaid or any of the other benefits available to a person with a disability. The most common are discussed in Chapter 3 of this book.

It is imperative that the Trustee know exactly what benefits are being received and how much is being received from the various programs. This may be more difficult than a trustee will realize because oftentimes the beneficiary, their legal representatives, and their family do not know which benefits the beneficiary is receiving. The trustee must become 100-percent certain of which benefits the beneficiary is receiving to do an effective SNT administration. In Chapter 19, suggestions are offered on how best to determine which benefits the beneficiary is receiving.

STEP SEVEN – KNOW THE OTHER PROFESSIONAL/ FIDUCIARIES INVOLVED

An SNT beneficiary typically has other professionals or fiduciaries involved with his or her life such as a conservator/guardian of the person or estate, SSA Representative Payee, care manager, licensed clinical social worker, or agent acting under a power of attorney. Be familiar with the extent and limits of the authority for each, and the trustee's responsibility as it concerns the beneficiary as these are the people the trustee will most often interact on behalf of the beneficiary.

STEP EIGHT – DETERMINE WHETHER TRUST ADVISORY COMMITTEE OR TRUST PROTECTOR ARE INCLUDED IN SNT AND OBTAIN INFORMATION

Many SNTs include a trust advisory committee and trust protector. It is important to get everyone's name, contact information and the extent of his or her authority over the beneficiary. The extent of the authority of members of a trust advisory committee and trust protector is entirely set forth in the terms of the trust agreement. The trustee should make sure he or she understands the full authority because a trustee must comply with the terms of the trust and failure to do so is a breach of fiduciary duty.

STEP NINE – UNDERSTAND TYPE OF SNT DISTRIBUTION PROVISION

Read and understand the distribution standard of the SNT. The distribution provision will inform the trustee whether it is acceptable for a distribution to cause a loss or reduction in benefits or not. A distribution standard that allows a trustee the discretion to make a distribution that may or may not cause a public benefit reduction is often called a Discretionary Distribution standard. A distribution standard that does not allow a distribution that will cause any reduction in public benefits is often called a Supplemental Distribution Standard. This is discussed in much more detail in Chapter 9. Failing to understand the proper SNT distribution standard will cause the trustee to improperly administer the SNT.

STEP TEN – PROVIDE A SYSTEMATIC PROCEDURE FOR REQUESTING DISTRIBUTIONS

Develop a written system for the beneficiary (or advisory committee members if provided this power) to contact the trustee requesting that a distribution be made. The disbursement procedure should determine whether disbursements can be made, *e.g.*, only during business hours, on weekdays, or after 24 hours from a written request.

It is in the trustee's interest to clearly communicate these policies to the beneficiary. This will go a long way in eliminating future friction during the administration. One good suggestion is for the trustee to purchase a fax machine or scanner for a beneficiary or his or her caregiver. This way, disbursement requests can be faxed or scanned and emailed directly to the trustee's office and the trustee will have a written record of requests. A sample form for distributions is in Appendix G of this book.

STEP ELEVEN – PREPARE A SPENDING PLAN FOR EXPECTED DISTRIBUTIONS

Prepare a spending plan for expected expenditures of SNT assets. A monthly spending plan should be established from this meeting so that monthly expenses may be paid without constant requests.

Many entities such as Merrill Lynch or Mass Mutual have sample spending plan worksheets for persons with disabilities on their websites. The trustee should meet with the beneficiary, any legal guardians, and those friends and family willing to participate. This is discussed in detail in Chapter 9 of this book.

STEP TWELVE – SET DATE TO PROVIDE ACCOUNT AND REPORT

Unless waived by the trust document, the trustee is legally required to provide an account and report. Schedule an account on an annual basis for non-court supervised trusts and for court-supervised trusts, schedule account one year after establishment and every two years thereafter. It is important to know who is entitled to an account and report from the trustee. Depending on the terms, an account and report is generally always required for the SNT beneficiary and his or her legal representatives. It may also be required of remainder beneficiaries and possibly the members of the trust advisory committee or trust protector. This is discussed in detail in this book in Chapter 8.

This is a step that if the Trustee is not comfortable handling should hire an experienced professional to assist.

STEP THIRTEEN – SUCCESSFULLY ONBOARD THE SNT BENEFICIARY AND LEGAL REPRESENTATIVE

The best thing an SNT trustee can do for a successful SNT administration is to have a successful "onboarding" of the beneficiary. Onboarding is the description of the process for familiarizing the beneficiary of how the SNT will be administered. The SNT trustee should expect to communicate this information in writing and reviewed verbally with the beneficiary in a way he or she can understand. As soon as the SNT trustee knows administration will begin, the following topics should be discussed with the beneficiary:

- Beneficiary's current public benefits, the rules the SNT trustee must work within, and what the trust can pay for: for example, the POMs which govern SSI impose severe consequences for any cash distributions to the beneficiary, so to avoid this issue the SNT trustee will not issue any cash disbursements directly to the beneficiary.
- Trust terms, purpose of the trust, and what the beneficiary hopes to accomplish (it could be as simple as relief of anxiety that they will not lose their benefits, consistently have access to the internet or cell service, or make the funds last as long as possible).

- How the SNT trustee gets paid consistent with trust terms-it may be hourly, on a percentage, or the trust may state that the SNT trustee is expected to serve without payment.
- How to best communicate with the SNT trustee:
    - If the SNT trustee is a family member who travels for work, email may work best.
    - If the SNT trustee is a professional, a standing appointment may work best, or request that the beneficiary schedule a phone conference, or an email may be sufficient.
    - How quickly will calls be returned
    - Set boundaries if necessary and discuss any limitations on the volume of communications and frequency of calls
    - Are there any accommodations the beneficiary will require in order to effectively communicate with the trustee?
- How to request disbursements:
    - How should the beneficiary forward these requests?
        * Fax
        * Email
        * First-class mail
        * Hand-delivery
    - Does the beneficiary or their legal representative have any limitations that need to be accommodated in order to submit disbursement requests?
    - Is there any equipment that needs to be purchased to facilitate disbursement requests, such as a scanner or fax machine?
    - What is the processing time for disbursement requests?
    - Identify parties authorized to make disbursement requests
    - Any documentation requirements, such as copies of receipts to support credit card purchases.
    - Discuss the beneficiary's responsibilities in gathering documents, record keeping, or obtaining information, such as obtaining a minimum of three quotes for a new roof to be installed at beneficiary's home
    - Identify any barriers to access and discuss how to use tools like TrueLink or ABLE accounts

- – How decisions regarding disbursement are made
- If the SNT trustee needs to purchase a pre-paid irrevocable funeral contract (which is a first-party SNT issue).
- Discuss the spending plan
  - – Explain why the financial information is necessary
  - – The purpose of the spending plan
  - – How it helps the trustee and beneficiary plan for the beneficiary's future and make the trust last as long as possible
  - – Address any unrealistic beneficiary and family expectations with regard to spending
- Investment policy
- Disclose any potential conflicts of interest
- Who is entitled to receive the annual accounting of the SNT trustee, and how should they best receive it-a beneficiary who resides in a group home may not want their financial information being sent to them at the group home

The language the SNT trustee uses to communicate with the beneficiary and government agencies is important. As you read this book, you may notice that the authors use what is called, "people first" language. In other words, we reference the person, not the disability, first. People with disabilities are, first and foremost, people. People with their own interests, abilities, and needs. The beneficiary may not care how you describe them, but by emphasizing the person first in your verbal and written communications, it honors the person the SNT trustee serves and counters the perpetuation of stereotypes that people are defined by their disability. Below are some examples of language to use and what to avoid:

Do Not Use	Preferred Language
Confined to wheelchair	Uses a chair for mobility
Retarded	Developmentally disabled
Mental handicap	Intellectual disability
Vegetable	Person in a vegetative state

Avoid words such as "stricken with" "suffers from" "victim of"

STEP FOURTEEN – IDENTIFY SNT TRUSTEE'S FEES

Determine in the document where fees are authorized and make sure you understand how fees are calculated for the trustee. In certain cases, the trust document will set a maximum fee or sometimes says no fee is allowed. If that is the case, then the trustee is agreeing to do this work for free. If the trustee is not willing to do so, he or she should not agree to serve or only agree if there is a court order allowing him or her to be paid. Trustee's compensation is discussed in more detail in Chapter 6.

CHECKLIST: Needed Documents and Immediate Actions When Setting Up SNT Administration

BENEFICIARY DOCUMENTS NEEDED

Proof of Identify

- Birth Certificate
- Driver's License
- Passport

Proof of Health Insurance

- Medi-Cal card
- Medicare card
- Private health insurance card

Proof of Authority of Professionals

- Representative Payee
- Guardianship/Conservatorship
- Power of Attorney
- Advance Health Care Directive

Proof of Public Benefits
- Medi-Cal
- In Home Supportive Services
- CalFresh – food stamps
- Supplemental Security Income (SSI)
- Social Security Disability Insurance (SSDI)
- Childhood Disabled Beneficiary (CDB)
- Social Security (SS) from retirement

Obtain Statement of SSA benefits by calling 800-772-1213 or having beneficiary set up personal account at https://secure.ssa.gov/RIL/SiView.action

Existing estate planning documents, including Wills, Living Trusts, Powers of Attorney, or Advance Health Care Directives

PRE-FUNDING

Obtain complete copy of signed trust document (with any amendments and ancillary documents like a Memorandum (or Letter) of Intent)

Confirm receipt of any Court Order that established or modified the SNT's terms (if necessary)

Obtain trustee's surety bond (if necessary)

Obtain signed trustee services agreement with required parties

Send copies of executed trust agreement to all interested parties, *e.g.* SSA, DHCS etc.

Obtain EIN (tax id number) for trust from IRS

Review beneficiary's situation to determine if any emergency or immediate needs

Determine the SNT's documents distribution standard

Supplementary distribution standard

Discretionary distribution standard

Select special needs planning attorney to advise on administration issues

Select financial advisor to advise on investment and on spending plan

Select tax advisor to assist with tax planning and preparation

POST-FUNDING

Establish trust bank account.

Establish trust Investment account. - include a written investment policy and ACH transfer link to bank checking account.

Set up accounting file on accounting system (*e.g.,* Quicken/Quickbooks) including download links to financial institutions

Prepare Initial Inventory

Initial meeting with beneficiary to introduce trustee, his or her team, discuss needs and wants, and setting appropriate expectations

Schedule care evaluation (if necessary)

Establish a spending plan with financial advisor, beneficiary, family, and others

Prepare and execute agreements with providers such as caregiver, landlord/tenant, etc. (if necessary)

Establish vendor relationships and set-up billing accounts

Review any pre-paid funeral arrangements and determine if one is needed

Obtain necessary insurance

Property

Umbrella

Workers' comp

Vehicle

Trustee's Errors and Omissions

SUMMARY: California Laws Outlining Trustee's Fiduciary Duties

Duty	Probate Code Section	Brief Description
Duty to administer trust	§16000	Duty to follow the terms of the trust and the law governing the administration of trusts.
Duty of loyalty	§16002	Duty to administer the trust solely for the benefit of the beneficiaries of the trust.
Duty to deal impartially with beneficiaries	§16003	Duty not to favor the interests of one beneficiary over another, except to the extent trust provides to the contrary.
Duty to avoid conflict of interest	§16004	Duty to avoid transactions with the trust that benefit you personally.
Duty not to require beneficiary to relieve the trustee of liability	§16004.5	Cannot require a beneficiary to waive rights as a condition of distribution.
Duty not to undertake as trustee an adverse trust	§16005	May not act as trustee of any other trust that has a competing interest with this trust.
Duty to take control and preserve trust property	§16006	Must marshal trust assets and take reasonable steps to preserve them.

Duty to make trust property productive	§16007	Subject to certain exceptions, duty to make the trust assets profitable.
Duty to keep trust property separate and identified	§16009	This is one of the most important duties. Duty to keep the assets and debts of the trust separate from trustee's own. In other words, do not commingle funds.
Duty to enforce claims	§16010	Must take reasonable actions to pursue amounts that may be owed to the trust.
Duty to defend actions	§16011	Duty to take actions to prevent a loss to the trust, such as by defending a lawsuit.
Duty not to delegate; exception	§16012; §16052	Subject to certain exceptions, must personally perform actions on behalf of the trust rather than having others act on behalf of the trust.
Duty with respect to cotrustees	§16013	If serving with a cotrustee, each have a duty to participate in the administration and prevent the other from committing a breach of trust.
Duty to use special skills	§16014	In managing the trust property, must use at least ordinary business ability. However, if one has special skills, will be held to a higher standard of care.
Duty to comply with Prudent Investor Rule	§16045	Duty to invest as a prudent investor would considering purposes, terms, distribution requirements and circumstances of the trust.
Duty to diversify	§16048	In making investment decisions, duty to diversify the investments unless it is not prudent under the circumstances
Duty to provide information to beneficiaries	§16060	There are duties relative to providing financial and other information to beneficiaries (and in some cases, the settlor's family members).
Discretionary powers to be used reasonably	§§16080; 16081	Even if trust says a particular action is entirely within discretion, trustee's duty is to act reasonably

SUMMARY: SSA and DHCS Reporting Guidelines

SOCIAL SECURITY ADMINISTRATION (SSA)

1. **Persons Responsible for Reporting:** The person responsible for maintaining the special needs trust (SNT) beneficiary's eligibility for public benefits will have the responsibility for making certain disclosures to the Social Security Administration (SSA). It is nearly always the public benefits recipient who is responsible for making these reports to the SSA. However, if that person lacks the capacity to manage his or her own financial matters, a "Representative Payee" may be appointed by the SSA to be the person responsible for reporting. The Representative Payee is the person designated by SSA to receive the Supplemental Security Income (SSI) payment on behalf of the SNT beneficiary. In certain cases, if a special needs trust, by its terms, requires the trustee to make sure that beneficiary maintains eligibility for public benefits. If the SNT's terms so require a trustee may have this requirement.

2. **Basic Requirements:** The reporting party has an obligation to report to the SSA the existence of the SNT if the SNT beneficiary is receiving SSI benefits. The report should note that the SNT beneficiary is not receiving trust income unless the trustee decides to distribute income, which is in the absolute and sole discretion of the trustee. The SSI computer system will pick up any income generated by the SNT. This comes from the K-1 issued by the SNT. Medi-Cal has a computer match with the IRS and will learn of these income distributions. It

will be incumbent upon the reporting party to show that payments were made to third-party providers and not directly to the SNT beneficiary. SSI has a right to inquire as to the amount and purpose of distributions from the SNT. The SNT trustee must respond honestly and completely to any such inquiries. SSI is concerned that income not be used to provide food or shelter. The trustee should keep excellent records and receipts for SSI and Medi-Cal.

3. **What Must Be Reported:** The individual responsible for reporting must report all of the following to the SSA:
   A. **Address.** Change in SNT beneficiary's address.
   B. **Employment.** Change in employment status.
   C. **Living arrangements.** Change in the arrangements (such as adding or losing a roommate).
   D. **Income.** All income (including the receipt of any direct income or ISM from the SNT).
   E. **Resources.** Any change in countable resources.
   F. **Marital status.** Any change in the SNT beneficiary's marital status. **Physical or medical condition.** Changes or improvements in the SNT beneficiary's physical or mental condition (for example, the SNT beneficiary improves so much that he or she is no longer considered disabled). **Medical facility.** Admission to or discharge from any health facility or public facility (such as a hospital or nursing home).
   G. **Travel.** Any trip outside the United States.

4. **How and When to Make a Report:**
   A. **Written.** The report must be in writing to the Social Security Administration. See https://secure.ssa.gov/apps6z/FOLO/fo001.jsp to obtain the local SSA office by inputting the SNT beneficiary's zip code.
   B. **Name.** The report must include the SNT beneficiary's name.
   C. **Social Security Number.** The report must include the SNT beneficiary's Social Security Number.
   D. **Event.** A description of the event that triggered the report and the date of the event. The report is due within ten days after the month in which the event took place.

5. **Penalty for Not Filing Report.** If reports are not made on a timely basis, SSA may seek reimbursement for benefits incorrectly paid and assess a penalty for up to $100 for a late filing. Failure to respond to correspondence from SSA may result in a loss of benefits.

6. **Appeals.** If SSA or Medi-Cal notifies the SNT beneficiary that it intends to reduce or eliminate benefits, there is a ten-day right of appeal. The appeal must be in writing. If the appeal is filed within ten days, the benefits continue. If the appeal is not filed within ten days, there is a sixty-day window to appeal an SSI decision and a ninety-day period to appeal a Medi-Cal notice of action or decision. However, benefits will be discontinued if the appeal is not filed within ten days.

DEPARTMENT OF HEALTH CARE SERVICES (MEDI-CAL)

1. **Medi-Cal.** Notice must be given to the Department of Health Care Services or a division thereof if the trust is self-settled.

2. **Timing of Notice.** Recipients must report any changes in status within ten days of the event. This is different from SSI's reporting requirement.

3. **What Must Be Reported.** The benefits recipient is under a general duty to report any change in circumstances such as,

   (A) Change of address

   (B) Change in property or income

   (C) Change in family composition

   (D) Change in other health-care coverage

   (E) Change in residence from one county to another within the state and apply for a redetermination of eligibility within the new county of residence (promptly notify the county department that initially established Medi-Cal eligibility in this case)

4. **Establishment or Funding of Trust.** When the SNT is established or funded the local Medi-Cal agency that provided funding must be notified of the establishment of the SNT. A copy of the signed trust must also be sent to this agency.

5. **Death of SNT Beneficiary.** The local Medi-Cal agency that provided medical assistance must be notified upon the death of the beneficiary. It can be done online at https://apps.dhcs.ca.gov/AutoForm2/Page/AutoForm2.aspx or notice may be sent by mail to the following addresses:

Office of Director
Department of Mental Health
1600 Ninth Street, Room 151
Sacramento, CA 95814

Office of Director
Department of Developmental Services
1600 Ninth Street, Room 240
Sacramento, CA 95814

Department of Health Care Services
Third-Party Liability and Recovery Division
Estate Recovery Section—MS 4720
PO Box 997425
Sacramento, CA 95899-7425

6. **Notification of Accounting.** Trustee should furnish DHCS with accountings to begin the triggering of the statute of limitations.
7. **Change of Trustee.** The DHCS must be notified of any change of trustee.

SAMPLE FORM: Special Needs Trust Summary Form for First Party SNTs and Third Party SNTs

FIRST PARTY SPECIAL NEEDS TRUST SUMMARY

1. Name of Trust: _____

2. Date of Trust: _____

3. Beneficiary's Contact Information

   _____

4. Beneficiary's Disability:

   _____

   _____

   _____

5. Beneficiary's Public Benefits:

   SSI $_____/month

   Medi-Cal Yes/No [circle one]

   If received Medicaid list other States _____

   IHSS Yes/No [circle one]

   CalFresh Yes/No [circle one]

   SSDI $_____/month

   Medicare Yes/No [circle one]

Veteran Benefits Yes/No [circle one]

Type of VA Benefit _____

Section 8 Yes/No [circle one]

What County _____

Regional Center Benefits Yes/No [circle one]

Name of Regional Center _____

Other Benefits

Describe _____

6. Date of Accounting _____

COURT ACCOUNT REQUIRED YES/NO [CIRCLE ONE]

7. Bond Required Yes or No [circle one] – Amount of bond $ _____

8. Trust Advisory Committee Yes or No [circle one].

If Trust Advisory Committee, list the names and contact information for Advisory Committee

Name	Relationship	Address and phone number

9. Trust Protector Yes or No [circle one]. If Yes Name and Contact Information

_____

10. Distribution Standard – [circle one]

    A. Supplemental Standard – Only allows disbursements that do not reduce or eliminate public benefits

    B. Discretionary Standard – Allows disbursements that may reduce or eliminate public benefits if in beneficiary's best interests

11. Any specific distributions authorized in Court Order

_____

_____

12. Responsibility To Report To SSA or DHCS For Beneficiary's Eligibility for Public Benefits Trustee/Beneficiary/Other _____[circle one]

13. List Successor Trustees

Name	Relationship	Address and phone number

14. List Remainder Beneficiaries

Name	Relationship	Address and phone number

15. Power of Appointment – Allows Beneficiary To Change Remainder Beneficiaries Yes or No [circle one]

16. If Yes, who may be appointed Anyone/Relatives Only/_____ [circle one or add unique appointment power]

COMMENTS

THIRD PARTY SPECIAL NEEDS TRUST SUMMARY

1. Name of Trust: _____

2. Date of Trust: _____

3. Beneficiary's Contact Information

   _____

   Beneficiary's Disability:

   _____

4. Beneficiary's Public Benefits:

   SSI $ $_____/month

   Medi-Cal Yes/No [circle one]

   If received Medicaid list other States

   _____

   IHSS Yes/No [circle one]

   CalFresh Yes/No [circle one]

   SSDI $_____/month

   Medicare Yes/No [circle one]

   Veteran Benefits Yes/No [circle one]

   Type of VA Benefit _____

   Section 8 Yes/No [circle one]

   What County _____

   Regional Center Benefits Yes/No [circle one]

   Name of Regional Center _____

   Other Benefits

   Describe _____

   Date of Accounting $_____

   Trust Advisory Committee Yes or No [circle one]. If Trust Advisory Committee,

list the names and contact information for Advisory Committee

Name	Relationship	Address and phone number

1. Trust Protector Yes or No [circle one]. If Yes Name and Contact Information

   _____

   _____

2. Distribution Standard – [circle one]
   a. Supplemental Standard – Only allows disbursements that do not reduce or eliminate public benefits
   b. Discretionary Standard – Allows disbursements that may reduce or eliminate public benefits if in beneficiary's best interests
3. Memorandum of Intent Yes or No [circle one]
4. Responsibility to Report to SSA or DHCS For Beneficiary's Eligibility for Public Benefits Trustee/Beneficiary/Other $_____ [circle one]
5. List Successor Trustees

Name	Relationship	Address and phone number

6. List Remainder Beneficiaries

Name	Relationship	Address and phone number

7. Power of Appointment – Allows Beneficiary to Change Remainder Beneficiaries Yes or No [circle one]
8. If Yes, who may be appointed Anyone/Relatives Only/_____ [circle one or add unique appointment power]

COMMENTS

WORKSHEET: Developing Beneficiary's Spending Plan

Beneficiary's Name:

INCOME	Monthly Amount
Salary and Wages	$_____
Structured settlement payments	$_____
Child support	$_____
Tax refund	$_____
Interest on savings	$_____
Investment income	$_____
Rental income	$_____
Unemployment compensation	$_____
Public assistance	$_____
Sources of funding related to the beneficiary's disability:	
State programs	$_____
Public benefits, such as SSI or SSDI	$_____
Assistance from fraternal and civic organizations	$_____
Other	$_____
Total Monthly Income:	$_____

EXPENSES

House payment or rent	$_____
Property taxes	$_____
Homeowners' or renters' insurance	$_____
Homeowners' association fees	$_____
Home repairs/improvements	$_____
Household goods/furniture	$_____
Lawn care/snow removal	$_____
Natural gas or heating fuel	$_____
Electricity	$_____
Water	$_____
Telephone (cell and land line)	$_____
Computer and internet services	$_____
Computer hardware and software	$_____
Other Electronic devices	$_____
Groceries	$_____
Meals eaten out	$_____
Automobile payments	$_____
Automobile insurance	$_____
Gas and Oil	$_____
Automobile repair	$_____
Costs for disability-related adaptations to vehicle	$_____
Bus/Taxi/Train/Air/Public transportation	$_____
Other transportation	$_____
Clothing costs	$_____
Dry cleaning	$_____
Life insurance premiums	$_____
Pet care	$_____
Camps	$_____
Memberships/Club Dues	$_____
Movies, Netflix, books, newspapers, magazines	$_____

Vacation costs	$_____
Sports/Hobbies	$_____
Other Entertainment	$_____
Church or charitable donations	$_____
Loan payments	$_____
Credit card payment(s)	$_____
Personal (toiletries, allowances, etc.)	$_____
Miscellaneous (classes, etc.)	$_____
Dental bills (non reimbursable)	$_____
Care giving Costs	$_____
Medical costs (non reimbursable)	$_____
Medical insurance co-payment	$_____
Prescription medications (non reimbursable)	$_____
Therapy (e.g., physical, not covered by insurance)	$_____
Lodging and meals incurred during treatment away from home	$_____
Child care/nursing care (if not covered by insurance)	$_____
Adaptive technology	$_____
Legal fees	$_____
Other costs	$_____
Total Monthly expenses	$_____
Spending plan Totals:	$_____
Total income	
(Total Monthly expenses)	($_____)
Monthly Amount	$_____

NOTE: Please give careful thought to the questions below. They assist us in determining your specific monthly supplemental needs. Answer the questions below accurately to avoid causing delays for your requested distributions.

Estimate the total monthly cash needed to meet the supplemental needs of the Beneficiary:

_____

_____

Do you feel these monthly costs will increase? ☐Yes ☐No

If you answered yes, please indicate when you expect the costs to increase and by approximately how much.

_____

_____

Do you feel these monthly costs will decrease? ☐Yes ☐No

If you answered yes, please indicate when you expect the costs to decrease and by approximately how much.

_____

_____

Will here be any extra one-time costs in the future? ☐Yes ☐No

If you answered yes, please indicate what the expense will be and when the funds will be needed.

_____

_____

Below, please provide us with any additional information you think might be helpful in providing for the supplemental needs of the Beneficiary.

_____

_____

SAMPLE FORM: Beneficiary Disbursement Request Form

THIRD PARTY SNT DISBURSEMENT REQUEST FORM
When Completed Fax or Email to ( )___-_____
Today's Date _____

Beneficiary's Last Name _____ First Name _____

Requester's Last Name _____ First Name _____

Relationship to Beneficiary _____

Requester's Contact Information _____

Payee Name _____ Payee Account #_____

Payee Address _____ Amount $ _____

Distribution Purpose

_____

_____

Original invoices from payee/creditors "must" be faxed/emailed
with this form
All disbursements must be payable to a 3rd party

Beneficiary's Last Name _____ First Name _____

Requester's Last Name _____ First Name _____

Relationship to Beneficiary _____

Requester's Contact Information _____

Payee Name _____ Payee Account #_____

Payee Address _____ Amount $ _____

Distribution Purpose

Original invoices from payee/creditors "must" be faxed/emailed with this form

All disbursements must be payable to a 3rd party

FIRST PARTY SNT DISBURSEMENT REQUEST FORM

When Completed Fax or Email to (   )____-_____

Today's Date _____

Beneficiary's Last Name _____ First Name _____

Requester's Last Name _____ First Name _____

Relationship to Beneficiary _____

Requester's Contact Information _____

Payee Name _____ Payee Account #_____

Payee Address _____ Amount $ _____

Distribution Purpose

Original invoices from payee/creditors "must" be faxed/emailed with this form

All disbursements must be payable to a 3rd party and for beneficiary's primary benefit

---

Today's Date _____

Beneficiary's Last Name _____ First Name _____

Requester's Last Name _____ First Name _____

Relationship to Beneficiary _____

Requester's Contact Information _____

Payee Name _____   Payee Account #_____

Payee Address _____   Amount $ _____

Distribution Purpose

**Original invoices from payee/creditors "must" be faxed/emailed
with this form**

**All disbursements must be payable to a 3rd party and for
beneficiary's primary benefit**

APPENDIX H

FLOWCHART: Effect on Public Benefits When Making SNT Distributions

1. SNT Beneficiary makes a request to buy item or service[563]
2. SNT Trustee determines if item or service is illegal
   If No, go to Step 3
   If Yes, stop and deny request

3. SNT Trustee checks terms of trust to see if item or service is acceptable
   If No because of specific prohibition, then stop and deny request
   If Yes because trust is silent or specifically allows then go to Step 4

4. SNT Trustee determines if SNT is Third-Party or First-Party SNT
   If Third- Party go to Step 5
   If First-Party, consider whether item or service is for sole benefit of beneficiary
   If No stop and deny request
   If Yes go to Step 5

---

563 This list was inspired by David Lillesand, Florida special needs and elder law planning attorney

5. SNT Trustee determines effect of item or service on beneficiary's public benefits

    If Beneficiary receives SSI consider if item or service will be counted as an available resource or as unearned income of beneficiary

    > If No, go to next sentence
    >
    > If Yes, stop and deny request

    If Beneficiary receives SSI consider if item or service is considered food or shelter

    > If No, go to Step 6
    >
    > If Yes, consider In-Kind Support and Maintenance (ISM) Rules and whether loss of Presumed Maximum Value (PMV) amount of SSI is okay
    >
    > > If No, stop and deny request
    > >
    > > If Yes, go to Step 6

    If Beneficiary does not receive SSI but receives Medi-Cal consider if item or service is equipment or service that Medi-Cal will purchase

    > If No, go to Step 6
    >
    > If Yes, stop and deny request

    If Beneficiary receives In-Home Supportive Services (IHSS) consider if request is to supplement IHSS workers' pay

    > If No, go to Step 6
    >
    > If Yes, stop and deny request

    If Beneficiary does not receive either SSI or Medi-Cal go to Step 6

6. SNT Trustee determines whether purchase of item or service is within SNT spending plan

    > If No, stop and deny request
    >
    > Yes, go to Step 7

7. Purchase Item or service

CHECKLIST: Interviewing a Financial Advisor

The best approach in hiring a financial advisor is to talk to multiple candidates, check backgrounds, call references, and maintain objectivity.

Below, are some sample questions and general advice in the selection of a competent financial advisor.

Prior to meeting with a prospective advisor, the trustee should review the advisor's website and review any promotional material the advisor has. The website and written packet should include:

* information on the advisory firm
* financial planning and investment approaches and philosophies
* the advisor's résumé
* compensation methods and fee schedules
* registration Form ADV

There are certain types of advisers that must be licensed to sell different financial products.

Planner's Name: _____

Company: _____

Address: _____

Phone: _____

Fax: _____

E-mail: _____

Website: _____

1. Please tell us about your education and credentials.

2. Tell us about your experience in serving Fiduciary & Trust Clients. How many years have you served?

3. Do you have experience in providing advice on Special Needs Financial Planning? If yes, indicate the number of years.

4. How long have you been offering financial planning advice to clients?
   - Less than one year
   - One to four years
   - Five to 10 years
   - More than 10 years

5. How did you get involved in Special Needs Financial Planning as a profession?

6. What are your total Assets Under Management (AUM)? What is your AUM related to specialized trust/fiduciary clients? What percentage does that represent of your total client base?

7. What is the total number of clients that you serve related to Special Needs Financial Planning?

8. What professional financial planning designation(s) or certification(s) do you hold?
   - CERTIFIED FINANCIAL PLANNER™ or CFP®
   - The Chartered Special Needs Consultant® (ChSNC®)
   - Certified Public Accountant-Personal Financial Specialist (CPA-PFS)
   - Chartered Financial Consultant (ChFC)
   - Other

9. Have you produced any publications, presentations or training seminars related to this market?

10. What financial planning continuing education requirements are you required to attend?

11. Are you or your firm licensed as a Registered Investment Advisor? Will you provide me with your disclosure document Form ADV Part II or its state equivalent?
    - Yes
    - No, If no, why not?
12. How are you paid for your services?
    - Fee
    - Commission
    - Fee and Commission
    - Salary
    - Other
13. What do you typically charge?
    A)   Fee:
    Hourly Rate _____
    Flat Fee (range) $ _____ to $ _____
    Percentage of AOM _____ percent
    B)   Commission:
14. Are there any hidden internal fees related to mutual funds or other products?
15. What is the cost to exit your program?
16. Do you have open architecture for various investment products?
17. Do you receive disparate compensation for any particular products?
18. What restrictions preclude you from any particular product area, type or vendor?
19. Who/What institution stands behind you and what is their financial strength?
20. What insurance covers you and to what limits?
21. Explain your firm's supervision and oversight process.
22. Explain your firm's Legal and Compliance review process and supervision methods.
23. Do you provide a written client engagement agreement?
    - Yes
    - No. If no, why not?

24. How often do you meet with your clients to review performance and any changes that might be appropriate the Investment Policy Statement (IPS)? How are they scheduled and executed? Please include a sample report.

25. Can you provide 3 families as a reference that you have provided Special Needs Financial Planning advice to? May I contact them?

26. Can you provide 3 other professionals in the disability community as a reference? May I contact them?

Unspoken questions:

- Do you "rationally trust" this person to advise you on your financial affairs?
- Do you believe that this person is among of the best advisers available?
- If not, you should keep looking, until you find one who is.
- Are you comfortable with the manner of your interactions?
- Do you always understand what the advisor says? Is he or she able to explain things to you clearly?
- Do you feel that you could learn something valuable from working with this advisor?
- Do you feel that this advisor will treat you like his/her best clients or do you feel like you will be treated differently?
- Every advisor will have a direct or indirect cost to you. Your advisor's value to you must be substantially greater than his cost.

SAMPLE FORM: Trustee Accounting Letter to Beneficiary for Informal Account

_____, Trustee
(Address)
(Address)

(Date)

(Beneficiary Name)
(Address)
(Address)

Re: _____ Special Needs Trust Accounting

Dear _____:

As a beneficiary of the _____ Special Needs Trust, you are entitled to a periodic accounting that contains a report of the receipts and distributions of principal and income that have occurred over the past year. Additionally, you are entitled to know the assets and liabilities of the trust as of the beginning and the end of the accounting period, as well as the names of those agents that I, as trustee, have hired to assist me in my duties as trustee, or you in your daily life. I have also included a list of all named remainder and contingent beneficiaries with their last known addresses. Enclosed with this letter are the schedules that reflect all of this information.

[Information regarding the status of trust activities (i.e., claims, major transactions, relationship w/ agents and/or beneficiary(ies), unusual events, termination, etc.) should be included here.]

The specific information regarding fees paid to agents hired by me can be found in the "disbursements" schedule. Unless indicated otherwise, agents of the trustee are neither related to nor are affiliated with the trustee.

I should also advise you that you are entitled to petition the court under Probate Code Section 17200 to obtain a review of the account and of the acts f the trustee. Claims against the trustee for breach of trust may not be made after the expiration of three (3) years from the date you receive an account or report disclosing facts giving rise to the claim. Please refer to Probate Code Section 16063.

[Trustee may insert the following if SNT document allows it, otherwise it should not be included (See Chapter 7 for a discussion of this additional provision):]

"Please note that this three-year period is shortened under Probate Code 16461(c) by the following:

YOU HAVE [180 DAYS [*or longer if specified in the trust instrument*] FROM YOUR RECEIPT OF THIS ACCOUNT OR REPORT TO MAKE AN OBJECTION TO ANY ITEM SET FORTH IN THIS ACCOUNT OR REPORT. ANY OBJECTION YOU MAKE MUST BE IN WRITING; IT MUST BE DELIVERED TO THE TRUSTEE WITHIN THE PERIOD STATED ABOVE; AND IT MUST STATE YOUR OBJECTION. YOUR FAILURE TO DELIVER A WRITTEN OBJECTION TO THE TRUSTEE WITHIN THE PERIOD STATED ABOVE WILL PERMANENTLY PREVENT YOU

FROM LATER ASSERTING THIS OBJECTION AGAINST THE TRUSTEE. IF YOU DO MAKE AN OBJECTION, THE 3-YEAR PERIOD PROVIDED IN SECTION 16460 OF THE PROBATE CODE FOR COMMENCEMENT OF LITIGATION WILL APPLY TO CLAIMS BASED ON YOUR OBJECTION AND WILL BEGIN TO RUN ON THE DATE THAT YOU RECEIVE THIS ACCOUNT OR REPORT."

Should you have questions or concerns, please feel free to contact me at your convenience. Please be advised that if you wish to discuss your rights as a beneficiary, you should contact your own attorney.

Best regards,

Trustee

CHECKLIST: Hiring and Managing a Care Provider

A trustee should review the list below to review the overall responsibilities of hiring and managing a CARE PROVIDER:

Who is the CARE PROVIDER's employer?

_____HOME CARE AGENCY

CARE PROVIDERs are employed by the home care company.

_____EMPLOYMENT SERVICES ORGANIZATION CARE PROVIDERS are employed by the employment services organization.

_____REGISTRY

Depending on the arrangement, the trustee will likely have employer responsibilities.

_____**TRUSTEE HIRE**

CARE PROVIDERs are employed by the SNT trustee.

Who screens the CARE PROVIDER's references and performs criminal background checks?

_____HOME CARE AGENCY

Company does all screening. SNT trustee should ask for copy of any and all background check documents of specific employees.

However, the employer may only be able to release these documents with authorization of employee.

_____EMPLOYMENT SERVICES ORGANIZATION
Organization does all screening.

_____REGISTRY
Some registry agencies will do background check this and other will not. Trustee should make sure.

_____**TRUSTEE HIRE**
Trustee must do all screening.

Who pays the CARE PROVIDER?

_____HOME CARE AGENCY
CARE PROVIDERs are paid by the company.

_____EMPLOYMENT SERVICES ORGANIZATION
CARE PROVIDERS are paid by the organization

_____REGISTRY
Trustee usually pays a combined referral agency fee and CARE Providers' wages into a trust account of the referral agency, or separately pays the referral fee to the agency and wages to the CARE PROVIDER. Trustee and CARE PROVIDER negotiate wages and raises.

_____**TRUSTEE HIRE**
CARE PROVIDERs are paid by the SNT trustee.

Who handles CARE PROVIDER's overtime and vacation pay?

    ____ HOME CARE AGENCY

CARE PROVIDERs are paid by the company.

    ____EMPLOYMENT SERVICES ORGANIZATION

CARE PROVIDERS are paid by the organization

    ____ REGISTRY

SNT trustee is responsible.

    ____ **TRUSTEE HIRE**

SNT trustee is responsible.

Who is responsible for withholding and paying Federal and State Income taxes?

    ____ HOME CARE AGENCY

Company prepares and files quarterly and annual employer payroll tax returns.

    ____ EMPLOYMENT SERVICES ORGANIZATION

Organization prepares and files quarterly and annual employer payroll tax returns.

    ____REGISTRY

Trustee is responsible for preparing and filing quarterly and annual employer payroll tax returns, except when the registry uses 1099 workers.

    ____ **TRUSTEE HIRE**

Trustee is responsible for preparing and filing quarterly and annual employer payroll tax returns.

Who is responsible for withholding and paying Social Security and Medicare taxes?

       ____HOME CARE AGENCY

Company pays employer's share of these taxes.

       ____EMPLOYMENT SERVICES ORGANIZATION

Organization pays employer's share of these taxes.

       ____REGISTRY

Trustee is responsible for paying employer's cost of these taxes.

       ____**TRUSTEE HIRE**

Trustee is responsible for paying employer's costs of these taxes

Who is responsible for unemployment taxes?

       ____HOME CARE AGENCY

Company pays these taxes.

       ____EMPLOYMENT SERVICES ORGANIZATION

Organization pays these taxes.

       ____REGISTRY

Trustee is responsible for paying these taxes.

       ____**TRUSTEE HIRE**

Trustee is responsible for paying these taxes

Who is responsible for providing insurance (other than workers' compensation insurance) to cover the CARE PROVIDER?

       ____HOME CARE AGENCY

Company will generally provide; trustee should check to make sure agency will cover.

_____ EMPLOYMENT SERVICES ORGANIZATION
Organization will provide this.

_____ REGISTRY
SNT trustee or homeowner where the beneficiary resides. SNT trustee should contact homeowner or renter's insurance carrier for details - may need to seek rider on policy for "household employee." Typical insurance should cover when the CARE PROVIDER injures another.

_____ **TRUSTEE HIRE**
SNT trustee or homeowner where the beneficiary resides. SNT trustee should contact homeowner or renter's insurance carrier for details - may need to seek rider on policy for "household employee." Typical insurance should cover both when the CARE PROVIDER is injured and if the CARE PROVIDER injures another.

Who is responsible for providing workers compensation insurance to cover the CARE PROVIDER?

_____ HOME CARE AGENCY
Company will generally provide this, trustee should check to make sure agency will cover.

_____ EMPLOYMENT SERVICES ORGANIZATION
Organization will provide this.

_____ REGISTRY
SNT trustee or homeowner where the beneficiary resides. SNT trustee should contact homeowner's insurance carrier for details.

_____ **TRUSTEE HIRE**
SNT trustee or homeowner where the beneficiary resides. SNT

trustee should contact homeowner's insurance carrier for details.

Who coordinates services, including replacements when CARE PROVIDERs are sick or need time off?

____ HOME CARE AGENCY

Company will provide this service.

____ EMPLOYMENT SERVICES ORGANIZATION

Organization relies on trustee and other persons concerned for the beneficiary to refer CARE PROVIDERS. It is helpful to have people hired on an on-call basis to deal with these situations and to have a care manager who can coordinate staffing.

____ REGISTRY

Day-to-day coordination is worked out between the CARE PROVIDER and the SNT trustee. A substitute may be available through the agency.

____ **TRUSTEE HIRE**

Day-to-day coordination is worked out between the CARE PROVIDER and the SNT trustee.

Who resolves any issues with the CARE PROVIDER?

____ HOME CARE AGENCY

Company's supervisors or case managers usually do this will provide this service.

____ EMPLOYMENT SERVICES ORGANIZATION

The Human Resources Department of the organization will work with the beneficiary, the family, and the trustee

_____ REGISTRY

SNT trustee and CARE PROVIDER generally need to resolve day-to-day problems themselves.

_____ **TRUSTEE HIRE**

SNT trustee and CARE PROVIDER generally need to resolve day-to-day problems themselves.

SAMPLE FORM: Caregiving Agreement

Note: Caregiving contracts can take many approaches. Terms will vary with individual circumstances. The following Form represents one approach. It is strongly recommended that prior to entering into such an agreement that the trustee consult with an experienced employment attorney.

Warning: An SNT beneficiary's caregiver will nearly always be an employee and not an independent contractor. Failing to understand this distinction could have drastic consequences for the trustee. It is important to understand what this means before hiring a caregiver for beneficiary. This is discussed in more detail in Chapter 15 of this book.

CAREGIVING AGREEMENT

This Agreement is entered into by and between [*name of SNT trustee or SNT beneficiary*] ("EMPLOYER") and [*name of CARE PROVIDER*] ("CARE PROVIDER") this [date]. It sets forth the terms under which CARE PROVIDER will provide personal assistance to [*name of SNT beneficiary*] ("BENEFICIARY"). Although the trustee or the power of attorney have fiduciary responsibilities to the BENEFICIARY and are authorized to act on Beneficiary's behalf, [*name of SNT trustee or SNT beneficiary*] is the CARE PROVIDER'S employer for all purposes

1. *DUTIES OF CARE PROVIDER.* CARE PROVIDER will provide care-giving services for BENEFICIARY at BENEFICIARY's residence or other facility where BENEFICIARY is living. [*Include specific details of type of care to be provided. Some suggested functions are indicated below.*]

1.1 EMPLOYER contracts to pay and CARE PROVIDER agrees to provide the following services on an "as needed" basis for benefit of BENEFICIARY:

(1)   Attend to needs of BENEFICIARY, including preparation of nutritious, appropriate meals and snacks; house cleaning; laundry;

(2)   Assist BENEFICIARY with grooming, bathing, dressing, laundry, and personal shopping, as needed;

(3)   Purchase, with funds made available by EMPLOYER, or assist BENEFICIARY in purchasing clothing, toiletries, and other personal items for BENEFICIARY as needed, taking into account EMPLOYER's ability to pay for such items;

(4)   Purchase, with funds made available by EMPLOYER, or assist BENEFICIARY in purchasing hobby, entertainment or other goods for BENEFICIARY's use and enjoyment, as needed, taking into account EMPLOYER's ability to pay for such items;

(5)   Monitor BENEFICIARY's physical and mental condition and nutritional needs on a regular basis in cooperation with health-care providers;

(6)   Arrange for transportation to health-care providers and to the physician of BENEFICIARY's choice. CARE PROVIDER will also arrange for assessment, services and treatment by appropriate health-care providers, including but not limited to, physicians, nurses, nursing home services, physical therapists, and mental health specialists as needed for BENEFICIARY;

(7) Assist BENEFICIARY in carrying out the instructions and directives of BENEFICIARY's health-care providers;

(8) Arrange for social services by social service personnel as needed by BENEFICIARY;

(9) Even if additional services are not needed, visit at least weekly with BENEFICIARY and encourage social interaction;

(10) Arrange for outings and walks in keeping with BENEFICIARY's lifestyle, if reasonable and feasible for BENEFICIARY;

(11) Interact with and/or assist any agent of BENEFICIARY in interacting with health professionals, long-term care facility administrators, social service personnel, insurance companies, and government workers in order to safeguard BENEFICIARY's rights, benefits, or other resources as needed.

CARE PROVIDER is not authorized to [*Include specific details of type of services the CARE PROVIDER should not provide. Some suggested functions are indicated below.*]

1. While CARE PROVIDER may make medications available to BENIFICIARY and assist BENEFICIARY with medication or provide assistance with medical devices as directed by BENEFICIARY'S medical professionals, CARE PROVIDER may not perform any medical services requiring a medical or nursing license.
2. Access BENEFICIARY's bank, credit card or other financial accounts.
3. Perform housekeeping duties, except as they are related to the independent living of BENEFICIARY, and then only on an occasional basis.

1.2 The privacy of BENEFICIARY shall be preserved and respected as to visitors, telephone conversations and personal mail. Family members shall be permitted to visit BENEFICIARY.

2. *DURATION.* EMPLOYER hires CARE PROVIDER on an at-will basis under the terms and conditions set forth herein. This Agreement may be terminated at any time for any reason or no reason. CARE PROVIDER agrees to provide no less than three days' notice of termination to provide sufficient time for EMPLOYER to locate a replacement if necessary. EMPLOYER may waive the notice requirement in writing. The "at-will" nature of CARE PROVIDER'S employment may not be modified except in writing signed by CARE PROVIDER and the EMPLOYER and only if reviewed and approved by the Power of Attorney or Trustee.

3. *COMPENSATION.* The parties stipulate that as of the execution of this Agreement, BENEFICIARY is [age] years of age. EMPLOYER agrees to pay, and CARE PROVIDER agrees to accept, in payment for the aforesaid services to be rendered by CARE PROVIDER, the compensation set forth below, which compensation the parties stipulate and agree to be fair and reasonable and commensurate with the quality and extent of the services and their fair market value.

3.1 The parties stipulate that court appointed conservators or guardians who render the aforesaid services in this county, generally receive $[amount] per hour under Court order. Professional geriatric care managers typically receive $[amount] per hour for performance of the services noted above. The parties stipulate and agree that the CARE PROVIDER shall receive $[amount] per hour.

3.2 CARE PROVIDER will receive overtime compensation in accordance with state, federal and local laws. CARE PROVIDER must accurately report all hours worked. CARE PROVIDER will be paid [every week/every other week/twice per month] on [*identify the pay days/dates*]

3.3 CARE PROVIDER is required to take a paid ten-minute rest break for every four hours worked. If CARE PROVIDER'S rest break is interrupted for any reason, CARE PROVIDER shall take the break at a later time.

3.4 CARE PROVIDER is entitled to a thirty-minute lunch break each day she works at least 5 hours. Due to the nature of the employment, CARE PROVIDER may not be relieved of all duties during CARE PROVIDER'S meal break. CARE PROVIDER agrees that the meals will be considered an on-duty meal period and CARE PROVIDER will be paid during this time. If CARE PROVIDER does not want to work an on-duty meal period CARE PROVIDER may notify EMPLOYER so that EMPLOYER can secure a different caretaker for BENEFICIARY during the meal period.

4. *SCHEDULE.* CARE PROVIDER'S typical schedule will be [*brief description of typical schedule, such as: 6 hours per day, 5 days per week; OR from 8:00 a.m. to 8:00 p.m. Monday through Saturday; etc.).* The actual days and hours may vary. CARE PROVIDER is free to leave the premises and engage in personal activities when not on duty.

5. *NONASSIGNABILITY.* This agreement is for services unique to BENEFICIARY. CARE PROVIDER agrees to personally perform the above services. CARE PROVIDER shall have no obligation to render services or otherwise be liable to any other person or entity.

6. *PERSONAL DAY/TIME OFF.* In the event that CARE PROVIDER decides to take a personal day or vacation, he or she will only do so if such an absence is feasible, practical, and responsible. Additionally, CARE PROVIDER will contact EMPLOYER to ensure that BENEFICIARY does not experience a lapse in care while CARE PROVIDER is away. Unless otherwise required by law, all time off is unpaid.

6.1. *SICK LEAVE.* CARE PROVIDER will accrue one hour of paid sick leave for every 30 hours worked, up to a maximum of 6 days of Paid Sick Leave [OR CARE PROVIDER will be entitled to take up to 3 days of Paid Sick Leave each year] in accordance with the Health Families Health Workplaces Act. CARE PROVIDER may not use more than 3 days of Paid Sick Leave per year. If CARE PROVIDER works in a city or county with higher sick leave requirements the higher requirements will apply.

7. *EXPENSES.* [OPTIONAL: Employee is provided with a credit card to be used for purchase of items on behalf of Employer. Employee is not authorized to, and shall not, use the credit card for any personal expenses. Employee must provide receipts for all purchases and provide an accounting of all expenses. Employee may use Employer's vehicle for all business-related travel. Any expenses or losses Employee incurs in the discharge of her duties or at the direction of the Employer must be submitted with receipts and proof of payment with Employee's time sheet. Employee is not to use the Employer-provided vehicle for personal reasons without permission.

8. *MEDICAL BENEFITS.* Medical care for the BENEFICIARY is to be provided at the expense of EMPLOYER. CARE PROVIDER shall not be liable for the cost of BENEFICIARY's care.

9. *MEALS AND LODGING.* CARE PROVIDER may be provided with meals and lodging while CARE PROVIDER is caring for BENEFICIARY, but the meals and lodging are not part of CARE PROVIDER'S compensation. CARE PROVIDER is not a tenant,

and therefore is not entitled to any notice prior to terminating CARE PROVIDER'S employment or lodging.

10. *EFFECTIVE DATE.* This Agreement shall take effect and be binding on the parties hereto upon payment of the agreed upon compensation set forth above for CARE PROVIDER.

11. *ARBITRATION CLAUSE.* The parties agree that any dispute between them regarding the services under this Agreement or any other aspect of this Agreement, will be determined by submitting it to arbitration under the laws of the State of [state], rather than by a lawsuit through the court process. [It may be desirable to be more detailed in identifying the arbitration mechanism, or it may be preferable to preserve the option of jury or court trial for the client.]

12. *REPRESENTATIONS.* The CARE PROVIDER represents to the EMPLOYER as follows:

    A.   The CARE PROVIDER's [state] Driver's License Number is [number]. It expires on [date].

    B.   The CARE PROVIDER has never been, and is not now, the subject of any claim or court action (civil or criminal) alleging criminal or dishonest activity.

    C.   The CARE PROVIDER is capable of performing the essential functions of the job, with or without reasonable accommodations, without subjecting CARE PROVIDER or BENEFICIARY to risk of harm or injury.

13. *MISCELLANEOUS.*

13.1 This Agreement contains the entire Agreement and understanding between the parties, surpassing all prior communications, either written or oral, concerning the subject matter of this Agreement. This Agreement may be changed only by a written instrument executed by both parties hereto.

13.2 This Agreement shall be governed by and construed in accordance with the laws of the State of California.

THIS IS A LEGALLY BINDING AGREEMENT. EACH PARTY HAS READ THE ABOVE AGREEMENT BEFORE SIGNING IT. EACH PARTY UNDERSTANDS THE AGREEMENT HE OR SHE IS MAKING, HAVING HAD THE OPPORTUNITY TO

ASK TO HAVE EACH TERM THAT THE PARTY DOES NOT UNDERSTAND FULLY EXPLAINED.

We, the CARE PROVIDER and the EMPLOYER, having read this Agreement, agree to its terms and sign it as our free act and deed on the date(s) set forth below.

EMPLOYER:

[name typed or printed] in his/her capacity as Trustee for the [*name of trust*]

[signature]

[date signed]

CARE PROVIDER:

[name typed or printed]

[signature]

[date signed]

[Notarial Acknowledgment]

APPENDIX M

SAMPLE FORM: Caregiver Timesheet

Date	Services Performed	$ per HR	Hours
4/1/11	Bathing/Grooming	$18.00	1 hour 30 minutes
	Cleaning and Laundry	$18.00	2 hours
4/2/11	Lawn care	$18.00	1 hour
4/3/11	Medication management & administration	$18.00	45 minutes
	Shopping	$18.00	1 hour
4/4/11	Bathing/Grooming	$18,00	1 hour 30 minute
	Transportation to appointment	$18.00	1 hour 45 minutes
4/6/11	Financial management	$18.00	1 hour
	Bathing/Grooming	$18.00	1 hour 30 minutes

4/7/11	Transportation to senior services	$18.00	1 hour
4/8/11	Cleaning	$18.00	2 hours 30 minutes
	Bathing/Grooming	$18.00	1 hour 30 minutes
	Transportation to and from doctors	$18.00	2 hours
4/9/11	Lawn care	$18.00	1 hour

Prepared from contemporaneous notes

_____

Dave Brown, Caregiver

APPENDIX N

CHECKLIST: Termination of Trust on Death of Beneficiary

The SNT will terminate for any of the reasons outlined in Chapter 18. This checklist is focused on termination upon the death of the beneficiary, not termination as a result of the depletion of trust assets.

Upon a beneficiary's death, the SNT trustee may also assist the family in carrying out the final wishes of the beneficiary. Occasionally, the SNT trustee is the only person in the beneficiary's life and must take on these duties. This checklist is designed to help the SNT trustee wrap up the affairs of the trust.

Dealing with Death of Beneficiary:

- Review the beneficiary's Advance Health Care Directive and Memorial Instructions form to discover any expressed wishes by the beneficiary or his parents or guardians/conservators regarding burial, cremation, services or other preferences.

- Review any beneficiary's nomination of Funeral Representative and any pre-paid funeral contract.

- Work with the surviving family and the health-care agent to provide an appropriate funeral or other service.

- Notify the beneficiary's employer, if applicable, and obtain benefits forms if life insurance, retirement planning or other survivor's benefits are in place.

- Request at least 6 certified copies of the death certificate

First-Party SNT Wrap Up Unsupervised Administration:

Send notices with copies of the Death Certificate

Social Security Administration

DHCS

Assess if beneficiary received Medicaid benefits from any other state. If so, send notice. Calendar follow up.

Remainder beneficiaries-include copy of trust along with death cert.

Publish notice to creditors

Request lien information from each state beneficiary received Medi-Cal/Medicaid benefits and calendar follow up:

May submit to DHCS by using https://apps.dhcs.ca.gov/AutoForm2/Page/AutoForm2.aspx.

Review lien information received from all state Medicaid agencies

Assess if any items should be eliminated. Look for improper or duplicative charges-especially if funds were from litigation proceeds and prior liens were resolved

Review with family or guardian knowledgeable of beneficiary's care

Negotiate payback if possible

Determine if beneficiary exercised power of appointment

Determine validity of claims presented and priority of remaining creditors

Pay allowable funeral expenses. Anticipate final administrative expenses.

Pay authorized creditors

Prepare, or arrange for, final tax return

Prepare final account of fiduciary

Issue final distributions to remainder beneficiaries along with final account. Obtain Receipt of Distributive Share from each remaindermen for your file.

First-Party SNT Wrap Up-Court Supervised Administration:

Send notices with copies of the Death Certificate

Social Security Administration

DHCS

Assess if beneficiary received Medicaid benefits from any other state. If so, send notice. Calendar follow up.

Remainder beneficiaries-include copy of trust along with death cert.

Request lien information from each state beneficiary received Medi-Cal/Medicaid benefits and calendar follow up:

**May submit to DHCS by using
https://apps.dhcs.ca.gov/AutoForm2/Page/AutoForm2.aspx.**

Review lien information received from state Medicaid agencies

Assess if any items should be eliminated. Look for improper or duplicative charges-especially if funds were from litigation proceeds and prior liens were resolved

Review with family or guardian knowledgeable of beneficiary's care

Negotiate payback if possible

Determine validity of claims presented and priority of remaining creditors

Determine if beneficiary exercised power of appointment.

Prepare final account of fiduciary with proposed final distribution schedule

Petition for Allowance of Final Account and proposed final distributions

Request approval of all fiduciary fees, including any anticipate final administrative expenses through completion

Include anticipated cost of preparation of final tax return and any anticipated tax owed to federal and state

Send notice of hearing and copies of all documents to all interested parties that apply:

- DHCS
- Remainder beneficiaries
- Creditors
- Bond Company

Issue Payments Pursuant to Court Order:

Pay allowable funeral expenses. Anticipate final administrative expenses through completion.

Pay authorized creditors

Pay remainder beneficiaries.

Obtain signed receipt of distributive share.

File signed Receipts with Court

Prepare, or arrange for, final tax return

Third-Party SNT Administration Wrap Up:

Send notices with copies of the Death Certificate

Social Security Administration

DHCS

Determine if beneficiary exercised power of appointment.

Send notice to remainder beneficiaries with copy of trust or governing instrument (if beneficiary exercised a power of appointment) and death certificate

If allowable, pay funeral expenses.

Prepare, or arrange for, final tax return

Prepare final account of fiduciary

Pay final administrative expenses

- Issue final distributions to remainder beneficiaries along with final account. Obtain Receipt of Distributive Share from each remaindermen for your file.

SUMMARY: No-Brainer SNT Distribution List

The following is an alphabetical list of generally permissible distributions from an SNT that will not reduce or eliminate SSI. It is not meant to be an exhaustive list.

- Automobile/van;
- Accounting services;
- Acupuncture/acupressure;
- Appliances (TV, microwave, stove, refrigerator, washer/dryer, etc.);
- Bottled water or water service;
- Bus pass/public transportation costs;
- Clothing;
- Clubs and club dues (record clubs, book clubs, health clubs, service clubs, zoo, advocacy groups, museums);
- Computer hardware, software, and programs;
- Conferences;
- Cosmetics;
- Courses or classes (academic or recreational), including books and supplies;
- Curtains, blinds, and drapes;
- Dental work not covered by Medi-Cal, including anesthesia;
- Down payment on home or security deposit on apartment;
- Dry cleaning and/or laundry services;
- Education expenses including tuition and related costs;
- Elective surgery;
- Erotic material (*i.e.*, videos, toys, etc.)

- Eyeglasses;
- Fitness equipment;
- Funeral expenses;
- Furniture, home furnishings (dishes, etc.);
- Gasoline or maintenance for automobile;
- Haircuts/salon services;
- Hobby supplies;
- Holiday decorations, holiday cards;
- Home alarm or monitoring/response system;
- Home improvements, repairs, and maintenance (not covered by Medi-Cal), including tools to perform home improvements, repairs, and maintenance;
- Home purchase;
- House cleaning/maid services;
- Insurance (automobile, home and/or possessions);
- Internet services
- Legal fees/advocacy;
- Linens and towels;
- Magazine and newspaper subscriptions;
- Massage;
- Musical instruments (including lessons and music);
- Nonfood grocery items (laundry soap, bleach, fabric softener, deodorant, dish soap, hand and body soap, personal hygiene products, paper towels, napkins, Kleenex, toilet paper, and household cleaning products);
- Over-the-counter medications (including vitamins and herbs);
- Personal assistance services not covered by Medi-Cal;
- Pet and pet supplies, veterinary services;
- Physician specialists if not covered by Medi-Cal;
- Private counseling if not covered by Medi-Cal;
- Repair services (*e.g.,* for appliances, automobile, bicycle, household, or fitness equipment);
- Snow removal/landscaping/gardening (lawn) services;
- Sporting goods/equipment/uniforms/team pictures;
- Stationery, stamps, and cards;
- Storage units;

- Taxicab/UBER/Lyft;
- Telephone service and equipment, including cell phone;
- Therapy (physical, occupational, speech) not covered by Medi-Cal;
- Tickets to concerts or sporting events (for beneficiary and an accompanying companion, if necessary);
- Transportation (automobile, motorcycle, bicycle, moped, gas, bus passes, insurance, vehicle license fees, gas, automobile repairs);
- Tuition and expenses connected with education
- Utility bills (satellite TV, cable TV, telephone—but not gas, water, or electricity);
- Vacation (including paying for companion to accompany the beneficiary if necessary)

APPENDIX P

SAMPLE FORM: Investment Policy Statement

[TRUST OR CLIENT's NAME][564]

1. *Introduction/Background*

BENEFICIARY is a 48-year-old female (DOB) with two young adult children. She is in good physical health, other than being recently diagnosed with schizophrenia. She is separated from her estranged husband and is currently going through a divorce. In the past she has not made prudent financial decisions, and she has a diagnosed gambling addiction.

The trust was set up by her father as a third-party SNT before he died to provide for her special needs. Currently BENEFICIARY is unemployed and has not managed her finances well. She lives a modest life in a rental house in the Sierra foothills. Her son just graduated from high school and is living with her while attending a community college. (The son has a trust that is supporting him while he is in school.)

Based on the IRS Publication 590 Single Life Expectancy table, Ms. BENEFICIARY's life expectancy is 84 years (an additional 36 years).

    A. *Income*: Ms. BENEFICIARY's income comes from SSI at $958.63 per month. Ms. BENEFICIARY'S SNT estimated annual income is from interest income from 4 deeds of trust (estimated annual income $12,000) and whatever interest or dividend income we can get from her investable assets.

---

564 This sample investment policy statement was developed from a statement provided to the author by Scott MacDonald, Merrill-Lynch special needs financial advisor.

B. *Expenses:* Ms. BENEFICIARY's living expenses, i.e. rent, auto insurance, health insurance, and utilities will be paid from the trust, if possible. Trust fees include professional services fees consisting of fiduciary, legal and tax accountant fees (estimated $8,000 annually).

C. *Assets:* Ms. BENEFICIARY's assets are a piece of property in TOWN, CA (appraised value as of 1/17/20 $135,000). Her SNT's assets are 4 deeds (installment notes) valued at $205,000 (appraised value as of 1/17/20), and cash for a total asset portfolio of approximately **$1,100,000.**

D. *Trust provisions:* The BENEFICIARY'S NAME Special Needs Trust was established on DATE at the time of her father's death. Per the terms of the trust, BENEFICIARY is entitled to discretionary distribution of income and principal based on the assets in the trust. In the trustee's discretion, BENEFICIARY may have as much as necessary for her special needs.

E. *Needs:* Ms. BENEFICIARY has significant need for income from this trust due to the fact she is unemployed. The trustee is considering putting a mobile or prefab home on the TOWN property to provide BENEFICIARY with a permanent residence.

2. *Measurable Investment Objectives:*

The objectives are to provide the income needs to the degree possible for Ms. BENEFICIARY's lifetime. The goal is to earn the highest rate of return with the least amount of risk in a diversified portfolio. Ms. BENEFICIARY's will need monthly distributions from the trust to support her living expenses.

A. *Minimum portfolio returns:* A reasonable objective is an average of 4-6% rate of return for the next five years. Per the UPIA this return is for the whole portfolio, not individual investments.

B. *Maximum acceptable portfolio risk:* Risk is to be measured as the potential for loss, rather than simple volatility using a semi-standard deviation scatter plot. The average risk should not exceed a moderate, or "average" risk class based on Morningstar's risk score on performance. This risk score compares funds in the same peer group and is a weighted, average of three, five and ten year performance. Defining and managing the risk levels are a key duty of a prudent professional fiduciary. The goal is to have the funds all in the northwest quadrant of the scatter plot.

3. *Investment Management Procedures:*

Investment managers are responsible for making investment decisions based upon their predetermined process and philosophy. The will use the same care, skill, prudence and diligence under the prevailing circumstances that experienced investment professionals, acting in like capacity, and fully familiar with such matters, would use in like activities for like portfolio, with like aims, in accordance and compliance with the Prudent Investor Rule and all applicable laws, rules and regulations. As a prudent investor, day trading and short sales would not be acceptable methodologies.

4. *Classes of Investments:*

Asset allocation and diversification are the keys to successful investment portfolio management. No classes of investments are excluded if they meet the risk and return objectives. The UPIA specifically does not exclude certain types of investments, leaving it up to particular risk versus return goals set forth in the trust.

5. *Asset Manager/Fund Hiring and Firing Criteria:*

A careful analysis of the asset manager or fund should be conducted prior to investing. Criteria includes tenure (at least 5 years with the fund), local references (at least two, and one from another professional fiduciary or attorney), and better than the peer group benchmark (S&P 500, MSCI EAFE, Bloomberg Barclays U.S. Intermediate Government/Credit Bond Index, 3-month T-bill) for the prior 5 years. Not meeting the minimum acceptable earnings objective or the maximum acceptable risk objective over the previous year will be the criteria for firing.

6. *Investment Advisor:*

As a professional fiduciary it is my duty to thoroughly review and evaluate an investment advisor before delegating the investment responsibilities. Normally, an investment advisor would be chosen based on a review of their investment approaches, their knowledge and experience with the UPIA, their past performances, their years in the field and their professional degrees. Also, the advisor would be expected to inspire confidence in what they do and be readily available to answer questions from the professional fiduciary. Fees and/or transaction costs would be evaluated compared to their value versus return. A substandard performance that doesn't meet the average minimum earnings objective and maximum risk tolerance over a year timeframe would be grounds for dismissal.

7. *Reporting*:

Periodic reviews include receiving monthly statements of accounts and quarterly summary reviews of the performance compared to the appropriate benchmark. The reviews should include a breakdown by asset class, sector and size. Twice a year in-person meetings will be conducted so there is a direct opportunity to discuss questions or issues. The adviser is to add the notes from the meeting in the file. The notes should include any significant changes to your current financial condition, net worth, employment situation, changes in risk tolerance, tax jurisdiction, family situation and any other considerations that may have an impact on how your portfolio is managed.

8. *Rebalancing*:

From time to time rebalancing the portfolio is required to continue to meet the return/risk objectives. This reallocation should be reviewed at a minimum of once a year. The actual investments may at times fall outside of these ranges for a variety of reasons. In determining whether to rebalance we will assess the current situation and take appropriate action consistent with the investment authority of the account. Rebalancing timing and magnitude will reflect considerations that may include (1) tactical targets that may be titled toward the upper or lower end of the stated range (2) the expected risk and return characteristics of the portfolio (3) liquidity terms of subject investments (4) tax considerations (5) distributions needs in the portfolio and (6) other appropriate factors.

Acknowledged by:

Investment Manager _____
Date _____

Prepared by:
[FIDUCIARY FIRM NAME]
LICENSED FIDUCIARY
DATED _____

SAMPLE FORM: Petition of Petition for Court Account and Report

KEVIN URBATSCH, SBN 168380

THE URBATSCH LAW FIRM, P.C.

3478 Buskirk Avenue, Suite 300

Pleasant Hill, CA 94523

Tel: (415) 593-9944

Fax: (925) 940-9588

Kevin@Urbatsch.com

Attorneys for Roger Zelazny,

Petitioner and Trustee

IN THE SUPERIOR COURT OF THE STATE OF CALIFORNIA

IN AND FOR THE CITY AND COUNTY OF SAN FRANCISCO

In re the matter of:	CASE NO.: 1-11-PR-123456
THE CORWIN AMBER SPECIAL NEEDS)	FIRST ACCOUNT & REPORT OF TRUSTEE;
TRUST)	PETITION TO SETTLE ACCOUNT; TO REDUCE
)	BOND; AND TO FIX & ALLOW TRUSTEE AND
)	ATTORNEY FEES (Probate Code § 1060)
)	DATE:
)	TIME:
)	DEPT:

ROGER ZELAZNY, trustee of the CORWIN AMBER SPECIAL NEEDS TRUST, presents his verified First Account and Report and Petition to Settle the Account; to Reduce Bond; and to Fix and Allow Trustee and Attorney Fees and Costs; (Probate Code § 1060). Petitioner alleges:

Jurisdiction and Venue. This Court has jurisdiction over this matter pursuant to Probate Code §17000, et seq.

Venue is proper in that this court approved the underlying settlement, under case number 1-08-CV-105511 and established the trust in this jurisdiction.

Parties. Pursuant to an Order of the Superior Court of San Francisco dated April 14, 2015, the Corwin Amber Special Needs Trust was established for Corwin Amber.

ROGER ZELAZNY (hereinafter referred to as "Trustee") is the current Trustee of the Trust.

CORWIN AMBER, the beneficiary of the Trust, is 14 years of age (Date of Birth 10/04/1995). He suffers from a disability that impairs his ability to provide for his own care and constitutes a substantial handicap.

First Account & Report of Trustee. Petitioner's account of the Corwin Amber Special Needs Trust covers the period from April 14, 2018 through April 30, 2020. A Summary of Account is attached hereto, and a full, true and correct account setting forth all credits and charges of petitioner as trustee is attached as Exhibit A.

During the account period, all cash of the trust estate was invested and maintained in interest bearing accounts or investments authorized by law or the governing instrument, except for an amount of cash that is reasonably necessary for the orderly administration of the estate.

Unusual Disbursements.

a. **Caregiver Fees.** Throughout this account period, the trustee disbursed trust funds to Fred Saberhagen for caregiver fees. Mr. Saberhagen is the employer of the caregivers. Payments were made directly to him, and he then disbursed the funds accordingly to the caregivers. True and correct copies of the invoices submitted to the trustee for payment of caregivers are attached hereto as **Exhibit B.** Pursuant to the court order establishing the special needs trust (which was filed under this case number on April 14, 2015, as an attachment to the Declaration of Kevin Urbatsch Regarding Establishment of Special Needs Trust) the trustee is authorized to hire a caregiver for Corwin Amber for $35 an hour. As noted by his doctor reports, Corwin requires 24-hour care. He functions at a level of a small infant, yet he continues to grow physically making his care increasingly difficult for his family. While the cost of care is large, finding safe and reliable people from a private agency would cost even more than is being expended by the trust now. Paying for a family caregiver is also accepted by the Social Security Administration (SSA). The SSA is the agency that runs the Supplemental Security Income (SSI) program that an SNT is designed to preserve. The federal policies governing SNTs originate from the SSA's Program Operation Manual System ("POMS"). In the context of SNTs, the POMS provide SSA field office personnel with operating instructions on evaluating trusts for eligibility purposes. As the Eighth Circuit Court of Appeals noted, "the POMS provisions demonstrate valid reasoning; that is, the detailed process required for establishing qualifying special-needs trusts contained in the POMS is consistent with 'Congress's command that all but a narrow class of an individual's assets count as a resource when determining the financial need of a potential SSI beneficiary.'" *Draper v. Colvin* (8th Cir 2015) 779 F.3d 556, 561. The POMS, states that while "[f]amily members may normally [provide care] without compensation, ... that does not prohibit the trust paying for these services." POMS SI 01120.201F.3.a. The POMS also specify that the policy allowing payments for caregiving should be applied uniformly regardless of who provides caregiving services (family member, non-family member, or professional services company). *Id.* Family caregivers are often the most likely candidates to be caregivers. They are most aware of the needs of the person with a disability, provide better care, and cost less than a third party hired through an agency. Provided this background, the Trustee exercised its discretion and used trust funds to pay for his caregiving services.

No capital changes occurred during the account period.

The trust has no liabilities.

Petitioner has managed and administered the beneficiary's estate frugally and without waste, collecting income and principal, investing the sums available for investment, retaining and disposing of property and investments, and applying or disposing of the income or corpus of the trust estate as required by law, the governing instrument and the orders of this Court, as detailed in the schedules attached to this petition.

The original bank statements will be filed prior to the hearing on this matter.

Bond. Per court order dated April 14, 2018, petitioner filed a bond in the amount of $1,008,982.82. Based on the ending value of the estate ($653,770.74), the estimated annual annuity payments ($120,000), the estimated annual income to be earned ($15,475–based on a 2% return), and the reasonable amount for the cost of recovery on the bond ($84,709), petitioner requests that the amount of bond be reduced by $134,982.80, for a total bond amount of $874,000,000. (Probate Code section 2320 (c)(4); Calif. Rule of Court 7.206.)

No Affiliate Relationships. During the accounting period, neither the trustee nor her attorney of record, KEVIN URBATSCH, Esq., had any family or affiliate relationship with any agent hired by petitioner as trustee.

Fix and Allow Attorney Fees. Petitioners retained the services of KEVIN URBATSCH, Esq., as their attorney in all matters concerning the trust administration in which it was necessary to have advice of counsel in the proper administration and conduct of the trust and in connection with preparing the First Account and Report of petitioner as trustee. Mr. Urbatsch received $4,922.00 in attorney's fees during this account period, pursuant to an order made by this court on April 14, 2018. Petitioner now seeks an order of this court to authorize and direct the Trustee of the CORWIN AMBER SPECIAL NEEDS TRUST to pay to Kevin Urbatsch the amount of $3,397.50 for his attorneys' fees all as set forth in the Declaration of Kevin Urbatsch attached hereto as Exhibit C.

Fix and Allow Trustee Fees. Pursuant to an order made by this Court on April 14, 2018, Petitioner is entitled to receive payment of interim fees based upon his then yearly rate to be divided equally throughout the year. During this account period, the trustee received a total of $7,029.00. Interim fees were based upon 1% of the trust assets under management, as allowed in this court's order approving this trust. Petitioner asks the court to confirm these fees, and to approve additional fees, based on the trustee's actual services provided. During this account period, the trustee has spent a total of 112.40 hours in managing the trust estate. Based on an hourly rate of $100.00, the trustee is entitled to $11,240. Therefore, Petitioner asks the court to allow payment of additional trustee fees in the amount of $4,211 (the difference between $11,240 and $7,029.00). In support of this request, the trustee's itemized time sheets are attached hereto as Exhibit D. By endorsing his name to this Petition, Petitioner represents that this is a reasonable value of the services as Trustee. In the management of the Trust estate during the period of this account, Petitioner has performed the following services:

> Petitioner has managed and administered the trust estate frugally and without waste, collecting income and principal, investing the sums available for investment including investing in interest-bearing accounts, retaining and disposing of property and investments, and applying or disposing of income or corpus of the estate as required by law.

Notice. The persons entitled to notice of hearing on this petition include the beneficiary and members of the trust advisory committee, as follows:

Corwin Amber, Beneficiary, 125 Logos, Amber, CA 95111

Oberon Amber, Father of Beneficiary and Trust Advisory Committee member, 125 Logos, Amber, CA 95111

Harry Dresden, Trust Advisory Committee Member, 125 Logos, Amber, CA 95111

Department of Health Services, Director, MS 0000, P.O. Box 997413 Sacramento, CA 95899-7413

Department of Mental Health, 1600 9ᵗʰ Street, Room 151, Sacramento, CA 98614

Department of Developmental Services, P.O box 944242, Sacramento, CA 94244-2020

There are no requests for special notice on file.

WHEREFORE, Petitioner requests that:

1. The court find that notice of hearing has been given as required by law;
2. The court make an order approving, allowing, and settling the attached first account and report of the CORWIN AMBER SPECIAL NEEDS TRUST as filed;
3. That bond be reduced by $134,982.80, for a total bond amount of $874,000;
4. The court confirm payment of interim trustee fees in the amount of $7,029.00;
5. The court authorize and direct petitioner to pay Leo Bautista, as trustee, $4,211 for trustee services.
6. The court authorize and direct petitioner to pay KEVIN URBATSCH, Esq., $3,397.50 for legal services rendered to the petitioner during the account period; and
7. For such other relief that the Court deems proper.

Date: _____, 2020   By: _____

ROGER ZELAZNY,
Petitioner and Trustee

Date: _____, 2020   _____

By: KEVIN URBATSCH
Attorney for Petitioner

VERIFICATION

I, ROGER ZELAZNY, declare:

I am the petitioner in the above-entitled matter and I declare that I have read the foregoing account and petition, and the requests designated therein, and know its contents. The account, which includes the report and the supporting schedules, is true of my own knowledge, except for the matters stated therein on our information and belief, and as to those matters, I believe them to be true. The account contains a full statement of all charges against us and all credits to which we are entitled in the estate during the account period.

I declare under penalty of perjury under the laws of the State of California that the foregoing is true and correct. Executed in the City of _____, California.

Date: _____, 2020

_____

Roger Zelazny

SAMPLE FORM: Trustee's Time Log

A trustee should keep a time log of all the tasks performed on behalf of trust. The following time log is a sample. There are additional suggestions in Chapter 6 dealing with Paying Trustee's Fees on how to properly fill out a time log. A lot of case management software systems will include a function where a trustee can contemporaneously keep their time and it will print out a time log that can serve as an invoice for the trustee.

Date	Time Expended	Biller	Rate	Amount Billed	Explanation
01/23/2016	.5	KU Trustee	$150/ hour	$75	Telephone call from beneficiary about request for trip and documents needed
01/24/2016	.5	MF Trustee Admin Ass't	$90/hour	$45	Pay gardener; pay accountant and request service for upcoming year

01/30/2016	.8	KU Trustee	$150/ hour	$120	Contacted Sunnyside Funeral Home to purchase pre-need funeral
Totals	1.8 hours	KU – 1.3 MF - .5		$240	Billed on 02/01/2016

SAMPLE FORM: Trustee's Declaration Supporting Request for Fees

The following two examples come from real cases when a trustee was required to provide sufficient evidence for a just and reasonable fee. The first example involves a corporate trustee and the second example involves a California licensed private professional fiduciary.

FEE NARRATIVE OF CORPORATE TRUSTEE

REGARDING TRUSTEE'S REQUEST FOR COMPENSATION FOR SERVICES RENDERED

In the paragraphs that follow, trustee briefly applies the relevant factors described in Rule of Court 7.776 to the present matter:

- **Gross Income of the Trust Estate.** The trust earned $181,383.34 in gross income over the three-year period. This is an amount significantly greater than the amount requested for fees.

- **Success or Failure of the Trustee's Administration.** The trustee successfully managed over $2,000,000 in SNT assets, causing no loss in public benefits to the beneficiary, which is one of the primary purposes of placing assets into a special needs trust. The parents who are very involved in the oversight over this SNT have not objected to the fee. There should be no reduction in compensation to the Trustee out of concern that the trust was not managed successfully.

- **Unusual Skill, Expertise or Experience.** Trustee used unusual skill and experience in managing SNT. The Trustee manages numerous special needs trusts. The purpose of a special needs trust is to maintain public benefits, the Trustee must manage, disburse, and invest SNT assets in such a manner that these benefits are not jeopardized. Given the byzantine laws and regulations on benefits for recipients of Medi-Cal and Social Security, the Trustee's management of special needs trusts can be extremely challenging and requires a nuanced understanding of the public benefit laws. The Trustee must ensure the suitable investment of SNT's assets, and works closely with financial advisor, a specialist in investments in special needs trusts, to maintain an appropriate range of investments that comply with Rule of Court 7.903 and Probate Code § 2614.

- **The Fidelity or Disloyalty Shown by The Trustee.** Petitioner managed and administered the SNT for the sole benefit of the beneficiary. There is no evidence that Petitioner showed any disloyalty or infidelity to beneficiary.

- **Amount of Risk and Responsibility Assumed by The Trustee.** Trustee assumed an enormous risk when agreeing to serve as trustee of a California court supervised special needs trust. Very few corporate trustees or private professional fiduciaries agree to serve as special needs trust trustees due to the federal and state public benefit rules and regulations. This extra layer of law and regulation on top of the added complexity of managing a court supervised trust means these types of trusts are very difficult to find placement. In order to succeed, a trustee must be diligent in keeping current with the ever-shifting landscape of public benefit laws. If a trustee does not stay current, distributions that were authorized one month might be forbidden the next month due to a change in the Social Security Administration (SSA) Program Operations Manual Systems (POMS) (SSA's guidebook to SNTs). Due to these uncertainties, and potential for liability, few corporate fiduciaries agree to take these cases.

- **Time Spent on Trustee's Duties**. Trustee carefully tracked the time spent administering the SNT. An exhaustive description of the tasks required for its administration of SNT, and the approximate time spent in completing these tasks, is documented in the declaration of trustee, filed concurrently with this petition.

- **Local custom**. The Court may consider local custom and the charges of similar professional trustees when reviewing the appropriateness of trustee fees under Rule of Court 7.776. Corporate trustees consistently charge a percentage rate for services. Further, other professional trustees in the area charge higher rates than that of trustee. Its fee is cost-effective when compared to the cost of other local professional trustees or a private professional fiduciary. The Trustee's fees of 0.90% on the first $2 million and 0.70% on the next $3 million are over a half a percent less than comparable fees charged by Big Bank, which charges 1.5% per year in trustee fees for Trusts up to $2,000,000. The parents of beneficiary asked that a fee schedule be prepared that they could sign memorializing this lowering of the Trustee's normal fee. See **Exhibit D** a true and correct copy of the signed fee schedule.

- **Required more than ordinary skill and judgment in managing the trust.** Trustee is one of the few corporate trustees who will agree to manage a court supervised special needs trusts. There are benefits to having a corporate fiduciary familiar with the administration of special needs trusts serve as trustee. One of the main concerns with any type of trust administration is familiarity with all of the fiduciary obligations of managing a trust. Any corporate fiduciary or private professional fiduciary should have knowledge of these fundamental fiduciary requirements. However, in addition to understanding all of the fiduciary requirements in managing any trust, a special needs trust trustee must also understand public benefits laws and how disbursements may affect these benefits. Many corporate fiduciaries and private professional fiduciaries are wholly unfamiliar with the laws of Social Security (along with the accompanying regulations and policies set forth in the Program Operation Manual System (POMS)) as it relates to Supplemental Security Income (SSI) eligibility or the California and federal law (along with accompanying regulations and policy memorandums) as it relates to Medi-Cal eligibility.

The second example comes from a declaration from a private professional trustee.

FEE NARRATIVE OF PRIVATE PROFESSIONAL FIDUCIARY

REGARDING TRUSTEE'S REQUEST FOR COMPENSATION FOR SERVICES RENDERED

Private professional fiduciary declares:

1. I, Private Professional Fiduciary of the trustee of the SNT. As trustee, I performed services during the period from December 24, 2018 to December 31, 2019 as set forth in the attached invoices. Attached hereto as Exhibit A are true and correct copies of the invoices. The rates of the staff involved at Private Professional Fiduciary Office are referenced in the Schedule of Fees attached hereto as Exhibit B.

2. **The success of the administration of the trust**: At the end of this period assets of the trust managed amounted to $900,000 (carry value) as of December 31, 2019. During this period all of the assets of the trust have been invested and maintained in interest bearing accounts or in investments authorized by law, except for an amount of cash that is reasonably necessary for the ordinary administration of the trust. Specific activities during the period of account include:

   • Background: The SNT is funded with the proceeds of a litigation settlement approved through a minor's compromise petition in a personal injury matter. Beneficiary, born on January 1, 2015 and was injured in an automobile accident. Beneficiary has a traumatic brain injury. The trust is a special needs trust in order to preserve beneficiary's eligibility for SSI and Medi-Cal.

- General Trust Administration: I reviewed and diagramed the trust in order to follow the terms of the trust. I provided input to the petition to establish the trust and signed the document as trustee. I qualified and secured the required bond. An EIN was obtained for the trust. The primary goal of the trust is to enhance beneficiary's quality of life; the secondary objective is to provide for beneficiary's special needs not taken care of by public benefits. The beneficiary's parents indicated that there would be minimal need for distributions from the trust at this time.

- Financial: I monitored the personal injury settlement status and received the funds in March 2018. Once funds were available a checking account was opened, and outstanding bills were paid. QuickBooks and case files were set up. Ongoing activities include reviewing and paying all of the bills and reconciling all financial statements. On a monthly basis data was analyzed and added to the accounting program in order to prepare the first accounting on time.

- Investment of Assets: In my duties as trustee I follow the Uniform Prudent Investor Act (UPIA) with the basic principles of diversification to minimize risk and maximize return. The goal is to earn a reasonable rate of return with prudent risk in a diversified portfolio that supports the beneficiary's lifetime needs. I worked closely with the Trust Protectors (beneficiary's parents) to choose an investment advisor, Investment Advisor, who they suggested and would be an asset to the team. Again, with support from the Trust Protectors I prepared an Investment Policy Statement (IPS) in which I outlined the background, the parameters and the needs to be met. This provides direction to the investment advisor to develop a portfolio asset allocation and modeling projections. A financial custodian account was set up.

Monthly financial statements are monitored, and quarterly reports are reviewed with the investment advisor. Copies are also provided to the Trust Protectors. Based on the volatile equity market dynamics in the second half of 2019, we took advantage of tax loss harvesting and swapped some funds that declined into similar positions of different securities. I continue to believe that the equity markets are going to be the best source of return given the long-term timeline for the trust.

- Communication with Trust Protectors: Due to the beneficiary's age, communication is with his parents, who are also the SNT's Trust Protectors. During the initial stages of setting up the trust and investing the funds, I sought input and kept them informed as to the decisions made and directions taken. They receive duplicate copies of the investment portfolio statements and can participate in investment reviews as desired. They receive copies of my monthly professional fiduciary invoices and to date, have not had any questions about the costs and effort expended. I am readily available to answer questions or provide support when requested.

3. **Special skill and experience brought to the trust by the trustee.** I am a California Licensed Professional Fiduciary (#9999 with an expiration date of 10/31/20. I have been actively providing services as a private professional fiduciary since 2000. I specialize in special needs trust administration, conservatorship of the person or estate, probate administration and payee services. I currently manage over $100,000,000 in conservatorship and trust accounts. I am a General Member of the Professional Fiduciary Association of California (PFAC), of the National Guardian Association, and is well respected and thought of in the community. I have completed all courses in fiduciary management at California State University, Fullerton and received Certificates in Professional Fiduciary Management for both Conservators and Trustees. I am a member of my local PFAC group and am an officer in the group. I have a Bachelor of Science in History from Truman University. I have over 20-years of management experience in the health care field. My experience includes managing financial plans, assessing and

analyzing health care needs, managing multi-level projects and organizing cross-sectional team efforts. A true and correct copy of my resume is attached as **Exhibit C**.

Others who worked on this case and their qualifications are as follows: Trust and Estate Manager. She has a Bachelor of Arts in Sociology from St. Mary's College. She has 10 years of experience in marketing and communications. Accounting Manager who is a QuickBooks Certified ProAdvisor. She has 5 years' experience in the accounting field working for a wide range of small companies. Trust and Estate Manager who has a Bachelor of Science in Statistics from the University of Iowa. She is an EA and has over 6 years of experience in the accounting field focusing on taxation of Trusts.

4. **The fidelity and loyalty of the trustee**: All actions have been focused on the management and protection of the assets of the trust and providing for the beneficiary per the terms of the trust. There have been no complaints from the Trust Protector about actions taken by the trustee.

5. **The risk and responsibility assumed**: I have taken full responsibility for garnering and managing all of the assets. I take personal responsibility for reviewing and paying all of the bills in a timely manner and reconciling the financial statements. I take responsibility for preparing an investment strategy and working with the investment advisor and Trust Protectors to invest the funds appropriately. I work closely with the Trust Protectors on defining distributions needs and being available for questions on the trust.

6. **The time spent in carrying out the fiduciary duties**: My office has spent a total of 28.9 hours in the administration of the trust. The total fees for the services performed during the accounting period of this declaration is $4,000. Of the total hours, 1.6 hours were worked and not charged for a total of $101.50. A detailed explanation of the work performed is attached hereto as Exhibit A (invoices) and are incorporated herein by this reference. Rates of the staff involved are explained in detail in the two Schedule of Fees attached hereto as Exhibit B and incorporated herein by this reference.

7. **The custom in the community regarding payments to fiduciaries**: Based on our experience, expertise, and skills the fees charged in this fee

declaration are in line with, and in many cases less than many professional fiduciaries in the area. I believe the compensation is fair and reasonable.

8. **The character of the work performed**: I have prudently managed all of the assets, paid all of the bills, reconciled all bank statements and invested the settlement funds appropriately. I have worked diligently and efficiently on the trust administration.

9. **The estimate of the value of our own services**: Based on the time expended, the responsibility assumed, the expertise of the Declarant, and the size of the estate, I believe that this is a reasonable compensation for the services performed and the costs incurred.

I declare under penalty of perjury under the laws of the State of California that the foregoing is true and correct.

DATED: _____
PRIVATE PROFESSIONAL FIDUCIARY

SAMPLE FORM: Motor Vehicle Ownership and Maintenance Contract

The _____ Special Needs Trust may, from time to time, maintain a motor vehicle for the use and benefit of _____. To comply with the provisions of the Trust, this memorandum outlines the standards for the purchase and operation of the motor vehicle.

1. The vehicle purchased by the _____ Special Needs Trust (hereinafter "the Trust") will be suitable for _____, and will be fitted for use by individuals who use a wheelchair for mobility.

2. The Trust will maintain valid registration of the vehicle. The vehicle will be registered in the state of _____.

3. The Trust will maintain bodily injury liability, property damage, collision and comprehensive ($500.00 deductible) and uninsured and unknown motorist insurance coverage for the motor vehicle while it is in the care and custody of any authorized driver. The Trust may maintain collision and comprehensive coverage for the vehicle at the discretion of the Trustee of the _____ Special Needs Trust (hereinafter "the Trustee").

4. The Trustee shall have care and custody of the motor vehicle, except for such periods when the vehicle is placed in the care and custody of one or more authorized users. If the vehicle is placed in the care and custody of an authorized user, the Trustee shall have the right to assume repossession

of the vehicle as deemed necessary by the Trustee in the best interests of the Trust.

5. The Trustee will determine the authorized users of the vehicle. It is expected that, for as long as _____ is in the physical care and custody of [INSERT NAME(S) HERE, that person [those persons] will be authorized users].

6. The Trust will maintain a copy of a current valid driver's license, and residential and employment addresses and telephone numbers for any authorized user.

7. The authorized user(s) is encouraged to be responsible for the operating costs of the vehicle during such time as the vehicle is in the possession of that authorized user(s) and without an absolute right of reimbursement from the Trust; such operating costs to include gas, oil, coolant, washer fluid, exterior and interior cleaning supplies, etc.

8. During such periods of time that the vehicle is in the possession of an authorized user, the authorized user(s) shall have the following duties and responsibilities:

   A. Provide the Trustee with his or her current residential and business address and telephone number, and any change thereof within seven days of the date of such change.

   B. Advise the Trustee promptly of any change in circumstances concerning _____ residence or [his/her] ability to make use of the vehicle.

   C. Advise the Trustee promptly of any change in circumstances concerning an authorized user's ability to safely operate the vehicle or which adversely affects the insurance underwriting rating or coverage of the vehicle including, but not limited to:

      i. Any serious or incapacitating illness or injury, or any medical condition which, on advice of a physician or other health care professional, prevents the authorized user from safely driving a motor vehicle;

      ii. The receipt by any authorized user of a motor vehicle law violation, citation, traffic ticket, involvement in a motor vehicle collision or accident (whether involving the Trust's motor vehicle or some other motor vehicle), or arrest for any violation of law.

D. Operate the vehicle in a safe, prudent and responsible manner and in conformance with law.

E. Advise the Trustee promptly if the vehicle is involved in any collision, accident, incident of vandalism or is otherwise damaged, or if any person is injured in, on, or in relation to the use of the vehicle.

F. Pay any parking ticket or citation issued with respect to the vehicle promptly, but in no event later than the due date of the citation.

G. Immediately advise appropriate law enforcement authorities and the Trustee of theft of, vandalism to, or involvement in criminal activity of the vehicle.

H. Advise the Trustee promptly of any major malfunction of the vehicle, breakdown of the vehicle, need for major repair, or any damage of any type to either the exterior or interior of the vehicle.

I. Ensure that the vehicle is maintained in accordance with the terms and conditions of the manufacturer's warranty and any other warranty covering the vehicle or any component parts thereof or additions thereto, including handicapped conversion devices or apparatus (hereinafter collectively referred to as "the warranty"). To affect this provision, the authorized user(s) will:

    i. Maintain both the exterior and interior of the vehicle in a clean, orderly, sanitary and safe condition.

    ii. Operate the vehicle in conformity with the terms and conditions of the warranty and vehicle owners' manual.

    iii. Ensure that the vehicle is brought for regular service as provided in the warranty and vehicle owners' manual. Such service shall be performed at a dealership of the manufacturer of the vehicle.

    iv. Promptly arrange for all servicing and repairs as needed or as recommended by the servicing dealership.

    v. Maintain tires with appropriate inflation and replace worn tires as recommended by the tire manufacturer or servicing dealership.

vi. The authorized user(s) will provide to the Trustee a record of the maintenance and servicing of the vehicle, including all servicing or repair invoices and receipts upon request.

vii. Make the vehicle available for inspection by the Trustee, or any person designated by the Trustee, upon reasonable notice.

9. The vehicle will be driven not more than 3,000 miles in any calendar quarter, exclusive of any vacation or other travel outside of the San Francisco metropolitan area. In the event of any vacation or other travel outside of the San Francisco metropolitan area, the authorized user(s) will advise the Trustee of such travel.

10. The authorized user(s) shall ensure that the vehicle shall be operated only by a person designated by the Trustee as an authorized user and shall in no event permit any person other than an authorized user to operate the vehicle without prior permission of the Trustee, except for emergency circumstances involving the health and physical well-being of persons occupying the vehicle at the time of the emergency.

11. The Trustee will be responsible for ensuring compliance with the terms of these Ownership and Operations Standards. The Trustee shall be required to forthwith reclaim possession of the vehicle in the event the Trustee determines that there has been non-compliance with any provision of these Ownership and Operations Standards. Any authorized user(s) will cooperate with the Trustee in reclaiming possession of the vehicle.

12. Any person who is an authorized user shall first agree in writing to be bound by the terms and conditions of these Ownership and Operations Standards.

Made this _____ day of ____, 20 __.

[Name of Trustee]

Trustee of the _____ Special Needs Trust

Agree to this _____ day of ____, 20 __.

_____

[Name of Authorized User]

_____

[Name of Authorized User]

SAMPLE FORM: Loan to SNT Beneficiary when Loss of SSI During Appeal

LOAN AGREEMENT

This loan agreement is made and will be effective on _____, 20 __.

BETWEEN

[*Name of SNT Beneficiary*], now referred to as "Borrower" located at [*Address of SNT Beneficiary*]

and

[*Name of Trustee*], Trustee of the [*Name of SNT Beneficiary*] Special Needs Trust, dated [*Date*], now referred to as "Lender" located at [*Address of SNT Beneficiary*]

THE TERMS AND CONDITIONS ARE AS FOLLOWS:

Amount of Loan: [*Amount of Loan, e.g., $958.63*] per month for as long as Borrower is not receiving Supplemental Security Income (SSI) and as long as the Lender has sufficient funds to continue payments.

The "Borrower" will repay the "Lender" the Amount of Loan paid upon receipt of Borrower's accrued SSI payments from the appeal submitted in which Borrower's SSI benefits were wrongfully denied.

The interest rate shall be the lowest legally acceptable rate for a loan of this sort, even if 0%.

Borrower and Lender both agree to follow the above-mentioned terms and conditions.

_____

[*Name of SNT Beneficiary*]
"Borrower"

_____

[*Name of Trustee*],
Trustee "Lender"

SAMPLE FORM: Beneficiary Waiver of Trustee Action

_____ **Special Needs Trust**

WAIVER AND ACKNOWLEDGEMENT

I, _____ ("Beneficiary") am the beneficiary of the
_____ Special Needs Trust.

As of the date of this waiver, my current trust balance is around $_____. I
have requested the Trustee authorize the purchase of [*Describe item or service wishing to purchase*], for a total purchase price of $.

The Trustee has advised me and my legal representative, that the distribution requested is not advisable for the following reasons:

- ☐ The requested distribution is a large percentage of my trust account and my available funds will be depleted at a fast rate.
- ☐ The requested distribution is not for my sole benefit.
- ☐ The requested distribution is contrary to federal or state policy(ies).
- ☐ The Trustee is concerned about my ability to maintain the property.
  - ☐ The Trustee has further advised me and my legal representative, that my trustee shall not be liable for ongoing costs, utilities, upkeep, maintenance, taxes, or insurance associated with the property.
- ☐ Other:

_____

☐ I acknowledge that the Trustee has advised me and my legal representative, of their concerns that if distribution is made it will have the impact described above or have unexpected consequences not disclosed.

The Trustee has agreed to consider this request for a disbursement if I agree to acknowledge the disclosure of adverse consequences and agree to waive any claim against the trustee for agreeing to the purchase of [*Describe item or service wishing to purchase*].

I waive, release, hold harmless, and indemnify the Trustee from any claim arising from the Beneficiary's loss of benefits, or reduction of income, which results from this distribution.

I understand that this is a legal document. The Trustee has encouraged me and my legal counsel, to seek independent, professional advice before signing this document.

*****

Agreed to and signed on_____.

_____
[*Beneficiary's Name*]

SAMPLE FORM: Beneficiary's Waiver Acknowledging Refusal to Accept Purchase of a Pre-Paid Funeral Contract

DISCLOSURE AND WAIVER ACKNOWLEDGING BENEFICIARY'S REFUSAL TO THE PURCHASE OF A PRE-PAID FUNERAL CONTRACT

Client Name: *[Name of SNT Beneficiary]*

Client Address: *[SNT Beneficiary's Address]*

[Name of Trustee] is the trustee of the *[Name of SNT Beneficiary]* Special Needs Trust.

[Name of SNT Beneficiary] has been advised by *[Name of Trustee]* in writing of the necessity of having a pre-paid funeral contract for *his/her* own benefit. *[Name of Trustee]*, Trustee has disclosed the importance of the purchase of a pre-paid funeral contract because of a Social Security Administration ("SSA") policy. The SSA's

current policy is that a first-party special needs trust trustee must pay the Medi-Cal/Medicaid claim before [*Name of Trustee*] is able to pay [*Name of SNT Beneficiary*]'s burial and funeral expenses. This means there may be no money left in trust after paying the Medi-Cal/Medicaid claim. This means there would be no money left to pay [*Name of SNT Beneficiary*]'s burial and funeral expenses. The better way to handle this issue is to allow [*Name of Trustee*] to purchase a pre-paid funeral contract. Yet, [*Name of SNT Beneficiary*] has stated that *he/she* does not want a pre-paid funeral contract.

By signing this Disclosure and Waiver, [*Name of SNT Beneficiary*] specifically acknowledges receiving [*Name of Trustee*]'s advice to purchase a pre-paid funeral contract. [*Name of SNT Beneficiary*] has chosen to NOT have [*Name of Trustee*] purchase a pre-paid funeral contract on *his/her* behalf.

_____

[*Name of SNT Beneficiary*]

SAMPLE FORM: Notice of Proposed Action

NOTICE OF PROPOSED ACTION
SALE OF PARTIAL INTEREST IN REAL PROPERTY

111 37TH AVENUE, SAN FRANCISCO

JOHN JONES SPECIAL NEEDS TRUST

Pursuant to Probate Code §§ 16500-16504, the trustee, Private Professional Trustee ("Trustee"), hereby gives notice to all beneficiaries of the above referenced trust that she intends to take the following proposed action.

On or after June 30, 2020, Trustee of the John Jones Special Needs Trust (the "Trust") intends to sell the one-half (1/2) interest in the real property commonly known as 111 37th Avenue, San Francisco, California (the "Property") held by the Trust without prior Court authorization.

THIS NOTICE IS BEING GIVEN PURSUANT TO PROBATE CODE § 16502. If you do not object in writing or obtain a court order preventing the action described herein, you will be treated as if you consented to the proposed action and you may not object after the proposed action is taken. If the trustee receives a written objection within the applicable period, either the trustee or a beneficiary may petition the court to have the proposed action taken as proposed, taken with modifications, or denied. Probate Code §16501(d) lists certain actions for which this notice may not be used.

Jim Jones executed the Trust on March 14, 2010. The Trust holds title to the Property. In consideration for the one-half (1/2) interest in the Property to be sold to Jim Buyer, the Trust will receive $600,000. If this proposed transaction were to occur, the Trust would realize substantial cash in order to meet John Jones special needs. John Jones does not reside in the home and is only obtaining a small amount of monthly rent in the amount of $800 per month due to San Francisco Rent Control Guidelines. The Trust will be better situated to care for John Jones the rest of his life if the Property were sold.

1. The name and address of Trustee is:

   Private Professional Fiduciary
   1234 Main Street
   San Francisco, CA 94100

2. If you require additional information concerning the proposed action, please contact:

   Kevin Urbatsch
   The Urbatsch Law Firm, P.C.
   3478 Buskirk Avenue, Suite 300
   Pleasant Hill, CA 94523
   Telephone: (415) 593-9944
   Fax: (925) 940-9588

Date: _____

_____
Kevin Urbatsch
Attorney

1. IF YOU OBJECT OR CONSENT TO THE TRANSACTION, YOU MAY INDICATE YOUR OBJECTION OR CONSENT BY SIGNING AND

RETURNING THIS FORM TO THE TRUSTEE AT THE ADDRESS LISTED IN ITEM 1 ABOVE NO LATER THAN _____.

YOU MAY SEND YOUR OWN WRITTEN OBJECTION OR CONSENT. BE SURE TO IDENTIFY THE PROPOSED ACTION AND STATE THAT YOU OBJECT OR CONSENT TO IT.

OBJECTION TO PROPOSED ACTION

I OBJECT to the proposed action described above.

Date: _____   _____(Sign)

_____(Print Name)

_____(Address)

_____(Phone Number)

CONSENT TO PROPOSED ACTION

I CONSENT to the proposed action described above.

Notice: You may indicate your consent by signing and returning this form (both pages) to the trustee at the address in item 1. If you do not object or obtain a court order before the date specified above, you will be treated as if you consented to the proposed action.

Date: _____   _____(Sign)

_____(Print Name)

_____(Address)

_____(Phone Number)

Notice: If you do not object or obtain a court order before the date specified above, you will be treated as if you consented to the proposed action.

CHECKLIST: Purchase of Home for Beneficiary

This form can be used or modified by an SNT trustee to inform the beneficiary of all the responsibilities a home purchase will involve. It can also be used by the trustee to determine how future expenses will be paid, especially if there are other people living in the home.

_____ Special Needs Trust
Beneficiary Checklist for Purchase of Home

Please complete form by initialing each blank to the left of the request and fill out each blank completely. If a blank is not applicable, write in "N/A". Requests for purchase of home will not be considered until form is completed.

____ Name of Beneficiary _____

____ Name of Beneficiary's Legal Representative _____

____ Name and relationship of person(s) requesting disbursement for home purchase

    a.   Name _____ Relationship: _____

    b.   Name _____ Relationship: _____

___ Acknowledge that Beneficiary has sufficient mental capacity to manage his or her own home (circle one) Yes No

___ If Beneficiary does not have sufficient mental capacity to manage his or her own home, then acknowledge that his or her legal representative has legal authority to manage Beneficiary's home.

    a.   Provide copy of Power of Attorney with real property authority

    b.   Provide copy of Letters of Conservatorship of Estate

Summary of Request for Home Purchase

___ Provide address of proposed home _____

___ Current amount of Beneficiary's trust estate is _____

    c.   Requested distribution amount from Sub-Account for purchase of home by Beneficiary is $_____

    d.   Percentage of Beneficiary's trust estate requested is _____%

___ Acknowledge that no more than [*select amount of trust estate Trustee is willing to use, e.g. one-half*] of Beneficiary's trust estate may be used for home purchase

___ Acknowledge that in order to obtain disbursement for home request that home will be used by Beneficiary as his or her primary residence

___ Acknowledge that it is solely within the trustee's discretion to disburse trust funds (or refuse to disburse trust funds) so Beneficiary can purchase home in his or her own name even when no more [*select amount of trust estate Trustee is willing to use, e.g. one-half*] of Beneficiary's trust estate is used

____ Acknowledge that in month of purchase of home, the beneficiary if an SSI recipient will trigger SSA income called In-Kind Support and Maintenance (ISM) that may reduce the SSI check for that month, but as long as real property continues as Beneficiary's primary residence, the Beneficiary will be able to live rent-free in the primary residence

____ Acknowledge that the Beneficiary or his or her Representative Payee provides notice to the Social Security Administration and Department of Health Care Services as required

____ Provide name and number of real estate broker who is assisting you and name of real estate broker assisting seller

      e.   Name of your broker _____

      f.   Phone number of your broker _____

      g.   Name of seller's broker _____

      h.   Phone number of seller's broker _____

____ Acknowledge that Beneficiary or Beneficiary's Legal Representatives have personally inspected home for suitability for Beneficiary

____ Schedule a home appraisal or provide comparable sales near home

____ Send copy of home appraisal to Trustee once completed or comparable home sale information

____ Provide home inspection report to trustee

____ Acknowledge that if Beneficiary owns home in his or her own name the Department of Health Care Services has a right to recover against the Beneficiary's "estate" for all Medi-Cal services provided to beneficiary after they die, the situation may not arise if the Beneficiary owns the home in a living trust, Beneficiary is encouraged to seek an attorney knowledgeable in this area to provide advice on the best way to manage home transfer after the death of the Beneficiary

Home Expenses and Sustainability

____ State estimated annual cost of property tax for home
$_____

____ Obtain homeowners insurance for home

      i.   Provide annual cost of home insurance
           $_____

      j.   Name of insurance broker _____

      k.   Name of home insurance company _____

____ List estimated cost to Beneficiary:

      l.   Moving expenses $_____

      m.   Accessibility modifications or repairs to home
           $_____

      n.   Monthly utility costs

           i. Gas $_____

           ii. Electricity $_____

           iii. Water $_____

          iv.   Sewer $_____

          v.   Garbage $_____

          vi.   Cable $_____

          vii.   Internet $_____

o.   Landscaping $_____

p.   Furnishings

          i.   Kitchen $_____

          ii.   Living Room $_____

          iii.   Dining Room $_____

          iv.   Master Bedroom $_____

          v.   Guest Bedroom(s) $_____

          vi.   Other room $_____

____ Acknowledge that [*Name of SNT Trustee*] of the [*Name of Special Needs Trust*] and Beneficiary or Beneficiary's Legal Representatives must agree on which party is responsible for paying foregoing expenses and trustee is under no obligation to pay for any such items

Others Living in Home

____ List names and relationship of all persons expected to live in home:

q.   Name _____ Relationship: _____

    r.   Name _____ Relationship: _____

    s.   Name _____ Relationship: _____

    t.   Name _____ Relationship: _____

    u.   Add additional sheet if necessary

____ Describe how much each person will pay of the monthly home expenses, describe:

____ Acknowledge that if other persons living in the home pay rent while home is owned by Beneficiary that if Beneficiary is an SSI recipient will cause a dollar-for-dollar reduction of his or her SSI check (after first $20) as unearned income. For example, if Beneficiary charges rent of $500 a month, it will reduce the SSI check by $480 a month.

____ Acknowledge that if Beneficiary does not pay for his or her fair market share of utilities and Beneficiary is an SSI recipient will cause a reduction of the SSI check based off of In-Kind Support and Maintenance (ISM) income

I declare under penalty of perjury that the information provided in this form is true and correct.

Dated: _____

_____

[Print Name]

Glossary of Commonly Used SNT Administration Terms

250% California Working Disabled Medi-Cal: This program provides full-scope Medi-Cal to persons with disabilities who work and have income that is too high to qualify for other Medi-Cal categories such as Categorically Eligible, Medically Needy or Aged & Disability Federal Poverty Level Medi-Cal. For this program, the recipient may have up to 250 percent of the federal poverty level in countable income and still receive Medi-Cal benefits. Enrollees pay a monthly, sliding-scale premium for this health coverage.

ABLE (Achieving a Better Life Experience): An account that can be established and funded once a year at the annual gift exemption amount (currently $15,000 a year) that can grow up to $100,000 and not disqualify a person from SSI that is used for Qualifying Disability Expenses and can be controlled by a person with a disability.

Accounting (Account) (See Also Simplified Account and Standard Account): A trustee must account for the trustee's actions. Generally, an account may be done informally at least once a year and a copy provided to the beneficiary or his or her legal representatives. An account will include all actions taken by the trustee including an explanation of all disbursements, investments, and purchases made by trustee. If the trust is court supervised, this account is a much more formal procedure and requires a petition and hearing in a local probate court. The petition must follow a set procedure. It is recommended that an attorney assist with all court accounting filings.

Aged & Disability Federal Poverty Level Medi-Cal: This program provides free Medi-Cal services for persons with disabilities who meet the income and asset requirements of the A&D FPL program. It covers individuals and couples whose income is slightly higher than the SSI eligibility requirements.

Agent: An agent is typically someone who has been appointed by the person with a disability to manage his or her own personal or financial care under a power of attorney or an advance health-care directive. The person with a disability can only sign such a document when the person with a disability has legal capacity.

Basis (sometimes called Cost Basis): The amount of money used to purchase an asset. For example, if a home was purchased for $50,000 its cost basis in the property is $50,000. It is important for the trustee to keep this information in its records. The basis is typically most important when a trust asset is being sold because it will set the capital gains tax on that asset.

Beneficiary (Primary, Remainder and Contingent): This is the person or persons who are to receive the benefit of the trust. The primary beneficiary of a SNT is the person with a disability. Oftentimes, they will only be called a "beneficiary." There may also be named "remainder beneficiaries" or sometimes "contingent beneficiaries," these are the persons who would receive the trust assets once the primary beneficiary either dies or there is a provision in the trust that would cause the assets to go to someone else. For example, an SNT could say, I leave my assets to be administered for the benefit of my child with a disability for as long as he is alive but, on his death, or upon his no longer being disabled, the assets of the trusts shall be distributed to my grandchildren. In this example, the remainder beneficiaries would be the grandchildren.

Bond: A bond is in essence an insurance policy purchased using trust assets that will pay the trust back if the trustee steals the money from the trust. Most trusts do not require a bond of a trustee because the trustee is someone who the beneficiary respects. However, if a court order established the trust, a trustee bond may be required. To qualify the trustee must have excellent credit and a decent sized net worth or enough of a net worth to cover the amount of the bond that is based on the amount of assets in the trust. If interested in being bonded, check http://www. phillipsbonding.com/ to see if the trustee would qualify.

Breach of Trust: A breach of trust is a violation by the trustee of any duty that the trustee owes the SNT beneficiary.

CalWORKS (TANF)-linked Medi-Cal: This program provides free, full-scope Medi-Cal services for California residents who qualify for CalWORKS (California Work Opportunity and Responsibility to Kids Program), *i.e.* individuals who care for financially needy children, grandchildren, or other minor relatives. Individuals who are over 60 or disabled are exempt from the Welfare to Work requirements. (CalWORKS is also known under its federal name as Temporary Aid to Needy Families or TANF (formerly known as Aid to Families with Dependent Children or AFDC.

Categorically Eligible Medi-Cal: Categorically needy individuals are automatically eligible for Medi-Cal if they receive Supplemental Security Income (SSI) or California Work Opportunity and Responsibility to Kids (CalWorks).

Conservator: This is a person who has been appointed by a court to manage the personal or financial care of a person with a disability who lacks the legal capacity to manage it themselves. Generally, the roles are divided between Conservator of the Person (who is responsible for things like making medical decisions or deciding where the person with a disability will live) and the Conservator of the Estate (who is responsible for managing the person with a disability's assets not in the special needs trust).

(d)(4)(A) SNT: Another name for an individual first-party special needs trust named after the federal statute that authorizes it, 42 U.S.C. 1396p(d)(4)(A).

(d)(4)(C) SNT: Another name for a pooled first-party special needs trust named after the federal statute that authorizes it, 42 U.S.C. §1396p(d)(4)(C).

Deeming (SSI): A concept where a minor's parents' assets and income are counted as the minor's when trying to qualify for SSI. Likewise, if an SSI eligible person is married, the spouse's assets and income are counted as the SSI eligible person. See Chapter 3 for further discussion.

Department of Health Care Services (DHCS): This is the California agency that runs Medi-Cal in California. They issue All County Welfare Letters that provide guidance on how the agency interprets its role in running the Medi-Cal program.

Disbursement: This is the process by which money or assets are spent from the trust for the benefit of the person with a disability who is the beneficiary of an SNT.

Distributable Net Income (DNI): DNI is a tax term that is generally applicable on third-party SNTs. Third-party SNTs are taxed at trust tax rates (rather than at individual tax rates) which are much harsher (meaning that more tax is paid on smaller amounts of income). DNI allows the trustee to make distributions of trust income for the benefit of the beneficiary and lower the amount of tax paid to the beneficiary's tax rate rather than the trust tax rate.

Earned Income (SSI): An SSI type of income that results in one-dollar reduction of SSI for every two dollars earned after the first $65 received of income earned by the SSI recipient.

Expanded Medi-Cal: A type of Medi-Cal eligibility that is not dependent on an asset test. If an individual is under age 65 and has an income of less than 138% of the Federal Poverty Limit (FPL), he or she can qualify for full scope Medi-Cal that can include IHSS and nursing home level health care.

Estate Tax: The tax owed by an individual's estate or trust on death. This may arise in situations where an SNT is funded with significant assets. There are generally large exemptions that may pass estate tax free. For example, in 2020 an individual may pass $11.58 million estate tax free. Note, in California there is no estate tax.

Fiduciary: From the Latin fiducia, meaning "trust," a person (or a business like a bank) who has the power and obligation to act for another (often called the beneficiary) under circumstances which require total trust, good faith and honesty. The most common is a trustee of a trust, but fiduciaries can include business advisers, attorneys, guardians, administrators of estates, real estate agents, bankers, stockbrokers, title companies or anyone who undertakes to assist someone who places complete confidence and trust in that person or company.

Fiduciary Duty: This is the legal definition for the type of duty a trustee owes to the beneficiary. It is the highest duty one person can owe another under the law. It is much like the duty a parent owes to a minor child. Thus, the trustee must take better care of trust property and look out for the interests of the beneficiary better than they would take care of their own money or person.

Financial Planner: A financial planner evaluates the finances and helps develop a financial plan to meet both the immediate needs of a beneficiary of a special needs trust and his or her long-term goals. Some, but not all, planners have credentials from professional organizations. Some well-known credentials are certified financial planner (CFP), chartered financial consultant (ChFC), certified investment management analyst (CIMA), and personal financial specialist (PFS). A PFS is a certified public accountant (CPA) that has passed an exam on financial planning. Some planners are also licensed to sell certain investment or insurance products. Fee-only financial planners charge by the hour or collect a flat fee for a specific service, but don't sell products or earn sales commissions. Other planners don't charge a fee but earn commissions on the products they sell to you. Still others both charge fees and earn commissions but may offset their fees by the amount of commission they earn.

First-Party SNT: A first-party SNT is funded with the assets of the person with a disability and may also be called a (d)(4)(A) SNT or a (d)(4)(C) SNT.

Franchise Tax Board: The California version of the IRS. It is responsible for collecting the amount of tax revenue in California.

Funding: The process of placing money or assets into a trust. Generally, this is done by either changing the title to property to the name of the trust or making a beneficiary designation to the name of the trust if for example the asset is a life insurance policy or retirement account.

Grantor Trust: A tax term that defines how a trust will be taxed. In SNTs, a first-party SNT is nearly always a grantor trust, meaning that it will be taxed at the beneficiary's tax rate. See Chapter 17 for a further description and nongrantor trust on alternative way to tax trusts.

In-Kind Support and Maintenance (ISM): An SSI type of income that results (in 2020) of $281 reduction of SSI payment if the SSI recipient receives food or shelter from a third-party or SNT. The amount of reduction will be based on the presumed maximum value (PMV) rule or the value of the one-third-reduction rule (VTR). For further discussion, see definitions of PMV and VTR in this glossary and see Chapter 3.

Impairment-Related Work Expenses (IRWE): An IRWE is an out-of-pocket expense related to an impairment that is needed to be able to work. These expenses paid for by the individual may be deducted from earnings when Social Security calculates the SSI payment. See Chapter 3.

Irrevocable Trust: A trust that cannot be terminated or modified except in certain very narrow circumstances which usually requires a court order.

Judicial Council Form: The Judicial Council is a part of the California judiciary that creates sample form documents to be used in court filings. Sometimes these forms are mandatory and sometimes they are optional. Many times when trustees go to court they can find relatively easy simple fill in the blank forms for their court filings. The forms are located at http://www.courts.ca.gov/forms.htm.

Medi-Cal: The Medicaid program (called Medi-Cal in California) is the primary provider of medical benefits for low-income persons with disabilities. In addition to the optional services Medi-Cal covers, California's Medi-Cal program must provide:
- Primary medical care coverage, such as outpatient hospital services and emergency services, physician services, diagnostic testing, emergency services, laboratory and X-ray services, surgery, inpatient hospital services, pregnancy-related services, and family planning.
- Ongoing care and recovery, such as in-home medical care services, personal care services, nursing facility stays, and adult day health care.

- Early and Periodic Screening, Diagnosis, and Treatment (EPSDT) for children under the age of 21.
- Other related costs, such as medical supplies, durable medical equipment, and transportation for doctor visits.

Medi-Cal Waiver Program: A Medi-Cal Waiver allows the Department of Health Care Services (DHCS) to waive Medi-Cal criteria for persons who would not be able to receive these Medi-Cal benefits otherwise. Services provided under a waiver are typically not part of the available benefit package under Medi-Cal or may be an extension of an existing benefit when there are predetermined limits such as with therapy services. An example is the Home and Community Based Service (HCBS) waivers which are creative alternatives, allowed under the federal law for states participating in Medi-Cal, to be implemented in the home community for certain Medi-Cal beneficiaries to avoid hospitalization or nursing facility placement.

Medically Needy Medi-Cal (sometimes called Share-of-Cost Medi-Cal): This program provides full-scope Medi-Cal services to aged, blind, or disabled people with income above the eligibility levels of no-cost Medi-Cal programs (such as SSI and A&D FPL). The program usually requires that individuals incur a monthly share of cost, which functions like a monthly copayment.

Medicare: Medicare is a federal program with no income or resource requirements. It provides health insurance for individuals who are age 65 or over, disabled, or have end-stage kidney disease or amyotrophic lateral sclerosis. Medicare does not provide complete coverage for all health-care needs. It only covers medically "reasonable and necessary" services. For example, it will not pay for many routine or preventive services such as annual physical exams, eyeglasses, dental care, hearing aids, or long-term care at home or in a nursing home.

Memorandum of Intent: Sometimes called a Letter of Intent or Letter of Understanding, is a document prepared by a parent (or grandparent) of a person with a disability that may describe the person with a disability, provide a summary of their disability and ongoing care and advocacy, give guidance on the best way to work with the person, and discuss how the parent or grandparent intends the trustee to use trust assets to enhance the quality of life of a person with a disability. It is generally not legally binding, meaning that a trustee can ignore it and not be sued, but most trustees will review the document when deciding if an SNT distribution should be done.

Miller Trust: A type of first-party SNT that is not in use in California. See Chapter 1 for more information.

Negligence: Negligence is the failure of the trustee to meet the applicable standard of care set forth under California law or by the trust document.

Nongrantor Trust: A tax term that defines how a trust will be taxed. In SNTs, a third-party SNT is nearly always a nongrantor trust, meaning that it will be taxed at the more onerous trust tax rates rather than at the individual tax rates. However, using distributable net income (DNI) a trustee is allowed to shift the burden of taxes to the typically lower beneficiary tax rate by making distributions on beneficiary's behalf. See Chapter 17 for a further description and grantor trust on alternative way to tax trusts.

Overpayment (SSI): An SSI overpayment occurs when the SSA determines that it has been improperly paying SSI benefits and seeks to have its money returned. For example, if the SSA has been paying SSI benefits of $600 per month for two years and then determines that it should not have been paying $300 of that amount, it will seek repayment of $7,200 ($300 times 24 months) by overpayment. This can be repaid either in a lump sum or (more typically) the SSA will reduce the ongoing SSI payments until the amount is repaid.

Pickle Amendment: The 1976 Pickle Amendment to the Social Security Act requires states to maintain SSI-linked Medi-Cal eligibility for SSI recipients who lose their SSI due to Social Security cost of living allowance. Eligibility extends to those who would have been eligible for SSI in the past, even if they never received it.

Pooled SNT: A type of first-party SNT that is already in existence that is managed by a nonprofit or charity. A person with a disability who has capacity can join this type of trust. Generally, the costs of pooled SNTs are very expensive. An individual will not be a trustee of an SNT. See Chapter 1 for more information.

Presumed Maximum Value (PMV): An SSI applicant will lose a certain amount of his or her SSI check if someone pays for his or her food or shelter and doesn't live in the home. This type of income is called "in-kind support and maintenance." The amount of reduction in 2020 is $281 per month or the actual amount if less than this amount. If both food and shelter are paid for by someone living in the home, then the reduction is under the value of the one-third-reduction rule (VTR). See VTR in this glossary and a further discussion in Chapters 3.

Prudent Investment Standard: The investment standard required in most trusts which states that a trustee shall invest and manage trust assets as a prudent investor would, by considering the purposes, terms, distribution requirements, and other circumstances of the trust. In satisfying this standard, the trustee shall exercise reasonable care, skill, and caution.

Qualified Disability Trust (QDT): This is a tax term that means if a trust qualifies it will increase the personal exemption of a trust (currently $100) up to the personal exemption amount of an individual (in 2020 $4,200). This really only applies to third-party SNTs because first-party SNTs typically are grantor trusts and do not need to utilize the exemption increase. However, unless specifically drafted this way, the third-party SNT may not qualify unless it was established for the "sole benefit" of the person with a disability who is under age 65, which is rarely the case for a third-party SNT. For a further discussion see Chapter 17.

Registered Investment Advisor (RIA): Investment advisers who register with the Securities and Exchange Commission (SEC) and agree to be regulated by SEC rules are known as registered investment advisers. Only a small percentage of all investment advisers register, though being registered is often interpreted as a sign that the advisor meets a higher standard.

Representative Payee: A person who has been appointed by the Social Security Administration to manage a person with a disability's SSI or SSDI's monthly checks. See 42 USC §405(j)(1)(A), (j)(3)(A).

Revocable Trust: A Trust that can be modified or amended by the settlor. An example of a revocable trust is a living trust designed for the purpose of avoiding probate.

Seed Trust: A type of first-party SNT that is established by a parent or grandparent using the assets of the person with a disability for a person with a disability who has legal capacity to manage his or her own financial affairs. See Chapter 1 for more information.

Settlor, Trustmaker, Grantor, Trustor: These are different names for the person or entity that created or established the trust. For example, if a parent created a trust for a child with a disability, then the parent would be named the settlor, grantor, trustmaker, or trustor of the trust depending on the drafting attorney's own convention of use. In California law, the term *settlor* is used however there is no difference in treatment if a trust document uses a different name.

Share-of-Cost: The amount of money that an individual must pay in order to qualify for medically needy Medi-Cal. The share of cost is all income over the "monthly maintenance need" level (MMNL), *i.e.*, the minimum amount necessary to meet basic living expenses as determined by DHCS and based on federal poverty level figures.

Share-of-Cost Medi-Cal: See Medically Needy Medi-Cal.

Shelter: SSI defines shelter to include room, rent, mortgage payments, real property taxes, heating fuel, gas, electricity, water, sewerage, and garbage collection services.

Simplified Accounting: A type of account that may be used for a SNT that is under continuing court jurisdiction. It lists transactions chronologically. If this method is used, the accounting must use the Judicial Council form as described in Chapter 17.

There are certain types of trusts that may not use the simplified account method and instead must use the standard account method described below.

Social Security Administration (SSA): The federal agency that runs the Social Security system. This includes running the Social Security Disability Income (SSDI) and the Supplemental Security Income (SSI) programs.

Sole Benefit: A legal requirement for the type of disbursement that can be made from a first-party SNT. It means that disbursements must be made for the primary benefit of the person with a disability only and that disbursements cannot be made to third parties. California and the SSA has interpreted to mean that others may derive some benefit from the disbursement but the primary benefit must be derived by the beneeficiary with a disability.

Standard Accounting: A type of account that may be used for a SNT that is under continuing court jurisdiction. It lists transactions by subject matter. There are certain SNTs that must use the standard accounting—for example, if the trust estate includes real estate. If this method is used, the accounting must use only one Judicial Council form but may use the remaining 33 forms as described in Chapter 17. The alternative is that the trustee may create his or her own forms, but they must substantially be similar to the Judicial Council forms.

Statute of Limitations: Laws setting deadlines for filing lawsuits within a certain time after events occur that are the source of a claim. For example, if a SNT account provides information to a beneficiary that shows the trustee was negligent, the beneficiary only has 3 years to sue on the claim or be forever prevented from filing a lawsuit. This example is called a 3-year statute of limitations. The length of time will vary depending on different statutes.

Substantial Gainful Activity (SGA): SGA is a level of work that is substantial and gainful. It is defined as "work activity that involves doing significant physical or mental activities" even if you only do it part-time. Monthly countable earnings of more than $1,260 (in 2020) usually demonstrate SGA. If the SGA is over this amount, it may affect eligibility for SSI and SSDI. The SSA uses SGA to determine the individual's initial and continuing eligibility for SSDI and initial eligibility for SSI (except for individuals who are blind). See Chapter 3 for more information.

Surcharge: If an SNT trustee breaches his or her duty and it causes the SNT money damages, the trustee can be surcharged which is a monetary penalty the trustee must pay to the SNT from his or her own funds.

Third-Party SNT: A third-party SNT is typically part of a parent or grandparent's estate plan for a child with a disability. However, it is not limited to them; any person other than the person with a disability can fund this type of trust. Such a trust is funded with the assets of a "third-party," that is, parents, grandparents, or anyone else other than the person with a disability whom the trust benefits.

Trustee: This is the person responsible for administering the trust once it is established. A trust may also name successor trustees who would be the persons responsible for managing the trust if the originally named trustee can no longer serve. A trust can have more than one trustee at a time. Be aware that a cotrustee can be held responsible for another cotrustee's breach of a fiduciary duty. Thus, it is important that all cotrustees pay close attention to everything that is done in the administration of the trust. If there is any question or problem, that should be communicated to the other cotrustee or cotrustees immediately. As a general rule, where there are two cotrustees, both have to agree on all matters of trust administration, and where there are three or more cotrustees, the majority rules. In order to minimize the chances of being held responsible for someone else's poor judgment or breach of duty, a cotrustee should be sure to make a written record of any points of disagreement about trust business. In extreme cases, a cotrustee may be required to blow the whistle on other cotrustees' activities.

Trust Advisory Committee: In some SNTs, there will be a group of persons called a trust advisory committee. Typically, the committee will have the authority to speak on behalf of the beneficiary and make requests for disbursements. They may also have the authority to remove and replace a trustee. As with nearly all questions surrounding trust administration, it is very important to read the document to understand what role the committee will serve.

Trust Protector: As with the trust advisory committee, a trust protector is used in some SNTs. The protector will be given a series of responsibilities as spelled out in the trust document. Typically, these include the right to remove and replace trustees and the right to amend the trust if there are changes in the law that will require an amendment to the trust to keep it current.

Unearned Income (SSI): A type of SSI income that results in a dollar for dollar reduction of SSI after the receipt of $20 of money by an SSI recipient. Unearned income is cash given to an SSI recipient that has not been earned.

Value of One-Third Reduction Rule (VTR): The VTR applies when the SSI recipient lives in another's house throughout a month, receives both food and shelter from inside the household, and does not meet his or her pro rata share of cost of the food and shelter expenses for the household. The SSI recipient will lose 1/3 of the federal portion of his SSI check. In 2020, the loss would be $261. See Presumed Maximum Value (PMV) and Chapter 3 for further discussion